Rethinking American Grand Strategy

Rethinking American Grand Strategy

Edited by

ELIZABETH BORGWARDT,
CHRISTOPHER McKNIGHT NICHOLS,
AND
ANDREW PRESTON

OXFORD
UNIVERSITY PRESS

Oxford University Press is a department of the University of Oxford. It furthers
the University's objective of excellence in research, scholarship, and education
by publishing worldwide. Oxford is a registered trade mark of Oxford University
Press in the UK and certain other countries.

Published in the United States of America by Oxford University Press
198 Madison Avenue, New York, NY 10016, United States of America.

© Oxford University Press 2021

Library of Congress Cataloging-in-Publication Data
Names: Borgwardt, Elizabeth, 1964– editor. | Nichols, Christopher McKnight, editor. |
Preston, Andrew, 1973– editor.
Title: Rethinking American grand strategy / edited by Elizabeth Borgwardt,
Christopher McKnight Nichols, and Andrew Preston.
Description: New York, NY : Oxford University Press, [2021] | Includes index.
Identifiers: LCCN 2020036111 (print) | LCCN 2020036112 (ebook) |
ISBN 9780190695668 (hardcover) | ISBN 9780190695675 (paperback) |
ISBN 9780190695699 (epub) | ISBN 9780190093143
Subjects: LCSH: National security—United States—History. |
Strategy—History. | United States—Foreign relations. |
United States—Military policy.
Classification: LCC E183.7 .R38 2021 (print) |
LCC E183.7 (ebook) | DDC 355/.033073—dc23
LC record available at https://lccn.loc.gov/2020036111
LC ebook record available at https://lccn.loc.gov/2020036112

DOI: 10.1093/oso/9780190695668.001.0001

1 3 5 7 9 8 6 4 2

Paperback printed by LSC Communications, United States of America
Hardback printed by Bridgeport National Bindery, Inc., United States of America

To those we love and have lost recently
Carolyn Nichols, Rodney Nichols, Kevin Preston

Contents

Acknowledgments   xi
Contributors   xiii

Introduction   1
Christopher McKnight Nichols and Andrew Preston

I. FRAMEWORKS

1. Getting Grand Strategy Right: Clearing Away Common Fallacies in the Grand Strategy Debate   29
   Hal Brands

2. The Blob and the Mob: On Grand Strategy and Social Change   49
   Beverly Gage

3. Turning the Tide: The Application of Grand Strategy to Global Health   63
   Elizabeth H. Bradley and Lauren A. Taylor

II. HISTORICAL GRAND NARRATIVES

4. Extending the Sphere: A Federalist Grand Strategy   83
   Charles Edel

5. Grand Strategy of the Master Class: Slavery and Foreign Policy from the Antebellum Era to the Civil War   106
   Matthew Karp

6. A Useful Category of Analysis? Grand Strategy and US Foreign Relations from the Civil War through World War I   123
   Katherine C. Epstein

7. Grand Strategies (or Ascendant Ideas) since 1919   143
   David Milne

III. RECASTING CENTRAL FIGURES

8. Woodrow Wilson, W. E. B. Du Bois, and Beyond: American
Internationalists and the Crucible of World War I   175
Christopher McKnight Nichols

9. Franklin Roosevelt, the New Deal, and Grand
Strategy: Constructing the Postwar Order   201
Elizabeth Borgwardt

10. Foreign Policy Begins at Home: Americans, Grand Strategy,
and World War II   218
Michaela Hoenicke Moore

11. National Security as Grand Strategy: Edward Mead Earle
and the Burdens of World Power   238
Andrew Preston

12. The Misanthropy Diaries: Containment, Democracy, and the
Prejudices of George Frost Kennan   254
David Greenberg

13. Implementing Grand Strategy: The Nixon-Kissinger
Revolution at the National Security Council   272
William Inboden

14. George H. W. Bush: Strategy and the Stream of History   292
Jeffrey A. Engel

IV. NEW APPROACHES

15. Foreign Missions and Strategy, Foreign Missions as Strategy   311
Emily Conroy-Krutz

16. The Unbearable Whiteness of Grand Strategy   329
Adriane Lentz-Smith

17. Rival Visions of Nationhood: Immigration Policy, Grand
Strategy, and Contentious Politics   346
Daniel J. Tichenor

18. Disastrous Grand Strategy: US Humanitarian Assistance and
Global Natural Catastrophe   366
Julia F. Irwin

19. Denizens of a Center: Rethinking Early Cold War Grand
    Strategy   384
    Ryan Irwin

20. Reproductive Politics and Grand Strategy   401
    Laura Briggs

V. REFLECTIONS FROM THE AMERICAN CENTURY

21. Casualties and the Concept of Grandness: A View from the
    Korean War   427
    Mary L. Dudziak

22. American Grand Strategy: How Grand Has It Been? How
    Much Does It Matter?   447
    Fredrik Logevall

Index   459

Acknowledgments

For their support of this project and the international conference at Oregon State University in 2016 that helped to generate this book, we thank the OSU College of Liberal Arts and Dean Larry Rodgers, the OSU School of History, Philosophy, and Religion, and Directors Ben Mutschler and Nicole von Germeten, as well as the OSU Center for the Humanities. We are very grateful for the support of Patrick and Vicki Stone, the Andrew Carnegie Corporation, and our other sponsors and collaborators. We want to recognize C-SPAN's coverage of the conference, and we extend special thanks to Robert Peckyno, Natalia Bueno, and Dougal Henken for exceptional design and conference support.

We deeply appreciate the superb team at Oxford University Press who helped to shepherd this volume to completion. In particular, we owe a personal and professional debt of gratitude to Susan Ferber. Thank you, Susan, for sticking with this project over several years. The project has benefitted enormously from your keen editorial eye, sharp analysis, and friendly enthusiasm.

We thank our families for their support and forbearance through the many twists and turns of this project. Conceiving and orchestrating this conference and developing and revising this book project helped to generate intellectual community, which sustained and distracted us over a number of years during which we experienced significant suffering and loss. We dedicate this book those we love and have lost recently: to Kevin Preston, to Carolyn Nichols, and to Rodney Nichols.

Finally, his fellow editors would like to thank Chris Nichols for carrying this project forward when challenges presented themselves and difficulties mounted. After hosting the conference that got this book off the ground, Chris's drive and focus, but even more importantly his optimism and good humor, kept us on target. It is no exaggeration to say that without his efforts this book would not have been published.

Contributors

Elizabeth Borgwardt is Associate Professor of History at Washington University in St. Louis. She is the author of *A New Deal for the World: America's Vision for Human Rights* (Harvard University Press, 2005).

Elizabeth H. Bradley, PhD, is President of Vassar College in New York. She was previously the Brady-Johnson Professor of Grand Strategy and Professor of Public Health at Yale University. She is the co-author of the *American Health Care Paradox: Why Spending More Is Getting Us Less* (PublicAffairs, 2013) and is a member of the National Academy of Medicine and the Council on Foreign Relations.

Hal Brands is the Henry Kissinger Distinguished Professor of Global Affairs at the Johns Hopkins School in Advanced International Studies, a scholar at the American Enterprise Institute, and a Bloomberg Opinion columnist. He is writing a book about the Cold War and long-term competition.

Laura Briggs is Professor of Women, Gender, Sexuality Studies at the University of Massachusetts, Amherst. She is the author of a number of books, including *Reproducing Empire: Race, Sex, Science, and US Imperialism in Puerto Rico* (University of California Press, 2002), and, most recently, *Taking Children: A History of American Terror* (University of California Press, 2020).

Emily Conroy-Krutz is Associate Professor of History at Michigan State University and the author of *Christian Imperialism: Converting the World in the Early American Republic* (Cornell University Press, 2015).

Mary L. Dudziak is the Asa Griggs Candler Professor of Law at Emory University, past president of the Society for Historians of American Foreign Relations, and the author of *War Time: An Idea, Its History, Its Consequences* (Oxford University Press, 2012), among other books.

Charles Edel is a senior fellow at the University of Sydney's United States Studies Centre; previously, he was Associate Professor at the US Naval War College and served on the US Secretary of State's policy planning staff from 2015 to 2017. He is co-author of *The Lessons of Tragedy: Statecraft and World Order* (Yale University Press, 2019) and author of *Nation Builder: John Quincy Adams & the Grand Strategy of the Republic* (Harvard University Press, 2014).

Jeffrey A. Engel is the founding director of the Center for Presidential History at Southern Methodist University. Author or editor of twelve books on American foreign policy, politics, and the American presidency, his latest are *Impeachment: An American History* (Modern Library, 2018) and *When the World Seemed New: George H. W. Bush and the End of the Cold War* (Houghton Mifflin Harcourt, 2017).

Katherine C. Epstein is Associate Professor of History at Rutgers University-Camden and the author of *Torpedo: Inventing the Military-Industrial Complex in the United States and Great Britain* (Harvard University Press, 2014). She studies technology transfer, the intersection of national security and intellectual property regimes, and the political economy of power projection.

Beverly Gage is Brady-Johnson Professor of Grand Strategy and Professor of History at Yale University. She is the author of *The Day Wall Street Exploded: A Story of America in Its First Age of Terror* (Oxford University Press, 2009) and a forthcoming biography of J. Edgar Hoover.

David Greenberg is Professor of History and of Journalism & Media Studies at Rutgers University. His books include the prize-winning *Nixon's Shadow: The History of an Image* (W.W. Norton, 2003) and, most recently, *Republic of Spin: An Inside History of the American Presidency* (W.W. Norton, 2016).

Michaela Hoenicke Moore is Associate Professor of History at the University of Iowa and the author of *Know Your Enemy: The American Debate on Nazi Germany, 1933–1945* (Cambridge University Press, 2009), which won the 2010 SHAFR Myrna Bernath Book Prize.

William Inboden is the William Powers Jr. Executive Director of the Clements Center for National Security and Associate Professor at the LBJ School of Public Affairs at the University of Texas at Austin. Earlier he was Senior Director for Strategic Planning on the National Security Council.

Julia F. Irwin is Associate Professor of History at the University of South Florida. She is the author of *Making the World Safe: The American Red Cross and a Nation's Humanitarian Awakening* (Oxford University Press, 2013) and is now working on a second book tentatively entitled *Catastrophic Diplomacy: A History of U.S. Responses to Global Natural Disaster*.

Ryan Irwin is Associate Professor of History at the University at Albany-SUNY and the author of *Gordian Knot: Apartheid and the Unmaking of the Liberal World Order* (Oxford University Press, 2012).

Matthew Karp is Associate Professor of History at Princeton University and the author of *This Vast Southern Empire: Slaveholders at the Helm of American Foreign Policy* (Harvard University Press, 2016).

Adriane Lentz-Smith is Associate Professor of History and African & African-American Studies at Duke University as well as Senior Fellow in Duke's Kenan Institute for Ethics. The author of *Freedom Struggles: African Americans and World*

War I (Harvard University Press, 2009), she has published in *American Quarterly, Southern Cultures*, and elsewhere.

Fredrik Logevall is Laurence D. Belfer Professor of International Affairs at Harvard University. His newest book is *JFK: Coming of Age in the American Century* (Random House, 2020).

David Milne is Professor of Modern History at the University of East Anglia. He is the author of *America's Rasputin: Walt Rostow and the Vietnam War* (Hill and Wang, 2008) and *Worldmaking: The Art and Science of American Diplomacy* (Farrar, Straus and Giroux, 2015); currently he is writing a biography of the trailblazing journalist Sigrid Schultz.

Christopher McKnight Nichols is Associate Professor of History and Director of the Center for the Humanities at Oregon State University. An Andrew Carnegie Fellow and frequent commentator of the historical dimensions of American politics and foreign relations, Nichols is the author, co-author, or editor of six books, most notably *Promise and Peril: America at the Dawn of a Global Age* (Harvard University Press, 2011).

Andrew Preston is Professor of American History and a Fellow of Clare College at the University of Cambridge. His most recent book is *American Foreign Relations: A Very Short Introduction* (Oxford University Press, 2019).

Lauren A. Taylor is a post-doctoral fellow in the Department of Population Health at NYU Grossman School of Medicine. She holds a PhD in Health Policy and Management and a Masters of Divinity from Harvard.

Daniel J. Tichenor is the Philip H. Knight Chair of Political Science and Program Director at the Wayne Morse Center of Law and Politics at the University of Oregon. His most recent book is *Rivalry and Reform: Presidents, Social Movements, and the Transformation of American Politics* (University of Chicago Press, 2019).

Rethinking American Grand Strategy

Introduction

Christopher McKnight Nichols and Andrew Preston

What is grand strategy? What does it aim to achieve? Does it have relevance—and, if so, applicability—beyond questions of war and peace? And what differentiates it from normal strategic thought—what, in other words, makes it "grand"?

In recent years, historians and other scholars have offered useful definitions, most of which coalesce around the notion that grand strategy is an amplification of the "normal" strategic practice of deploying various means to attain specific ends.[1] "The crux of grand strategy," writes Paul Kennedy, co-founder of the influential Grand Strategy program at Yale University, "lies . . . in *policy*, that is, in the capacity of the nation's leaders to bring together all the elements, both military and nonmilitary, for the preservation and enhancement of the nation's long-term (that is, in wartime *and* peacetime) best interests."[2] John Lewis Gaddis, the program's co-founder with Kennedy, defines grand strategy succinctly as "the alignment of potentially unlimited aspirations with necessarily limited capabilities."[3] Hal Brands, an alumnus of Yale's program and a contributor to this volume, observes that grand strategy is best understood as an "intellectual architecture that lends structure to foreign policy; it is the logic that helps states navigate a complex and dangerous world."[4] Peter Feaver, who followed Yale's model when establishing a grand strategy program at Duke University, is somewhat more specific: "Grand strategy refers to the collection of plans and policies that comprise the state's deliberate effort to harness political, military, diplomatic, and economic tools together to advance that state's national interest."[5] International Relations theorist Stephen Walt is even more precise: "A state's grand strategy is its plan for making itself secure. Grand strategy identifies the objectives that must be achieved to produce security, and describes the political and military actions that are believed to lead to this goal. Strategy is thus a set of 'contingent predictions': if we do A, B, and C, the desired results X, Y, and Z should follow."[6]

While clear about grand strategy's purpose, these definitions do not explicitly address its proper scope and focus. Why? In spite of recognizing the complexity of their subject, the generators of these definitions and other noted scholars of grand strategy have often limited their analytic framework to moments of conflict and the "purposeful employment of all the instruments of power available to a security community"—in other words, war.[7] Tackling episodes from antiquity to the present, in many cases with remarkable depth and sophistication, scholars of grand strategy have examined the relationship between armed conflict and the peace that follows. Many theorists argue that it should continue to be this way.[8] The tight focus on policy and warfare, they suggest, provides precision, particularly considering that the scope of their work tracks millennia—from Herodotus and Thucydides to Kennan and Kissinger. Even those otherwise insightful studies that look beyond the conduct of warfare still perceive grand strategy as falling strictly within the realm of high diplomacy, deterrence, macroeconomic power, and other measures that fall just short of war—a perspective broader than warfare, perhaps, but not by much.[9]

Because these scholars focus on statecraft as it has been conventionally understood, they omit much else that could be considered political. However, as the definitions by Kennedy, Gaddis, and others demonstrate, it is possible to consider, and even reach, a more capacious understanding of grand strategy, one that still includes the battlefield and the negotiating table but can also expand beyond them. While the concept of strategy is undoubtedly military in origin, and although strategic culture retains a high degree of its original military character, there is no reason to confine grand strategy solely to the realm of warfare. Scholars have similarly located the origins of sovereignty, law, and statehood in the realm of warfare, yet it is hard to think of these topics as falling exclusively within the domain of military history.[10] Just as contemporary world politics is driven by a wide range of non-military issues, the most thorough considerations of grand strategy must examine the bases of peace and security as broadly as possible.[11] As one recent survey of the topic puts it, "An exclusive focus on military force appears inconsistent with the contemporary environment of world politics."[12] A theory that bears little resemblance to the reality around us every day—in which gender, race, the environment, public health, and a wide range of cultural, social, political, and economic issues are not only salient but urgently pressing—can only be so useful.

For this reason, among others, some scholars have doubted the usefulness or even very legitimacy of studying grand strategy. Skeptics tend to mount criticisms in roughly three key areas: definitions, discipline, and scope. One argument that combines definitional and disciplinary criticism argues that "the more the output of grand strategists is examined, the more the enterprise comes down to a desire by statesmen, and their would-be tutors, not so much to understand the world as to stake their place in it."[13] Other critics suggest that those who make as well as those who study grand strategy are likely to find the grandiosity they seek. Richard Betts, for example, admonishes scholars that "it is good to step back and realize that there is less in the idea of this voguish concept than meets the eye." Actual policy is just too messy to be the product of a coherent advanced planning, and grand strategy is not "what actually drives governments' actions."[14]

Taking the modern United States as a nation-state case study, *Rethinking American Grand Strategy* instead argues for the relevance and usefulness of grand strategy; and, in doing so, demonstrates that grand-strategic analysis can be much more capacious than the usual politico-military framework of international history. To encompass the fullest dimensions of grand strategy, scholarship must include the forgotten voices that contributed to the intellectual architecture, plans, policies, and aspirations of US foreign policy, especially those voices that traditional scholarship has neglected. Not only have these understudied and undertheorized figures and topics long factored into US strategic thought, but they have actively shaped it.[15] One of the principal aims of this book is to integrate these forgotten voices into the broader contours of American grand strategy.

Case Study I: The Unexpected Grand Strategy of George W. Bush

Sometimes the most effective and farsighted grand strategy has little to do with armed conflict. By way of illustration, consider the policies of President George W. Bush.[16]

It is clear that many people in the Bush administration saw the attacks of September 11, 2001, as an opportunity to deal with Iraq once and for all. Their view carried the day, in the teeth of opposition from national security officials and anti-war protestors alike. But despite Bush's determination for a showdown with Saddam Hussein, and despite later perceptions, there was no rush to war—a full eighteen months passed between 9/11 and the invasion of Iraq. In that time, Bush convened many National Security Council (NSC) meetings on Iraq. Key members of the administration spent countless hours explaining both the nature of what they saw as an Iraqi threat and the regional and international benefits of removing that threat. Most notable was the National Security Strategy, a thirty-one-page document released in September 2002 that explicitly laid out Bush's vision for prosecuting the "global war on terror."

What is particularly striking about those eighteen months of planning and deliberation, however, is how un-strategic the Bush administration's thinking was: its highly ambitious ends bore almost no relationship to realistic means. For example, in early March 2003, shortly before they would oversee the invasion of Iraq, military commanders met with Secretary of Defense Donald Rumsfeld and predicted a quick victory that would see US forces occupying Baghdad within a matter of weeks. But those plans, focused narrowly on defeating the Iraqi army, did not come close to matching up with, let alone achieving, the administration's almost limitless regional and global objectives. At an NSC meeting the day after Rumsfeld's consultation with the generals, Under Secretary of Defense for Policy Douglas Feith laid out a wish list, including the preservation of Iraq's territorial integrity, an improved quality of life for the Iraqi people, international support for the US invasion, international participation in Iraq's reconstruction, and the development of "democratic institutions" in Iraq that would serve "as a model for the region" and perhaps even pave the way for a final settlement of the Israel-Palestine conflict. Bush left the meeting uneasy with Feith's abstractions, but when he met with a Vatican envoy sent to Washington to convey the pope's opposition to war, he simply repeated Feith's platitudes.[17] Right on the eve of war, then, the architects of a war entirely of their own making had little grasp of how they were going to complete their design. Unsurprisingly, the war failed to meet its goals and instead caused new problems for American security.

Nearly four years later, Bush launched another strategic initiative to deal with Iraq. Since its start, the war had gone disastrously wrong. Only one of Feith's objectives, preserving the territorial integrity of Iraq, had been achieved, at unimaginable cost—but even that was simply a status quo objective, not the kind of transformation for which Bush had launched the war in the first place. Bush then fired Rumsfeld after the Republican Party suffered a heavy defeat in the 2006 midterm elections in which the Iraq War was the main issue. Instead of beginning a withdrawal from Iraq, however, Bush convened a series of high-level, top secret meetings designed to turn the war around. The meetings were, observed Secretary of State Condoleezza Rice, being conducted separately, in "atomized fashion," and needed coordination.[18] Bush placed National Security Adviser Stephen Hadley in charge, who by all accounts brought order to the Bush administration's chaos. Planning under Hadley was both extensive and intensive, and an administration notorious for its dysfunctional infighting reached a pragmatic consensus. The result was the so-called Surge, a deployment of 30,000 additional troops, combined with new efforts to win over Sunni opposition fighters in Iraq. The new approach, implemented in January 2007, stabilized the war, and Bush and his supporters were quick to claim it as a victory. But while the Surge may have stabilized an ever-deteriorating operational situation, it could not secure a strategic victory in any meaningful sense. The original objectives that Feith had outlined four years earlier still remained well out of reach, and America's reputation still lay in tatters.[19]

In these two episodes, the same people devoted significant time and resources to forward strategic planning to solving, more or less, the same problem. In 2002–3, the Bush administration's planning on Iraq was haphazard and unrealistic, and the result was humiliating defeat. In 2006–7, the administration's planning on Iraq was well coordinated and tightly focused, yet while the result was a tactical success the United States was still no closer to achieving even its most limited, modest goals. The Surge succeeded in the short term by focusing on the small details that would win battles, not wars, and it did not create a peace to follow the fighting. Admiral William J. Fallon, head of US Central Command, put it bluntly a few months after the Surge had been launched. "Nobody's doing any strategic thinking," he complained. "They're all tying their shoes. Now I understand why we are where we are. We ought to be shot for this."[20]

Now consider what might well turn out to be, in the long run, Bush's most enduring strategic endeavor. As two contributors to this volume, Elizabeth H. Bradley and Lauren A. Taylor, explain, Iraq was not the only focus of Bush's planning. In a series of secret meetings in 2002, running alongside the administration's meetings on Iraq, Bush and some of his advisers discussed ways of tackling the AIDS crisis in Africa. The result was an ambitious but realistic plan to fight an epidemic that was ravaging the African continent and had the potential to spread far beyond. Non-traditional foreign policies, including humanitarian causes like health care, are not usually included in analysis of grand strategy. Yet they should be, not simply for the sake of inclusivity but because they meet the test of grand-strategic objectives: creating the conditions for an enduring peace, fostering international stability, advancing US ideals and interests, and reducing anti-Americanism. Bradley and Taylor illustrate that the successful implementation of the President's Emergency Plan for AIDS Relief (PEPFAR) owed much to the principles of grand strategy. In doing so, they also show that the boundaries of grand strategy extend far beyond the conduct of warfare.

What Is Grand Strategy?

So, to return to our opening question, what is grand strategy? This is unsteady theoretical and historiographical ground, for there are virtually countless definitions in existence, including many not quoted here. "No simple, clear definition of grand strategy can ever be fully satisfactory," observes military historian Williamson Murray, while others have noted that it is "hard to overstate how much questions of definition bedevil contemporary studies of grand strategy."[21] These reservations may be true, but they should not mean that definitions should be avoided altogether. If analysts do not provide high definition to what they claim to be investigating, why should anyone pay attention to their conclusions?[22] For a volume on how scholars and practitioners should rethink grand strategy, it is therefore incumbent upon the editors to make clear what we talk about when we talk about grand strategy.[23]

By engaging with various dimensions of the historical record, this volume argues that grand strategy is best understood as a holistic and interconnected system of power, encompassing all aspects of society in pursuit of international goals "based on the calculated relationship of means to ends."[24] While it is, as Barry Posen puts it in a now-classic formulation, "a state's theory about how it can best 'cause' security for itself," how states cause their own security is often down to the actions of non-state actors who produce their own theories of power and security.[25] In a representative democracy like the United States, grand strategy helps answer the underlying question, "What is our power for?"[26] Capacious and far-sighted (long-term) perspectives differentiate a higher-order (grand) strategy from more proximate strategies, or lower-level operational pursuits and tactics. Grand strategy is not simply about winning wars or attaining specific foreign-policy objectives, important as these priorities are; it is not only an answer to the question of what power is meant to achieve. Grand strategy is also about creating a durable peace that follows a war and then maintaining the stability of that peace long after the war has faded into a distant memory. It is, and has been, about making or preventing large-scale change. It is—for the United States especially, with its global ambitions, widespread commitments, and enormous capabilities in all forms of power—about trying to shape world conditions so as to ensure the protection of national security and the flourishing of national values.[27] If "normal" strategy is pragmatic, essentially an exercise of short-term problem solving, "grand" strategy is ideological, a programmatic vision of reshaping a state's external environment and reordering, to the extent that it's possible, the people who live in it.

While strategy has a conceptual lineage stretching back to antiquity, grand strategy has a decidedly more modern pedigree. Although the label of "grand strategy" might be applied to the statecraft of leaders from before the modern period,[28] only in the last two centuries or so have strategic thinkers explicitly conceptualized strategy on a "grand" scale, and only in the last hundred years has strategy been codified as "grand."[29] Even the great Prussian strategist Carl von Clausewitz did not write about "grand" strategy in what is probably the most important strategic treatise in diplomatic and military history, *On War*; nor did his influential contemporaries, such as Antoine-Henri Jomini. In fact, nobody did until the first era of modern globalization, in the late nineteenth and early twentieth centuries, when the mass armies and nationalist movements of the nineteenth century were joined to the industrial economies, innovative technologies, and ideological visions of the twentieth century. Shortly before World War I, two naval strategists, American Alfred Thayer Mahan and Briton Julian Corbett, offered a totalistic conception of strategy that reached far beyond the military, including its economic, political, and, at times, cultural and ideological dimensions. In 1911, Corbett even distinguished between forms of "minor" and "major" strategy. But it was not until after the Great War that "grand strategy" came into existence in a formal and theoretical way.[30]

It was entirely fitting, then, that grand strategy was forged as a separate discipline during the global conflicts of the twentieth century. The phrase "grand strategy" first appeared with some recurrence in English-language writing in the 1860s, but it does not appear to have been much used until the World War II era, with an explosion of use of the term in 1936 reaching a peak in 1944. That there appears to have been a dramatic rise in references, debates, and discussions of grand strategy from 1936 to 1949, with the greatest usage in the 1939–46 period, should come as no surprise.[31] Indeed, grand strategy as a phrase mirrors the wartime intellectual deliberations and planning not just for the conflict but also the postwar peace; it thus maps onto the mid-century "American Century" moment as surely as any declaration by Henry Luce or Franklin Roosevelt. The United States aimed to devise a grand strategy for enduring global power in those years, and everyone knew it. Through these crises, from two world wars and into the global Cold War, intellectual innovators such as Briton Basil Liddell Hart and American Edward Mead Earle made strategy "grand." Liddell Hart and Earle—the latter the subject of a chapter in this volume—argued that grand strategy encompassed the new dimensions of power in the modern age. Their visions were flawed, but they were visionaries all the same, and they exerted a profound influence on later historians of grand strategy.[32]

These figures were not alone in rethinking the best way for states to engage with the new world order. Warfare had always been rooted in politics and policy, but the unprecedented social scale of warfare led to a widespread reconceptualization of those wars. Even before the advent of nuclear weapons in 1945, nation-states had begun devising ways of limiting and perhaps even eliminating warfare itself. But the failure of these ambitions, and the persistent threat of total war in the nuclear age, meant that states had to consider their place in the world in a more comprehensive fashion. The ability of states to project awesomely destructive power far beyond their borders meant that threats had to be identified long before they became imminent.

Because grand strategy is a creature of modern warfare, developed in an increasingly interconnected and interdependent world, it took a broad view of the factors involved in world security and a robust view of its own role in contributing to it. States also had to consider the emergence of threats from more unconventional sources. Disease, migration, access to foodstuffs and raw materials, the status of women, racism and racial conflict—by the middle of the twentieth century, all these issues and more had to be evaluated as legitimate threats to peace and security. Strategy, which before the twentieth century had been primarily operational and military in focus, could no longer be effective if it ignored the increasingly complicated and integrated modern world system. Grand strategists had to see the whole picture, not just the battlefield, and they had to peer into the future, not just solve the problems of the present. For this reason, it is probably better to think of plural grand strategies rather than a singular grand strategy.

While it is clear that strategy was born of military and political necessity, grand strategy was born of the need to fit military and political matters into a larger framework. As the case of PEPFAR demonstrates, developing strategies designed to win wars has not been enough to ensure a state's national security or international standing. Strategic studies must therefore take a wider accounting of what is considered "effective" or successful beyond military effectiveness on the battlefield and diplomatic success in the corridors of power.[33]

Recent events underscore the point: strategic thinking in realms other than military security, such as public health, might be even more important in the long run. In the midst of the COVID-19 pandemic, science commentator Anjana Ahuja lamented "the skewed risk-benefit calculations that see bottomless riches apportioned to anti-terrorism measures and a begging bowl to disease control."[34] History is instructive here, too: the global scale and scope of the coronavirus pandemic of 2020 are eerily reminiscent of the experience of the influenza pandemic of 1918–19. That pandemic infected 20 to 30 percent of the world's population, accounting for as many as 50 million deaths (estimates range from nearly 18 million to over 100 million), including roughly 675,000 Americans. In the United States, induction camps, cramped quarters, wartime transport, and industry generated optimal conditions for the flu to spread.

Around the world, global interconnection had reached an apex in world history allowing the flu to reach much of the world in a scant four months and to circumnavigate the globe within a year.[35] Though it came to be known as the "Spanish flu," that epithet was the product of political and racial rhetoric rather than science. It emerged in weaponized nationalist form in the British and American press because of skepticism about the pro-Austro-Hungarian leanings of neutral Spain, where the press covered the flu in ways the combatant nations did not permit when Spain's King Alfonso XIII became ill in the spring of 1918. Still, there was no monopoly on wrapping the virus in national stigma: the Spanish sometimes called it the "French flu," while the Germans termed it the "Russian pest." In the United States, Woodrow Wilson's administration took no preemptive public health actions. In correspondence with wartime allies, US military leaders minimized the risk of illness, deriding it at first as a "three-day fever" throughout spring and summer 1918. Wilson never even addressed the American people publicly about the pandemic. Perhaps most shockingly, even in the wake of the pandemic the United States did not develop an internal national public health infrastructure or collaborate with the new League of Nations on a multinational strategy to prevent future outbreaks.

The very martial language of combating the virus was a product of the politico-racial antagonisms of the wartime environment and was generated by the ways in which modern, industrial nations came to muster their resources to confront enormous challenges, be they war or infectious disease. Among the historical insights we can derive from 1918–19 is that without a cohesive public health strategy, both national and international, the devastation was amplified. Wartime and hyper-patriotic pressures in the United States and Britain prevented the adoption of non-pharmaceutical interventions such as school closures, bans on gatherings, enhanced hand hygiene, quarantine, and social distancing that public health officials knew would help prevent spread and ameliorate suffering. The strategic priorities of war took precedence over a cohesive public health strategy, and as a result, six times as many Americans died from influenza than died in the war, and more American soldiers succumbed to the flu and other diseases than died in combat. The supposedly novel interconnectedness of our globalized world is actually not so different from the conditions of 1918–19; now, as then, those connections magnify the problem of pandemics and necessitate longer-term national and international planning.[36]

In peacetime, or simply in moments of relative peace, grand strategists (and grand strategies) balance priorities, calibrate means to ends, and preserve essential interests not simply against enemies and competitors but also in relation to allies and neutrals, all of which requires marshaling a society's military, economic, diplomatic, cultural, and even ethical resources. In the current international climate, states take a larger view than developing policies to ensure "victory" in current or prospective future armed conflicts. Having a grand strategy for peace means finding alternatives to armed confrontations in order to secure positive outcomes and, if no other alternative presents itself and war ensues, ensuring that a state will be better off in victory than it had been before the war. The most effective grand strategists plan for a postwar settlement in which their state's external environment is conducive not just to that state's interests but to the interests of entire regions and blocs of nations as well. Conversely, the most notorious episodes in modern history have often come as the result of badly conceived grand strategies in which unrealistic ends outpaced available means.

In approaching grand strategy, scholars and policymakers therefore need to consider phenomena—such as race, religion, health, and culture—that are essential to comprehending the world around them but have nonetheless been neglected from traditional grand-strategic analysis. Just as neglected in the American grand-strategic canon are historical and contemporary actors who have usually been kept at arm's length from the policymaking process. According to one study, in the making of strategy, "the playing field is skewed, dominated by powerful, mainstream voices. . . . Policy options that do not fit neatly into an established story are treated as beyond the pale, rarely heard and easily dismissed."[37] Those often-ignored phenomena and people are addressed in the chapters of *Rethinking American Grand Strategy*.

To be sure, sweeping visions of relations between peoples must, on some level, consider the state and interstate relations.[38] Strategy sits, as military historian Hew Strachan notes, in the interstices between war and politics; at certain moments, it connects war and politics in order to achieve immediate goals and make possible long-term objectives.[39] Inescapably, strategy is, and always has been, an act of statecraft. But it is not *only* that. Either in practice or in analysis, grand strategy need not be limited to formal statecraft, and by expanding our frame of reference beyond the state and interstate relations we aim to arrive at a fuller, richer understanding of the sources and mechanisms of human relations in a global age.

Toward a New Definition of Grand Strategy

As a complement to the perspective on grand strategy that has dominated the field, this book proposes to build on the concept of strategic culture.[40] Premised on the inherent relationship between culture and strategy, this perspective reflects political scientist Jack Snyder's call to explore "the body of attitudes and beliefs that guides and circumscribes thought on strategic questions, influences the way strategic issues are formulated, and sets the vocabulary and perceptual parameters of strategic debate."[41] As military theorist Colin Gray argues, an intimate and intricate bond exists between strategic culture and the decisions made by those in positions of responsibility within a security community. Strategic culture "can be conceived as a context out there that surrounds, and gives meaning to, strategic behavior" and "should be approached both as a shaping context for behavior and itself as a constituent of that behavior." According to Gray, "Everything a security community does, if not a manifestation of strategic culture, is at least an example of behavior effected by culturally shaped, or encultured, people, organizations, procedures, and weapons."[42] Although the impact of strategic culture is often subtle, it is ubiquitous and applies to groups, ideas, and beliefs operating outside of formal politics and policymaking. As such, we propose to include the widest possible range of cultural conditions that "shape the perceptions strategists have of material conditions" as well as the outcomes they seek.[43] Doing so yields surprises that deepen as well as broaden our understanding of grand strategy. As the chapters in this book illustrate, hidden grand strategies and strategists abound in the historical record.

Following the insights of Nina Silove, this book highlights three main types of grand strategy: "grand plans," "grand principles," and "grand behavior." Each of these types, she argues, has its own value, and they all need not be seen in opposition; indeed, viewed comprehensively, they allow for a more thoroughgoing understanding of what grand strategy is in theory and has been, historically, in practice. While we hope to offer conceptual clarity in the study of grand strategy, we also want to emulate Silove's broad thinking and avoid the strict policing of disciplinary boundaries she rightly critiques.[44]

Consequently, a key intervention of *Rethinking American Grand Strategy* is to approach grand strategy as an epistemology—that is, as a theory of knowledge of international history that organizes outcomes around methods, means, and desired ends. When viewed as a way of organizing knowledge, situated within and emanating from a distinct historical and cultural context, the idea of grand strategy becomes more mobile, its content and operation more readily apparent. Such an approach recognizes the diagnostic, philosophic, prescriptive, historical, and programmatic elements of grand strategy. It expands our reach beyond military means or high-level state actors, both of which have dominated a literature concerned primarily with the applications of hard power and the conduct of warfare.

If global power is to some extent diffuse, it follows that, as historian Akira Iriye suggests, the world is "created and recreated as much by individuals from 'lesser powers' as by the great powers." In contrast to the traditional power-politics narrative, Iriye observes that "individuals and groups of people from different lands have sought to develop an alternative community of nations and peoples on the basis of their cultural interchanges and that, while frequently ridiculed by practitioners of power politics and ignored by historians, their efforts have significantly altered the world community and immeasurably enriched our understanding of world affairs."[45] In this volume, the contributors heed Iriye's call to broaden the conceptual frame of international history. This new conception comprises sweeping strategic visions of race, gender, religion, law, transnational activism, international organizations, and core values. This more expansive view does not downplay the centrality of traditional "hard" power, and it does not ask us to ignore the world of high politics, great powers, and international orders. Yet it does call on those who study and practice grand strategy to broaden their perspective and situate unconventional issues alongside the more conventional concerns.

Yet while power can be diffuse, there are parts of the world in which power is more concentrated than others. The United States is one of those places, and for this reason this volume uses it as a benchmark to rethink grand strategy in history.[46] While some scholars insist that only great powers can, by definition, have a grand strategy,[47] we have not chosen to focus on the United States for this reason. For one thing, the contemporary United States is home to a disproportionate number of university grand-strategy programs, which in turn provide much of the recent scholarly work on the topic. But as a topic in its own right, the study of American grand strategy offers a wide range of complementary benefits: few states in the international system project power like the United States. More to the point, very few, if any, other states deploy virtually all forms of social power—military, economic, intellectual, and political—in their engagement with the wider world as the United States does.[48] Moreover, few states have a foreign policy that imbricates, but is also bedeviled by, such a wide array of social and cultural phenomena ranging from race and religion to gender and sexuality. And few states have generated and participated in a vast range of strategic projects that might be understood as "grand." The United States is a large, diverse country with an active, complex foreign policy that is both globally active but also deeply rooted in domestic politics; it provides scholars with a suitable laboratory for experimenting with the concept of grand strategy. Thus the scale and reach of American power, both hard and soft, make it an ideal subject for a revisionist study such as this.

If the United States provides a good focus for rethinking grand strategy, history provides an ideal discipline. Indeed, it is no coincidence that historians of American foreign relations have in recent years pursued an ever-widening array of diverse subjects, along the way innovating new methodologies and theories and blazing new disciplinary trails for international history as a whole.[49] Political scientists and theorists of international relations occupy a prominent place in the study of grand strategy, but for the most part even they approach the topic historically—that is, with qualitative methods and with a deep engagement with the past. This is not a coincidence. "The study of history seems almost written into the DNA of the field," concludes one study of grand strategy by three political scientists.[50] Grand strategy is endlessly complex, which makes studying it with quantitative methods difficult; it is more a branch of political thought or political theory, both of which are deeply historical, than other aspects of political science. Similarly, history is usually the preferred method in teaching grand strategy.[51] For these reasons, the contributions to *Rethinking American Grand Strategy* come predominantly from historians, and they have approached the subject by way of examining the past.

Case Study II: Barack Obama, Reluctant Strategist

For all its power and range, the United States is hardly omnipotent. In fact, conducting US grand strategy has become so complex that attempting to do so is close to being mission impossible.[52] Seeking a way through this complexity by reducing his overriding approach to one concise, explicit statement, Barack Obama chose four simple words: "Don't do stupid shit."[53] Obama was not simply warning against ill-considered policies and half-baked operations in the wake of the Iraq War—he was also expressing his disdain for grand-strategic thinking of any kind.

But Obama and his closest advisers went further with their critique. They refused to countenance the national security intellectuals and architects from think tanks and universities who had agitated for regime change in Iraq and who now offered the administration their own visions for America's purpose in the world. One of Obama's closest aides, Deputy National Security Advisor Ben Rhodes, memorably described this Washington-based foreign-policy elite as "the Blob," an amorphous group of centrist Republicans and Democrats, many with area expertise, who were suspected of having a vested interest in keeping America active in the world. The Blob, Obama and Rhodes implied, was an undifferentiated and unthinking mass with unstoppable force but little actual purpose in the practical formulation of US foreign policy. Americans had to be more realistic, Obama and Rhodes argued. They had to deal with "the world as it is," as Rhodes titled his memoir of his time in the Obama administration, and not try in vain to remake it how they wished it to be.[54]

Despite Obama's repudiation of the national security establishment, his administration did not shirk the intellectual work essential to the policy-making process. In fact, Rhodes helped preside over the largest NSC staff in US history.[55] And Obama's foreign policy did not lack for ambition—witness his attempted rapprochement with Cuba, his nuclear deal with Iran, and his pivot to East Asia. Rather, Obama's concern focused in particular on those grandiose initiatives—the kind that led the nation into Iraq—in which the nation's aims greatly exceeded its means. Instead of remaking the world, Obama wanted to avoid the Blob's "stupid shit" which, inevitably, led to tragedy.

As Obama discovered, though, avoiding stupid shit is not as straightforward as it sounds. After all, shit happens.[56] Following the outbreak of civil war in Syria, in March 2011, he came under increasingly heavy domestic pressure to intervene in support of the rebels fighting the government of Bashar al-Assad. At the very least, many of his advisers wanted him to authorize the sale of US weapons to the rebels. Obama refused to do either, but this only brought him greater criticism at home. In August 2012—during the escalating Syrian civil war but, more crucially, in the midst of a presidential election campaign—he declared at a press conference that the United States would intervene if Assad or his allies crossed "a red line" by using chemical weapons. When Assad's forces openly crossed that line a year later, by using chemical weapons in an attack on Eastern Ghouta, Obama did not respond by deploying American power. He instead sought congressional approval for military strikes against Syria, and, while Congress debated intervention, Russian President Vladimir Putin filled the breach by brokering a settlement with Assad that made US intervention unnecessary. In his attempt to avoid repeating Bush's mistakes in Iraq, Obama had boxed himself in on Syria. He side-stepped one pile of stupid shit only to step right in another.

Few Americans wanted to repeat their misadventure in Iraq. But while Obama's desire to avoid foreign entanglements was widespread, it was not universal, and his critics, including some inside his own national security team, took him to task for avoiding grand strategy. For these critics, the Obama administration's commitment to a more deliberative, realism-driven foreign policy was itself a failure. Samantha Power, a passionate advocate of humanitarian intervention and a key member of Obama's national security team, frequently tried to goad the president into doing more.[57] Hillary Clinton, who served as Obama's first secretary of state and nearly became his successor as president, chafed at the administration's strategic lethargy.

"Great nations need organizing principles," she told an interviewer after leaving the State Department and during the long run-up to the 2016 presidential election. Attempting to avoid making mistakes "is not an organizing principle."[58] Others chimed in. "This administration is notable for its lack of grand strategy—or strategists," the *Washington Post* intoned in 2010. In his *Newsweek* column, historian Niall Ferguson blamed Obama's struggles in the Middle East on a "lack of any kind of a coherent grand strategy, a deficit about which more than a few veterans of US foreign policymaking have long worried."[59]

The contrasting strategic problems of two recent presidents, Bush and Obama—one criticized for doing too much, the other too little—seem to suggest that the key problem lies not with the principle of having a grand strategy. Indeed, as Obama discovered in the wake of his non-intervention in Syria, a president cannot be without a grand strategy.[60] Nor can the president simply appear to be "leading from behind," as one of his advisers put it when the British and French took the initiative during the 2011 invasion of Libya.[61] Obama learned from these mistakes. After his Libyan and Syrian debacles, he devised a more coherent—and successful—grand strategy of restrained engagement designed to reduce tensions and normalize relations with historic enemies like Cuba and Iran.

Obama's journey to discovering his grand strategy was painful but hardly unusual. Leaders of the most powerful state in the international system have found it difficult to avoid thinking strategically even when they have wanted to. Presidents, who sit at the very center of that power, need to conceive of ways in which that power can be projected efficiently, effectively, and morally, factoring in American ideals alongside national interests. As political scientist and foreign-policy columnist Daniel Drezner observes, national security officials must strike a delicate balance when devising a grand strategy. On one hand, they must do enough strategic planning to chart a successful path in the world and not entangle the United States in lost causes and unnecessary wars. On the other, they have to guard against the common tendency of strategizing too grandly and leading the nation, and the world, into interventionist disasters, such as the wars in Vietnam and Iraq.[62] Sometimes formalizing and codifying strategy has had a stultifying effect on foreign policy; at other times, in its quest to find solutions, grand strategy has created problems where none had existed.[63] David Milne reminds us, in his contribution to this volume and elsewhere, that diplomacy is as much an art as it is a science.[64] Getting it right is difficult.

Rethinking American Grand Strategy

Generally, courses in grand strategy have tended to exalt far-sighted individuals, usually decision makers from elite backgrounds struggling against the shortsighted constraints of the small-minded. Though there is less of that thinking today, as contributor Beverly Gage reveals all too often such coursework or scholarship has been a kind of "Great Man" theory of history on steroids, with the Great Man serving simultaneously as a detached analyst and the object of study—for example, Henry Kissinger's classic work *Diplomacy*, along with his more recent book, *World Order*.[65] Laws and norms, culture and collaboration, economic development, gender, race, sexuality, public health, social movements, and non-governmental organizations are all eclipsed by Kissinger's more concentrated understanding, however erudite it may be, of the historical development and utility of grand strategy. Nonetheless, these neglected subjects contribute to the capacious vision of twenty-first-century security that Kissinger's work, in fact, aims to achieve.

Such latent notions of "rethinking," or "re-conception," serve as grand strategy's historical leitmotif. Methodologically, then, *Rethinking American Grand Strategy* builds on the previous literature in two ways. First, it broadens the range of topics treated historically, as well as the range of scholars from outside the field of conventional diplomatic and military history. Second, it offers specific, empirically detailed case studies to demonstrate why history matters in developing new thematic approaches to a more expansive understanding of grand strategy. The main purpose of the chapters in this volume is to expand the boundaries of what constitutes grand strategy, who the actors are, and how one engages with the field.

While keeping statecraft as a central focus, these new interventions undermine and complicate the definitions of state interests and enhance our appreciation of the "intermestic"—the interaction and overlap between domestic and international affairs.[66] At the intersection of race and grand strategy in this volume, for example, Adriane Lentz-Smith explores historically marginalized actors who articulated their own alternative visions of the United States in the world that continue to resonate today. Christopher Nichols's chapter similarly traces W. E. B. Du Bois's black-nationalist worldview as it adapted elements of the language of "self-determination" advanced by Woodrow Wilson and turned it against articulations of US democracy promotion. Other chapters complicate the "intermestic" in similarly provocative ways. Emily Conroy-Krutz's chapter on foreign missions makes a case not just for the importance of religion in the history of US foreign relations but in the very ways we conceptualize grand strategy. Daniel Tichenor shows that the sweep of immigration policy can be categorized and understood in grand-strategic terms. Laura Briggs argues that transnational adoption, and reproductive politics more broadly, must be understood as key elements in a broader US grand strategy.

The complexity of grand strategy as an analytic problem is also reflected in a measure of disagreement among our contributors on matters of scope, scale, and valence. There is even a good deal of skepticism about the very legitimacy of the concept itself. By contrast, others question the need to expand the parameters of grand strategy. The scholars in this volume therefore do not unanimously agree on exactly what constitutes grand strategy, let alone its dimensions and scope. They nonetheless concur that we should continue to study grand strategy even as we expand its terms. In the end, this volume does not claim to offer a definitive answer to what grand strategy absolutely is, or has been. Indeed, asking questions and offering new possibilities, rather than providing a dispositive settlement to a large and growing field, is the mission that lies at the heart of this book.

Rethinking American Grand Strategy is organized into five parts. It begins by establishing a firm foundation of definitions, debates, and key ideas before moving on to situate them historically from the late eighteenth century to the present. It then shifts to focus on (re)assessments of key figures and groups before concluding with a dynamic set of new approaches and reflections for rethinking the history of American grand strategy in new and even radical ways.

Part I, "Frameworks," offers new perspectives on some fundamental debates about American grand strategy. It opens with Hal Brands making the case for doing grand-strategic historical analysis properly by highlighting several fallacies scholars should avoid. Beverly Gage then proposes a theory of social movements as a new lens through which to perceive grand strategy. Bradley and Taylor's analysis of PEPFAR follows as an example of how the principles outlined in the first two chapters can be applied.

Part II, "Historical Grand Narratives," provides a sweeping chronological overview of American grand strategy from the nation's founding to the current era. The chapters move from the grand-strategic calculus embedded in the Federalist Papers to the role of Southerners and slavery in US foreign policy before the Civil War, and from grand strategies related to naval power to the most ascendant ideas at work in America's rise as to become a global power and then superpower since the end of World War I.

Part III, "Recasting Central Figures," examines some of the most familiar historical actors in the study of American grand strategy: Woodrow Wilson, W. E. B. DuBois, Franklin D. Roosevelt, Edward Mead Earle, George F. Kennan, Richard Nixon, Henry Kissinger, and George H. W. Bush. But as Michaela Hoenicke-Moore illustrates, ordinary Americans, central figures in a foreign policy conditioned by democratic politics and popular opinion, must also be considered. In these chapters, scholars reconsider these central figures by shedding new light on their principles, policies, and context.

The fourth part, "New Approaches," builds on the foundations established by the previous chapters to propose a range of new ways to study grand strategy. Many of these approaches, such as reproductive rights, public health, the environment, humanitarianism, immigration, and race, have not featured much in the voluminous existing literature. Other topics, such as war, law, domestic politics, and religion, may have appeared in previous scholarship but not necessarily in the ways presented here. Collectively, these chapters are informed by social history's emphasis on the importance of voices from below. This bottom-up perspective is not intended to supplant grand strategy's usual top-down focus on strategic leaders and thinkers. Instead, it is meant to offer complementary approaches that will make the study of grand strategy more rounded, better informed, and more consistent with how the world actually operates.

The final part offers two chapters that use the halcyon days of American grand strategy—the mid-twentieth-century moment when victory in World War II and the first years of the Cold War saw the United States become the most powerful state in the world—to reflect on the meaning and limits of grand strategy's history.

Ultimately, this book argues that the strategic-cultural umbrella provided by an epistemological way of conceiving of the history of grand strategy has tremendous potential. It forces us toward a broader vision of the national, international, and transnational dimensions of the United States and the world. Our more expansive view does not downplay the centrality of traditional "hard" power, nor does it ignore the world of high politics, great powers, and international orders. But it does call on those who study and practice grand strategy to expand their perspective and situate unconventional issues alongside the more traditional concerns. This book therefore presents a challenge to which we hope future scholars and policymakers will respond in surprising and exciting ways.

Notes

1. Scholars routinely note that there is no single, authoritative definition of "grand strategy." For the most thoughtful of the recent analyses, see Lukas Milevski, *The Evolution of Modern Grand Strategic Thought* (Oxford: Oxford University Press, 2016); Nina Silove, "Beyond the Buzzword: The Three Meanings of 'Grand Strategy,'" *Security Studies* 27 (2018), 27–57; and Thierry Balzacq, Peter Dombrowski, and Simon Reich, "Is Grand Strategy a Research Program?" *Security Studies* 28 (2019), 58–86. While it is true that grand strategy lacks an agreed definition, this is also true for many concepts (such as "ideology" or "liberalism") as well as for seemingly self-evident categories of analysis (such as "religion" or "gender"), all of which are nonetheless subjects of intensive study.
2. Paul Kennedy, "Grand Strategy in War and Peace: Toward a Broader Definition," in *Grand Strategies in War and Peace*, ed. Paul Kennedy (New Haven, CT: Yale University Press, 1991), 5. Emphasis in original.
3. John Lewis Gaddis, *On Grand Strategy* (New York: Penguin Press, 2018), 21.
4. Hal Brands, *What Good Is Grand Strategy? Power and Purpose in American Statecraft from Harry S. Truman to George W. Bush* (Ithaca, NY: Cornell University Press, 2014), 1. This is the definition many of the contributors to this volume use or adapt themselves.
5. Peter Feaver, "What Is Grand Strategy and Why Do We Need It?," *Foreign Policy*, April 8, 2009, http://shadow.foreignpolicy.com/posts/2009/04/08/what_is_grand_strategy_and_why_do_we_need_it.
6. Stephen M. Walt, "The Case for Finite Containment: Analyzing US Grand Strategy," *International Security* 14 (Summer 1989), 6.
7. Colin S. Gray, *War, Peace and International Relations: An Introduction to Strategic History*, 2nd ed. (New York: Routledge, 2012), 349.
8. Most notably, see Edward Luttwak, *Strategy: The Logic of War and Peace* (Cambridge, MA: Harvard University Press, 1987); and Hew Strachan, *The Direction of War: Contemporary Strategy in Historical Perspective* (Cambridge: Cambridge University Press, 2013). The IR theorist Robert J. Art holds a slightly more expansive view of grand strategy, but still rests it on a foundation of warfare—why, when, how to fight them, and how to win them—because this is the main way to distinguish "grand strategy" from "foreign policy." See Robert J. Art, "A Defensible Defense: America's Grand Strategy after the Cold War," *International Security* 15 (Spring 1991), 5–53; and Robert J. Art, *America's Grand Strategy and World Politics* (New York: Routledge, 2009). In a similar vein, see Patrick Porter, "Why America's Grand Strategy Has Not

Changed: Power, Habit, and the US Foreign Policy Establishment," *International Security* 42 (Spring 2018), 9–46.

9. See, for example, Williamson Murray, "Thoughts on Grand Strategy," in *The Shaping of Grand Strategy: Policy, Diplomacy, and War*, ed. Williamson Murray, Richard Hart Sinnreich, and James Lacey (Cambridge: Cambridge University Press, 2011), 6.

10. The literature here is endless, but for a recent, succinct, and above all persuasive overview, see Jens Bartelson, *War in International Thought* (Cambridge: Cambridge University Press, 2018).

11. Following Kennedy's definition, quoted above, scholars have explored how grand strategy aims to shape the peace following a major war. For example, see G. John Ikenberry, *After Victory: Institutions, Strategic Restraint, and the Rebuilding of Order after Major Wars* (Princeton, NJ: Princeton University Press, 2001); and Williamson Murray and James Lacey, eds., *The Making of Peace: Rulers, States, and the Aftermath of War* (Cambridge: Cambridge University Press, 2008).

12. Balzacq, Dombrowski, and Reich, "Is Grand Strategy a Research Program?," 69.

13. Thomas Meaney and Stephen Wertheim, "Grand Flattery: The Yale Grand Strategy Seminar," *The Nation*, May 28, 2012, 27–31.

14. Richard K. Betts, "The Grandiosity of Grand Strategy," *Washington Quarterly* 42:4 (Winter 2020), 7.

15. The literature, published mostly in the last two or three decades, illustrating how gender, sexuality, and race were a part of the history of American foreign relations, is too vast to cite here. But for leading examples, see Kristin L. Hoganson, *Fighting for American Manhood: How Gender Politics Provoked the Spanish-American and Philippine-American Wars* (New Haven, CT: Yale University Press, 1998); Thomas Borstelmann, *The Cold War and the Color Line: American Race Relations in the Global Arena* (Cambridge, MA: Harvard University Press, 2001); Carol Anderson, *Eyes Off the Prize: The United Nations and the African American Struggle for Human Rights, 1944–1955* (New York: Cambridge University Press, 2003); Mary Dudziak, *Cold War Civil Rights: Race and the Image of American Democracy* (Princeton, NJ: Princeton University Press, 2000); David K. Johnson, *The Lavender Scare: The Cold War Persecution of Gays and Lesbians in the Federal Government* (Chicago: University of Chicago Press, 2004); and Robert Vitalis, *White World Order, Black Power Politics: The Birth of American International Relations* (Ithaca, NY: Cornell University Press, 2015).

16. On considering the Bush administration in grand-strategic terms, see two articles by John Lewis Gaddis: "A Grand Strategy of Transformation," *Foreign Policy* 133 (November–December 2002), 50–57; and "Grand Strategy in the Second Term," *Foreign Affairs* 84 (January–February 2005), 2–15.

17. Bob Woodward, *Plan of Attack* (New York: Simon & Schuster, 2004), 325–332.

18. Quoted in Bob Woodward, *The War Within* (New York: Simon & Schuster, 2008), 174.

19. For the most thorough appraisal of the Surge, which includes praise as well as criticism, see Timothy Andrews Sayle, Jeffrey A. Engel, Hal Brands, and William Inboden, eds., *The Last Card: Inside George W. Bush's Decision to Surge in Iraq* (Ithaca, NY: Cornell University Press, 2019).

20. Quoted in Woodward, *The War Within*, 343.

21. Murray, "Thoughts on Grand Strategy," 5; Balzacq, Dombrowski, and Reich, "Is Grand Strategy a Research Program?," 66.

22. A penetrating insight gleaned from Silove, "Beyond the Buzzword."

23. With apologies to Raymond Carver and Nathan Englander.

24. Charles Edel, *Nation Builder: John Quincy Adams and the Grand Strategy of the Republic* (Cambridge, MA: Harvard University Press, 2014), 5.

25. Barry R. Posen, *The Sources of Military Doctrine: France, Britain, and Germany between the World Wars* (Ithaca. NY: Cornell University Press, 1984), 13. For a more recent, slightly revised version—this time applied specifically to the United States—see Barry R. Posen, *Restraint: A New Foundation for US Grand Strategy* (Ithaca, NY: Cornell University Press, 2014), 1.

26. Jennifer Mitzen, "Illusion or Intention? Talking Grand Strategy into Existence," *Security Studies* 24 (2015), 62.

27. This formulation of grand strategy is based on the authoritative definition of "national security" as devised by Melvyn P. Leffler. See his *A Preponderance of Power: National Security, the Truman Administration, and the Cold War* (Stanford, CA: Stanford University Press, 1992); and *Safeguarding Democratic Capitalism: US Foreign Policy and National Security, 1920-2015* (Princeton, NJ: Princeton University Press), 317-335.

28. As insightfully achieved by Gaddis in *On Grand Strategy*, and as many grand strategy courses challenge students to do.

29. Perhaps this is why two important historical overviews of strategy as practiced around the world since antiquity more or less ignore grand strategy. See Peter Paret, ed., *Makers of Modern Strategy: From Machiavelli to the Nuclear Age* (Princeton, NJ: Princeton University Press, 1986); and Williamson Murray, Alvin Bernstein, and MacGregor Knox, eds., *The Making of Strategy: Rulers, States, and War* (Cambridge: Cambridge University Press, 1994).

30. For the most thorough of recent accounts of this conceptual history, see Beatrice Heuser, *The Evolution of Strategy: Thinking War from Antiquity to the Present* (Cambridge: Cambridge University Press, 2010); and Lawrence Freedman, *Strategy: A History* (Oxford: Oxford University Press, 2013). But for a condensed version, split into two parts, see Lawrence Freedman, "The Meaning of Strategy, Part I: The Origins," *Texas National Security Review* 1 (December 2017), 90–105; and "The Meaning of Strategy, Part II: The Objectives," *Texas National Security Review* 1 (February 2018), 34–57.

31. These observations, courtesy of Google Books NGram Viewer, come from searches of the phrase "grand strategy" (accessed August 11, 2019).

32. Kennedy, "Grand Strategy in War and Peace," 2–7.

33. Among the best of such studies, however, are Allan R. Millett and Williamson Murray, eds., *Military Effectiveness*, 3 vols. (Cambridge: Cambridge University Press, 1988); John Lewis Gaddis, *Strategies of Containment: A Critical Appraisal of American National Security Policy during the Cold War*, rev. ed. (New York: Oxford University Press, 2005); William C. Martel, *Victory in War: Foundations of Modern Military Policy* (Cambridge: Cambridge University Press, 2007); Williamson

Murray, *War, Strategy, and Military Effectiveness* (Cambridge: Cambridge University Press, 2011); Williamson Murray and Richard Hart Sinnreich, eds., *Successful Strategies: Triumphing in War and Peace from Antiquity to the Present* (Cambridge: Cambridge University Press, 2014); and Ann Hironaka, *Tokens of Power: Rethinking War* (Cambridge: Cambridge University Press, 2017).

34. Anjana Ahuja, "The War on Germs," *Financial Times*, April 11–12, 2020, Books section, 8. Her observation here was drawn from Michael T. Osterholm and Mark Olshaker, *Deadliest Enemy: Our War against Killer Germs* (New York: Little, Brown, 2020).

35. This era of globalization now has a large scholarly literature, but a good place to start is Emily S. Rosenberg, ed., *A World Connecting: 1870–1945* (Cambridge, MA: Harvard University Press, 2012).

36. On the US reaction to the 1918–19 flu pandemic, see Christopher McKnight Nichols, "President Trump's Desire to Reopen Businesses Quickly Is Dangerous," *Washington Post*, March 25, 2020, https://www.washingtonpost.com/outlook/2020/03/25/president-trumps-desire-reopen-businesses-quickly-is-dangerous/; Christopher McKnight Nichols, "Oregon Response to Flu in 1918 Offers Insights for Coronavirus Fight in 2020," *The Oregonian*, April 5, 2020, https://www.oregonlive.com/opinion/2020/04/opinion-oregon-response-to-flu-in-1918-offers-insights-for-coronavirus-fight-in-2020.html; Christopher McKnight Nichols et al., Roundtable, in the *Journal of the Gilded Age and Progressive Era* (October 2020). See also John Barry, *The Great Influenza: The Story of the Deadliest Pandemic in History* (New York: Viking, 2004); and Nancy Bristow, *American Pandemic: Lost Worlds of the 1918 Influenza Epidemic* (New York: Oxford University Press, 2012).

37. Ronald R. Krebs and David M. Edelstein, "Delusions of Grand Strategy: The Problem with Washington's Planning Obsession," *Foreign Affairs* 94 (November/December 2015), 109–116, 116.

38. Charles Hill, *Grand Strategies: Literature, Statecraft, and World Order* (New Haven, CT: Yale University Press, 2010), prologue, 88.

39. Strachan, *Direction of War*, 20–23.

40. Alastair Johnston, "Thinking about Strategic Culture," *International Security* 19 (Spring 1995), 32–64.

41. Jack L. Snyder, *The Soviet Strategic Culture: Implications for Limited Nuclear Operations* (Santa Monica, CA: Rand Corporation, 1977), 9.

42. Colin S. Gray, "Strategic Culture as Context: The First Generation of Theory Strikes Back," *Review of International Studies* 25 (January 1999), 50–52.

43. Johnston, "Thinking about Strategic Culture"; Darryl Howlett, "Strategic Culture: Reviewing Recent Literature," *Strategic Insights* 6 (November 2005), http://hdl.handle.net/10945/11212

44. Silove, "Beyond the Buzzword," 55–57.

45. Akira Iriye, *Cultural Internationalism and World Order* (Baltimore: Johns Hopkins University Press, 1997), 2.

46. On the value of US-centric approaches, see Daniel Bessner and Fredrik Logevall, "Recentering the United States in the Historiography of American Foreign

Relations," *Texas National Security Review* 3 (Spring 2020), https://tnsr.org/2020/04/recentering-the-united-states-in-the-historiography-of-american-foreign-relations/

47. See, for example, Murray, "Thoughts on Grand Strategy," 1.

48. This follows the classic typology of power developed in Michael Mann, *The Sources of Social Power*, 4 vols. (Cambridge: Cambridge University Press, 1986–2013).

49. Americanists are not the only innovators within international history, but no other grouping of international historians has reflected or innovated as much. For a primer, see the essays in Frank Costigliola and Michael J. Hogan, eds., *Explaining the History of American Foreign Relations*, 3rd ed. (New York: Cambridge University Press, 2016).

50. Balzacq, Dombrowski, and Reich, "Is Grand Strategy a Research Program," 83. See also Williamson Murray and Richard Hart Sinnreich, *The Past as Prologue: The Importance of History to the Military Profession* (Cambridge: Cambridge University Press, 2006); Hill, *Grand Strategies*; Peter R. Mansoor and Williamson Murray, eds., *Grand Strategy and Military Alliances* (Cambridge: Cambridge University Press, 2016); and Gaddis, *On Grand Strategy*.

51. Robert Ralston et al, "Teaching Grand Strategy," *H-Diplo Roundtable* 21 (April 2020), https://issforum.org/roundtables/PDF/Roundtable-XXI-35.pdf.

52. Robert Jervis, "US Grand Strategy: Mission Impossible," *Naval War College Review* 51 (Summer 1998), 22–36.

53. Jeffrey Goldberg, "The Obama Doctrine," *The Atlantic*, April 2016.

54. Ben Rhodes, *The World as It Is: A Memoir of the Obama White House* (New York: Random House, 2018).

55. According to the *Washington Post*, "Obama's NSC staff has been widely criticized for its size—at least 400 people at its zenith, more than half of them policy advisers, with the rest in administration and technology support—and for what some of his former Cabinet officials have called excessive "micromanagement" of their departments." When Susan Rice joined the Obama administration in July 2013, "she reduced the overall staff size by 15 percent and cut policy and senior staff positions by 17 percent, to fewer than 180." "Rice Favors 'Mean but Lean' National Security Council," *Washington Post*, January 17, 2017, www.washingtonpost.com/world/national-security/rice-favors-mean-but-lean-national-security-council/2017/01/16/6244aa3c-dc49-11e6-ad42-f3375f271c9c_story.html?utm_term=.cbf9292494a8. On Rhodes and the "blob," see David Samuels, "The Aspiring Novelist Who Became Obama's Foreign-Policy Guru," *New York Times*, May 5, 2016, https://www.nytimes.com/2016/05/08/magazine/the-aspiring-novelist-who-became-obamas-foreign-policy-guru.html?_r=0.

56. As pointed out, by way of reference to the strategic thought of Napoleon and Clausewitz, in Gaddis, *On Grand Strategy*, 203 (see also 308–309). On the unavoidable importance of contingency in strategy, see Strachan, *Direction of War*, 235–252. There is considerable irony in the fact that Donald Rumsfeld made this very same observation—sanitized as "stuff happens"—as Iraq was descending into chaos shortly after the 2003 US invasion. "Rumsfeld on Looting in Iraq: 'Stuff Happens,'" *CNN*, April 12, 2003, https://edition.cnn.com/2003/US/04/11/sprj.irq.pentagon/. For an

explanation, see Stephen Benedict Dyson, "'Stuff Happens': Donald Rumsfeld and the Iraq War," *Foreign Policy Analysis* 5 (October 2009), 327–347.

57. "We've all read your book, Samantha," an agitated Obama retorted during one meeting when Power was agitating for intervention. The book was her Pulitzer Prize-winning *A Problem from Hell: America and the Age of Genocide* (New York: Basic Books, 2002). Power herself investigates these tensions at some length in *The Education of an Idealist: A Memoir* (New York: Dey Street, 2019). For a penetrating critique of Power's worldview, see Daniel Bessner, "The Fog of Intervention," *New Republic*, September 4, 2019, https://newrepublic.com/article/154612/education-idealist-samantha-power-book-review.

58. Jeffrey Goldberg, "Hillary Clinton: 'Failure' to Help Syrian Rebels Led to the Rise of ISIS," *The Atlantic*, August 2014.

59. Both quoted in Daniel W. Drezner, "Does Obama Have a Grand Strategy? Why We Need Doctrines in Uncertain Times," *Foreign Affairs* 90 (July/August 2011), 57.

60. For contrasting views on this issue, see Daniel W. Drezner, Ronald R. Krebs, and Randall Schweller, "The End of Grand Strategy: America Must Think Small," *Foreign Affairs* 99 (May/June 2020), 107–117; and Andrew Ehrhardt and Maeve Ryan, "Grand Strategy Is No Silver Bullet, but It Is Indispensable," *War on the Rocks*, May 19, 2020, https://warontherocks.com/2020/05/grand-strategy-is-no-silver-bullet-but-it-is-indispensable/.

61. Ryan Lizza, "The Consequentialist," *New Yorker*, May 2, 2011, https://www.newyorker.com/magazine/2011/05/02/the-consequentialist. The remark was highly controversial and Obama himself both denied and disavowed it: David Jackson, "Obama Never Said 'Leading from Behind,'" *USA Today*, October 27, 2011, http://content.usatoday.com/communities/theoval/post/2011/10/obama-never-said-lead-from-behind/1#.XZEriC2ZOik.

62. Drezner, "Does Obama Have a Grand Strategy?" 57–68.

63. For an incisive assessment of whether devising a strategy is actually good strategic practice, see especially Richard K. Betts, "Is Strategy an Illusion?," *International Security* 25 (Fall 2000), 5–50. But see also Steven Metz, "Why Aren't Americans Better at Strategy?," *Military Review* 77 (January–February 1997), 187–190; Jervis, "US Grand Strategy: Mission Impossible"; Colin Gray, "Why Strategy Is Difficult," *Joint Force Quarterly* 22 (Summer 1999): 6–12; Krebs and Edelstein, "Delusions of Grand Strategy"; and Drezner, Krebs, and Schweller, "End of Grand Strategy."

64. David Milne, *Worldmaking: The Art and Science of American Diplomacy* (New York: Farrar, Straus and Giroux, 2015).

65. Beverly Gage, "'Strategy' May Be More Useful to Pawns Than Kings," *New York Times*, September 3, 2018, https://www.nytimes.com/2018/09/03/magazine/strategy-may-be-more-useful-to-pawns-than-to-kings.html; Henry Kissinger, *Diplomacy* (New York: Simon & Schuster, 1994); Henry Kissinger, *World Order* (New York: Penguin, 1994).

66. The term is from Campbell Craig and Fredrik Logevall, *America's Cold War: The Politics of Insecurity* (Cambridge, MA: Harvard University Press, 2009). While the

contributions in this volume add new aspects to our understanding of how national societies shape international grand strategies, they are not the first to draw this connection. See, for example, Richard Rosecrance and Arthur A. Stein, eds., *The Domestic Bases of Grand Strategy* (Ithaca, NY: Cornell University Press, 1993); and Kevin Narizny, *The Political Economy of Grand Strategy* (Ithaca, NY: Cornell University Press, 2007).

PART I
FRAMEWORKS

1

Getting Grand Strategy Right

Clearing Away Common Fallacies in the Grand Strategy Debate

Hal Brands

Grand strategy is a growth industry these days. Books, articles, and other public commentaries on the subject have proliferated in recent years; college and university programs in grand strategy are legion. Yet the concept of grand strategy remains contested and even polarizing. Disagreements about how to define grand strategy persist; disputes about whether grand strategy actually exists remain common, as some of the chapters in this book demonstrate.

No less contentious than the debate over grand strategy as a concept is the debate over American grand strategy today. Core questions about America's role in the world are at issue: Is America in irreversible decline, or can it reassert its international primacy? Can Washington pivot from one region to another, or do losses in one region undermine gains elsewhere? Will the American public bear the burdens of global leadership in coming years? How has the presidency of Donald Trump shifted America's approach to global affairs, and what will the long-term effects be for US grand strategy? More broadly, analysts debate whether it is even possible for the United States to articulate and implement a coherent grand strategy in a domestic environment characterized by bitter partisanship and an international environment characterized by myriad and diverse challenges and considerable geopolitical complexity.

Debate is all to the good, of course. But these debates over grand strategy in general, and American grand strategy in particular, are clouded by fundamental misconceptions about the basic nature and purpose of grand strategy. Accordingly, this chapter seeks to bring greater clarity to these debates by reviewing ten common fallacies in the study of grand strategy, and clarifying the misconceptions underlying them. Clearing away this conceptual confusion can lead to more productive debates about grand strategy writ large; it can also better inform discussions about the prospects for American grand strategy today.[1]

Fallacy #1: Defining Grand Strategy Too Broadly or Too Narrowly

The first common fallacy in the study of grand strategy is a definitional one. Some analysts ask the concept of grand strategy to bear more weight than it should be expected to carry, by defining it as "the alignment of national ends, ways, and means."[2] Such a grand strategy would be truly, breathtakingly grand, bringing together—in coherent fashion—all aspects of foreign *and* domestic policy. It is not clear that the United States has ever really done strategizing on this scale, except in the tautological fashion that defines strategy as the sum total of all policy on all dimensions. If we are looking for great powers that have done this sort of strategizing, the best examples might be the Soviet Union or Communist China, with the elaboration of their encompassing five-year plans. At any rate, this is an unsatisfying definition, for it tells policymakers little about how they should actually *do* grand strategy in practice.

Others set the criteria for qualifying as a grand strategy too narrowly, requiring a label that commands consensus political support before acknowledging that a grand strategy exists. This might be called the "containment fallacy," reflecting the notion that America had a coherent grand strategy during the Cold War because US foreign policy had a pithy label during those decades, and the failure to settle on a similar label since 1991 means that there has necessarily been no grand strategy. In reality, the containment label was used throughout the Cold War, but what it meant changed markedly over time. Some administrations even shunned or modified that label altogether. Moreover, the general acceptance of "containment" as a label hardly resolved the intense—even vitriolic—debates about what containment actually meant in practice: which areas to defend, what instruments to prioritize, how American military forces should be structured, and so on.[3]

With respect to the post–Cold War era, reasonable observers can debate whether the United States has consistently followed a coherent grand strategy since the fall of the Berlin Wall.[4] It is equally reasonable to question whether the presidency of Donald Trump constitutes a significant pivot in America's grand strategic orientation. Yet to base this judgment on whether there has been a universally accepted "bumper sticker" would be wrong. If grand strategy has analytic utility, it rests not in the label but in the underlying coherence of the concepts, and in the effectiveness of the policies that flow therefrom. A definition acknowledging that grand strategy can exist even absent a bumper sticker is therefore more useful.

Fallacy #2: Grand Strategy Is Whatever Post-Hoc Rationalization One Can Induce from the Data

A second and closely related fallacy is also definitional. Some historians and political scientists set the threshold for the existence of a grand strategy too low: if an analyst can discern even a very broad pattern amid the myriad events, then there must have been a grand strategy.[5] Admittedly, there is a kernel of insight in this argument. A grand strategy does not necessarily require a formal label or an elaborate public rollout. And historically speaking, most American grand strategies have been both "deliberate" and "emergent"—they have been informed by pre-hoc planning, but also by an iterative process of adaptation.[6]

Properly understood, however, grand strategy is more purposeful, intentional, and self-aware than the post-hoc approach implies. Officials who engage in grand strategy are not just responding to crises or handling events one-by-one in hopes that their actions will eventually add up to some well-defined whole. Rather, they are acting on a more coherent and forward-looking idea of what their country aims to achieve and how it plans to get there. Grand strategy requires policymakers to have a clear understanding of the international environment, a rough ranking of the threats and opportunities their country faces within that environment, a sense of how finite resources can be deployed across various opportunities and threats, and at least an initial plan of action derived from these concepts. Above all, the grand strategist must have a theory of how the world works, which provides an integrative logic linking diverse actions taken across time and space. In this sense, grand strategy is the conceptual architecture that lends structure and purpose to foreign policy; it is the theory, or logic, that links a country's long-term objectives to its everyday dealings with the world. As such, it requires systematic, pre-hoc effort.

Looking at the history of US grand strategy helps clarify this point. Those administrations that have viewed themselves as taking grand strategy seriously have almost always conducted some formal planning process, even though the resulting lines of action have inevitably evolved as feedback is processed and reality intervenes. Think, for instance, of the seminal policy papers written by George Kennan at the Policy Planning Staff in 1947–48 or the drafting and implementation of NSC-68 during Truman's second term. Think of the Solarium exercise under Eisenhower, or the preparation of NSDD-32 and NSDD-75 under Reagan.[7] In each case, these administrations were consciously seeking to "do" grand strategy in real time, and this intentionality can be seen from the historical documents.

Since the mid-1980s, of course, grand strategic planning has often taken the form of the preparation and release of formal *National Security Strategy* reports mandated by the Goldwater-Nichols act of 1986. The *NSS* is a perennially derided document, in part because administrations never release these reports as frequently or quickly as the law technically mandates, and in part because the reports often bear the scars of being written by committee.[8] These criticisms do have some merit, but they should not obscure the fact that the writing of the *NSS* is essentially a formal, legally mandated exercise in grand strategy. The *NSS* forces the president to outline a basic vision for American statecraft and to begin relating that vision to individual policies. It usually occasions an administration-wide debate about priorities and areas of emphasis, even if the public nature of the document ensures that priorities are not ranked as clearly as some observers might like. Finally, the document signals to the bureaucracy, the Congress and the public, and both allies and adversaries abroad the general direction US policy will follow. If grand strategy is a deliberate and purposeful endeavor, then the crafting of the *NSS* represents an essential part of that undertaking.

Fallacy #3: Thinking of Grand Strategy as a Principle or a Doctrine Rather than a Process

None of this is to argue that grand strategy should be thought of as some immutable blueprint from which policy must never deviate. In public parlance, grand strategy is often conflated with the promulgation of official doctrines, pronouncements that lay down—in advance—what the US response will be to a specified action or circumstance.[9] The Truman Doctrine, for instance, proclaimed that it would be US policy "to support free peoples who are resisting attempted subjugation by armed minorities or by outside pressure" in the context of the emerging Cold War.[10] The Eisenhower Doctrine expanded on the Truman Doctrine by stating that the United States would intervene militarily to halt potential communist advances in the Middle East. More recently, demands for an "Obama Doctrine" often took the form of calls for a definitive pronouncement on US policy toward crises such as the "Arab Spring." Doctrines can be quite useful, of course, because they signal resolve and provide audiences at home and abroad with an easily understandable expression of American goals. Grand strategy, however, should be something different.

Because foreign policy deals with a dynamic environment, flexibility and adaptation are central to any good grand strategy. If a grand strategy is soundly conceived, then the overall goal (containing Soviet power, or maintaining American primacy) may remain the same over years or even decades. But the various sub-components—decisions on how best to allocate resources, judgments about what mix of policies is most likely to produce the desired outcome—must come up for reassessment as conditions change and friends and enemies react to US initiatives. In this sense, grand strategy is best seen as a process—something iterative and even continual—rather than any single doctrine or principle.

The course of American statecraft during the Cold War illustrates this point. The long-term goals of US policy—the containment of Soviet influence; the preservation of a favorable global balance, particularly in Eurasia; the eventual "breakup or mellowing of Soviet power"—were evident as early as 1946–47 and provided a basic intellectual guide for decades to follow. Yet what these goals actually meant for policy was subject to continual revision and recalibration. What was the proper level of defense spending for meeting the Soviet threat? Should America practice "symmetrical" or "asymmetrical" containment? What emphasis should be placed on negotiations with the Soviet Union or other communist states? What areas of the globe were central to American security and what areas were peripheral? The answers to these questions varied over the course of the Cold War; they had to be worked out—and reworked out—amid the myriad crises of the era.[11] Indeed, Dwight Eisenhower may have begun with his famous Solarium planning exercise, but he subsequently had his administration's major planning papers revised almost annually to ensure that US policies kept pace with events. As Eisenhower understood, grand strategy requires purpose and a willingness to look ahead, but it demands significant tactical flexibility as well.

Fallacy #4: Only Certain Types of Grand Strategy Are Worthy of the Name

Another fallacy is the idea that only certain *types* of grand strategies are worthy of the label. This mistake is made even by very insightful observers. In an article published in 2010, former policy planning staff director Stephen Krasner argues that grand strategy must be truly transformative in its ambitions—it must envision some fundamental change in the international system and in the domestic structures of other countries—or it is no grand strategy at all.[12] The prominent strategic analyst Barry Watts takes a different, but similarly restrictive, approach. In Watts's view, a proper grand strategy is necessarily a competitive, asymmetric strategy designed to exploit the weaknesses of a particular rival or enemy.[13]

Watts's definition is useful, in the sense that grand strategy occurs in an inherently competitive international environment. Indeed, as numerous observers have noted, if nations did not have enemies, they would have little need of grand strategy.[14] Furthermore, insofar as a country faces a single, defining rivalry with another key actor, then adopting an asymmetric approach that pits one's own strengths against an opponent's weaknesses may make good sense. This was, of course, the ethos of Ronald Reagan's "cost-imposing" strategy during the 1980s, the goal of which was to force the Soviets either to compete in areas in which they had little chance of winning or else give up the game altogether. The results Reagan achieved testify to the potential utility of the competitive, asymmetric approach.[15]

Yet this view of grand strategy is also problematic, precisely because it is so restrictive. By its nature, this definition applies mainly to dyadic rivalries such as the Cold War and provides little guidance for how states should behave in periods in which their foreign policy is not dominated by a consuming rivalry. The United States, for example, currently confronts a situation in which it faces not a single, overriding challenge, but a range of different challenges from actors as diverse as the Islamic State, Iran, North Korea, Russia, and China (not to mention "non-actors" such as pandemics, global climate change, and economic crises). It is not clear that American policymakers could, even in theory, devise a grand strategy that would simultaneously give it asymmetric advantages against all of these actors. Nor is it clear that such an approach would be an appropriate way of handling individual relationships that are often characterized not by explicit, Cold War–style rivalry, but by an ambiguous mix of competition and cooperation. By restricting what qualifies as grand strategy, Watts limits the overall utility of the concept, as well.

The same is true of Krasner's approach. In one sense, Krasner's view is unhelpful because it fuels the perception that grand strategy is necessarily a grandiose, hubristic undertaking. More to the point, Krasner's definition excludes the possibility that a country could have a grand strategy premised on maintaining an advantageous status quo or conducting a selective retrenchment in order to improve long-term prospects. This is an ahistorical perspective, for it implies that British statesmen were necessarily not doing grand strategy when they sought to manage relative decline in the late nineteenth and early twentieth centuries, or that Henry Kissinger was not doing grand strategy when he sought to uphold a creaking Cold War order during the Nixon-Ford years. Moreover, it is a perspective that poorly informs the current debate about America's goals and policies. It implies that the United States will not be doing grand strategy unless it aims at systemic transformation, while also implying that the tasks that make up the intellectual core of grand strategy—setting priorities, balancing means and ends, linking short-term actions to long-term interests and goals—are devalued if American officials seek something less ambitious. In reality, the opposite is closer to truth. These intellectual tasks, and grand strategy in general, become all the more important when resources are stretched and hard choices must be made.

The essence of grand strategy lies not in the ambition of its desired end-state, nor in the particular approach (whether asymmetric or otherwise) taken to achieving that goal. Rather, the essence of grand strategy lies in the struggle to make sense of complexity and impart coherence to policy. When analysts over-specify grand strategy, they obscure more than they illuminate.

Fallacy #5: Grand Strategy Is a Pipe Dream

A fifth common fallacy is that grand strategy is an illusion—that it is impossible to achieve the unity of effort, correspondence between goals and outcomes, and overall coherence of policy that is necessary for grand strategy to work. From this perspective, grand strategy is a nice idea, but there are simply too many confounding variables: the limits of human rationality and wisdom, the uncertainty and ambiguity that cloud the international environment, the vagaries of bureaucracy and politics. In these conditions, grand strategy is a post-hoc rationalization at best and a pipe dream—"an elusive holy grail"—at worst.[16]

This view is not uncommon among scholars, and it has even been found in the Oval Office.[17] In his memoirs, Strobe Talbott recalls a conversation with Bill Clinton. Clinton had been reading biographies of Roosevelt and Truman that convinced him that neither had grand strategies for how to exert American leadership against the global threats posed by Hitler and Stalin. Rather, they had "powerful instincts about what had to be done, and they just made it up as they went along." Strategic coherence, he said, was largely imposed after the fact by scholars, memoirists, and "the chattering classes."[18]

Whatever one thinks of Clinton's statecraft, his underlying critique of grand strategy cannot be dismissed out of hand. Richard Betts and other scholars have excellent points about the limits of strategic thought and action in a chaotic world.[19] Likewise, even George Kennan, who is frequently revered as America's archetypal strategic thinker, often talked about the problems inherent in strategic planning in his famous National War College lectures.[20] As Kennan understood, Clausewitzian friction was a constant in grand strategy: "Countless minor incidents—the kind you can never really foresee—combine to lower the general level of performance, so that one always falls far short of the intended goal."[21]

It is thus unreasonable to expect that any administration can achieve flawless strategic foresight or seamless coherence of policy, especially on a day-to-day basis. Yet to argue that grand strategy is therefore impossible is to misunderstand what grand strategy is meant to achieve. The proper aim of grand strategy is not to achieve flawless foresight and seamless coherence all of the time. It is to achieve enough foresight and coherence enough of the time that a nation can protect its vital interests and accomplish its basic purposes. Grand strategy is not a game of perfect; it is a game of good enough.

Once this more reasonable standard for success is established, then grand strategy becomes more plausible. One could certainly argue that America got its grand strategy right enough over the course of the Cold War, despite missteps and oscillations along the way. One could make the same argument about British grand strategy over a period of decades or even centuries. Grand strategy is difficult, but it is hardly a pipe dream.

Fallacy #6: Democracies Can't Do Grand Strategy

A corollary to the foregoing fallacy is the idea that democracies in particular just can't get grand strategy right. This argument has been around as long as democracy itself. Thucydides's *History of the Peloponnesian War* is replete with examples of the allegedly baleful influence of mass politics on statecraft. Written some 2,000 years later, Alexis de Tocqueville's *Democracy in America* takes much the same tone:

> Foreign politics demand scarcely any of those qualities which are peculiar to a democracy; they require, on the contrary, the perfect use of almost all those in which it is deficient. . . . A democracy can only with great difficulty regulate the details of an important undertaking, persevere in a fixed design, and work out its execution in spite of serious obstacles. It cannot combine its measures with secrecy or await their consequences with patience.[22]

More recently, this basic critique—that democratic systems lack the discipline, unity of purpose, and steadiness that are essential to grand strategy— has been given voice by some of America's most gifted policymakers. George Kennan was famously skeptical of whether the United States could execute a coherent grand strategy, and he spent his later years arguing that America had to choose between its global ambitions and its democratic institutions.[23] Similarly, amid the traumas of Vietnam and Watergate, Henry Kissinger remarked that "I sometimes despair . . . whether it is possible in a democracy any more to conduct a thoughtful foreign policy."[24] Since then, other prominent observers have contended that Washington was or is inherently disadvantaged vis-à-vis the Soviet Union, China, or other authoritarian regimes. These days, this sentiment often takes the form of "Putin envy"—the idea that the Russian president can be a master strategist because he holds the reins of power firmly in his own hands, whereas American officials are handicapped not just by their own limitations but by the basic character of the democratic system.

At first glance, these arguments do have some plausibility. It is easy to think of ways in which raucous partisan politics, executive-legislative discord, the vagaries of public opinion, and other notable features of American democracy can militate against effective grand strategy. It is easier still to cite historical examples of this phenomenon, from the era of the nation's founding to the present.

It does not follow, however, that democracies are incapable of doing grand strategy, or that they are less capable of doing it than their authoritarian rivals. For one thing, this argument ignores the fact that authoritarianism entails its own set of strategic pathologies. Authoritarian leaders are no less prone to bad decisions or ideologically blinkered thinking than their democratic counterparts; the difference is that authoritarian systems contain fewer checks on a leader's ability to turn those bad ideas into policy. In studying the Cold War, for instance, John Lewis Gaddis found that the Soviet Union and People's Republic of China consistently underperformed compared to their democratic foes. The reason, he argues, was that "authoritarian systems reinforce, while discouraging attempts to puncture, whatever quixotic illusions may exist at the top."[25] Similarly, Gaddis found that authoritarian governments were ill-suited to forging organic alliances, because their authoritarian tendencies at home carried over into their behavior abroad.[26] Nor were these pernicious outcomes of authoritarianism limited to the Cold War. One can see similar trends in German and Japanese strategic behavior during World War II, Cuban foreign policy under Castro, or Iraqi conduct under Saddam Hussein.[27]

Democracy, conversely, brings a number of key grand strategic benefits. Gaddis and G. John Ikenberry have argued that democratic states have significant advantages in managing alliances and forging international regimes.[28] Going further, Ikenberry contends that the primacy of a democratic country is less likely to seem inherently threatening than that of an authoritarian power.[29] At a different level of analysis, Walter Russell Mead has made the case that democracy is good for the long-term health of foreign policy, because it provides mechanisms for aggregating interests, correcting flawed concepts, and replacing ineffective leaders.[30] The list of democratic advantages could go on; the point is that there is much reason to doubt that democracies are congenitally handicapped in grand strategy.

In fact, the United States actually has a very good historical record when it comes to doing grand strategy over the medium- and long-term. For all the political and bureaucratic intrusions that so horrified Kennan during the late 1940s, the Truman administration managed to define achievable grand strategic priorities—containing Soviet influence and maintaining a favorable configuration of power on the Eurasian landmass—and then to construct the various institutions and initiatives that allowed it to achieve those objectives.[31] The same pattern held for the Cold War as a whole: containment is now generally considered to have been one of the most successful grand strategies in modern history. Reaching farther back, one could argue that America executed successful grand strategies during much of the nineteenth century and during World War II as well. As Mead puts it, "The rise of American power has been consistent, striking, sustained over the long term, and accomplished at an astonishingly low cost considering the size and range of the power the country has amassed."[32] Democracy certainly makes grand strategy messy, but it does not make good grand strategy impossible.

Fallacy #7: Grand Strategy Is Irrelevant or Even Dangerous in a World with no Single Grand Threat

Is grand strategy even a useful concept in a world in which the United States no longer faces a single, overriding threat to its security? Since the end of the Cold War, a number of leading commentators have answered this question in the negative. They contend that the complexity of the post–Cold War world precludes—and renders counterproductive—the effort to devise any useful "grand theory" of foreign policy. "Given the divisions and uncertainties of the contemporary environment," writes Krasner, "it is impossible to frame a responsible grand strategy."[33] Proponents of this view often adduce the travails of George W. Bush as evidence of their assertions. "As Bush has so painfully demonstrated," wrote James Goldgeier and Derek Chollet in 2008, "the quest to define a simple, Kennan-esque concept to guide US foreign policy is fruitless, overrated and even dangerous in the complex world of the 21st century."[34]

There is no disputing that the world is complicated and dynamic and that this makes grand strategy hard. Yet for several reasons, the idea that grand strategy has become anachronistic does not hold water. First, this argument misunderstands what grand strategy actually is (or should be). If one thinks of it strictly as a formally enunciated doctrine or a one-size-fits-all approach to the world, then it is almost certainly a quixotic and even pernicious pursuit. Yet grand strategy is best seen as something less dogmatic. It involves systematically thinking about the future, establishing hierarchies of goals and priorities, and outlining a realistic course of action for realizing those objectives. But it is also a process that can—indeed, must—allow for adaptation as time passes. It is worth remembering that the "golden age" of American grand strategy—the Truman years—was characterized by repeated reassessments of what mix of means and commitments was required to contain Soviet power, even as that overarching goal remained constant.[35] If one thinks of grand strategy in this manner, then it no longer appears so foolish an undertaking.

Second, the idea that the security environment is infinitely more complex now than it was during the Cold War is highly debatable.[36] Admittedly, the presence of the Soviet threat did focus America's attention and provide a "north star" in discussions of grand strategy. But it did not exempt American policymakers from dealing with complexity, unpredictability, or nasty shocks. Such developments were the rule rather than the exception throughout the Cold War, from the Soviet A-bomb test of 1949, to rapid decolonization and the emergence of the Third World during the 1950s and 1960s, to the Soviet invasion of Afghanistan, and so on. As one article notes, "Complexity, or the perception of complexity, is the timeless companion of the national security strategist."[37] If America could maintain a more or less coherent grand strategy amid all this, it can probably do so today.

Third and finally, even if one concedes the point that the world is more complicated now than it was in the past, the response should be to place more emphasis on grand strategy rather than less. "Strategic nihilism" will not allow us to escape the complexity that makes grand strategy so hard to do; it will only compound the problems besetting American foreign policy.[38] In fact, the more challenging the circumstances, the higher the premium should be that one should place on doing the intellectual legwork associated with grand strategy: setting priorities, thinking systematically about resource constraints, establishing general strategic ideas that can serve as conceptual anchors amid the geopolitical squalls. Doing all of this will not remove the imperative of recalibration and improvisation, but it can increase the chances that these adjustments will be made intelligently, in ways that are more consistent than not with long-term national objectives. As Dwight Eisenhower used to say, "The plans are nothing, but the planning is everything."[39] The Cold War may be over, but the relevance of grand strategy remains.

Fallacy #8: Politics Must Be Adjourned When Grand Strategy Is in Session

As the Cold War began, Senator Arthur Vandenberg—a Republican— explained that he would support key aspects of Truman's containment

strategy because meeting the grave challenges that America faced required "stopping partisan politics at the water's edge."[40] Since then, it has
become all too common for pundits and other observers to argue that politics actually did "stop at the water's edge" during the Cold War and to
infer that politics must again be adjourned if successful grand strategy is
to take hold.

Neither idea holds up to much scrutiny. There was bipartisan support
for certain pillars of Truman's foreign policy—Truman Doctrine aid, the
Marshall Plan—during a brief two-year period from 1947 until 1949. But the
good feelings faded fast. In 194951 alone, there were furious debates over
who lost China, accusations that the State Department was infested with
treasonous communists, the conduct of the war in Korea, and other matters.
From that point onward, such debates—over Cuba and the missile gap, windows of vulnerability and the nuclear freeze—were more the norm than the
exception. Politics most certainly did not stop at the water's edge during the
Cold War; policy was more often used as a political bludgeon by Democrats
and Republicans alike.[41]

This history matters because it gives us a more realistic standard for
thinking about the relationship between politics and grand strategy. Aspects
of today's political climate, particularly the high levels of tribalism and partisan polarization, are indeed worrying when it comes to the steadiness of
American policy and the perceptions of that policy abroad. But perspective
helps here, because if the real history of the Cold War is taken as a point of
comparison, then the level of foreign policy rancor and disagreement since
1991—or since 9/11—does not seem so elevated. And if we allow that the
United States pursued a generally successful grand strategy—or perhaps a
string of cumulatively successful grand strategies—during the Cold War,
then there is less reason to think that the country cannot do likewise today.
Partisan politics certainly make grand strategy messy, but the two can coexist
nonetheless.

Fallacy #9: Grand Strategy Is Only About the Future

Grand strategy is a forward-looking discipline—it involves setting long-term
goals and crafting ideas that will carry policy ahead. Yet as political scientist Peter Feaver has pointed out, it is also a backward-looking discipline, informed as much by insights from the past as predictions about the future.[42]

Franklin Roosevelt's strategy for fighting World War II, as well as his wartime planning for the postwar period, was shaped by what he perceived to be Woodrow Wilson's mistakes during and after World War I. Truman's grand strategy during the early Cold War, in turn, was influenced by the experience of World War II. It aimed to prevent Stalin from accomplishing what the Axis powers had nearly done—dominating Eurasia—without starting another global war in the process. At the end of the Cold War, Ronald Reagan's grand strategy was shaped by his judgments about the apparent failures of détente, as well as by his own sense of the long-running historical trends at play, namely, US resurgence and Soviet decline. Similarly, George W. Bush's grand strategic choices after 9/11 stemmed from the conviction that the United States must never allow another such catastrophe, and they drew on the long-standing American tendency to mount expansive responses to severe security threats.[43] In this sense, the past is always present in grand strategy.

Grand strategy is about looking backward in other ways, as well. It is impossible to understand which way the world is moving without understanding how things came to be as they are, just as it is impossible to comprehend a country's position without comprehending how it arrived at this point. Moreover, grand strategy is a discipline that necessarily involves as much reassessment as forecasting. Setting out on a long-term journey requires self-confidence that one is ultimately headed in the right direction, but the only way to test that belief is to evaluate (and reevaluate) whether one's policies are producing the desired short- and medium-term results. In a way, then, grand strategy depends on the rigorous study of the recent past to determine what mix of perseverance and flexibility constitutes the proper way forward.

What all of this suggests is that grand strategy is—and must be—sensitive to history. To be sure, grand strategy cannot be *purely* backward-looking; it must also flow from a firm understanding of the present and an ability to anticipate, if only very broadly, the shape of the future. Yet a country's grand strategy is inevitably a reflection of its own history, both recent and more distant, and good grand strategies are those that exploit the insights the past has to offer.

Fallacy #10: Day-to-day Policy Debates Don't Matter to Grand Strategy

In many ways, the history of American grand strategy is a story of continuity—the fact that certain key ideas or approaches have been far more durable than one might initially presume. For much of the nineteenth century, for example, the United States followed a fairly consistent approach involving European diplomatic non-entanglement, determined westward expansion, and pursuit of hemispheric preeminence. Since World War II, America has maintained a broad commitment to shaping the global order through economic and diplomatic engagement, forward deployment of military forces, and other efforts to preserve an eminently favorable balance of power. Call it "deep engagement" or "American empire," but the underlying continuity is difficult to deny.[44]

This impression of continuity is only reinforced—albeit unintentionally—by the frequently exaggerated nature of political debates on grand strategy. Presidential candidates tend to claim that there is a night-and-day difference between their policies and those of their opponent, but the rhetoric is often more striking than the reality. Eisenhower and his secretary of state, John Foster Dulles, initially condemned containment as immoral and defeatist; they ended up adopting the vital essence of that policy. More than fifty years later, Barack Obama portrayed himself as the "anti-Bush" (just as George W. Bush had initially tried to be "anything but Clinton"), but he embraced and even intensified a number of his predecessor's national security policies.[45]

There are thus good reasons to think that grand strategy does not change as much, or as quickly, from president to president as is sometimes assumed. After all, some of the key determinants of America's approach to the world—its geography, its national identity and values—evolve slowly, if at all. It makes sense, then, that American grand strategic debate actually occurs within a framework of substantial continuity and that those presidents who promise dramatic departures usually revert toward the mean.

Change does happen, though, and choices do matter. The heated political debates of the Cold War *did* involve important forks in the road, and had different choices been made, they would have mattered immensely. Imagine how different the course of the Cold War might have been had Truman heeded calls by Douglas MacArthur—and the general's Republican supporters—to expand the Korean War into China. Or imagine how foreign policy might have looked had certain elections or events gone differently. Would a President Hubert Humphrey have approached Vietnam, or US relations with Moscow and Beijing, in the same manner as Richard Nixon and Henry Kissinger did? How would the course of the Iraq war—with all of its strategic implications—have differed had John

Kerry won the 2004 presidential election? For that matter, how would the history of American grand strategy have developed if John F. Kennedy had not been assassinated or Woodrow Wilson not suffered an incapacitating stroke?[46]

This line of argument can be extended to the numerous policy issues and decision points that have, collectively, characterized debates over American grand strategy in recent years. Should the United States spend 2 percent, 3 percent, or 4 percent of gross domestic product (GDP) on defense? How strongly should Washington support its Asian allies in their maritime and territorial disputes with China? What level of American intervention, if any, is warranted in the Syrian civil war or other conflicts in the Middle East? Individually, these decisions may not have transformative effects on US grand strategy today or tomorrow. But collectively, and over time, they can exert a significant influence over the circumstances that Washington confronts and the path that it follows. Even relatively small decisions or shifts made now can, over time, build into something more substantial. The rhetoric of policy debates can be misleading, but the consequences that specific policy choices have for the trajectory of American grand strategy are real indeed.

The same point can be made about the debates surrounding Donald Trump's foreign policy that were raging as of this writing. It may be, as some supporters of Trump's foreign policy have argued, that the president has made fewer concrete policy departures than his campaign rhetoric might have led one to predict. But some of those departures—withdrawal from the Trans-Pacific Partnership trade agreement, for instance—may have a significant downstream effect on the competitive environment the United States faces in the Asia-Pacific region a decade hence. Even where policies have not shifted dramatically, President Trump has shifted the intangibles of US grand strategy—the rhetoric, the motivating ideas, the relationships of deep respect and cooperation with allies, the general appearance of America before the world—in ways that seem likely to trigger destabilizing geopolitical adjustments if continued over time.[47] The least conventional president in US history may thus be demonstrating an old truth about grand strategy—that changes today can have outsize effects in the future.

The debate over what grand strategy is, and what it should be, will undoubtedly continue—as will debates about the purpose and nature of contemporary American grand strategy. But the quality of both debates can be improved by dispelling some of the more common misconceptions and fallacies that afflict these discussions and by infusing them with greater analytical clarity. If we want to have informed arguments about the value of grand strategy, we have to know what we are talking about. And if we want to help policymakers get America's grand strategy right today, we must first get grand strategy right as a concept.

Notes

1. Some ideas expressed here are developed at greater length in Hal Brands, *What Good Is Grand Strategy? Power and Purpose in American Statecraft from Harry S. Truman to George W. Bush* (Ithaca, NY: Cornell University Press, 2014); and Hal Brands, *The Promise and Pitfalls of Grand Strategy* (Carlisle Barracks, PA: Strategic Studies Institute, 2012).
2. Adam Grissom, "What Is Grand Strategy? Reframing the Debate on American Ends, Ways, and Means," RAND Corporation Working Paper, April 2012.
3. On Cold War–era grand strategy, see John Lewis Gaddis, *Strategies of Containment: A Critical Appraisal of American National Security Policy during the Cold War* (New York: Oxford University Press, 2005).
4. For contrasting views, see Hal Brands, *From Berlin to Baghdad: America's Search for Purpose in the Post-Cold War World* (Lexington: University Press of Kentucky, 2008); Peter Feaver, "American Grand Strategy at the Crossroads: Leading from the Front, Leading from Behind, or Not Leading at All," in *America's Path: Grand Strategy for the Next*, ed. Richard Fontaine and Kristin M. Lord (Washington, DC: Center for a New American Security, 2012).
5. See Kevin Narizny, *The Political Economy of Grand Strategy* (Ithaca, NY: Cornell University Press, 2007).
6. On emergent and deliberate strategies, see Ionut Popescu, "Design and Emergence in the Making of American Grand Strategy," PhD dissertation, Duke University, June 2013.
7. NSDD-32, NSDD-75, and Reagan-era strategy are described in Hal Brands, *Making the Unipolar Moment: U.S. Foreign Policy and the Rise of the Post–Cold War Order* (Ithaca, NY: Cornell University Press, 2014), chapter 2. NSC refers to National Security Council and the documents it produced; NSDD stands for National Security Decision Directive.
8. For criticism, see Stephen M. Walt, "Why We Don't Need Another 'National Strategy' Document," http://walt.foreignpolicy.com/posts/2009/09/27/why_we_dont_need_another_national_strategy_document. For a defense, see Peter Feaver, "Holding Out for the National Security Strategy," http://shadow.foreignpolicy.com/posts/2010/01/20/holding_out_for_the_national_security_strategy

9. For instance, Fareed Zakaria, "Stop Searching for an Obama Doctrine," *Washington Post*, July 6, 2011; Derek Chollet and James Goldgeier, "Good Riddance to the Bush Doctrine," *Washington Post*, July 13, 2008.

10. "President Harry S. Truman's Address before a Joint Session of Congress," March 12, 1947, http://avalon.law.yale.edu/20th_century/trudoc.asp.

11. Gaddis, *Strategies of Containment*; Melvyn Leffler, *A Preponderance of Power: National Security, the Truman Administration, and the Cold War* (Stanford, CA: Stanford University Press, 1992).

12. Stephen Krasner, "An Orienting Principle for Foreign Policy: The Deficiencies of 'Grand Strategy,'" *Hoover Policy Review* 163 (October 2010).

13. Barry Watts, *Why Strategy? The Case for Taking It Seriously and Doing It Well* (Washington, DC: Center for Strategic and Budgetary Assessments, 2007), esp. 2.

14. Colin Dueck, *Reluctant Crusaders: Power, Culture, and Change in American Grand Strategy* (Princeton, NJ: Princeton University Press, 2008), 10.

15. John Arquilla, *The Reagan Imprint: Ideas in American Foreign Policy from the Collapse of Communism to the War on Terror* (Chicago: Ivan R. Dee, 2006).

16. Krasner, "Orienting Principle for Foreign Policy."

17. Steve Yetiv, *The Absence of Grand Strategy: The United States in the Persian Gulf, 1972-2005* (Baltimore: Johns Hopkins University Press, 2008); Marc Trachtenberg, "Making Grand Strategy: The Early Cold War Experience in Retrospect," *SAIS Review* 19:1 (1999), 33–40.

18. Strobe Talbott, *The Russia Hand: A Memoir of Presidential Diplomacy* (New York: Random House, 2002), 133–134.

19. Richard Betts, "Is Strategy an Illusion?" *International Security* 25:2 (Fall 2000), 5–50; Melvyn P. Leffler and Jeffrey W. Legro, "Conclusion: Strategy in a Murky World," in *In Uncertain Times: American Foreign Policy after the Berlin Wall and 9/11*, ed. Melvyn P. Leffler and Jeffrey W. Legro (Ithaca, NY: Cornell University Press, 2011).

20. Kennan, "Where Do We Stand?" National War College Lecture, December 21, 1949, Box 299, Kennan Papers, Seeley Mudd Manuscript Library, Princeton University.

21. Carl von Clausewitz, *On War*, ed. and trans. Michael Howard and Peter Paret (Princeton, NJ: Princeton University Press, 1984), 119.

22. Quoted in Miroslav Nincic, *Democracy and Foreign Policy: The Fallacy of Political Realism* (New York: Columbia University Press, 1992), 3.

23. George Kennan, *Memoirs, 1925–1950* (Boston: Little, Brown, 1967); George Kennan, *The Cloud of Danger: Current Realities of American Foreign Policy* (Boston: Little, Brown, 1977), esp. 8, 229.

24. Memorandum of Conversation between Kissinger and Golda Meir, May 2, 1974, Box 7, Henry A. Kissinger Records, Record Group 59, National Archives and Records Administration. See also Will Inboden's essay in this volume.

25. John Lewis Gaddis, *We Now Know: Rethinking Cold War History* (New York: Oxford University Press, 1997), 291.

26. Gaddis, *We Now Know*, 189–220, 288–289.

27. As an example, see Hal Brands and David Palkki, "Conspiring Bastards: Saddam Hussein's Strategic View of the United States," *Diplomatic History* 36:3 (April 2012), 625–629.

28. Gaddis, *We Now Know,* passim, esp. 288–289; G. John Ikenberry, *After Victory: Institutions, Strategic Restraint, and the Rebuilding of Order after Major Wars* (Princeton. NJ: Princeton University Press, 2001), esp. chapters 3 and 6.

29. Ikenberry, *After Victory,* 76–79.

30. Walter Russell Mead, *Special Providence: American Foreign Policy and How It Changed the World* (New York: Knopf, 2001), chapters 2–3.

31. Leffler, *A Preponderance of Power.*

32. Mead, *Special Providence,* 34.

33. Krasner, "Orienting Principle for Foreign Policy"; Fareed Zakaria, "Stop Searching for an Obama Doctrine," *Washington Post,* July 6, 2011; R.W Apple, "A Domestic Sort with Global Worries," *New York Times,* August 25, 1999.

34. Derek Chollet and James Goldgeier, "Good Riddance to the Bush Doctrine," *Washington Post,* July 13, 2008; also Zakaria, "Stop Searching for an Obama Doctrine."

35. Leffler, *Preponderance of Power.*

36. For an example of this argument, see Robert Gates, "That Was Amateur Night" (interview by John Barry), *Newsweek,* October 25, 2008.

37. Michael J. Gallagher, Joshua A. Geltzer, and Sebastian L.V. Gorka, "The Complexity Trap," *Parameters* 42, 1 (Spring 2012), 5–16, esp. 9.

38. Phrase borrowed from Betts, "Is Strategy an Illusion?" 16.

39. Robert Bowie and Richard Immerman, *Waging Peace: How Eisenhower Shaped an Enduring Cold War Strategy* (New York: Oxford University Press, 1998), vii.

40. The precise provenance of the quote is difficult to determine. In February 1947, Henry Cabot Lodge reportedly said that partisan politics "stops at the water's edge." See "Lodge Says Parties See Abroad as One," *New York Times,* February 13, 1947. Regardless, the saying is generally traced back to the period when Vandenberg assumed the chair of the Senate Foreign Relations Committee that same year.

41. See Campbell Craig and Fredrik Logevall, *America's Cold War: The Politics of Insecurity* (Cambridge, MA: Harvard University Press, 2009); Julian Zelizer, *Arsenal of Democracy: The Politics of National Security from World War II to the War on Terrorism* (New York: Basic Books, 2010).

42. Peter Feaver, "Eight Myths about American Grand Strategy," in *Forging American Grand Strategy: Securing a Path Through a Complex Future,* ed. Sheila R. Ronis (Carlisle Barracks, PA: Strategic Studies Institute, 2013), 42–43; also Williamson Murray, MacGregor Knox, and Alvin Bernstein, "Introduction: On Strategy," in *The Making of Strategy: Rulers, States, and War,* ed. Williamson Murray, MacGregor Knox, and Alvin Bernstein (Cambridge: Cambridge University Press, 1994), 1–23.

43. On Bush and historical patterns, see John Lewis Gaddis, *Surprise, Security, and the American Experience* (Cambridge, MA: Harvard University Press, 2004).

44. Stephen Brooks, G. John Ikenberry, and William Wohlforth, "Don't Come Home, America: The Case against Retrenchment," *International Security* 37:3 (Winter 2012/2013), 7–51.

45. Immerman and Bowie, *Waging Peace*; Andrew Bacevich, "Different Drummer, Same Drum," *National Interest* 64 (Summer 2001), 67–77; Peter Feaver, "Obama's National Security Strategy: Real Change or Just 'Bush Lite'?" *Foreign Policy*, May 27, 2010.

46. On how US policy in Vietnam might have differed had JFK lived, see Fredrik Logevall, *Choosing War: The Lost Chance for Peace and the Escalation of War in Vietnam* (Berkeley: University of California Press, 1999).

47. This interpretation is offered in Hal Brands, *American Grand Strategy in the Age of Trump* (Washington, DC: Brookings Institution Press, 2018).

2

The Blob and the Mob

On Grand Strategy and Social Change

Beverly Gage

On February 15, 2003, the world witnessed the largest mass demonstration in global history. That day, an estimated 6 to 11 million people on six continents took to the streets to try to prevent a looming catastrophe: the American invasion of Iraq. This was also the largest failed demonstration in global history. Little more than a month later, the United States invaded Iraq, and US troops have remained there, in greater and lesser numbers, ever since.

This moment suggests two important points for anyone interested in grand strategy, either as a field of study or as a form of practice. The first is that America's foreign policy elites might do well to broaden their horizons and to pay more attention to voices bubbling up from below; in this case, the protesters turned out to be right and the policy establishment turned out to be wrong. The second is that citizens and activists inclined to social protest might spend more time thinking about how to be effective and about the limits and possibilities of protest in the twenty-first century. The art of doing that—of channeling collective grievances into effective action—is known as social movement strategy. Although grand strategists and social movement strategists often view each other as opposites (or even enemies), they have more to learn from each other—and more in common—than either group might think.

The intersections between these ways of thinking now form a significant part of Yale's Brady-Johnson Program in Grand Strategy. Founded in 2000, the program began with a focus on war and statecraft, the traditional realms of "grand strategy." Over the past few years, however, it has evolved to consider strategy as a category encompassing a growing range of thinkers and political endeavors—not just strategies of world order, but also strategies of how to change the world. This has entailed engagement with thinkers, activists, and writers whose interests often fall as much on the side of dissenters and changemakers as policymakers and statesman. Think of it as grand strategy for an age of global democratic crisis and mass action, in which the old categories—like the center itself—cannot hold.

Means and Ends

As other essays in this collection demonstrate, the idea of "grand strategy" emerged out of the world of military affairs. Under the famous rubric identified by British historian B. H. Liddell Hart, "strategy" was what generals did, while "grand strategy" fell to politicians and statesmen, charged not only with winning the war but also with securing a viable and sustainable peace. Far-sighted civilian leaders were tasked with thinking through how to amass a nation's vast resources (economic, cultural, social, military) toward those ends. In this construct, grand strategy was an elite enterprise, undertaken by the daring, powerful, and visionary few, a game of power politics played on a map of the world.[1]

Social movements, by contrast, are often thought to be radically democratic and people-centered, spontaneous uprisings with little cohesion or central direction. Unlike states, movements have no formal power— no standing army or tax-collecting agency to carry out their will. They often have no formal hierarchy or designated leadership, at least not one that can claim widespread legitimacy. By definition, "movements" exist at some remove from established political institutions, outside of parties and governments and official agencies. Their power, if they can get it, comes through mass action rather than through back-room games played by a handful of participants. Partly as a result, they often appear to lack any strategy whatsoever, much less a strategy that could rise to the august label of "grand."

Such differences can be deceptive, however. Far from lacking in a strategic tradition, the realm of social change over the past two centuries has given rise to an extensive literature in which activists and thinkers have debated which forms of organizing might best fit which situations.[2] Much of that literature focuses what my colleague John Gaddis identifies as the central concern of any grand strategy: "the alignment of potentially unlimited aspirations with necessarily limited capabilities."[3] If one conceives of grand strategy exclusively as something that states do, there may be little reason to bring these two literatures together. But if one considers it as something more like a methodology, a way of thinking through large-scale questions of means and ends, timing and scale, then there is a robust conversation to be had.

This is the assumption now guiding Yale's grand strategy program, which has maintained its original focus on statecraft and foreign policy while opening up space for different forms of engagement with large-scale strategic thinking, including exploration in the realms of domestic politics and social movements. The course still includes what might be considered the grand strategy canon: Thucydides, Machiavelli, Clausewitz. In addition, it now incorporates thinkers from a long tradition of dissenting and social-movement thought, beginning with the abolitionists of the nineteenth century. The goal in doing this is not only to make space for creative thinking about what grand strategy is and does, but also to engage a set of questions crucial for understanding the challenges of the twenty-first century, when no competent statesman can afford to ignore populist and people's movements, and no effective activist can avoid the question of how to engage with and influence institutions of power.

My own interest in grand strategy emerged at the intersection of these areas. My scholarly field is American political history, not statecraft or foreign policy, though I have written a good deal on national security topics such as terrorism and domestic intelligence. As a citizen, I have, for better or worse, been as likely to be a protester as a policymaker. (During the run-up to the Iraq War, I was one of those hapless dissenters, aghast at what seemed like an obvious imperial misadventure but, as it turned out, helpless to stop it.)

So why grand strategy? I encountered the program not long after arriving at Yale in 2004, a newly minted assistant professor curious about what was then a small, experimental venture. The campus was already buzzing about its virtues and vices, polarized between those who believed the program offered a visionary correction to the many ills of academic life and those who questioned its methodologies and politics. As Stephen Wertheim and Thomas Meaney have suggested, one of the most frequent critiques was that it engaged in a form of power politics that was less about strategy than about "flattery," encouraging already over-confident Yale students to see themselves as part of a lineage of statesmen and power brokers stretching back to the classical world.[4] Another critique was more immediate: that the forms of analysis and habits of thought promoted by the program contributed to grand mistakes the war in Iraq.

As I got to know the program, however, I found unexpected points of intellectual crossover and resonance, along with an intriguing experiment in historical pedagogy. First among them was the program's claim that history and the humanities have something distinctive to offer future public servants, forms of knowledge that provide a perspective fundamentally different from what one might encounter in a policy lab or at a school of international affairs. For academic purists, this might be dismissed as "instrumentalizing" the humanities. Less ominously, it might be seen as creating space within universities for different forms of engagement with history and humanistic thought, a complement to rather than a detraction from the academic research mission. In an age of declining history majors and crisis within the humanities, it seems puzzling (and strategically inadvisable) to insist that historians and humanists sit apart from the world, fiddling with journal articles while the republic burns.

The grand strategy program appeared to be a place to do something that isn't often done in academic history circles but that happens to be the way many people relate to history and the humanities: it allowed for learning lessons and making imaginative connections across vast differences of culture and context. The grand strategy program also embraced the idea that the university and the "real world" were not mutually exclusive realms— that policymakers and practitioners might have something to learn from academics, and vice versa. This entailed more than bringing a diplomat or politician or activist to campus for a talk. It meant co-teaching: sitting together week after week, reading the same texts and discussing the same problems. At its best, this approach required everyone—students, practitioners, professors—to acknowledge the value but also the limits to their ways of knowing the world.

Perhaps most provocatively, the program insisted on generalization, on pushing past boundaries of discipline and expertise in order to take on breathtakingly large—or, if you will, grand—questions about both the past and the present. At its most extreme, this might be interpreted as the rejection of a scholarly mission that favors careful specialization over synthesis. Seen in the context of a modern university education—just two of the thirty-six credits required of Yale students—the program appears more modest in its aims, a counterweight to rather than a replacement for more specialized classes.

Finally, and perhaps most obviously, the program offered a place to think about, well, *strategy*—not simply the "what" of policy but the "how" of getting things done. In the program of 2004, this mostly meant studying challenges faced by world leaders: statesmen, diplomats, presidents, princes. Today, it also means thinking about the actions of social movement leaders and ordinary people, faced with ambitions and visions for changing the world but all too often at a loss about how to do it.

Running the World and Changing the World

There is some peril in the effort to join these two worlds together. As many of the chapters in this collection note, "grand strategy" is already an amorphous term, at once a subject and a methodology, a form of planning that questions the ultimate utility of planning itself. Adding in another category of analysis further muddies the waters: If grand strategy is not primarily a matter of statecraft and national security, then what is it? There may be good reasons that policymakers and activists often view each other as adversaries rather than allies—the "blob" versus the "mob." Certainly these divisions seem to be relevant to students on campus, who tend to self-sort into one group or the other. Students who want to run the world take classes like Grand Strategy and vie for internships at the State Department, eager to make their way up through the established order. Students who want to change the world, by contrast, often renounce allegiance to institutions and formal politics, looking with scorn on less imaginative strivers who aim to exercise power over their fellow citizens.

Within the realm of strategic thought, however, there has long been significant intellectual overlap between military, political, and social-movement approaches. Far from standing apart from questions of war and peace, stability and instability, conflict and diplomacy, nearly every significant movement for social change has actively engaged these questions, including the real or potential use of violence. Beginning in the early nineteenth century, abolitionists hotly debated means and ends and tactics, from "nonresistance" through "terrorism" and on up to total war. The woman suffrage movement wrestled with its own daunting strategic challenge: how to exercise power within a system that excluded women from traditional political methods but also from the skill and ability to bear arms. The labor movement of the nineteenth century employed a wide variety of violent and non-violent tactics aimed at the grand end of altering the balance of power between employers and employees, even of transforming capitalism itself. Around the world, still more radical movements, many of them at least nominally Marxist in orientation, produced vast literatures on the virtues and vices of revolutionary strategy as well as the complex task of transforming members and leaders, after victory, from revolutionaries into statesmen.

In modern Western democratic societies, social-change strategists tend to favor non-violent methods, but debates rage nonetheless: How ambitious or limited should a movement's ends be? What are the best means of achieving those ends: litigation, street protest, persuasion, electoral power? How can leaders best promote resilience and discipline in the face of resistance, friction, and unexpected events? Who are those leaders and how do they maintain legitimacy? Who is their enemy, and how should the conflict be framed? Such questions take particular forms in the mass organizing context of the twenty-first century but they resonate strongly with the concerns that statesmen and generals have faced for centuries—a fact that many social-change strategists have long recognized.

Machiavelli for the Have-Nots

Take Saul Alinsky, the veteran radical and movement theorist best known as the father of "community organizing." Toward the end of his life, Alinsky published *Rules for Radicals* (1971), the distillation of more than four decades of experience as an organizer and front-line strategist for grassroots organizations. Alinsky's career began in the labor movement of the 1930s, where he was schooled in both direct-action tactics and patient institution-building under the auspices of the Congress of Industrial Organizations (CIO). By the 1940s, he started to consider how those lessons might be applied to the plight of poor and disfranchised people more broadly. The result was what came to be known as the "Alinskyite" model of organizing, which combined brash messaging and confrontational tactics with the slow, diligent work of building organizations over the long term. Alinsky wrote *Rules for Radicals* as a guide to implementing this particular vision and method, and it has remained a touchstone for activists ever since. But he also intended it as a broader work of strategy reflecting on "certain central concepts of action in human politics that operate regardless of the scene or time," very much in conversation with the works of statesmen, politicians, and military leaders, and with precisely those issues most often taught and contemplated in the field of grand strategy.[5]

From the first sentence of the first chapter, Alinsky placed himself within a canon recognizable to any grand strategy scholar. "*The Prince* was written by Machiavelli for the Haves on how to hold power," he proclaimed. "*Rules of Radicals* is written for the Have-Nots on how to take it away." Like Machiavelli, Alinsky presented himself as a hard-headed realist, concerned with "the world as it is and not as we would like it to be." He aimed his book at young activists, warning them against the dual temptations of utopianism and despair, both of which seemed to be in ample supply in the late 1960s. "They have no illusions about the system, but plenty of illusion about the way to change our world," he wrote of the student New Left. "It is to this point that I have written this book." Rather than succumb to either fantasy or hopelessness, Alinsky urged them to turn to strategy and to think about "pragmatic" ways to create the world they want to see.[6]

Alinsky insisted that social activists—no less than statesmen or military leaders—operated in an arena of power politics, in which interest and coercion rather than abstract morality ultimately shaped the course of events. He feared that grassroots organizers were often hampered by their inability to recognize this fact, and by the misguided idea that they occupied a different plane of existence. "Political realists see the world as it is: an arena of power politics moved primarily by perceived immediate self-interests," he wrote. The challenge was to adopt a "realistic" approach to social change while not entirely losing sight of high ideals and noble aspirations.[7]

In Alinsky's view, this fundamental dilemma was no different in grassroots organizing than in any other area of strategy. "Whenever we think about social change, the question of means and ends arises," he wrote. "The man of action views the issue of means and ends in pragmatic and strategic terms." Alinsky avoided describing any particular end to his methods, beyond a general faith in democratic openness and a belief that the "people," if empowered to take on their bosses and rulers, would produce a wiser and more virtuous society. Some of his vagueness on the subject came from an acknowledgment that ends would always have to be tied to means— that "you can miss the target by shooting too high as well as too low." But the vagueness was also deliberate, an effort to correct for what he saw as a pernicious imbalance within the realm of strategic literature. According to Alinsky, Marxist figures such as Lenin, Mao, and Che Guevara so thoroughly dominated the literature on revolution and social change that the very concept of strategy had become tied to Marxist dogma. He hoped to provide an alternative for those who wanted to hold on to the idea of revolutionary strategy—whether literal or metaphorical—while jettisoning Marxism altogether.[8]

If Alinsky had relatively little to say on the subject of "ends," he had plenty to say when it came to assessing "means." Alinsky began from the obvious if daunting realization that most "Have-Nots" lacked the basic tools of power: money, arms, control of political institutions. Rather than wring his hands over that circumstance, however, he viewed it as a given, one of many factors to be considered in developing a range of strategic options. "The resources of the Have-Nots are (1) no money and (2) lots of people," he wrote. "All right, let's start from there." It was not, he argued, such a bad position to be in. After all, having "lots of people"—in reality or in potential—opened up a range of possibilities, from electoral campaigns to mass protest. Alinsky also counted among the means available to the "Have-Nots" the rights of assembly, speech, and petition, however limited those might sometimes be in practice. Organized effectively, he insisted, "lots of people" exercising such democratic rights could be enormously powerful—perhaps even more powerful than if money, arms, and influence were there for the asking. In any case, "lots of people" was what was available, and "in organizing, the major negative in the situation has to be converted into the leading positive."[9]

Alinsky devoted the bulk of *Rules for Radicals* to thinking strategically about this hard situation—in particular, the challenge of translating mass action (or the potential for mass action) into concrete political gain. He paid special attention to the study of "tactics," the crucial set of practices that turned means and ends into action. Alinsky defined tactics as the simple but necessary proposition of "doing what you can with what you have." If ends had to be aligned with means, he wrote, then tactics had to be situated within both, a careful calculus of what was possible and of how a given action might or might not yield a particular outcome. The book offered a range of entertaining examples, from theatrical direct confrontation to the painstaking work of planning meetings and persuading participants. It also offered more than a dozen "rules" of tactical maneuver, now among the most famous of Alinsky's aphorisms. Rule number one declared, "Power is not only what you have but what the enemy thinks you have," arguing that deception and evasion could be vital tools for organizers. Rule number three emphasized surprise and innovation. "Wherever possible go outside of the experience of the enemy," he wrote, thus encouraging "confusion, fear, and retreat."[10]

If some of Alinsky's language resonates with what might be found in any manual on military strategy, that was no mistake. While Alinsky aimed *Rules for Radicals* at anguished young organizers, he also aimed to situate his insights and experiences within a broader strategic conversation, much of it developed within geopolitics and warfare rather than grassroots organizing. Though Alinsky occasionally drew on social movements to illustrate his arguments, far more often he reached for examples from military and political history, citing figures such as Churchill and Lincoln, Jefferson and Disraeli. While this may betray a certain grandiosity to Alinsky's self-conception, it also suggests that he understood himself to be acting and thinking within those traditions, actively engaged in a dialogue about means and ends, strategics and tactics, morality and ethics.[11]

And he hoped that future generations would follow this eclectic example. In the late 1960s, as he was writing *Rules for Radicals,* Alinsky launched a training school organized around many of the book's key ideas. As part of their curriculum, students were required not only to gain hands-on organizing experience and learn Alinsky's theories but also to read Thucydides's *History of the Peloponnesian Wars* and act out the famed Melian dialogue, that classic set piece of realist negotiation. In assigning this text, Alinsky was doing something not so dissimilar from what ought to happen in today's grand strategy programs: holding on to a rich and valuable canon of strategic thought while adapting it for the exigencies of a new audience and a new historical moment.[12]

Leading the Leaderless

The point of examining Alinsky at some length is not to argue for a single inviolable tradition of "grand strategy" or to assert that all tricky situations—from war to labor conflict—can be managed with a little help from the strategic masters. Nor is it to suggest that Alinsky's text holds the best and only vision of social-change strategy to come along in recent decades. Too often, the "grand strategy" approach tends to reify certain texts rather than truly examine them, as if a dash of Machiavelli and a bit of Clausewitz will produce a set of fixed insights to be applied at will. As many critics have pointed out, Alinsky's emphasis on institution-building guided by professional organizers offered but one way to approach the sweeping challenge of creating bottom-up social change. To a 21st-century reader, the paternalistic racism in sections of Alinsky's book also offers reason to pause. Like any other work, Alinsky is best read in its historical context and with a critical sensibility. Indeed, Alinsky himself warned against following his prescriptions too closely, urging readers to remember that his book offered only templates and gestures and reminders, not hard-and-fast solutions.

Alinsky's writing nonetheless suggests that there is plenty of room in even the most canonical view of grand strategy to engage with new voices and concerns, and to use the concept as a platform not for rigidity but for experimentation. To do so is not to construct a false intellectual tradition, cherry-picking aphorisms across time. It is to reflect real continuities as strategists themselves often understood them, many of whom saw no hard and fast distinctions between the worlds of war, politics, and social change. While academics may have sorted themselves into disciplines and discrete areas of expertise, strategists have not necessarily followed suit. Indeed, many would argue that to do so would be to miss an essential lesson of good strategy: the need to be nimble and broad-minded even in moments of crisis, and to take inspiration and instruction wherever it might be found.

If this is true of Alinsky, it is also true of the literature on "strategic non-violence," a term coined by scholar and activist Gene Sharp. As described by Mark Engler and Paul Engler in their book *This Is an Uprising*, Sharp experienced an epiphany of sorts as a young peace activist, when he observed many sympathizers choosing non-violence as an act of moral purity rather than as the approach that would get the job done. Sharp made a case for non-violence as a strategic rather than a moral choice, and he attempted to reinterpret figures such as Gandhi not only as spiritual leaders, but as expert strategists and tacticians, self-consciously choosing the means that would best suit their ends. Like Alinsky, Sharp used martial language to make his case and often borrowed from military strategy. The practice of non-violence, he wrote, entails "waging of 'battles,' requires wise strategy and tactics, and demands of its 'soldiers' courage, discipline, and sacrifice." He also made the case that non-violence, rather than being a form of passive resistance, required "the use of psychological, social, economic and political power," all concentrated toward a particular end. This insistence on non-violence as a hard-headed strategic choice rather than a weak form of virtue signaling earned him nicknames as both the "Machiavelli of non-violence" and the "Clausewitz of unarmed revolution."[13] No less a figure than Thomas Schelling, the father of game theory, recognized the commonalities between systems of war and Sharp's theory of non-violent action. "The difference is not like the difference between prayer and dynamite," Schelling wrote in the introduction to Sharp's *The Politics of Nonviolent Action*. "Political violence, like political nonviolence, usually has as its purpose making somebody do something or not do something or stop doing something."[14]

Like Alinsky, Sharp presented himself as a realist, concerned not with moral purity but with whether a given strategy would be effective to achieve a particular end. He had grand visions and aspirations for the higher good. At the same time, he argued that "feeling good . . . when you have not achieved the goals of your struggle, does not change the fact that you have failed."[15] This set him apart from more idealistic colleagues. As Engler and Engler note, no less a figure than the Reverend Dr. Martin Luther King Jr. waffled on whether it was permissible to adopt a purely strategic position even as he helped to design the successful strategies of civil rights activism, arguing that "nonviolence in the truest sense is not a strategy that one uses simply because it is expedient in the moment."[16]

Such debates are not merely the province of history, remnants from a lost age of revolutionary aspiration and social-justice idealism. Today, there are passionate strategic debates under way as mass movements topple governments, force corporate titans from power, and transform entrenched laws and social ideas. In 2017, for instance, the influential left thinkers Michael Hardt and Antonio Negri published *Assembly*, a book that attempts to puzzle through how to conduct strategy in the context of "leaderless" or "horizontal" movements and how to sustain such movements beyond their initial bursts of enthusiasm. Their answer, borrowing somewhat awkwardly from Machiavelli, is to create a "New Prince" based not on the knowledge of a single aristocratic adviser but on "the power of the multitude."[17]

There are many other recent examples of writers and activists grappling with questions of means and ends, timing and scale, power and tactics. Jane McAlevey's *No Shortcuts* describes the difference between advocacy, mobilizing, and organizing, calling for a strategic assessment of which means might be best suited to which ends.[18] Eric Liu's *You're More Powerful than You Think* offers a guide for "how to understand power" in an age of mass action—a primer for "anyone who wants to make change, large or small," in the words of political scientist Anne-Marie Slaughter.[19] Micah White, one of the creators of Occupy Wall Street, has proclaimed "the end of protest," arguing that street protest, as traditionally conceived, has outlived its strategic utility.[20] All three of these authors have visited Yale's grand strategy program in recent years, offering advice and engagement, in addition to more traditional guests such as General John Hyten, commander of US Strategic

Command (USSTRATCOM), and General H. R. McMaster, former national security adviser to President Donald Trump.

The point is not that all of these practitioners and writers agree with each other or even see themselves operating in the same world. It is simply that they have enough of a shared language and outlook and set of challenges to make for an interesting conversation. In recent years, historians have increasingly emphasized the enmeshed histories of movements and foreign policy, from the Cold War's impact on the civil rights movement (and vice versa) to the influence of the 1968 rebellions on the policy of détente (and vice versa once again).[21] It is long past time that such insights made their way into both scholarly and practical discussions of grand strategy.

This may be especially true in the present moment, when the advent of social media and new technologies has upended both spheres of action. As sociologist Zeynep Tufekci notes, social media has made it easier than ever before to gather large groups of people quickly, whether in Tahrir Square or for the Women's March in Washington.[22] At the same time, those technologies pose a host of new problems, including the potential for surveillance, infiltration, manipulation, and disruption of domestic movements by hostile governments. Perhaps the most significant challenge is figuring out how to move forward after the flash and fire of the demonstration itself, how to exercise long-term power and influence when the commitments of participants may be shallow and when everything is moving so fast. Consider the case of Egypt, where a non-violent protest movement ousted one government from power only to see it replaced by something close to a military regime. Social media may have made it easier to start the war, or at least the battle, but it has made it even harder to secure a desirable peace.

Much of the more theoretical discussion of such dilemmas has been occurring on the left, among pro-democracy and progressive activists. But the dilemmas themselves are hardly limited to that sphere. At its peak in 2010, the Tea Party borrowed heavily from Saul Alinsky, encouraging members to read *Rules for Radicals* and adopt its tactics where relevant.[23] After Trump's election, the liberal group Indivisible borrowed it back from the Tea Party, embracing its example of "local advocacy tactics that work."[24] History is replete with examples of such exchanges. As Eric Liu notes, "Occupy begat We Are the 99 percent begat Fast Food Forward begat $15 Now begat the Bernie Sanders campaign. The Tea Party harnessed a radical anti-establishment spirit that seized and then consumed the Republican Party, fueled Donald

Trump's election, [and] unleashed a new populism."[25] Movements have always learned from each other—and from their enemies as well.

Scholars, practitioners, and teachers interested in grand strategy should learn from them too. Some have argued that the concept of grand strategy no longer has a place in the post–Cold War world, when its very expansiveness threatens to do more harm than good. But it is precisely the capaciousness of the term, the desire to take in everything, that may make it most useful in this moment. Whatever else one may say of the early twenty-first century, it is a moment to think big rather than small. The sprawling, strange, amorphous, sometimes troubling, and always difficult category known as "grand strategy" can be a prod to do just that.

Notes

1. B. H. Liddell Hart, *Strategy* (New York: Meridian Books, 1991).
2. Since the 1970s, a vast scholarly literature has also developed to challenge the idea of movements or other forms of protest as "spontaneous" or "disorganized." This includes recent scholarship on "contentious politics," a term meant to encompass a wide range of non-institutionalized political action, ranging from revolution to protest to ethnic conflict, of which traditional social movements are just one part. On "contentious politics," see esp. Doug McAdam, Sidney Tarrow, and Charles Tilly, *Dynamics of Contention* (New York: Cambridge University Press, 2011); Charles Tilly and Sidney Tarrow, *Contentious Politics*, 2nd ed. (Boulder, CO: Paradigm, 2015); Sidney Tarrow, ed., *Power in Movement: Social Movements and Contentious Politics* (New York: Cambridge University Press, 2011). For recent works with a focus on strategy, see esp. Marshall Ganz, *Why David Sometimes Wins: Leadership, Organization, and Strategy in the California Farm Worker Movement* (New York: Oxford University Press, 2010) and Erica Chenoweth and Maria J. Stephan, *Why Civil Resistance Works: The Strategic Logic of Nonviolent Conflict* (New York: Columbia University Press, 2011). For a recent study of movements in the context of foreign policy, see Joshua W. Busby, *Moral Movements and Foreign Policy* (New York: Cambridge University Press, 2010).
3. John Gaddis, *On Grand Strategy* (New York: Penguin Press, 2018), 21.
4. Stephen Wertheim and Thomas Meaney, "Grand Flattery: The Yale Grand Strategy Seminar," *The Nation*, May 9, 2012.
5. Saul Alinsky, *Rules for Radicals: A Pragmatic Primer for Realistic Radicals* (New York: Vintage Books, 1971), xviii.
6. Ibid., 3, 12, xiii.
7. Ibid., 12.
8. Ibid., 24, xviii, 8–10.
9. Ibid., 138, 42.
10. Ibid., 126, 127.

11. Ibid., 29, 31, 14, 32.

12. Sanford D. Horwitt, *Let Them Call Me Rebel: Saul Alinsky, His Life and Legacy* (New York: Vintage Books, 1989), 531.

13. Mark Engler and Paul Engler, *This Is an Uprising: How Nonviolent Revolt Is Shaping the Twenty-first Century* (New York: Nation Books), 2–8.

14. Thomas C. Schelling, "Introduction," in Gene Sharp, *The Politics of Nonviolent Action*, vol. 1 (Boston: P. Sargent Publisher, 1973), xx.

15. Engler and Engler, *This Is an Uprising*, 7; Gene Sharp, *Waging Nonviolent Struggle: 20th Century Practice and 21st Century Potential* (Manchester, NH: Extending Horizons Books, 2005), 436.

16. Engler and Engler, *This Is an Uprising*, 11.

17. Michael Hardt and Antonio Negri, *Assembly* (New York: Oxford University Press, 2017), 227–228.

18. Jane McAlevey, *No Shortcuts: Organizing for Power in the New Gilded Age* (New York: Oxford University Press, 2016).

19. Eric Liu, *You're More Powerful Than You Think: A Citizen's Guide to Making Change Happen* (New York: PublicAffairs, 2017), 15, back cover.

20. Micah White, *The End of Protest: A New Playbook for Revolution* (Toronto: Alfred A. Knopf Canada, 2016).

21. For two examples among many, see Mary Dudziak, *Cold War Civil Rights: Race and the Image of American Democracy* (Princeton, NJ: Princeton University Press, 2011); Jeremi Suri, *Power and Protest: Global Revolution and the Rise of Détente* (Cambridge, MA: Harvard University Press, 2005).

22. Zeynep Tufekci, *Twitter and Tear Gas: The Power and Fragility of Networked Protest* (New Haven, CT: Yale University Press, 2017).

23. Kenneth P. Vogel, "Right Loves to Hate, Imitate Alinsky," *Politico*, March 22, 2010.

24. "Advocacy Tactics," in *The Indivisible Guide*, https://indivisible.org/resource/local-advocacy-tactics-work (accessed February 13, 2019).

25. Liu, *You're More Powerful Than You Think*, 3–4.

3

Turning the Tide

The Application of Grand Strategy to Global Health

Elizabeth H. Bradley and Lauren A. Taylor

> Ladies and gentlemen, seldom has history offered a greater opportunity to do so much for so many. . . . And to meet a severe and urgent crisis abroad, tonight I propose the Emergency Plan for AIDS Relief, a work of mercy beyond all current international efforts to help the people of Africa. This comprehensive plan will prevent seven million new AIDS infections, treat at least two million people with life-extending drugs, and provide humane care for millions of people suffering from AIDS and for children orphaned by AIDS. I ask the Congress to commit $15 billion over the next five years, including nearly $10 billion in new money, to turn the tide against AIDS.
>
> —President George W. Bush, 2003 State of the Union address[1]

With these sentences, President George W. Bush stunned officials inside and outside the beltway and around the world. His announcement marked the largest commitment by any nation in history to address a single disease.[2] Developed largely in secret and placed outside the traditional bureaucracy of the US Agency for International Development (USAID), the president's Emergency Plan for AIDS Relief (known as PEPFAR) pole vaulted the United States into a leadership role in global health. The purpose of this chapter is to describe the principles of grand strategy as applied to global health and analyze President Bush's PEPFAR program through the lens of these principles. We will highlight how the use of grand strategic principles resulted in a highly successful, if still limited, global health intervention.

A Framework for Studying Grand Strategy

The study of grand strategy, growing out of military history and political science, involves examining the deployment of all existing resources—including diplomatic, economic, military, and other resources—to attain political objectives.[3] Although the study of grand strategy has often focused on the ends and means of military action and international security, the principles and methods of grand strategy are relevant to a broad array of ends and means.[4] In addition to security, ends might include economic and political stability, health, climate sustainability, technological advancement, and other national or global interests. Given this broader definition of grand strategy, is it appropriate to refer to PEPFAR as a grand strategy? On what basis would one make that determination?

To address this question, we propose a framework for exploring human endeavors to achieve desired ends with existing resources. The framework suggests a progression in time from the *current state* (the present landscape) to the *desired state* (the aspiration) and can be understood as occurring at multiple levels: an individual decision maker, a group of decision makers, a nation, or even global entities. The *strategy* is the means by which the entity moves from the current to the desired state (the end), and the implementation *tactics* are the mechanisms by which the strategy is executed. As described by Hal Brands, strategy is the "what" and the implementation tactics are the "how" of grand strategy.[5] Importantly, in effective grand strategies, a proportionality of means and ends is apparent, and both the "what" and the "how" of the means fit with, or are adapted to, the existing ecology broadly conceived. The framework is marked by double-headed arrows, connoting dynamic processes in which a change in knowledge and perspectives in any stage of the grand strategic process may cause a recalibration of other aspects of the strategy. As an example, in the celebrated text of grand strategy *On War*, Carl von Clausewitz noted that "friction" experienced in the field during implementation phases may feed back to cause revisions to either the description of the current states or the vision of the desired future state.[6] Ideally, the process allows for the improvisation and adaptation from what may have been the ideal strategy on paper to what is the effective strategy in practice.

Critical to grand strategy is recognition of the *ecology* in which strategy is developed and implemented, including the historical, political, economic, physical, psychological, and social forces that shape national and global actions and reactions. For the astute grand strategist, analysis of the ecology not only outlines capabilities, available resources, and possible alliances, but also highlights prioritized problems or threats that successful strategies must correct or overcome. For instance, in the case of PEPFAR, the problem might have been framed as a runaway epidemic of HIV/AIDS (human immuno-deficiency virus/acquired immunodeficiency syndrome) in several countries of southern Africa, with potential for pandemic spread. The ecology sur-rounding the problem included growing international pressure on wealthy countries to contribute to achievement of the Millennium Development Goals (MDGs) formulated by the United Nations (UN), a US Congress and Republican administration that were typically lukewarm about supporting humanitarian development assistance, and increasing international security threats presumed to be fomented within nations with extreme poverty and largely failed states.[7]

Furthermore, the ecology includes not only present-day forces but also a historical perspective on the current state. The historical view is essential to uncovering precedents of the current state and *root causes* of the pressing problems or threats. Root causes refer to the beginning or at least earlier stages in the chain of events that produced the current problem. Although a perfect understanding of the causal chain is unattainable, careful histor-ical research can uncover facets of the problem that may be masked by the current environment but are nonetheless central to both causing and hence potentially mitigating existing threats. Through our analysis, we sought to examine the value of grand strategy as a framework for understanding global health efforts.

The President's Emergency Program for AIDS Response (PEPFAR): A Narrative

Introduced in President Bush's 2003 State of the Union address, PEPFAR ini-tially focused on rapidly scaling up treatment and prevention services in fifteen low-income countries where more than half of the HIV infections worldwide occurred. The first authorization, the *United States Leadership against HIV/ AIDS, Tuberculosis and Malaria* Act of 2003 (P.L. 108-25), shortly followed the State of the Union address, allocating $15 billion over five years. The desired state was to have "turned the tide" on the HIV/AIDS epidemic in Africa by attaining unequivocally ambitious targets: 2 million people on anti-retroviral medication treatment by 2006, 10 million infected and affected people under some kind of care by 2008, and 7 million prevented infections by 2008.[8]

President Bush's motives in establishing PEPFAR were manifold. First, the investment in PEPFAR would meet the international call for increasing humanitarian support to further progress toward the Millennium Development Goals[9] but would do so through a bilateral mechanism rather than the multilateral one (the Global Fund to Fight AIDS, TB, and Malaria)[10] proposed by the UN. Second, in 2000, the UN Security Council passed Resolution 1308,[11] which declared HIV to be a threat to security and stability around the world. Even though PEPFAR called for a doubling of US spending for international humanitarian aid for health, President Bush viewed the sum as trifling compared with the $72.5 billion spent on the War on Terror in fiscal year 2003 (the United States spent some $900 billion on the War on Terror between 2001 and 2008).[12] Third, the president saw an opportunity to deploy practical, effective tools to stem the tide of the lethal HIV/AIDS epidemic. Anti-retroviral treatment, first made available on a larger scale in 1996, had been shown to work in Africa through a small but impressive program in Uganda.[13] With this case serving as a proof of concept, President Bush felt confident that PEPFAR would stand on firm scientific footing. Fourth and seemingly most central, President Bush's public statements and reflections from those close to him during the decision in 2003 reflect a deep moral underpinning to address what was seen as a humanitarian disaster.[14] As an evangelical Christian, the president was supported by figures such as Senator Jesse Helms and the Reverend Franklin Graham, both of whom were frequent interlocutors in the lead up to PEPFAR's unveiling.[15] Repeatedly, Bush also made the case that helping people suffering from HIV/AIDS around the world aligned with American values:

> When I visit Africa, I will reaffirm our Nation's commitment to helping Africans fight this disease. America makes this commitment for a clear reason directly rooted at our founding: We believe in the value and dignity of every human life. We're putting that belief into practice.[16]

The confluence of Bush's deep sense of moral responsibility and the opportunity to demonstrate effectiveness in foreign humanitarian aid led to the creation of a legacy project for the Bush administration. Additionally, once informed about the scope of the HIV/AIDS epidemic and the credible strategy to effectively stem the epidemic, the president feared that inaction on the HIV/AIDS epidemic would be judged poorly by history.[17] The president was therefore eager to do something that Washington and the world would recognize as *big*.[18]

President Bush wanted to define PEPFAR as a new way of deploying American resources for humanitarian assistance, aligning it with his vision of reforming US approaches to development assistance more broadly. To confidants, the president revealed doubts about the effectiveness of traditional foreign development assistance. In his view, development efforts were non-strategic, lacked clear outcomes and accountability, and had become paternalistic as recipient countries had been treated as victims rather than as partners in development. Reflecting these concerns, Bush wrote in his autobiography:

> Another problem was that the traditional model of foreign aid was paternalistic: A wealthy donor nation wrote a check and told the recipient how to spend it. I decided to take a new approach in Africa. . . . We would base our relationships on partnership, not paternalism. We would trust developing countries to design their own strategy for using American taxpayer dollars. In return, they would measure their performance and be held accountable. The results would be that countries felt invested in their own success, while American taxpayers could see the impact of their generosity.[19]

Although President Bush heralded PEPFAR as a departure from the past, in fact, its approach mirrored tactics used in the Marshall Plan sixty years earlier, in which US dollars rebuilt Western Europe through the European Recovery Plan (ERP) after the devastation of World War II through a partnership model of aid. Each PEPFAR focal country was required to develop a detailed plan of activities—an approach that echoed the insistence of Truman, Secretary of State George Marshall, and Ambassador George Kennan that European countries draw up their own plans before receiving funds from the Marshall Plan.[20] As described by Kennan's biographer, John Lewis Gaddis, "It made sense . . . to let the Europeans take the lead in shaping the Marshall Plan, because this would encourage unity among them" without appearing to promote "American imperialism," which would give Moscow a target of attack.[21] Thus, the Europeans wrote their own report, totaling $22 billion of requests, which they prioritized, not as American satellites but independent nations.[22] In 2007, Ambassador Mark Dybul, US Global AIDS coordinator, characterized PEPFAR as modeled on the effort to rebuild Europe after the Second World War; speaking before the House Committee on Foreign Affairs, he said, "Fundamentally, this new philosophy rejects the failed 'donor-recipient' approach developed during the Cold War and returns to the vision of the Marshall Plan."[23]

Consistent with his goal of demonstrating better returns on investment for US development assistance, Bush sought expert scientific counsel from then head of the National Institute of Allergy and Infectious Diseases (NIAID), Anthony Fauci. Increased investment in research for an HIV/AIDS vaccine would have benefited NIAID, but Fauci suggested that the best use for available funds was in prevention and treatment of existing cases through the use of now available anti-retroviral drugs. The administration understood that prevention efforts alone, without also offering treatment, could not be successful, as individuals would be unlikely to get tested for HIV/AIDS if an affirmative result only confirmed an immutable death sentence. With the new AIDS drugs now more available and some (albeit limited) evidence that treatment adherence in Africa was possible, Fauci convinced the architects of PEPFAR to commit to treatment and care for existing cases and increased education and counseling (as well as testing) for people at risk of HIV/AIDS.[24] Abstinence education, thought to be an effective prevention strategy that aligned well with conservative values, was integrated into the funded activities.[25]

Bush wove both Democratic and Republican values into the fabric of PEPFAR in order to ensure enough congressional support to fund his enormous aspirations. Prominent members of the left, including ACT UP, the singer-philanthropist Bono, and the Global AIDS Alliance had previously critiqued the president's commitments to the Global Fund as insufficient and motivated by politics rather than genuine commitment.[26] In response, Bush commissioned his closest allies to think "big" about their next move in the fight against HIV/AIDS—even going so far as to "assume money is no object."[27] Officials held design meetings in the Situation Room of the White House in an effort to avoid derailment by opponents, media skepticism, and being captured by the existing bureaucratic machinery of US humanitarian and development aid.[28] Conservative critique of the PEPFAR program came later, following the State of the Union announcement that PEPFAR would promote an "ABC" (abstinence, be faithful, condoms) approach. Republican members of Congress quickly leaped on the administration with concerns that condom distribution was not to be federally funded per previous federal regulations.[29] Ultimately, Congress passed a bill that required at least one-third of prevention funding be spent on abstinence-until-marriage programs, although condom distribution could be funded.[30] PEPFAR funds could not support groups that advocated legalization of the sex trade, but the public law was explicit that this exclusion should not be construed to prevent individuals who participated in the sex trade from receiving condoms and HIV/AIDS treatment. PEPFAR won enough congressional support to pass the House on May 1 and the Senate on May 23, 2003. In the words of one of PEPFAR's architects, Bush made a "previously polarized line into a circle, or almost a circle. He made a bigger coalition."[31] With support from both the left and right, the president and his team created a new organizational structure to match the "emergency" language used in his political strategy.

Even with broad-based political support and an attainable end in mind, PEPFAR was limited in its impact by the realities of the day, which the study of grand strategy dubs "friction."[32] For many of the fifteen countries chosen for PEPFAR funding, other priorities—such as emergency maternal and obstetrics care or basic infrastructure that served a general population—ranked above HIV/AIDS in health priorities. The lack of essential commodities and health care workers continually stymied the roll out of auspicious PEPFAR programs.[33] Cultural taboos surrounding an AIDS diagnosis undermined efforts to make the disease a political priority in countries such as South Africa, one of the hardest hit by the epidemic.[34] Public health experts experienced more setbacks than anticipated as they worked to scale up treatment strategies. UN agencies, public health experts, and AIDS activists consistently critiqued the "ABC approach" to prevention for being unrealistic and overly defined by religious mores of conservatives in the Republican Party.[35]

The haste with which the US government mobilized PEPFAR resources also had drawbacks. The relentless workload burned out staff quickly, the emphasis placed on working with small civil society organizations resulted in money often being left unspent in US accounts,[36] and experienced experts such as the leadership at the US Center for Disease Control and Prevention were omitted from PEPFAR design meetings.[37] The impact of HIV funding on the delivery of health services for ailments other than HIV/AIDS remains an open debate and likely varied by country.[38] For instance, immunization efforts may have been crowded out, while maternal health services may have been enhanced.[39]

Despite these shortcomings, the global health community has generally converged around a positive view of the program's impact.[40] PEPFAR represents the largest investment to date by any country to address a single disease, resulting in wide-ranging impacts. PEPFAR has been credited with saving more than 18 million lives, in no small part by proiding for 15.7 million people to have access to antiretroviral treatment. [41] Since the peak of the AIDS epidemic in 2004, global deaths have decreased 60%. Rigorous research demonstrated that between 2004-2008, all-cause mortality in PEPFAR focus countries declined more than non-focus countries. [42]

PEPFAR was reauthorized in 2008; an additional $48 billion was allocated, of which $38 billion was targeted for HIV/AIDS and $10 billion was made available for tuberculosis and malaria treatment, using a "Partnership Framework" agreement with the US. government regarding priorities and allocation of resources. The continued investment and commitment also has inspired a generation of young adults interested in the science, policy, and strategy of global health, and many of the global health institutes and initiatives are based at US universities. The global reputation of the United States may also have benefited from the US engagement in global health. [43] In 2009, five years after the initial PEPFAR investments (which funded 95 percent of all AIDS-related care in some countries), Africa was the global region with the most positive view of US leadership. [44]

In short, PEPFAR has greatly expanded the US footprint abroad and has transformed global health into an instrument of diplomacy and statecraft. Kathleen Sebelius, at that time secretary of the Department of Health and Human Services, underscored the statecraft that underlies the current US Global Health Initiative, [45] remarking, "We can no longer separate global health from America's health." [46] One of several principles defined in the Global Health Strategy [47] of the US Department of Health and Human Services (HHS) was to "advance health diplomacy" based on the PEPFAR experience. In a commentary on the strategy, Nils Daulaire, director of the HHS Office of Global Affairs, wrote:

> PEPFAR is the leading example of how a health intervention can serve to support US credibility and influence in other parts of the world. Notably in Africa, PEPFAR has become the cornerstone of bilateral relationships with host governments and civil society. HHS' work internationally is an emerging arena of US influence and impact that starts with better health across national borders but has a major effect on encouraging and securing constructive relationships with foreign governments. [48]

PEPFAR in Light of Historical Ambivalence
toward International Health Efforts

Although President Bush framed PEPFAR as part of his new approach to development assistance, a grand strategic perspective must consider PEPFAR within the historical context of 150 years of US engagement in international health efforts. On one hand, PEPFAR remains unique in a long line of US international health efforts due to its size and speed of implementation. On the other hand, PEPFAR emerged from and was shaped by a historical ambivalence toward international health promotion efforts. This history illustrates a deep suspicion of multilateral efforts and a clear preference for medically focused programs that directly serve American interests.

The United States did not participate in the earliest modern efforts to foster international collaboration on health, which were largely fueled by ambitions of European imperialism and nineteenth-century economic development. Motivated by concerns that the spread of infectious diseases (such as plague, yellow fever, and cholera in the context of increased population mobility) would dampen commerce, representatives from eleven European states and the Ottoman Empire convened as the International Sanitary Conference in Paris in 1851–52 for the first modern intergovernmental meeting on health. The conference aimed to create uniform international quarantine regulations to replace existing excessive precautions that hindered international commerce.[49] Over seven conferences and more than forty years, participants found agreement on international standards and regulations difficult to achieve, particularly given the scientific disputes about the etiology of infectious diseases. In 1892, the 7th International Sanitary Conference, held in Venice, adopted the first international quarantine convention, and even then, narrowly focused on cholera and only for westbound shipping from the East.[50]

Not until 1907—more than fifty years after the initial convention in Paris—did a unified organization emerge to integrate all previous International Sanitary Conferences with support from the United States and twelve other governments who signed the treaty known as the Arrangement de Rome.[51] This new organization, named Office International d'hygiene Publique or OIHP, would convene future International Sanitary Conferences focused on a limited number of infectious diseases prioritized because of their potential to interfere with maritime trade. Furthermore, it was clear in its mandate that the OIHP could not interfere in any way with the administration of states.[52]

By 1920, thirty-nine governments had signed the Arrangement de Rome, and all business was conducted in French.

After World War I, the League of Nations embarked on a parallel path to influence international health efforts. Article 23(f) of the Covenant of the League of Nations indicated, however, that the League would undertake a broader agenda in health than merely establishing international quarantine standards. Instead, Article 23(f) indicated that the League would "endeavor to take steps in matters of international concern for the prevention and control of disease."[53] Moreover, Article 24 suggested that the League of Nations would integrate all former international health agreements (including the OIHP) under one umbrella—the Health Organization of the League. The United States, now an influential force in the OIHP, had no intention of joining the League, and hence, refused to accept the dissolution of OIHP.

During the interwar years, the two organizations—the OIHP and the Health Organization of the League—persisted as separate bodies, although many of the same individuals participated in both. The OIHP continued to focus on specific infectious diseases that could impede international commerce, while the Health Organization of the League, led by Polish scientist Ludwik Rajchman, sought to tackle broader issues regarding the social and economic determinants of health. Within his scope of focus were working and living conditions of those who became sick as well as the development of statistical comparisons to track progress in health promotion across countries.[54] Although US medical scientists participated as individuals in the Health Organization of the League, the US government remained absent from international health cooperation other than those efforts sponsored by the narrower, disease-focused OIHP.[55]

Even after World War II, when international collaboration allowed the creation of a single, international health organization, the World Health Organization (WHO) of the United Nations, divisions over its purview and goals persisted. Different views about the determinants of disease and health (with the United States endorsing a more biomedical focus and the Soviet Union adopting a more social and economic focus) meant that countries struggled to agree on the appropriate scope and obligations of the WHO.[56] At the Technical Preparatory Committee for the International Health Conference in Paris 1946, which would establish the WHO, US Surgeon General Thomas Parran successfully advocated relatively narrow functions of the WHO. These functions emphasized quarantine standards, drug and biological product labeling and safety, and disease nomenclature.[57] Activities that might address the social and economic conditions that accelerated the spread of disease were left to nations themselves.

Within the United States, policymakers have been ambivalent about the WHO since its inception. At the opening assembly in 1948, participants from the United States were seated in the public gallery because the US Congress had reserved the right to withdraw membership in the WHO rather than fully endorsing US membership. Ironically, it was N. A. Vinogradradov, the deputy minister of health from the Soviet Union, who spoke in favor of accepting the United States for membership. The nation was thus admitted to the WHO "by the back door"[58] despite the US congressional reservations. The controversy reflected a more general US uncertainty about participating in international health collaborations. The US interventions in international health had historically sidestepped working on social and economic conditions that influence health broadly and instead opted for focused efforts to address infectious diseases for which medical treatments were available.

This American proclivity toward short-term, medically motivated interventions presents a persistent challenge to modern-day strategies to promote health globally. Divergent views on the most effective approaches to produce health coupled with potential conflicts between national and global interests challenge US efforts to develop a grand strategy for global health as the grandest of all strategies would require substantial international collaboration. As illustrated by the unfolding of the WHO as well as the design of the US PEPFAR program, achieving an effective balance between focused, medical fixes and broader, system-building activities will be essential to the creation of sustainable, modern approaches to health.

Evaluating PEPFAR

We conclude that PEPFAR met many of the criteria of a grand strategy in global health for the Bush administration. Certainly, the Bush administration articulated explicit goals, or ends, and connected those to the larger ecology of national interests related to demonstrating American morality and protecting the United States from the threat of pandemic HIV/AIDS. The brilliance of PEPFAR was in creating an ambitious but "intellectually graspable"[59] end onto which key stakeholders, including policymakers, advocates, and the public, could latch. Impressive targets could be enumerated (2 million treated with anti-retroviral medicines, 10 million in care, and

7 million cases prevented) and tracked. Moreover, the means were proportional to those ends. Detailed plans were made about targets and distribution channels for the interventions, and recipient countries were involved in these plans, accepting that the plans were attached to the financial support.

Nevertheless, PEPFAR as a strategy was incomplete. The largest commitment to a single disease failed to address critical root causes of the spread of HIV/AIDS—the social and economic conditions in which such pathogens emerge and spread. Although PEPFAR saved and continues to sustain millions of lives, PEPFAR focused largely on a medical approach to address HIV/AIDS, an approach reminiscent of the cautious US engagement in international health efforts for decades. In failing to address root causes, PEPFAR can be analogized to a "whack-a-mole" strategy. The strategy addressed what could be seen (cases of HIV/AIDS) but largely neglected the more fundamental causes of the infectious diseases that spread in high-poverty environments.

This analysis ultimately raises key strategic questions for the United States looking forward. America's values and interests as well as its ambivalence about its role in promoting health internationally strongly shaped the PEPFAR strategy toward HIV/AIDS in Africa. Some of the defining features of PEPFAR—the focus on a single disease and bilateral rather than multilateral engagement—reflect a realistic understanding of the political environment on the part of the Bush administration and were essential for garnering congressional and popular support. In contrast, strengthening the international system to deal with the root causes of such infectious diseases would have been necessary to prepare nations for similar, subsequent threats. To the degree that these root causes involve sociopolitical and economic conditions, the United States has been loath to intervene in what is viewed as the purview of sovereign nation-states. This leaves open the question: What constitutes a grand strategy in US global health?

Conclusion

In this chapter, we aimed to make an affirmative argument for the value of grand strategy as a framework for understanding global health efforts. We began by outlining the key components of analysis—including not only the strategy itself but also the tactics, the current and desired states, and the ecology within which a strategy operates. We then applied this understanding of grand strategy to one of the United States' signature global health achievements, PEPFAR, illustrating that policymakers outside the realms of diplomacy and defense have been strategizing in a way that aligns with the existing literature on grand strategy. We described a strategy that was able to achieve substantial health impacts and raise the profile of the United States in large part because it was well tailored to American politics, history, and values. This case underscores the relevance of grand strategy in domains beyond military strategy where the requirement is to achieve large ends with limited means.

In applying the concept of grand strategy to PEPFAR, we also uncovered ways in which the traditional definitions and concepts used to characterize grand strategy are imperfect and sometimes unclear. In particular, the question of what makes a strategy grand posed a challenge. PEPFAR continues to be critiqued for not being ambitious enough given the scale and urgency of the human need for HIV/AIDS prevention and treatment. Our analysis thus confronted the following challenge: How large must the problem be for the strategy to be considered a *grand* strategy? In other words, how deep into the root causal chain must a grant strategist go? We suspect the pragmatic answer is "as far as possible given available resources and sociopolitical will." Unfortunately, without being in the seat of leadership at the time the strategy is being developed, it is difficult to fully appreciate the constraints and resources that may reasonably affect the scope of the problem definition and subsequent strategy choices. Experts debate what might have happened had the PEPFAR strategy been designed to address the root causes of the HIV/AIDS epidemic more thoroughly. Without the counterfactual, analysts like ourselves are hampered in our judgment of PEPFAR's proportionality, one of the most elusive but important criteria for judging the success of a grand strategy.

This challenge underscores the critical import of leadership in designing and implementing a grand strategy. It falls on those in leadership to assess the scope of the problem and its root causes and then calibrate the desired ends with the availability of resources and capabilities. In so doing, grand strategists recognize that means and ends are interdependent; a reframe of the objective (or end) may change the availability of resources (or means), or vice versa. The complexity of this task defies reliance on simple ledgers and underscores institutions' continued reliance on leadership, even as clearer articulations of the strategy development process and enhanced technological aids emerge.

As we found in the case of PEPFAR, often a grand strategy is not able to tackle the most fundamental causes of the problem. Bush was not in a position to deploy aid programs that could fully remedy the social determinant of health deficits occurring in dozens of countries around the world. Some grand strategists may feel disappointed to realize that their ecology will not withstand the most ambitious and impactful strategy possible. In such cases, we encourage these leaders to recognize their place in a history that has yet to be written. Moreover, as we analysts and commentators judge impact, we would do well to also recognize strategies as part of the larger span of history, evaluating them not only based on what they achieve but also on what groundwork they lay on which future strategists can build. One generation's grand strategy becomes the following generation's inherited ecology. Avoiding the foreclosure of a successor's ability to pursue a still *grander* strategy may itself be a strategic success.

Notes

1. "President Delivers 'State of the Union,'" White House Archives, President George W. Bush, January 28, 2003.
2. "The U.S. President's Emergency Plan for Aids Relief (PEPFAR)," Henry J. Kaiser Family Foundation, Washington, DC.
3. B. H. Liddell Hart, *Strategy* (California: Faber & Faber, 1967).
4. See Williamson Murray and Mark Grimsley, "Introduction: On Strategy," in *The Making of Strategy: Rulers, States, and War*, ed. Williamson Murray, MacGregor Knox, and Alvin Bernstein (Cambridge: Cambridge University Press, 1994), 1–23; Hal Brands, *What Good Is Grand Strategy? Power and Purpose in American Statecraft from Harry S. Truman to George W. Bush* (Ithaca, NY: Cornell University Press, 2014); Charles Hill, *Grand Strategies: Literature, Statecraft, and World Order* (New Haven, CT: Yale University Press, 2011); Liddell Hart, *Strategy*; and Paul Kennedy, *Grand Strategies in War and Peace*, reprint (New Haven, CT: Yale University Press, 1992).
5. Brands, *What Good Is Grand Strategy?* 200.
6. Carl von Clausewitz, *On War*, trans. Michael Eliot Howard and Peter Paret, reprint (Princeton, NJ: Princeton University Press, 1989), 119–121.
7. "About Mdgs: What They Are," Millennium Project, http://www.unmillenniumproject.org/goals/.
8. "Celebrating Life: Latest PEPFAR Results," ed. US President's Emergency Plan for AIDS Relief (2008), https://preview.state.gov/wp-content/uploads/2019/08/PEPFAR-2009-Annual-Report-to-Congress.pdf.
9. "About Mdgs: What They Are," Millennium Project, http://www.unmillenniumproject.org/goals/.

10. "About the Global Fund," Global Fund to Fight AIDS, TB and Malaria. 2016. http://www.theglobalfund.org/en/.

11. "UN Security Council Resolution 1308, HIV/AIDS," edited by United Nations Security Council, July 17, 2000.

12. Josh Bolton, interview by Elizabeth Bradley, January 23, 2016; Amy Belasco, "The Cost of Iraq, Afghanistan, and Other Global War on Terror Operations since 9/11," (Congressional Research Service, December 8, 2014).

13. S. M. Hammer et al., "A Controlled Trial of Two Nucleoside Analogues plus Indinavir in Persons with Human Immunodeficiency Virus Infection and Cd4 Cell Counts of 200 Per Cubic Millimeter or Less. Aids Clinical Trials Group 320 Study Team," *New England Journal of Medicine* 337:11 (September 11, 1997), 1394–1395; John Donnelly, "The President's Emergency Plan for AIDS Relief: How George W. Bush and Aides Came to 'Think Big' on Battling HIV," *Health Affairs* 31, no. 7 (2012).

14. George W. Bush, *Decision Points* (New York: Crown, 2010), 335.

15. Franklin Graham, "The Age of AIDS: Interview with Franklin Graham," *Frontline*, January 31, 2005.

16. "Remarks Announcing the Nomination of Randall Tobias to Be Global Aids Coordinator and an Exchange with Reporters," ed. Administration of George W. Bush (Washington, DC: US Government Printing Office, July 2, 2003).

17. Donnelly, "The President's Emergency Plan for AIDS Relief," 1395.

18. Ibid., 1390.

19. Bush, *Decision Points*, 335.

20. John Lewis Gaddis, *George F. Kennan: An American Life* (New York: Penguin Group, 2011), 276–297.

21. Ibid., 278.

22. Ibid., 283.

23. Ambassador Mark Dybul, "President Bush's Emergency Plan for AIDS Relief (PEPFAR): Testimony before the House Committee on Foreign Affairs," news release, April 24, 2007, http://2001-2009.state.gov/p/af/rls/rm/83616.htm.

24. Bolton, "Interview Snippets from Josh Bolton."

25. Donnelly, "The President's Emergency Plan for AIDS Relief," 1392.

26. Jay P. Lefkowitz, "AIDS and the President—an inside Account," *Commentary Magazine*, January 1, 2009.

27. Ibid.

28. Ibid.; Bolton, Josh, interview by Elizabeth Bradley, January 23, 2016; Amy Belasco, "The Cost of Iraq, Afghanistan, and Other Global War on Terror Operations since 9/11," (Congressional Research Service, December 8, 2014).

29. George W. Bush, "Memorandum for the Administrator of the United States Agency for International Development," news release, January 22, 2001, http://web.archive.org/web/20010604032136/http://www.whitehouse.gov/news/releases/20010123-5.html; Lefkowitz, "AIDS and the President."

30. *H.R. 1298—United States Leadership against HIV/AIDS, Tuberculosis and Malaria Act of 2003*, 108–125, 108th Congress.

31. Gary Edson, interview by Elizabeth Bradley, January 27, 2016.

32. Clausewitz, *On War*, 119–121.

33. Committee on the US Commitment to Global Health, "The U.S. Commitment to Global Heath: Recommendations for the Public and Private Sectors" (Washington, DC: Institute of Medicine of the National Academies, 2009), 65–67.

34. Nicoli Nattrass, *The Moral Economy of AIDS in South Africa* (Cambridge: Cambridge University Press, 2004), 41.

35. Jonathan Cohen and Tony Tate, "The Less They Know, the Better: Abstinence-Only HIV/AIDS Programs in Uganda," *Reproductive Health Matters* 14:28; Scott H. Evertz, "How Ideology Trumped Science: Why PEPFAR Has Failed to Meet Its Potential" (Washington, DC: Council for Global Equality: Center for American Progress, January 2010); "President Bush Signs H.R. 5501, the Tom Lantos and Henry J. Hyde United States Global Leadership against HIV/AIDS, Tuberculosis and Malaria Reauthorization Act of 2008," news release, July 30, 2008.

36. R. J. Simonds, Constance Carrino, R. J. Simonds, and Michele Moloney-Kitts, "Lessons from the President's Emergency Plan for AIDS Relief: From Quick Ramp-up to the Role of Strategic Partnership," *Health Affairs* 31:7 (July 2012).

37. Gregg Gonsalves, interview by Elizabeth Bradley, 2016.

38. Karen A. Grépin, "HIV Donor Funding Has Both Boosted and Curbed the Delivery of Different Non-HIV Health Services in Sub-Saharan Africa," *Health Affairs* 31:7 (2012); "Evaluation of PEPFAR," Washington, DC, Institute of Medicine of the National Academies, 2013.

39. "HIV Donor Funding Has Both Boosted and Curbed the Delivery of Different Non-HIV Health Services in Sub-Saharan Africa."

40. "Evaluation of PEPFAR," Institute of Medicine of the National Academies, 2013; E. Bendavid and J. Bhattacharya, "The President's Emergency Plan for AIDS Relief in Africa: An Evaluation of Outcomes," *Annals of Internal Medicine* 150 (2009), 688–695.

41. "PEPFAR." HIV.gov Accessed 10/7/2020. https://www.hiv.gov/federal-response/pepfar-global-aids/pepfar#:~:text=Since%20PEPFAR's%20inception%20in%20 2003,50%20countries%20around%20the%20world.

42. Bendavad E et al. "HIV development assistance and adult mortality in Africa," JAMA, 2012. https://pubmed.ncbi.nlm.nih.gov/22665105/.

43. Constance Carrino, R. J. Simonds, and Michele Moloney-Kitts, "Lessons from the President's Emergency Plan for Aids Relief: From Quick Ramp-up to the Role of Strategic Partnership," ibid. (July 2012).

44. James W. Curran Michael H. Merson, Caroline Hope Griffith, and Braveen Ragunanthan, "The President's Emergency Plan for Aids Relief: From Successes of the Emergency Response to Challenges of Sustainable Action," ibid. (2012).

45. "US Global Health Programs," US Government Global Health Initiative, https://www.ghi.gov/.

46. Nils Daulaire, "The Importance of the Global Health Strategy from the U.S. Department of Health and Human Services," *American Journal of Tropical Medicine and Hygiene* 87:3 (2012); Kaiser Family Foundation, "Kaiser Newsroom: Exploring HHS' Role in Global Health & New Global Health Strategy," (2012), https://www.kff.org/wp-content/uploads/2012/01/hhs_-role-in-global-health-transcript-010512.pdf.

47. Department of Health and Human Services, "The Global Health Strategy of the US Department of Health and Human Services" (2012), http://www.hhs.gov/sites/default/files/hhs-global-strategy.pdf.
48. Daulaire, "The Importance of the Global Health Strategy from the U.S. Department of Health and Human Services."
49. Norman Howard-Jones, "The Scientific Background of the International Sanitary Conferences, 1851–1938," *World Health Organization* (1975).
50. Ibid.; "The World Health Organization in Historical Perspective," *Perspectives in Biology and Medicine* 24:3 (1981).
51. "The World Health Organization in Historical Perspective."
52. Iris Borowy, *Coming to Terms with World Health: The League of Nations Health Organization, 1921–1946* (New York: Peter Lang, 2009).
53. "Covenant of the League of Nations," ed., League of Nations (1919).
54. Francesca Piana, "Humanitaire et Politique, in Medias Res: Le Typhus en Pologne et L'organisation Internationale D'hygiène de la Sdn (1919–1923)," *Relations internationales* 138:2 (2009).
55. Howard-Jones, N., "The World Health Organization in historical perspective," *Perspectives in Biology and Medicine* 24:3, 467–82; Piana, "Humanitaire et Politique, in Medias Res."
56. Kelley Lee, *Global Institutions: The World Health Organization* (Abingdon, UK: Routledge, 2008).
57. "Minutes of the Technical Preparatory Committee for the International Health Conference Held in Paris from 18 March to 5 April 1946," paper presented at the International Health Conference, Paris, 1946.
58. Howard-Jones, "The World Health Organization in Historical Perspective."
59. Gary Edson, interview by Elizabeth Bradley, January 27, 2016.

PART II
HISTORICAL GRAND NARRATIVES

4

Extending the Sphere

A Federalist Grand Strategy

Charles Edel

In the beginning, there was an ocean. Actually, two. Or, depending on how one counted, three. The traditional story of America's growth centers on this geographical fact. With distance came safety, and with safety an opportunity for the young nation to expand its territory, capitalize on its abundant resources, and develop its republican institutions free from threat of invasion. Writing in 1960, the distinguished historian of the American South, C. Vann Woodward, took up the question of how security affected the American character. "Nature's gift of three vast bodies of water," Woodward observed, counting not only the Atlantic and the Pacific, but the Arctic as well, "interposed between this country and any other power that might constitute a serious menace to its safety" provided it with "free security."[1]

Describing Adam and Eve's banishment from the Garden of Eden, John Milton ended *Paradise Lost* with the hopeful phrase "the world was all before them, where to choose their place to rest, and Providence their guide."[2] Though written in the midst of the English Civil War, Milton's words capture precisely the view that Woodward reflected in his glance back at the nation's early years. According to this reading of history, all America had to do was march west into the sunlight. Of course, it did not take a historian writing in the midst of the Cold War to realize the significance of these fundamental geographic facts. From the very beginning of American history, American statesmen understood that circumstance and geographic realities afforded them certain opportunities.

To be sure, from the very beginning of American history, there were reasons for moderate optimism—a wide ocean separating America from Europe, a rapidly expanding population with a commercial spirit, and a new government designed to safeguard the liberty of its inhabitants. But those were aspirations rather than established facts; believing in a powerful

America that set an example with its republican conduct did not make it so. Of course, the story was considerably more complicated. From the late fifteenth century onward, the great European imperial powers had been engaged in a struggle for mastery on the European continent. Much of that competition took place overseas as colonial possessions and commercial trade conferred on their possessors economic wealth and political power. After nearly a hundred years of sustained competition with the British, a French foreign ministry report noted in 1779 that "the discovery of the New World has transformed the political system of Europe."[3] According to this logic, whoever controlled the new world would come to dominate the old.

A similar logic shaped early American strategic thinking. As Alexander Hamilton articulated in the *Federalist 11*, the goal of the newly formed United States was "to become the arbiter of Europe in America, and to be able to incline the balance of European competitors in this part of the world as our interests may dictate."[4] The more the United States was able to project its power in the Western Hemisphere, the less European imperial powers would dictate the limits of America's ambitions. This was no mean task. Europe, dominated by monarchies hostile to the concept of republicanism and greedy for further colonial possessions in the new world were likely to threaten the United States—a small, divided, and defenseless republic with immature, if not non-existent, institutions—in both territorial and ideological terms. From its very founding, America had to compete with British, French, Spanish, and Russian claims to North American territory, in addition to those of the indigenous peoples who already inhabited those lands.

Moreover, those external dangers were hardly the only ones that America faced in its early years. Internally, the twin dangers of slavery and political faction had the potential to tear the nation apart, even if neither danger seemed particularly acute at the founding. Finally, as John Quincy Adams perhaps most acutely understood, in addition to threats posed to the nation by these external and internal problems, Americans often wanted to support democratic revolutions abroad before they had even finished establishing their own. Adams saw the danger of US missionary zeal outstripping American capabilities and thought this would leave the nation highly vulnerable.

The commonly held objectives of all early American statesmen were to preserve, expand, and strengthen the republic and the idea of republicanism in the face of all these threats. From Washington's Neutrality Proclamation and Farewell Address, to the varied responses of John Adams, Thomas Jefferson, and James Madison to the Napoleonic Wars, to the Monroe Doctrine, through to the expansionist policies of Andrew Jackson and James Polk, the broad contours of a consistent and largely consensual grand strategy emerge. While American statesmen fiercely debated the nature of the threats facing the republic, and the timing and sequence of various strategies, a core set of principles was embraced to varying degrees by the first generation of American statesman.

The authors of the *Federalist Papers* offered the first conceptualization of American grand strategy. But the relevance, the coherence, and ultimately the impact of this conceptualization can only be evaluated against the unfolding of subsequent American policy choices. This chapter evaluates the development of early American grand strategy by examining the context in which the *Federalist Papers* were written, drawing out the grand strategy for America's rise to power as articulated by its authors, and evaluating the impact of, and departure from, those ideas on subsequent American statecraft.

In doing so, it makes several arguments. First, there existed a coherent set of ideas guiding American grand strategy from the outset, even as those ideas evolved over time. Second, the *Federalist Papers* are usually read as a defense of the United States Constitution and in a largely domestic political context for what they have to say about the structure of the government, the powers and limitations of its component parts, and the nature of federalism. But, even by a numerical count, the requirements of national security clearly played a dominant role in the minds of the drafters. Third, grand strategy, conceived in this manner, can be understood as the integration of foreign policy and domestic developments; politics and the economy play as much a part in grand strategy as do diplomacy and military force. Finally, evaluation of a grand strategy entails charting its successes and failures, consistencies and inconsistencies, internal tensions and unintended consequences.

Avoiding Tyranny at Home and Abroad: The Creation of American Security

Victories on the battlefield and diplomatic recognition earned American independence from Great Britain. But the question of what was to follow this independence was less clear. While the war had forged deep bonds between the thirteen states, it had not resolved whether the American people were to form one sovereign nation or a confederation of sovereign nations. Furthermore, America went from being a privileged member of the world's most powerful trading empire to an insignificant and emerging state of its own. These outstanding issues meant that the United States was unable to fulfill many of the basic functions of a state, including defending its borders, paying its soldiers, reimbursing its creditors, and establishing a trade policy.

To deal with these problems, American leaders drafted a Constitution establishing a unified government. But drafting was not the same as establishing a new, centralized, though federated, state. The Constitution called for ratification in nine of the thirteen states, but without the endorsement of the large states, the new government would be severely weakened. The subsequent debate between Federalists and Antifederalists took on its sharpest shape in New York. In response to a series of Antifederalist essays, Alexander Hamilton, James Madison, and John Jay, collectively writing under the pseudonym Publius, published eighty-five essays for New York newspapers that argued in favor of the Constitution. These essays were collected into two volumes and given the name *The Federalist*.

Conceived in a moment of failing national security, the Constitution, as Hamilton, Madison, and Jay explained throughout the *Federalist*, was designed to create American security. That security, they argued, would derive from a strengthened union that used geography and time to develop its capabilities. Hamilton, Madison, and Jay explore how best to grow the United States' sources of strength, examining the interrelationship between economic, military, and political power.

The vision that emerges is one where the United States needed to act like its former imperial master Great Britain. A central concept running through the *Federalist* is that America must avoid the fate of Europe. Europe, after all, was a crowded place where the proximity of hostile states meant that, in the search for security, civil liberties and political liberalism fell to the imperative of maintaining large, standing armies. The only nation that had escaped the vicious cycle of perpetual arms races was Great Britain. So long as the United States took advantage of its geographical assets it would derive "from our situation the precious advantage which Great Britain has derived from hers," Hamilton argued in *Federalist 41*. Due to the natural barrier that the English Channel afforded, England could insulate itself from the grasp of continental Europe, so long as it maintained a sufficiently powerful navy. "It must, indeed, be numbered among the greatest blessings of America," Hamilton held, "that . . . in this respect our situation bears another likeness to the insular advantage of Great Britain."[5]

During the Seven Years War, William Pitt the elder had put such a grand strategy into place, simultaneously orienting Britain toward the Continent to trim and adjust the balance of power and directed toward the sea to strengthen her maritime dominance. In practice, this meant that Britain required continental allies that could pin down France's resources in a land war, so that France could not challenge Britain on the seas. Such a strategy was dependent on having enough material and financial resources to underwrite a long and expensive war. For the British, a key, if not the key, element of their strategy was to figure out how to increase their finances as the foundation of their power. As the British ambassador to Prussia was informed by British Secretary of State Lord Holderness in 1757, "We must be merchants while we are soldiers. . . . [T]rade and maritime force depend upon each other, and . . . the riches which are the true resources of this country depend upon its commerce."[6] Commerce was extremely important to the British because it allowed them to pay for a superior navy, maintain a decent expeditionary army, and subsidize any European land power that would keep France's attention firmly rooted in Europe and not on the Atlantic.

While this history might seem tangential to early American grand strategy, and certainly there were no American formal alliances or subsidizing of European powers until the twentieth century, this was the history with which the founding generation was most intimately familiar. The lessons of this history, at least to the authors of the *Federalist*, were clear. America, like Britain before it, was a maritime power. And successful grand strategy for a maritime power depended on possessing and maintaining a strong economy, a strong navy, and strong allies.[7] Similarly, the strategic vision that emerged from the *Federalist* was of a robust commercial and naval power, protected from the imposition of tyranny either from abroad or at home. As Hamilton, Madison, and Jay argued, land borders were inherently threatening to a republican government because they required large, expensive, and oppressive standing armies, which necessarily circumscribed a nation's liberty and wealth.

The dangers to the republic were multiple and overlapping. Disunion meant that the new world would look ever more like the old—divided, armed to the teeth, and frequently at war. Moreover, without a national trade policy, different states would develop differing commercial interests which would, in all likelihood, lead to differing alliances. The more divided the nation was, the more likely it was to become a plaything of the European powers. The gravest danger to the young nation's ideology and nascent institutions was the emergence of multiple sovereign states in North America. In such an eventuality, North America would become Europe: an arena where many states jostled for supremacy in a limited geographical space. The result was a constant balancing of power that demanded permanent military establishment and left no room for human flourishing.

Extending the Sphere: A Federalist Grand Strategy

To offset these dangers, the *Federalist* advanced several strategies that would shape the contours of American foreign policy for the foreseeable future. The first of these was domestic unity, within a federated state structure. Ensuring that America's political development stood in stark contrast to Europe's, the authors of the *Federalist* proposed an alternative path forward for their country. Jay laid this out most clearly in *Federalist 5*, arguing that if America were to divide itself into several distinct nations, "they would always be either involved in disputes and war, or live in the constant apprehension of them," underscoring that this was the fate of "most other BORDERING nations."[8] The answer was simple; the nation needed to ensure it had no bordering nations. The best chance they had of doing so was to unify their confederation of states into a federated nation. Echoing Jay, Hamilton contended that "A FIRM Union will be of the utmost moment to the peace and liberty of the States, as a barrier against domestic faction and insurrection."[9]

If union was the first strategy, and indeed the underlying logic that the *Federalist* advanced as a whole, then expansion was the second. Hamilton and Madison held that territorial expansion of the Union was the means best suited to secure the republican character of their state. In *Federalist 9*, Hamilton advocated "the ENLARGEMENT of the ORBIT within which such systems are to revolve," and in Madison's most famous essay, *Federalist 10*, he advanced a theory that expansion was the best cure for factionalism.[10] Or, as he more succinctly put it, "extend the sphere" and you expand the republic and the cause of republicanism itself.[11] To a certain extent, both were talking about enlarging the republic to include all thirteen states as one sovereign, federated entity.

The third strategy the *Federalist* laid out was that the republic must become, like Britain before it, a great commercial power that grew in wealth, power, and influence. Particularly pronounced in Alexander Hamilton's essays, the commercial and financial foundations of American power were analyzed from a number of angles. While Hamilton examined all the parts of America's mixed and growing economy—"the assiduous merchant, the laborious husbandman, the active mechanic, and the industrious manufacturer"—it is commerce that is of paramount importance to the creation of national wealth. In order to expand the sinews of state power, Hamilton argued, the state must be able to extract revenue without retarding the growth of the overall size of its economy. In this, Hamilton concluded that commerce was "the most powerful instrument in increasing the quantity of money in a state."[12]

In his view, as commerce grew, so too would the revenues and power of the state. The net effect of this increase in wealth would be a vastly stronger nation able to influence the course of international events. Hamilton believed that the American character was both adventurous and entrepreneurial, and that these qualities, combined with America's abundance of natural resources, had "already excited uneasy sensations in several of the maritime powers of Europe."[13] European concerns, thought Hamilton, were well founded as commerce and a strong navy were "a resource for influencing the conduct of European nations toward us."[14] Here Hamilton suggests that commerce would not only increase the wealth and power of the nation. Perhaps more important was its ability to influence the conduct of European states that would vie for access to this dynamic emerging market. In this, Hamilton suggested using trade as a tool of foreign policy.

Another, related strategy suggested in the *Federalist Papers* was the policy of neutrality in European affairs. While this policy would come to dominate much of the antebellum period and was embraced by Federalist, Republican, Democratic, and Whig administrations alike, it is in the *Federalist Papers* that its benefits were first articulated. Hamilton advanced the view that a strategic use of commercial and political neutrality would allow America time to build its strength and eventually project its power abroad. Neutrality, which would best be achieved through a unified and powerful nation, meant that the republic could prevent itself from being "gradually entangled in all the pernicious labyrinths of European politics and wars."[15] Neutrality would allow the young country to trade time for space, expanding territorially because it had avoided, or at least, postponed a clash with a great power.

A more fully formed version of this strategy was articulated in Hamilton's later defense of the Jay Treaty. In an essay defending the 1795 treaty between the United States and Great Britain, Hamilton argued that the imperfect treaty was merely a means to "defer to a state of manhood a struggle to which infancy is ill-adapted. . . . We ought to be wise enough to see that this is not the time for trying our strength."[16] As Hamilton understood, neutrality's value did not reside in its cause but in its effects. The Anglo-French conflict dominated America's formative years. As it drew more of Europe into its vortex, virtually all the belligerents' commercial ships, save England's, were swept from the seas. What was Europe's distress quickly became neutral America's advantage, exponentially increasing America's carrying trade, creating a vast European market for its shipbuilding and related industries, and growing its domestic economy.

Related to neutrality was the necessity of having the power to maintain America's political independence and commercial growth. This was particularly true in an international system dominated by an Anglo-French colonial and maritime rivalry. If America wanted to maintain its neutral commerce on the high seas and be able to ignore both British and French objections, it would need the means to do so. This, specifically, meant having a powerful navy.

The authors of the *Federalist* understood the supreme importance of this point. A navy could protect the nation's commercial activities, preserve its republican character, and ensure that the wide moat separating the old world and new limited the power projection capabilities of Europe's imperial powers. "A further resource for influencing the conduct of European nations toward us," Hamilton asserts in his essay discussing the interwoven nature of commerce and maritime power, "would arise from the establishment of a federal navy." A sufficiently large naval force, which only a united nation could provide, would safeguard the republic as it promoted commercial growth and enabled a policy of neutrality toward Europe's warring states. Without one, America lay vulnerable to Europe's imperial ambitions. In world politics, this was the norm. According to Hamilton, while the world could be divided into four geographical and political regions—Africa, Asia, America, and Europe—it was Europe that dominated the other three by force of her arms and allowed Europeans to fashion themselves "the Mistress of the World." Such "arrogant pretentions" were antithetical to republican ideology. But Hamilton was well aware that independence of action came not from the country's unique form of republican government but rather from the real power of its armed force. "The rights of neutrality will only be respected when they are defended by an adequate power," Hamilton concluded. "A nation, despicable by its weakness, forfeits even the privilege of being neutral."[17]

Naval power, however, was part of a larger strategy raised in the *Federalist*. Controversial at the time it was proposed and ever after in American politics, the *Federalist* called for a consolidation of state power, especially in the realm of national security. Intended to offset the enfeebled government of the Articles of Confederation, the Constitution sketched a powerful and centralized state. Discussing in *Federalist 41* how union of the states was the surest safeguard against foreign invasion, Madison made the point that security could never be absolute. Rather, it must always be judged relative to the intentions and capabilities of other states. This meant that the means allocated to that security must be evaluated on an iterative basis that responded accordingly to the fluid international environment. In practical terms, this meant that national defense capabilities must be set not at the preferred level of "the most pacific nations," but rather in response to more militantly inclined states.[18]

Because the requirements of national security needed to be calibrated against a constantly shifting external environment, Hamilton held an expansive view of the power the Constitution afforded the executive branch of government. Explaining in *Federalist 23* why a national government required a strong executive, Hamilton argued that "the circumstances that endanger the safety of nations are infinite, and for this reason no constitutional shackles can wisely be imposed on the power to which the care of it is committed. This power ought to be coextensive with all the possible combinations of such circumstances."[19] This genius of the Constitution, according to this interpretation, was that it gave the executive the power to expand and contract with the exigencies of the times. Arguments over the appropriate size, scale, and scope of the federal government drove the ratification debate and indeed much of American political history from that point forward.

While clearly advocating a powerful government, Hamilton also articulated a basic strategic principle which could not "be made plainer by argument or reasoning. It rests upon axioms as simple as they are universal; the MEANS ought to be proportioned to the END; the persons, from whose agency the attainment of any END is expected, ought to possess the MEANS by which it is to be attained."[20] This was the eighteenth-century version of Walter Lippmann's 1943 plea for "solvency" that called for "bringing into balance, with a comfortable surplus of power in reserve, the nation's commitments and the nation's power." Sounding strikingly like Hamilton, Lippmann demanded that "the nation must maintain its objectives and its power in equilibrium, its purposes within its means and its means equal to its purposes, its commitments related to its resources and its resources adequate to its commitments."[21] While Lippmann pleaded for solvency, for the proper calibration between means supplied and objectives desired, Hamilton made the point throughout the *Federalist* that the requirements of national defense ought to be more than sufficient to the demands of security and prosperity.

The whole point of these collected essays was to examine the advantages that union offered, while considering the dangers and evils of dissolution. For the most part, the *Federalist* argued the negative—that if the Constitution were not ratified, a "dismemberment of the union" would likely follow. But, woven into the eighty-five essays was a positive vision of what the young country might achieve if united. If the strategic vision was to preserve, expand, and strengthen the republic and the idea of republicanism, the infant nation needed time to grow and develop its capabilities. It could do so through pursuing five distinct, though linked strategies.

First, the nation must unite into a much strengthened federation, shedding individual sovereignty for greater collective security, wealth, and liberty. Second, expanding the size of the republic would offer physical security. Originally intended as an argument for consolidating the thirteen states into one nation, this strategy also portended securing American hegemony on the North American continent, if not the entire Western Hemisphere. A third strategy was intended to promote the growth of America as a commercial nation, capable of influencing the rest of the world as much through the weight of its economy as through the power of its republican ideology. Fourth was the strategy of neutrality in European affairs. Although the young nation would alternatively lean toward London or Paris at various moments over the subsequent quarter century, it essentially preserved its independent foreign policy. Finally, the authors of the *Federalist* promoted the growth of defense capabilities that would allow the republic to defend its trade, its territory, and its honor. Specifically, this came in a call for an enlarged maritime presence and, more generally, in an expansive national security capability. In a narrow sense, these interrelated strategies were intended to stave off dismemberment and promote the ratification of a more powerful union.

The development of American grand strategy over the next several decades saw these policies move from conception to execution. Sufficiently elastic to fit the dictates of changing circumstances, these principles formed the basis of American grand strategy. While successive administrations often deviated in how they sought to apply these basic principles, the underlying ideas remained remarkably consistent.

Greater than the Sum of Its Parts: The
Supremacy of the Union

Take the idea of a strengthened union, where national cohesion would supersede regional, state, and individual interests, and forge a country that was greater than the sum of its individual parts. Of course, union meant many things to many different people, and it was a sufficiently elastic term to take on multiple meanings.[22] But the idea of a union that could provide collective security dated at least as far back as the Albany Plan of 1754. In the aftermath of the outbreak of hostilities between the French and British during the French and Indian War, Benjamin Franklin had suggested a plan that would neutralize French advantages against the thirteen separate British colonies in North America by creating a unified colonial government that could appropriately coordinate defense and expeditiously allocate needed funds. This was the same sentiment driving unity some twenty years later during the American War for Independence, when, during the signing of the Declaration of Independence, Franklin supposedly admonished his fellow delegates that "we must, indeed, all hang together, or most assuredly we shall all hang separately."[23] It was the same rallying cry of those, like James Madison, who called for a Constitutional Convention that would remedy the weaknesses of the Articles of Confederation with a stronger national government capable of defending Americans against Indian raids, Spanish intrigues, and British provocations.

George Washington devoted much of his presidency to forging a political culture that stressed national unity. Yet, this hardly meant that subsequent American history was endowed with Daniel Webster's later call for "Liberty and Union, now and forever." While the federal government grew in its ability to control both foreign and commercial policy, calls for unity of purpose were undercut by the development of partisan politics and by the overlapping state and federal sovereignty that the Constitution had enshrined into law. Politically, it was Washington's vision that the nation would transcend factionalism in the interest of the state. This highly idealized vision of politics was undercut almost from the start, as different factions fought to define what, exactly, was the national interest and how it could best be achieved. While this ideal of national unity appealed to most of Washington's successors, it proved easier to call for than to achieve. Washington, of course, understood this, making his Farewell Address a warning that competing political interests could tear the nation apart and an admonition against the spirit of factionalism. But democracy, even in the partial and exclusionary form it assumed in late eighteenth-century America, hardly lends itself to internal unity apart from adherence to several expansively defined concepts. And so, as partisan politics took off, embedded itself within the system, and became more formalized, national political unity became a concept often invoked and seldom achieved.

Nowhere was this challenge clearer than in the relationship between the federal and state governments. One of the most innovative concepts of the Constitution was the introduction of dual sovereignty, which was divided between the federal government and the individual states. Born out of America's colonial experience dealing with a distant—and seemingly disinterested—government and intended to appease anti-Federalists concerned about the potential accumulation of power in a remote seat of government, the Constitution drew overlapping lines that were never quite defined. The closest the framers got was in the Tenth Amendment, which reserved to the state governments all powers not expressly delegated to the federal government, but it refrained from explicitly defining what those powers were.

This ambiguity invited legal challenge to the supremacy of the Union as a governing entity. The Kentucky and Virginia Resolutions of 1798–99, composed by Thomas Jefferson and James Madison in response to the Alien and Sedition Acts, argued that ultimate sovereignty lay in the states and granted the states power to declare void what they deemed unconstitutional federal laws. Angered by the War of 1812, delegates from New England states who met at the Hartford Convention discussed seceding from the United States. They issued a report in which they argued that any individual state had both the right and the duty "to interpose its authority" between the federal government and its own inhabitants to protect against what it deemed unconstitutional acts. In response to the Tariff of 1828, or the Tariff of Abominations, as Southerners referred to it, John C. Calhoun built on earlier nullification sentiments to argue that each state reserved the power of "veto" and the "right of interposition" to arrest federal encroachment.[24] Most drastically, this culminated in the secession of the southern states in 1860–61 on the premise that the federal government did not possess the right to impose its will on non-compliant state governments. The Civil War resolved the legal question of supremacy, but it hardly answered it politically. The aggregation of resources at the national level made for a stronger nation, one that was more capable of exercising its power. The use of such power was never, however, uncontested.

Our Proper Dominion: The Push for Westward Expansion

If the idea of Union held a broad-based appeal but was challenged in practice, the concept of westward expansion was consistently embraced and pursued throughout this period. America's size and its capacity for growth meant that it had the potential to rival, and perhaps eventually supersede, the European states that had dominated world politics for the past several hundred years. But that would happen only if American statesmen prevented the emergence of an old world balance of power in the new. The best way to preserve America's independence was to reduce the menace of Europe in North America. And, it would do so by establishing itself as the dominant power on the North American continent, precluding the emergence of any power that might contest its dominion and, in effect, carving out its own sphere of influence. This meant undercutting British, French, Spanish, and Russian attempts to contain the young republic. Much of early American diplomacy therefore was predicated on simultaneously undermining European powers' claims to sovereignty in North America while strengthening Washington's hold.

The original conception of this, as laid out in the *Federalist*, meant enlarging the republic to include all thirteen states as one sovereign, federated entity. But there can be little doubt that the authors' vision was considerably more ambitious. The Constitution they were so robustly defending included Article Four, which granted Congress the authority to admit new states to the Union. Given that the Constitution allowed for territorial expansion, and given that the authors of the *Federalist Papers* distinctly feared the emergence of powerfully armed neighbors, both the objective and the logic were clear. In order to avoid Europe's fate, America must eventually unify the New World landmass, replacing European influence in North America. If this did not occur, North America would end up looking like the warring states of Europe, which meant no liberty. As John Quincy Adams observed in 1819, "The world shall [have] to be familiarized with the idea of considering our proper dominion to be the continent of North America."[25]

The United States spent most of the nineteenth century preventing anyone else from establishing a continental sphere of influence, but that eventually expanded to encompass, at least in theory, the entire Western Hemisphere. From the creation of the Northwest Territories in 1787 to the Louisiana Purchase of 1803 to the Transcontinental Treaty of 1819, westward expansion dominated early American foreign policy. With the Monroe Doctrine of 1823, American declaratory policy proclaimed that henceforth the Western

Hemisphere would serve as America's exclusive sphere of interest and was off limits to European colonization. The 1840s saw the United States double in size with the annexation of Texas in 1845, the Mexican War of 1846, the subsequent acquisition of California and most of the Southwest in 1848, and the 1846 Oregon Treaty which established the Pacific Northwest border between British North America and the United States. In 1853 the Gadsden Purchase of Arizona and New Mexico continued this trend, and ultimately the Civil War consolidated America's control of much of the North American continent and ensured that the country's sovereignty was uncontested.

Even though territorial expansion was fervently pursued by American policymakers, its pursuit challenged and, in the run up to the Civil War, increasingly came into conflict with other goals—none more so than union. James Madison had famously argued in *Federalist 10* that only a territorially expansive republic, with a multitude of competing power centers and interest groups, could mitigate the negative effects of factionalism and prevent a majority from becoming a monolithic tyranny. According to this logic, the only way to stave off the division and dismemberment of the country was to subsume the rest of the continent under a single and unified republican system of government. But, contrary to the hopes of many of the Constitution's signers, as the United States grew, slavery became more, not less, firmly entrenched in the political DNA of the country.

In the antebellum period, territorial expansion simultaneously helped establish the United States as the preponderant power in North America *and* exacerbated its internal tensions. What had previously been thought of as a safety valve to alleviate contending interests seemed increasingly to inflame sectional tensions and sow discord into the political fabric of the country. This issue was thrown into stark relief when Missouri applied for federal statehood in 1820, prompting a congressional debate on whether Congress possessed the power to regulate slavery in the territories and revealing the enormous gulf of opinion that had arisen between northern and southern interests. So violent was the debate that Thomas Jefferson observed that the division of the country created by the Missouri Compromise line would eventually lead to the destruction of the Union: "This momentous question, like a fire bell in the night, awakened and filled me with terror. I considered it at once as the knell of the Union. It is hushed indeed for the moment. But this is a reprieve only, not a final sentence."[26] Jefferson's concerns proved prescient as each subsequent territorial expansion triggered an increasingly violent debate over the wisdom and viability of political unity.

We Ranked as the Most Commercial Nation: The Expansion of American Trade

Like territorial expansion across the North American continent, the growth of American commercial power was intended to advance the global influence of the United States. Long before America became an independent nation, its potential to shape the rest of the world—particularly through its commercial reach—had been noted by European observers. According to a French report of the 1750s, "the true balance of power really resides in commerce and in America."[27] In an age of contending European empires, whichever state could secure the lion's share of American resources—either through conquest or commerce—would have the ability to dominate its rivals. The American founders had attempted to turn this logic on its head, arguing that it was American power—in the form of commercial prowess and a strong navy—that could make it "the arbiter of Europe in America, and to be able to incline the balance of European competitors in this part of the world as our interests may dictate."[28]

While Alexander Hamilton and James Madison could agree in *The Federalist* on the need to utilize American resources and remain firmly integrated into global markets, their visions increasingly differed on the role that commerce should play in the nation's development. Hamilton saw the future as one of industrial manufacture where America was firmly integrated into global markets, whereas Madison championed a Jeffersonian vision of domestic agrarian production and foreign market acquisition.[29] Both, however, agreed on the overwhelming importance of advancing American trade overseas. This mission has depended on access to the world's seas and markets. When that access was circumscribed—by the British in 1812 and later by the Germans in 1917—Americans went to war to preserve it. It is unsurprising, then, that Americans also looked askance at efforts by other powers to establish areas that might be walled off from trade and investment—and from the spread of America's capitalist ideology.[30]

By any measure, foreign trade grew exponentially in the antebellum period. For example, domestic exports to Britain doubled between 1790 and 1807 and re-exports increased from $300,000 to $59,643,558 during the same period, with the overwhelming growth occurring after the Jay Treaty between Great Britain and America was ratified in 1795.[31] Once the United States was on favorable terms with London and its vessels largely free from the menace of the Royal British Navy, American trading ships were soon found in Asian, European, South American, and West Indian ports. As an early American politician and economist keenly observed, "A new era was established in our commercial history. . . . In proportion to our population we ranked as the most commercial nation; in point of value, our trade was only second to that of Great Britain."[32] During this period, American statesmen differed markedly on how best to ensure that material basis of American power, with Thomas Jefferson's Embargo of 1807 standing out as perhaps the least effective attempt to protect American commerce. But all believed that stimulating domestic production, protecting the country's infant industries, harnessing technological improvements, enhancing regional connectivity, and promoting America's commercial interests abroad served the national interest.

Not the Time for Trying Our Strength: The Appeal of Neutrality

The neutrality advocated in *The Federalist* was a strategy intended to avoid being dragged into war by Europe's various warring parties, buy time for the United States to develop its republican institutions, build up its commercial and military power, and forestall further European encroachment in the Western Hemisphere. But as American policymakers discovered, neutrality would be increasingly challenging to maintain as they attempted to navigate between the Scylla and Charybdis of growing British and French rivalry. Moreover, as the country grew in power, and as its external circumstances changed, the appeal and value of neutrality faced increasing scrutiny from policymakers and from the American public. Nevertheless, most early American statesmen believed neutrality held particular advantages for the country.

Policymakers knew that as a weak and relatively defenseless country, the nation profited from friendly relations with the major powers.

Neutrality would only work, however, if it were profitable and respected by other nations. This was the impetus for Washington's Proclamation of Neutrality when Britain and France went to war in 1792, despite much American enthusiasm for the nascent French Revolution. This policy was reinforced with Washington's Farewell Address of 1796, where he held that abstention from European politics was in America's interests and warned that it would be ill-advised to tie American fortunes to the vicissitudes of European politics. When American neutrality was flagrantly violated by the French in the 1790s and later by the British, it became the rationale for the (non-declared) Quasi War with France and the declaration of war against the British in 1812. Adherence to this policy culminated in the Monroe Doctrine of 1823, in which the United States declared a commitment to neutrality in European Affairs and non-interference in the internal concerns of European colonies. While policymakers often conflated the concepts of an independent non-aligned foreign policy, non-interference, and neutrality, all were predicated on the belief that to do otherwise would invite intervention in the Western Hemisphere.

Despite the appeal of neutrality, multiple factors complicated its implementation. First, neutrality depended on American policy taking a disinterested approach to the causes of foreign quarrels and a dispassionate attitude toward the interested parties. When events seemed to echo America's own revolt against its former colonial master and when rebels consciously modeled their cause on America's fight for independence, the emotional pull became harder to resist. In his famous July 4 Address of 1821, John Quincy Adams famously declared that for America "wherever the standard of freedom and Independence, has been or shall be unfurled, there will her heart, her benedictions and her prayers be," before concluding that America would refrain from actively supporting such movements. This stance was tested each time a foreign revolution broke out and its leaders asked for American support, as American responses to the French Revolution, the Haitian Revolution, the Greek fight for independence from the Ottoman Empire, and the South American colonial revolt against Spain all make clear.[33]

Moreover, as American power grew and as geopolitical pressures eased, the temptation to cast aside American neutrality increased. John Quincy

Adams himself advocated a decidedly less neutral approach to hemispheric affairs just three years after drafting the Monroe Doctrine, arguing that both domestic and international circumstances had changed since Washington's time and contending that Washington's position was never intended to serve as the immutable law governing America's foreign relations. Such a reading of Washington's advocacy for neutrality and counsel against permanent alliances implied that both should be understood as enablers of American growth. As subsequent American history would bear out, when America had grown sufficiently powerful, it would possess the ability and often the intent to act otherwise.

Neutrality was neither a natural nor an inevitable state, and it could only be accomplished if the country were strong enough not to be forced into taking sides. Neutrality, most understood, could only become a workable policy if it stood a realistic chance of being enforced.

Defended by an Adequate Power: The Growth of American Military Power

The robust defensive capability called for in the *Federalist Papers* was, in many ways, the necessary component supporting a strengthened union, aiding expansion, facilitating commerce, and enabling neutrality. If the country lacked a sufficiently powerful deterrent, American policymakers feared it would invite European aggression. Possessing a strong military and demonstrating a willingness to use it would allow the nation to pursue its own course and safeguard its commercial activity. This would entail a buildup of military forces, support for their professionalization, and ensuring their effectiveness.

It was necessity, though, more than it was a coherent plan that enabled the growth of American defensive capabilities and military power.[34] Following the Revolutionary War, the American army was reduced to a single regiment.[35] But in the mid-1790s, in response to the growing European conflict and the Barbary threat to American commercial interests in the Mediterranean, Congress voted to expand coastal fortifications and voted appropriations for six frigates. Even though there was a temporary naval buildup during the quasi-War with France, the military strategy of the United States was almost wholly defensive.[36]

While Federalist military policy called for at least sufficient force to deter any overreaching European powers, Republican policy, ideologically inclined toward suspicion of powerful standing armies, took a different tack. In power since 1800, the Jeffersonian Republicans drastically cut the defense budget. They reduced the national debt 43 percent by slashing defense appropriations, which had accounted for 50 percent of the federal budget in 1799. Under Jefferson, the army shrank from 14,000 to 3,287 soldiers and the navy's budget was reduced 67 percent.[37] Jeffersonian military strategy, acutely conscious of the threat standing armies could pose to civil liberties, called for a small regular army, a loosely organized militia still officially controlled by the states, and a tiny navy. Jefferson was aware that this could prove disastrous in the face of an invasion, writing Madison in 1809 that "I know no government which would be so embarrassing in wars as ours."[38]

Chastened by the burning of Washington and the country's underwhelming stalemate with British forces during the War of 1812, American policymakers attempted to put the nation's security on sounder footing, calling for an enlarged peacetime army, an expanded navy, an improved coastal fortification system, a better disciplined militia, and an investment in professional military schools.[39] While these initiatives received different levels of support, it became increasingly clear that the war had fundamentally shifted Republican thinking and created the conditions necessary for a robust peacetime military establishment.[40]

The growth of American military power through much of early American history faced several ongoing challenges. Fears of a large standing army, born out of the country's colonial experience and ideological disposition, persisted despite the decidedly mixed record of America's militias. Another challenge stemmed from the size, prowess, and power-projection capabilities of Europe's large militaries. Even as America's military power grew in absolute terms, it did not always do so in relative terms. Additionally, a robust military establishment—in war or in peacetime—required a public willingness to expend revenues. Americans' enthusiasm for taxing themselves was never high, and most policymakers understood that, absent a national emergency, most Americans would remain unwilling to do so at a level sufficiently high to support a ready military. Finally, American professional military education and efficient organizational structure lagged behind European standards throughout much of early American history.

The Fate of an Empire: Conception, Implementation, and Adaptability

The Grand Strategy of the *Federalist* was designed to put the United States on a path to power and global influence by determining "the fate of an empire in many respects the most interesting in the world."[41] Union, expansion, commerce, neutrality, and power combined to chart a path for America as a rising power among nations. But these, of course, were ideas more than they were actual policies. The authors of the *Federalist* possessed a clear idea of what they wanted the nation to accomplish as it rose to power, as well as a general plan of how it could best utilize the resources at its disposal. But the *Federalist* was not holy writ; nor was it enshrined in law or statute, having preceded the ratification of the Constitution. It was, merely, a mostly coherent and interlocking set of ideas about how the young republic could provide for its security, promote its prosperity, and develop and protect its own unique system of republican government. What makes it compelling as a blueprint for America's rise is that the broad contours of American grand strategy stayed remarkably consistent over the next several decades. It also remained flexible enough to adapt to changing domestic and international circumstances.

What it did not possess was internal consistency. Some of its successes—notably continental expansion—undercut other objectives, such as unity. How then to account for this seeming discrepancy, if not outright failure? A common critique of the idea of grand strategy is that a true grand strategy would mean that the whole strategy would have to be developed in advance and executed flawlessly. This, however, is neither realistic nor useful. Grand strategy is not figuring everything out perfectly in advance but rather responding and recalibrating along the way. In his classic work *On War*, Carl von Clausewitz writes that "theory should be study, not doctrine."[42] That is, theory, and in this case strategy, is best understood as a verb and not a noun. It is something that needs to be done on an iterative basis so that as the strategic environment shifts, so too does the approach. As circumstances changed, so too did policymakers' conception of what the nation could realistically accomplish.

While context might explain the success or failure of a grand strategy, it is not the only measure of success. The practice of grand strategy must necessarily include both conception and execution, which involves both context and circumstance. But success may also be judged by a longer time horizon.

If this is the standard, establishing adaptable and transferable strategies is as important for judging the success of a grand strategy as is successful implementation.[43]

Notes

1. C. Vann Woodward, "The Age of Reinterpretation," *American Historical Review* 66 (October 1960), 3. See also John Lewis Gaddis, *Surprise, Security and the American Experience* (Cambridge, MA: Harvard University Press, 2004), 7ff.
2. John Milton, *Paradise Lost* (New York: Norton, 2004), Book 12, lines 646–647.
3. Quoted in Robert Tombs and Isabelle Tombs, *That Sweet Enemy: The French and the British from the Sun King to the Present* (New York: Alfred A. Knopf, 2007), 108.
4. Hamilton, *Federalist 11*, "The Utility of the Union in Respect to Commercial Relations and a Navy," https://www.congress.gov/resources/display/content/The+Federalist+P apers#TheFederalistPapers-11. All subsequent citations to the *Federalist Papers* take the form of Hamilton, *Federalist 11*.
5. Hamilton, *Federalist 41*.
6. Tombs and Tombs, *That Sweet Enemy*, 108.
7. Alfred Thayer Mahan would articulate such a formulation more than a century later when he examined the rise of British maritime power. But Mahan was hardly the first American to call on the British experience as a maritime power as a useful guide for the American development of its maritime power and commercial power.
8. Jay, *Federalist 5*.
9. Hamilton, *Federalist 9*.
10. Hamilton, *Federalist 9*.
11. Madison, *Federalist 10*.
12. Hamilton, *Federalist 12*.
13. Hamilton, *Federalist 11*.
14. Hamilton, *Federalist 11*.
15. Hamilton, *Federalist 7*.
16. Alexander Hamilton, The Defense No. II, July 25, 1795, *The Papers of Alexander Hamilton Digital Edition*, Founding Era Collection, Rotunda Database, http://rotunda.upress.virginia.edu/founders/ARHN-01-18-02-0310.
17. Hamilton, *Federalist 11*.
18. Madison, *Federalist 41*.
19. Hamilton, *Federalist 23*.
20. Hamilton, *Federalist 23*.
21. Walter Lippmann, *U.S. Foreign Policy: Shield of the Republic* (Boston: Little, Brown, 1943), 9, 7.
22. See, Paul C. Nagel, *One Nation Indivisible: The Union in American Thought, 1776–1861* (Oxford: Oxford University Press, 1964).

23. Jared Sparks, *The Life of Benjamin Franklin* (Boston: Tappan, Whittemore and Mason, 1840), I: 408, ch. 9.

24. This section draws from Charles Edel, *Nation Builder: John Quincy Adams and the Grand Strategy of the Republic* (Cambridge. MA: Harvard University Press, 2014), 260–261. The quotations come from, respectively, Theodore Dwight, *History of the Hartford Convention: With a Review of the Policy of the United States Government, Which Led to the War of 1812* (New York: N. & J. White, 1833), 361; and John C. Calhoun, "Exposition and Protest," November 1828, in *John C. Calhoun Selected Writings and Speeches*, ed. H. Lee Cheek (Washington, DC: Regnery, 2003), 299.

25. John Quincy Adams, Diary 31, November 16, 1819, 205 [electronic edition], *The Diaries of John Quincy Adams: A Digital Collection* (Boston: Massachusetts Historical Society, 2004), http://www.masshist.org/jqadiaries.

26. Thomas Jefferson to John Holmes, April 22, 1820, http://www.loc.gov/exhibits/jefferson/159.html (accessed May 6, 2010).

27. French foreign ministry report, 1759, quoted in Tombs and Tombs, *That Sweet Enemy*.

28. Hamilton, *Federalist 11*.

29. Drew R. McCoy, *The Elusive Republic: Political Economy in Jeffersonian America* (Chapel Hill: University of North Carolina Press, 1980).

30. Hal Brands and Charles Edel, "The Disharmony of the Spheres," *Commentary*, December 2017.

31. Douglass C. North, *The Economic Growth of the United States 1790–1860* (Englewood Cliffs, NJ: Prentice-Hall, 1961), 25. See also Edel, *Nation Builder*, 77.

32. Adam Seybert, *Statistical Annals: Embracing Views of the Population, Commerce, Navigation, Fisheries, Public Lands, Post-Office Establishment, Revenues, Mint, Military and Naval Establishments, Expenditures, Public Debt, and Sinking Fund of the United States of America: Founded on Official Documents: Commencing on the Fourth of March Seventeen Hundred and Eighty-Nine and Ending on the Twentieth of April Eighteen Hundred and Eighteen* (Philadelphia: Thomas Dobson & Son, 1818), 59ff.

33. See Caitlin Fitz, *Our Sister Republics: The United States in the Age of American Revolutions* (New York: Liveright, 2016).

34. The following section draws on Edel, *Nation Builder*, 100ff.

35. The best summary of the growth of the American military can be found in Russell F. Weigley, *The American Way of War: A History of United States Military Strategy and Policy* (Bloomington: Indiana University Press, 1973). For this period, see esp. Chapter 3, "The Federalists and the Jeffersonians," 40–55. Weigley links foreign policy to military strength and concludes that during the early national period—at least through the War of 1812—"obviously any sort of assertive national policy was impossible" (41).

36. Weigley concludes that throughout this period "the military policy of the United States prepared the country for little more than a strategy of passive defense against any adversary stronger than Indian tribes" (46).

37. Michael D. Pearlman, *Warmaking and American Democracy: The Struggle over Military Strategy, 1700 to the Present* (Lawrence: University Press of Kansas, 1999), 73.

38. Quoted in Pearlman, *Warmaking*, 75.

39. Special message to Congress (accompanying Treaty of Ghent), February 18, 1815, *The Writings of James Madison*, vol. 8, 1808–1819, ed. Gaillard Hunt (New York: G.P. Putnam's Sons, 1908), 325.

40. Peter Maslowski, "To the Edge of Greatness: The United States, 1783–1865," in *The Making of Strategy: Rulers, States, and War*, ed. Williamson Murray, MacGregor Knox, and Alvin Bernstein (Cambridge: Cambridge University Press, 1994), 205–241.

41. Hamilton, *Federalist 1*.

42. Carl von Clausewitz, *On War*, trans. and ed. Michael Howard and Peter Paret (Princeton, NJ: Princeton University Press (1976 [1993]), Book 2, Chapter 2.

43. These concluding thoughts draw off from my responses to both Christopher Nicholas and Andrews Preston's review of my book in roundtables that appeared in *H-Diplo* and *Passport*: https://networks.h-net.org/node/28443/discussions/110994/h-diplo-roundtable-xvii-13-nation-builder-john-quincy-adams-and#_Toc442566757, and https://shafr.org/sites/default/files/passport-01-2016.pdf.

5

Grand Strategy of the Master Class

Slavery and Foreign Policy from the Antebellum Era to the Civil War

Matthew Karp

The specter of secession haunts the history of mid-nineteenth-century America. No other moment in the American past is so powerfully defined by an event that came afterward: we have several "postwar" eras, but in 200 years of national history, only the 1840s and 1850s are considered an "antebellum" period. The fact that the slave South fled the Union in 1861—and was defeated in the Civil War by 1865—encourages a narrative of the sectional crisis that regards the South, encumbered with its peculiar institution of slavery, as a renegade section, while the free North represents a kind of nation in utero. Nowhere, perhaps, is this tendency more pronounced than in the history of US foreign relations—and, especially, the history of US foreign relations as told by writers who emphasize American grand strategy.

For the policy analysts, national security experts, and scholars of international relations who dominate the discourse of grand strategy, this teleological view of antebellum politics makes a certain kind of sense. Understanding American history primarily as a fund of instructive examples for the use of present-day actors, these writers tend to skirt past the slaveholders who betrayed the Union and lost the Civil War, and who are almost nobody's idea of useful role models today.[1] Occasionally a more daring or polemical analyst will mount a brusque defense of the strategic vision of James K. Polk, whom former National Security Council adviser William C. Martel has called "a focused, successful one-term grand strategist."[2] But for the most part, policy-focused treatments of American grand strategy tend to leap straight from the very early republic—occasionally pausing to linger over John Quincy Adams—to the outbreak of the Civil War. In this scheme, it is easy to depict northern leaders like Adams and Abraham Lincoln as fundamentally American—and part of a recognizable American grand strategic tradition—while southern slaveholders like John C. Calhoun and Jefferson Davis are cast as disruptive outsiders, if not essentially un-American enemies.[3]

Often this marginalization is quite explicit. Along with the four schools of American foreign policy that Walter Russell Mead identifies in *Special Providence*—Hamiltonian, Jeffersonian, Jacksonian, and Wilsonian—a fifth and "now defunct" grouping appears. This, in Mead's treatment, is the "Davisonian" tradition, led by Jefferson Davis and his allies, who prioritized slavery above all other questions and "ended up, literally, as a school of treason as they rushed to meet their doom." Unlike his other schools, Mead understood the "Davisonians" as essentially strangers to the continuous and long-standing currents of American strategic thought, and therefore they receive virtually no attention over the course of the rest of his book.[4]

In *Dangerous Nation*, on the other hand—in some ways the shrewdest single-volume survey of nineteenth-century US foreign policy—Robert Kagan devotes considerable space to a discussion of "the foreign policy of slavery" in the years between 1840 and 1860. Yet Kagan's framework for understanding antebellum politics falls into the familiar trap of making the South sectional and the North national. Viewing the conflict between the free and slave states as a kind of Cold War, Kagan likens northern anti-slavery politics to George Kennan's strategy of containment during the US-Soviet conflict. Kagan insists on seeing slaveholders, even when they were at the height of their national power, as a domestic Other. In its ideological and strategic worldview, he writes, the South merits comparison not to the antebellum North but to "the despotic regimes of nineteenth-century central and Eastern Europe," or even "the totalitarian societies of the twentieth century."[5]

Not all scholars of American foreign relations are so keen to exoticize the slave South. Yet larger narratives grounded in the national or imperial growth of the early United States still tend to look forward to the second half of the nineteenth century, often implicitly demoting the antebellum South to a kind of sectional status. From this perspective, slavery appears primarily as an explosive factor in American politics that divided leaders into fights over various proposed territorial expansions—an essentially domestic problem that was solved in bloody but decisive fashion by the Civil War.[6] Those studies that do explore slavery's specific impact on foreign policy, meanwhile, have generally confined themselves to the ways that slaveholders worked to secure fugitive slave laws, enact restrictions on black sailors, or, at most, fight to add new slave states to the Union.[7] Scholars of US foreign policy have not quite come to terms with Richard Hofstadter's classic insight about John C. Calhoun: "What he wanted was not for the South to leave the Union, but to dominate it."[8]

The kind of domination Calhoun and like-minded slaveholders desired went beyond the need to reinforce their narrow property rights, or even the desire to expand the amount of territory under slave cultivation. The very extent of slaveholders' power within the American foreign policy establishment suggests something of their larger ambitions. "Since the slavery agitation," Iowa congressman Josiah Grinnell observed in 1865, slaveholders "have had the Secretaryship of State for two thirds of the time; and . . . for four fifths of the time have the Secretary of War and the Secretary of the Navy been from the South." W. E. B. Du Bois later calculated that before the Civil War 80 out of 134 US ministers abroad hailed from the slaveholding states.[9] Relative to its small free white population, of course, the South held disproportionate influence in virtually every branch of the antebellum federal government. From contemporary Republican complaints about the scope of the "Slave Power" to careful modern scholarship on the pro-slavery bias of the antebellum Union, few observers have doubted the fact of southern influence in Washington.[10] Still, it is notable that slaveholders maintained especially firm control over the "outward state"—the sector of the federal government responsible for foreign relations, military policy, and the larger role that American power assumed outside American borders.[11]

Looking back after four years of civil war, Grinnell suggested that the South had sought to control the antebellum military, "as if it were to be ready for this conflict of arms."[12] (The Iowan was an early victim of the historical tendency to view the 1850s through the lens of 1865.) But antebellum slaveholders like Secretary of State Calhoun and Secretary of War Davis did not assume national Cabinet posts to strengthen the South for a coming war with the North. Instead they sought to command the power of the entire United States, and then, crucially, use that power to strengthen slavery in world politics. If grand strategy, as Hal Brands has pithily defined it, is "the intellectual architecture that gives form and structure to foreign policy," slaveholding leaders were not merely provincial sectionalists but bold and cosmopolitan strategic thinkers. Their profound ideological commitment to slavery did not merely affect domestic politics within a divided republic; it left a deep imprint on the "strategic culture" of American foreign policy.[13]

From 1841 to 1860, after all, pro-slavery southerners sat atop the policy-making apparatus of the federal government. In the two decades before the

Civil War, it was the grand strategy of the master class, more than any other rival vision, that set the course of US foreign relations.

American Slaveholders, American Power

To what extent does it even make sense to speak of the antebellum "master class" as a single political unit? For generations, historians have emphasized the powerful regional, economic, and partisan fault lines that divided the antebellum South.[14] On many matters of antebellum politics, a Whiggish lawyer from tidewater Virginia, a Democratic cotton planter from middle Tennessee, and a states' rights theorist from upland South Carolina may have had little in common. Nevertheless, on the largest questions of foreign policy John Tyler, James K. Polk, and John C. Calhoun proved impressively cohesive. For all the important divisions within the antebellum South, it is misleading to view master class foreign policy as a chaos of regional splits, partisan feuds, or colliding individual egos. In the 1840s, domestic rivals Tyler, Polk, and Calhoun joined forces to mount an aggressive defense of slave institutions in Texas. In the 1850s, longtime Democrats like Jefferson Davis and former Whigs like Alexander Stephens were united not only on the fugitive slave law and the status of slavery in the western territories but also on the enhanced funding and expansion of the US military. On the most crucial questions of foreign and military policy, slavery brought southern statesmen together far more than it pulled them apart.

To be sure, a few scattered southern dissenters—mostly border-state Whigs—refused to place slavery at the absolute center of national grand strategy. On the other end of the spectrum, in the 1850s a growing number of Lower South extremists rejected the notion of the Union altogether and either opposed or offered ambivalent support to pro-slavery foreign policy efforts at the national level. Yet across the antebellum decades, each of these factions was dwarfed in size and influence by the slave South's political leadership in Washington. This group included presidents like Tyler and Polk, Cabinet officers like Calhoun and Davis, and a less well-known cadre of national statesmen who came to dominate US foreign policy under the presidencies of Franklin Pierce and James Buchanan. From the Lower South came Stephen Mallory, longtime Florida senator and Naval Affairs Committee chairman; Alabama's William Rufus DeVane King, minister to France, president pro tempore of the Senate, and vice president under Pierce;

and Louisiana senator John Slidell, a New York native who became the political kingmaker of New Orleans, Polk's first envoy to Mexico, and Buchanan's
most important southern ally. Even more influential, perhaps, were a trio of
powerful Virginians: Henry A. Wise, outspoken pro-slavery congressman
and Tyler's minister to Brazil; James Murray Mason, veteran Senate Foreign
Affairs Committee chairman; and Robert M. T. Hunter, longtime chair of the
Senate Finance Committee and a leading voice on foreign policy questions.

Beyond these elected leaders stood the southern diplomats, military
officers, journalists, and scholars who formed a kind of strategic intelligentsia for the master class. They included the Virginia navy lieutenant
Matthew Fontaine Maury, a leading nautical scientist and an aggressive
champion of naval reform; Duff Green, a roving businessman whose official
and unofficial travels from Paris to Mexico City led John Quincy Adams to
dub him America's all-purpose "ambassador of slavery"; New Orleans editor James D. B. De Bow, whose *Review* was the South's most widely circulated periodical; and William Henry Trescot, an urbane, well-connected
Charlestonian whose many published books and essays after 1846 made him
perhaps America's foremost foreign policy thinker in the decade before the
Civil War.[15] As much as the South's powerful politicians, these pro-slavery
intellectuals set the course for antebellum US grand strategy. To return to
Brands's formulation, it was they who developed the "integrated scheme of
interests, threats, resources, and policies" that helped statesmen like Calhoun
and Davis manage the "concrete initiatives" that amounted to American foreign policy.[16]

Three basic principles defined the grand strategic vision of these slaveholding leaders and intellectuals. The first was a close attention to the international politics of slavery and abolition. Historians of antebellum America
are accustomed to discussing the sectional balance of power in the Senate between free and slave states, but southern statesmen also tracked the balance
of power between free and slave states across the Atlantic world. The British
abolition of slavery in the West Indies after 1833 encouraged slaveholders to
see the entire Atlantic basin as a kind of strategic checkerboard of enslaved
and emancipated societies. If Great Britain had determined "to become the
great Apostle of emancipation," one Charleston newspaper declared in 1840,
"let those countries largely interested in Slave property know the fact that
they may be prepared to resist a pretension so extravagant."[17]

In the face of ongoing British abolitionism, by the early 1840s
southern leaders insisted that the other slave countries in the Western

Hemisphere—chiefly the Spanish colony of Cuba, the Empire of Brazil, and the Republic of Texas—were the natural allies of the slaveholding United States. Between America and Brazil, Secretary of State Calhoun wrote US minister Henry Wise, "there is a strict identity of interests on almost all subjects, without conflict, or even competition, on scarcely one." The strongest Brazilian-American bond involved "the important relation between the European and African races as it exists with [Brazil] and in the Southern portion of our Union." To abolish slavery in one country, Calhoun explained, "would facilitate its destruction in the other. Hence our mutual interest in resisting her interference with the relation in either country." For Calhoun and other southern statesmen in the 1840s, a threat to slavery anywhere was a threat to slavery everywhere. [18]

This kind of nineteenth-century domino theory sometimes drove Southerners to ravenous acts of expansion. The Tyler administration's tireless effort to annex Texas in 1844–45, largely as a means to fend off British abolitionism, is the paramount example.[19] But just as frequently, an attention to the international balance of power between slavery and abolition dulled rather than quickened expansionist impulses. In 1854, rumors about Cuba's imminent "Africanization"—that is, emancipation—prompted some slaveholders, led by Mississippi's John Quitman, to plan a filibuster expedition against the Spanish colony. But when the Spanish colonial government backed away from its anti-slavery measures and threatened to free Cuba's slaves in the event of an invasion, the most powerful southern statesmen in Washington expressed their doubts. An over-hasty filibuster attack might result in the accidental destruction of Cuban slavery. Ultimately President Franklin Pierce—backed by his influential secretary of war, Jefferson Davis—decided to shut down the Quitman expedition.[20]

Some Southerners even contended that an independent Cuba—free from Spain, but still possessed of its slaves—represented the optimal outcome for the United States. "A kindred and slave-holding republic," argued William Henry Trescot, would exercise a benevolent influence over the "community of islands in the Gulf."[21] Perhaps its flourishing example might even encourage a reestablishment of slavery in the British and French West Indies. To be sure, Davis and most other southern leaders still hungered for an eventual American annexation of Cuba. But as with earlier emancipation panics, the preservation of overseas slave institutions proved a higher strategic priority than the desire for new slave territory. As Alexander Stephens admitted, he would even prefer to see England take possession of Cuba, with its slave system intact, than let the island fall to "Guinea negroes and African savages." The balance of power between slavery and abolition, in southern eyes, was often more decisive than the balance of power between the United States and other powers in the hemisphere.[22]

This does not imply that southern leaders believed their country should play a quiet or subordinate role in foreign affairs. The second major principle of master class grand strategy was that the United States itself must serve as the Western Hemisphere's chief defender of slave institutions. Slaveholders agreed that the rising power of the American republic was the defining feature of geopolitical struggle across the Atlantic basin. The "young Hercules of America," declared James D. B. De Bow, was destined to play a great part in "the great race for position and for empire." Trescot, who for tactical reasons preferred Cuban independence to immediate annexation, nevertheless presumed that the whole of the Caribbean came under America's strategic purview. As "the leading power of this western world," Trescot declared, "we will assign Cuba her place. . . . She is our Belgium."[23]

In their belief in the present significance and future grandeur of American power, slaveholders were no different from many of their northern peers in the exuberant 1840s and 1850s, the golden decades of "manifest destiny." What distinguished the master class was a firm sense that American power should and must be harnessed to serve the ends of American slavery—not just within US borders, but across the entire "western world." In a hemisphere threatened by the anti-slavery influence of Great Britain, it was the duty of the rising United States to act as the protector and champion for slave institutions throughout the Americas. Sometimes the hemispheric defense of slavery required a policy of direct annexation. By absorbing the vulnerable Republic of Texas into the American fold, slaveholders consolidated the institution on both sides of the Sabine River: "The slave interest is too small in N. America to be maintained without molestation if held by two governments," as one Texas government official wrote to Duff Green in 1844. "To make it secure one government should protect it all."[24] In other circumstances, as in Cuba in 1854, the overseas defense of slavery demanded a more restrained policy of pro-slavery solidarity and strategic cooperation. But in every case, slaveholders assumed that the United States, and no other power, would play a leading role in protecting slave institutions from both their foreign and domestic enemies.

This second principle of pro-slavery grand strategy encouraged slaveholders to embrace the power of the American state. In many areas of domestic politics, of course, slaveholders opposed the creation of a vigorous federal government. A powerful central state might threaten the sovereignty of masters over the enslaved people they held as property. It might also undermine the security of state governments managed exclusively by slaveholders. On a wide variety of domestic issues, southern elites often claimed the mantle of states' rights and insisted on a strict construction of the Constitution. Yet in international politics, the playing field was larger, and next to avowedly anti-slavery nations like Great Britain and Mexico, the United States itself appeared as the world's largest sovereign slave state. As Southerners in an American union, Calhoun and Davis genuinely feared many aspects of a strong central government. But as Americans in the wider world, they understood US national power as the strongest possible mechanism to advance the international interests of the slaveholding class.[25]

The result was that states' rights Southerners often acted as aggressive champions of American state power in foreign and military affairs. As Tyler's secretary of the navy, the Virginia Calhounite Abel P. Upshur called in 1841 for a massively expanded naval force—effectively an eightfold increase in American sea power—in large part to match the anti-slavery threat of the British navy. (In his struggle for naval expansion and reform, Upshur drew heavily on the strategic ideas developed by the pro-slavery intellectual Matthew Fontaine Maury.) In the Pierce administration, naval secretary James Dobbin of North Carolina oversaw the largest shipbuilding program in the antebellum era, while in the War Department, Davis successfully pushed for new infantry and cavalry regiments.[26] Compared to contemporary European military establishments, the antebellum armed forces remained quite small, although under Pierce the US Army probably surpassed that of Great Britain as the largest military power in North America. By national standards, Davis and Dobbin's achievements were considerable. From 1853 to 1857, they produced the largest peacetime military increase in pre–Civil War American history.[27]

To be sure, slavery alone cannot explain this mid-nineteenth-century effort to strengthen the army and navy. The master-class grand strategy of Upshur and Davis, insofar as it involved the armed forces, was compatible with a range of non-slaveholding imperial visions and won the support of key non-slaveholding allies, from commercial New England to the western frontier. Nevertheless, it was notable that the executive leadership for these ambitious military initiatives did not come from the purportedly "national" North but from the adamantly pro-slavery South. The key legislators who procured the funds for these expansive programs and defended them on the floor of Congress, too, were pro-slavery southerners: above all Stephen Mallory in the Senate, but also Virginia's Charles Faulkner and Thomas Bocock, who led the House Military and Naval Affairs Committees in crucial sessions.[28]

In the same years, another group of Southerners in government led a successful campaign for the reform and enlargement of the US diplomatic corps. Congressman John Perkins of Louisiana and Assistant Secretary of State A. Dudley Mann of Virginia collaborated to produce an 1855 bill that increased the number of ministers abroad, added a secretary of legation to each mission, and raised diplomatic and consular salaries around the world. Six years later, Perkins would chair Louisiana's state secession convention, but for now, he argued that America's "great advances in wealth and power" demanded an expansion and overhaul of the State Department. De Bow, who gave the consular reforms much attention in his *Review*, agreed: a powerful, modern nation like the United States required an army, navy, and foreign service to match.[29]

This emphasis on diplomatic reform was no accident. For all their military zeal, few antebellum Southerners wanted to risk war with a major power. "Peace," John C. Calhoun often insisted, "is indeed our policy."[30] More than mere policy, it amounted to a third major strategic principle of the master class. Amid the various northeastern boundary clashes with Britain in the early 1840s, southern leaders generally urged calm diplomacy and military preparation, not provocative action. During the Oregon border negotiations of 1845–46, President Polk indulged in some Anglophobic saber rattling, but before long he readily agreed to a peaceful compromise. In the various diplomatic imbroglios of the 1850s—principally over British interference in Central America—some pro-slavery hotspurs urged military action, but in every case they were overruled by a more cautious and more powerful southern mainstream. A suitably strong armed establishment, declared Robert M. T. Hunter in 1856, added to the American "sense of security. . . . I desire to see this country placed in such a condition that no foreign Power shall ever direct a gun in menace upon our coast without feeling that they do it under the responsibility of aiming at those who have guns enough pointed in return." For like-minded southern leaders, peace, strength, and slavery were mutually reinforcing. A powerful, well-armed American state, at ease with Europe and dominant in its own hemisphere—this was the surest possible guarantee for both the South and its slave institutions.[31]

The prospect of a major war, by contrast, gave slaveholders bad dreams. During the Revolutionary War and the War of 1812, masters rightly feared that their slaves would run to British lines. But in those years Great Britain was still a major slaveholding power. After 1833, the possibility of an Anglo-American war took on a different cast. "We are on the eve of hostilities with that very country which is the center and source of antislavery fanaticism," warned a contributor to the *Richmond Enquirer* in 1840. "In such an event, will not an appeal be made to our slaves, and arms put in their hands?" The whole of the slaveholding states, argued one South Carolina congressman, might be turned into "a howling wilderness . . . wrapt in conflagration." War with Britain would involve not merely the risk of battlefield defeat but also the nightmarish possibility of slave rebellion and mass emancipation. It was no wonder that slaveholders from Calhoun to Davis consistently resisted military and diplomatic activities that would trigger a major Anglo-American conflict. [32]

At first glance, the Polk administration's war with Mexico might appear as the great exception to slaveholders' strategic preference for peace. Yet in 1846, southern elites did not view Mexico as a foreign power of dangerous consequence. Although it was strong enough to threaten slave property in the weak republic of Texas, slaveholders were confident that Mexico lacked the capacity to resist the United States, "the leading power of this western world." Much of Calhoun's initial opposition to the war derived from a fear that it would involve Great Britain. After the Oregon dispute was finally settled, and it became clear that Britain would not enter the fray, Calhoun's position evolved: "The war has opened with brilliant victories on our side," he told his son-in-law. "I give it a quiet, but decided support, as much as I regret the occurrence." [33]

Ultimately Polk's war divided southern leaders along partisan lines, with Whigs denouncing the conflict while a larger group of slaveholding Democrats cheered on the US conquest of Mexico. Calhoun appeared to join the opposition in 1847 when he criticized Polk's invasion of the Mexican heartland and briefly delayed the passage of war funds in the Senate. Yet under the appearance of conflict, Calhoun continued to provide quiet but decided support for Polk's war. On all the major war measures that passed through Congress, Calhoun expressed a degree of dissent, yet he went ahead and supported the administration anyway.[34] In some ways, Polk and Calhoun represented opposite ends of the antebellum South's strategic spectrum. Independently, they construed their foreign policy goals in very different ways, with Polk emphasizing national expansion, pushy diplomacy, and the vigorous prosecution of war, while Calhoun stressed the security of slavery, free trade, and the avoidance of dangerous conflict. In practice, their visions proved easy to reconcile. Between 1845 and 1848 the United States successfully protected slavery in Texas, escaped a conflict with Great Britain, waged a victorious war against Mexico, and tailored its continental expansion to gain the maximum amount of territory with the minimum possible risk to slave labor. For the slaveholders who exercised a decisive influence on US foreign policy during the 1840s, American hemispheric power and the security of hemispheric slavery were congruent objectives. Ultimately, the war with Mexico enhanced both of them.[35]

To the Civil War and Beyond

The end of the war with Mexico marked a turning point in the evolving grand strategy of the master class. For more than a decade after 1833, when Great Britain passed the Slavery Abolition Act, pro-slavery strategic thinkers had generally believed they were acting on the defensive in international politics. Within the American union, anti-slavery forces remained weak and marginal. But on the world stage, with the global power of the British empire officially hostile to slave institutions, American slaveholders had to scramble to counteract it. Between 1841 and 1848, the Southerners in and around the Tyler and Polk administrations did just that: the annexation of Texas and the conquest of Mexico capped a larger strategic effort to strengthen and consolidate the forces of slavery within the hemisphere.

After 1848, however, slavery's international and domestic fortunes began to reverse themselves. Northern opponents of bondage gained new impetus from the debate over the future of the western territories seized from Mexico; through the next decade they grew continually stronger within American domestic politics. On an international plane, however, the strategic position of hemispheric slavery was much improved. Falling global tariffs and soaring demand for cotton left southern planters flush with wealth and ecstatic about the dependence of the industrial world on a commodity that only American slaves seemed able to produce with profit. In the 1850s, the collapse of staple exports in the emancipated British West Indies—and the emergence of enslaved Cuba and Brazil as the world's leading producers of sugar and coffee—appeared to dampen Great Britain's moral and strategic commitment to abolition. Moreover, slaveholders believed, the spread of European empires in Africa and Asia, the rise of "coolie" bound labor systems in the tropics, and the latest discoveries of modern science all seemed to affirm the global necessity of racial hierarchy and coerced labor. In this emerging world order, as one contributor to *De Bow's Review* declared, it seemed clear that "modern civilization" itself depended on "compulsory black labor."[36]

Across the 1850s, the underlying principles of master-class grand strategy remained the same as ever. The balance of power between slavery and abolition still demanded attention; the United States still figured as the hemisphere's indispensable defender of slave property. Yet the favorable international environment gave pro-slavery foreign policy a ruddier complexion than it had previously assumed. Before 1845, the forces troubling the hemispheric balance of power still carried the anti-slavery impetus of the Age of Revolution: the real and imagined rebellions, reforms, and diplomatic meddling that disturbed existing slave regimes in Cuba, Brazil, and Texas. After 1848, the major destabilizing forces came from slaveholders themselves—filibuster invasions of Cuba and Nicaragua, assertive diplomacy to secure transit across the Central American isthmus, and a drumbeat of boasts about the reenslavement of all tropical America.[37] Not all slaveholding statesmen participated in these efforts; sometimes they sought to restrain their most aggressive forms. But the international grand strategy of slavery had, in effect, moved from defense to offense.

On the domestic front, however, slaveholders proved unable to hold their position. The emergence of the anti-slavery Republican Party threatened the partisan alignment that had given slaveholders such disproportionate power since the founding of the republic. The election of Abraham Lincoln in 1860 constituted a revolution in American politics and promised a revolution in American grand strategy. Suddenly slaveholding elites, who had understood themselves as the leading architects of US international power for the past three decades, found that they had no access to their creation. "So is the nation gone—forever over to Black Republicanism," brooded Henry Wise. "That breaks the charm of my life."[38]

Even worse, the mighty organism that Southerners had built now threatened to turn its formidable energies against their own institutions. The whole of America's outward state—its armed forces, its diplomatic corps, its entire capacity for overseas action—could be mobilized by a Republican administration to undermine slavery across the western hemisphere.

When compromise negotiations in Washington collapsed, even the South's most committed pro-slavery nationalists lent their strength to the cause of disunion. After secession had triumphed, these same nationally experienced leaders assumed command of the new Confederate regime. In February 1861, the Montgomery convention chose Davis as president and Stephens as vice president. Robert Hunter served as secretary of state (1861–62) and then president pro tempore of the Confederate Senate (1862–65); Stephen Mallory as secretary of the navy (1861–65); James Mason as minister to England (1862–65); and John Slidell as minister to France (1862–65).[39]

Davis and his allies did not entirely forget the antebellum master-class's strategic preference for peace. At his inaugural address in February 1861, the new southern president channeled Calhoun: "As an agricultural people," he declared, "our true policy is peace."[40] In April, however, Davis proved unable to secure his sovereign slave republic without bombarding United States troops in Charleston harbor. Amid the intoxications of independence, statehood, and nation-making, Confederates lost their grip on strategic reality. Violating a central principle of the antebellum master class, the Davis administration triggered a war with a much larger, much stronger, and very determined anti-slavery foreign power.

By 1865, that war had destroyed slavery and the Confederate republic alike. Southern elites were virtually cut off from national power for over half a century, encouraging future students of American foreign policy to neglect the once-mighty antebellum master class. Yet the grand strategy of slavery left a profound imprint on the history of the United States. For decades, pro-slavery leaders controlled the chief levers of power within the American state. Their intense focus on the balance of power between slavery and abolition decisively shaped the course of national expansion in the mid-nineteenth century. They anticipated, in substantial ways, the strategic assumptions behind US hemispheric hegemony in the late nineteenth century and the ideological assumptions behind US global imperial power in the twentieth. And they contributed to the development of a powerful tradition in American strategic thought, still influential in the twenty-first century, that has simultaneously sought limited government at home and a muscular foreign policy abroad. The ultimate horizon of master-class grand strategy—the preservation of slave institutions—was a dead end. But historians of American foreign relations and American grand strategy neglect slaveholders at the peril of their own understanding.

Notes

1. Even foreign relations scholars otherwise closely attuned to domestic politics tend to ignore slavery and brush past the antebellum era: see, for example, Peter Trubowitz, *Politics and Strategy: Partisan Ambition and American Statecraft* (Princeton, NJ: Princeton University Press, 2011); and Peter Trubowitz, *Defining the National Interest: Conflict and Change in American Foreign Policy* (Chicago: University of Chicago Press, 1998).

2. William C. Martel, *Grand Strategy in Theory and Practice: The Need for an Effective American Foreign Policy* (Cambridge: Cambridge University Press, 2015), 194. See also Patrick J. Buchanan, "Jimmy Polk's War," *National Interest* 56 (Summer 1999), 97–105.

3. For a representative and revealing example, see John Lewis Gaddis, *Surprise, Security, and the American Experience* (Cambridge, MA: Harvard University Press, 2004), 7–35. The fact that the early republic's single most important international statesman and strategist was an anti-slavery New Englander has certainly encouraged the South's demotion in this literature: see Samuel Flagg Bemis, *John Quincy Adams and the Foundations of American Foreign Policy* (New York: Knopf, 1949); William Earl Weeks, *John Quincy Adams and American Global Empire* (Lexington: University Press of Kentucky, 2002); Charles Edel, *Nation Builder: John Quincy Adams and the Grand Strategy of the Republic* (Cambridge, MA: Harvard University Press, 2014).

4. Walter Russell Mead, *Special Providence: American Foreign Policy and How It Changed the World* (New York: Knopf, 2001), 92–93.

5. Robert Kagan, *Dangerous Nation: America's Foreign Policy from Its Earliest Days to the Dawn of the Twentieth Century* (New York: Vintage, 2006), 181–264, quoted 186.

6. George C. Herring, *From Colony to Superpower* (New York: Oxford University Press, 2005), 176–223; Kinley Brauer, "Economics and the Diplomacy of American Expansion," in *Economics and World Power: An Assessment of American Diplomacy since 1789*, ed. William H. Becker and Samuel F. Wells Jr. (New York: Columbia University Press, 1984); William Earl Weeks, *The New Cambridge History of American Foreign Relations*, vol. 1, *Dimensions of the Early American Empire, 1754–1865* (New York: Cambridge University Press, 2013).

7. See, for instance, Don E. Fehrenbacher, *The Slaveholding Republic: An Account of the United States Government's Relations to Slavery* (New York: Oxford University Press, 2001), 89–134, 231–294; Michael A. Schoeppner, "Status across Borders: Roger Taney, Black British Subjects, and a Diplomatic Antecedent to the Dred Scott Decision," *Journal of American History* 100:1 (June 2013), 46–67; Robert E. May, *The Southern Dream of a Caribbean Empire, 1854–1861* (Gainesville: University Press of Florida, 2002 [1973]). Joseph Fry's monograph on Southerners and foreign policy likewise tends to define the South as a sectional rather than a national space: Fry, *Dixie Looks Abroad: The South and U.S. Foreign Relations, 1789–1973* (Baton Rouge: Louisiana State University Press, 2002).

8. Richard Hofstadter, *The American Political Tradition and the Men Who Made It* (New York: Vintage, 1948), 70.

9. Josiah Grinnell, speech in House, *Congressional Globe,* 38th Cong., 2nd Sess., 199 (January 10, 1865); W. E. B. Du Bois, *Black Reconstruction in America* (New York: Russell and Russell, 1935), 47.

10. Henry Wilson, *The History of the Rise and Fall of the Slave Power in America,* 3 vols. (Boston: J. R. Osgood & Co., 1872–1877); Fehrenbacher, *The Slaveholding Republic;* David F. Ericson, *Slavery in the American Republic: Developing the Federal Government, 1791–1861* (Lawrence: University Press of Kansas, 2011); Adam Rothman, "The 'Slave Power' in the United States, 1783–1865," in *Ruling America: A History of Wealth and Power in a Democracy,* ed. Steve Fraser and Gary Gerstle (Cambridge, MA: Harvard University Press, 2005), 64–91.

11. On the notion of an "outward state," and its relative strength in a later nineteenth-century period, see Andrew W. Cohen, "Smuggling, Globalization, and America's Outward State, 1870–1909," *Journal of American History* 97:2 (September 2010), 371–398. See also Matthew Karp, *This Vast Southern Empire: Slaveholders at the Helm of American Foreign Policy* (Cambridge, MA: Harvard University Press, 2016); Robert E. Bonner, *Mastering America: Southern Slaveholders and the Crisis of American Nationhood* (New York: Cambridge University Press, 2009), 3–40.

12. *Congressional Globe,* 38th Cong., 2nd Sess., 199 (January 10, 1865).

13. Hal Brands, *What Good Is Grand Strategy? Power and Purpose in American Statecraft from Harry S. Truman to George W. Bush* (Ithaca, NY: Cornell University Press, 2014), 3; Alastair Johnston, "Thinking about Strategic Culture," *International Security* 19 (Spring 1995), 32–64.

14. An emphasis on these divisions has predominated in accounts of the South's relationship to US foreign policy: see Fry, *Dixie Looks Abroad,* 66–70; William W. Freehling, *The Road to Disunion,* vol. 2, *Secessionists Triumphant, 1854–1861* (New York: Oxford University Press, 2007), 145–167; Douglas A. Ley, "Expansionists All? Southern Senators and American Foreign Policy, 1841–60," PhD dissertation, University of Wisconsin-Madison, 1990.

15. Adams speech at Dedham, Massachusetts, quoted in *Niles' Register,* November 4, 1843.

16. Brands, *What Good Is Grand Strategy?,* 4.

17. [Charleston, SC] *Southern Patriot,* February 29, 1840. On the South's ideological and strategic reaction to British emancipation, see Edward B. Rugemer, *The Problem of Emancipation: The Caribbean Roots of the American Civil War* (Baton Rouge: Louisiana State University Press, 2008).

18. Calhoun to Henry Wise, May 25, 1844, in William R. Manning, ed., *Diplomatic Correspondence of the United States: Inter-American Affairs, 1831–1860,* 12 vols. (Washington, DC: Carnegie Endowment for International Peace, 1936–39), vol. 2, 126–128. On antebellum Southerners and other slave societies, see Matthew Pratt Guterl, *American Mediterranean: Southern Slaveholders in the Age of Emancipation* (Cambridge, MA: Harvard University Press, 2008); Gerald Horne, *The Deepest South: The United States, Brazil, and the African Slave Trade* (New York: New York University Press, 2007).

19. Frederick Merk, *Slavery and the Annexation of Texas* (New York: Knopf, 1972); Karp, *This Vast Southern Empire*, 81–102.

20. May, *Southern Dream*, 59–76; Karp, *This Vast Southern Empire*, 186–198; David M. Potter, *The Impending Crisis: America before the Civil War, 1848–1861* (New York: Harper and Row, 1976), 198.

21. William Henry Trescot, *A Few Thoughts on the Foreign Policy of the United States* (Charleston, SC: John Russell, 1849), 19–23.

22. Stephens, "Speech in Reply to Mr. Campbell of Ohio," *Alexander Stephens, in Public and Private, with Letters and Speeches, Before, During, and Since the War*, ed. Henry Cleveland (Philadelphia: National Publishing Co., 1866), 440.

23. De Bow, "The South American States," *De Bow's Review* (July 1848), 8; De Bow et al., "The Memphis Convention," *De Bow's Review*, March 1850, 217–232; Trescot, "Mr. Everett and the Cuban Question," *Southern Quarterly Review*, April 1854, 462.

24. Memucan Hunt to Duff Green, March 11, 1844, Duff Green Papers, Southern Historical Collection, University of North Carolina-Chapel Hill; Bonner, *Mastering America*, 21–29.

25. On the pro-slavery embrace of different forms of state power, see Douglas Ambrose, "Statism in the Old South," in *Slavery, Secession, and Southern History*, ed. Robert L. Paquette and Louis A. Ferleger (Charlottesville: University Press of Virginia, 2000), 101–125; John Majewski, *Modernizing a Slave Economy: The Economic Vision of the Confederate Nation* (Chapel Hill: University of North Carolina Press, 2009).

26. On antebellum southern navalism, see John H. Schroeder, *Shaping a Maritime Empire: The Commercial and Diplomatic Role of the American Navy, 1829–1861* (Westport, CT: Greenwood Press, 1985), 57–78; Matthew Karp, "Slavery and American Sea Power: The Navalist Impulse in the Antebellum South," *Journal of Southern History* 77, no. 2 (May 2011), 283–324.

27. John Muldowny, "The Administration of Jefferson Davis as Secretary of War," PhD dissertation, Yale University, 1959; John Darwin, *The Empire Project: The Rise and Fall of the British World-System, 1830–1870* (New York: Cambridge University Press, 2009), 34; Matthew Karp, "Arsenal of Empire: Southern Slaveholders and the U.S. Military in the 1850s," *Common-place* 12:4 (July 2012).

28. Karp, *This Vast Southern Empire*, 199–225.

29. *House Reports*, 33 Cong., 1 Sess., No. 348: *Diplomatic and Consular System* (Serial 744, Washington, 1854); Perkins, speech in Senate, *Congressional Globe*, 33 Cong., 2 Sess., 356–366 (January 11, 1855; February 6, 1855); "The Consular System," *De Bow's Review* (January 1854), 1–16; "The New Diplomatic and Consular System of the United States," *De Bow's Review* (May 1855), 578–82. See also Wilbur J. Carr, "The American Consular Service," *American Journal of International Law* 1:4 (October 1907), 891–913.

30. Calhoun, "Speech on the Treaty of Washington," in Senate, August 19, 1842, *Papers of Calhoun*, vol. 16, 393–410.

31. Hunter, speech in Senate, *Congressional Globe*, 34 Cong., 1 Sess., 620 (March 10, 1856).

32. *Richmond Enquirer*, April 14, 1840; Francis Pickens, speech in House, *Congressional Globe*, 25 Cong., 3 Sess., Appx., 299–300 (March 1, 1839).

33. Calhoun to James Henry Hammond, August 30, 1845, *Papers of Calhoun*, vol. 22, 100–101; Calhoun to Thomas Clemson, June 11, 1846, *Papers of Calhoun*, vol. 23, 96, 171–172; Bruno Gujer, "Free Trade and Slavery: Calhoun's Defense of Southern Interests against British Interference, 1811–1848," PhD dissertation, University of Zurich, 1971, 271–282.

34. An account that stresses the rupture between Calhoun and Polk is Ernest McPherson Lander, *Reluctant Imperialists: Calhoun, the South Carolinians, and the Mexican War* (Baton Rouge: Louisiana State University Press, 1980). But on Calhoun's failure to disrupt Polk's war effort, and his quiet cooperation with Polk, see *The Diary of James K. Polk during His Presidency, 1845 to 1849*, ed. Milo Milton Quaife, 4 vols. (Chicago: A.C. McClurg & Co., 1910), vol. 2, 463; vol. 3, 236; vol. 4, 19–21; William Cooper, *The South and the Politics of Slavery, 1828–1856* (Baton Rouge: Louisiana State University Press, 1978), 236–238; Karp, *This Vast Southern Empire*, 103–124

35. On southern enthusiasm for the war in Congress, see Joel Silbey, *The Shrine of Party: Congressional Voting Behavior 1841–1852* (Pittsburgh: University of Pittsburgh Press, 1967), 76–78.

36. Anonymous [Thomas P. Kettell], "The Future of the South," *De Bow's Review* (February 1851), 137. For further discussion, see Matthew Karp, "The World the Slaveholders Craved: Proslavery Internationalism in the 1850s," in *The World of the Revolutionary American Republic*, ed. Andrew Shankman (New York: Routledge, 2014), 414–432.

37. See May, *Southern Dream*; Walter Johnson, *River of Dark Dreams: Slavery and Empire in the Cotton Kingdom* (Cambridge, MA: Harvard University Press, 2013), 330–420.

38. Wise to Caleb Cushing, October 13, 1860, quoted in Craig M. Simpson, *A Good Southerner: The Life of Henry A. Wise of Virginia* (Chapel Hill: University of North Carolina Press, 1985), 236. See also Michael E. Woods, *Emotional and Sectional Conflict in the Antebellum United States* (New York: Cambridge University Press, 2014), 206–231; William J. Cooper Jr., "The Critical Signpost on the Journey toward Secession," *Journal of Social History* 57:1 (February 2011), 3–16.

39. On the dominance of mainstream politicians in the formation of the Confederacy, see William C. Davis, *"A Government of our Own": The Making of the Confederacy* (New York: Free Press, 1994), 44–261; Emory M. Thomas, *The Confederate Nation, 1861–1865* (New York: Harper Perennial, 2011 [1979]), 37–66.

40. Davis, Inaugural Address, February 18, 1861, Lynda L. Crist et al., eds., *The Papers of Jefferson Davis*, 14 vols. (Baton Rouge: University of Louisiana Press, 1971-2015), vol. 7, 47.

6

A Useful Category of Analysis?

Grand Strategy and US Foreign Relations from the Civil War through World War I

Katherine C. Epstein

Few historians would dispute that US foreign relations were transformed in the period from 1865 to 1918. The nature of this transformation is another matter, however. One influential interpretation, propagated initially by the "Wisconsin school" but adopted in modified form by many other historians, characterizes it as a purposeful effort to project US industrial and naval power on a global scale. As historian Walter McDougall put it, "Raw statistics prove that the United States became a world power in the generation after the Civil War. . . . The industrial revolution matured to the point that by 1900 Americans produced 244 million tons of coal per year (an output equal to Britain's) and 10 million tons of steel, nearly twice the total of second-place Germany."[1] Walter LaFeber, a leading member of the Wisconsin School, made the industrial revolution, the search for markets for surplus manufactured goods, and the growth of the battleship navy in the late nineteenth century major themes of his story in *The New Empire*.[2] In such accounts, industrial power and naval power are closely linked: the rapid industrialization of the United States vaulted it past the first industrial nation, Great Britain, as the world's leading manufacturer, while its growing industrial base both enabled and benefited from the construction of an oceangoing steel battlefleet. Thanks to these developments, by the turn of the century— years before the outbreak of World War I—the United States had taken its place among the great powers of the world.

Some historians, particularly those with an interest in the ideas of Alfred Thayer Mahan, have explicitly analyzed the transformation of US foreign relations from 1865 to 1918 in terms of "grand strategy."[3] Others who have not (and probably would not) use the concept as an analytical tool have nevertheless offered interpretations that can be easily assimilated by the concept's enthusiasts and, if so desired, given a different ideological edge. Whether the emergence of the United States as a great power is to be welcomed or lamented, both celebrants and critics can agree that it happened, and that it happened largely as a result of the deliberate peacetime melding of industrial and naval power. If the influential definitions of "grand strategy" by Edward Mead Earle or B. H. Liddell Hart are adopted, then the key components of a grand strategy would appear to have been in place: there was an intentional effort, in peacetime, to coordinate both military and non-military elements of national power (the means) in order to improve the relative position of the United States in the global balance of power (the end).[4]

This interpretation of US foreign relations during this period is problematic, however, and attempting to analyze the subject in terms of "grand strategy" exacerbates the problems. The critique offered here is based on certain convictions about the study of history. Although historical evidence does not create or interpret itself, it has an integrity to which historians should do as little violence as they can. To the best of their ability, historians are obliged to try to understand and explain the past on its own terms, not on their own. Thus the test of any historical interpretation should be how well it explains the relevant evidence, not how well it conforms to contemporary policy concerns.

By this standard, the application of the concept of "grand strategy" often produces worse rather than better historical scholarship. It tempts historians to commit the cardinal grand strategic sin of confusing ends and means. The end should be a contribution to our understanding of the past, and the application of the concept of grand strategy the means. Instead, the end can become a contribution to "grand strategy studies," and the study of the past the means. Thomas Meaney and Stephen Wertheim have described and decried this confusion of ends and means as "the overt instrumentalization of the humanities."[5] Historians should not abet this process.

Although the concept of grand strategy cannot be blamed for creating the problems with the existing literature on US foreign relations from the Civil War through World War I, it tends to worsen them, in two related ways. First, the concept of grand strategy privileges the nation-state as the unit of analysis, when no less important units in this case are the sub-national and the global. Second, the "grandness" of grand strategy encourages scholars to neglect critically important details of US economic and naval power. These details are more than isolated anomalies: taken together, they compel a new explanatory paradigm.

Why the Unit of Analysis Matters

The theorists and users of the concept of grand strategy typically regard the nation-state as the appropriate unit of analysis. In one famous formulation, for instance, Liddell Hart defined the purpose of grand strategy as the "co-ordinat[ion] and direct[ion of] all the resources of a nation, or band of nations."[6] To understand US foreign relations between 1865 and 1918, however, interest in the national scale of analysis must be supplemented by attention to sub-national and global scales. The sub-national includes the sectional (or regional), the sectoral (as in economic sector), and the partisan. The global should be conceived not as the international (or accumulation of the national) but as a level at which certain processes occur independent of the control of nation-states. A global phenomenon of particular relevance to US foreign relations in these decades was what scholars now refer to as the first era of globalization, often dated from about 1870 to 1914—or largely coincident with the period under review. Then as now, globalization was defined chiefly by extraordinary increases in the volume of world trade, the growing economic interdependence of the world, and the convergence of global commodity prices.[7] Within the US political economy, sub-national and global processes fed each other in ways that reshaped US foreign relations.

As scholars Richard Franklin Bensel and Elizabeth Sanders have argued, the US political economy after the Civil War was fractured along regional, sectoral, and partisan lines. These lines overlapped to a considerable degree. Regionally, the United States consisted of four principal sections: the Northeast, the Midwest, the West, and the South. Each of these regions specialized in certain economic sectors: the Northeast in industry, finance, and commerce; the Midwest in industry, agriculture (mainly corn), and ranching (mainly hogs); the West in agriculture (mainly wheat and, to a lesser degree, sugar beets), ranching (mainly cattle and sheep), mining, and logging; and the South in agriculture (mainly cotton). Together, the West and the South comprised the "extractive periphery" to the more developed northeastern and midwestern core. In partisan terms, the North, Midwest, and West tended to vote Republican, while the South voted Democratic.[8]

Globalization exacerbated this sub-national variation within the domestic political economy of the United States. In the globalizing world economy, the United States could not make whatever policies it wanted but had to adapt them to international market discipline, the gold standard being the prime example. But the national policies necessary to prosper within a globalized world economy did not have a uniform national impact; rather, they had differential regional impacts. Within the United States, the economies of the South and West were the most directly dependent on international trade and the least capable of providing for local needs. Much of the alcohol in western saloons was brought in by rail.[9] Thus, while the financial Northeast and industrial Midwest were dependent on Britain once over, the South and West were dependent twice over, on both their richer American and their richer British cousins. This double dependence helps to explain their hatred of the gold standard. The preeminent requirement of the international financial order dominated by Britain and the national financial order dominated by the Northeast, it served as a symbol of their dual dependence.[10]

Given these regional, sectoral, and partisan fractures, there was no unified national interest for a putative grand strategy to advance. Rather, there were a series of sub-national interests competing with each other to secure control of national policymaking and then to redefine by synecdoche their sub-national interest as the national interest. Policies ostensibly geared toward the United States' external relations had as much to do with its internal relations. The political scientist Peter Trubowitz has shown that regional positions on three major foreign-policy questions of the era—a battleship navy, economic and territorial expansion, and the tariff—correlated closely to the sectional structure of the domestic political economy.[11] Most of the policies being touted to aid the expansion of the United States—a tariff to strengthen its industrial base, a merchant marine built in US shipyards to carry its goods, a navy to protect its commerce, a stronger financial services industry—were (correctly) perceived by many Americans on the extractive periphery, especially in the South and especially in the Democratic Party, as tilting the domestic political-economic balance further in favor of the Republican economic core. The revenues to build the ships would come from the hated tariff and be built mainly in northern yards, while a stronger financial services industry would enrich the northeastern capitalists who kept the periphery in peonage.[12] As the historian Antony Hopkins notes, "Town and country did not form a natural, harmonious alliance" when it came to the projection of US power abroad.[13] The first question to be asked by historians of US foreign relations studying this period should be, therefore, not how the United States pursued its national interest, but how certain groups gained control of national policy at the expense of others.

The concept needed to answer this question is not grand strategy but po-litical economy. To be clear, a political-economic approach does not rule out the argument that US policymakers acted strategically in the decades before World War I. What it rules out is the argument that they acted "grand" stra-tegically. It shows that they acted strategically—but their strategies were as much partisan, sectoral, and regional as they were national. As the Wisconsin School historian Lloyd Gardner put it, rejecting the "realist" critique of policymakers as strategically impaired moralists, "American policy makers knew what they were about."[14] They had strategies—just not the strategies that "grand" strategy looks for.

For understanding these strategies, the work of the Wisconsin School remains unsurpassed though incomplete. As Hopkins astutely notes, the Wisconsin School contains "two versions that were never fully integrated."[15] One focused on industry as the key sector of the political economy driving overseas US power projection. Brilliantly elaborated by LaFeber in *The New Empire*, this version nevertheless tends to flatten internal political-economic disputes into an expansionist consensus. The other, put forward by William A. Williams (the doyen of the Wisconsin School) in *The Roots of the Modern American Empire*, focused on agriculture as the key sector driving overseas power projection and kept its sights firmly trained on tensions between farmers and other interest groups. Although Hopkins fairly judges that the agricultural version "remained undeveloped and is now neglected," this judgment does not absolve scholars for the subsequent lack of development or neglect.[16] However incomplete their work, Wisconsinite authors formu-lated a series of original, important questions about US foreign relations from 1865 to 1918 and carried out a staggering quantity of intensive pri-mary source research that no historians, whatever their ideological persua-sion, have come close to matching. The Wisconsin School did an enormous amount; they cannot be expected to have done everything. Minimization of the value of their work on the grounds that it was "Marxist" (debatable and irrelevant) and "economically determinist" (it was not) has prevented it from receiving its scholarly due. According to John Gaddis, who taught at the Naval War College during Stansfield Turner's overhaul of the "Strategy and Policy" curriculum and who co-founded the Grand Strategy program at Yale, he was told that Williams's work had been on the "Strategy and Policy" reading list "but had to be taken off because the war college students found it too convincing."[17] Perhaps the time has come to put the scholarship of this decorated naval officer—Williams—back on the syllabus.

Why the Economic and Naval Details Matter

Enabling US expansion in the decades following the Civil War, the standard narrative goes, was the growth of its industrial and naval power. These two forms of power, in turn, are understood to have been the results of industrialization and the construction of an oceangoing steel battleship navy, respectively. Viewed from the perspective of US history, both of these developments truly constituted significant departures from the national past. The United States was not a mature industrial power before the Civil War, and Americans had a long tradition of opposing standing naval forces because of the taxation necessary to support them.[18] US industrial output after the Civil War was also significant viewed from the perspective of the global great powers, not only in terms of US history. However, US economic growth and naval growth were much less impressive when compared to the real great powers than is generally appreciated by historians of US foreign relations. Flattering US strategy with the moniker "grand" only strengthens the mistaken belief that the United States became a great power before World War I.[19]

It is true that the United States became a great industrial power between 1865 and 1918. But this statement requires several qualifications. First, despite the oft-cited growth in industrial exports as a share of overall exports, agricultural exports continued to dwarf industrial exports in value. Moreover, it was the former (especially raw cotton), not the latter, which allowed the United States to earn foreign exchange, maintain its international creditworthiness, and thereby ensure a continuing flow of foreign investment capital into industrial development. In 1913, the value of raw cotton exports was just under $550 million, while the *total* value of all exports of iron and steel-mill products, copper and manufactures, and all classes of machinery was just over $460 million—less than the value of raw cotton alone.[20] Second, aggregate statistics on industrial exports must be carefully scrutinized. They say a great deal about the United States' raw manufacturing power but very little about the quality of its manufactured goods. The United States was the China of its day: quantity and cost were its great advantages. British steel from Sheffield, for instance, generally remained a higher-quality product.[21] Third, again like China, the United States relied heavily on the transfer—or confiscation—of European intellectual property to develop industrially.[22] As the secretary of the navy put it ingenuously (if a touch euphemistically) in 1886, "I think our true policy is to borrow the ideas of our neighbors so far as they are thought to be in advance of ours."[23] Fourth, British and continental

European talk of an American commercial "invasion," often cited as evidence of the United States' industrial maturation, should not automatically be taken at face value. This "invasion" talk (like so much invasion talk) primarily reflected the desire of interest groups abroad to prosper within their own domestic political economies rather than a disinterested commitment to empirical accuracy.[24]

Finally, and most important, industrialization was not the only great global economic phenomenon of the era. When it came to the other—globalization—the United States lagged behind France, Germany, and especially Britain. Indeed, Britain, notwithstanding its relative industrial decline, remained the hegemon of the globalized world economy. Its power rested on its effective monopoly control of the infrastructure of globalization: naval power, oceangoing (as distinct from coastal) merchant shipping, global communications (cables and wireless), and financial services (banking and insurance).[25] Because so much of the world's trade was carried in British ships, negotiated over British communications, financed in London, and denominated in sterling, Britain accrued substantial invisible earnings even when it was not the importer or exporter.[26] This is not to say that Britain's economic sovereignty was unlimited—like every other nation, it had to adapt its policies to international market discipline—but as hegemon of the global economy, it enjoyed relatively greater economic sovereignty than any other nation.

The United States barely dented British control of the infrastructure of globalization before World War I. Its merchant marine had not recovered from the flight of the flag from the world's oceans during the Civil War. A law requiring that any ship registered under the American flag be built in the United States was largely responsible for the merchant marine's persistent weakness, since US shipbuilders had higher labor and operating costs than their competitors.[27] The United States possessed no global communications grid. Its financial services sector was backward compared to those of other industrialized nations. Until 1913, the United States had no discount market for bills of exchange, while US banking laws prohibited American banks from establishing foreign bank branches.[28] US lenders were able to establish a financial toehold in several Latin American nations but were unable to compete in Asia.[29] US anti-trust laws prohibited firms from combining vertically or horizontally to penetrate foreign markets.[30] Sterling was *the* international currency; trade between the United States and Latin America was denominated in sterling, and bills of exchange between them cleared through London, not New York. US capital markets remained considerably less developed than some historians have assumed. Although it is true that they were more mature than before the Civil War and that the United States was becoming a capital exporter to Latin America and Asia, its economy, like those of other developing nations, remained critically dependent on capital imports from Europe, especially from Britain—and those capital imports depended on the export of agricultural goods far more than industrial products.[31] Even as the United States was becoming a creditor nation vis-à-vis weaker powers, it remained a debtor nation vis-à-vis its aspirant peers.

Viewed in this light, episodes on which US historians lavish attention as evidence of the United States' arrival on the world scene take on a different hue. The Open Door Policy appears not to have been the expression of new-found American industrial might that it is sometimes portrayed as, but the plea of a financially, commercially, and militarily weaker nation for others to let it make acquisitions that it lacked the power to force.[32] Neither it nor the Roosevelt Corollary intimidated Britain, which had sought the maintenance of an Open Door in China for decades and was delighted to have the United States assume responsibility for Latin American nations' payment of their debts.[33] A leading historian of British diplomacy bluntly writes, "America was of secondary importance. The main focus of British thinking was on the relations with the major European Powers."[34] The United States was a problem for Britain only in the context of multiple simultaneous threats to the British position around the world, not by virtue of its own power alone. None of this is to say that Wisconsin School authors were wrong to detect a sense among Americans of their nation's rising power. The Olney Note to Britain of 1895, for instance, which declared that the United States "is practically sovereign upon this continent [so much for Canada or Mexico], and its fiat is law upon the subjects to which it confines its interposition," improbably made Kaiser Wilhelm II's "Kruger telegram" of several months later look statesmanlike by comparison.[35] But there was a large gap between the rhetoric and the reality—a gap of which many policymakers were aware. As observed by John Hay, author of the Open Door Notes, the United States had no army, and talk "about 'our preeminent moral position giving us authority to dictate to the world' is mere flap-doodle."[36] Marilyn Young was right to hear a "mingled note of fear and triumph"—not just triumph—in American rhetoric of the period.[37]

As for the US Navy, most diplomatic historians have been seduced by its steel exoskeleton and have neglected to inquire into its supplies, logistics, and prospects against peer competitors.[38] Navies require more than battleships to be effective fighting forces. They need repair and fueling facilities, an advanced industrial base, communications systems, targeting technologies, tactical doctrine, political support, and funding, to name a few requirements. The United States lacked a global basing infrastructure and was particularly weak in dry docks, the most expensive and important part of any naval base.[39] Overseas, the United States had eight yards, while Britain had twenty-one. These overseas British bases and dry-docks included several in Canada and the Caribbean—notwithstanding the United States' self-declared sovereignty over the continent and hemisphere. Commodore George Dewey had to use the facilities at the British base of Hong Kong on his way to found the modern American empire in 1898, while the Great White Fleet, that symbol of the United States' arrival on the world scene nine years later, had to stop at British bases to refuel.[40]

Reflecting the immaturity of the United States' naval-industrial base, equipment for constructing armor plate and ordnance had to be imported wholesale from France and England.[41] The US Navy was top-heavy in capital ships, lacking the smaller vessels necessary to perform myriad functions— protection from submarine attacks, refueling, and so on—required to make a fleet effective. In 1916, after some thirty years of striving to construct a modern fleet, the US Navy had a ratio of battleships to other warships of one to three. By contrast, the Royal Navy had a ratio of one to eight.[42] The navy's ability to cope with enemy torpedo attacks, to fire accurately at likely battle ranges, and to communicate in battle was severely limited.[43] At the Battle of Manila Bay, the hitting rate of its gunnery against the stationary Spanish fleet under extraordinarily favorable firing conditions was 2.42 percent.[44] Although the navy was adequate to defeat the navies of weaker nations, it was not a serious rival to the Royal Navy in terms of capability, performance, or reach.

What political support did exist for the US Navy followed the contours of the domestic political economy. Southerners generally opposed or supported less enthusiastically than did others expenditures on the navy.[45] When they did vote to support naval spending, their votes should not automatically be interpreted as endorsements of a "grand strategy" to increase US power in the world. As Senator "Pitchfork" Ben Tillman (D-SC) explained his vote in support of expenditures on a dry-dock at Port Royal, "If you are going to steal, I want my share."[46] Thanks to the traditional US fear of a European-style fiscal-military state, which remained especially strong in the South, the federal government had far less power to extract financial resources from society than did the British government. In a challenging budgetary environment, the US Navy could not have everything it wanted. Forced to choose among its priorities, it invariably chose battleships, even as naval officers bemoaned the lack of bases and support vessels.[47] For their part, when growth in the budget for bases was on the table, congressmen habitually prioritized home bases, where they had constituents to reward them, rather than overseas bases.[48] Lacking political and financial support, the US Navy was not the navy of a great power.

It took World War I to make the United States into a great power, and even then a fragile one. While weakening Britain abroad, the war reshaped the domestic politics surrounding the construction of an infrastructure to challenge Britain as global hegemon. Support for such a US-dominated infrastructure grew because the war redistributed the costs and benefits of global financial and commercial weakness within the country. Before the war, the American political-economic sectors most dependent on the smooth functioning of the British-dominated global economic infrastructure—namely, the southern and western periphery—were the most opposed to the construction of an alternative US-dominated global economic infrastructure. This opposition made compelling sense in peacetime, when British interests in the smooth functioning of the system aligned with those of the American export-oriented extractive periphery. The opposition made less sense in wartime, when Britain's perception of its own interests vis-à-vis the infrastructure of globalization changed. On the outbreak of war, Britain implemented a plan to deny Germany access to the British-dominated infrastructure of globalization in an effort to rapidly collapse the German economy and will to fight.[49] Although this effort was directed against Germany, neutrals suffered collateral damage, none more severe than the United States. The cotton South—the political base of President Woodrow Wilson's Democratic Party—found itself unable to move its crop to Europe, and the nation faced the prospect of mass financial default three months before midterm elections.[50]

A political realignment ensued. The last proposal for strengthening the US merchant marine before the war had come, predictably, from a Massachusetts Republican; the first proposal after the war began came from a Mississippi Democrat.[51] In the 1916 Naval Appropriations Act, passed at a time when relations with Britain were particularly strained, Wilson committed himself to building "a navy second to none." With the 1918 Webb-Pomerene Act, the Wilson administration removed the anti-trust restrictions on business combinations for the purposes of foreign trade, to enable American firms to compete with their foreign counterparts.[52] Wilson also initiated efforts to build a US-centric global communications grid.[53] Seen from this perspective, Wilson's commitment to freedom of the seas was not idealistic; access to the global commons was an economic and strategic necessity for the United States and for Wilson's Democratic base.[54] Breaking the political-economic logjam blocking efforts to construct a US-controlled global economic infrastructure required the crisis of World War I. Even then, support for these efforts declined at the end of the war.[55]

Why have US historians and strategic studies scholars so badly overstated the degree of American economic and naval power relative to the great powers before World War I? There are several reasons, but one of the most important is their unwillingness to grapple with the details of the day-to-day workings of either the international economy or navies. Making steel is not the same as shipping it, financing its sale, or insuring its carriage. Building battleships is not the same as constructing an operationally deployable navy. If grand strategies require grand means as well as grand ends, then the means seem to have been lacking. It will take a major conceptual shift for historians to ask, let alone to answer, questions about these details—and the "grandness" of grand strategy will only get in the way.

Conclusion

Fixing the problems with the existing master narrative of US foreign relations between 1865 and 1918 requires the approach of the historian, not of the strategic studies scholar. What is needed is not an effort to bang the square pegs of history into the round holes of grand strategy studies but a willingness to grapple with historical complexity as much as possible on its own terms. To be clear, this approach does not fetishize complexity for its own sake: it just acknowledges that the past was complex. Nor is it antiquarian or scholastic. It does not treat presentism and relevance as sources of scholarly corruption but rather accepts them as necessary and even desirable elements of scholarship, the merits or demerits of which should be judged according to whether they help or hinder the effort to answer historical questions. Ironically, in regarding contemporary policy usefulness—the holy grail of grand strategy studies—as incidental to the primary objective of greater scholarly understanding, this approach is more likely to produce policy-relevant results than the self-conscious search for relevance that dominates the field of strategic studies today, because it does not reflect policymakers' existing categories of analysis back at them.

When strategic studies scholars think about the sources of national power, they rely on a model that reduces economic power to industrial capacity. This model can be traced back at least to the turn-of-the-century British geo-strategist Halford Mackinder, who predicted that industrialization (especially the spread of the railroad) would vault continental Russia past insular Britain to the top of the global power rankings.[56] Mackinder's ideas were rooted in a particular historical context: namely, a cluster of anxieties among reform-minded Edwardians, including advocates of a protectionist trade policy and others concerned about the island nation's place in a world of industrializing land powers, who believed that Britain must abandon its commitment to free trade and reform its empire in order to compete in the modern world.[57] The Mackinderian link between industrial strength and national power was then rediscovered, in a different historical context, by Edward Mead Earle at Princeton in the 1930s. Earle was alarmed by the ability of totalitarian states to command the industrial resources of their nations for military purposes, and he determined that the American academy should help policymakers to navigate this dangerous new world.[58] Bringing his own training as a historian to bear on the problem, he sought to explain totalitarianism as a modernized form of early modern mercantilism. In his seminal edited volume *Makers of Modern Strategy*, Earle's own chapter, subtitled "The Economic Foundations of Military Power," drew a more or less straight line to Adolf Hitler from Friedrich List, whom Earle explicitly described as a proto-Mackinderian and praised for his ability to understand the strategic significance of railroad development.[59] From different starting points, then, both Mackinder and Earle came to define economic power in terms of industrial strength, and both adopted this definition not in the disinterested search for scholarly truth but in their attempts to influence contemporary policy. Each, moreover, advocated a "grand strategy" that sought to shape his society at home as much as to shape its relations with the outside world, and each feared his country's weaknesses as much as he celebrated its strengths—much like American policymakers at the turn of the century.[60]

While Earle introduced a Mackinderian model of economic power into strategic studies, the two naval historians in Earle's circle at Princeton—Harold and Margaret Sprout—contributed a complementary model of naval power defined in terms of battleships, which was equally intended to influence contemporary policy debates. In their 1940 study *Toward a New Order of Sea Power*, they presented Mahan as a neo-mercantilist thinker who derived from his study of the seventeenth- and eighteenth-century British empire "the doctrine of battle-fleet supremacy."[61] They paired an emphasis on the US Navy's "Mahanian" transition from cruisers to battleships with a Mackinderian narrative about late nineteenth-century British decline due to the loss of industrial supremacy.[62] Thus, while their understanding of economic power was not as explicit as Earle's, it informed their interpretation of naval power, which they defined in terms of battleships.

The most prominent modern exponent of this model of economic and naval power is Paul Kennedy, who, as a historian of Edwardian Britain and as one of the founders of the grand strategy program at Yale, effectively yoked the Mackinderian critique of British decline to Earle's demand for the American academy to supply work with contemporary strategic relevance. Kennedy's oeuvre argues that when nations lose relative industrial power, they decline in the global power rankings. He first developed this argument in his work on Edwardian Britain, in which he linked Britain's industrial decline vis-à-vis continental Germany to the rise of the German dreadnought challenge and to the Royal Navy's abandonment of global reach. He then applied his "rise and fall" model to other nations at other times, achieving an extraordinary degree of perceived contemporary relevance at a moment of great concern in the United States over decline in the face of a then-rising Japan.[63]

Working in yet another historical context, Wisconsin School authors exploring the industrial (rather than agricultural) drivers of overseas US power projection converged on a strikingly similar understanding of national power. Like strategic studies scholars, they hoped to achieve contemporary policy relevance, but they had relevance of a different sort in mind. Whereas Earle hoped to cooperate with the state to meet foreign-policy threats, Wisconsin School scholars, distressed by US foreign policy in the early Cold War, took an essentially critical attitude toward the state. Nevertheless, in their quest to understand the historical roots of a foreign policy they deplored, they adopted the same definitions of economic power in terms of industrial strength and naval power in terms of battleships that Kennedy was working toward. Indeed, they produced essentially the inverse of Kennedy's interpretation of Edwardian Britain for the turn-of-the century United States. While Britain declined in industrial terms, the United States rose. While Britain's naval reach contracted, the United States' naval reach expanded. While Britain's strategic gaze narrowed from overseas empire to continent, the United States' strategic gaze widened from continent to overseas empire. The two national narratives mirrored each other.

Mackinder, Earle, the Sprouts, Kennedy, and Wisconsin School authors offered interpretations that were not wrong so much as incomplete. They were all correct to regard industrial strength as an important component of national power. They were also correct in arguing that Britain was experiencing relative industrial decline, and the United States was experiencing relative industrial growth, at the turn of the century. But they missed other, equally significant stories. Most important, with respect to globalization—a phenomenon to which these scholars paid almost no attention—Britain was not experiencing relative decline, and the United States was not experiencing relative rise. This lacuna in their work presumably has a good deal to do with the fact that the concept of globalization did not come into vogue until the 1980s and especially the 1990s, too late to be of help to them.[64] Earle and the Sprouts focused on mercantilist, not globalized, periods of history. Moreover, they, along with Kennedy and Wisconsinite authors, all formed as scholars during a period of deglobalization, that is, when the world was less economically integrated than it had been in Mackinder's Edwardian era. Globalization was not a contemporary problem for them to address, nor was the concept available even if they had wanted to address it.

Globalization is a reality today, however, and historians (and others) have produced an extensive body of work on it in the past three decades. This work has led to a rethinking of British power in the Edwardian era. As historian Martin Daunton has written, "The context for thinking and writing about British economic growth has changed: the late nineteenth century can now be interpreted less as a period of decline and more as an era of globalization."[65] Yet no such rethinking has occurred for the narrative of US power in the period from 1865 to 1918, or for the model of economic and naval power on which the field of strategic studies relies.[66] For instance, the flagship strategy course at the Naval War College, with which the Yale program has historically maintained strong links, continues to rely on Kennedy's work for an understanding of turn-of-the-century Britain and the international balance of power in the module on the World War I–era.[67]

One way that the field of strategic studies could try to update its model would be to pursue relevance for the sake of relevance in a world characterized by globalization as well as industrialization. But a better way to achieve relevance would be to study globalization in history as much as possible on its own terms. Historians have somehow managed to produce better and more policy-relevant work on the history of globalization than have strategic studies scholars, not by attempting to cater to the Pentagon's needs but by immersion in their chosen historical subjects. Contemporary strategic usefulness must be permitted to emerge, if it is to emerge, by letting the past speak in its own language. The search for policy applicability forces the past to speak in our language and thereby reduces our chances of hearing what it might be able to teach us. Indeed, what passes for sound historical analysis in the strategic studies field often compares unfavorably to genuinely sound historical scholarship. It is difficult to see how bad scholarship can be any more relevant to policymakers than historical fiction.

Put differently, would-be grand strategists should not go rummaging around history in search of "lessons" or "principles" to guide policymakers. John Gaddis, whose grand strategic credentials are impeccable, has made the case against this approach very cogently.[68] If we take seriously Gaddis's insistence that history is non-linear, then we should be skeptical of our ability to know the past or the present in sufficient detail to derive lessons or identify principles. They require one-to-one ratios—X led to Y in the past, and the equivalent of X exists today, so the equivalent of Y will follow—but the whole logic of non-linearity is that causes are so interdependent that they cannot be isolated and potentially so small that they cannot be identified. As Sir Michael Howard, who also knew something about grand strategy, described his response when he was asked for the "lessons" of history, "I was conscious above all of the unique quality of an experience that resulted from circumstances that would never, that *could* never, be precisely replicated."[69] The correct scholarly response in the face of complexity is epistemological humility, a sense of how difficult it is to know anything. When grand strategy encourages the opposite, the time has come to put away grand strategy and focus on being historians.

To be clear, this is not a call for historians to abandon the search for relevance or a denunciation of presentism. Like any group of professionals, historians need to stay relevant to the public that makes their livelihoods possible. Even without this imperative, historians cannot avoid being influenced by the historical contexts in which they live, any more than the subjects of their study can. This unavoidable influence is not necessarily corrupting: it can enrich scholarship, by leading historians to ask productive new questions about the past. But to stand the test of time—to persuade future scholars who were not influenced in the same way—the influence of the present must be disciplined by scholarly craft. Accepting this discipline does not mean a retreat into the ivory tower. On the contrary: it is a profound form of activism, because it seeks the expert interpretation of the most valuable database of human behavior that we have, and it refuses to let that database be used as a political football in contemporary debates. People will always be tempted to instrumentalize the past in order to claim its authority; they may even seek, as Howard noted, to "abolish" the past altogether when it proves inconvenient.[70] By checking instrumentalization and preserving the past, historians perform the vital public service entrusted to them. It is perfectly consistent with this trust for historians to seek relevance by using their special knowledge of the past to suggest questions for policymakers to ask about the present. But they undermine this trust when they go beyond their competence and undertake to provide answers about the present under the cloak of their expert credentials. The goal of achieving relevance by protecting history and by offering perspective on the present is ambitious, not modest. It should be enough.

Notes

1. Walter A. McDougall, *Promised Land, Crusader State: The American Encounter with the World since 1776* (Boston: Houghton Mifflin, 1997), 102.
2. Walter LaFeber, *The New Empire: An Interpretation of American Expansion, 1860–1898* (Ithaca, NY: Cornell University Press, 1998 [1963]), esp. 6–10, 121–127.
3. E.g., James Kurth, "America's Grand Strategy: A Pattern of History," *National Interest* 43 (Spring 1996), 3–19; Walter A. McDougall, "History and Strategies: Grand, Maritime, and American," *The Telegram* 6 (October 2011), downloaded from http://www.fpri.org/article/2012/08/history-and-strategies-grand-maritime-and-american/, March 19, 2016; Michael J. Green, *By More than Providence: Grand Strategy and American Power in the Asia Pacific since 1783* (New York: Columbia University Press, 2017), 56–110.
4. See B. H. Liddell Hart, *Strategy* (New York: Penguin, 1994 [1954]), 321–322; Edward Mead Earle, "Introduction," in *Makers of Modern Strategy: Military Thought from Machiavelli to Hitler*, ed. Edward Mead Earle (Princeton, NJ: Princeton University Press, 1948 [1943]), viii.
5. Thomas Meaney and Stephen Wertheim, "Grand Flattery: The Yale Grand Strategy Seminar," *The Nation* 294:22 (May 28, 2012), 27–31, at 31.
6. Liddell Hart, *Strategy*, 322. See also Michael Howard, "Grand Strategy in the Twentieth Century," *Defence Studies* 1:1 (Spring 2001), 1–10, at 1–2.

7. For an introduction, see Kevin H. O'Rourke and Jeffrey G. Williamson, *Globalization and History: The Evolution of a Nineteenth-Century Atlantic Economy* (Cambridge, MA: MIT Press, 1999).

8. Richard Franklin Bensel, *The Political Economy of American Industrialization, 1877–1900* (Cambridge: Cambridge University Press, 2000); Elizabeth Sanders, *Roots of Reform: Farmers, Workers, and the American State, 1877–1917* (Chicago: University of Chicago Press, 1999).

9. Richard White, *"It's Your Misfortune and None of My Own": A New History of the American West* (Norman: University of Oklahoma Press, 1993), 275–277.

10. See Bensel, *Political Economy of American Industrialization*, 355–456; Mira Wilkins, *The History of Foreign Investment in the United States to 1914* (Cambridge, MA: Harvard University Press, 1989), 574.

11. Peter Trubowitz, *Defining the National Interest: Conflict and Change in American Foreign Policy* (Chicago: University of Chicago Press, 1998), 31–95.

12. On the merchant marine, Democrats typically favored what was known as the "free-ship" position—that the US merchant marine could be built up through the purchase of ships built abroad—while Republicans favored a requirement that ships be built domestically, coupled with subsidies for US shipyards.

13. Antony Hopkins, *American Empire: A Global History* (Princeton, NJ: Princeton University Press, 2018), 341.

14. Lloyd Gardner, "A Progressive Foreign Policy, 1900–1921," in *From Colony to Empire: Essays in the History of American Foreign Relations*, ed. William A. Williams (New York: Wiley, 1972), 222.

15. Hopkins, *American Empire*, 341.

16. Ibid.

17. John Gaddis, "Maybe You *Can* Go Home Again," H-Diplo Essay 208 (March 27, 2020), 3n10, https://issforum.org/essays/PDF/E208.pdf, accessed May 12, 2020.

18. Denver Brunsmann, "De-Anglicization: The Jeffersonian Attack on an American Naval Establishment," in *Anglicizing America: Empire, Revolution, Republic*, ed. Ignacio Gallup-Diaz, Andrew Shankman, and David J. Silverman (Philadelphia: University of Pennsylvania Press, 2015), 205–225.

19. For further development of the arguments in this section, see Katherine Epstein, "The Conundrum of American Power in the Age of World War I," *Modern American History* 2:3 (November 2019), 345–365.

20. These numbers were calculated from figures in Table 1010, "Exports of United States Merchandise—Value of Selected Articles: 1821 to 1945," *Statistical Abstract of the United States*, 68th ed. (Washington, DC: US Department of Commerce, 1947), 904–905

21. Geoffrey Tweedale, *Steel City: Entrepreneurship, Strategy, and Technology in Sheffield, 1743–1993* (Oxford: Oxford University Press, 1995), 99–154.

22. See, e.g., Robert Angevine, "The Rise and Fall of the Office of Naval Intelligence, 1882–1892: A Technological Perspective," *Journal of Military History*, 62:2 (April 1998), 291–312; and Kathryn Steen, *The American Synthetic Organic Chemicals Industry: War and Politics, 1910–1930* (Chapel

Hill: University of North Carolina Press, 2014). This process lasted far later than most historians appreciate, as Michael Falcone shows in "The Rocket's Red Glare: Global Power and the Rise of American State Technology," PhD dissertation, Northwestern University, 2019.

23. Quoted in Angevine, "The Rise and Fall of the Office of Naval Intelligence," 299.

24. Séverine Antigone Marin, "Did the United States Scare the Europeans? The Propaganda about the 'American Danger' in Europe around 1900," *Journal of the Gilded Age and Progressive Era* 15:1 (January 2016), 23–44.

25. Nicholas Lambert, *Planning Armageddon: British Economic Warfare and World War I* (Cambridge, MA: Harvard University Press, 2012), 80–84, 111–116, 121–126, 164–175, 237–240.

26. Peter Cain and Antony Hopkins, *British Imperialism: Innovation and Expansion, 1688–1914* (London: Longman, 1994), 170–180.

27. Richard Sicotte, "Economic Crisis and Political Response: The Political Economy of the Shipping Act of 1916," *Journal of Economic History* 59:4 (December 1999), 864–865.

28. See Carl Parrini, *Heir to Empire: United States Economic Diplomacy, 1916–1923* (Pittsburgh: University of Pittsburgh Press, 1969), 9, 22–24; J. Lawrence Broz, *The International Origins of the Federal Reserve System* (Ithaca, NY: Cornell University Press, 1997), 36–54; Barry Eichengreen and Marc Flandreau, "The Federal Reserve, the Bank of England, and the Rise of the Dollar as an International Currency, 1914–1939," NBER Working Paper (July 2010), 3–5.

29. Cain and Hopkins, *British Imperialism*, 276–315, 422–446.

30. Parrini, *Heir to Empire*, 7–9, 27–31.

31. Wilkins, *The History of Foreign Investment in the United States to 1914*, 153–155, 587.

32. Marilyn Young, "American Expansion, 1870–1900: The Far East," in *Towards a New Past: Dissenting Essays in American History*, ed. Barton Bernstein (New York: Pantheon Books, 1968), 176–201.

33. D. C. M. Platt, *Finance, Trade, and Politics in British Foreign Policy, 1815–1914* (Oxford: Clarendon Press, 1968), 262–294, 346–351.

34. Thomas Otte, *The Foreign Office Mind: The Making of British Foreign Policy, 1865–1914* (Cambridge: Cambridge University Press, 2011), 233.

35. An exemplar of Wilhelmine tactlessness and the cause of a diplomatic crisis with Britain, the Kruger telegram was a note from the Kaiser congratulating the Boer leader Paul Kruger on repelling a raid seeking to establish British authority in the Transvaal.

36. Quoted in Young, "American Expansion," 195.

37. Young, "American Expansion," 183.

38. A striking exception is James A. Field, who criticized diplomatic historians' neglect of the nuts-and-bolts of naval power in his essay "American Imperialism: The Worst Chapter in Almost Any Book," *American Historical Review* 83:3 (June 1978), 644–668, esp. 652–656.

39. On the importance of dry-docks, see Sean Getway, "Supporting the Trident: US Naval Bases from 1898 to 1916," MA thesis, University of Maryland, 2015, 11. For an

overview of the different types of naval shore facilities, see Getway, "Supporting the Trident," 8–13.

40. Ibid., 14; John Maurer, "Fuel and the Battle Fleet: Coal, Oil, and American Naval Strategy, 1898–1925," *Naval War College Review* (1981), 60–77 at 68–69.

41. Benjamin Franklin Cooling, *Grey Steel and Blue Water Navy: The Formative Years of America's Military-Industrial Complex, 1881–1917* (Hamden, CT: Archon Books, 1978), 66–82.

42. Getway, "Supporting the Trident," 1.

43. Katherine Epstein, "'No One Can Afford to Say Damn the Torpedoes': Torpedoes, Battle Tactics, and U.S. Naval History before World War I," *Journal of Military History* 77:2 (April 2013), 491–520.

44. Christopher Havern Sr., "A Gunnery Manqué: William S. Sims and the Adoption of Continuous-Aim in the United States Navy, 1898–1910," MA thesis, University of Maryland, 1995, 9.

45. Trubowitz, *Defining the National Interest*, 37–52; Thomas H. Coode, "Southern Congressmen and the American Naval Revolution, 1890–1890," *Alabama Historical Quarterly* (Fall and Winter 1968), 89–110.

46. Quoted in Getway, "Supporting the Trident," 31, citing Daniel J. Costello, "Planning for War: A History of the General Board of the Navy, 1900–1914," PhD dissertation, Fletcher School of Law and Diplomacy, 1968, 180.

47. Getway, "Supporting the Trident," 43–44, 51–53.

48. Ibid., 15, 19–20, 25, 30–34, 41, 47, 49–50.

49. Lambert, *Planning Armageddon*, 185–231.

50. Arthur Link, *Woodrow Wilson and the Progressive Era, 1910–1917* (New York: Harper and Row, 1954), 149–150, 170–172; Sanders, *Roots of Reform*, 293–294, 300; Lambert, *Planning Armageddon*, 232–278.

51. Sicotte, "Economic Crisis and Political Response," 868–869.

52. Parrini, *Heir to Empire*, 8.

53. Jonathan Winkler, *Nexus: Strategic Communications and American Security in World War I* (Cambridge, MA: Harvard University Press, 2009).

54. A point made in Parrini, *Heir to Empire*; Lambert, *Planning Armageddon*; and Adam Tooze, *The Deluge: The Great War and the Remaking of Global Order, 1916–1931* (London: Allen Lane, 2014), esp. 33–67, 173–231, 255–304.

55. Epstein, "The Conundrum of American Power," 361–364.

56. The classic statement is Mackinder, "The Geographical Pivot of History," *Geographical Journal* 23:4 (April 1904), 421–437.

57. As points of entry into the rich literature on this context, see G. R. Searle, *The Quest for National Efficiency: A Study in British Politics and Political Thought, 1899–1914* (Berkeley: University of California Press, 1971); Cain and Antony Hopkins, *British Imperialism*, 202–225; and Duncan Bell, *The Idea of Greater Britain: Empire and the Future World Order, 1860–1900* (Princeton, NJ: Princeton University Press, 2007).

58. David Ekbladh, "Present at the Creation: Edward Mead Earle and the Depression-Era Origins of Security Studies," *International Security* 36:3 (Winter 2011/12), 107–141 (esp. 115–16); Dexter Fergie, "Geopolitics Turned Inwards: The Princeton Military

Studies Group and the National Security Imagination," *Diplomatic History* 43:4 (September 2019), 644–670.

59. "List foresaw what Sir Halford Mackinder was to elucidate more than half a century later, that there was nothing eternal about British maritime supremacy. The development of steam railways and steam navigation, he thought, might give the continental powers advantages in relation to the British Isles which they did not then possess" (Earle, "Adam Smith, Alexander Hamilton, Friedrich List: The Economic Foundations of Military Power," in *Makers of Modern Strategy: Military Thought from Machiavelli to Hitler* [Princeton, NJ: Princeton University Press, 1943], 148).

60. On Mackinder, see the references cited above; on Earle, see Fergie, "Geopolitics Turned Inwards."

61. Harold and Margaret Sprout, *Toward a New Order of Sea Power: American Naval Policy and the World Scene, 1918–1922* (Princeton, NJ: Princeton University Press, 1940), 12. This interpretation of Mahan was basically similar to that appearing in their jointly authored book *The Rise of American Naval Power, 1776–1918* (Princeton, NJ: Princeton University Press, 1939), and in Margaret Sprout's chapter on Mahan ("Mahan: Evangelist of Sea Power") in Earle, *Makers of Modern Strategy*.

62. Sprout and Sprout, *Toward a New Order of Sea Power*, 16–19.

63. See esp. Kennedy, "Mahan versus Mackinder: Two Interpretations of British Sea Power," *Militärgeschichtliche Mitteilungen* 2 (January 1974), 39–66; *The Rise and Fall of British Naval Mastery* (London: Allen Lane, 1976); *The Rise of the Anglo-German Antagonism, 1860–1914* (London: Allen and Unwin, 1980); and *The Rise and Fall of the Great Powers* (New York: Random House, 1987).

64. In Kennedy's and LaFeber's case, too late to be of help to their early work dealing with the turn of the century. Both have subsequently written about the current, second wave of globalization.

65. Martin Daunton, *Wealth and Welfare: An Economic and Social History of Britain, 1851–1951* (Oxford: Oxford University Press, 2007), 166.

66. For an attempt at such a rethinking, see Epstein, "The Conundrum of American Power."

67. Naval War College, Strategy and Policy Department, "Strategy and Policy," syllabus for March 2020–June 2020, pp. 56–58, available for download at https://usnwc.edu/Faculty-and-Departments/Academic-Departments/Strategy-and-Policy-Department (scroll to the bottom of the page).

68. See Gaddis, *The Landscape of History: How Historians Map the Past* (New York: Oxford University Press, 2002), esp. chapters 4–6.

69. Michael Howard, "The Lessons of History," *History Teacher* 15:4 (August 1982), 489–501 at 490.

70. Ibid., 500–501.

7

Grand Strategies (or Ascendant Ideas) since 1919

David Milne

Segmenting US foreign policy since 1919 by "grand strategy" would seem to require grand simplification—a willful assault on complexity. Even those administrations commonly identified as practicing quintessential grand strategy appear more inchoate when approached from the protagonists' perspectives at the time. To give one such example, the sequence of foreign policy innovations that the United States spearheaded from 1945 to 1949—the creation of the United Nations, the Bretton Woods agreements, the Marshall Plan, NATO—were collectively possessed of considerable foresight. But they were also a series of strategies (plural) advocated by various actors at different times with motives that do not necessarily reduce to a mono-strategic essence. Led by the efforts of memoirists and historians, a sequence of discrete, single-shot initiatives spanning a presidency is often reconceived as something larger and more deliberate—a creation moment.[1] But this omniscient narrator is not always there in the archival record.

Even in regard to post-1945 US foreign policy, a period that has been sub-divided by many distinguished scholars, it is difficult to identify clearly demarcated grand strategies that provide overarching clarity.[2] And this, needless to say, asks some hard questions of the historian commissioned to impose order. Hal Brands describes "grand strategy" as "the intellectual architecture that gives form and structure to foreign policy."[3] This definition can be applied to many twentieth-century presidencies, but not to all. This chapter focuses instead on the "ascendant ideas" that have informed policymaking, shaped public discourse, forced other ideas into decline, and that can perhaps even be identified as "representative" of particular eras. It is harder to hold "ideas" to the light for inspection than the plans of an architect. But they do provide a less reductive way to order a sequence of messy realities.

Economic Expansion and Identity Crises, 1919–1939

Sometimes it is difficult to detect a grand strategy *or* an ascendant idea. This certainly seems to be the case from 1919 to 1939, when confusion reigned about what constituted the appropriate role for the United States in the world. In many respects it was Woodrow Wilson's failed attempt to implement a "grand strategy" that contributed to this uncertainty. The planning process commenced in earnest in September 1917, when Wilson established "The Inquiry," an advisory committee of intellectuals, drawn mainly from the professoriates of the Ivy League and the University of Chicago, to help him develop an architecture for the postwar world. From October 1917 to Germany's formal surrender on November 11, 1918, the Inquiry's membership produced nearly 2,000 reports. Twenty-three members of the Inquiry accompanied Wilson to Paris. This was strategy on a grand scale.

The Inquiry's influence on Wilson's foreign policies was significant. The territorial portions of Wilson's famous "Fourteen Points" address of January 1918—which set out America's war aims—were drawn from the Inquiry's recommendations. As Edward "Colonel" House noted in his diary, "We actually got down to work at half past ten and finished remaking the map of the world, as we would have it, at half past twelve o'clock."[4] Many of the most important articles of the Treaty of Versailles relating to Western Europe, Poland, the Balkans, the Middle East, and the creation of the League of Nations–governed mandate system also had their origins in the Inquiry. And yet Wilson failed to achieve a balanced peace based on the Fourteen Points. In fact, his grand strategy disintegrated on first contact with reality. At the Paris peace conference, the French president Georges Clemenceau was determined that Germany should suffer for provoking the war as Berlin bore sole responsibility for this human tragedy. France alone had lost 2 million men, Britain nearly a million, Russia over 3 million. America's contribution to the Allied victory was critical in regard to its battlefield timing and execution, but Washington had entered the war late in the day, suffering just over 100,000 battlefield deaths. In those circumstances Wilson's case for "peace without victory" withered in the face of France and Britain's greater blood sacrifice.

Despondent at seeing their carefully laid plans outgunned in negotiation by Clemenceau, the Inquiry's membership met with like-minded British civil servants to explore ways in which systemic, scholarly thinking on foreign affairs might be woven into the policymaking fabric of their respective nations. The British returned home and made swift progress in establishing the Royal

Institute for International Affairs—better known as Chatham House, the grand Georgian townhouse in which it is based—in 1920. A year later the Americans followed suit in forming the Council on Foreign Relations (CFR), which counted twenty-one members of the Inquiry among the founding members. The Council became and remains a hugely influential forum through which policy ideas are formulated, scrutinized, and sometimes even nudged into the stream of policymaking. Yet CFR's mark on the grand strategic thinking of the 1920s and much of 1930s was slight. Many Americans through these two decades appeared to be immersed in the process of figuring out what it was precisely that Woodrow Wilson had sought to achieve, and for whose benefit.

"Isolationist" is the term most commonly used to describe US foreign policy and public opinion from 1919 to the Japanese attack on Pearl Harbor. Reacting against the idealistic overreach of Wilson at the Paris Peace Conference, so the narrative goes, US policymakers thereafter focused narrowly on the nation's economic interests and kept the nation at arm's length from the League of Nations and the World Court. "Contra-Wilson" was the grand strategy of presidents Warren Harding, Calvin Coolidge, and Herbert Hoover. Following the Wall Street crash and the onset of the Great Depression, the nation turned further inward as sensational exposés—such as H. C. Engelbrecht's and F. C. Hanighen's *Merchants of Death* and Gerald P. Nye's investigative Senate committee—suggested that it was munitions makers, northeastern bankers, and proto-imperialists who recklessly pushed Wilson to wage war for reasons far removed from making "the world safe for democracy."[5] At a time of grave economic uncertainty, Wilson's foreign policies appeared in retrospect as either fantastical in their detachment from the nation's interests or driven by cynical motivations that enriched established elites. This narrative, which places disappointment with Wilson at the center of things, arguably obscures as much as it reveals—but it does reveal something.

Some historians have argued that, grand strategy-wise, the interwar years were little different from what preceded them and what came next— the wants of big business were always paramount and were invariably met. William Appleman William in 1954 noted that "isolationism" was a legend and the 1920s was a period "marked by express and extended involvement with—and interventions in the affairs of—other nations." It was simply that the most brazen US interventionism occurred in Latin America, where it usually did, and so few really noticed. The Marines were deployed in the Western Hemisphere, an Open Door was proclaimed in East Asia, and a shaky European economic system was propped up via the Dawes and Young Plans, among other things, for the benefit of US business.[6]

Or perhaps the interwar years were principally a period of self-reckoning, where questions of culture and identity—as John A. Thompson argues in *A Sense of Power*—mattered a great deal.[7] A hinge moment arrived in the late 1930s, when US politicians were engaged in heated debate over whether to align the nation more closely with France and Great Britain in resisting Nazism. Franklin Delano Roosevelt (FDR) made his own position clear in September 1939 in observing, "Destiny first made us, with our sister nations on this Hemisphere, joint heirs of European culture. Fate seems now to compel us to assume the task of helping to maintain in the Western world a citadel wherein that civilization may be kept alive." This perspective, of course, was not unanimously shared. For many Americans, the United States was not the heir of European culture but its repudiation.

For a while, at least, the notion that Woodrow Wilson had betrayed the continentalist vision of the Founding Fathers was ascendant. Charles Beard's *A Foreign Policy for America*, published in 1940 but building on a decade of scholarship that sought to develop his theory of "continental Americanism," portrayed the debate on his nation's proper world role as one for the soul of the United States. For Beard, George Washington's farewell warning against "foreign entanglements" was not, in his view, "light words, spoken angrily," but "weighed and winged words directed to his contemporaries and the coming ages." He thought Thomas Jefferson similarly wise to adhere to the maxim, "while they tear down . . . let us build and improve here." Beard argues that this tradition of restraint was destroyed by admiral and historian Alfred Thayer Mahan—"the most successful propagandist ever produced in the United States"—and Woodrow Wilson, who promised "a program for world peace" that was fantastically utopian. Beard's grand strategy was one of "Americans First."[8] President Roosevelt's rejection of this narrow conception of the nation's self-interest—that neutrality was no longer an appropriate option—set the United States on a very different course.

Lancing Threats and Establishing Primacy, 1940–1950

When once asked which factors were most likely to shape his policies, British prime minister Harold Macmillan replied, "Events, dear boy, events." It's become a rather hackneyed phrase in British political discourse, but it does capture the principal difficulty facing policymakers hoping to construct intellectual architecture—namely, that events do not always play along with the blueprints drawn to master them. But when considering the origins of the Second World War and Roosevelt's decision to ally the United States closely with the United Kingdom, after the fall of France, in resisting fascism in Europe—and to chart a course in the Pacific that was almost certain to lead to conflict with Japan—one must pay close attention to events, in general, and enemies in particular. In the period from 1940 to 1950, Germany, Japan, and the Soviet Union represented adversaries more formidable than any that had faced the United States since Great Britain in the first three decades of nation's existence. That these enemies asserted themselves at a time in which the United States became globally preeminent compelled a step change in the nation's world role.

FDR's presidency is of vast significance in the history of US foreign relations, yet identifying a grand strategy or strategist that defined his presidency is difficult. That this might be said of this most consequential of foreign policy presidents—who bequeathed an enduring legacy—invites hard questions regarding the utility of grand strategy as a concept. Roosevelt was adept at improvisation and placed great store in the importance of personal diplomacy; he danced around fixed principles, blurring lines where he believed it served the greater good.[9] "You know, I am a juggler," FDR observed in 1942, "and I never let my right hand know what my left hand does. . . . I may have one policy for Europe and one diametrically opposed for North and South America. I may be entirely inconsistent, and furthermore I am perfectly willing to mislead and tell untruths if it will help me win the war."[10]

Roosevelt juggled and used whatever ideas best served his goals at a particular time. But the president knew precisely what he was doing in a larger sense—he would work to shape a world that was optimally receptive to the characteristics and advantages that the United States possessed. He was also an internationalist and understood that the United States was economically and culturally interwoven with the rest of the world. In this respect, Woodrow Wilson was both an instructive example and a cautionary tale. This was the Wilson that FDR hoped to emulate, a leader whose principal goal was to make a world in which the United States was best poised to thrive economically.[11] Yet Roosevelt knew that Wilson had lost sight of narrow self-interest in those moments of overreach, particularly as they pertained to his most cherished project, the League of Nations. FDR sought to decisively apply US power to defeat enemies as Wilson had done, and his ideal postwar world was similarly one in which free trade reigned and the British imperial preference system was gone. But he understood that his nation had to lead this system, not turn inward, and that this meant pursuing policies with strong bipartisan support while not vesting excessive hope that a successor organization to the League of Nations would be pivotal in keeping the postwar peace.

In this sense, FDR had a strong and influential ally in journalist Walter Lippmann, whose foreign policy views were influential from 1940 to 1944. The most read, revered, and trusted print journalist in America from Calvin Coolidge to Lyndon Johnson, Lippmann performed multiple roles during the Second World War. He helped FDR formulate a persuasive rationale for providing Great Britain with material support, the "Destroyers for Bases" deal.[12] From 1939 he identified through his syndicated *Today and Tomorrow* columns a compelling strategic rationale for facing down Germany. Of prime concern to Lippmann was the necessity that no hostile power be permitted to assume naval dominance of the Atlantic Ocean. Then in 1943 Lippmann published *U.S. Foreign Policy: Shield of the Republic*, a book that sold close to half a million copies and gathered even broader readership through syndication in *Reader's Digest*.[13]

As the war progressed, however, his ideas lost their luster. Lippmann believed that while FDR should disagree with Moscow where necessary, he should always keep an eye on the ultimate goal of avoiding another global war. To make this happen, Lippmann advised that the United States should work with the world's other powerful nations to ensure postwar stability and give the United Nations short shrift. Roosevelt, he believed, should resist making grandiose claims connecting the spread of democracy to the maintenance of peace. In the service of avoiding another global war, contentious issues of smaller stake—such as Soviet domination of Eastern Europe—could be sacrificed.

Ultimately, Lippmann believed that his 1943 thesis, that "a foreign policy consists in bringing into balance, with a comfortable surplus of power in reserve, the nation's commitments and the nation's power," also applied to Josef Stalin, a rational actor acutely conscious of his nation's strengths and weaknesses, meaning the Soviet leader was unlikely to overstep the mark in projecting power if dispassionate analysis flagged the dangers of such a course. Yet Lippmann's grand strategic formulation—for this *is* what it was— missed a great deal. While Stalin's goals in the early Cold War were not as expansionary as some have portrayed, ideology did play a causal role in shaping

Soviet foreign policy.[14] Lippmann's theory blinded him to the possibility that Marxism-Leninism was not merely a wall of sanctimony deployed to dupe the people and lend grandiosity to a brutal despot, but rather that it animated Soviet action. This made a modus vivendi between the two nations difficult to achieve.

Of course, the fact that liberal-capitalism and Marxism-Leninism represented rival Universalisms, each theoretically conditioned to extinguish the other, placed a strain on US-Soviet relations too. In this respect, the financial architecture that was developed in Bretton Woods, New Hampshire, in July 1944, to facilitate the rehabilitation, stability, and prosperity of the liberal-capitalist world, was vitally important. Again, members of the Roosevelt administration were determined to avoid Woodrow Wilson's errors of a previous generation. The Bretton-Woods system was designed to avoid the short-sightedness and narrow sectionalism that had made the interwar period so economically volatile. It did this by placing the United States at the very center of the global economy. The agreements made in New Hampshire had a grand purpose in mind—to regulate the financial and monetary order of the world once the war had been won by the Allies. There the rules of international finance were entirely rewritten.[15]

In the economic sphere, it is of course ironic that this grandest of strategies—making the dollar the world's reserve currency and establishing the International Monetary Fund (IMF) and the World Bank—was shaped principally by Harry Dexter White, a man believed by many scholars to be a Soviet spy.[16] The negotiating process also turned out to be a bruising one for John Maynard Keynes, the world-renowned economist charged with arguing Great Britain's corner and protecting his nation's own interests in regard to the imperial preference system, which proved a forlorn task. The *Battle of Bretton Woods* depicted by historian Benn Steill was one-sided. Keynes was more brilliant than White, but the United States held the most important cards. While Keynes was unable to mask his nation's slip from the first rank of great powers, he and White did concur on the virtues of stable currency exchange rates, global financial cooperation, and the necessity to impose some restrictions on short-term, speculative investments that so bedeviled the interwar period. They agreed that the system should be closely regulated and managed. Perhaps it is not so surprising after all that White, a dedicated statist, worked in concert with Keynes to shape such a system. But whatever else it was, the Bretton-Woods system was decisively shaped by and for the United States.

Yet as historian Geir Lundestad has noted, centrist politicians in Western Europe were quite willing to concede a dominant role to the United States and voluntarily join an "Empire by Invitation."[17] Lundestad demonstrates that Western Europe, not the United States, was the originator of many of the policies that are often bundled together as representative of a golden era in US grand strategy. To give one such example, Great Britain, operating from a position of weakness and trepidation, was the principal force behind the creation of the North Atlantic Treaty Organization (NATO). According to Lundestad, NATO's raison d'être is still most accurately expressed as to "keep the Russians out, the Germans down, and the Americans in"—the quip attributed to Lord Ismay, the Briton who served as NATO's first secretary general.[18]

And yet it is to George Kennan's "Long Telegram" and "X-Article" that we invariably turn when identifying the totemic documents of early US Cold War strategy. Why? The answer, put simply, is that before Kennan's telegram, nobody in the employ of the US government had articulated a cohesive US strategy toward Moscow in the postwar world; policy had been piecemeal. As Truman's aide, George Elsey, remarked: "Kennan tied everything together, wrapped it in a neat package, and put a red bow around it."[19] Kennan's gift to American grand strategy was circulated quickly and widely on its arrival and was read by the secretaries of war and the navy, and, later, by President Truman himself. Secretary of the Navy James Forrestal was persuaded by its logic and clarity. He had the telegram copied and sent to other members of the Cabinet, also insisting that it became required reading for senior members of the armed forces.

In regard to the actual threat posed to American interests, Kennan believed that Stalin was naturally cautious, taking what was possible where it "is deemed timely and promising," but temperamentally disinclined to push to the point of open conflict: "Thus these efforts are restricted to certain neighboring points conceived of as being of immediate strategic necessity, such as Northern Iran, Turkey, possibly Bornholm." Give Stalin an opening and he will ruthlessly exploit it. Communicate a clear sense of boundaries, however, and the postwar world could be as peaceable as the era that followed the Congress of Vienna.[20]

As a non-military barrier against communist expansion, the Marshall Plan was the closest realization of logic contained in the Long Telegram. Tottering on shaky economic and political foundations in 1947, Western Europe would regain its footing and embark on a remarkable period of sustained growth.

Historians and economists continue to debate the actual utility of the plan. Western Europe had greater latent economic potential than any other region on earth and could only rise steeply from that war-induced trough. But one need not enter this scholarly debate to observe that the Marshall Plan made a significant contribution—psychologically at the least, transformatively at the most.[21]

In July 1947, Kennan published an article, "The Sources of Soviet Conduct" in *Foreign Affairs*, under the letter "X," which covered much of the same ground as the long telegram. Notably it deployed the term "containment" for the first time:

> In these circumstances it is clear that the main element of any United States policy toward the Soviet Union must be that of a long-term, patient but firm and vigilant containment of Russian expansive tendencies.[22]

Kennan's article stirred a strong reaction in Walter Lippmann, who published twelve successive *Today and Tomorrow* columns in the late summer of 1947 criticizing X's rationale, prescriptions, and predictions. In the most damning indictment, Lippmann accused Kennan of authoring a "strategic monstrosity" that was likely to cause geopolitical exhaustion: "The Americans themselves would probably be frustrated by Mr. X's policy long before the Russians were."[23]

Lippmann was effective in identifying the faulty logic contained in Kennan's advocacy of the "adroit and vigilant application of counter-force at a series of constantly shifting geographical and political points." "The Eurasian continent is a big place," wrote Lippmann, "and the military power of the United States, though it is very great, has certain limits which should be borne in mind if it is to be used effectively." Of particular concern to Lippmann was containment's apparently broad application, unencumbered in presentation by any clearly established hierarchy of American interests: "The policy can be implemented only by recruiting, subsidizing and supporting a heterogeneous array of satellites, clients, dependents and puppets." The problem with lavishing resources, and vesting credibility, on such areas and regimes is that "satellite states and puppet governments are not good material out of which to construct unassailable barriers. We shall have either to disown our puppets, which would be tantamount to appeasement and defeat and loss of face, or must support them at incalculable cost on an unintended, unforeseen and perhaps undesirable issue."[24] Lippmann had peered into the future.

All the World's America's Stage, 1950–1968

That future was not written by George Kennan, however—who later conceded that Lippmann's critique had been largely fair and expressed regret for the ambiguous way he had defined containment—but by Paul Nitze and the other authors of NSC-68, a seminal policy document first presented to President Truman in April 1950. NSC-68's manner of threat assessment was influenced by Nathan Leites, a RAND social scientist who would publish an important book in 1951 titled *The Operational Code of the Politburo*.[25] Nitze came to know Leites's work through his connections with RAND and was impressed by his insights, drawn mainly from psychology, regarding the relentless expansionary instincts of the Politburo. NSC-68 follows Leites in identifying a series of "rules" or "codes" that drives Soviet behavior—referred to in the document as the drivers behind a cohesive Soviet "design." Indeed, the word "design" is used some fifty times in NSC-68 and is deployed to imply malevolence, rather than "purpose" or "strategy" (or indeed "grand strategy") which suggests normality in diplomatic intention. So the third section of NSC-68, titled "Fundamental Design of the Kremlin," describes Soviet intentions in the following terms:

> The design . . . calls for the complete subversion or forcible destruction of the machinery of government in the countries of the non-Soviet world and their replacement by an apparatus and structure subservient to and controlled from the Kremlin. . . . The United States, as the principal center of power in the non-Soviet world and the bulwark of opposition to Soviet expansion, is the principal enemy whose integrity and vitality must be subverted or destroyed by one means or another if the Kremlin is to achieve its fundamental design.[26]

"The assault on free institutions is worldwide now," Nitze wrote, "and in the context of the present polarization of power a defeat of free institutions anywhere is a defeat everywhere." The Cold War had been truly transformed into a zero-sum game, in which few Soviet provocations—real or perceived—could be ignored. NSC-68 maintained that US credibility was at stake everywhere, for ignoring minor transgressions would invite subsequent aggression on a larger scale. All citizens needed to realize that "the cold war is in fact a real war in which the survival of the free world is at stake."[27] North Korea's invasion of the South in June 1950 appeared to vindicate NSC 68's dark portrayal of Moscow's design. The US defense budget quadrupled from 1950 to 1951, from $13.5 billion to $48.2 billion.[28] NSC-68 truly created what Dwight Eisenhower would later identify and disparage as the "military-industrial complex."

This expansive view of where US vital interests lay was not shared by Eisenhower even if his inaugural address echoed NSC-68's maximalist crisis logic: "Conceiving the defense of freedom, like freedom itself, to be one and indivisible," he declared, "we hold all continents and peoples in equal regard and honor. We reject any insinuation that one race or another, one people or another, is in any sense inferior or expendable." Uttering a sentiment that chimed with Nitze's worldview, and jarred with Kennan's, Eisenhower reinforced the universalism of his inaugural address six months later: "As there is no weapon too small, no arena too remote, to be ignored, there is no free nation too humble to be forgotten." [29]

These sentiments cheered Nitze but they were not followed by increased defense spending. Fearing the creation of a garrison state, Eisenhower sought to deter the Soviet Union at a minimal cost. Eisenhower had told Senator Robert Taft, his main challenger through the Republican primaries, that he planned to cut $5 billion from the Truman defense budget in 1954—the reverse of what Nitze had recommended in NSC-68 and NSC-141. Indeed, Eisenhower was as good as his word, cutting the defense budget from $41.3 billion to $36 billion through his first year in office, taking the largest share from the Air Force. Eisenhower's public stance was that America's foreign policy interests were theoretically limitless. Privately, he opposed increasing the defense budget "excessively under the impulse of fear" which "could, in the long-run, defeat our purposes by damaging the growth of the economy and eventually forcing it into regimented controls."[30]

The president and his hawkish secretary of state, John Foster Dulles, viewed the Soviet threat in similar terms to those presented in NSC-68. Indeed, Dulles went further than Nitze (and much further than Kennan) in arguing that "liberation" should replace "containment" as America's default goal. But Eisenhower's frugality ensured that the administration's bark would be worse than its bite. At the Council on Foreign Relations on January 12, 1954, Dulles presented the logical conclusion of strong anticommunism on the cheap. Recounting the substance of a meeting called to survey the Eisenhower administration's first year in office, Dulles said:

The President and his advisers, as represented by the National Security Council, had to take some basic policy decisions. This had been done. The basic decision was to depend primarily upon a great capacity to retaliate, instantly, by means and at places of our choosing.

Nitze was seated next to banker and diplomat—and later John F. Kennedy's treasury secretary—Douglas Dillon during Dulles's speech. He recalled, "We looked at each other in amazement as his words sunk in."[31] Dulles had unveiled the policy of "massive retaliation," whereby the United States seemed to promise to confront all gradations of Soviet provocation—from meddling in a civil war in Congo to invading West Germany—with a massive American nuclear response.

Nitze was relieved to discover that massive retaliation was merely the scariest hollow threat in history. In fact, Dulles allegedly told Nitze and Kennan, in separate meetings, that "rollback," "liberation," and "massive retaliation" were political slogans designed to distinguish Eisenhower from his much-maligned predecessor but that they shouldn't be taken too seriously. The truth of the matter was that Eisenhower's foreign policies were not so different from Harry Truman's. In October 1953, for example, Eisenhower approved NSC-162/2, which affirmed many of NSC-68's precepts—though not those that vastly increased the defense budget. As Nitze himself observed, "By 1955 it became clear that Foster's doctrine of massive retaliation was merely a declaratory policy, whilst our action policy was graduated deterrence."[32] In deploying the CIA to effect regime-change in Iran and Guatemala in 1953— in the case of the former, with particularly dire long term consequences— Eisenhower was following NSC-68's line that perceived threats everywhere should be treated with equal seriousness.

It was during the presidencies of John F. Kennedy and Lyndon Johnson, though, that NSC-68 was most fully realized. In Kennedy's oft-quoted inaugural address, it took just two and a half minutes for him to commit US foreign policy to anything and everything:

> Let every nation know, whether it wishes us well or ill, that we shall pay any price, bear any burden, meet any hardship, support any friend, oppose any foe, to assure the survival and the success of liberty. This much we pledge— and more.[33]

The speech was one of the most gracefully written inaugurals in history, pledging assistance to "those people in the huts and villages of half the globe struggling to break the bonds of mass misery" and inviting Americans to remember that "civility is not a sign of weakness, and sincerity is always subject to proof. Let us never negotiate out of fear, but let us never fear to negotiate." Yet lurking behind the ornate words was a fierce commitment to Cold War interventionism redolent of NSC-68. "In the long history of the world" Kennedy said near the end of the speech, "only a few generations have been granted the role of defending freedom in its hour of maximum danger. I do not shrink from this responsibility—I welcome it." The inaugural synthesized Woodrow Wilson's idealism—"defending freedom"—and Paul Nitze's alarm-fueled pugnacity—"its hour of maximum danger." The United States had arrived at a high point in its confidence in muscular foreign policy idealism. For Kennedy to remain true to his inaugural word, America's foreign policy commitments would have to expand in precisely the way NSC-68 had proposed. One can draw a clear line of continuity from NSC-68 to 1968, when half a million American troops were deployed in Vietnam. Superpower tension had dissipated in Europe, thanks in part to the Soviet Union's installation of the Berlin Wall in 1961, but for much of the developing world the Kennedy and Johnson administrations represented peak "Cold War Time," to borrow from the title of Mary Dudziak's book.[34] Historian Paul Chamberlain aptly describes the devastating human cost wreaked by asinine proxy conflict in the postcolonial world as the *Cold War's Killing Fields*.[35]

Détente, Credibility, and the Resilience of the Cold War Prism, 1969–1976

Henry Kissinger and Richard Nixon believed that the United States had to step sharply back from the unsustainable commitments that Nitze's NSC-68 had encouraged. Through his tenure as national security adviser and secretary of state, Kissinger encouraged a policy of détente, or a relaxation of tensions, with the Soviet Union; an all-guns-blazing withdrawal from the Vietnam War; a reduction in America's overseas commitments through delegating roles to regional powers; and the merits of formally recognizing the People's Republic of China. Kissinger was a polarizing figure, to put it lightly. George Kennan applauded his efforts and advised him to ignore his detractors, once remarking that "Henry understands my views better than anyone at State ever has." Paul Nitze abhorred Kissinger's worldview, which he viewed as unnecessarily declinist and as posing grave dangers to the nation's (still dominant) world position.

Kissinger would complain that Americans "never fully understood that while our absolute power was growing, our *relative* position was bound to decline as the Soviet Union recovered from World War II."[36] In August 1971 Kissinger met with a collection of conservative intellectuals including William Rusher, editor of the *National Review*, and Allan Ryskind, editor of *Human Events*. Finding them locked in quite a different era—when Paul Nitze's expansionary doctrine retained luster—Kissinger reminded them that Nixon was elected following "the collapse of foreign policy theory. A new frontier of the 1960s had ended in the frustration of Vietnam, a divided country, and vicious isolationism clamored [for] by liberals."[37]

While Nitze and his ilk had erred badly, Kennan's notion of containment, though admirable in certain ways, lacked the specifics for effective diplomacy in a multipolar world. As Kissinger observed in *White House Years*, "Containment treated power and diplomacy as two distinct elements or phases of policy. It aimed at an ultimate negotiation but supplied no guide to the content of these negotiations. It implied that strength was self-evident and that once negotiations started their content would be self-evident."[38]

Like Kennan, Kissinger believed in the necessity of negotiating with America's enemies—ignoring powerful nations was reckless and pointless, while engagement brought significant rewards. But Kissinger was more comfortable than Kennan in urging the deployment of the military—to maintain and enhance US "credibility," a geo-strategic attribute he valorized above all others—where he deemed it necessary. So America intervened forcefully, and in many cases calamitously, in North Vietnam, Cambodia, and Laos, and significant credibility was vested in the outcome of conflicts on the Indian sub-continent, sub-Saharan Africa, and Latin America. Kissinger longed to liberate American foreign policy from the expensive demands of waging the global Cold War along the lines suggested in NSC-68. But he struggled to liberate himself from a tendency to view all conflicts through a zero-sum lens, which artificially inflated the stakes involved. Kissinger's Cold War perspectives were conventional in many respects.

The administration's greatest achievement was undoubtedly the decision to begin the process of normalizing relations with the People's Republic of China—and Nixon deserves more credit than Kissinger as the principal force behind this process. In his memoir, Kissinger effusively summarizes the impact of the China opening: "In one giant step we had transformed our diplomacy. We had brought new flexibility to our foreign policy. We had captured the initiative and also the imagination of our own people."[39] This observation is hard to dispute. Downplaying ideological differences and restoring relations with a nation of China's size and economic potential was a deft diplomatic move. Moscow was horrified, and Soviet fears of what this unexpected rapprochement portended added value to American diplomacy. It allowed Nixon and his successors to play the communist antagonists against each other. It gave China a direct stake in the timely resolution of the Vietnam War. For Kissinger, a devotee of balance of power of diplomacy, China's entry to the concert of nations was a gift.

Ultimately, though, the grand strategic course charted from 1969 to 1976, when Kissinger was the dominant figure in foreign policy, was ephemeral—the shadow that Kissinger cast on subsequent presidencies was not nearly as marked or dark as historian Greg Grandin has suggested.[40] With Ford's defeat, America's curious relationship with European balance of power politics came to a swift and ignominious end. It was a passionate and volatile affair. After the fling ended, however, the nation sheepishly returned to its long-standing spouse: Woodrow Wilson. Historian Mario Del Pero's description of Henry Kissinger as an "eccentric realist" still appears to capture him the best.[41] He sought to normalize the Cold War through détente and a de-escalation of the ideological stakes, yet beyond bilateral relations with Moscow and Beijing, Kissinger was a conventional and often blinkered Cold Warrior.

Wilsonianism Redux and the Allure of Unipolarity, 1977–2008

In the presidential campaign of 1976, Jimmy Carter sharply criticized Kissinger, Nixon, and Ford for too narrowly defining the US national interest, instead insisting that the country's foreign policy should pay greater heed to democracy and to human rights. Carter pointedly exchanged warm letters with the Soviet dissident physicist Andrei Sakharov, encouraged post-Helsinki dissidents across the Soviet bloc, and established a Bureau of Human Rights and Humanitarian Affairs at the State Department that graded each nation on how well they treated their citizens. During his inaugural address in 1977, Carter declared, "Our commitment to human rights must be absolute."[42] The new president's words and actions reassured an ambitious young foreign policy intellectual named Paul Wolfowitz who had been unimpressed by Nixon's and Ford's narrowness of vision and who accepted the position of deputy assistant secretary for defense for regional programs.

In the summer of 1976, Wolfowitz had ruminated on the strengths and limitations of Henry Kissinger's doctoral thesis, *A World Restored*, with a graduate student named Francis Fukuyama. It was a well-researched and interesting book, Wolfowitz said, but Kissinger had identified the wrong exemplar. That craftsman of Realpolitik, Klemens von Metternich, projected a vision that was lacking in scruple and substance; the "peace" he helped secure was unsustainable in the long term. Tsar Alexander I, who had advocated fierce resistance to Napoleon Bonaparte on moral and religious grounds, was the true hero of the tale. Fukuyama later recalled, "I remember him saying the thing that's wrong with Kissinger is that he does not understand the country he is living in, that this country is dedicated to certain universalistic traditions."[43] On Kissinger's preference for amoral, balance of power diplomacy, Wolfowitz was fond of quoting a sardonic Polish phrase that emphasized its insidiousness: "the stability of the graveyard."[44] Wolfowitz's values-led universalism marked a clear break with Kissingerian retrenchment, owed a large debt to Woodrow Wilson, and would be a central force in the debate about foreign policy for the next thirty years. Wolfowitz, like Paul Nitze, did not assume the most prominent foreign policy positions in the administrations he served. But like Nitze, his ideas shaped the parameters and contours of US foreign policy in this period like those of no other individual.

There were other significant contributions to foreign policy thinking through this period, of course. In 1979, Jeane Kirkpatrick, a noted professor of international affairs at Georgetown University, published an influential article in *Commentary* magazine titled "Dictatorships and Double Standards." While her preference in ideal conditions was the Wilsonian proliferation of pure and virtuous democracies, Kirkpatrick cautioned that the Cold War world was not so simple. Her article launched a strong attack on the Carter administration for pushing autocratic leaders, such as the shah in Iran and Anastosio Somoza in Nicaragua, to liberalize and democratize their governments too quickly. Kirkpatrick faulted Carter for encouraging far-reaching changes only in nations "under pressure from communist guerrillas. We seem to accept the status quo in Communist nations (in the name of 'diversity' and national autonomy) but not in nations ruled by right wing dictators or white oligarchies [such as South Africa]." Here was the double standard of Kirkpatrick's title. Instead of pursuing laudable but self-defeating pipe dreams, she recommended that political leaders be more patient with authoritarian governments that supported US policy. These regimes would be more likely to evolve gradually in the direction of liberal-democracy than Marxist-Leninist "totalitarian" varieties. Accompanying this was Kirkpatrick's contempt for ahistorical wishful thinking. Wilsonianism was clearly the intended target.[45]

Kirkpatrick's article made an immediate impression on Ronald Reagan, the former governor of California and GOP presidential frontrunner, who read it soon after publication and sent her a note expressing admiration for her logic. After his election as president, Reagan appointed Kirkpatrick his ambassador to the United Nations, the first woman to serve in that position. Yet Reagan was highly selective in how he applied Kirkpatrick's ideas. In Guatemala and El Salvador, for example, the administration supported murderous right-wing, but reliably anti-communist, dictatorships perpetrating awful crimes against their people. But in the Philippines, Reagan eventually came around to the idea of pressuring the autocratic Ferdinand Marcos to step down from power, repudiating a key element of Kirkpatrick's thesis. Indeed, Marcos had once offered an after-dinner toast to Kirkpatrick that quoted verbatim from "Dictatorships and Double Standards"—for all the good it did him.[46]

In a sense, Kirkpatrick shared a trait with Henry Kissinger, whose support for anti-communist strongmen mirrored her own. Indeed, Kissinger registered strong disapproval of Marcos's ousting in Kirkpatrickian terms in March 1986: "Whatever else may be said about the Marcos regime, it contributed substantially to American security and had been extolled by American presidents, including President Reagan, for nearly two decades." From the perspective of Kirkpatrick and Kissinger, those of Reagan's foreign policies that were informed by a neo-Wilsonian commitment to democratization weren't just a disappointment—they were naïve and dangerous.

But Reagan accomplished something in his second term that Kirkpatrick thought impossible: he formed a close working relationship with a Marxist-Leninist who implemented policies—glasnost and perestroika—that served to mellow a "radical totalitarian" regime. The leadership of Mikhail Gorbachev was the very thing that Kirkpatrick's theory held as implausible. When Senator Ted Cruz said in a speech in January 2016 that "we could do worse, in my opinion, than adopting the Reagan-Kirkpatrick philosophy today," he neglected to note the massive gulf that separated the two. Indeed, the president turned out to be far from doctrinaire. The title of James Graham

Wilson's history of the end of the Cold War, *The Triumph of Improvisation*, captures how inconstant US foreign policy was in the 1980s. He marshals compelling evidence to sustain his assertion that "grand strategies did not shape the end of the Cold War."[47]

As Mikhail Gorbachev continued to benignly lead the Soviet Union toward oblivion, how the United States should regard and shape the post–Cold War world became a highly contested subject. The oracles of grand strategy assumed center stage. Would civilizations clash, as political scientist Samuel Huntington warned, or would history end with the universal triumph of liberal-capitalism, as Francis Fukuyama reassured? Both interpretations capture elements of truth, but it fell to a journalist to really nail down America's foreign policy future. In an article published in *Foreign Affairs* in 1990, titled "The Unipolar Moment," Charles Krauthammer observed that the "immediate post–Cold War world is not multipolar. It is unipolar. The center of world power is the unchallenged superpower, the United States, attended by its Western allies."[48] It was this triumphalist formulation—not the Realist scholar John Mearsheimer's belief that the world would revert to multipolarity—that most accurately foresaw what would happen next.[49] The actual world was not nearly as unipolar as Krauthammer had suggested, but the United States began to behave as if it were.

Wolfowitz agreed with Krauthammer that the time was opportune for the United States to truly impose its will. He directed a study that created the Defense Policy Guidance (DPG) document of 1992, although its drafting was delegated to political scientist Zalmay Khalizad, who in turn took advice from the hawkish foreign policy advisers Richard Perle, Albert Wohlstetter, and I. Lewis "Scooter" Libby.[50] The DPG resembled NSC-68 in that it was a collective enterprise inspired by the vision of one individual. It also assumed worst-case scenarios to emphasize the necessity that the United States maintain an insurmountable lead in military and power-projection capabilities. Someone in the Pentagon, desirous of a wider debate, leaked the document to foreign affairs journalist Patrick Tyler, who published excerpts in the *New York Times* on March 8, 1992. Tyler reported that the forty-six-page document stated, "America's political and military mission in the post-cold-war-era will be to insure that no rival superpower is allowed to emerge in Western Europe, Asia, or the territory of the former Soviet Union."[51]

The DPG offered a clear-cut repudiation of the collectivist aspirations of the United Nations—"ad hoc coalitions" was the preferred alliance model. This was the principal policy area where Wolfowitz disagreed fundamentally with Woodrow Wilson. The former feared that America's enemies would use a well-intentioned but dangerous institution like the UN to curtail the nation's freedom of action. Wilson was more hopeful that the proclivities and interests of nations could harmonize, instilling vitality and unity of purpose into his cherished League of Nations; he had been more optimistic, ultimately, than Wolfowitz that the world could have a peaceable future. The DPG identified a whole series of threats to American interests, whether they be "European allies, Arab dictatorships, Muslim terrorists, resurgent Russians, Chinese and North Korean communists, weapons proliferators," as the New Yorker writer George Packer described them.[52]

Tyler's article provoked outrage among America's allies, who were not thrilled at the vassal status bestowed upon them by Wolfowitz and his colleagues. The reaction from old-school Republicans and mainstream Democrats was similarly hostile. Patrick Buchanan, a retrenchment-inclined Republican who struggled to identify many "good" wars in American history, observed that the DPG was "a formula for endless American intervention in quarrels and war when no vital interest of the United States is remotely engaged." Bush's national security adviser, Brent Scowcroft, later remarked of the DPG: "That was just nutty. I read a draft of it. I thought, 'Cheney, this is just kooky.' It didn't go anywhere. It was never formally reviewed."[53] Scowcroft is correct on the absence of presidential imprimatur but wrong to observe that it "didn't go anywhere." It went through various drafts and emerged as a remarkable and durable strategy document. On May 5, 1992, Wolfowitz sent the final draft to Secretary of Defense Dick Cheney and added a PS: "We have never had a defense guidance this ambitious before."[54] While the document fell into abeyance for the next eight years, the next President Bush resuscitated it. And his administration would introduce the Wilsonian dimension that Wolfowitz felt was lacking in the original DPG drafts: a strong emphasis on America's role in fostering democratization.[55]

During George H. W. Bush's presidency, then, Wolfowitz argued strongly against reducing defense spending following the collapse of the Soviet Union and made the case, unheeded, that regime change in Iraq should have followed the ejection of Saddam Hussein's forces from Kuwait. Through the Clinton era, Wolfowitz assumed the role of fierce critic, although there was much in that era for him to admire. Clinton's foreign policies proved to be multifaceted and irreducible to a single word or concept. How could they be otherwise in the absence of an enemy like the Soviet Union? One theme emphasized repeatedly was that of the necessity of "democratic enlargement"—that the United States (and NATO) should extend security and political commitments to the emerging democracies in Eastern and Central Europe. A renewed dedication to free and open trade was also stressed as vital. On January 1, 1994, Clinton presided over the creation of a North American Free Trade Area (NAFTA) encompassing Canada, the United States, and Mexico. So far so Wilsonian. The collapse of the Soviet Union was akin to the collapse of the Hapsburg Empire. Clinton, like Wilson, welcomed a significant increase in the number of independent nation-states—and encouraged their long-suppressed democratic aspirations.

But purposeful American leadership of this democratically enlarged and economically liberalized world was taken as given. There would be no ceding of US sovereignty in the manner Wilson envisioned in 1918. Bill Clinton did not view the United Nations as a practicable conduit through which to realize specific US goals or indeed to keep the peace more generally—here Clinton hewed more closely to Wolfowitz than to Wilson. Clinton promised to lead "an America with the world's strongest defense, ready and willing to use force when necessary."[56] During Clinton's second term Secretary of State Madeleine Albright declared herself comfortable "with the projection of American power." She pointedly observed that the historical analogy that motivated her worldview took place in the 1930s, not the 1960s:

> My mind-set is Munich; most of my generation's is Vietnam. I saw what happened when a dictator was allowed to take over a piece of a country and the country went down the tubes. And I saw the opposite during the war when America joined the fight. For me, America is really, truly, the indispensable nation.[57]

Wolfowitz warmed to Albright's sentiments, observing that she "represents the best instincts of this administration on foreign policy."[58] Indeed, the Clinton administration appeared to be closely following the recommendations presented in the controversial 1992 DPG. Defense spending scarcely dipped in real terms from the Reagan-era levels, the maintenance of primacy remained the principal goal, and the United States reserved the right to undertake unilateral action when necessary to protect its interests or right wrongs.

In 1999, for example, the United States spearheaded NATO airstrikes against Slobodan Milosevic's Serbia to defend Kosovo against a brutal assault motivated by ethnic cleansing. The UN was not willing to authorize such an action, due to Russian objections, but Clinton paid no heed, operating through NATO instead. Serbia eventually desisted and Milosevic's odious regime collapsed. But the United States had indeed acted as "the indispensable nation" in sidestepping the UN when it deemed action necessary. Much of Clinton's foreign policy vindicated a document that had roused such ire on its publication in 1992.

His admiration for Albright notwithstanding, Wolfowitz did identify serious flaws in the Clinton administration's policies toward certain regions. First among them was Saddam Hussein's Iraq, where Clinton's containment strategy comprised the enforcement of "no-fly zones" through intermittent air strikes and the maintenance of stringent UN sanctions. Wolfowitz viewed this combination as not up to the task of applying sufficient pressure on Hussein. In a 1996 *Wall Street Journal* article, glaringly titled "Clinton's Bay of Pigs," Wolfowitz lambasted the "pinprick" Tomahawk cruise missile attacks favored by Clinton and accused the administration of "betraying the Kurds" in permitting Iraqi forces to strike northward against that restive region with impunity.

This was clearly bad news for America's reputation as a guarantor and for its hard-won reputation as a military power without equal, but it also emboldened Iraq, whose military might pose a threat to the United States itself. Wolfowitz believed the stakes in Iraq could scarcely be higher: "Saddam is a convicted killer still in possession of a loaded gun—and it's a pointed at us." Here was one of the first public references to Hussein's chemical and bacteriological weapons programs and the potential that he might either use them against the United States or sell or gift them to a terrorist organization to do the same. To prevent the realization of such a possibility, Wolfowitz urged Clinton to "go beyond the containment strategy and confront the Iraqi dictator once and for all."[59] This was of course the policy course that Wolfowitz urged upon Clinton's successor.

Wolfowitz, whom Bush appointed deputy (to Donald Rumsfeld) secretary of defense, was broadly impressed by the first eight months of the George W. Bush presidency. Bush withdrew the United States from the 1972 Anti-Ballistic Missile (ABM) treaty and moved forward with the development of a national missile defense program, resurrecting Reagan-era hopes of invulnerability to missile attack. He immediately repudiated Clinton's engagement policy and unveiled a hard line toward North Korea, undermining Seoul's so-called sunshine policy of courting Pyongyang with the prospect of greater economic interaction. On a personal level, Wolfowitz admired

Bush's simple, direct style. During a discussion about the relative merits of economic interests-focused engagement versus principled opposition to an authoritarian regime, Wolfowitz recalled (although he did not disclose the identity of the nations under discussion) that Bush interjected with real moral clarity: "We're talking about them as though they were members of the Chevy Chase Country Club. What are they really like? How brutal are these people?" In Wolfowitz's opinion, Bush's words brought to mind Reagan at his best.

In the immediate aftermath of the 9/11 attacks, Wolfowitz forcefully re-made the case that removing Saddam Hussein from power was impera-tive. In these crucial and chaotic days, he was the only person to present a "grand strategy" for how to respond to this audacious and brutal attack: re-move Hussein from power and then democratize, and hence pacify, the wider Middle East. Wolfowitz had no particular enthusiasm for using weapons of mass destruction as the primary justification for invading Iraq. As he later recalled, "For bureaucratic reasons we settled on one issue, weapons of mass destruction, because it was the one reason everyone could agree on."[60] So what did Wolfowitz truly believe? Certainly he thought that Saddam Hussein and al-Qaeda were linked in ways that the CIA had not substantiated. CIA director George Tenet later observed: "Wolfowitz genuinely believed there was a connection between Iraq and 9/11."[61] But there was a measure of doubt on this issue—as even he recognized. Rather, Wolfowitz believed that an American invasion of Iraq could rid the world of a brutal despot, provide the United States with a strategic foothold in this pivotal, oil-rich region, and lead ultimately to the creation of a dem-ocratic and prosperous Iraq, which would serve as a model for the rest of the Middle East and make Israel's place in the region more secure. Scholar Andrew Bacevich observes that Wolfowitz also wanted to "establish new norms regarding the use of force. . . . [T]he objective was to lift any and all restrictions on the use of armed force by the United States."[62] There were potential "wins" right across the board. As the foreign policy writer James Mann notes, Wolfowitz's plan for regime change in Iraq "represented one of the most ambitious programs to transform a region in U.S. history." Colin Powell's chief of staff, Lawrence B. Wilkerson, identified in Wolfowitz's plans a more dismal future: "I call them utopians. . . . I don't care whether utopians are Vladimir Lenin in a sealed train going to Moscow or Paul Wolfowitz. Utopians I don't like. You're never going to bring utopia, and you're going to hurt a lot of people in the process trying to get it."[63]

The potential for democratizing the Middle East appeared limitless in 2002—before Wolfowitz's theories made acquaintance with reality. This came through clearly in the Bush administration's most important policy document: The National Security Strategy of the United States, 2002—or NSS 2002, as it became commonly known. The first sentence declared that there was "a single sustainable model for national success: freedom, democracy, and free enterprise." Thereafter the words "freedom" and "democracy" recur every third or fourth sentence—a frequency that might have made Wilson blush. Wolfowitz did not draft the document, but he can lay good claim to be its spiritual author. "We will defend the peace by fighting terrorists and tyrants. . . . We will extend the peace by encouraging free and open societies on every continent." NSS 2002 fleshed out the Wilsonian elements that Wolfowitz believed were lacking in the 1992 DPG. It also provided a rationale for invading Iraq in the absence of a direct, verifiable threat to the American homeland.[64]

The concept of preemptive or preventive defense thus entered the foreign policy lexicon. American presidents had always reserved the right to unilaterally neutralize a threat before its realization. John F. Kennedy's policy of "quarantining" Cuba loosely falls into this category, and John Lewis Gaddis claimed historical precedent for the Bush administration in the unilateral and preemptive foreign policy doctrines of John Quincy Adams.[65] But reserving the privilege to strike before being struck—or not, as the case may be—had never been proclaimed so baldly. NSC-68, for example, viewed preventive defense as a step too far.

On February 26, 2003, just a few weeks prior to the invasion of Iraq, President Bush delivered a speech at the American Enterprise Institute, a think tank that had provided Wolfowitz and his ideological allies an institutional home in which to think and strategize about foreign policy during the Clinton years. Through the course of a remarkable address, Bush rationalized the planned invasion of Iraq as a war to make the Middle East safe for democracy. It was informed by Wolfowitz's deeply felt belief in humanity's innate perfectibility (to a Western blueprint):

> There was a time when many said that the cultures of Germany and Japan were incapable of sustaining democratic values. Well, they were wrong. Some say the same of today. They are mistaken. The nation of Iraq—with its proud heritage, abundant resources and skilled and educated people—is fully capable of moving toward democracy and living with freedom.

Bush, delighting his rapt, like-minded audience, riffed on this Wilsonian theme through the course of the address. "The world has a clear interest in the spread of democratic values," the president continued, "because stable and free nations do not breed the ideologies of murder. . . . A new regime in Iraq would serve as a dramatic and inspiring example of freedom for other nations in the region."[66]

From Pragmatism to Transactional Nationalism, 2008–

The US campaign to realize such Wilsonian dreams in the Middle East did not end well. On December 18, 2007, Barack Obama, then a candidate for the Democratic presidential nomination, observed: "I am running to do more than end a war in Iraq. I am running to change the mindset that got us into that war."[67] He had identified that mindset in his most significant speech on foreign policy prior to his winning the presidency, delivered at an "anti-war rally" in Chicago in 2002. Obama lambasted the move to war against Saddam Hussein as a "dumb war. A rash war. A war based not on reason but on passion, not on principle but on politics." "What I am opposed to," said Obama, "is the cynical attempt by Richard Perle and Paul Wolfowitz and other armchair, weekend warriors in the administration to shove their own ideological agendas down our throats, irrespective of the costs in lives lost and in hardships borne."[68]

Barack Obama's foreign policies were shaded by this aversion to ideology and a reluctance to proclaim a grand strategy. Indeed, in March 2008, Obama's national security advisory team recommended that "pragmatism over ideology" should serve as his bumper sticker.[69] The president was opposed to declaring allegiance to a fixed foreign policy principle, although the "Pivot" to Asia comes closest. He declined to consult Congress over the intervention in Libya in 2011 but did so in regard to Syria in 2013. He ordered a troop surge in Afghanistan in 2009—which he now seems to view as his gravest foreign policy error—and then retreated from America's commitments with alacrity. Obama drew a red line on Syria regarding the use of chemical weapons, invited Congress to decide what to do when Bashar al-Assad crossed it, and then ceded a starring role in finding a solution to Vladimir Putin. "Folks here in Washington like to grade on style," Obama told ABC news; "I'm much more concerned about getting the policy right."[70] The president appears to concur with Ralph Waldo Emerson (and FDR) that "a foolish consistency is the hobgoblin of little minds, adored by little statesman and philosophers and divines."[71]

This intellectual method has a name: pragmatism—a word often misinterpreted to solely mean excessive compromise in pursuit of any given goal. In his classic series of lectures on the meaning of pragmatism, William James observed that "at the outset, at least, it stands for no particular results. It has no dogmas, and no doctrines save its method ... the attitude of looking away from first things, principles, 'categories,' supposed necessities; and of looking towards last things, fruits, consequences, facts."[72] Intellectual historian James Kloppenberg argues persuasively that Obama's worldview and diplomatic method were informed by Jamesian pragmatism, writing admiringly that it is "a philosophy for skeptics, a philosophy for those committed to democratic debate and the critical assessment of the results of political decisions, not for true believers convinced they know the right course of action in advance of inquiry and experimentation. Pragmatism stands for openmindedness and ongoing debate."[73] The aftermath of the Second Iraq War rendered otiose grand Wilsonian thinking about America's ability to bend nations, regions, and indeed history to its will. The rise to power of Barack Obama, as well as America's diminished capacity and appetite to project power, vitalized America's principal contribution to world philosophy as a guide to foreign policy. Well, for a while at least.

Donald Trump's resuscitation of "America First" springs from multiple sources. One of them is clearly frustration at the reigning Wilsonian conception of the United States as the principal guarantor of the liberal order and as a force for the global advancement of democracy. Trump's hostility toward free trade agreements, his unease when interacting with allies (and alliance systems), his praise for authoritarian rulers, and his repeated insistence that the "liberal world order" represents a bad deal for the United States marks a clear break with the core ideas that have driven United States foreign policy since 1919. Locating intellectual architects for Trump's worldview is a serious challenge, though perhaps *Breitbart News*' Steve Bannon—who once compared himself to Thomas Cromwell in the Tudor court of Henry VIII—is perhaps the strongest candidate.[74] Trump is no isolationist, as increased defense spending and continued recourse to drone and cruise missile strikes suggest. Trump *is* a nationalist, narcissist, and unilateralist whose actions have dispelled the notion that the president of the United States is the "leader of the free world." Advisers who disagree with Trump but choose to serve in the hope of gaining some traction and blunting the president's worst instincts—like H. R. McMaster—tend not to last long.

The ascendant ideas in the Age of Trump are narrowly transactional and avowedly anti-Wilsonian. This means that these are dismal times for foreign policy wonks from both parties, as the notion that America owes the world its leadership is simply not shared by President Trump. It seems likely that America's grand strategists will remain sequestered in think tanks such as the Brookings Institutions and policy schools like SAIS (Johns Hopkins School for Advanced International Studies) until a new president takes office. Global perceptions of the United States will continue to evolve, likely in a downward direction, during these four or eight years. Whether the United States will find itself able to easily restore itself to a post-Trump world leadership role—as if the Trump presidency never happened—remains to be seen. The worldmaking presumptions of "grand strategy" have never felt more detached from the reality.

Notes

1. Dean Acheson, *Present at the Creation: My Years at the State Department* (New York: W. W. Norton, 1969).
2. See, for example, James Goldgeier and Jeremi Suri, "Revitalizing the U.S. National Security Strategy," *Washington Quarterly* 38:4 (Winter 2016), 35–55.
3. Hal Brands, *What Good Is Grand Strategy? Power and Purpose in American Statecraft from Harry S. Truman to George W. Bush* (Ithaca, NY: Cornell University Press, 2014).
4. "From the Diary of Colonel House," January 9, 1918, Arthur S. Link, ed., *The Papers of Woodrow Wilson*, vol. 45, 551.
5. H. C. Engelbrecht and F. C. Hanighen, *Merchants of Death: A Study of the International Armament Industry* (New York: Dodd Mead, 1934).
6. William Appleman Williams, "The Legend of Isolationism in the 1920s," *Science and Society*, Winter 1945, 1–20.
7. John A. Thompson, *A Sense of Power: The Roots of America's Global Role* (Ithaca, NY: Cornell University Press, 2015).
8. Charles A. Beard, *A Foreign Policy for America* (New York: Alfred A. Knopf, 1940), 39, 47.
9. On Roosevelt's personal diplomacy, see Frank Costigliola, *Roosevelt's Lost Alliances: How Personal Politics Helped Start the Cold War* (Princeton, NJ: Princeton University Press, 2012).
10. Warren F. Kimball, *The Juggler: Franklin Roosevelt as Wartime Statesman* (Princeton, NJ: Princeton University Press, 1994), 7.

11. Adam Tooze, *The Deluge: The Great War, America, and the Remaking of the Global Order, 1916–1931* (New York: 2014).

12. See Ronald Steel, *Walter Lippmann and the American Century* (Boston: Little Brown, 1980), 385, and "The Reminiscences of Walter Lippmann," Columbia University Rare Books Library, New York City, 178.

13. Walter Lippmann, *U.S. Foreign Policy: Shield of the Republic* (Boston: Little Brown, 1943).

14. Vladislav M. Zubok's *Failed Empire: The Soviet Union in the Cold War from Stalin to Gorbachev* (Chapel Hill: University of North Carolina Press, 2008) is particularly effective in tracing the way in which ideology influenced Stalin's ambitions. Geoffrey Roberts's *Stalin's Wars: From World War to Cold War, 1939–1953* (New Haven, CT: Yale University Press, 2008) lends support to Lippmann's portrayal of Stalin as a pragmatic and rational actor.

15. Additionally, as Elizabeth Borgwart has shown in *A New Deal for the World*, the international negotiations at Bretton Wood, in combination with those that led to the creation of the United Nations and the Nuremberg Trials, built logically on the Atlantic Charter and Franklin Delano Roosevelt's Four Freedoms and inaugurated "a transformation in the ideas and institutions underlying the modern human rights regime." Elizabeth Borgwart, *A New Deal for the World: America's Vision for Human Rights* (Cambridge, MA: Harvard University Press, 2005), 5.

16. See, most recently, Benn Steil, *The Battle of Bretton Woods: John Maynard Keynes, Harry Dexter White, and the Making of a New World Order* (Princeton, NJ: Princeton University Press, 2013).

17. Geir Lundestad, "Empire by Invitation? The United States and Western Europe, 1945–1952," *Journal of Peace Research* 23:3 (September 1986).

18. Geir Lundestad, *The United States and Western Europe since 1945: From Empire by Invitation to Transatlantic Drift* (Oxford: Oxford University Press, 2003), 13.

19. Thompson, Nicholas, *The Hawk and the Dove: Paul Nitze, George Kennan, and the History of the Cold War* (New York: Henry Holt and Co., 2009), 60.

20. http://www.gwu.edu/~nsarchiv/coldwar/documents/episode-1/kennan.htm.

21. See Michael J. Hogan, *The Marshall Plan: America, Britain, and the Reconstruction of Western Europe, 1947–1952* (New York: Cambridge University Press, 1989). The full text of the speech can be accessed at http://www.americanrhetoric.com/speeches/georgecmarshall.html.

22. X, "The Sources of Soviet Conduct," *Foreign Affairs*, July 1947. http://www.foreignaffairs.com/articles/23331/x/the-sources-of-soviet-conduct.

23. Walter Lippmann, *The Cold War* (New York: Harper and Row, 1972; first published by Little, Brown in 1947).

24. Ibid., 11, 14–16.

25. Nathan Leites, *The Operational Code of the Politburo* (New York: McGraw Hill, 1951).

26. The full text of NSC-68 can be found at http://www.fas.org/irp/offdocs/nsc-hst/nsc-68.htm.

27. Ibid.
28. Fred Kaplan, *The Wizards of Armageddon* (New York: Simon and Schuster, 1983), 140–141.
29. John Lewis Gaddis, *Strategies of Containment: A Critical Appraisal of American National Security Policy*, revised and expanded (New York: Oxford University Press, 2005), 127–128.
30. Fred Kaplan, *The Wizards of Armageddon* (Palo Alto, CA: Stanford University Press, 1991), 145.
31. Ibid, 151.
32. Paul Nitze, *From Hiroshima to Glasnost: At the Center of Decision* (New York: Grove Press, 1989), 152.
33. For the full text of Kennedy's speech, see *Public Papers of the Presidents of the United States, John F. Kennedy, 1961* (Washington, DC: US Government Printing Office, 1962), 1–3.
34. Mary Dudziak, *War Time: An Idea, Its History, Its Consequences* (New York: Oxford University Press, 2012).
35. Paul Thomas Chamberlin, *The Cold War's Killing Fields: Rethinking the Long Peace* (New York: Harper, 2018).
36. Jeremi Suri, *Henry Kissinger and the American Century* (Cambridge, MA: Belknap Press of Harvard University Press, 2007), 161.
37. Julian Zelizer, *Arsenal of Democracy: The Politics of National Security from World War II to the War on Terrorism* (New York: Basic Books, 2009), 240.
38. Henry A. Kissinger, *White House Years* (Boston: Little, Brown, 1979), 62.
39. Ibid., 787
40. Greg Grandin, *Kissinger's Shadow: The Long Reach of America's Most Controversial Statesman* (New York: Metropolitan Books, 2015).
41. Mario Del Pero, *The Eccentric Realist: Henry Kissinger and the Shaping of American Foreign Policy* (Ithaca, NY: Cornell University Press, 2011).
42. Zelizer, *Arsenal of Democracy*, 275.
43. James Mann, *Rise of the Vulcans: The History of Bush's War Cabinet* (New York: Viking, 2004), 75–76.
44. Richard H. Immerman, *Empire for Liberty: A History of American Imperialism from Benjamin Franklin to Paul Wolfowitz* (Princeton, NJ: Princeton University Press, 2010), 202.
45. Jeane Kirkpatrick, "Dictatorships and Double Standards," *Commentary* 68:5 (November 1979), 41, 37.
46. Mann, *Rise of the Vulcans*, 92.
47. James Graham Wilson, *The Triumph of Improvisation: Gorbachev's Adaptability, Reagan's Engagement, and the End of the Cold War* (Ithaca, NY: Cornell University Press, 2015), 198.
48. Charles Krauthammer, "The Unipolar Moment," *Foreign Affairs* 70:1 (1990).
49. John J. Mearsheimer, "Back to the Future: Instability in Europe after the Cold War," *International Security* 15:1 (Fall 1990); Francis Fukuyama, "The End of History?" *National Interest* (Summer 1989).

50. Immerman, *Empire for Liberty*, 217. For the various drafts of the DPG, see the website of the National Security Archive based at George Washington University: http://www.gwu.edu/~nsarchiv/nukevault/ebb245/index.htm (accessed February 7, 2013).

51. http://www.nytimes.com/1992/03/08/world/us-strategy-plan-calls-for-insuring-no-rivals-develop.html?pagewanted=all&src=pm.

52. George Packer, *The Assassins' Gate: America in Iraq* (New York: Farrar, Straus and Giroux, 2005), 21.

53. Derek Chollet and James Goldgeier, *America between the Wars: The Misunderstood Years between the Fall of the Berlin Wall and the Start of the War on Terror* (New York: Public Affairs, 2008), 45.

54. Memorandum from Paul Wolfowitz to Secretary of Defense Dick Cheney, May 5, 1992, http://www.gwu.edu/~nsarchiv/nukevault/ebb245/doc14.pdf.

55. Immerman, *Empire for Liberty*, 218.

56. Mann, *Rise of the Vulcans,* 219.

57. Christopher Preble, *The Power Problem: How American Military Dominance Makes Us Less Safe, Less Prosperous, and Less Free* (Ithaca, NY: Cornell University Press), 31.

58. Mann, *Rise of the Vulcans*, 395, fn. 40.

59. Paul Wolfowitz, "Clinton's Bay of Pigs," *Wall Street Journal*, September 27, 1996, quoted in Chollet and Goldgeier, *America Between the Wars*, 188.

60. Stefan Halper and Jonathan Clarke, *America Alone: The Neoconservatives and the Global Order* (New York: Cambridge University Press, 2004), 202.

61. George Tenet, *At the Center of the Storm: My Years in the CIA* (New York: Harper Collins, 2007), 306.

62. Andrew Bacevich, *The Limits of Power: The Limits of American Exceptionalism* (New York: Metropolitan Books, 2008), 117.

63. Mann, *Rise of the Vulcans*, 24, 7.

64. http://www.state.gov/documents/organization/63562.pdf.

65. John Lewis Gaddis, *Surprise, Security and the American Experience* (Cambridge, MA: Harvard University Press, 2004).

66. James Traub, *The Freedom Agenda: Why America Must Spread Democracy—Just Not the Way George Bush Did* (New York: Farrar, Straus and Giroux, 2008), 118.

67. Quoted in Stephen Wertheim, "A Solution from Hell: The United States and the Rise of Humanitarian Interventionism, 1991–2003," *Journal of Genocide Research* 12:3-4 (September–December 2010).

68. Partial audio of the speech (and a full transcript) is available at http://www.npr.org/player/v2/mediaPlayer.html?action=1&t=1&islist=false&id=99591469&m=99603945.

69. Jo Becker and Scott Shane, "Secret Kill List Proves a Test of Obama's Principles and Will," *New York Times*, May 26, 2012, http://www.nytimes.com/2012/05/29/world/obamas-leadership-in-war-on-al-qaeda.html?pagewanted=2&hp.

70. Zachary A. Goldfarb, "Obama Says Iran Shouldn't Misinterpret U.S. Response to Syria," *Washington Post*, September 15, 2013, http://www.washingtonpost.com/politics/obama-says-iran-shouldnt-misinterpret-us-response-to-syria/2013/09/15/fd6f27cc-1e05-11e3-8459-657e0c72fec8_story.html.

71. Ralph Waldo Emerson, with preface by Thomas Carlyle, *Essays* (London: James Fraser, 1841), 58.

72. William James, *Pragmatism*, edited and introduced by Bruce Kuklick (Indianapolis: Hackett, 1981), 29.

73. James T. Kloppenberg, *Reading Obama: Dreams, Hope, and the American Political Tradition* (Princeton, NJ: Princeton University Press, 2011), xiii.

74. See Brendan Simms and Charlie Laderman, *Donald Trump: The Making of a Worldview* (London: I. B. Tauris, 2017).

PART III
RECASTING CENTRAL FIGURES

8

Woodrow Wilson, W. E. B. Du Bois, and Beyond

American Internationalists and the Crucible of World War I

Christopher McKnight Nichols

Woodrow Wilson looms over the landscape of modern American foreign relations like a colossus, "the dominant personality, the seminal figure," as historian George Herring puts it.[1] Yet, though Wilson's diplomacy and ideas represent such a strong force in US foreign relations, scholarship on grand strategy tends to omit or minimize his contributions.[2] This literature often (and incorrectly) disregards Wilson's initiatives because they did not appear to have had immediate results in his period. Diplomat-turned-grand-strategy expert Charles Hill emphasizes outcomes. For Hill what is most significant is that the main points of Wilson's postwar agenda "all failed."[3] The Senate rejected US membership in the League of Nations, and Republican isolationism dominated foreign policy during the following decade; thus, this line of interpretation suggests, Wilsonian internationalism might have been grand but it was not much of a strategy given its lack of success in directing the nation's foreign policy. Despite the fact that Wilson's conceptualization of a new world order interlocked with—and helped to set in motion— the strategic theories of internationalism that shaped the US's relations with the world after his lifetime, the term "grand strategy" remains indelibly linked to the World War II era, when usage of the term peaked in applications to wartime as well as postwar planning. The significance of World War I seems to pale in comparison with the Second World War and the Cold War era, since the US developed and applied the American grand strategy of hegemony in that later period, as political scientist Christopher Layne and historian Paul Kennedy have consistently argued.[4]

For nearly a century, scholars framed the First World War as arising out of a system of international relations in which great powers developed networks to mediate and moderate conflict and facilitate cooperation, before devolving into catastrophic confrontations in Western Europe. Such a perspective has not only lost its originality but also much of its appeal. In place of stale debates about war guilt and conflictual security system, historians and political scientists have recently constructed more nuanced accounts of how, why, when, and where nations went to war, epitomized by historian Christopher Clark's popular *Sleepwalkers*.[5] Recent research, such as that undertaken by historians David Reynolds, Susan Pedersen, and Adam Tooze, also has revealed the ways in which new political formulations and new internationalisms took shape in the World War I period.[6] These works argue convincingly that this war—and, particularly, the US role in it and the peace that followed—effectively "remade" the global order.

In addition, recent accounts of World War I now emphasize other regions, such as the Eastern front, looking more in-depth at transnational movements of peoples, ideas, and goods and contextualizing the war in the historiographies of decolonization and capitalism.[7] Cutting-edge global-historical analysis, such as Douglas Boyd's *The Other First World War* and Eugene Rogan's *The Fall of the Ottomans*, situate Europe alongside, for example, the involvement of colonies in the Middle East, Russia and the Eastern Front, or Japan's expansionism and territorial growth in the period. Many of these newer transnational histories do not restrain their focus to the national level, starting with one state and moving on to others. Rather, they take multiple levels of historical experience as given and make analytic interventions by focusing on organizations and events that existed both below and above the apparatus of a nation-state. One example of such phenomena lies with pre-war non-governmental organizations (NGOs), such as the Red Cross, which operated effectively below the nation-state, until it eventually became the US government's official voluntary aid agency and an arm of the state during the war. Another case would be international conferences, such as the Edinburgh world missionary conference in 1910, which gathered thousands of missionaries seeking to advance a global mission, or the Hague Conferences/Conventions of 1899 and 1907 on international peace and the conduct of warfare. These operated above the nation-state, with significant impacts on the avenues for intervention, mediation, humanitarian relief, and exchange before, during, and after the war.[8]

Innovative new historical work has also emphasized the under-appreciated global intersections of ideas, peoples, and groups during and immediately following the conflict. Erez Manela's pathbreaking efforts, for example, have helped reconceptualize the transmission and reception of Wilsonian ideals.[9] Demonstrating that Wilsonian notions of self-determination played a role in China's May Fourth movement, in Korea, India, Egypt, Vietnam, and elsewhere, Manela underscores the reasons that grand strategy scholars must take Wilsonianism seriously.

By centering his narrative outside the Euro-American framework, Manela's *Wilsonian Moment* opens new arenas of analysis for measuring the diffuse strands of strategic ideas beyond facile binaries of success or failure, war or peace. Instead of narrating the interplay of great-power nation-states—the classic domain of narrowly defined grand strategy—Manela describes the ways in which non-Europeans adopted, adapted, and/ or invented their own versions of Wilson in nationalist and anti-colonial projects with international scope and ambition. He brings in nationalists such as India's Jawaharlal Nehru and Mahatma Gandhi, Korea's Syngman Rhee, Vietnam's Ho Chi Minh, and China's Mao Zedong, and portrays them as quasi-Wilsonian grand strategists. In invoking Wilsonianism, Manela argues, these figures searched for their own kind of "self-determination" that Wilson, Britain's David Lloyd George, France's Georges Clemenceau, and Italy's Vittorio Orlando were absolutely unprepared and unwilling to offer them at the time. In effect, Manela simultaneously emphasizes the lost promise and the tremendous significance of Wilson's idealistic message of self-determination, as well as the potential of US leadership among nationalist anti-colonial movements around the world.[10]

The mismatch of rhetoric and reality in formal US foreign policy and the consequences of its unfulfilled pledges did not deter a range of thinkers, politicians, activists, regular citizens and subjects from strategically adapting Wilson to their own ends. They made this intellectual-strategic turn even as it estranged them from embracing the United States as the paragon of those ideals.[11] Indeed, while Wilson "faded from the international arena," Manela shows that anti-colonial movements "embraced the language of self-determination that he brought to prominence, refashioning their goals and identities in its image even as they recast its meanings in theirs."[12] As they struggled to be recognized as sovereign actors in the international community, they extrapolated from Wilsonian internationalism a grand strategy of anti-colonial, revolutionary proportions that shaped the ensuing decades and continues to define the contemporary world.

Recent scholarly interest in assessing the First World War's global nature and its catalyzing effects on foreign relations—much of it timed to the centennial anniversaries from 2014 to 2018—functioned more as a rediscovery than a new intervention. Only in the post-1945 period did historians and politicians come to depict this war as primarily a European conflict, compared to the all-pervading Second World War. For most people in Europe and the United States at the time, however, these decades were "postwar" years, emphatically so for the internationalists who devoted their lives to disarmament and preventing the next war. Similarly, what came to be known as The Great War revealed another insight: the utter unpredictability of the future.

At the dawn of the twentieth century, Europe had not fought a major conflict for a hundred years. Most political and military experts predicted a war of mere months and little bloodshed. World War I, a war few wanted or expected, shattered their belief in the cresting tide of human progress. The war was thus a fundamental challenge to strategic thought and the assumptions that might undergid the effort to strategize for the future, given the unknowable consequences of modern state violence, in meaningful ways. In addition to recasting Wilson, then, the choice to reframe the war as a crucible moment disrupts the notion of the 1920s and 1930s as "interwar" years and exposes the true (and truly radical) dynamics of postwar internationalisms in this period.

With a new, broadened understanding of grand strategy as an epistemology, Wilson reenters the frame. Wilson's case also provides clarity about the strategic role that non-state actors and ideologies have played in global politics and in American involvement in the world. The devastation of the Great War exposed the underlying frameworks of the world system; joining the war altered the United States' foreign relations calculus, as it had never before fought and joined with European powers on their continent; this, in turn, propelled new visions for the reconstruction of international relations, generating four transformative theories of internationalism that shaped the contours of US global engagement for the rest of the twentieth century. Though these internationalisms and their advocates sometimes diverged, they generally intersected in compatible ways, developing capacious, long-term strategies to transform both US foreign policy and worldwide systems and organizations through shared values.

First, Wilsonianism, premised in large part on a vision of American exceptionalist leadership, represented a liberal scheme of moral and legal internationalism best expressed in brief in Wilson's Fourteen Points and institutionally in the League of Nations. Globally influential from 1918 through 1919, the Wilsonian vision dramatically collapsed when the League failed. Still, it rapidly inspired new movements (even non- or anti-Wilsonian ones) that rearticulated and translated Wilsonian internationalism into forms, functions, and meanings beyond those expressed or advocated by Woodrow Wilson himself. The ramifications of such a worldview, if not a set of concrete policies, precipitated what one scholar termed the ensuing "Wilsonian Century."[13]

Second, settlement house pioneer and peace activist Jane Addams and a host of associates (most notably Emily Balch) advanced and applied a feminist-moral vision for peace internationalism through organizations such as the Women's Peace Party (WPP) and Women's International League for Peace and Freedom (WILPF). As part of the burgeoning Outlawry of War movement, they promoted international disarmament, most prominently during the Washington Naval Conference (1921–22). They also aimed at broader anti-colonial, anti-imperial activism designed to diagnose and root out the role of militarism and bellicosity in capitalism. These efforts culminated symbolically in the Kellogg-Briand Pact (1928), signed by more than forty nations, including virtually all the belligerents, which sought to "outlaw war as an instrument of national policy" and to have nations "settle their disputes by peaceful means."

Third, intellectual W. E. B. Du Bois and a range of allies developed and directed a new black internationalism premised on a critique of the "global color line" and racist-imperialist Western capitalism. Du Bois articulated key elements of this grand strategic analysis of the "African Roots of the War" (1915), which came to fruition in his anti-colonial and pan-African activities in the 1920s. During the war, Du Bois had notoriously advocated a compromise position, encouraging African Americans to "Close Ranks" with their "white fellow citizens" and join in "fighting for democracy" in exchange for postwar fulfillment of civil rights. Through his leadership of the NAACP and his postwar travels to Africa, however, Du Bois gradually developed a more revolutionary internationalism.

Fourth, the war crystallized the isolationist unilateralism of figures such as Idaho Republican senator William Borah, who helped spearhead the Senate rejection of the League of Nations. Borah and his fellow "Irreconcilables" insisted that the United States retain a "free hand" at home and abroad. As another alternative, it developed an approach to US foreign relations that rejected multilateralism and collective security (the League, the World Court) but embraced the principle of moral suasion via international law. Along these lines, we find anti-war, anti-interventionist affinities with aspects of black internationalism and with peace internationalists, such as the WILPF and a range of so-called peace progressives, alongside whom Borah advocated anti-colonialism and non-binding internationalism, embodied in multinational agreements such as the Kellogg-Briand Pact.[14]

The four faces of American internationalism show how and why we might benefit from a new definition of grand strategy, grounded in the First World War. Wartime experience formed a crucial—even central—basis for American internationalism and for subsequent models of international relations. If the term "grand strategy" has any meaning, Woodrow Wilson's liberal internationalism (epitomized in his Fourteen Points) must be understood in the context of the conflict as a radically ambitious and capacious postwar plan. Wilson's conception of a world order—based on democratic values and directed by American leadership—recalibrated US foreign policy in its moment and for generations to come. It marked an American-centric drift that later internationalists resisted, using similar tactics to those laid out by Addams, Du Bois, and Borah.

This chapter's emphasis is largely on the first three of these focal areas, given that the fourth is better known as an alternative to Wilsonianism. The point here is to be suggestive, rather than exhaustive. As the chapter gestures to the depth and development of these intersecting American internationalisms, the historical cases explored here urge us to see the First World War as the cradle of new internationalisms and they provide the basis for a larger analytical-definitional intervention in how scholars, students, and practitioners can understand the path of American grand strategy in the twentieth century.

By revisiting Woodrow Wilson and moving beyond his Fourteen Points and tragic death, this chapter aims to move beyond the man and to shed new light on his long-term impact on internationalism. This examination of the unique influences of Wilsonianism during and after the war focuses on figures who cannot be said to have been Wilsonian champions; they took up aspects of his concept of American internationalism, reshaped it to their own ends, and carried these ideas to guide visions for American foreign policy and world relations into the 1920s and beyond. Resituating the history of grand strategy around a crucible moment and centering its analysis on non-state actors and ideologies, this chapter puts forward a cultural-intellectual and transnational model for grand strategy.

The New Model and Grand Strategy

Historically, grand strategy had focused on policies that ensured victory in armed conflicts, but the First World War proved that focus too narrow to secure the nation-state's vital ends. At the time, anti-interventionist, isolationist, and internationalist thinkers observed that conflict-centered grand strategies tended to produce confrontations that invariably undercut international security. But they argued that grand strategies for peace might reasonably create the conditions to avoid the cataclysm and instability of war in the first place, and grand strategies that extended beyond military means and state actors might avert the dangers endemic to formal politics and policymaking on the national and international stage.

Historians have only recently begun to explore the grand strategic and transnational dynamics at play during and after the peace process concluded at Versailles. According to Jay Winter, the Paris Peace revealed that the war was both "the apogee and the beginning of the end of imperial power, spanning and eroding national and imperial boundaries."[15] The world conditions that gave rise to the Great War and the unfortunate consequences of its peace settlement generated a need for new ideas, strategies, and systems that would have wide-ranging influences.

During and after the lengthy negotiation in Paris, Wilson put into play an expansive internationalist vision of grand strategy that opened the realm of possibility for supra-state, non-state, and para-state institutions, actors, and groups. As historian Frank Ninkovich pointed out, Wilson "recognized one of modernity's most prominent and paradoxical features: as the world became more industrialized and integrated, it became more orderly and predictable; at the same time, breakdowns of the system, though perhaps less frequent, were more calamitous."[16] As a consequence, Wilson and other unconventional international figures such as Du Bois, Addams, and Borah, many of whom operated in the interstices of those systemic ruptures, constructed alternative strategies of resistance and coexistence that should rightly be labeled as "grand."[17]

Like more traditional grand strategists, figures like Du Bois, Addams, Borah, and their allies developed comprehensive, integrated plans of action, "based on the calculated relationship of means to ends," often seeking non-state and para-state solutions, and always taking the long view.[18] In Akira Iriye's words, they each formulated a vision of cultural internationalism that sought "to reformulate the nature of relations among nations through cross-national cooperation and interchange" or to transcend nation-states altogether.[19] Although sweeping programmatic visions of the relations between peoples must be about the state on some level, as Charles Hill has argued, the new American internationalisms of this era involved a wide swath of actors, groups, and approaches.[20] Faced with the breakdown of traditional institutions and approaches to international relations, they struggled to find a grand strategy for peace that would avoid the devastation of another world war.

In this way, they modeled a cultural-intellectual-transnational approach to grand strategy that the narrow scholarly focus on moments of conflict has largely missed. Through their work, they joined other "individuals and groups of people from different lands" that "have sought to develop an alternative community of nations and peoples on the basis of their cultural interchanges." As Iriye argues, "[w]hile frequently ridiculed by practitioners of power politics and ignored by historians, their efforts have significantly altered the world community and immeasurably enriched our understanding of world affairs."[21] Taken together, their actions informed the "security imaginary," the "structure of well-established meanings and social relations out of which representations of the world of international relations are created."[22] In addition to the concrete impact that Wilson, Addams, Du Bois, and Borah had on world affairs through their institutional, intellectual, and legal accomplishments, then, they also contributed to the strategic culture on which future state actors built their own grand strategies.

As historian Glenda Sluga has persuasively established, the arc of internationalism as it developed through the 1910s really took shape in the World War I wartime period and found its apogee at the end of World War II. Although organizations such as the League of Nations and later the United Nations stood for the sovereignty of nation-states, they often sought to transcend national allegiances through alternative solidarities. In this way, according to Sluga, they created the conditions under which women, subject populations (e.g., American people of color), and marginalized colonial subjects could make their voices heard in an international arena.[23] The grand strategists who propelled the internationalisms of the Great War era set the stage not only for internationalisms ascendant in the interwar years but profoundly shaped internationalist ideologies and movements through the present.

Wilsonianism and Postwar Internationalism

By the time the United States entered the war in April 1917, Wilson considered the conflict a permanent rupture in historical time and precedent. In articulating his plan for the postwar order, therefore, he promulgated a substantively different vision from his earlier oratorical commitments to "peace without victory" and "no annexations, no indemnities." In place of a peace designed to restore the antebellum status quo, he asserted an internationalist framework that provided the foundation for grand strategies of peace based on international collaboration, international law, and self-determination. Catalyzed by the war, Wilsonian internationalism expressed the broader transformations in political thought and international governance decades in the making that would also give rise to Addams's peace internationalism and Du Bois's black internationalism.[24] At once lofty, idealistic, and strategically vague, Wilson's Fourteen Points raised and dashed expectations in nearly equal measure. Over time, they exerted a powerful influence on world politics, framing the postwar world as much as the peace settlement they informed. As Wilson declared in 1918:

> The day of conquest and aggrandizement is gone by; so is also the day of secret covenants entered into in the interest of particular governments and likely at some unlooked-for moment to upset the peace of the world. It is this happy fact, now clear to the view of every public man whose thoughts do not still linger in an age that is dead and gone, which makes it possible for every nation whose purposes are consistent with justice and the peace of the world to avow now or at any other time the objects it has in view.[25]

The most comprehensive account of belligerent war aims emanated not from Europe, then, but from the United States, a nation that took almost three years to enter the war and, at this point in history, had not yet developed a comprehensive foreign policy program.[26] Wilson's words—the grounds upon which Germany sued for peace—represented nothing less than a sea change in American (and global) internationalism.[27]

In the Fourteen Points, Wilson outlined a liberal internationalist program for peace designed to serve as a blueprint for orderly progress that would orchestrate and amplify harmony between nations. Crucially linked to a worldview that prioritized universalist notions of the link between political and economic freedoms, the Wilsonian project also manifested a commitment to expanding capitalist market economies around the world. Nevertheless, enduring scholarly debates often miss the main points of the speech. Glossing over or ridiculing its sweeping aims, they neglect its development in the late wartime geopolitical environment, particularly its relationship to other nascent internationalisms and to contemporary economic thought. As Stephen Wertheim has put it, the charged intellectual controversy over Wilsonianism has "reduced early twentieth-century internationalism to a caricature: one-dimensional, polarizing, and, not least, inaccurate."[28]

The historical record, however, amply suggests that nearly all observers at the time recognized the myriad challenges and complexities of the moment and the problems of creating vibrant new internationalist solutions. Despite the rhetoric that Wilson "kept us out of war" during the 1916 presidential election, many Americans acknowledged the phenomenon that Europeans and other keen watchers of international relations from around the world had long noted: the fluctuating alliances among European nation-states, alongside the realities of asymmetrical interests and strength, had finally and fatally undermined the Concert of Europe balance-of-power system that had endured in principle since the 1648 Treaty of Westphalia. So, what would replace the old system?

The self-assured progressive intellectual Wilson had all the answers. He was confident that open diplomacy, freedom of the seas for navigation and commerce, lowered trade barriers, disarmament, and national self-determination would restabilize Europe, and a properly organized League with US leadership would fix the rest. Wilson culminated his fourteen-point prescriptions with his well-known *cri de coeur* for a postwar organization of collective security and international governance that would become the League of Nations.[29]

Wilson's proposal was hardly unprecedented. Continuing the pre-war trend, a large and powerful body of internationalists worked both inside and outside of government toward broader internationalist outreach and engagement. Former presidents Theodore Roosevelt and William Howard Taft, for example, alongside leading legal-internationalist thinkers such as former Secretary of State Elihu Root, championed the League to Enforce Peace (LEP, established 1915), an international regime based on a legally binding model of collective security that combined economic sanctions with military force to ensure the compliance of member states.[30] Sometimes these internationalists favored legalism and sanctions as the LEP did, but in most cases they did not.[31]

The same year that Taft took the helm of the LEP, peace-activist Jane Addams and a group of like-minded women gathered for the International Congress for Women at the Hague, where they established the International Committee of Women for Permanent Peace and, later, WILPF, an international organization that envisioned a world devoid of violence. In her prewar monograph *Newer Ideals of Peace* (1906), Addams prefigured an idea later propounded by cultural critic Randolph Bourne that "war is the health of the state." In this work and her later writing, speaking, and activism, she aimed to make the case not simply for pacifism or for cooperative feelings between peoples, but also to explain war as a symptom of a broader disease in the international community.

Addams described militarism as a pathology that destructively regulated relations among nations and also within them, simultaneously ordering and benefiting from a conflict-based system of international relations. In its place, she advanced a more active, dynamic ideal of peace that required people to recognize their interdependence and replace the military models for organizing internal and international relations with an "enlightened" industrialism that would benefit broader swaths of society.[32] She supported the American Union Against Militarism (in which Bourne was involved as were fellow settlement house pioneers Lilian Wald and Florence Kelley). Whereas isolationist figures like William Borah initially voted for the United States to enter the war on nationalist-patriotic grounds, Addams maintained her pacifism absolutely. Unlike instrumentalist pacifists such as John Dewey, who joined the Wilsonian war as a progressive project "to make the world safe for democracy," Addams never wavered.

Toward the end of the 1920s, Jane Addams characterized international interdependence as an international "consciousness" that had matured into fullness only after the war, a view widely shared by other internationalist and pacifist activists. Applying the lessons she learned in the settlement-house movement and through her international peace initiatives, Addams concluded that "the modern world is developing an almost mystic consciousness of the continuity and interdependence of mankind."[33] The new internationalism of the post-Wilson years did, in fact, rely on world consciousness and world opinion, shared, at the very least, by elite politicians, activists, and intellectuals.

The League that Wilson "eventually asked Americans to join reflected the cultural prejudices of its designers," as historian Trygve Throntveit notes, but "its capacity for self-correction under the pressure of world opinion was, in fact, its defining feature."[34] This vision aimed to measure means to grand-strategic ends and even in its "failure" served to increase popular discussion and debate. The limited collapse of formal Wilsonianism generated a deepening urgency to find alternative solutions that would successfully ensure peace and enhance the world community. Rather than destabilizing or discouraging new international connections and movements, the disillusionment with aspects of Wilsonianism fed them.[35] In this way, Wilson both authored and inspired an "integrative internationalism," to borrow Throntveit's term, epitomized by the deliberative, egalitarian elements of the League, which demanded meaningful concessions of sovereignty from its members.[36]

The racist, segregationist Wilson—who authorized interventions in Mexico, Haiti, the Dominican Republic, and the Virgin Islands—might seem an unlikely progenitor of a new diplomacy based on transparency, self-determination, and collective security among democratic nations. But, as historian Emily Rosenberg has pointed out, he also maintained "deep ties to international circles that advocated for labor rights, feminism, anti-imperialism, and even socialism." In spite of Wilson's failings, his "blueprint for a conflict-free world of self-determining democracies and laws informed the agendas of many reformers around the world, including anti-colonial leaders in China, India, Egypt, Korea, and elsewhere," and "his belief in the concept of a league of self-determining states" inspired "internationalists at home and abroad" to recognize their potential to transform the world.[37] As they struggled for anti-colonial, anti-imperialist, and disarmament projects, and guided the American public toward a more cosmopolitan sensibility, these internationalists often kept faith with or worked with the League because it provided a potent conduit for transnational connections and advocacy. For instance, as historian Ian Tyrrell has chronicled, the US-led global effort for prohibition in the 1920s briefly gained traction worldwide in part because its advocates worked through the League to constrain the international trafficking of narcotic substances.

Another example of the contours of Wilsonianism after the war that I cannot fully address due to space contraints but that bears mentioning here is the case of the League mandate system, which sought to administer and transform the imperial order. As shown by Susan Pedersen, the League's Mandates Commission and system became symbolic of new international governance for an interdependent, interconnected, multipolar postwar world with the potential to reify colonial injustices or to right them. In short, and unexpectedly, it made Geneva the nexus for debates over claims to national self-determination; it also made the League a key site for collaboration and co-optation by imperial powers. This was the peculiar intellectual-institutional offspring of Wilson, the very embodiment of only-partly-intended consequences of the Fourteen Points, interconnected inherently to the era's rising black internationalism and peace internationalism. The mandates system, like black internationalism and the Outlawry of War peace movement that led to the toothlessly transcendent Kellogg-Briand Pact in 1928, were the engines driving various global "internationalisms" long after Wilson. These efforts represented the pushes and pulls of wartime inspired processes "by which political issues and functions [we]re displaced from the national or imperial, and into the international realm."[38] This became both intellectual and institutional. By 1926, more than 1,200 organizations joined together for the study of international questions, whereas in 1914 that number was a mere 120.[39]

War, Race, Empire, and Internationalism

Because World War I cast the relationship between war and empire into stark relief, W. E. B. Du Bois focused some of his most trenchant analysis on the relationship between imperial nations, their international objectives, and oppressed peoples during and immediately after the war. It was clear, he suggested, that the colonial and capitalist conflicts between large European powers—epitomized by the colonial "scramble for Africa" and the search for markets for industrial goods—had helped spark an arms race. For the prior four decades, the major powers (particularly France, Germany, Austro-Hungary, England, Russia, and the Ottoman Empire) had accelerated their commercial and imperial competition with each other, leading to a series of alliances and mutual defense pacts that further destabilized world relations. In their rush to dominate, they made war more likely. As military-industrial capacities grew alongside commercial-colonial reach, these developments ensured that any future war would be larger and worse.

Like Addams and Balch, Du Bois described how empire, racism, and conflict were inextricably interconnected. In his remarkable 1915 essay, "The African Roots of the War," Du Bois detailed the enormous profits that imperial nations generated from a feminized Africa, "prostrated, raped, and shamed," even as they advanced an agenda of "Africa for the Africans."[40] In a related set of wartime writings, Du Bois developed this analogy of colonial devastation on the body of Africa while emphasizing Africa's potential for rejuvenation through international agencies. In contrast with Addams's outright rejection of militarism, however, Du Bois initially viewed the war as an opportunity for "black folk" to prove their worth as citizens. After 1917, he embraced the war effort as a plastic juncture for black citizenship, controversially publishing a series of editorials encouraging enlistment (most notably "Close Ranks," published in 1918) in *The Crisis*, the magazine of the National Association for the Advancement of Colored People (NAACP). At the urging of the NAACP's chairman, Du Bois even applied for a commission in US military intelligence.

As it did for many public figures, the reality of war and its apparent incapacity to secure the rights of marginalized people radicalized Du Bois, leading him to reject the nation-state as arbiter of those rights. Du Bois did not realize his internationalist mission, as he put it, until his 1923 visit to Africa as an official envoy of Liberia. On that trip, Du Bois reported, he discovered that the "income-bearing value of race prejudice was the cause and not the result of theories of race inferiority" in the colonized world as well as in the United States.[41] As a result, he rejected (current or former) formal colonial state involvement in Africa but left the option open for unspecified non-governmental and activist groups to intercede.

Rather than rely on national institutions and his prior nationalist position to achieve his desired ends, Du Bois turned toward transnational means. In his immediate postwar thought and action, Dubois constructed alternative visions of international action in which he formulated a grand strategy for racial justice. In this effort, many other Black people joined him, including activists who had not considered themselves his allies, such as Marcus Garvey and the United Negro Improvement Association (UNIA). In their work, they created international networks and alliances, matched resources and methods to their long-term geopolitical goals, and established a comprehensive theory of knowledge that justified and reinforced their aims.

Thus, this effort entailed all the core components of a grand-strategy epis-temology. Du Boisian black internationalism, as historian Keisha Blain per-suasively argues, "centers on visions of freedom and liberation movements among African descended people worldwide," aiming "to forge transnational collaborations and solidarities with other people of color" and to move to-ward freedom for oppressed populations around the world.[42]

Du Bois's shift toward internationalist and non-state solutions informed his work with the NAACP and his anti-colonial advocacy. In hemispheric and US terms, it amounted to efforts to ensure race equality in American democracy and to pull American Marines out of Haiti and the Caribbean. In world terms, articulated in his 1940 "autobiography of a race concept" *Dusk of Dawn*, Du Bois pivoted his black internationalist turn around the Russian Revolution. The revolution, he said, "was the foundation stone of my fight for black folk; it explained me."[43] Initially Du Bois supported Garvey's Black Star Line and UNIA as ways to link the African diaspora and encouraged sim-ilar black internationalist feminist intellectual and internationalist efforts.[44] As sociologist Roderick Bush succinctly explains, Du Bois's core vision was widely shared. He "illuminat[ed] the vast scope of the problem of the color line in class analysis; the history of social stratification in the United States and the world-system; the politics of the United States, people of African de-scent, and the world-system; and the quest for a democratic, just, and egali-tarian world order."[45] By diagnosing the many ways in which the Great War represented an extension of European imperial competition and an expan-sion of the Euro-American world economy, Du Bois made a piercing case for the fundamental moral function that whiteness and Western hierarchies served in justifying Euro-American hegemony.

Du Bois's analysis of the role of Africa in the war combined with his expe-rience after the failed "Closing Ranks" moment, his participation at the First (1919) and Second pan-African Congresses (1921) as well as the events of Red Summer in 1919 all propelled him to even more explicitly and publicly link the war to racial violence, arguing "there can be little doubt but that the [Ku Klux] Klan in its present form is a legacy of the World War." [46] Du Bois is-sued a resolution for the League to appoint more people of color and directly tackle issues of labor and inequality, to little result. Yet again this confirmed for him that no effective national or European-led international solution existed to the problem of the color line, which he famously referred to as "belting the world." As Mary Dudziak, Carol Anderson, and other historians have shown, the analysis linking US domestic racism with international racial imperialism and competition took new form in the Cold War in what we might best depict as grand strategies operating at the intersection of national and international policy and law.[47]

These developing internationalisms inflected with Du Boisian anti-imperialism, anti-capitalism, and pan-Africanism took shape at the 1955 Bandung Conference (a collaboration of twenty-nine African and Asian countries committed to anti-colonialism) and the subsequent Non-Aligned Movement, with its rejection of power politics and its declaration of principles and activities "for world peace and cooperation."[48] Such an effort is rarely depicted in grand strategic terms and yet it very clearly had the world-shaping aims and many of the effects of those more often depicted as grand strategy. In an era of worldwide Black Lives Matter protests and dawning mass consciousness of the enduring effects of systemic racism, anti-blackness, and settler colonialism, Du Bois's black internationalist grand strategic aspirations and critiques resonate powerfully in and for contemporary American politics and foreign policy as well as international relations more broadly.

"The Pressure of World Opinion"

Ultimately, Wilson's vision for a world order based on a partial (but genuine) relinquishment of sovereignty by even the most powerful nations—including the United States—was more radical than any plan seriously pursued by policymakers before or since. Politicians and pundits recognized the radical implications of Wilsonianism and related American internationalisms and rejected them for their reliance on multilateralism and "self-correction under the pressure of world opinion."[49] Indeed, as historian Adriane Lentz-Smith has found, this was the crucial, radical nexus of domestic and foreign—leveraging Wilson and his ideas to presen a vivid challenge for the United States to live up to its democratic ideals. At the Paris peace talks "as they took up the language of Wilsonian internationalism," working alongside women's peace activists and through venues like the pan-African Congress "race reformers navigated the mixed terrain between the local and the global." As Lentz-Smith explains, "revamping and reinvigorating [Wilsonianism] to make it their own, black civilians had their mind set on freedom in the United States."[50]

Christopher Hemmer, whose recent book was the first to center on Wilson as a seriously "grand strategist," argued that Wilson's proposal for the League of Nations "was perhaps the most distinctive part of his grand strategic agenda."[51] So, too, Trygve Throntveit elucidates Wilson's ideas in the context of pragmatism. He reveals the world-shaping yet thoroughly "American" ambitions of Wilson's grand strategies, depicting Wilson's "pragmatist internationalism [as] facilitat[ing] a direct response to anarchy and the security dilemma by acknowledging the simultaneously real and constructed nature of each."[52] Wilson, after all, sought to propel a cooperative international reconfiguration, which, in his own words, was premised on "common counsel" yet would be "of the American type—of governments joined with governments for the pursuit of common purposes, in honorary equality and honorable subordination."[53]

In spite of its thoroughgoing reformulation of the world system, its prominence in the period, and its impact on US grand-strategic thought in subsequent decades (even in its postwar repudiation), the best recent scholarship on grand strategy has just begun to take stock of Wilsonianism and the related American internationalists and internationalisms of Wilson's era. The mismatch between Wilsonian rhetoric (the idealism, moralizing, and altruism that inflected his foreign policy vision) and practice, in addition to Wilson's sometimes vague or obscure intentions, makes it hard to precisely pinpoint Wilsonian internationalism in the historical record. Still, Wilsonian notions—often cast by proponents and opponents as forms of internationalist "idealism"—continue to inform essential components of US grand strategy, manifesting in foreign policies devoted to humanitarianism, racial justice, foreign aid, international law, and economic sanctions, to name just a few.

The Wilsonian perspective was never fully discarded in practice, much less in thought. Despite fairly strict limits on formal US diplomatic policy during the 1920s and 1930s, signaled by an isolationist aversion to binding collective security agreements and formal participation in major multilateral organizations, Wilsonian internationalism was far from dead. Indeed, there were Americans on virtually every major League of Nations committee; there are countless examples of private and public US engagement in transnational commercial and cultural arenas. These internationalist efforts exposed the fissures in—and also helped to shape—new configurations of isolationism as it crystallized into a more coherent set of political positions in the 1920s and 1930s. In addition to the strategies built by the para-state and non-state internationalism—exemplified in the WILPF and Addams's writing—these new configurations of isolationism also constituted a robust grand strategy for American growth, prosperity, and national security through domestic development and limited global military and hard diplomatic commitments. Unexpectedly, these developments created what I have called a new "isolationist internationalism."[54]

The new face of American nationalism in the postwar period was surprisingly international in nature. William Borah expressed this limited—yet globally engaged—political philosophy for US foreign relations most dramatically in the 1920s, although he gradually backed away from it during the following decade.[55] A leader in the Senate and one of the nation's principal articulators of foreign policy, Borah reassessed how and why the United States had entered the conflict. In so doing he grounded his grand strategy in the bedrock beliefs of Washington and Jefferson and the injunction to steer clear of foreign entanglements. Yet he and fellow advocates of global involvement updated these notions without significant commitments. Essentially, for Borah, this meant a redoubling of the value of local autonomy as best, what I call "autonomism," so long as it did not transgress criminally against other entities; this included people and businesses, as well as cities, states, and nations. In this way Borah was not simply "anti-treaty" or a mere "great opposer," as his opponents often claimed. He and his allied Irreconcilables, indeed much of the Republican Party in the 1920s and 1930s, could get behind a principle of maintaining US authority to take unilateral action as a global economic and military power while not being bound to commit troops or material abroad. In this, Borah went a step further: he firmly opposed American expansion and imperial policies, yet he staunchly advocated strict American policing of the hemisphere in keeping with the tenets of the Monroe Doctrine; at the same time he rejected interference in the governments of Latin America on behalf of US commercial interests. In the case of US intervention in Nicaragua, for example, in 1922 Borah proclaimed, "The people of Nicaragua are being exploited in shameless fashion by American corporations protected by United States Marines."[56]

Indeed, American anti-colonialism and the ruling of peoples against their will sat at the center of Borah's isolationist internationalism, making him an unlikely but staunch ally of the NAACP and the WILPF in their anti-war, anti-interventionist initiatives. Borah consistently argued against what he called the "fetish of force" in the nation's rise to power and in the international system. In the wake of World War I, he called for moral US leadership by example, not deed, declaring that his country "ought to be ashamed to stand before the world . . . with all our professions of peace and against military power in the attitude of keeping a military heel upon a helpless people."[57] Given limited resources, especially in light of the United States' economic power, "Why stand abroad when we can stand at home?" Borah asked rhetorically, paraphrasing Washington. This set of positions prioritizing democratic ideals, moral suasion over force, and involvement without commitment abroad found widespread support across a vast swath of American society after the war, when an inward focus seemed essential to ensure progress, and then, during the Depression, to mitigate dire domestic conditions. Such arguments also resonated across political lines, with alliances that included socialist internationalists such as Norman Thomas.

Plural in form, new visions of American international leadership tended to be cooperative enough to satisfy many internationalists (including peace internationalists and the advocates of pan-Africanism), while remaining "non-entangled" enough to placate unilateralist-oriented isolationists who reflexively opposed binding security alliances and organizations. At the end of 1928, a startlingly heterogeneous group of internationalists achieved a great symbolic triumph. Bringing together prominent women and former suffragists, high-profile African American activists and internationalists, and the remaining "Irreconcilables" who had opposed US involvement in the League of Nations, they galvanized support for the idealistic internationalism of the Kellogg-Briand Pact to outlaw war.

The culmination of over a decade of internationalist peace activism and a vastly popular policy achievement at the intersection of state and non-state actors, the Kellogg-Briand Pact of 1928 compelled the United States, France, Great Britain, Italy, Japan, Weimar Germany, and other countries to renounce the use of war as an "instrument of national policy." As historian Robert Johnson has shown, virtually the entire peace bloc in Congress and the vast majority of the American population strongly supported an effort to "outlaw war" despite having significant concerns about its effectiveness. Johnson has found that isolationist anti-war thought was part of a broader effort to find an "alternative to corporatism," noting that "the peace progressives who favored Kellogg-Briand argued that the treaty embraced anti-imperialism.[58] Moral internationalism of this kind did not lead to legal strictures in practice, of course, and the non-binding nature of the pact posed deep problems for its implementation. Nevertheless, the considerable American efforts during the interwar period to promote European political and economic security, general disarmament, and, specifically, reductions in the world's navies combined elements of competing strands of internationalism at least in part inspired by or in opposition to Wilson's integrative internationalism.

As Elizabeth Borgwardt has shown, the specter of World War I and the "ghost of Wilson" haunted international developments in the 1920s, 1930s, and particularly the Second World War era. The emergence of so many dynamic forms of internationalism in this period, as historian Mark Bradley has suggested, provided the base on which a global civil society and new international organizations would rise later in the century.[59] If grand strategic analysis seeks to understand this period and its later influences, it must more fully examine American internationalists, internationalism, and the crucible moment of the First World War.

Hal Brands observes that grand strategy is best understood as an "intellectual architecture that lends structure" to foreign policy and, I would add, also lends structure and direction to relations beyond the scope of the conventional nation-state.[60] Once they move beyond a narrow understanding of grand strategy as practiced by world leaders or viewed in terms of military force, analysts must continue to develop and weigh the salient factors involved. In keeping with other scholars in this volume, those seeking to analyze grand strategy would do well to keep historical circumstances and contingency firmly in mind. We need to integrate a deeper understanding of any given historical moment, examining hard and soft power approaches and high policy, as well as new figures and groups.

By chronicling the powerful influence of Wilsonianism—and even more of the variously interpreted political, economic, and social "lessons" of World War I—on internationalist as well as on isolationist ideas, this chapter has gestured toward some of the ways in which an expanded definition of grand strategy should apply to Wilson, Addams, Du Bois, and even Borah. This analysis reminds us of the centrality of the "moment" from roughly 1914 through 1920 and into the 1920s in the development of varied internationalisms. In turn, these insights suggest three related interventions: first, most basically, the lessons of the Great War profoundly shaped wartime and postwar internationalism(s) (specifically, the war inspired Wilsonianism, which influenced concurrent and subsequent internationalisms); second, an expanded definition of grand strategy applies to these internationalisms and their advocates; and third, to understand the history of grand strategy, we must look at the crucible moment of World War I and the internationalisms it inspired. Peace internationalism, black internationalism, isolationist-internationalism, and of course Wilsonian internationalism amounted to grand strategies aiming to remake the organization of the world, nations, and peoples, war as well as peace, with the added pressure of world opinion of what most of those living at the time considered the most cataclysmic event in human history: the Great War. That these and other internationalist ideologies, primarily aimed at finding solutions to nationalist rivalry and conflict, did not prevent another world war should in no way undermine our understanding of the power and ambitions of these competing as well as complementary internationalisms.

Notes

1. George Herring, *From Colony to Superpower: US Foreign Relations since 1776* (New York: Oxford University Press, 2009), 379. This quote was selected in part because it also reminds us of how intensely gendered the language, even deployed by the most exceptional scholars, continues to be about "great" politicians and diplomats.
2. "Wilson" and "Wilsonianism" do not appear in most iconic grand-strategy scholarship, such as the work of Paul Kennedy, John Lewis Gaddis, and Charles Hill. Much recent writing by Hal Brands, for example, tends to begin in 1940 or 1945 and centers on World War II or the Cold War. Other efforts miss Wilson and gloss the First World War in an attempt at covering the vast sweep of world history from antiquity to the present (Hill, Brands, Lawrence Freedman, Williamson Murray). To be fair, Kennedy has extensively explored European Great War grand strategies, and most grand-strategy courses, if they focus on the United States, do include Wilson or Wilsonian internationalism.
3. Charles Hill, *Grand Strategies: Literature, Statecraft, and World Order* (New Haven, CT: Yale University Press, 2010), 222.
4. Another way to describe this might be as "modes of internationalism." This is essential to the analysis of Christopher Layne, *The Peace of Illusions: American Grand Strategy from 1940 to the Present* (Ithaca, NY: Cornell University Press, 2006) and it fits for the classic Paul Kennedy, *Grand Strategies in War and Peace* (New Haven, CT: Yale University Press, 1991), esp. ch. 10.
5. Christopher Clark, *The Sleepwalkers: How Europe Went to War in 1914* (New York: Harper Perennial, 2014).
6. David Reynolds, *The Long Shadow: The Legacies of the Great War in the Twentieth Century* (New York: W.W. Norton, 2014); Susan Pedersen, *The Guardians: The League of Nations and the Crisis of Empire* (New York: Oxford University Press, 2015); Adam Tooze, *The Deluge: The Great War, America, and the Remaking of the Global Order, 1916–1931* (New York: Viking, 2014).
7. Clark, *Sleepwalkers*, see framing sections.
8. Julia Irwin, *Making the World Safe: The American Red Cross and a Nation's Humanitarian Awakening* (New York: Oxford University Press, 2013); Michael

Thompson, *For God and Globe: Christian Internationalism in the United States between the Great War and the Cold War* (Ithaca, NY: Cornell University Press, 2015); Benjamin Trueblood, *The Two Hague Conferences and Their Results* (Boston: American Peace Society, 1914).

9. Erez Manela, *The Wilsonian Moment: Self-determination and the International Origins of Anticolonial Nationalism* (New York: Oxford University Press, 2007).

10. Here I intend the wide-openness of meaning, similar to how Wilson's message was heard and interpreted in vastly different ways. For example, this could be taken to suggest that US leadership carries with it a certain promise among nationalist anti-colonial movements; or that it has the potential to shape those nationalist anti-colonial movements; or as it regards the "potential work" that "US leadership does" around the world. Indeed, in this sense US leadership could be taken as inspirational, active, both, or even to some extent, neither.

11. In this case we can better see that by privileging the post–World War II era—and such Cold War organizing concepts as containment—as archetypal strategies, I argue that we miss perhaps the central feature of state and non-state internationalist thought during and even despite the "Wilsonian moment."

12. Manela, *Wilsonian Moment*, 225. Here I am most heavily indebted to Manela's conclusion, which makes this point far better than I can, as well as to Winter's comments on the stakes of the Wilsonian Moment. In terms of the epoch ushered in by the war, Jay Winter asks a great question: "Who could have imagined that the decision these men took to award rights to Shandong Province, formerly held by Germany, not to China but to Japan would lead to major rioting and the formation of the Chinese Communist Party?"

13. Frank Ninkovich, *The Wilsonian Century: US Foreign Policy since 1900* (Chicago: University of Chicago Press, 1999).

14. Christopher McKnight Nichols, *Promise and Peril: America at the Dawn of a Global Age* (Cambridge, MA: Harvard University Press, 2011), chs. 5–6; Robert Ferrell, *Peace in Their Time: The Origins of the Kellogg-Briand Pact* (New York: W.W. Norton, 1969); Oona Hathaway and Scott Shapiro, *The Internationalists: How a Radical Plan to Outlaw War Remade the World* (New York: Simon and Schuster, 2017).

15. See the great Jay Winter interview and remarks related to the global World War I: Zeithistorische Forschungen/Studies in Contemporary History 2014, "Global Perspectives on World War I, a Roundtable Discussion," http://www.zeithistorische-forschungen.de/?q=node/5009 (accessed November 4, 2015).

16. Ninkovich, *Wilsonian Century*, 66–67.

17. Charles Hill, *Grand Strategies: Literature, Statecraft, and World Order* (New Haven, CT: Yale University Press, 2010), prologue, 88.

18. Charles Edel, *Nation Builder: John Quincy Adams and the Grand Strategy of the Republic* (Cambridge, MA: Harvard University Press, 2014), 5.

19. Akira Iriye, *Cultural Internationalism and World Order* (Baltimore: Johns Hopkins University Press, 1997), 2–3.

20. Charles Hill, *Grand Strategies: Literature, Statecraft, and World Order* (New Haven, CT: Yale University Press, 2010), prologue, 88.

21. Iriye, *Cultural Internationalism*, 2.

22. Jutta Weldes, *Constructing the National Interest: The United States and the Cuban Missile Crisis* (Minneapolis: University of Minnesota Press, 1999), 10. See also Carnes Lord, "American Strategic Culture," in *Legal and Moral Constraints on Low-Intensity Conflict*, ed. Alberto R. Coll, James S. Ord, and Stephen A. Rose (Newport, RI: Naval War College Press, 1995), 266. For another brief rendering of my view of the work that an expanded understanding of "grand strategy" can do at the intersection of intellectual history and the US role in the world, Nichols, "The US in the World: The Significance of an Isolationist Tradition," ch. 13 in *American Labyrinth: Intellectual History for Complicated Times*, ed. Raymond Haberski Jr. and Andrew Hartman (Ithaca, NY: Cornell University Press, 2018).

23. Glenda Sluga, *Internationalism in the Age of Nationalism* (Philadelphia: University of Pennsylvania Press, 2013), chs. 1–2.

24. Thanks for insights on this to Trygve Throntveit and Lloyd Ambrosius, as well as Thomas Knock, John Milton Cooper Jr., John Thomson, and Arthur Link.

25. Woodrow Wilson, Fourteen Points Address to Joint Session of Congress, January 8, 1918, *PPWW: War & Peace*, 1: 162. This speech, its overriding worldview, the World War I crucible moment that gave it shape, and the American internationalisms it informed are peculiarly absent from most thinking about grand strategy. It is also notable in its absence from Michael Hunt's erudite *Ideology and US Foreign Policy* (New Haven, CT: Yale University Press, 1987) and from some newer work on global intellectual history as well.

26. See John Thompson, *Woodrow Wilson* (London: Pearson, 2002), ch. 6, esp. 160–168, for a good brief assessment of this historical context and how Wilson conceived of his program and how, in turn, his proclamation came to be regarded as the singular comprehensive statement of war aims.

27. David Milne astutely depicts Wilson's Fourteen Points within a nuanced view of how Wilson blended both diplomatic art and elements of science: *Worldmaking: The Art and Science of American Diplomacy* (New York: Farrar, Straus and Giroux, 2015), 112.

28. Stephen Wertheim, "The League That Wasn't: American Designs for a Legalist-Sanctionist League of Nations and the Intellectual Origins of International Organization, 1914–1920," *Diplomatic History* 35 (November 2011), 798. See also Stephen Wertheim, "The Wilsonian Chimera: Why Debating Wilson's Vision Hasn't Saved American Foreign Relations," *White House Studies* 10 (2011), 343–359. Indeed, historians of internationalism, all too often have missed an essential point that Wertheim's several articles have clarified: namely, that international law was relatively eclipsed in the founding of the League.

29. To Henry Kissinger, this amounted to a grand strategy, though he did not use the term, remarking in *Diplomacy* that the grand-scale US entry into the world system was epochal. "Woodrow Wilson told the Europeans that, henceforth, the international system should be based not on the balance of power but on ethnic self-determination, that their security should depend not on military alliances but on collective security, and that their diplomacy should no longer be conducted secretly

by experts but on the basis of 'open agreements, only arrived at.'" Henry Kissinger, *Diplomacy* (New York: Simon & Schuster, 1994), 19–20.

30. Foreseeing the insights developed in Charles Edel's chapter in this volume, the League to Enforce Peace (LEP) even modeled one key postwar document embodying their legal-international grand strategy on the Federalist papers: see *The Covenanter: An American Exposition of the Covenant of the League of Nations* (1919). The LEP also was a transnational movement more than it was national, or at least parochially national for the British and French "league" societies and unions.

31. For my take on the Wilson legacy, see Christopher McKnight Nichols, "The Wilson Legacy, Domestic and International," in *A Companion to Warren G. Harding, Calvin Coolidge, and Herbert Hoover*, ed. Katherine A. S. Sibley (Malden, MA: Wiley-Blackwell, 2014), 9–33.

32. Louise Knight, *Citizen: Jane Addams and the Struggle for Democracy*. (Chicago: University of Chicago Press, 2005).

33. Jane Addams, *The Second Twenty Years at Hull House* (New York: Macmillan, 1930), 7.

34. Trygve Throntveit, "The Fable of the Fourteen Points: Woodrow Wilson and National Self-Determination," *Diplomatic History* 35 (June 2011), 446.

35. The examples detailed in Manela's *Wilsonian Moment* are indicative of what Wilsonianism helped to generate worldwide; here we must also add emergent forms of black internationalism and peace internationalism as well as renewed efforts at religious mission and moral reform. See Ian Tyrrell, *Reforming the World: The Creation of America's Moral Empire* (Princeton, NJ: Princeton University Press, 2010).

36. Trygve Throntveit, *Power without Victory: Woodrow Wilson and the American Internationalist Experiment* (Chicago: University of Chicago Press, 2017).

37. Emily S. Rosenberg, *A World Connecting, 1870–1945* (Cambridge, MA: Harvard University Press, 2012), 839–840.

38. Tyrrell, *Reforming the World*, 219. See also Ian Tyrrell, *Woman's World/Woman's Empire: The Women's Christian Temperance Union in International Perspective, 1880–1930* (Chapel Hill: University of North Carolina Press, 1991). Susan Pedersen, *Guardians*, 4–5.

39. Merle Curti, *Peace or War* (New York: W.W. Norton, 1936), 273

40. W. E. B. Du Bois, "African Roots of the War" (1915), in *The Oxford W.E.B. Du Bois Reader*, ed. Eric Sundquist (New York: Oxford University Press, 1996), 520.

41. Du Bois, *Reader*, 30–32. Because of the wartime controversy, Du Bois's reputation as an "unbending opponent of racial discrimination" was damaged alongside what Mark Ellis depicts as the "deepened divisions between various factions in the increasingly vigorous black political vanguard." See "'Closing Ranks' and 'Seeking Honors': W. E. B. Du Bois in World War I," *Journal of American History* 79 (June 1992), 96. See also my analysis of Du Bois in World War I as allied with the *New Republic* pro-war progressive intelligentsia, and the longer trajectory of his anti-imperialism since the late nineteenth century, in *Promise and Peril*.

42. Keisha Blain, "Teaching Black Internationalism and Americanah," essay originally appearing on the blog of the African American Intellectual History Society (AAIHS), November 2014, available on the Blog of the American Studies Journal: https://amsj.

blog/2015/01/27/teaching-black-internationalism-and-americanah/ (accessed June 8, 2020); see also, Keisha Blain, *Set the World on Fire: Black Internationalist Women and the Global Struggle for Freedom* (Philadelphia: University of Pennsylvania Press, 2018).

43. W. E. B. Du Bois, "Dusk of Dawn," in *The Oxford W.E.B. Du Bois Reader*, ed. Eric Sundquist (New York: Oxford University Press, 1996), 285.

44. Keisha Blain, "For the Rights of Dark People in Every Part of the World: Pearl Sherrod, Black Internationalist Feminism, and Afro-Asian Politics during the 1930s," *Souls* 17:1–2 (June 2015), 90–112; Joyce Blackwell, *No Peace without Freedom: Race and the Women's International League for Peace and Freedom 1915–1975* (Carbondale: Southern Illinois University Press, 2004).

45. Roderick Bush, *The End of White World Supremacy: Black Internationalism and the Problem of the Color Line* (Philadelphia: Temple University Press, 2009), 51.

46. W. E. B. Du Bois, "The Shape of Fear" (1926), in *The Oxford W.E.B. Du Bois Reader*, ed. Eric Sundquist (New York: Oxford University Press, 1996), 386.

47. Mary Dudziak, *Cold War, Civil Rights: Race and the Image of American Democracy* (Princeton, NJ: Princeton University Press, 2000); Carol Anderson, *Eyes Off the Prize: The United Nations and the African American Struggle for Human Rights, 1944–1955* (Cambridge: Cambridge University Press, 2003).

48. David Levering Lewis, among others, also makes this point. On nonalignment and black internationalism, see Robert Rakove, *Kennedy, Johnson, and the Nonaligned World* (Cambridge: Cambridge University Press, 2012); Christopher Lee, ed., *Making a World after Empire: The Bandung Moment and Its Political Afterlives* (Athens: Ohio University Press, 2010). See also Keisha Blain's forthcoming book on black internationalism, and two online essays of Blain's on the website of the African American Intellectual History Society, "Teaching Black Internationalism and Americanah": http://www.aaihs.org/teaching-black-internationalism-and-americanah/ and "Bibliography of Black Internationalism": http://www.aaihs.org/a-bibliography-of-black-internationalism/ (both accessed April 2, 2016).

49. Paraphrasing from Wilson, Throntveit argued that "the League he eventually asked Americans to join reflected the cultural prejudices of its designers—including Wilson—its capacity for self-correction under the pressure of world opinion was, in fact, its defining feature." "Fable of the Fourteen Points," 446.

50. Adriane Lentz-Smith, *Freedom Struggles: African American and World War I* (Cambridge, MA: Harvard University Press, 209), 139.

51. Christopher Hemmer, *American Pendulum: Recurring Debates in US Grand Strategy* (Ithaca, NY: Cornell University Press, 2015), 26

52. Trygve Throntveit, *Power without Victory: Woodrow Wilson and the American Internationalist Experiment* (Chicago: University of Chicago Press, 2017), 13.

53. Cited in Trygve Throntveit, *Power without Victory Woodrow Wilson and the American Internationalist Experiment* (Chicago, IL: University of Chicago Press, 2017), 306.

54. Nichols, *Promise and Peril*, ch. 6, conclusion.

55. Ibid., ch. 6.

56. Report in *New York Call*, December 8, 1922.

57. Borah, "The Fetish of Force," *Forum* 74 (August 1925), 240–45. See Claudius Johnson, *Borah of Idaho* (Seattle: University of Washington Press, 1967 [1936]), ch. 17, "Anti-Imperialist," 336–353; *New York Times*, January 9, 1930, not long before American forces left Haiti.

58. Robert Johnson, *The Peace Progressives and American Foreign Relations* (Cambridge, MA: Harvard University Press, 1995), 178.

59. Mark Philip Bradley, *The World Reimagined: Americans and Human Rights in the Twentieth Century* (New York: Cambridge University Press, 2016).

60. Hal Brands, *What Good Is Grand Strategy? Power and Purpose in American Statecraft from Harry S. Truman to George W. Bush* (Ithaca, NY: Cornell University Press, 2014), 1, http://plato.stanford.edu/archives/spr2014/entries/epistemology/ (accessed March 15, 2016).

9

Franklin Roosevelt, the New Deal, and Grand Strategy

Constructing the Postwar Order

Elizabeth Borgwardt

"There should have been a Secretary of the Future," observed novelist, social critic, and World War II veteran Kurt Vonnegut. Any putative secretary of the future in the US executive branch would in effect be a "grand strategist"— gaming out long-term, big-picture scenarios not only linked to a vision of the national interest but also designed to shape the responses of allies and rivals alike.[1]

Yet President Franklin Delano Roosevelt (FDR), often criticized as a hasty, improvisational, and short-term thinker, served in certain ways as his own secretary of the future in the World War II era. By 1941, FDR and his key advisers were distilling some hard-won wisdom from their trial-and-error approaches in devising what had become known as the New Deal and applying them to the world's burgeoning international crises. These policymakers and analysts were also seeking to sidestep many of the perceived mistakes of President Woodrow Wilson at the end of the First World War.[2]

The key, for Roosevelt, was a New Deal–inspired set of ideas and institutions that animated a capacious reframing of the national interest.[3] Internationalizing the New Deal meant reconfiguring the playing field of world politics in three broad, institutional realms:

Collective security through the United Nations, especially the UN Security Council;

    Economic stability through the Bretton Woods institutions as originally conceived (including the International Monetary Fund and the World

Bank), and also through subsidiary organizations of the UN such as the International Labor Organization; and finally,

Rule of law institutions addressing concerns about accountability—notably through the Nuremberg and Tokyo War Crimes Trials, at one point intended to pave the way for a permanently sitting International Criminal Court, as well as through a revived International Court of Justice (for inter-state disputes not of a criminal nature).

These three institutional pillars—collective security, economic stability, and accountability through rule of law—are usually what contemporary international relations specialists mean when they refer to "the postwar international order."[4] What made this institutionally focused scaffolding into "grand strategy"—as opposed to just a fancy term for long-term planning—was the way any resulting improvement to the functioning of the international order was dependent on negotiation and diplomacy. The strategic element was the necessity of anticipating and accommodating how others would likely—or even just possibly—react. Proposals needed to be crafted in order to advantage one's own side, to be sure, but also to benefit other players enough for them to say "yes."[5]

All three sets of institutions also involved what social scientists like to call a certain "cabining" or constraining of sovereignty for the sake of such coordination and cooperation. It is precisely these three postwar pillars that were energetically hewed away by the policies and personnel of the early Trump administration. While conservative Republicans in the United States have long been intent on shredding the fabric of the domestic New Deal, the Trumpian order of Republican operatives are equally as focused on ending the New Deal as grand strategy, with its attendant institutional expressions of US leadership worldwide.[6]

There is no claim here that this liberal institutional ordering is in any way ideal. As any number of critics have been quick to highlight, by the 1970s, New Deal social liberalism had evolved into free market neoliberalism, quite explicitly abandoning any kind of aspirational economic justice orientation along the way. Nevertheless, Trumpian attacks from 2017 through 2020 on these three institutional pillars were still a terrible idea, as our study of history suggests here.

Grand Strategy as "Security"

Many of the programs of FDR's New Deal had sought to expand the boundaries of security at home, based on the perceived lessons of the early years of the Great Depression. For example, one explicit purpose of "Social Security" was to help to short-circuit civil unrest. Yet for the most creative New Deal administrators, security meant much more than simply stability. Expanding the capacity of a widening swath of Americans to participate in a more prosperous and hopeful future may indeed have served to stabilize capitalism. But widening these circles of inclusion was also intended to entrench—and even to improve upon—the practice of democracy. Many of these New Deal programs were designed to sand down some of the sharpest edges of the spiking inequalities generated by the free enterprise system.[7]

To be sure, the domestic New Deal programs aimed at expanding opportunities and improving standards of living also starkly reflected the limits of the American social imagination. Social Security programs made a point of excluding agricultural and domestic workers, for example—that is to say, segments of the economy with high proportions of African American participation. Electrification programs tended to benefit rural areas while many youth employment programs generally assisted urban dwellers, but in both cases black exclusion was the norm, and by design. Southern senators, in particular—virtually all of them Democrats in this era—often explicitly demanded fencing out African American citizens as a price of "party solidarity" and white political participation in FDR's reformist initiatives.[8]

Just because New Deal programs sought to expand the idea of "security" to encompass economic and social security—within the arguably rather crabbed demographic confines referenced above—did not mean that the concept was therefore confined to domestic dimensions, however. Such a perspective would discount the powerful anxieties glowering on the international horizon in the unsettled strategic landscape of the late 1930s. Whether Americans looked out over the Atlantic or the Pacific late in the interwar era, the idea of "security" had never exclusively been economic or domestic.[9]

By the time the United States joined the ongoing war effort, devastation across the European landscape and the economic leverage offered by America's wartime boom combined to make the United States a willing leader in designing New Deal–style models for multilateral institutions for the postwar era. As Charles Merriam, a political science professor working for the National Resources Planning Board observed in 1941,

There are two great objectives of democracies in the field of world relationships:

I. The security of a jural order for the world in which decisions are made on the basis of justice rather than violence.
II. The fullest development of the national resources of all nations and the fullest participation of all peoples in the gains of civilization.[10]

The linkage of these two sets of objectives in "world relationships" as a matter of public policy was a direct outgrowth of the perceived lessons of the New Deal.

Lawyers and other Roosevelt administration officials who participated in drafting and negotiating the terms of the UN charter, the Bretton Woods charters, and the Nuremberg charter later in the war often communicated among themselves and with other departments and officials, both in the United States and overseas, about what they thought they were doing and why. They tended to describe themselves as architects drawing up constitutive blueprints that would fill in concrete content behind abstract statements of freedoms and rights, using institutions to entrench and extend order, prosperity, and legitimacy. As a 1944 editorial in *The Nation* proclaimed, "Only a New Deal for the world, more far-reaching and consistent than our own faltering New Deal, can prevent the coming of World War III."[11]

"Freedom from Fear and Want"

As early as the summer of 1940, FDR had been asked at a press conference how he might "write the next peace." He began to speak about this New Deal–infused agenda as a set of war aims, most notably in his January 1941 "Four Freedoms" address and over six months later in his joint statement with Prime Minister Winston Churchill of Britain, the "Atlantic Charter" of early August 1941.

In his State of the Union address, Roosevelt had described "four essential human freedoms"—freedom of speech and expression, freedom from want, and freedom from fear—as needing to take effect "everywhere in the world" for true security to be possible. He called for "the protection of human rights—everywhere in the world." FDR elaborated, "Freedom means the supremacy of human rights everywhere. Our support goes to those who struggle to gain these rights or keep them."[12]

One noteworthy dimension of the four freedoms address was accordingly its international scope. Presidential adviser Harry Hopkins noted, in conversation with FDR, that the repeated phrase "everywhere in the world" was perhaps too ambitious, "cover[ing] an awful lot of territory, Mr. President." He warned, "I don't know how interested Americans are going to be in the people of Java." "I'm afraid they'll have to be someday, Harry," a ruminative Roosevelt reportedly replied. "The world is getting so small that even the people in Java are getting to be our neighbors now."[13]

Later that year, Roosevelt was seeking to capitalize on the favorable attention the four freedoms speech had generated by propounding, in his words, "some kind of public statement of the objectives in international relations in which the Government of the United States believed." The president indicated he was seeking to use the framework of the four freedoms to advance the cause of "keeping alive some principles of international law, some principles of moral and human decency," in both the United States and world public opinion. Although Roosevelt was himself a lawyer, this was unusual language, as he rarely spoke about international law explicitly.[14]

The resulting Atlantic Charter soon became best known for its resonant evocation of the earlier four freedoms address, a phrase about establishing a particular kind of postwar order—a peace "which will afford assurance that all the men in all the lands may live out their lives in freedom from fear and want." An early British draft of the proposed joint declaration described the document as a list of "certain principles which they [Roosevelt and Churchill] both accept for guidance in the framing of their policy and on which they base their hopes for a better world." The Atlantic Charter purported to sketch a postwar world in broad strokes, calling for self-determination of peoples, freer trade, and several New Deal–style social welfare provisions. Released as a 400-word telegram, the document also mentioned a future "wider and permanent system of general security"—the first reference in a bilateral document at this "high political" level to what would become the United Nations organization—as well as arms control and freedom of the seas.[15]

One of the more eyebrow-raising aspects of these proclamations was simply their timing: it was a risky step to be meeting with a foreign leader and invoking a postwar world, however aspirational, months before the United States was actually in the war. FDR was mindful that "the isolationists at home were screaming bloody murder," and he was concerned enough to leave behind a decoy Secret Service officer fishing on the Cape Cod Canal—complete with cigarette holder, pince-nez, and Fala the dog—while the president departed in secret for the site of the Atlantic Conference off the coast of Newfoundland. Sensitive to these American political constraints, British negotiators offered successive drafts that avoided formal treaty language or the suggestion of a military alliance.[16]

What legal scholar Edward Laing has called the Atlantic Charter's "flexible constitutional essence" also served as a focal point for movements promoting an expanded role for multilateral institutions. The Atlantic Charter prefigured the collective security articulated in the UN charter, the rule-of-law orientation of the Nuremberg charter, and even the Keynesian approach of the Bretton Woods charters. As noted, early planning memos for subsequent, detailed blueprints such as the charters of the United Nations, Nuremberg, and Bretton Woods all drew their inspiration and in many cases their broad provisions from the Atlantic Charter.[17]

The Atlantic Charter was part of an effort on Roosevelt's part to prepare the American public for an increasingly activist, multilateralist foreign policy. In 1943 Roosevelt expressed exasperation with what he perceived as his critics' literalism and negativity: "I am everlastingly angry at those who assert vociferously that the four freedoms and the Atlantic Charter are nonsense because they are unattainable," commented FDR, in a peroration he wrote himself for a speech marking the end of the First Quebec Conference in August 1943. The president continued testily: "If these people had lived a century and a half ago they would have sneered and said that the Declaration of Independence was utter piffle."[18]

A number of US postwar planners did indeed seek to siphon off some drams of legitimacy from America's founding documents, at least rhetorically. Some analogized the Atlantic Charter to the Declaration of Independence, and the subsequent set of more detailed institutional charters to the US Constitution. Just as the young FDR had been an avid consumer of the strategic seapower theories of Alfred Thayer Mahan (which drew heavily on analogies with ancient Rome), so too were these young New Dealers designing roadmaps for the future by tracing over parchments from the past.

By contrast, Roosevelt-hating journalist John Flynn wrote scornfully that the Atlantic Charter was a "fake document" that was "nothing more than a publicity stunt." Anti-New Dealers and anti-interventionists were by no means the only critics. By the end of the war, images of "war aims" and "what we are fighting for" had contributed to creating and raising expectations about the justice and legitimacy of any proposed postwar order, in the United States and abroad. People around the world who heard or read FDR's words were inspired by them and often adapted the speech's underlying ideas to support their own struggles against racism, in favor of economic justice, or in support of more thoroughgoing international cooperation.[19]

As with the programs of the domestic New Deal, these initiatives aimed at a new postwar architecture may be defined as much by their omissions as by their inclusions. Capacious designs and ambiguous rhetoric ducked problems of colonial legacies and economic justice, as various energized constituencies had of course noted from the very beginning. The editor of a West African newspaper asked, "Are we fighting for security of Europeans to enjoy the four freedoms while West Africa continues on pre-war status? We naturally feel we are entitled to know what we are fighting for, and are anxious to know what our position is to be in the coming new world order."[20]

This postwar institutional order may accordingly be framed as somewhat analogous to the domestic New Deal: it was both progressive and conservative, forward-looking and backward-looking, imaginative and hidebound, inflating and constricting global citizenship at the same time. Many critics of these postwar institutions have asserted that injustice and inequality were, in essence, baked into the cake of the postwar international order. Other skeptical voices in the United States—styling themselves "nationalists" or "unilateralists"—have continued to argue that these institutions simply gave away too much cake to others. Liberal internationalists, by contrast, have framed the shortcomings of these institutions as a kind of frosting that could somehow be scraped away and replaced. But the static image itself highlights where all of these approaches are somewhat off-kilter: international systems are dynamic. They are not cakes; they are systems. Their dynamics reflect values and leadership, and when the values, leadership, and surrounding cultures evolve, so do the workings of the systems.

The Maximalist Vision: "A New Deal for the World"

Political scientists Daniel Duedney and John Ikenberry have recently referenced these "liberal internationalist organizations and regimes" of the New Deal as a kind of "third founding" for the United States.[21] In their estimation, "the greatness of the United States during the 'American Century' rested on a set of institutional foundations, both domestically and internationally." They continue:

At home, the Roosevelt revolution forged the modernized government that re-established economic growth, political legitimacy, and social peace. Abroad, the Roosevelt Administration, in winning World War II, established the United States as the pre-eminent great power in the international system and started putting into place the panoply of international organizations and regimes that make up the postwar liberal international order.[22]

Historian Carol Anderson offers the important reminder that in addition to eliding the New Deal's exclusion of issues of racial justice on the domestic front, these kinds of sweeping assessments also map similar exclusions onto the Global South. It was nevertheless Roosevelt's personal vision, as well as the vision of others on the left wing of the New Deal, that such a social democratic system was premised on expanding to become more inclusive over time.[23]

More than this, ambitious international visions for security, stability, and accountability drew power from domestic ambitions. As legal scholar Cass Sunstein summarizes, "the threat from Hitler and the Axis powers broadened the New Deal's commitment to security and strengthened the nation's appreciation of human vulnerability." In another section of his four freedoms address, FDR had spelled out his ideas about the "basic things expected by our people of their political and economic systems." This list served as the basis for a more elaborate "Economic Bill of Rights" devised by one of the most aggressively progressive New Deal agencies, the National Resources Planning Board (NRPB), and widely reprinted in a pamphlet titled "Our Freedoms and Rights." Charles Merriam, the NRPB vice chair quoted earlier, offered a summary of these "fundamentals which underlie a democratic program guaranteeing social justice" in his 1941 Godkin Lecture on Democracy at Harvard University. This Economic Bill of Rights, which included a right to education, health care, "a job at a fair wage," and "equal access to minimum security," was summarized by Merriam with the pious hope that "some day it will dawn upon us that all of the clauses in the Preamble to the Constitution are worth fighting for."[24]

Such a "renewed summation of the New Deal," in the words of another one of Roosevelt's speechwriters, marked what Sunstein explained as "a basis for a broadened understanding of what a nation would do if it were genuinely committed to ensuring the 'security' of its citizens. The threat to security from abroad was a reason to strengthen and rethink the idea of security at home." And vice versa: the maximalist multilateralist vision in the early World War II years had included a robust UN system capable of repelling aggression and a full World Trade Organization; also, the Nuremberg and Tokyo trials were meant to lead the way to a permanently sitting International Criminal Court. FDR saw the postwar UN as possibly having its own air force to constrain and punish aggressors. John Maynard Keynes's early drafts of the Bretton Woods institutions envisioned the World Bank and the International Monetary Fund as a global engine to reduce economic injustice. Francis Biddle, the American judge at the main Nuremberg trial, wrote to President Truman in 1946 that "the time has now come to set about drafting a code of international criminal law" that would "reaffirm the principles of the Nuremberg Charter" and lay the groundwork for a permanently sitting international criminal court.[25]

By 1949, however, this maximalist multilateral vision had diminished considerably, at home and abroad. In one sense, perhaps this is a tale of institutional declension. On the international plane, grandiose visions such as a robustly functioning United Nations based on the sovereign equality of all states, a Bretton Woods system that would actually support development, and a permanently sitting International Criminal Court had given way to a series of paler and less ambitious measures, often bounded in both time and scope.

A set of miniaturized institutions had emerged as muffled echoes of these ambitious wartime klaxons: an ambitiously multilateral UN Relief and Rehabilitation Association was wrapping up by 1947; substantial Marshall Plan aid to former European Allies (and not including the Soviet Union) was US-based and as much an instrument of geopolitical dominance as an aid to postwar reconstruction. Twelve slightly anemic subsequent Nuremberg trials were run exclusively by the Americans in 1946–49, in the wake of the flagship International Military Tribunal. The Bretton Woods agreement ginned up a wheezing General Agreement on Tariffs and Trade (GATT) mechanism instead of Keynes's earlier vision of a more robust World Trade Organization and regional security organizations such as the North Atlantic Treaty Organization (NATO) growing up alongside the universalist United Nations as a partial replacement for an increasingly sclerotic UN.[26]

The expansive briefs of these organizations quickly fell victim to rapidly changing postwar political configurations—notably the Cold War, of course—as well as some of the consequences of rapid decolonization. The United Nations Charter, for example, was out of date before the ink was dry on its fifty signatures. Bluntly, the Charter and resulting United Nations Organization was unable either to anticipate or to respond in agile ways to three of the most tectonic shifts of the immediate postwar era. First, as noted, the advent of the most virulent phase of the Cold War—which might be dated from Winston Churchill's 1946 "Iron Curtain" speech—quickly reconfigured the international diplomatic landscape. Second, rapid decolonization meant that the initial pro-US majority in the UN General Assembly soon evaporated with the proliferation of unaligned and anti-colonial nation-states. International legal scholar José Alvarez has noted the irony of how "the United Nations, intended to institutionalize an effective collective security system, [became] the greatest state-producing device in the history of the world." A third factor was the advent of the nuclear age, with its attendant high stakes and disproportionate destructive power. The design of the UN had been hobbled by the unwillingness of its great-power founders to address the legacies of colonialism, economic injustice, or other violations of human rights with any vision of what it might mean for "democratizing" winds to blow both at home and abroad.[27]

Ambitions for the social democratic provisions of the New Deal were shrinking on the home front as well. The aspirations of the Economic Bill of Rights, discussed above, collided with the realities of an increasingly Republican-dominated Congress. Rather than an expansion of democracy—improving well-being and the prospect for participation for an ever-wider swath of US citizens—the key provisions of the Economic Bill of Rights emerged instead as a social welfare program: the 1944 GI Bill. Veterans were an easier sell among conservatives as they were "deserving" citizens who had sacrificed for the homeland, compared to ordinary citizens who had made no similar sacrifices. The "GI Bill of Rights" included mortgage assistance, funding for education, business loans, medical care, and extended unemployment assistance. The GI Bill was in effect a shriveled version of the New Deal Economic Bill of Rights, with an echo of the latter's mission of increasing economic stability through reducing inequality. Roosevelt had envisioned various categories of civilians becoming eligible for GI-type benefits over time in an ever-widening circle of inclusion, a process labeled "social citizenship" by the sociologist T. H. Marshall. To be sure, the veterans' program was a significant commitment: by 1948, almost half of US enrollees in higher education were GI Bill beneficiaries. As Ira Katznelson summarizes it, "No other New Deal initiative had as great an impact on changing the country."[28]

Nevertheless, part of the point of the GI Bill as enacted was exclusion. The price of its approval had been appeasing southern legislators with a system of local administration for the benefits, for example, which meant in practice that assistance to African American veterans was slowed to a trickle. Women veterans as well as those discharged dishonorably, or those discharged on an "undesirable" basis (often homosexuals), were also routinely denied. As historian Margot Canaday has argued, the workings of the GI Bill reinforced the image of the normative "first class" American citizen as male, white, and straight.[29]

Even this constricted demographic was a wee bit suspect, at least if recipients were poor. Anxieties lingered from the World War I era that returning servicemen might turn into "roving armies of jobless veterans" like the ill-fated Bonus Army veterans camping out in Hoovervilles during the Depression. Conservative legislators believed that rewarding veterans for their roles as breadwinners and family men would domesticate these returning servicemen in desirable ways, whereas extending benefits to others in need risked undermining the "moral fiber" of the country, in the words of one opponent of the New Deal, by encouraging "laziness," in the words of another such skeptic. Just as the Marshall Plan symbolized how far the United States had moved on from true multilateralism, so too the GI Bill suggested "how much further [Congress] had moved from New Deal aspirations to distribute state resources broadly among its citizenry," in Canaday's incisive assessment.[30]

Present at the Destruction

The twenty-first-century incarnations of FDR's domestic opponents have been focused on dismantling the enduring legacies of the New Deal. What former Trump presidential adviser Steve Bannon has called the "deconstruction" of the administrative state has long been a feature of some Republican agendas. Early examples have included inaugurating a poorly designed "Muslim ban," hollowing out the State Department, cutting various cabinet-level agencies, cutting taxes for the super wealthy, eviscerating public health and education programs, gutting the Voting Rights Act, deregulating polluters and predatory lenders, and stressing the signature initiative of building a wall to exclude outsiders—including asylum-seekers.[31]

Reducing equality and access to resources while turning a blind eye to corruption is part of a process that is of course not limited to the United States. The United Kingdom, Hungary, Poland, Brazil, the Philippines, Nicaragua, Venezuela, and Russia, among others, are also slipping downward in what one investigative non-governmental organization (NGO) calls their "Freedom Index." Rather than a post–Cold War vision of democracy triumphant, the breakup of the Soviet Union seems to have resulted of rivulets of corruption and oligarchic practices seeping throughout the industrialized world—or perhaps more accurately, in such practices becoming more widespread and acceptable where they already existed. That these aspects of the Russian model would prove to be more generalizable than the much-vaunted spread of democratizing forces is one by-product of abandoning equality as a focus for domestic policy.[32]

In the United States, this anti-governmentalism and whole-cloth opposition to the New Deal order at home is also reflected in a rending of the institutional fabric abroad. Ikenberry notes that "as their prospects dim, the willingness of the American public to support an ambitious American role in the world is understandably in decline." Once again, the outside reflects the inside. Fighting "globalists" has entailed withdrawal from the Paris Climate Accord, the Iran Nuclear deal, and the INF arms control treaty with Russia, as well as expressing a generalized hostility to multilateral institutions such as the UN, the International Criminal Court, and even NATO. Under the banner of "America First"—once the title of anti-semite Gerald L. K. Smith's 1943 political party—Trump officials moved quickly to spin a narrative reframing human rights concerns as obstacles to national security interests, promoting what reporter Jackson Diehl has called "values-free foreign policy." Yet it is increasingly clear that support for perpetrators of massive human rights abuses further fuels anti-Americanism and highlights the role of the United States as an ever-more-unreliable ally. Or, as Ikenberry tartly summarizes it: "All across the horizon of international problem-solving and institution-building, the radical Right has diminished America's ability to lead."[33]

The pillars of collective security, economic stability, and rule of law—however wobbly or weak—supported the structure of the postwar order throughout the Cold War. Political scientists write of the "stickiness" of institutions, and for all their flaws these institutions have had a certain staying power. It is precisely this stickiness that Trump and his associates are working to unglue. In their avid degradation of norms, institutions, and the even the careers of experienced personnel, Trump's policies are not serving to "drain the swamp," in the words of another well-known campaign slogan. Rather, this eager undermining of diplomacy and collaboration is rapidly draining away the very resource that one of FDR's Republican opponents, Wendell Willkie, described as "a gigantic reservoir of good will" toward the American people. "As I see it," Willkie elaborated over seventy-five years ago, "the existence of this reservoir is the biggest political fact of our time."[34] A parched and polluted puddle may soon be all that is left.

"Immune from the Great Cataract of Nonsense"

The Greek historian Dionysius famously asserted that "history is philosophy teaching by examples." In addition to helping us expand our own political imaginations, the study of history may also offer some analytic distance and perspective on our own contemporary assumptions, approaches, and aspirations.

In what might serve as a kind of book-end to the Vonnegut quote about planning for the future that opened this chapter, the British novelist, poet, and literary critic C. S. Lewis wrote: "Most of all, perhaps, we need intimate knowledge of the past." He continued:

> A man who has lived in many places is not likely to be deceived by the errors of his native village: the scholar has lived in many times and is therefore in some degree immune from the great cataract of nonsense that pours from the press and microphone of his own age.[35]

In other words, studying the past may help citizens, scholars, and officials alike to serve as our own "secretaries of the future." Vonnegut's quote opening this essay was actually part of a drawing in some hitherto unpublished notebooks. As part of the self-same image, the novelist and political commentator also offered a sobering reminder of the costs of failing to factor in the perceptions of other parties who will inevitably affect the outcomes of any strategic planning, however intricate or bold. His admonition about how "there ought to have been" a secretary of the future is etched on the side of a bomb plummeting toward earth—too late for the planning, too late for the future.

Notes

1. Kurt Vonnegut, *Armageddon in Retrospect: New and Unpublished Writings on War and Peace* (New York: G. P. Putnam's Sons, 2008), n.p. but near p. 47.

2. On FDR as improvisational, see Warren F. Kimball, *The Juggler: Franklin Roosevelt as Wartime Statesman* (Princeton, NJ: Princeton University Press, 1994). On FDR as seeking to avoid the perceived mistakes of Woodrow Wilson, see Elizabeth Borgwardt, *A New Deal for the World: America's Vision for Human Rights* (Cambridge, MA: Belknap Press of Harvard University Press, 2005) (hereafter *NDFW*), especially chapter 1, "The Ghost of Woodrow Wilson."

3. Roosevelt and his advisers tended to use the term "New Deal" very loosely—as did their many enemies—to refer to "the duty of government to use the combined resources of the nation to prevent distress and to promote the general welfare of all the people." *NDFW* at p.7ff; also see *NDFW* for a discussion of the expanding idea of national security.

4. See, for example, Or Rosenboim, *The Emergence of Globalism: Visions of World Order in Britain and the United States, 1939–1950* (Princeton, NJ: Princeton University Press, 2017); Daniel Deudney and G. John Ikenberry, "Unraveling America the Great," *American Prospect*, March 15, 2016.

5. Making formal and detailed estimates of the thinking of "the other side" is an integral part of the approach to bargaining and negotiation closely associated with legal scholar and practitioner Roger Fisher, whose work included negotiation simulations and other exercises forcing diplomats to "stand in the other side's shoes." See especially Fisher's: *Beyond Machiavelli: Tools for Coping with Conflict*, co-authored with Elizabeth Borgwardt and Andrea Schneider (Cambridge MA: Harvard University Press, 1994), an elaboration on the approaches presented in *Getting to Yes: Negotiating Agreement without Giving In*, 2nd ed., co-authored with William Ury and Bruce Patton (New York: Penguin, 1991) and based on Fisher's consulting experience on conflicts in El Salvador, Guatemala, Cyprus, Iran, and elsewhere.

6. See the articles referenced below on Trump administration attacks on norms and institutions. On the cabining of sovereignty, see Kal Rustiala, "Sovereignty and Multilateralism," *Chicago Journal of International Law* 1 (2000) (revised as UCLA School of Law, Law-Econ Working Paper No. 2000-01). On the early days of the Trump administration's relationship to the neoliberal world order, see Wolfgang Streeck, "Trump and the Trumpists," *Inference: International Review of Science* 3 (2017).

7. See generally Kiran Klaus Patel, *The New Deal: A Global History* (Princeton, NJ: Princeton University Press, 2016). In supplying what is in effect the missing last chapter of Daniel Rodgers's *Atlantic Crossings*, Patel reminds us that many of these New Deal social welfare programs were inspired by European models. See also Wolfgang Schivelbusch, *Three New Deals: Reflections on Roosevelt's America, Mussolini's Italy, and Hitler's Germany, 1933–1939* (New York: Picador, 2006); Daniel Rodgers, *Atlantic Crossings: Social Politics in a Progressive Age* (Cambridge, MA: Belknap Press of Harvard University Press, 1998).

8. Patel, *New Deal*, 74; Ira Katznelson, *Fear Itself: The New Deal and the Origins of Our Time* (New York: Liveright, 2013); Barton J. Bernstein, "The Conservative Achievements of Liberal Reform," in *Toward a New Past: Dissenting Essays in American History*, ed. Barton J. Bernstein, ed. (New York: Pantheon, 1968).

9. *NDFW*, 7; Schivelbusch, *Three New Deals* (on projecting power as part of a New Deal aesthetic), introduction and chapter 5, "Public Works."

10. Quoted in *NDFW*, 52.

11. Freda Kirchwey, "A Program of Action," *The Nation* 158, March 11, 1944, 300.

12. FDR, "Annual Message to Congress, Jan. 6, 1941," available online in text and audio at http://www.americanrhetoric.com/speeches/fdrthefourfreedoms.htm. For text of the 1941 Atlantic Charter, see the Appendix to *NDFW*.

13. Robert E. Sherwood, *Roosevelt and Hopkins: An Intimate History* (New York: Harper, 1948), 231.

14. Hadley Cantril, letter of March 20, 1941 (to Anna Rosenberg for the president), quoted in *NDFW* at 21, 29.

15. Sherwood, *Roosevelt and Hopkins*, 350.

16. "1st British Draft" in FDR's handwriting, dated August 10, 1941, FDR, Papers as President, President's Secretary's Files, Safe File, Box 1, Franklin D. Roosevelt Library, Hyde Park, NY (hereafter FDRL).

17. Edward A. Laing, "The Relevance of the Atlantic Charter for a New World Order," *Indian Journal of International Law* 29 (July-December 1989), 298; George B. Galloway, *Postwar Planning in the United States* (New York: Twentieth Century Fund, 1942). On the Bretton Woods charters as Keynesian, see, for example, Benn Steil, *The Battle of Bretton Woods: John Maynard Keynes, Harry Dexter White and the Making of a New World Order* (Princeton, NJ: Princeton University Press, 2013).

18. FDR quoted in Samuel I. Rosenman, *Working with Roosevelt* New York: Harper, 1952), 387.

19. John T. Flynn, *The Roosevelt Myth* (New York: Devin-Adair, 1948), 386. On various groups adopting FDR's rhetoric for their own purposes, see *NDFW*, 34–35; for a discussion of some analogous expectations raised in various quarters around the world by Woodrow Wilson's World War I–era aspirational rhetoric, see Erez Manela, *The Wilsonian Moment: Self-Determination and the International Origins of Anticolonial Nationalism* (New York: Oxford University Press, 2007).

20. From the editor of the *West African Pilot* to Mr. Winston Churchill, November 15, 1941, Prime Minister's Office Records 4/43A/3, The National Archives, Kew, London, UK; George Padmore, "Nigeria Questions Intent of Atlantic Charter," *Chicago Defender*, January 31, 1942, 12. See also Carol Anderson, "A New Deal for (Most of) the World," H-Peace, H-Net Reviews, August 2006.

21. Daniel Duedney and G. John Ikenberry, "Unraveling America the Great," *American Interest*, March 15, 2016.

22. Ibid.: the first two foundings were the framing of the Constitution, premised on the sovereignty of the people, and the expansion of citizenship heralded by the Reconstruction Amendments in the wake of the US Civil War.

23. Anderson, "A New Deal for (Most of) the World." On Roosevelt's preferences, see Margot Canaday, *The Straight State: Sexuality and Citizenship in Twentieth-Century America* (Princeton, NJ: Princeton University Press, 2012), 143–144.

24. Cass Sunstein, *The Second Bill of Rights: FDR's Unfinished Revolution and Why We Need It More than Ever* (New York: Basic Books, 2004); National Resources Planning Board, "After the War—Toward Security: Freedom From Want," September 1942, President's Secretary's Files, Postwar Planning, Box 157, FDRL; see also James T. Kloppenberg, "Franklin D. Roosevelt: Visionary," *Reviews in American History* 34 (December 2006), 509–520; *NDFW* 51–52.

25. Rosenman, *Working with Roosevelt*, 264; Sunstein, *Second Bill of Rights*; Biddle, quoted in Elizabeth Borgwardt, "'Constitutionalizing' Human Rights: The Rise and Rise of the Nuremberg Principles," in *The Human Rights Revolution: An International History*, ed. Akira Iriye, Petra Goedde, and William Hitchcock (New York: Oxford University Press, 2012), 75.

26. On UNRRA, see Jessica Reinisch, "Internationalism in Relief: The Birth (and Death) of UNRRA," *Past & Present* 210, Supplement 6 (January 2011), 258–289. On the Marshall Plan, see Benn Steil, *The Marshall Plan: Dawn of the Cold War* (New York: Simon & Schuster, 2018). On the subsequent Nuremberg trials, see Kevin Jon Heller, *The Nuremberg Military Tribunals and the Origins of International Criminal Law* (Oxford: Oxford University Press, 2012). On the Bretton Woods institutions, see Steil, *Battle of Bretton Woods*; and Eric Rauchway, *The Money Makers: How Roosevelt and Keynes Ended the Depression, Defeated Fascism, and Secured a Prosperous Peace* (New York: Basic Books, 2015). On NATO, see Timothy Andrews Sayle, *Enduring Alliance: A History of NATO and the Postwar Global Order* (Ithaca, NY: Cornell University Press, 2019).

27. Winston S. Churchill, "The Sinews of Peace" (Iron Curtain Speech), Westminster College, Fulton, MO, March 5, 1946, audio available at www.winstonchurchill.org; José E. Alvarez, "Multilateralism and Its Discontents," *European Journal of International Law* 11 (2000), 393–411, at 395; Mark Mazower, *No Enchanted Palace: The End of Empire and the Ideological Origins of the United Nations* (Princeton, NJ: Princeton University Press, 2009). See, generally, Ibrahim J. Gassama, "A World Made of Violence and Misery: Human Rights as a Failed Project of Liberal Internationalism," *Brooklyn Journal of International Law* 37 (2012), 407–458. Analysts such as Martti Koskenniemi are starting to reframe some of their earlier critiques as somewhat overstated. See, for example, Martti Koskenniemi, "The Many Faces of Sovereignty: Introduction to Critical Legal Thinking," *Kutafin University Law Review* 4 (2017), 282–291.

28. On "deserving" citizens, see Canaday, *Straight State*, 142, 144; T. H. Marshall quoted in Koskenniemi, "The Many Faces of Sovereignty," at 140; Katznelson quoted in Koskenniemi, "The Many Faces of Sovereignty," at 141. See also Kathleen J. Frydl, *The GI Bill* (New York: Cambridge University Press, 2009).

29. Canaday, *Straight State*, 141.

30. Quoted in Canaday, *Straight State*, at 152, 168, in a chapter which includes an extensive discussion of the "domestication" of returning servicemen.

31. See Brian Beutler, "Steve Bannon Is Not Your Friend," *New Republic*, August 22, 2017; Roger Cohen, "The Desperation of Our Diplomats: Why Is Trump Hollowing Out the State Department?," *New York Times*, July 28, 2017.

32. "Democracy in Retreat 2019," with the subsection "The United States in Decline," noting that the countries with the closest tallies to the United States on Freedom House metrics are Belize, Croatia, Greece, Latvia, and Mongolia. Freedom House Report, freedomhouse.org/report/freedom-world/freedom-world-2019. See also Franklin Foer, "Russian-Style Kleptocracy Is Infiltrating America," *The Atlantic*, March 2019.

33. Diehl quoted in Sarah B. Snyder, "Is the Trump Administration Abandoning Human Rights?" *Washington Post*, July 2, 2017; Duedney and Ikenberry, "Unraveling America the Great."

34. Wendell L. Willkie, *One World* (New York: Simon & Schuster, 1943), 284.

35. C. S. Lewis, *The Weight of Glory and Other Addresses* (New York: Macmillan, 1949), 50–51; the excellent essay by Cian O'Driscoll, "Divisions within the Ranks? The Just War Tradition and the Use and Abuse of History," *Ethics & International Affairs* 27 (2013), 47–65 led me to the Lewis quote and the quotation from Dionysius.

10

Foreign Policy Begins at Home

Americans, Grand Strategy, and World War II

Michaela Hoenicke Moore

"Foreign Policy Begins at Home," argued presidential adviser James P. Warburg at the end of World War II. By this he meant that the domestic support that President Franklin D. Roosevelt had mobilized for America's role in the war would be crucial in maintaining the peace. At the same time, Warburg warned of a narrowly conceived nationalism backing the newly found internationalism. It was important to steer away from "dangerous . . . thinking in terms of unilateral action for security and selfish national interest." Instead, Warburg emphasized Roosevelt's theme of interdependence: "Just as we must always remember that our economic prosperity is indivisible from the prosperity of other nations, so we must regard our military power as part of the united power for peace to be exercised by and for the benefit of all peace-loving nations."[1] Warburg's book, published before the November election of 1944, carried a partisan message. For the Jewish German-American banker, the ongoing war was not just a military conflict between the Allies and the Axis but a political crusade against fascism abroad and at home. A committed interventionist by 1940 and deputy director of the Office of War Information's (OWI) Overseas Branch since 1942, Warburg fully embraced Roosevelt's multilateral-cooperative internationalism. His postwar ideas echoed Vice President Henry A. Wallace's progressivist vision of the Century of the Common Man, in turn a rejection of media mogul Henry Luce's nationalist-internationalist American Century. Warburg's book *Foreign Policy Begins at Home* was part of a broader effort to keep Americans alert to the international scene and their country's role in it. While this ultimately bipartisan campaign contributed to a new internationalist consensus, the term internationalism obscures just how divergent the underlying postwar visions were, ranging from the wartime, humanitarian-cooperative spirit to an exceptionalist-triumphalist Cold War mentality.

This chapter offers another look at World War II and its legacies with a view to broader societal debates about America's role in the world, highlighting the tension between grand strategy and democracy. Ordinary citizens were part of these debates to a much greater extent than is generally acknowledged. Apart from opinion and election polls, citizen voices have often been shunned by politicians and scholars, who have dismissed them as ineffective and marginal, deplored them as racist or sectarian, and criticized them as isolationist or detrimental to American strategic interests. Attending to what citizens had to say about their country's international role, especially over the course of the transformative 1940s, brings unsettling questions into clearer focus: What purpose and whose interests do grand visions of foreign policy serve?

World War II holds a near mythical status in American public memory and foreign policy discourse. The "good war" is remembered as a time of national unity and celebrated for the achievements of the "greatest generation." According to conventional understanding, the war brought about a new internationalist consensus that was subsequently used to support the country's new global military role in the Cold War. It produced the anti-appeasement, Munich lesson that portrays diplomacy as weak, ineffectual, at times even immoral, and, correspondingly, validates the use of military force, even preemptive strikes, as effective and necessary. Yet this conventional rendition does not do justice to US wartime strategies and the deeper underlying contestations over ideas and values that America stands for at home and abroad.

World War II and Grand Strategy

The premise of the following exploration is that the 1940s saw not one but two significant shifts in American grand strategy. From 1938 through 1941, Roosevelt led the country from a policy of formal neutrality and staying out of the war to an alliance-based, time-bound war effort against the Axis, giving priority to the defeat of Nazi Germany, requiring significant mobilization at home, and resulting in a global military campaign that kept US casualties comparatively low. From 1945 on, Harry Truman, building on his predecessor's strategy, shifted it once more, transforming it into a long-term American readiness, militarily and politically, to assume global leadership, with allies in supporting roles, against a new enemy, world communism. How did citizens respond to these two versions of American internationalism?

There is no agreement in the literature on whether the foreign policy of Roosevelt—the fox, the juggler, the sphinx—actually amounted to a grand strategy. Yet the dispute over this is more illuminating than the verdict. Definitions of grand strategy identify several rocks on which modern US foreign policies have foundered. Historian John Lewis Gaddis, highlighting the tension between ideas and their realization, defines grand strategy "as the alignment of potentially unlimited aspirations with necessarily limited capabilities." Awarding Roosevelt high marks for being guided by confidence rather than fear, Gaddis observes that what makes a strategy grand is a matter of what is at stake. In World War II, he argues, it was the survival of democracy and capitalism and "it was Roosevelt, more than anyone else, who rescued [both]."[2] David Milne, by contrast, doubts that Roosevelt was capable of grand strategy. Instead Milne shows how those who had grand visions and plans for America's role in the world often failed to calibrate the balance between goals and means.

Christopher Layne's definition, finally, points to a different realm of tension. For him grand strategy is the "meeting point where the international system's geopolitical constraints intersect with a state's domestic political culture and its sense of national identity."[3] In this respect, Roosevelt proved adept as he responded to external events and cobbled together foreign and domestic alliances for shifting and evolving foreign policy goals. The New Deal–inspired Four Freedoms—a recognition of the socioeconomic underpinnings of liberal democracy and an updated version of "life, liberty, and the pursuit of happiness"—served as the ideological centerpiece of the anti-Axis military campaign. But it did not keep the president from working with a white supremacist regime in the American South or a totalitarian dictator abroad.[4]

Two further aspects are of relevance. The demos, that is, the people, in democracy have often been a challenge to grand strategists, provoking wariness or outright mistrust. Roosevelt's pre-war and wartime policies, by contrast, showed a clear recognition of the limits of American power and political will. In other words, the president acted as realist both in terms of grand strategy and with regard to American democracy. Finally, Milne warns about the 1940s American-created postwar liberal world order, ranging from the United Nations and Bretton Woods to European recovery and the Atlantic community, that what looks like a brilliant masterplan was in fact "a series of strategies, plural, advocated by various individuals at different times with different motivations and goals."[5] Historical inquiry thus throws doubt on the concept of grand strategy from two directions: grand plans, more often than not, were not implemented as intended, and what looks like over-arching strategy was, in hindsight, often a hodgepodge of competing plans and agendas.

What Polls Don't Show

Polls are a first and indispensable resource to probe the relationship be-tween the public and foreign policy, between democracy and grand strategy. Political scientist Adam Berinsky confirms in his study of public opinion *In Time of War* that World War II was no exception in the history of how Americans responded to mobilization and war, namely, with patriotic loyalty as well as reasoned skepticism and reluctance. The "good war" was *not* recog-nized at the time as a necessary campaign against evil, it had *not* been a very popular war, and the attack on Pearl Harbor did *not* have a decisive effect of turning an isolationist public into a pro-war public.

The myth of the "good war" obscures the reality of US intervention: that it was preceded by intense intellectual conflicts and political divisions over the wisdom of intervening militarily in Europe—for a second time within a generation. Skepticism and rejection of the interventionists' arguments were fueled by deep and widespread disillusion with Wilsonianism that ranged from pacifist-socialist, through liberal and conservative, to exclusionary-nationalist. The conflict was over conscription, the incompatibility of war and (American) democracy, and the rejection, in hindsight surprisingly pop-ular and principled, of any kind of renewed overseas crusade for democracy, which was decried as a hypocritical cloak for old world–style militarism and imperialism.[6]

Yet there are limits to what surveys can tell us, with their pre-formulated questions aimed at gauging support for official policies. In the 1940s, pollsters were often more interested in interviewing white educated males than a true cross-section of American society.[7] Moreover, elite cue and partisan iden-tification theories do not reveal how deeply and confusingly domestic and foreign policy positions were entwined. There was no clear alignment of pro- and anti-war opinion with Democrats and Republicans. Letters to the pres-ident show New Deal supporters beseeching him "to keep the United States out of this European war," while others assured him that "thousands like me, who may disagree with you on domestic questions, turn with all our faith to

you as the leader of our Country and hope that you with calm determination will continue to lead us in the paths of peace." Conversely, self-identified
Republicans and critics of the administration congratulated Roosevelt on
moving toward military intervention by 1940.[8]

Much of the great debate from 1938 through 1941, ostensibly over US international engagement, was, in fact, over the very nature of the American way of
life.[9] Americans found themselves in marked disagreement on this issue. The
political spectrum was considerably broader than it would be after the war and
included a large and complex left wing, from agrarian populists through urban
Trotskyites, that would soon fall victim to another red scare. Conservatives
began to combine their hostility toward the Roosevelt administration with
a warning to steer clear of the gathering European conflict. Associating the
Roosevelt administration with "communistic," socialist, national-socialist,
"collectivist," and other foreign and un-American systems became a recurring
accusation in Congress. Not only Martin Dies and the House Committee on
Un-American Activities, but also former president Herbert Hoover, Senator
Robert A. Taft, and Congressman Hamilton Fish, who did "not like dictators of
any kind, here or abroad," pounded away at this theme.[10]

Research based on qualitative data shows that domestic arguments over
shifts in grand strategy were entangled with arguments over domestic
order—and were not limited to elites. Public mail, that is, citizen letters to
the president, to the editor, to elected officials, and to civic organizations,
document the grassroots level at which Americans vigorously participated
in these domestic controversies, expressing their views on the need, expe-
diency, or futility of fighting overseas. Citizens responded to official, especially presidential, rhetoric but also adapted critiques offered by dissenting
experts and opinion makers. They affirmed, resisted, and challenged official
versions, all the while articulating their own conceptions of "what America is
all about," underscoring an intricate connection between domestic agendas
and grand strategies. As the sheer volume of public correspondence in presidential and other archives shows, letter writing was immensely popular at
mid-century, and correspondents included women, minorities, the poor,
and the less educated. Public mail reveals strong and often well-informed
views on international affairs and America's role in them, views that many
may not have shared with "those official-looking interviewers who rang their
doorbells asking about the war."[11]

Setting aside official propaganda and elite discourse and digging deeper
into records that reveal the perspectives of private citizens, historian

Brooke Blower finds that in the aftermath of the Great War, Americans were deeply disillusioned with any military effort to make the world safe for democracy. Instead, a highly heterogeneous society with conflicting interests converged on a preference for neutrality: "what has often been characterized as Americans' desire to keep the United States isolated from international politics was more accurately a profound ambivalence about their quite well-developed sense of engagement with foreign affairs."[12] Instead of Wilsonianism, which ostensibly had failed, an internationally engaged policy of neutrality, that is, trade but not war, seemed to serve America's collective national interest best. Yet, as the postwar period threatened to turn into an interwar period, even neutrality was seen increasingly as inadequate. Different motivations and reasons sorted citizens not primarily into Democrats or Republicans, interventionists or isolationists, but into "antifascist idealists, opportunistic unilateralists, traditional law advocates, pacifists, pragmatic businessmen, and those who did not find the Nazis all that objectionable as long as they stayed on the other side of the Atlantic."[13] By 1937, 70 percent of Americans regarded their country's entry into the Great War as a mistake. Before the interventionists succeeded with their version of a second chance, weary citizens wondered: "Why make the same mistake twice?"[14]

To Go to War or Not to Go to War

Returning to the president and grand strategy: Why did he lead the country into war? Four reasons converged over time, highlighting the dynamic, flexible quality of Roosevelt's strategy. In line with Layne's definition, he responded to foreign and domestic realities, and following Gaddis's criteria, he matched ideas and values with material resources. First, Roosevelt, like many in his administration, abhorred the Nazi regime and tracked the Axis's expansionist aggression with increasing concern. Second, the president committed the country to war only after all other options had been exhausted or had run their course. Even after the Japanese attack on Pearl Harbor, he waited for Adolf Hitler to declare war on the United States. But when his propagandists suggested slogans like "the people's war," FDR insisted on his preference of "the survival war," rhetorically capturing (and exaggerating) the concern that the country's economic and political system would not survive in a world militarily dominated by the Axis power.[15]

Finally, the United States entered the war because it could: successful political mobilization, economic productivity, and increasingly military-tech-
nological advantage allowed the country to make a decisive contribution to
the Allied victory.[16]

Studying public and private arguments on "the nature of the enemy"
and "why we fight"—in the OWI's phrasing—it is hard not to root for the
interventionists, admire the prescience and courage of those who were
maligned as premature anti-fascists and warmongers, and those who
worked tirelessly to stall Germany's genocidal policies. But in considering citizens' views in general, we should be mindful of their lived historical context: What historical precedents and analogies were on their
minds, what experiences and concerns did they bring to various policy
options, what was their horizon of expectation? This horizon did not yet
include genocide and the extraordinary, dystopian German war aims that
made the war against Nazi Germany in hindsight exceptional and a moral
crusade. The concepts of humanitarian intervention or Responsibility-
to-Protect had not yet been invented. Setting aside for a moment the subsequent, problematic, and largely unsuccessful record of these two policy
options, the United States had not yet reached military superpower status
and Nazi policies were carefully and viciously crafted to prevent most outside rescue operations. On a more strategic level, it is somewhat of an intellectual shortcut to suppose that the United States should have or could
have averted the genocide. The history of World War II does not lend itself
to this US-centered approach.[17]

Rather than confusion or ignorance, citizen commentaries expressed an
understandable ambivalence. Against going abroad in search of monsters
to destroy, popular historian Will Durant argued that "Democracy,
Communism and Fascism are merely the molds in which diverse people
in diverse conditions have been organized to pursue similar ends in diverse ways; they are the products of different geographical and historical
conditions; they are not forms of national virtue or vice. . . . Only the simple,
then, can see in these varied forms of political and industrial organization
cause to go to war." For the interventionist side, Jewish émigré Toni Sender
acknowledged that "in this world of social upheaval, military action, and
psychological confusion, the task of a citizen in a free country is a most per-
plexing and complicated one." But after laying out the domestic and foreign
policies of the Third Reich she had barely escaped, she warned against "considering fascism the best ramparts against bolshevism. . . . We are sitting on a

volcano and those who have actually experienced the eruption have a greater knowledge of the crater."[18]

After the German attack on Poland, Americans experienced their own phony war with both interventionists and non-interventionists using historical lessons to infuse the debate with a greater sense of urgency. Organized isolationist and interventionist positions were diametrically opposed "but," historian Susan Brewer laconically concludes, "most Americans continued to agree with both. . . . [T]hey did not want to go to war and they did not want Hitler to win." Similarly, Roosevelt joked that his job was to "steer a course . . . between the wish of 70 percent of Americans to keep out of [the] war . . . [and] the wish of 70 percent of Americans to do everything to break Hitler, even it if means war."[19]

Interventionist-minded citizens responded to Roosevelt's theme of an interdependent world and neighborly solidarity (garden hose simile for Lend-Lease) with a Christian notion of extending charity to people outside one's immediate circle. As one Oregon farmer put it: "When a Chinaman's home is not secure, an American home cannot be secure. The world is our country and we are our brother's keeper."[20] The humanitarian interventionists' indictment of the anti-interventionists' alleged callousness brings to mind Dr. Seuss's cartoon showing the America First (AF) Committee as an elderly schoolmarm reading the fairy tale of Little Red Riding Hood to horrified American children, primly concluding: "and then Adolf, the Wolf chewed up the children and spit out their bones. . . . but those were Foreign Children and it really didn't matter."[21] Against these emotional appeals for international solidarity, America First supporters insisted on clear-headed, rational policies based on national interest, proffering a kind of proto-realist argument. Historian David Goodman usefully characterizes America First as a democratic populist nationalist movement. Convinced that the majority of their fellow Americans did not want to go to war (again), AF proponents understood the war debate as really about democracy. The seemingly inexorable drift toward war only fueled their anti-government and anti-semitic conspiracy theories.

The War Itself—Fought by a Conflicted Nation

Pearl Harbor did not put an end to popular skepticism regarding the war. Neither on the question of the nature of the enemy nor on the problem of what we are fighting for did the government, let alone its liberal, anti-fascist supporters, succeed with their more inspirational messages. More than half of the people in wartime surveys admitted they did not have a clear idea of what the war was about.[22] The army, which conducted its own systematic studies, reported that "the usual term by which disapproval of idealistic exhortation was invoked was 'bullshit.'" The "main reason" soldiers cited for fighting this war was "that we <u>had</u> to because we were attacked." Those who wallowed in "idealistic values and patriotism" were seen as "hypocritical." Over 40 percent of the troops admitted to feeling "very often" (11 percent) or "sometimes" (32 percent) that "this war is not worth fighting."[23] While a pious wartime patriotism made it no longer appropriate to criticize the government directly, frustration and anger manifested in malicious rumor campaigns targeting vulnerable groups, such as immigrants, American Jews, and African Americans, seen as surrogates of the Roosevelt administration.[24] The reluctance on the part of many Americans to fight the Germans, a people with whom they felt a kinship in this racial war, remained a challenge throughout the war.[25]

The image of a highly fractured nation is confirmed in historian Nancy Beck Young's study of congressional wartime politics, a crucial intersection of democracy and grand strategy. The legislature reflected grassroots political, racial, and social consciousness as "lawmakers held the same range of values and prejudices as did average Americans ... [and] acted on constituency priorities." Congress encapsulated a divided nation and represented a cross-section of the national, mainly white male, cacophony. It often proved a thorn in the administration's liberal, multilateral-internationalist side, and yet this branch of government was instrumental in debating, modifying, rejecting, and funding its grand strategy and many war-essential initiatives. It worked at the heart of American democracy and, as such, contributed to an internationally recognized sense of the United States as an exceptional nation that saved liberal democracy.

But Congress did so by negotiating compromises and passing bills that were marked by white supremacist attitudes, anti-immigration sentiment, and a determined effort to resist social-democratic, civil rights (anti-lynching), and fair employment legislation. Southern Democrats, key to Roosevelt's domestic alliance, ensured that an often violent racial regime in the South remained intact. Right-wing populists carried their campaign against the New Deal government, under the banner of "anti-communism," all the way into a proto-fascist realm. Thus, democratic politics in the legislature led, at times, to undemocratic policies that violated the spirit of America's declared war aims.[26] Young's study illustrates with many striking examples Blower's observation that "the arguments and alliances became even more counterintuitive once the war broke out in Europe."[27]

The darker side of the populist discontent with an apparently inexorable trend toward war included American societal anti-semitism which, fueled by prominent public figures, reached its high-water mark during this period.[28] In retrospect, this can only be seen in the context of the contemporaneous but notably different, singularly virulent, and murderous German anti-semitism. Accordingly, activists at the time and scholars subsequently have worried about anti-semites' role in undermining and impeding efforts to save and protect European Jews from the Third Reich's eliminatory anti-semitism.[29] Yet, responsibility for the genocide lies with Germans, not Americans, and possibilities for rescue of the Jews were tragically limited by Nazi design.

Moreover, American anti-semitism has to be seen alongside other contemporaneous forms of white American racism, resulting in the violation of constitutional, civil, and human rights of African Americans (violence, segregation) and Japanese Americans (internment). It was one of the many ironies of Roosevelt's wartime domestic coalitions that the most fervently and reliably interventionist region was also the most violently racist.[30] The dual challenge of grasping a foreign reality and determining its significance for one's own country and community was brought into sharp relief in African American responses to Nazi Germany and avowed US war aims. African Americans were quicker to recognize and articulate the centrality of racial anti-semitism to Nazi politics than many whites. For them the brutal persecution and, later, mass murder of Jews by the Nazi state were not "beyond belief." Many black civil rights leaders joined forces with American Jewish and anti-fascist organizations to raise awareness of the interlinked threat of fascism and racism. But, especially in the South, African American leaders also insisted—in a manner reminiscent of the non-interventionist argument to promote democracy at home rather than abroad—that the "cancer" of anti-democratic racism had to be addressed at home not only, or primarily, elsewhere in the world. As a 1938 *Crisis* editorial put it, "The South approaches more nearly than any other section of the United States the Nazi idea of government by a 'master race' without interference from any democratic process."[31] Still, three years later, as part of the Double V campaign, African American soldiers understood their wartime service as a contribution "to secure real democracy." Poignant expressions of loyalty by African Americans abound in the archives, complete with promises "to serve anytime."[32]

The prominent place of American soldiers in government mobilization efforts as well as in public memory has eclipsed the range of their real-life experiences and memories.[33] Youthful patriotism, an appetite for adventure, but mainly a strong sense of communal obligation animated young men as they entered the military. Like much of the country, they proved remarkably resistant to government propaganda. For the most part they understood their role in defeating the Axis enemy as a job that had to be done so they could return home and resume their civilian lives. Historian Gerald Linderman examines the agonizing and soul-destroying realities of American combat soldiers in World War II by tracing their journey from this decidedly sober, pragmatic, and somewhat resigned attitude through the intense camaraderie of battle, learning strategies of survival and coping with trauma, to finding a final refuge in fatalism. The number of US combat soldiers was small, less than 1 percent of the US population. Yet their casualty rate was high. Infantrymen suffered 70 percent of casualties, though they were only 14 percent of US troops overseas.[34] Not surprisingly, approval of the proposed United Nations Organization, high among general citizens at 81 percent, reached 99 percent among GIs in 1945. Soldiers were nearly unanimous in support of their country's "active participation in an international organization to keep the peace"—so they wouldn't have to.[35]

Public memory of war is meant to smooth over, even to help forget, experiences of violence and trauma. As a result, memory of war is "invariably contested."[36] Private narratives of loss and sorrow compete with public ones of victory and patriotism. While official lessons from World War II were often enabling, personal experiences and memories were more often cautionary and reflected critically on the imperfect domestic scene back home. Not surprisingly, some of the most passionate and principled arguments against war came from former combat soldiers.[37]

Resistance against World War II–Inspired Cold War Internationalism

In his last Fireside Chat in January 1945, Roosevelt, acknowledging the public's intense hope for peace, proclaimed, "We Americans of today, together with our Allies, are making history—and I hope it will be a better history than ever has been made before." Nine months later, with Germany and Japan defeated, his successor, President Truman, appealed to a sense of national accomplishment: "The United States now has a fighting strength greater than at any other time in history. It is greater than that of any other nation in the world." But Truman cautioned that "we can ensure . . . peace only so long as we remain strong. We must face the fact that peace must be built upon power. . . . [W]e must relentlessly preserve our superiority on land and sea and in the air." He warned "not to make the same mistake that we made after the first World War when we sank back into helplessness."[38]

The term "internationalism" obscures the significant shift from the time-bound war effort, based on burden sharing and a recognition of the limits of US power, to a strategically more ambitious, global containment doctrine, rooted in a sense of national triumph and fear of a new enemy filling power vacuums.[39] At home, it was a pre-existing, domestically useful anti-communism—in conjunction with an extraordinarily propitious moment of US power—that shaped the domestic mobilization campaign for the new grand strategy of Soviet containment. The concept of totalitarianism proved crucial in this regard, "channel[ing] the anti-Nazi energy of the wartime period into the postwar struggle with the Soviet Union."[40] Within months after the end of the war, phrases that had described the Nazis were now applied to the Soviet Union in internal memoranda as well as public proclamations. This time, used to characterize the ideology, the master plan, and the world conquest intentions of the Soviet Union, they turned out to be more compelling than they had been as a propaganda blueprint characterizing the Nazi threat. The Munich lesson, postulating that aggression unchecked leads to general war, soon became the most enduring but also the most problematic historical lesson drawn from World War II.[41]

Even as the monolith of world communism solidified in official rhetoric, American public opinion did not. Postwar surveys show a majority of Americans longing for peace and placing their hope in the new international organization of the United Nations.[42] There was widespread and outspoken concern over blurring the line between war and peace and little readiness to put the United States on a permanent war footing. Letters to the Truman administration from 1945 to 1950 document that Americans had noticed at the time what Mary Dudziak highlights in *War Time*: there had been no formal declaration that ended World War II. Citizens worried about and objected to this open-endedness.[43] Similarly, the postwar debate over universal military training (UMT) caused an unusually large volume of protest mail demonstrating the breadth and depth of resistance to peacetime military training that was rejected as un-American, un-democratic, and un-Christian. Letters show that the lessons citizens drew from World War II were different from those of their political leadership. A common theme was the great disappointment that the sacrifice and victory of the recent war seemed to have been in vain, that the promises their government had held out were seemingly discarded by the current administration, that the focus on domestic priorities had been lost. Some warned of hubris and overreach as their country held an atomic monopoly and its economy outproduced much of the rest of the world; others feared that their country would play "Santa Claus to the world."[44] Foreign policy experts' critical reflections on America's new grand strategy of militarized containment found their counterpart in the comments of ordinary people.[45]

When the Cold War turned unexpectedly hot in Asia—not in Europe, toward which so much American postwar effort and investment had been directed—it only accentuated lingering popular preferences for peaceful cooperation or, alternatively, for retreat from military globalism. At the beginning of the Korean War, letter writers asked, "Why are our boys there? Why should our boys die so the [corrupt] Rhee government should survive?" Others agreed: "Korea is not our problem, and we have no business there." By December 1950, Iowa farmers advised the president that communist China should be admitted to the United Nations: "If we mean to shut out all representatives who don't agree with us, there's no reason to have a world organization." With regard to the war itself, they were "quite willing to give up in Korea, permanently." Two years into the conflict, citizens in Elyria, Ohio, felt "that the conflict is a useless murder of the best of our sons and that it should be terminated, even tho [sic] we may lose 'face.' " Jane Culbertson of St. Louis, whose husband was a prisoner of war (POW), told President Truman: "We, the little people, did not send our boys to Korea—it is time the men responsible bring them back."[46]

If reading World War II through a Cold War lens distorted its reality and significance, looking back at it from the vantage point of Vietnam yielded new insights. Veterans and citizens whom journalist and historian Studs Terkel interviewed in the early 1980s for his oral history of World War II, recall the prevalence of racism, anti-semitism, and bigotry as well as the brutality, the anguish, and the powerful camaraderie of actual war. Admiral Gene LaRocque, reflecting on the "senseless waste of human beings" he had seen in

Vietnam, concluded: "World War II has warped our view of how we look at things today. . . . [T]he twisted memory of it encourages the men of my generation to be willing, almost eager, to use military force anywhere in the world." The admiral, echoing George F. Kennan, thought that the Soviet Union had to be contained and that the United States had "to compete with communism wherever it appears. Our mistake is trying to stem it with guns."[47] Similarly, historian John Bodnar, examining the role that public memory of World War II played in the militarization of American culture and identity, reached this mournful conclusion:

> The land of the free increasingly became known as the home of the brave; acts of killing and dying were transformed into heroic deeds and cherished memories. . . . [T]he defense of the nation became as important as the old dream of uplift and equality. Americans talked not only about the pursuit of happiness but about the road to victory.[48]

In the mid-1950s, theologian Reinhold Niebuhr described "the anatomy of American nationalism" emerging on the political right as "an undue reliance on purely military power and an almost pathological impatience with the frustrations of forces beyond our control."[49] Nationalism is often thought of as feeding into aggressive foreign policy. For the American case, the reverse might be true. For generations, Americans, as citizens, volunteers, conscripts, and professional soldiers, have followed the call of duty and fought for their country. Yet they were often called on to fight for democracy and freedom in places far away from home. The rhetorical and emotional defense of having sent American soldiers to fight on behalf of others began to shape an American culture of patriotism.[50] Global reach and military strength became defining aspects of American identity. A corresponding patriotism served the function to overcome, indeed negate, any arguments to the contrary.[51] But the course of (American) history is not one-directional.

In his study of American nationalism and the origins of the Cold War, John Fousek finds that "the lack of fundamental public debate about the nature and purposes of US foreign policy after 1950 contributed to the development of an increasingly militarized foreign policy controlled by narrow ideological blinders that obscured fundamental international realities."[52] Of the realist trio George Kennan, Niebuhr, and Hans Morgenthau, it was the immigrant Morgenthau who first and poignantly spoke out publicly against the escalating war in Vietnam.[53] Many of the realists' philosophically and historically grounded warnings of militarized globalism were expressed in citizens' letters and personal reflections. This is not to argue that some inherent wisdom resides with "the people," but to strengthen the case for recognizing the public as a legitimate participant in foreign policy debates.[54] The absence of any meaningful contestation among the wider public or foreign policy elites in the 2002–3 run-up to the invasion of Iraq confirms that domestic conflict might be not only more democratic but also more beneficial for the foreign policymaking process itself.

Conclusion

In 2014 Richard Haass, president of the Council on Foreign Relations and foreign policy adviser under both presidents Bush, chose the same book title as James Warburg had in 1944 to advance a very different argument. Seventy years later, the title *Foreign Policy Begins at Home* served to make a case, one could almost say, to put America first, more specifically, as his subtitle suggests: to put America's house in order first. Like other voices across the political spectrum, Haass called for America to return home and warned against imperial overstretch. He observed that "the biggest threat to American security and prosperity comes not from abroad but from within," by which he meant that previously admired standards of education, immigration, infrastructure, and economic well-being were crumbling at home.[55] Just as Warburg had captured an internationalist-humanitarian moment, Haass's book coincided with another phase of disillusionment. Having grown wary of the military campaigns of a decade-long Global War on Terror, Americans were questioning the efficacy of war as a solution to the problems facing the nation and the world.[56] Haass's internationalist credentials are beyond doubt. What explains the difference in argument between Warburg and Haass is the impact that the accumulated legacy of American military globalism, part of successive, varying, and variously successful grand strategies, had on the nation itself and the situation at home.

Popular support for military interventions and an active engagement in international affairs has been forthcoming both from conservative nationalists and progressive internationalists, just as Americans across the political spectrum were also ready, for different reasons, motivations, and concerns, to endorse "staying at home" and "not do[ing] stupid things." In personal statements as well as polls, Americans expressed ambivalence, conflicting impulses of hope and caution, realistic assessments that the world would not easily submit to American ideas and ambitions, and preferences for working toward a just and equitable domestic order either ahead of or in tandem with overseas efforts. Warburg and Haass's respective positions of sharing in international responsibility and taking care of the nation at home are two sides of a scale that requires continuous rebalancing.

The most often deployed argument against plumbing the indomitable diversity of American civil society in relation to the country's foreign policy is that public opinion has little or no impact—certainly not on grand strategy. Indeed, Berinsky cautions that civil society, in spite of its often pacifist, antiinterventionist preferences, might not be able to rein in war-prone politicians. This conclusion matters if we are solely concerned with the impact of public opinion on foreign policy.[57] But this is too high a bar for civil society in the national security state and we should at least consider the opposite perspective as well and examine the impact of American grand strategy on civil society. It is precisely because the balance of state and civil society—never an equal one when it comes to foreign policy—has shifted even more dramatically toward the former that the task of including voices outside the officially sanctioned national security discourse has become all the more important.

Movements and arguments that have challenged American globalism and rejected calls for overseas intervention have appeared on the left as much as on the right, have been pacifist-humanitarian as often as chauvinist-exclusionary, racist as well as cosmopolitan—and thus they defy comfortable partisan appropriations while, on the other hand, lending themselves to partisan attacks. We should not be content with retracing the perspective of those in power: even though often marginalized, dissenting voices are both persistent and varied in their specific concerns at different junctures. They are for the most part the losers of (official US foreign policy) history, yet their arguments are clearly recorded in the government archives and in the public sphere, and they constitute an important part of American political culture. They deserve to be included in our history of American democracy and grand strategy.

Notes

1. James P. Warburg, *Foreign Policy Begins at Home* (New York: Harcourt, Brace, 1944), 295.

2. John Lewis Gaddis, *On Grand Strategy* (New York: Penguin Press, 2018), 21, 288.
3. David Milne, *Worldmaking: The Art and Science of American Diplomacy* (New York: Farrar, Straus and Giroux, 2015), 11 et passim. Christopher Layne, "Grand Strategy," *The Oxford Encyclopedia of American Military and Diplomatic History* (New York: Oxford University Press, 2013), 436–447, here 436.
4. Ira Katznelson, *Fear Itself: The New Deal and the Origins of Our Time* (New York: W.W. Norton, 2013). On FDR's foreign policy, seeDavid Reynolds, *From Munich to Pearl Harbor: Roosevelt's America and the Origins of the Second World War* (Chicago: Ivan R. Dee, 2001); Warren Kimball, *The Juggler: Franklin Roosevelt as Wartime Statesman* (Princeton, NJ: Princeton University Press, 1991).
5. Milne, *Worldmaking*, 526. Similarly, G. John Ikenberry, *After Victory: Institutions, Strategic Restraint, and the Rebuilding of Order after Major Wars* (Princeton, NJ: Princeton University Press, 2000), 164–214.
6. Justus Doenecke, *Storm on the Horizon: The Challenge to American Intervention, 1939–41* (Lanham. MD: Rowman and Littlefield, 2003).
7. Adam J. Berinsky, *In Time of War: Understanding American Public Opinion from World War II to Iraq* (Chicago: University of Chicago Press, 2009), 35–38. See also Steven Casey, *A Cautious Crusade: Franklin D. Roosevelt, American Public Opinion, and the War against Nazi Germany* (New York: Oxford University Press, 2001); and Michaela Hoenicke Moore, *Know Your Enemy: The American Debate on Nazism, 1933–1945* (New York: Cambridge University Press, 2010).
8. *The People and the President: America's Conversation with FDR*, ed. Lawrence W. Levine and Cornelia R. Levine (Boston: Beacon Press, 2002), 280ff, 283, also 269ff; 276, 282.
9. Wendy Wall, *Inventing the "American Way": Politics of Consensus from the New Deal to the Civil Rights Movement* (New York: Oxford University Press, 2008).
10. Michaela Hoenicke Moore, "The Idea of the Dictator and Totalitarianism in the 1930s," in *Oxford Handbook on the New Deal*, ed. Nancy Beck Young (New York: Oxford University Press, forthcoming).
11. Brooke Blower, "From Isolationism to Neutrality: A New Framework for Understanding American Political Culture, 1919-1941," *Diplomatic History* 38 (April 2014), 357; James Sparrow, *Warfare State: World War II America and the Age of Big Government* (New York: Oxford University Press, 2011), 29–32.
12. Blower, "From Isolation to Neutrality," 360, 362.
13. Ibid., 375.
14. Hoenicke-Moore, *Know Your Enemy*, 29–40, 64–75, 132, 197.
15. Ibid., 105f.
16. John A. Thompson, *A Sense of Power: The Roots of America's Global Role* (Ithaca, NY: Cornell University Press, 2015).
17. Mikkel Rasmussen, "The History of a Lesson: Versailles, Munich and the Social Construction of the Past," *Review of International Studies* 29 (October 2003), 499–519; Stephen Wertheim, "A Solution from Hell: The United States and the Rise of Humanitarian Interventionism, 1991-2003," *Journal of Genocide Research* 12 (2010), 149–172; Shlomo Aronson, *Hitler, the Allies and the Jews* (New York: Cambridge University Press, 2009).

18. Will Durant, "No Hymns of Hatred," *Saturday Evening Post*, June 4, 1938, 23, 48f, 51f; Toni Sender, "We Must Face the Issues," *Annals of the American Academy of Political and Social Sciences* 216 (July 1941), 16–23.

19. Susan Brewer, *Why America Fights: Patriotism and War Propaganda from the Philippines to Iraq* (New York: Oxford University Press, 2009), 93; Casey, *A Cautious Crusade*, 30.

20. David Goodman, "The Limits of the Sayable: Public Propaganda and Private Opinion in the Debate about U.S. Entry into World War II," paper presented at the June 2015 Annual Meeting of SHAFR in Arlington, VA.

21. Cartoon of October 1, 1941, emphasis in original, Richard Minear, ed., *Dr. Seuss Goes to War: The World War II Editorial Cartoons of Theodor Seuss Geisel* (New York: New Press, 2001), 45.

22. Hoenicke-Moore, *Know Your Enemy*, 107.

23. *The American Soldier: Combat and Its Aftermath*, vol. 2, ed. Samuel Stouffer et al. (Princeton, NJ: Princeton University Press, 1949), 150–153.

24. Sparrow, *Warfare State*, 89–109.

25. Hoenicke-Moore, *Know Your Enemy*, 105–155.

26. Nancy Beck Young, *Why We Fight. Congress and the Politics of World War II* (Lawrence: University of Kansas Press, 2013), 4f., 132. See also Katznelson, *Fear Itself*, 156–194.

27. Blower, "From Isolation to Neutrality," 355.

28. Myron I. Scholnick, *The New Deal and Anti-Semitism in America* (New York: Garland, 1990).

29. Hoenicke-Moore, *Know Your Enemy*, 72–74, 110f., 193f.

30. Glenda Gilmore, *Defying Dixie: The Radical Roots of Civil Rights, 1919–1950* (New York: Norton, 2008), 158–172, 189–192, 196–200; Joseph A. Fry, *Dixie Looks Abroad: The South and U.S. Foreign Relations, 1789–1973* (Baton Rouge: Louisiana State University Press, 2002), 188–221.

31. Quoted from Johnpeter Horst Grill and Robert L. Jenkins, "The Nazis and the American South in the 1930s: A Mirror Image?" *Journal of Southern History* 58 (November 1992), 689.

32. *The People and the President*, 330, 366, 371, 386.

33. Sparrow, *Warfare State*; Robert B. Westbrook, *Why We Fought: Forging American Obligations in World War II* (Washington, DC: Smithsonian, 2004).

34. Gerald F. Linderman, *The World within War: America's Combat Experience in World War II* (New York: Free Press, 1997), 48–89.

35. Current Opinions #12, May 10, 1945, OWI Research Division, Philleo Nash Papers, box 5, Harry S. Truman Library, Independence, MO.

36. John Bodnar, *The "Good War" in American Memory* (Baltimore: Johns Hopkins University Press, 2010), 3.

37. Yuen Foong Khong, *Analogies at Wa: Korea, Munich, Dien Bien Phu, and the Vietnam Decisions of 1965* (Princeton, NJ: Princeton University Press, 1992); Bodnar, *The "Good War,"* 34–57; Studs Terkel, *"The Good War." An Oral History of World War II* (New York: Ballantine Books, 1984), 117, 196, 233, 265.

38. FDR's Radio Address, https://www.presidency.ucsb.edu/node/210108 (accessed June 6, 2018); Harry S. Truman, Address before a Joint Session of Congress, October 23, 1945, https://www.trumanlibrary.org/publicpapers/index.php?pid=183 (accessed April 29, 2018).

39. John Fousek, *To Lead the Free World: American Nationalism and the Cultural Roots of the Cold War* (Chapel Hill: University of North Carolina Press, 2000), 7; Melvyn P. Leffler, *A Preponderance of Power. National Security, the Truman Administration, and the Cold War* (Stanford, CA: Stanford University Press, 1992). xxx

40. Abbott Gleason, *Totalitarianism. The Inner History of the Cold War* (New York: Oxford University Press, 1995), 3. Les K. Adler and Thomas G. Paterson, "Red Fascism: The Merger of Nazi Germany and Soviet Russia in the American Image of Totalitarianism, 1930s–1950s," *American Historical Review* (April 1970), 1046–1064.

41. Michaela Hoenicke Moore, "The Nazis and U.S. Foreign Policy Debates: History, Lessons, and Analogies," in *The Other in US History and Foreign Policy*, ed. David Ryan and M. Patrick Cullinane (New York: Berghahn, 2014), 142–162.

42. Walter LaFeber, "American Policy-Makers, Public Opinion, and the Outbreak of the Cold War, 1945–1950," *The Origins of the Cold War in Asia*, ed. Yonosuke Nagai and Akira Iriye (New York: Columbia University Press, 1977), 43–65; *The Gallup Poll: Public Opinion 1935–1971* (New York: Random House, 1972), 592, 622, 39, 672, 681, 691, 717; Elizabeth Borgwardt, *A New Deal for the World: America's Vision for Human Rights* (Cambridge, MA: Belknap Press of Harvard University Press, 2005), 81ff., 156ff., 289.

43. "Public Mail," in Harry S. Truman Papers, Official Files (OF) 190 (World War II), boxes 800, 801 and interspersed elsewhere, Harry S. Truman Library, Independence, MO; Mary Dudziak, *War Tim:. An Idea, Its History, Its Consequences* (New York: Oxford University Press, 2012), 36.

44. UMT letters are in boxes 284 and 285, President's Personal Files [PPF] 200, Truman Papers [HSTP],Harry S. Truman Library, Independence, MO [HSTL]. Santa Claus quote: Mr. and Mrs. F. Miller to Bourke B. Hickenlooper, July 17, 1947, Topical Files Foreign Policy, General 1947, box 24, Bourke B. Hickenlooper Papers, Herbert Hoover Presidential Library, West Branch, IA.

45. Michael Hogan, *A Cross of Iron: Harry S. Truman and the Origins of the National Security State* (New York: Cambridge University Press, 1998), 209 and 419–482; Thomas G. Paterson, ed., *Cold War Critics: Alternatives to American Foreign Policy in the Truman Years* (Chicago: Quadrangle Books, 1971).

46. Hardee Carr to President Truman [HST], July 15, 1950; Richard J. Chell to HST, July 7, 1950, Official Files [OF] 471-B, box 1476, HSTP, HSTL. Marilyn B. Young, "Hard Sell: The Korean War," in *Selling War in a Media Age: The Presidency and Public Opinion in the American Century*, ed. Kenneth Osgood and Andrew Frank (Gainesville: University Press of Florida), 113–139; V. H. Andrews of Elyria, OH, January 21, 1952, OF 471 B, box 1454, HSTP, HSTL; Mrs. Jane Culbertson to President Truman, January 21, 1952, *Dear Harry . . . Truman's Mailroom, 1945–1953*, ed. D. M. Giangreco and Kathryn Moore (Mechanicsburg, PA: Stackpole Books, 1999), 347.

47. Terkel, *"The Good War,"* 188f.

48. Bodnar, *The "Good War,"* 8.

49. Reinhold Niebuhr, "The Anatomy of American Nationalism," reprinted in *The World Crisis and American Responsibility* (New York: Association Press, 1958).

50. Brewer, *Why America Fights*, 277.

51. Paul T. McCartney, "American Nationalism and U.S. Foreign Policy from 9/11 to the Iraq War," *Political Science Quarterly* 119 (Fall 2004), 399–423.

52. Fousek, *To Lead*, 190.

53. Hans Morgenthau, "We Are Deluding Ourselves in Vietnam," April 18, 1965, and "Globalism: Johnson's Moral Crusade," July 3, 1965 in Michael Hunt, *A Vietnam War Reader: A Documentary History from American and Vietnamese Perspectives* (Chapel Hill: University of North Carolina Press, 2010), 166ff.

54. Daniel Bessner and Stephen Wertheim, "Democratizing U.S. Foreign Policy: Bringing Experts and the Public Back Together," *Foreign Affairs*, April 5, 2017, https://www.foreignaffairs.com/articles/united-states/2017-04-05/democratizing-us-foreign-policy (accessed April 7, 2017).

55. Richard Haass, *Foreign Policy Begins at Home: The Case for Putting America's House in Order* (New York: Basic Books, 2014), 1.

56. A 2013 Pew Research Poll on "America's Place in the World" showed for the first time in fifty years a record number of Americans in favor of their country "mind[ing] its own business internationally." Support for allies, international cooperation, and trade indicated the public's weariness of the Global War on Terror's *military* adventures, *not* a resurgent isolationism, http://www.people-press.org/2013/12/03/public-sees-u-s-power-declining-as-support-for-global-engagement-slips/ (accessed March 30, 2014). Benjamin Page, with Marshall Bouton, *The Foreign Policy Disconnect: What Americans Want from Our Leaders but Don't Get* (Chicago: University of Chicago Press, 2006).

57. Berinsky, *In Time of War*, 214ff.

11

National Security as Grand Strategy

Edward Mead Earle and the Burdens of World Power

Andrew Preston

With good reason, the historian Edward Mead Earle is widely credited with sanctifying the concept of "grand strategy" during World War II, at least to an American audience. In his introduction to *Makers of Modern Strategy*, a canonical collection of essays published in 1943, Earle defined strategy as "the art of controlling and utilizing the resources of a nation—or a coalition of nations—including its armed forces, to the end that its vital interests shall be effectively promoted and secured against enemies, actual, potential, or merely presumed." But the conditions of World War II—industrial warfare that mobilized entire societies fight on a global scale in the pursuit of ideological ends—demanded an even more expansive conception of strategic doctrine, which is what led Earle to the notion of grand strategy: "The highest type of strategy—sometimes called grand strategy—is that which so integrates the policies and armaments of the nation that the resort to war is either rendered unnecessary or is undertaken with the maximum chance of victory."[1]

Although Earle never returned to the idea of grand strategy in *Makers of Modern Strategy*, and although other strategists in Britain and the United States were also devising their own definitions around the same time, observers have marked Earle's pithy definition as a turning point in the evolution of strategic thinking in the United States.[2] According to John Lewis Gaddis, *Makers of Modern Strategy*—and with it Earle's definition—"immediately became the single most influential primer on grand strategy for American wartime and postwar planners."[3] But Earle did more than codify a term, "grand strategy," that most other strategists had missed. By making strategy "grand," he also broadened its scope from a Clausewitzian basis that had been exclusively military—about the waging and winning of wars—to one that incorporated all of statecraft, indeed, virtually all of politics.[4] "By such a definition," concludes Paul Kennedy, "Earle massively extended the realm of enquiry about 'grand strategy' to encompass national policies in peacetime as well as in wartime."[5] Strategy guided warfare; grand strategy not only helped guide warfare but it also aimed to shape an enduring peace that would follow the end of conflict.

However, Earle's programmatic work on redefining—and, more important, expanding—the boundaries of statecraft was not limited to strategic concepts. At precisely the same time he was codifying "grand strategy," he was also deeply involved in the construction of another new foreign-policy term, one that would become more frequently used and politically effective than grand strategy, at least in the United States: "national security."[6] Earle wasn't the first to deploy the term "national security," but he played an instrumental role in establishing its tenets and determining its uses. Not coincidentally, Earle's codification of "national security" involved the same expansionary impulse that gave rise to "grand strategy." In an age of industrialized warfare, air power, and a truly global politics of security, Earle believed that existing notions of safety and strategy needed to be stretched and broadened. His new definitions did precisely that.

The need to modernize the parameters of basic concepts such as strategy and security was especially acute for the United States of the late 1930s and early 1940s. Earle's project had genuine intellectual underpinnings, but its main purpose was to influence politics and policy. It aimed to go beyond scholarly inquiry: constructing both "grand strategy" and "national security" were political acts designed to facilitate a more active international role for the United States during the world crisis of the late interwar period. As David Ekbladh, the most thorough chronicler of Earle's exploits, aptly puts it, "Earle desired serious research, but from the start, he was out to create the means to influence the course of national policy."[7] Earle's stature as a respected academic and his decision to convene a seminar on national security comprised of academic experts, infused his initiative with legitimacy. While politicians such as Franklin Roosevelt also began invoking "national security" around the same time, Earle's efforts gave the concept a scholarly veneer of rigor and objectivity. In an era of intense political controversy over foreign policy, this was a significant contribution to the internationalist cause. Concealed in supposedly neutral academic theory, Earle's concepts were designed to carry an explosive potential to change the very terms on which Americans engaged with the rest of the world. He therefore must be understood, and his influence appreciated, as a policy activist and a political actor, and not simply as a scholar.

But how did Earle wield such influence? His impact didn't stem from a prolific body of work: for such a consequential thinker, Earle was surprisingly unproductive as a scholar, at least when it came to publications. He taught at some of the nation's leading institutions of higher education, such as Columbia (from where he also received his doctorate) and the Institute for Advanced Study in Princeton, yet he never authored a major book of history or political theory. Aside from quickly turning his doctoral dissertation into a specialist monograph on imperial maneuverings in the modern Middle East, and aside from publishing a small handful of articles in a select handful of journals, he actually wrote remarkably little for a scholar of his stature and intelligence.[8] This was almost certainly due in part to poor health—Earle suffered from tuberculosis, among other ailments—but it was also because of a deliberate focus on shaping policy rather than pursuing academic research. Narrow contributions to scholarship were not what Earle had in mind, at least not by the time Americans began debating their role in the world crisis of the late 1930s. He wanted to affect policy—and hopefully public opinion too.[9] Reaching a wide and diverse audience at a time of unusual importance in world affairs, then, was Earle's key ambition. His target audience was not fellow academics but policymakers and other influential Americans. With this in mind, at various times in the interwar period he contributed articles to the highbrow popular press, such as the *New Republic* and *Foreign Affairs*, and served in the leadership of the Foreign Policy Association, an elite organization that aimed to shape popular attitudes on America's role in the world.[10]

Earle's most important initiative, however, was a seminar of academic luminaries in Princeton that studied the terms of US foreign policy in a changing world; from there, he hoped his ideas could have an effect on policy planning in the State Department, the War Department, and perhaps even the White House. With generous funding from the Carnegie Corporation, Earle convened his seminar on foreign policy, strategy, and security from 1939 until 1943; it met at the Institute for Advanced Study in Princeton.[11] The seminar comprised a group of esteemed historians, political scientists, and economists, who engaged in wide-ranging discussions about America's engagement with the wider world. It was here where Earle and his colleagues hammered out the concepts of grand strategy and national security and put them in the service of state policy. Many of the seminar's participants, including Earle himself, joined the war effort of one of the Allies—not only the United States but also Britain, Canada, and France—where they applied their ideas to the conduct of warfare and wartime diplomacy. As Ekbladh observes, the "most powerful impact" the seminar made did "not come from drawing the government into the seminar but from insinuating the seminar into the government."[12] Another historian of Earle's intellectual work in service of the state puts it in similar terms. "The Princeton Group's interest in bringing military studies to academe," writes Dexter Fergie, "helped propel many of its members into the war itself."[13]

Whatever the enduring importance Earle's Princeton seminar had on the development of International Relations theory within the academy, it was undoubtedly a forum for the formation and dissemination of new views on grand strategy and national security. Earle and his seminarians weren't the only ones reconceptualizing these terms, but they were probably the only ones who did so in such a deliberate and self-conscious fashion, and they were unusual in arriving at definitions that conflated the purposes of strategy and security. Most important, they were pivotal in conceiving of new strategic and security concepts that could transform the United States into a superpower. Americans had long possessed the latent capacity and economic wherewithal to be the greatest of the great powers; what they lacked were the conceptual tools to build that power and wield it on a global scale. Earle's ideas about grand strategy and national security promised to furnish them.

Making the Danger Seem Clear and Present

Grand strategy was an important part of Earle's emerging new worldview, but in the febrile atmosphere surrounding the debate over American intervention in the early 1940s, national security took priority. The reason was simple: grand strategy would be helpful in winning a war the United States had not yet joined, while national security was essential in creating the political and ideological conditions for the United States to join it. As Earle put it in 1938, the burgeoning world crisis, and the growing threat of totalitarian states, introduced a completely new world order, one that hadn't been previously encountered by American statesmen. "It is of the utmost importance, therefore, that the United States reexamine its whole policy of national defense."[14] Grand strategy would become more relevant in the years after Pearl Harbor, but in 1941, when Earle convened the sessions on national security, the seminar's focus was on devising a rationale for American intervention without admitting that was the goal. Felix Gilbert, Earle's executive assistant for the seminar but himself a distinguished historian who later taught at Bryn Mawr before returning to the Institute in 1962 as Earle's successor, recalled that Earle wanted to come up with a definition of national security that was pragmatic, objective, and unemotional, one that couldn't be accused of bias or political intent.[15]

To be sure, the two concepts, grand strategy and national security, were not distinct in Earle's mind, and the seminar's work would seamlessly weave the two together, in particular by infusing in national security the bold expansiveness of grand strategy. But for the moment, immediate need prevailed, and that led the seminar to a concentration on national security. This was natural for two reasons, though both essentially boiled down to political necessity. First, the traditional justification for belligerence was self-defense. This was a generally recognized aspect of international law, one that carried over from the early-modern period to the twentieth century, but it was especially strong in the American legal tradition going back to Daniel Webster's *Caroline* standard of 1842 (which itself became an important basis for the international laws of war).[16] In order to justify a more interventionist approach to the world crisis, Earle and his seminar needed to broaden the scope of what exactly constituted "self-defense," which in turn meant defining national security as expansively as possible to include not just the defense of territorial sovereignty but also the protection of national interests and even national norms and values. If the United States was to react with armed force, it was essential that this action be on the grounds of self-defense—more precisely, a type of extended self-defense that became the hallmark of national security.

The second reason was similar to the first but even more compelling because of its political intensity: even as American public opinion turned decisively against Nazi Germany after the fall of France in June 1940, a solid majority continued to oppose outright military intervention in the war. If the American people were going to sanction entry into the war, they first needed to be convinced that it was not a matter of choice but an unavoidable response to a clear and present danger.[17]

To this end, taxonomy and classification were key, which is why Earle was so preoccupied with devising a new definition for—and with it a new way of perceiving—the security of the United States. Earle wanted American statecraft to be less static and reactive. "Defense is a much more far-reaching concept than mere sitting back and waiting until the enemy is at one's gates," he explained in an article published a few months before the seminar began considering the issue. "Perhaps a better word to use is security. The purpose of armed forces is not merely the defense of the nation in the sense of resisting attack on its territorial possessions; it is more than that." The similarities to grand strategy were uncanny: whatever one may call it, "defense or security was not merely a crisis phenomenon, but an obligation of statecraft at all times" requiring "the extension of our diplomatic and of indeed our military frontiers beyond our mere territorial possessions." Relabeling a term and rethinking words might seem pedantic, but for Earle the stakes could not be higher. "If defense is conceived as security in a larger sense," he concluded, "the initiative can be ours, and only by taking the initiative, only by being prepared, if necessary, to wage war offensively, can we in the last analysis make sure that defense is something more than a phrase and is in fact a reality."[18]

With all this in mind, Earle's Princeton seminar studied the revolutionary effects on world order produced by the collapse of the post–World War I settlement embodied in the 1919 Treaty of Versailles and the 1921–22 Washington Naval Conference treaties. As Earle put it in his introductory remarks at the first meeting of the seminar dedicated to the study of national security, defense was "not exclusively or even primarily a problem for the professional soldier" in the modern world because "the long arm of military affairs now reaches into virtually every phase of life including economics, psychology, education, public health." International relations was now in an unbounded era of "Total defense and Total War" in which it was unclear whether "conventional military standards any longer apply." The result was that "for the first time in over one hundred years we consider ourselves vulnerable." Earle was remarkably prescient in his initial recommendations to reorganize the conduct of US foreign and military policy: a "Council of National Defense" would advise the president, and a separate air force would stand alongside the War and Navy departments. And of crucial importance was "the political factor: Grand Strategy."[19]

In the autumn of 1941, Earle's Princeton seminar devoted its energies to devising a new definition of national security. The task of providing a first draft fell to Albert K. Weinberg, an American historian who taught political science at Johns Hopkins University but at the time was on a fellowship at the Institute for Advanced Study. Weinberg was both an apposite and an odd choice for the assignment. On one hand, as the author of a highly acclaimed study of nineteenth-century manifest destiny, Weinberg was an expert on tracing the ideological and cultural sources of the American worldview; he was especially sensitive to the ways in which interests beyond the protection of territorial sovereignty influenced the framing of America's role in the world.[20] He was also strongly critical of so-called isolationism, that is, of those who opposed American involvement in the world crisis and invoked a tradition of isolation to support their position.[21] On the other hand, Weinberg's very sensitivity to these cultural forces would presumably have made him wary of defining a new term, "national security," in a manner similar to "manifest destiny." His critique of manifest destiny, after all, was that it framed US interests and security concerns in broad, almost cosmic terms to the extent that under its rubric almost anything could qualify as a security threat or a matter of national interest. He was not simply a critic of American expansionism but of the self-serving nature in which increasingly capacious definitions of American interests were used—indeed, devised—to justify the great land grabs of the nineteenth century. Weinberg was thus a daring choice to lead Earle's effort to come up with a definition of national security that could facilitate a more activist foreign policy for the United States.

This perhaps explains the ambivalence with which Weinberg approached his task, for the definition he came up provided for a broad conception of American self-defense while simultaneously recognizing its limits and contradictions. In short, Weinberg sought to draft a reasonable and sensible definition of national security without providing it with the space to gain a life of its own. "National security," he proposed to the other members of the seminar, "is the condition in which external attack, direct or indirect, by armed force or other means, upon the nation's territorial domain, rights, or vital interests is not likely to be made or, if made, to succeed." Weinberg was careful to explain what this definition did, and did not, include. The threat of attack, he emphasized, had to be external; internal enemies did not count unless they were directly connected to a foreign enemy. And while "the most obvious form of attack is upon the territorial domain, the other forms are important as well," such as "economic pressure," a violation of America's maritime rights, or an encroachment on "America's preponderance in the Caribbean." It was paramount, Weinberg stressed, that true national security could only be achieved when the United States was able to have an effective deterrence of any prospect of an attack.[22]

Weinberg's definition purported to be applicable not just to the United States but to every great power. His training as a historian, however, especially as a historian of American expansionism, made him alert to the peculiarities of the United States. Due to a condition that would later be called "free security"—that is, the protection afforded by two oceans to the east and west and weak neighbors to the north and south—by 1941 Americans had grown accustomed to the implausibility of an attack being made against the continental United States. "America's geographical detachment," he wrote elsewhere, "together with her notion of a distinctive mission, had given rise to a feeling of preordained right to *ideal* security."[23] As a result, Americans placed much greater emphasis on the possibility of indirect attack, attack by means other than armed force, and ideological threats. "In sum," Weinberg concluded, "the American concept of security tends to be more extreme, more exigent, than does the concept of security among most other peoples." The implications were profound: if Weinberg's analysis was correct, "the *conditions* of American security . . . are conceived on a less modest scale than usual." In turn, this meant that the shocking events of 1940–41 had dealt a "blow . . . of unusual force" to Americans' sense of security.[24]

Weinberg's analysis, in part an exposé of exaggerated fears about America's place in the modern world but also in part a codification of a national security doctrine that validated the mental framework that gave rise to such fears, tried to have it both ways, and other members of the seminar weren't hesitant to point this out. The political scientist Étienne Dennery, who had joined the Free French after the imposition of the collaborationist Vichy regime in Paris, found Weinberg's invocation of rights and vital interests "very vague." The economist Albert T. Lauterbach went even further, pronouncing Weinberg's discussion of vital interests "dangerously vague," too susceptible to manipulation and misinterpretation, and oblivious to the regional and social diversity within the United States that made finding a consensus on exactly what constituted the nation's vital interests to be difficult if not impossible. The historian Herbert Rosinski, a German Jew who had fled first to Great Britain and then the United States, where he taught at the Institute, lamented that "an objective definition of the term 'National Security' is impossible *in principle*" because one nation's security usually resulted in another's insecurity. "For these reasons," Rosinski explained, " 'national security' seems to me to represent not so much a tangible fact capable of exact definition as an ever changing problem of national guardianship," one that had to take into account the socioeconomic concerns of the people as well as the grander exigencies of statecraft observed by policymakers in Washington. Richard P. Stebbins, another Institute scholar and later the editor of the Council on Foreign

Relations' annual review *The United States in World Affairs*, similarly felt that "national security is incapable of objective measurement" because it cannot be altogether divorced from the 'freedom from care, anxiety or apprehension.'" It was only by "picturing" an international environment that allowed for the alleviation of America's fears that a true condition of national security could exist; while Stebbins thought such a definition, or "picturing," was desirable, he doubted it was feasible. Alfred Vagts, another German émigré at the Institute, also found Weinberg's definition too subjective.[25]

Perhaps the most skeptical person was Felix Gilbert, whose interests ranged widely from early-modern European political thought to American diplomatic history to general theories of historiography and methodology. Gilbert was Earle's closest Institute colleague and, with Gordon A. Craig, helped edit the various editions of Earle's *Makers of Modern Strategy* published between 1943 and 1986.[26] Gilbert was deeply immersed in the history of ideas, but it was perhaps his experience as a Jewish refugee from Nazi Germany that provided the basis for his skepticism of Weinberg's definition of national security. Gilbert saw a paradox in American ideas about security, and from there in Weinberg's attempt to codify them in a single definition: the preoccupation with security was a product of the rise of popular democracy in an age of mass industrialization and profound economic uncertainty. In previous eras, one would have spoken of "freedom" or perhaps "sovereignty" as the nation's chief objective; now, in an age of dislocation and anxiety, it was "security." Perhaps, Gilbert wondered, America's "peculiar concept of security," more acute and expansive than that of other countries, arose "precisely because it is the most democratic country" and was therefore more prone to the excessive whims of popular opinion.[27]

Weinberg's colleagues had all praised his efforts, yet they all had reservations with the ambiguous capaciousness with which he had defined "national security." But these critical assessments were themselves ambivalent, just as Weinberg himself had been, because while they all criticized the American tendency to exaggerate national insecurity, they also all recognized that it would be difficult to devise a new standard of national security without taking this insecurity into account. As the political economist Maxim von Brevern shrewdly noted, Weinberg's "conditioned term 'national security' also constitutes the fountain source of another equally potent force, namely 'manifest destiny.' "[28] Or as DeWitt Poole, the Institute's diplomat-in-residence who would soon help found the Office of Strategic Services, put it in a praiseworthy assessment, Weinberg had improved on stale notions of "basic security" and come up with a codification of "extended security" that "goes beyond the bare fact of continued existence and embraces 'rights' and 'vital interests' of unlimited geographical scope."[29]

As Poole had realized, here was America's new way of thinking for the new world order. National security as "extended security" came exceedingly close to emulating grand strategy, at least conceptually, for it was at the point where defensive security concerns stopped and proactive ambitions to shape the international environment began where security became strategy. National security could forge the two separate concepts together. As Weinberg had put it six years earlier, in his magnum opus on manifest destiny, "immediate self-preservation and permanent security are logically distinct goals. Expansion in behalf of security is really a defense against a possible and future rather than an actual and immediate danger."[30] Weinberg's new definition of national security now effectively bridged the distance between security and strategy, blending the immediate need for protection with a visionary ambition to reshape the external environment in America's favor.

Earle realized this too, and despite some mild and minor reservations, he accepted Weinberg's definition. In fact, he hoped to make it even broader still. For Earle, as for the other members of the seminar, security was both relative and relational, and never absolute. "If the *belief* in security does not exist," he observed, "even the *substance* of security may easily be destroyed." Creating the conditions for such a belief to flourish included guarding against the "strategy of terror" the Nazis had perfected, but it also meant maintaining an external environment that was conducive to America's engagement with the wider world. As Earle put it, "it can hardly be denied" that a key US objective was "an interest in, or at least a concern for, an ordered world and a free world."[31]

A Grand Strategy for a Great Power (In Waiting)

Armed with the seminar's insights on a working definition of national security, Earle now moved to gain wider acceptance, beyond the academy, for his interventionist ideas.[32] If the United States was to create hospitable conditions for "an ordered world and a free world," it needed to have a more realistic appreciation for the new requirements of self-defense. In turn, that new way of perceiving national security would inherently provide for a new grand strategy that would allow American officials to create that world. In this sense, an expansive appreciation of national security would itself provide the basis for a great-power grand strategy—indeed, one that would enable the United States to become the greatest of great powers. As Earle explained to the poet and Librarian of Congress Archibald MacLeish, "If we are to understand where we are heading, it seems to me clear that we should examine the fundamental and controlling conditions of American security and the manner in which they have been affected by political and technological developments of the last twenty-five years."[33]

The seminar built on ideas Earle had already been formulating, particularly the sense that national security should be thought of in broader terms than Americans were accustomed to using. But the seminar also provided Earle with a platform to disseminate the new doctrine of national security more broadly. Events overseas seemed to corroborate Earle's alarmism, and he found it difficult to understand why anti-interventionists continued to resist a more active role for the United States in world affairs, specifically in resisting the spread of Nazism and fascism. His most notable effort in popularizing these ideas came in a fiercely and eloquently argued polemic, *Against This Torrent*, which used the new doctrine of national security as a benchmark for a new American role in the world.[34] Earle then synthesized the Princeton seminar's various ideas of national security, including Weinberg's, into a workable definition that was published in *The Annals of the American Academy of Political and Social Science* on the eve of the Japanese attack on Pearl Harbor. Here, Earle recycled many of the themes he himself had written on and his Princeton seminar had debated. In an age of revolutionary, mechanized warfare and in "a highly integrated world," national security meant protecting moral values and economic freedoms as well as physical territory; it called for extended defense and not just reactive self-defense; it required creating the external environment that would enable Americans "to live our lives with reasonable freedom from care, anxiety, or apprehension." Doing anything less would be fatal because America faced totalitarian enemies with ambitions "to which no limits have been set and which leave no margin for error on our part." In the end, Earle concluded, "peace and safety are indivisible."[35] Although he didn't say so, he had repackaged manifest destiny for a global age.

Earle and his seminar were not alone in professing the indivisibility of peace and security. Other intellectuals, most prominently the columnist Walter Lippmann and the theologian Reinhold Niebuhr, offered a similar message in service to the same cause of American intervention on the side of the Allies.[36] More important, so too did President Franklin D. Roosevelt. Beginning in 1937, in response to the Japanese invasion of China, Roosevelt gradually nudged the United States closer and closer into a more activist role in resisting Axis aggression in Europe and Asia. Public opinion remained strongly anti-interventionist until the fall of France in June 1940, however, and so the president had to tread carefully. His most effective way of promoting internationalism and interventionism without getting too far in front of a more reluctant public and Congress was to, as John Thompson has rightly put it, "exaggerate American vulnerability," and his most effective way to do that so was to invoke the new doctrine of national security in order to illustrate that the United States needed to defend itself in a new world of risks and threats. National security, and its more extensive criteria of the things that needed defending—not just territorial sovereignty but also core values and vital interests—was a powerful answer to the problems raised by a totalitarian menace in an increasingly interdependent world.[37] Earle believed it was so powerful that it would be the most effective force to mobilize Americans at home for the indefinite global, ideological struggles that were certain to characterize the world from then on.[38]

National security, then, was not simply a description of what the United States needed to defend, or why; nor was it just a plan for how to defend what needed defending. It was instead a kind of system, an integrated analysis of a wide range of factors in identifying the myriad ideological, economic, political, cultural, and of course military threats to the United States and how Americans should respond. National security was, in other words, a kind of grand strategy in that it asked fundamental questions of calibrating means to ends in times of both war and peace. As Edward Mead Earle's leadership of the Princeton seminar demonstrates, the emergence of national security as America's grand strategy was neither incidental nor natural. Instead, it was a deliberate construction, a plan for the projection of America on a global scale.

Notes

1. Edward Mead Earle, "Introduction," in *Makers of Modern Strategy: Military Thought from Machiavelli to Hitler*, ed. Edward Mead Earle (Princeton, NJ: Princeton University Press, 1943), viii. Earle had been working on this definition of "grand strategy" for several years before publishing it. See David Ekbladh, "Present at the Creation: Edward

Mead Earle and the Depression-Era Origins of Security Studies," *International Security* 36 (Winter 2011/12), 119.

2. See, for example, Beatrice Heuser, *The Evolution of Strategy: Thinking War from Antiquity to the Present* (Cambridge: Cambridge University Press, 2010), 25–26; and Hal Brands, *What Good Is Grand Strategy? Power and Purpose in American Statecraft from Harry S. Truman to George W. Bush* (Ithaca, NY: Cornell University Press, 2014), 2. The most famous and influential of Earle's contemporaries was the British strategic theorist Basil Liddell Hart. On Earle's forebears in the United States, who were active during the interwar period, see Lukas Milevski, *The Evolution of Modern Grand Strategic Thought* (Oxford: Oxford University Press, 2016). However, it should be noted that several major studies of the history of strategy, particularly but not exclusively those that have a mainly British and/or continental European focus, do not mention Earle at all, even in passing. See, for example, Edward N. Luttwak, *Strategy: The Logic of War and Peace* (Cambridge, MA: Harvard University Press, 1987); Williamson Murray, MacGregor Knox, and Alvin Bernstein, eds., *The Making of Strategy: Rulers, States, and War* (Cambridge: Cambridge University Press, 1994); Colin S. Gray, *Modern Strategy* (Oxford: Oxford University Press, 1999); Williamson Murray, Richard Hart Sinnreich, and James Lacey, eds., *The Shaping of Grand Strategy: Policy, Diplomacy, and War* (Cambridge: Cambridge University Press, 2011); and Lawrence Freedman, *Strategy: A History* (Oxford: Oxford University Press, 2013).

3. Quoted in Linda Kulman, *Teaching Common Sense: The Grand Strategy Program at Yale University* (Westport, CT: Prospecta Press, 2016), 53. Aside from contemporaneous reviews, the most sustained historical examination of *Makers* is found in Michael P. M. Finch, "Edward Mead Earle and the Unfinished Makers of Modern Strategy," *Journal of Military History* 80 (July 2016), 781–814.

4. This is the chief complaint Hew Strachan, the staunchest and most articulate critic of the idea that strategy can apply beyond the realm of warfare, has of Earle. See his *The Direction of War: Contemporary Strategy in Historical Perspective* (Cambridge: Cambridge University Press, 2013), 34.

5. Paul Kennedy, "Grand Strategy in War and Peace: Toward a Broader Definition," in *Grand Strategies in War and Peace*, ed. Paul Kennedy (New Haven, CT: Yale University Press, 1991), 2.

6. On the national security revolution, and Earle's influential role in it, see Robert Endicott Osgood, *Ideals and Self-Interest in America's Foreign Relations: The Great Transformation of the Twentieth Century* (Chicago: University of Chicago Press, 1953), esp. 395–396; Daniel Yergin, *Shattered Peace: The Origins of the Cold War and the National Security State* (Boston: Houghton Mifflin, 1977), 193–220; Andrew Preston, "Monsters Everywhere: A Genealogy of National Security," *Diplomatic History* 38 (September 2014), 477–500; John A. Thompson, *A Sense of Power: The Roots of America's Global Role* (Ithaca, NY: Cornell University Press, 2015), esp. 204–216; and Dexter Fergie, "Geopolitics Turned Inwards: The Princeton Military Studies Group and the National Security Imagination," *Diplomatic History* 43 (September 2019), 644–670.

7. Ekbladh, "Present at the Creation," 117.

8. The book is Edward Mead Earle, *Turkey, the Great Powers, and the Bagdad Railway: A Study in Imperialism* (New York: Macmillan, 1923). Most of the articles are cited below. A similar criticism of Earle's relatively meagre thin body of work is made in Robert Vitalis, "Review of David Ekbladh," H-Diplo-ISSF Article Review 14 (June 2012), 2–3: https://issforum.org/ISSF/PDF/ISSF-AR14.pdf.

9. This is one of the central contentions of Ekbladh, "Present at the Creation," seen especially in 117, 127, 131–133, 139–141.

10. David John Allen, "Every Citizen a Statesman: Building a Democracy for Foreign Policy in the American Century," PhD dissertation, Columbia University, 2019, 65–69.

11. Ekbladh, "Present at the Creation," 115–120, 123–127; Inderjeet Parmar, *Foundations of the American Century: The Ford, Carnegie, and Rockefeller Foundations in the Rise of American Power* (New York: Columbia University Press, 2012), 73–76.

12. Ekbladh, "Present at the Creation," 132.

13. Fergie, "Geopolitics Turned Inwards," 658.

14. Edward Mead Earle, "American Military Policy and National Security," *Political Science Quarterly* 53 (March 1938), 4.

15. Felix Gilbert, *A European Past: Memoirs, 1905–1945* (New York: W. W. Norton, 1988), 175–176.

16. On the transition of the legal bases for waging war from the early-modern period to the twentieth century, see Oona A. Hathaway and Scott J. Shapiro, *The Internationalists: How a Radical Plan to Outlaw War Remade the World* (New York: Simon & Schuster, 2017). On the *Caroline* standard, see John Fabian Witt, *Lincoln's Code: The Laws of War in American History* (New York: Free Press, 2012), 112–117, 137–138.

17. My analysis here, and indeed throughout this entire chapter, rests heavily on John A. Thompson, "The Exaggeration of American Vulnerability: The Anatomy of a Tradition," *Diplomatic History* 16 (January 1992), 23–43.

18. Edward Mead Earle, "Political and Military Strategy for the United States," *Proceedings of the Academy of Political Science* 19 (January 1941), 3, 5, 8, 9.

19. "Introductory Statement to Seminar," September 26, 1941, Edward Mead Earle Papers, Research Files—WWI–WWII, National Defense, box 32, Seeley G. Mudd Manuscript Library, Princeton University (hereafter EME Papers). He returned to some of these suggestions in the 1943 edition of *Makers of Modern Strategy*: see Earle, "Introduction," vii.

20. Albert K. Weinberg, *Manifest Destiny: A Study of Nationalist Expansionism in American History* (Baltimore: Johns Hopkins University Press, 1935).

21. Albert K. Weinberg, "The Historical Meaning of the American Doctrine of Isolation," *American Political Science Review* 34 (June 1940), 539–547.

22. A. K. Weinberg, "The Meaning of National Security (in General and in American History)," ca. September 1941, Research Files—WWI–WWII, Security folder, box 33, EME Papers.

23. Weinberg, *Manifest Destiny*, 385. Emphasis in original.

24. Weinberg, "Meaning of National Security," Research Files—WWI–WWII, Security folder, box 33, EME Papers. Emphasis in original. "Free security" was first coined by

C. Vann Woodward, "The Age of Reinterpretation," *American Historical Review* 66 (October 1960), 1–19. For subsequent scholarly analyses that use free security, see Campbell Craig and Fredrik Logevall, *America's Cold War: The Politics of Insecurity* (Cambridge, MA: Harvard University Press, 2009); Preston, "Monsters Everywhere, 481–484; and Fergie, "Geopolitics Turned Inwards," 647–649.

25. "Comments on Mr. Weinberg's definition of National Security," Research Files—WWI–WWII, Security folder, box 33, EME Papers.

26. Earle, who died in 1954, dropped off the masthead for only the final volume, which was the most significantly revised and updated version: Peter Paret, ed., with Gordon A. Craig and Felix Gilbert, *Makers of Modern Strategy: From Machiavelli to the Nuclear Age* (Princeton, NJ: Princeton University Press, 1986).

27. "Comments on Mr. Weinberg's definition of National Security," Research Files—WWI–WWII, Security folder, box 33, EME Papers.

28. Ibid.

29. D. C. Poole to Earle, October 22, 1941, ibid.

30. Weinberg, *Manifest Destiny*, 384.

31. "Comments on Mr. Weinberg's definition of National Security," Research Files—WWI–WWII, Security folder, box 33, EME Papers. Emphasis in original.

32. Reading the published work of some of the other members in light of their time with Earle, it is clear that the seminar had an influence on their scholarship. This was another effective way to disseminate the seminar's novel ideas about national security and grand strategy. See, for example, Alfred Vagts, "The United States and the Balance of Power," *Journal of Politics* 3 (November 1941), 401–449; and Albert T. Lauterbach, "Militarism in the Western World: A Comparative Study," *Journal of the History of Ideas* 5 (October 1944), esp. 477–478.

33. Earle to Archibald MacLeish, November 21, 1941, Writings, Articles—"American Security," box 37, EME Papers.

34. Edward Mead Earle, *Against This Torrent* (Princeton, NJ: Princeton University Press, 1941). For a more detailed analysis of the book, see Preston, "Monsters Everywhere," 494–496.

35. Edward Mead Earle, "American Security: Its Changing Conditions," *Annals of the American Academy of Political and Social Science* 218 (November 1941), 189, 192, 193.

36. The literature on the interventionist foreign policies of Lippmann and Niebuhr is now large, but for recent analyses see, respectively, Patrick Porter, "Beyond the American Century: Walter Lippmann and American Grand Strategy, 1943–1950," *Diplomacy & Statecraft* 22 (December 2011), 557–577; and William C. Inboden, "The Prophetic Conflict: Reinhold Niebuhr, Christian Realism, and World War II," *Diplomatic History* 38 (January 2014), 49–82.

37. Thompson, "Exaggeration of American Vulnerability." See also Thompson, *A Sense of Power*, 151–192. The dramatic events of 1940–41 have been chronicled extensively, but for the best concise account, particularly its analysis of the changing course of American public opinion, see David Reynolds, *From Munich to Pearl Harbor: Roosevelt's America and the Origins of the Second World War* (Chicago: Ivan R. Dee, 2001). For a more detailed outline of Roosevelt's use of "national security,"

see Preston, "Monsters Everywhere," 477–500. "Vital interests" is of course from Weinberg, but "core values" comes from what is the most authoritative definition of the concept: Melvyn P. Leffler, "National Security," in *Explaining the History of American Foreign Relations*, 3rd ed., ed. Frank Costigliola and Michael J. Hogan (New York: Cambridge University Press, 2016), 25–41.

38. Fergie, "Geopolitics Turned Inwards."

12

The Misanthropy Diaries

Containment, Democracy, and the Prejudices of George Frost Kennan

David Greenberg

On a hot dusty Sunday in early September 1959, George Frost Kennan, the retired diplomat and renowned Sovietologist, welcomed to his Pennsylvania farmhouse an unusual trio of intellectuals. Trekking out to see him that Labor Day weekend were the German-born psychologist Erich Fromm, the sociologist David Riesman, and the perennial Socialist Party nominee for president Norman Thomas. Their agenda: the creation of a new socialist party for the United States.

"What a strange quartet we were," Kennan reflected. Though Thomas's name was synonymous with socialism in America and Fromm also hewed to the left, Riesman—"brilliant, subtle, and hugely imaginative"—had never been enchanted "by the waning power of Marx's magic spell." More to the point, Kennan himself had never harbored, as he put it, the smallest mote of "sympathy . . . with the inherent self-pity of the socialist cause." Edmund Burke, Edward Gibbon, and the nineteenth-century Russian novelists all shaped his own thinking far more than any left-wing thinkers ever had. "All my Scottish-Protestant antecedents rose in protest against [Fromm's] egalitarianism," he wrote in his diary. "This really wild belief in the general goodness of man, this obliviousness to the existence of original sin, . . . this grievous Marxist oversimplification of the sources of aggressiveness and bad behavior in the individual as in the mass"—it was all too naïve and wooly minded. Predictably, the attempted meeting of the minds ended in incoherence, thrusting Kennan back into what he called "the organizational isolation where, evidently, I belong."[1]

This vignette is one of many gems in the fascinating edition of Kennan's diaries that the historian Frank Costigliola published in 2014. Kennan has long been acclaimed, of course, for having formulated the containment doctrine that guided American policymakers as they lurched through the Cold War, as well as for his significant role in shaping US foreign policy as both a diplomat and a thinker. It's hard to think of a non-elected official of the last century with a more august reputation. Over many decades biographers, foreign-policy hands, politicians, intellectuals, and journalists have showered Kennan with praise and hailed him as the prime example of a grand strategist. Both *The Wise Men*, the influential group portrait of America's Cold War architects by the magazine journalists Evan Thomas and Walter Isaacson, and *George F. Kennan: An American Life*, the Pulitzer Prize-winning life by the eminent historian John Lewis Gaddis, rendered admiring judgments about him.[2] He has been credited not only with conceiving of containment but also with raising his voice against McCarthyism, promoting Radio Free Europe, opposing the nuclear arms race, and speaking out against the Vietnam War. For all the scholarly disputes about Kennan, there is general agreement that he was correct about many (though certainly not all) of the most vital issues of his time, and his "realism" has been often treated as a model from which subsequent American policymakers departed at their peril.[3]

Still, as Kennanologists have long known, there is more to the story. His acclaimed 1951 study, *American Diplomacy*, included disparaging statements about democracy, and starting with his brooding memoirs, published in 1967, and proceeding through his dyspeptic ruminations of the 1990s—*Around the Cragged Hill* and *At Century's Ending*—his writing exhibited nasty, misanthropic, and aristocratic currents. Several of the books about him reckon, if fleetingly, with this ugly side. Still, the publication of the voluminous private diaries he kept laid bare Kennan's foulness in ways that his other writings simply hadn't. Costigliola's edition of the diaries may well have been the most damaging collection of published private writings of any American public figure since H. L. Mencken's.[4]

The precise relationship between Kennan's personal prejudices and his political ideas will occupy scholars for many years. There is no simple way to map one onto the other. But his diaries do make clear that his animosities were anything but peripheral to his thought. That makes them significant, because Kennan was anything but peripheral to the formulation of American grand strategy in the twentieth century. To this day, when politicians, policymakers, and scholars discuss grand strategy, it's common for them to invoke Kennan as *the* paradigmatic figure. It was not just the containment doctrine that made him important; long after he left the State Department, he would return to Washington and to the newspapers to dispense advice like an oracle, weighing in on foreign policy undertakings from the Vietnam War to the Persian Gulf conflicts to the expansion of NATO.

He remains pertinent in the twenty-first century, too. In 2014, Barack Obama, rejecting criticisms that he had failed to use America's immense power to shape the geopolitical landscape for the greater good, disdained the value of grand strategy by stating, "I don't really even need George Kennan right now." Obama indeed considered the very idea of a Kennan-style grand strategy to be overrated. He acted as if individual foreign policy decisions could be viewed in relative isolation from one another and showed little concern for the ways that action or inaction in one place might ramify somewhere else. Ironically, Kennan's hard-bitten realism might have provided Obama with justification for his own aversion to championing the movements for democracy and human rights among repressed peoples. From his coolness toward the Green Revolution of Iran in 2009 to his refusal to become more sincerely involved in the Syrian civil war, Obama disappointed humanitarians and internationalist liberals with his return to a small-minded realism.

Nonetheless, in ostentatiously spurning Kennan and his legacy, Obama was also in a backhanded way attesting to the diplomat's importance. His struggle to diminish the importance of strategy even as he shunned peaceful democracy promotion was in its own convoluted way a tribute to Kennan's enduring importance to the ways in which America practices its international relations.[5]

The Loner

Kennan's importance, indeed, was what invested the publication of his diaries in 2014 with such significance. Spanning the years from 1916, when he was eleven, to 2004, when he was ninety-nine, the diaries exude a pervasive, relentless gloom. As his misbegotten 1959 effort to forge a common agenda with Fromm, Riesman, and Thomas made clear, Kennan was a man whose ideas were central to American foreign policy in the twentieth century, and yet who also believed that he had no real home in its political system. Normally a supporter of Democrats—in the diaries he voices support for the presidential bids of Adlai Stevenson, John F. Kennedy, Eugene McCarthy, Frank Church ("promptly regretted it deeply"), and Bill Clinton ("without enthusiasm")—Kennan was at the same time soberly conservative in his worldview and ill at ease in his own country. His conservatism was neither the belligerent cultural populism bequeathed to today's Republicans by Richard Nixon nor the happy hawkishness championed by Ronald Reagan (both of whom, incidentally, Kennan abhorred). It partook, rather, of Burke's chastened view of human nature; the declinism of Gibbon; and the Social Darwinism of Herbert Spencer and William Graham Sumner, which often manifested in casual and appalling prejudices. Above all, it echoed the lugubrious anti-modernism and civilizational despair of Henry Adams, to whom Kennan likened himself in the winter of his life. The brains behind the policy of containment, it turns out, crafted the policy in defense of a country he never much liked, filled with citizens he mostly despised.[6]

So bleak was Kennan's worldview that even when ensconced with tenure for a half-century at the Institute for Advanced Study in Princeton, without so much as a few graduate students to interfere with his freedom to think, he would constantly wonder about the purpose of it all. For all his accomplishments, he forever despaired in his notebooks of influencing anyone or anything. Statesmen would seek his counsel, editors would solicit his articles, audiences would invite him to speak. But no one ever seemed to listen.

His Pennsylvania farm providing inadequate refuge from the vulgar society, Kennan even fantasized about retreating to New Hampshire or Vermont to farm. As the years passed, these fantasies shifted to ever more remote locales: Alaska, Norway, Antarctica. In his own mind, he was a relic of the nineteenth century, a misfit in modern times. The achievements of science, medicine, and technology left him cold. He saw only the defilement of nature wrought by the automobile and the corruption of the spirit brought on by consumer society, whose blight he lamented with numbing frequency. "With all due effort to avoid exaggerated pessimism and overdramatization," he wrote, in a typical passage, from 1978, "I can see no salvation for the U.S. either in its external relations nor in the development of its life internally." From urban decay to the decline of the schools, from the media's crass commercialism to sexual libertinism, he saw about him a decadent society—late Rome—offering grounds only for hopelessness.[7]

To Russia with Love

Kennan's fatalistic worldview was inculcated early in life. Born in 1904 to a family of Wisconsin Presbyterians, he lost his mother at two months old—the wellspring of his lifelong melancholy. Even late into his life, Florence Kennan would appear in George's dreams. Wallowing in his loneliness, the young Kennan developed a tragic sensibility that he carried with him as an undergraduate at Princeton, where he felt alienated from the student body's Fitzgeraldian wealth and whimsy. After graduation, he joined the Foreign Service and lived abroad for most of the next two decades. While overseas, he met his wife, a Norwegian named Annelise Sorensen, and developed his expertise in Russia—a subject that had also enchanted another George Kennan, an older cousin well known a century ago for his explorations in Siberia.

The younger Kennan found much to dislike about Russia, as he did about most places he visited, calling it, for example, "a filthy, sordid country, full of vermin, mud, stench and disease."[8] But he also came to love it, and he immersed himself in its history and culture. Early on, he discerned the exhaustion of the communist ideal. "Will the burly overalled worker, with his sleeves rolled up, brandishing a red flag and striding over the bodies of top-hatted capitalists, ever grasp the hearts of people as it did just after the war?" he wondered in 1935. "I doubt it."[9]

Kennan's historical studies gave him an appreciation as well of his host nation's need for a sphere of influence. With his tragic sensibility, Kennan accepted that this meant that the West should at the end of World War II forsake the freedoms of many Eastern Europeans. Most immediately, it meant abandoning the so-called London Poles, Poland's wartime government-in-exile, and with them the hopes of all Poles for self-determination. After dining in 1944 with Stanislaw Mikolajczyk, the leader of the London Poles, Kennan noted, "I wished that instead of mumbling words of official optimism, we had the judgment and the good taste to bow our heads in silence before the tragedy of a people who have been our allies, whom we have saved from our enemies, and whom we cannot save from our friends." The West could do little to stop Stalin from installing, in brazen violation of his commitments, a stooge regime.[10]

Kennan's knowledge of Russia and his inveterate pessimism led him, while serving in the American Embassy in Moscow after the war, to craft his famous "Long Telegram." This 5,500-word analysis of the Soviet regime held out only the most meager prospects for continuing the wartime alliance. It argued that Soviet leaders were "committed fanatically to the belief that with the U.S. there can be no permanent modus vivendi." Still, Kennan insisted, the relationship could be managed peaceably.[11] Circulated in Washington,

Kennan's missive "set out no fully conceived grand strategy," as Gaddis has emphasized.[12] But, along with an expanded articulation of Kennan's thoughts, "The Sources of Soviet Conduct," which was published the next year in *Foreign Affairs* under the pseudonym "X," the Long Telegram gave rise to the doctrine of containment. Steering a middle course between the folly of war and the futile Wallaceite hope of frictionless cooperation, Kennan counseled containing the Soviet drive to expand its influence through the strategic application of American power.

By the time Kennan wrote the "X" article, Secretary of State George C. Marshall had named him to run the State Department's newly created Policy Planning Staff. It is a testament to Kennan's legacy that the office has since been treated as a perch for the department's resident intellectual (although, truth be told, the most notable cultural document to emerge from the office since Kennan's day may well be Anne-Marie Slaughter's *Atlantic* article on motherhood and careerism, "Why Women Still Can't Have It All").[13] In his diaries, Kennan explains why, even during his own tenure, the Policy Planning office was consigned to ineffectuality. "It is time I recognized that my planning staff . . . has simply been a failure, like all previous attempts to bring order and foresight into the designing of foreign policy by special institutional arrangements," he groused in 1949. "The reason for this seems to lie largely in the impossibility of having the planning function performed outside of the line of command. . . . No one can regiment this institution in the field of ideas except the Secretary." Meaningful planning couldn't arise from an adjunct office, he understood; it had to flow from the top.[14]

Kennan—whose bouts of self-loathing alternated with egotistical claims about his unique prophetic powers—was underselling his contributions at State. In particular, the Marshall Plan, a praised pillar of Harry Truman's Cold War foreign policy, drew direct inspiration from Kennan's arguments about the need to bolster postwar Europe with economic assistance. But Kennan was correct that his influence had already peaked. He finished out Truman's presidency with a fruitless stint as ambassador to the Soviet Union before being rudely forced into retirement by the incoming president, Dwight Eisenhower, and his imperious secretary of state, John Foster Dulles, who vowed to replace containment with a more aggressive plan of "rollback," which Kennan deplored as reckless. Kennan repaired to the Institute of Advanced Study to think, write, and brood about the demise of Western civilization.

Containing Containment

Containment served American policymakers well, though it was not without costs. In later years, a simplistic critique of the doctrine would argue that it led the United States into terrible misadventures, especially in Vietnam. But there was nothing inherent in containment, as Kennan had first articulated it, that required intervening everywhere that communism was ascendant. Kennan himself, as is well known and as his diaries amply attest, opposed military intervention in Vietnam. He describes one of President Lyndon B. Johnson's first bombing raids, on February 7, 1965, as "petulant escapism" that "will, I fear, lead to no good results." Containment, Kennan always held, did not mandate intervention in non-strategic places as far away as Southeast Asia, nor was it primarily a prescription to use military force.[15]

But if Kennan found it easy to fault other policymakers' misinterpretations of containment, he didn't always make it easy for them to know what he meant by it. As with most grand doctrines, the devil was in the details, rendering the doctrine less than reliable in its specific applications. Famously, he called for the "adroit and vigilant application of counterforce at a series of constantly shifting geographical and political points, corresponding to the shifts and maneuvers of Soviet policy." But not every president or policymaker would identify the same pressure points, and the ground for interpretive disputation was sowed. As early as 1947, Kennan was critical of the Truman Doctrine—the president's pledge to help free peoples resisting communist subjugation—on the grounds that it was too expansive, even though he did favor helping Greece and Turkey to fight off Soviet efforts at subversion. In short, no sooner had he proposed the idea of containment than he feared it was being corrupted. When Walter Lippmann subjected the X article to a thoroughgoing critique in a series of columns for the *New York Herald Tribune*, Kennan found himself endorsing many of Lippmann's criticisms—or so he later said.[16]

Yet as the diaries remind us, Kennan was hardly averse to using military force, despite his later reputation among latter-day isolationists as something of a dove. He was hawkish, for instance, in support of the Korean War. After hearing news of the North Korean attack on the South in 1950, Kennan promptly revised his terms for the containment doctrine, extending from Europe to Asia the "defensive perimeter" he had previously called for. He adopted a hard-line stance against the North Koreans and their Soviet and Chinese sponsors, even if that required putting more American troops under arms than first planned. "We had to go through with our purpose in Korea, come what may," he wrote in July 1950, warning of the consequences should the Russians smell weakness. To his colleagues he argued that it "was a question of our will and not our ability."[17]

Kennan was a hawk on Suez, too. In 1956, when Israel, Britain, and France tried to stop Egypt—with Soviet backing—from nationalizing the Suez Canal, Kennan faulted Eisenhower and Dulles for capitulating to the Russians and "selling out French and British interests there." (He never cared much about Israeli interests.) He feared, he wrote, that the Russians might "dominate the area and use the oil, to the extent that they could control it, as an instrument of blackmail against the West." Given this shifting advice, depending on the "geographical and political points" at stake, it would be wrong to surmise crudely that containment applied in Egypt and Korea, but not Eastern Europe or Vietnam. But it is easy to wonder if containment, at least as Kennan intended it, applied pretty much wherever Kennan thought it applied at any given moment.[18]

Kennan's Heart of Darkness

While Kennan's private accounts of his dealings with his Russian counterparts, his arguments about Korean War strategy, and other such material amount to a tremendous historical resource, they are not the chief revelation of his diaries. Rather, what dominates the text—especially in the latter half of Kennan's life, when his interactions with power are fleeting and ceremonial—are the *pensées* about life, career, and humankind. Kennan himself said as much. "I have been reading over the diary entries from 1964–1984, and have derived little pride or satisfaction from the effort," he wrote in 1987. "Where they were not personally plaintive, they tended to be repetitive."[19]

Ironically, what spells the tedium—what compels a fascination despite Kennan's monotony—are the eye-popping outbursts of bigotry against all manner of ethnic groups. The value of these splendid rants was lost on the former *New Yorker* editor William Shawn, who after he had left the magazine had occasion to peruse them on behalf of what Kennan calls "the very Jewish firm of Straus & Farrar." As Kennan recorded, Shawn (who was Jewish) told Kennan's agent Harriet Wasserman (also Jewish) that Kennan's disparaging comments about Jews and the Jewish people, along with no visible trace of his having criticized the Nazi regime while stationed in Germany at the start of World War II, made publication inadvisable. Kennan denied any problem. "I have never been anti-Semitic," he insists, with a breathtaking lack of self-awareness, "but I must admit that this episode brought me as close as I have ever been to becoming one."[20] Ten years later, he would still see Jewishness as a salient trait as only an anti-Semite would. "The scandal of Mr. Clinton's relationship to his Jewish girl intern" begins one diary entry written during the Monica Lewinsky sex scandal that captivated that national news media for the better part of a year.[21]

The diaries establish beyond any doubt, and in starker relief than even his previous books, that Kennan was given to gross and derogatory generalizations about not only Jews but virtually all foreign peoples. His belief in national character was strong, and if it led him to useful insights about Russian behavior, much more often it led to mere prejudice. The shockers in the diaries start early. During his junior year at Princeton, he wrote about a conversation with a friend called Army. "He half-converted me to his 'extermination of the lower races' idea," Kennan writes. "I cannot see why it is wrong in principle." As a twenty-eight-year-old Foreign Service officer, he remained convinced that the world's problems were "essentially biological" in that "we have a group of more or less inferior races. . . . No amount of education and discipline can effectively improve conditions as long as we allow the unfit to breed copiously and to preserve their young." Nor did Kennan learn, in his long globetrotting career, to see this kind of talk as the rubbish that it is. At the age of eighty, he was still confiding to his diary his enthusiasm for eugenics. "If I had my way," he muses, "men having spawned more than 2 children will be compulsively sterilized. Planned parenthood and voluntary sterilization will be in every way encouraged." Immigration, too, "will be effectively terminated."[22] These pronouncements cannot be waved away as the typical prejudices of his day, or with the excuse that Kennan was simply a "creature of his times." That sort of explanation may be useful in contextualizing the prejudices held by many historical figures, but not Kennan's; his attitudes were extreme even for a time when bigotry was rampant, and he held onto them well past the time when the norms of society had dramatically changed.

So who were these "inferior races" whom Kennan deplored? Jews, to be sure. But the Jews were in good company. In fact, in the diaries it's hard to find an ethnic group that escapes his contempt. An Italian he meets while traveling is a "typical dago—wears a cap, a bushy, black moustache . . . talkative in a weak, ignorant, furtive, sneering way." The Georgians, he proclaims, are "a lazy, dirty, tricky, fiercely proud and recklessly brave people. They never seem to work unless they have to." The Iraqis he encounters on a 1944 trip to Baghdad? "A population unhygienic in its habits, sorely weakened and debilitated by disease, inclined to all manner of religious bigotry and fanaticism, condemned by the tenets of the most widespread faith to keep a full half of the population, namely the feminine half, confined and excluded from the productive efforts of society but a system of indefinite house arrest."[23]

No group is too small or too far outside Kennan's expertise to elude his confident condescension. Zambians are wracked by "suppressed anger" and "ostentatious cockiness." Lithuanians are "foolish." What he finds ugly about southern stretches of New England—the landscape "grown over by scrub forest"—he attributes to the "Italians and Portuguese, the tone set increasingly by the Catholic Church." Even the Norwegians—of whom his wife was one—"for all their admirable characteristics . . . have small regard for subtleties & refinement of thought."[24]

Unsurprisingly, blacks do not rank high in Kennan's estimation. In one lunatic rant, from 1978, he envisions all of humanity destined to "melt into a vast polyglot mass," with only the Chinese, Jews, and blacks remaining apart. "Could this mean that these three minorities are destined to subjugate and dominate all as an uneasy but unavoidable triumvirate the rest of society—the Chinese by their combination of intelligence, ruthlessness, and ant-like industriousness; the Jews by their sheer determination to survive as a culture; the Negroes by their ineradicable bitterness and hatred of the whites?" His racism toward African peoples extended to his evaluation of South African apartheid. "It is not my purpose here to appear as an apologist for the practices of the South African government in racial questions," he writes in 1967, "but . . . " He proceeds not only to excuse apartheid but also to warn that "a reversal of South African policy designed to force racial segregation on a reluctant white population" would produce results as bad as those "in many a number of great American cities." Even as late as 1990, with democratic change sweeping that country, he remains impassive. "I have no confidence in the prospects for anything like a mingling of the races in South Africa, nor can I permit myself to hope that whites will be permitted to retain very much of the quality of their own lives."[25]

Ethnic and racial bigotry, alas, did not exhaust Kennan's reservoir of prejudice. Equally backward were his attitudes toward women. He conceived of the sexes as wholly different creatures, with women subordinate. "A woman, as she grows older, should become more sociable," he reflected in midlife, "and should seek her compensation in service to others, without asking too much from them." Again, this was hardly an uncommon view among men of his generation, but here too Kennan's penchant for orotund pronouncements renders his precepts about women's roles exceptionally obnoxious—such as his argument that biblical injunctions against adultery were conceived when polygamy was the norm, and thus "it was easier to observe when you had 35 of them." (It's hard not to hear in such passages a justification for his own infidelity—a theme of Gaddis's biography.) Then there was homosexuality. Kennan saw the rising visibility of gays in American life as another sign of moral rot. "The weird efforts to claim for homosexuality the status of a proud, noble, and promising way of life," he grouped with "shameless pornography" and "the pathological preoccupation with sex and violence" as a mark of America's "unrestrained decadence" at the century's end.[26]

A Thoroughgoing Misanthropy

The more time one spends with Kennan, the more one sees that this disdain toward the various peoples of the world was part of a thoroughgoing misanthropy. Even as a young man, he expresses disgust with regular people. In one case it is a group of Rotarians with whom he shares an ocean crossing from Europe, whom he deems "nice people" but without "a real lady or gentlemen among them. . . . They are children, and it is a bore to have to protect children from their environment when you cannot discipline them and teach them to protect themselves." (Kennan was all of twenty-eight.) Any encounters with the masses leave him angry and scornful, complaining to his diary about Americans' love of television, cars (in ice storms, he takes pleasure from motorists sliding on the roadways), instant gratification, and—waxing lyrical—the culture's "wretched sexual encounters in the back-seats of cars, its proudly worn gonorrheas, its hangovers, its cruelties, its bad faith." Even when he seeks escape from America's vulgarity in the refined climes of old Europe, his countrymen annoy him. " 'These damned American tourists,' so goes my inner protest, 'with their lousy clothes—their exposed undershirts, their California-style "casual" shirts, their jeans and tennis shoes: Why do they have to be here in the Zurich airport?' "[27]

Kennan's contempt for his fellow Americans may be the most startling of all his hatreds. It is hard, after all, to reconcile his loyal career in government with the low opinion he held of the United States and its people. "For me this country presents no interest whatsoever," he wrote while on a train from Washington to Princeton in December 1953. "This is an infinitely boring country, which, though it has not the slightest idea about this, is condemned to a sad and pitiful fate." Or, a few years later: "For my own country, I have not a shred of hope, not one." Two decades later, more of the same: "More and more it is borne upon me how little I have in common with, how little I belong to, this polyglot accumulation of people in the meridial part of North America."[28]

Kennan's revulsion toward the mediocrity that he saw as endemic to America was connected ultimately to a hostility toward democracy itself, and here the personal views start to impinge on his political philosophy. (Kennan himself believed there was a connection; when he published *Around the Cragged Hill*, he gave it the subtitle *A Personal and Political Philosophy*.) Though he deplored Soviet communism and put his intellectual and diplomatic skills to use fighting it on his country's behalf, he never had much regard for the alternative. One price of loving democracy is tolerating—even enjoying—its messiness and conflicts, its interest-group jockeying, its coalitions and deal-making, its pluralism. Any citizenry can, of course, be ill-informed and short-sighted and make bad choices. We rely on sagacious leaders to respond to public opinion with not just respect and sensitivity but also independence of judgment. But Kennan never had any patience for the give-and-take of democracy, the struggles of engaging with public opinion to put public policy on a firm popular basis. "I believe in dictatorship," he wrote as a young man, during the Depression, "but not the dictatorship of the proletariat. The proletariat, like a well-brought up child, should be seen and not heard. It should be properly clothed and fed and sheltered, but not crowned with a moral halo, and above all not allowed to have anything to do with government."[29]

After his 1930s flirtation, Kennan stopped singing the praises of outright dictatorship. The United States wasn't about to abandon democracy. Throughout his life, however, he continued to imagine "better" alternatives, such as "hereditary oligarchy," which he believed history had shown to be a more reliable custodian of the public welfare than self-government. Later in life, as if resigned to the permanence of American democracy, he took pains to stipulate that he supported only "representative government" and not direct democracy. Moreover, the public, he held, should be restricted in its voting choices to a slate of candidates selected by some other elite body. "It is not in the election of representatives that our system fails; it is in the process of nomination. That is an extremely complicated problem."[30] By the time Kennan published *Around the Cragged Hill* in 1993, he had arrived at a solution that he called a "Council of State," an unelected body that would take over key government functions. Reviewers of the book, who treated the idea as eccentric but charming, failed to recognize that it was only the most gentle of Kennan's anti-democratic tendencies, one of the few he was willing to publish.[31]

But Kennan's dim view of democracy, of America, of humankind is of more than passing interest. It is more than a quirky sidelight to a distinguished intellectual career—like Vladimir Nabokov's lepidoptery or Dwight Macdonald's nudism. This isn't to say that these views should be used to dismiss his contributions to foreign policy. Innumerable thinkers and artists, diplomats and politicians, have enriched the world with their ideas despite holding some contemptible views. All the same, when currents of thought run so deep and so consistently through someone's worldview, they need to be reckoned with.

One place to begin might be in reconsidering Kennan's much-praised realism, the cold-eyed interest-based pragmatism that he prescribed for American foreign policymakers, which has since the Iraq War been enjoying a renaissance.

In his diaries, Kennan summarized this idea as he made notes for an article for *Foreign Affairs* in 1953. "What I would like to show," he wrote, "is that the conduct of the foreign relations of a great country is a practical, not a moral, exercise. What is at stake is the adjustment of conflicting interests."[32] This nostrum, or some version of it, has become an axiom of the realist current in international relations theory that has long been associated with Kennan and others—and shapes much thinking about grand strategy as well. The precept makes a certain amount of sense when thinking about the great-power politics that dominated Kennan's time: in the early Cold War, realism served as a brake on the extreme, religiously infused anti-communism of men like John Foster Dulles, and in the Vietnam years it birthed a critique of the war more temperate than that of the New Left and its moralism. The practice of diplomacy and international relations should always keep practical goals and constraints clearly in view. As Kennan's fellow Washington mandarin Joseph Alsop once observed, the sage was at his best when he could apply his chessboard thinking and pragmatic judgments to geopolitical realities. "Although he regards himself as a total contemplative," Alsop noted of his friend, "George makes his best sense as a man of action, when there is a good, loud cable machine at his elbow clanking out horrible problems all over the world. When George broods, he becomes a little silly." [33]

The Limits of Realism

The problem went deeper than Kennan's brooding. He and his disciples seldom acknowledged that any purely realist, interest-based philosophy has limitations. The shortcomings of realism have been especially evident when it comes to peoples whose interests aren't represented at the great powers' bargaining table: immigrants and refugees, minorities and subjugated classes in other sovereign states, citizens of weak or failing nations, people being persecuted or exterminated, and many others. Those interests, after all, are precisely the ones that are sacrificed when the great powers banish moral considerations from their calculus and seek only the adjustment of interests. Foreign policy shouldn't be sentimental, but neither should it be inhumane. Kennan, with his romantic sensibility, was hardly indifferent to feeling. Yet his realism was rooted in a personal contempt for other people, especially those not like him, which could translate into a callous willingness to let them suffer. "For my entire literary life, as I now see it," he wrote in his diaries, "has been one long effort to gain understanding for the outlooks of others and to reach their understanding for my own."[34] As long as he lived, he still had far to go on that journey.

Kennan's disregard for peoples unlike himself also hampered his ability to think productively about emerging nations of Africa and Asia. He may have been astute in assessing the superpower rivalry of the Cold War and the arms race, but he displayed little insight into the importance of decolonization and the proliferation of independent countries that also marked the late twentieth century.[35] In contrast, a less cramped thinker like Arthur M. Schlesinger Jr., in his role as a speechwriter for John F. Kennedy, argued that the Cold War conflict offered a chance to help improve both the material and political conditions of emerging nations: as decolonization proceeded, new nations would tend to prefer open political systems like America's because the free pursuit of knowledge about science and technology could help them develop and thrive in a liberal international order. Kennan's ideas about grand strategy rarely proceeded along such lines.[36]

In general, ideas about grand strategy are still typically associated with the amoral realism of men like Kennan. It can be easy to make too much of the impact of Kennan's prejudices, misanthropy, and discomfort with democracy on his strategic thinking. Yet his unsavory qualities affirm the need to broaden the basic elements that policymakers or analysts should consider in developing a foreign policy strategy that is effective, enlightened, and far-sighted. These elements include humanitarian considerations, human rights, cultural diversity, and the attractions that liberal democracy holds for all kinds of peoples. Barack Obama did not "need" a George Kennan to reinforce his realist instincts, but neither was he well served by an improvisational foreign policy devoted to merely "hitting singles and doubles," as he awkwardly put it in 2014.[37] What he needed was a strategy that took stock of both Kennan's insights and his blind spots.

Kennan liked to note those occasions on which he was astute or prescient in assessing big problems. "In the case of the Soviet Union, I was one of the first to recognize the essentiality of the ideology to the regime . . . that you cannot expect to have normal relations with people who have a great deal of blood on their hands." And again: "I was one of the first, and the few, to recognize that the weapons of mass destruction invalidated all previous thinking and doctrine concerning the value and uses of armed force."[38] Setting aside the immodesty (and dubious accuracy) of some of these boasts, Kennan was, without question, profoundly influential on these other important questions of the day. He was also often right. But one reason that America was spared the consequences of Kennan's uglier ideas was that he always played a subordinate role to men like Franklin Roosevelt, Harry Truman, and John F. Kennedy who, like most great politicians, possessed a love of their people—and a love of humanity—that George Kennan seemed unable to retrieve from within himself.

Notes

1. George F. Kennan, *The Kennan Diaries*, ed. Frank Costigliola (New York: Norton, 2014), 392–393.
2. Walter Isaacson and Evan Thomas, *The Wise Men: Six Friends and the World They Made* (New York: Simon & Schuster, 1986); John Lewis Gaddis, *George F. Kennan: An American Life* (New York: Penguin Press, 2011). These two books probably have done the most to shape Kennan's reputation. But the historiography is considerably larger, as the note below makes clear.
3. That Kennan has attained the status of a sage does not mean that scholars have been uniform in their admiration of him or his diplomacy. On the contrary, a

lively contentiousness characterizes the sizable literature on Kennan. Though the whole of that corpus is too large to summarize here, key works include not only the aforementioned books by Gaddis and by Isaacson and Thomas but also the following treatments of his life, career, and thought: Barton Gellman, *Contending with Kennan: Toward a Philosophy of American Power* (New York: Praeger, 1984); John Lukacs, *George Kennan: A Study of Character* (New Haven, CT: Yale University Press, 2007); David Mayers, *George Kennan and the Dilemmas of U.S. Foreign Policy* (New York: Oxford University Press, 1988); Wilson D. Miscamble, *George F. Kennan and the Making of American Foreign Policy, 1947–1950* (Princeton, NJ: Princeton University Press, 1992); Walter L. Hixson, *George F. Kennan: Cold War Iconoclast* (New York: Columbia University Press, 1989); Anders Stephanson, *Kennan and the Art of Foreign Policy* (Cambridge, MA: Harvard University Press, 1989); and Nicholas Thompson, *The Hawk and the Dove: Paul Nitze, George Kennan, and the History of the Cold War* (New York: Henry Holt, 2009). Also important are Kennan's *Memoirs* (Boston: Little, Brown, 1967–72). Notable, too, are two earlier works by Gaddis, *The United States and the Origins of the Cold War, 1941–1947* (New York: Columbia University Press, 1972); John Lewis Gaddis, *Strategies of Containment: A Critical Appraisal of Postwar American National Security Policy* (New York: Oxford University Press, 1982), as well as Michael J. Hogan, *The Marshall Plan: America, Britain, and the Reconstruction of Western Europe, 1947–1952* (New York: Cambridge University Press, 1987); and Melvyn P. Leffler, *A Preponderance of Power: National Security, the Truman Administration, and the Cold War* (Stanford, CA: Stanford University Press, 1992). Finally. this list does not include the many book introductions, essays, and book reviews about Kennan or the books about the Cold War, US diplomatic history, or US history in general in which Kennan plays a significant role.

4. George F. Kennan, *American Diplomacy* (Chicago: University of Chicago Press, 1951); George F. Kennan, *Around the Cragged Hill: A Personal and Political Philosophy* (New York: W.W. Norton, 1993); George F. Kennan, *At a Century's Ending: Reflections, 1982–1995* (New York: W.W. Norton, 1996). On Mencken, see "Mencken's Dark Side," *Washington Post*, December 5, 1989, C2; Edwin McDowell, "Book Notes," *New York Times*, December 6, 1989, C26; and H. L. Mencken, *The Diary of H. L. Mencken*, ed. Charles A. Fecher (New York: Alfred A. Knopf, 1989).

5. It remains an interesting question whether Obama lacked a grand strategy altogether or whether he followed a strategy that was rooted in a reluctance to assertively seek to shape the outcomes of foreign conflicts, even when unfavorable outcomes there might do harm to the United States. Voicing a common critique, the German editor and foreign policy thinker Josef Joffe told *New Yorker* editor David Remnick: "There is certainly consistency and coherence in his attempt to retract from the troubles of the world, to get the U.S. out of harm's way, in order to do 'a little nation-building at home,' as he has so often put it. If you want to be harsh about it, he wants to turn the U.S. into a very large medium power, into an XXL France or Germany." David Remnick, "Going the Distance: On and Off the Road with Barack Obama," *The New Yorker*, January 27, 2014. On the other hand, some saw Obama as simply eschewing grand strategy. As noted in this volume's introduction, Obama once inadvertently revealed the paucity

of his foreign policy vision by describing it as "don't do stupid shit"—a statement first reported in Mike Allen, "Playbook," *Politico*, June 1, 2014. This proved a liability to his former secretary of state Hillary Clinton in her 2016 presidential bid, and she disavowed it in an interview with the journalist Jeffrey Goldberg. Jeffrey Goldberg, "Hillary Clinton: 'Failure' to Help Syrian Rebels Led to the Rise of ISIS," *The Atlantic*, August 10, 2014.

6. Kennan, *Diaries*, 494, 629, 633.
7. Ibid., 509.
8. Ibid., 92.
9. Ibid., 109.
10. Ibid., 167.
11. Gaddis, *Kennan*, 220.
12. Ibid., 230.
13. Anne-Marie Slaughter, "Why Women Still Can't Have It All," *The Atlantic*, July/August 2012.
14. Kennan, *Diaries*, 236.
15. Ibid., 431.
16. Walter Lippmann, *The Cold War: A Study in U.S Foreign Policy* (New York: Harper's, 1947); Gaddis, *Kennan*, 274.
17. Kennan, *Diaries*, 258; Gaddis, *Kennan*, 395–397.
18. Kennan, *Diaries*, 362–363.
19. Ibid., 578.
20. Ibid., 585, 593–594.
21. Ibid., 662.
22. Ibid., 9, 78, 555.
23. Ibid., 34, 112, 163.
24. Ibid., 445, 609, 339.
25. Ibid., 508, 447, 607.
26. Ibid., 316, 335, 637.
27. Ibid., 76, 356, 386, 548.
28. Ibid., 337, 387, 503.
29. Ibid., 79.
30. Ibid., 309, 569.
31. George F. Kennan, *Around the Cragged Hill: A Personal and Political Philosophy* (New York: Norton, 1993), 239–248.
32. Kennan, *Diaries*, 333.
33. Quoted in Gaddis, *Kennan*, 397.
34. Ibid., 628.
35. On this, see Clayton R. Koppes, "Solving for X: Kennan, Containment, and the Color Line," *Pacific Historical Review* 82:1 (February 1, 2013), 95–118.
36. Schlesinger's role in Kennedy's 1962 University of California at Berkeley speech in which those ideas were expressed is discussed in Richard Aldous, *Schlesinger: The Imperial Historian* (New York: W.W. Norton, 2017), 285–286. The speech itself can be found online. John F. Kennedy, "Address in Berkeley at the University of California,"

March 23, 1962, The American Presidency Project, http://www.presidency.ucsb.edu/ws/?pid=8566.

37. "It avoids errors," he said at an April 2014 press conference in the Philippines. "You hit singles, you hit doubles; every once in a while we may be able to hit a home run. But we steadily advance the interests of the American people and our partnership with folks around the world." Juliet Eilperin, "Obama Lays Out His Foreign Policy Doctrine," *Washington Post*, April 28, 2014.

38. Kennan, *Diaries*, 518.

13

Implementing Grand Strategy

The Nixon-Kissinger Revolution at the National Security Council

William Inboden

Recent years have witnessed a renaissance of sorts in the study of grand strategy. It has been revived as a term of art used by scholars and policymakers, courses and programs in grand strategy have proliferated at colleges and universities across the nation, and writers have been producing an array of books and articles on many angles and permutations of grand strategy. Amid this revival, and as this volume illustrates, "grand strategy" remains a contested and malleable concept that raises as many questions as it answers. For example, it sits uneasily at the intersection of historical analysis and policy prescription. Should scholars, historians in particular, confine ourselves to employing grand strategy as a heuristic frame to help us understand the past actions of leaders and nations in the realm of statecraft? Or may we also employ grand strategy as a framework to help translate our historical insights into possible use by policymakers today?

Mindful of the abundant risks that beset the latter approach, I still believe it is warranted. Policy professionals and political leaders remain drawn to history more than perhaps any other academic discipline, and in their own efforts to formulate strategy at all levels they will often first turn to history. Here historians working on grand strategy have an opportunity—or even an obligation—to respond to this interest of the policymaking community.

Thus far scholars have largely neglected an essential dimension of grand strategy, one that especially preoccupies policymakers: How should a government be organized to implement and execute a particular grand strategy? For the president of the United States—ostensibly the most powerful person in the world—how does he (or potentially she) get the sprawling executive branch to carry out the presidential will? Strategic genius is of little consequence in the corridors of power if it is not integrated with the instruments of statecraft; grand designs are of little use divorced from implementation. These instruments include government organization, especially the National Security Council (NSC), and personnel choices.

Grand strategy, after all, exists not merely as a set of abstract ideas about aligning a nation's means with its larger ends in the world, developed in places like Aspen and Davos salons, or boardrooms in New York and London, or lecture halls in Cambridge, New Haven, Palo Alto, and Oxford. It exists just as much in the implementation of its principles and policies, whether in the Sixth Floor regional bureaus at the State Department, the D Ring at the Pentagon, America's far-flung embassies, consulates, and combatant commands, or the isolated outposts where Central Intelligence Agency (CIA) case officers and Special Operations Forces labor in the shadows.

To illuminate this challenge of connecting strategic ideas with implementation, this chapter explores the Richard M. Nixon administration, particularly in its early months. Nixon and his indispensable partner Henry Kissinger took office with a coherent and well-developed grand strategy, based on ideas they had been developing and articulating for years. Much scholarship has been devoted, and rightfully so, to the strategic principles and policies that Nixon and Kissinger pursued while in office.[1] Yet the way that Nixon and Kissinger organized their national security system and attempted to implement their strategy has received much less attention— despite the fact that Nixon and Kissinger themselves devoted considerable time and intellectual energy to these organizational issues. In other words, they were concerned not merely with *what* policies they wanted to pursue and *why* they would pursue them, but also *how* they would advance those policies.

In the case of Nixon and Kissinger, this "how" included the remarkable centralization of power in the National Security Council, often at the expense of the State and Defense Departments. This chapter explores how and why Nixon and Kissinger went about this, particularly focusing on how they connected their organizational decisions to their grand strategy. That story alone is complex and nuanced enough to dominate here; an evaluation of how that organization connected with actual policy decisions, and in what ways it succeeded and failed, awaits further research. Similarly, a case study of just one presidential administration will not provide dispositive conclusions about the relationship between strategy and implementation. But it can illustrate a method of inquiry into this essential yet neglected dimension of grand strategy and perhaps offer some useful insights.

A Determined President

As many other scholars have perceptively discussed, President Richard Nixon took office with a coherent grand strategic vision for how he wanted to reorient the geopolitical order. With an emphasis on stabilizing America's eroding international standing, restoring a balance of power equilibrium, reasserting American credibility, defusing tensions with the Soviet Union while arresting any further Soviet advances, unwinding America's disastrous and costly misadventure in Southeast Asia, and pursuing a strategic opening with Maoist China, Nixon attempted a profound reshaping of American national security policy. Undergirding each of these moves on the geopolitical chessboard he and Kissinger developed the concept of linkage, whereby America's interests on a particular issue in one part of the world were tied to corresponding moves in another. For example, they conditioned their offer of arms control talks and trade improvements to the USSR on increased Soviet pressure on North Vietnam to accept a negotiated settlement in the war.

Nixon had pondered and refined these strategic principles during his years in the political wilderness following his defeats in the 1960 presidential race and the 1962 California gubernatorial election, and as the 1968 presidential campaign approached he had begun to articulate them in a series of speeches, interviews, and publications. His 1967 essay in *Foreign Affairs* offers a prime example. Titled "Asia after Viet Nam," and written at the apex of American involvement in the war, Nixon's article described the broader dynamism of the region and argued that "these developments present an extraordinary set of opportunities for U.S. policy which must begin to look beyond Viet Nam." Taking its own advice, the article even looked beyond Asia as it sketched out a broader set of principles to guide American strategy, particularly the importance of constantly adjusting and balancing between stability and the dynamism of change. Here Nixon first publicly signaled what would become his strategic opening to China, writing that "taking the long view, we simply cannot afford to leave China forever outside the family of nations."[2] If ever a president did have a grand strategy, Nixon provides the archetype.

In turn, this grand design encompassed all of the tools of statecraft and all elements of national power: diplomatic, military, intelligence, economic. Yet along with his national security adviser Henry Kissinger, Nixon also employed an organizational model that marginalized and sidelined the very departments and agencies of the federal government that were nominally in charge of implementing those same tools of statecraft, especially the Departments of State and Defense, and the Central Intelligence Agency. To do this, Nixon and Kissinger elevated the National Security Council to an unprecedented level of influence, power, and control.

The fact that in hindsight Nixon and Kissinger succeeded in imposing their grand strategy on the US government and implementing their design should not obscure what a profound challenge they faced. Within the American government there had developed entire bureaucratic structures devoted to particular issues and policy commitments. Thus bureaucratic resistance to new initiatives did not just emanate from the individual and collective opinions of, say, foreign service officers at the State Department, analysts and case officers at CIA, or senior officers at the Pentagon, who may have occasionally differed with a particular Nixon foreign policy. Rather, when and where a particular policy or overall strategy advanced by Nixon clashed with bureaucratic preferences, as they often did, the bureaucratic resistance could be systemic and institutional—because the new policy was perceived as a threat to the existence of that department or agency. Thus the Arms Control and Disarmament Agency did not just have an institutional policy preference for continuing SALT talks with the Soviet Union; it possessed an existential commitment to such talks, for its very existence was predicated on maintaining the SALT negotiations. Similarly, the powerful Office of Soviet Affairs at the State Department possessed a cultural and institutional commitment to privileging the bilateral US-USSR relationship above all others. Thus it resisted a strategic concept such as linkage that introduced new complications into the US-USSR bilateral relationship, or outreach policies to Soviet satellites such as Romania or rivals such as China that were intended to throw the Soviet leadership off balance and increase American leverage in the relationship. Facing these entrenched bureaucratic interests that were institutionally opposed to his grand strategy, Nixon needed to centralize control in order to hold the reins of his own government and steer large swaths of it in directions toward which it was otherwise hardwired not to go.

Puzzles that immediately arise from Nixon's design of his national security system are to what extent it was shaped by a strategic vision, and to what extent it was shaped by Nixon's famously insecure, conspiratorial personality. While by the time of his election as president Nixon possessed considerable self-confidence and strategic clarity, he also maintained his wariness and low regard for the State Department and Central Intelligence Agency in particular. Ivy League patricians still dominated the ranks of both institutions, perpetually fueling Nixon's resentments and enmity. Disentangling the psychological from the organizational factors with any level of precision is elusive, perhaps impossibly so. At a minimum, the influence of presidential personality and character on the functioning of the White House and institutions of executive branch governance should not be underestimated.

Nor should Nixon's own background be neglected, especially his eight years as Eisenhower's vice president during which he participated in many NSC meetings. On the campaign trail he cited his past experience as a participant in (and occasionally chair of) NSC meetings. As Peter Rodman, a longtime Kissinger aide, observes, "Citing the wars in Vietnam and the Middle East, [Nixon] went so far as to blame 'most of our serious reverses abroad since 1960' on Kennedy's and Johnson's dismantling of the NSC system that they had inherited from Eisenhower and Nixon."[3]

The story of Nixon's selection of Kissinger to be his national security adviser (NSA) is well known.[4] What seems to have faded in time, however, is an appreciation for just how unorthodox a choice it was. In doing so, Nixon violated almost every rule in the book. The president should have a strong personal relationship with the NSA, but Nixon barely knew Kissinger at all. The NSA should be loyal to the president and to the party, but in the general election Kissinger had angled to work for Nixon's opponent Hubert Humphrey in the case of a Democratic victory, and he was very close to Nixon's main Republican rival Nelson Rockefeller. Given the job's almost impossible responsibilities of managing diplomacy, intelligence, and the military in coordinating national security policy, the NSA should have considerable prior government experience, yet Kissinger's entire professional life had been in academia, with only occasional policy consultations on the side.

Nor should it be forgotten that, just as Kissinger at the time would have appeared manifestly unfit for the NSA job, Nixon's choice of William Rogers as secretary of state would have seemed inspired and ordained for success. After all, Rogers was a longtime close personal friend of Nixon's, going back to their collaboration on the Alger Hiss case in the late 1940s and Rogers's assistance to Nixon on the "Checkers" speech in the 1952 presidential campaign (two of the most searing and formative experiences of Nixon's career). Their work together continued during the Eisenhower administration in which Rogers served as attorney general. Rogers had also enjoyed a luminous legal career. In short, Rogers would seem to embody many of the traits of a successful and influential secretary of state: the trust and confidence of the president, experience running a large cabinet department, and a professional legal pedigree reminiscent of influential previous secretaries of state such as Dean Acheson and John Foster Dulles. Any informed observer in December 1968 would have predicted that in the Nixon administration, Rogers and the State Department would be the dominant architects of American foreign policy, running bureaucratic circles around the inexperienced and ill-suited national security adviser Henry Kissinger.

Of course that was not to be. The question is why. Nixon, one of the most complex personalities ever to occupy the presidency, may have been beset by personal insecurities in some areas, but when it came to foreign policy he rested confident in his strategic acumen. In Kissinger he sought someone who, although not a political supporter of his, could function as an intellectual partner and alter ego. He also found someone who shared not only his geopolitical outlook but also—crucially—his convictions on how to reshape the national security machinery of the federal government. They found common cause in reasserting the power of the presidency and diminishing the influence of the permanent bureaucracy, especially the State Department and CIA, though not excluding the Pentagon.

Nixon and Kissinger's approach to consolidating control in the executive branch embodied an ambivalent, even paradoxical relationship with democracy. On the one hand, as other scholars have observed, both sought to insulate the conduct of statecraft and long-term design of strategy from the passions, vicissitudes, and often uninformed predilections of public opinion. In Hal Brands's apt description, both "shared a tendency to see foreign policy as a lonely, heroic endeavor. . . . [F]or Kissinger as for Nixon, grand strategy was about seizing hold of history—and escaping the limitations of one's own society, as well."[5] On the other hand, Nixon in particular saw himself as much more aligned with public opinion and the values of ordinary Americans than the elite career officials at State and the CIA who were the frequent objects of his fulminations. As Robert Dallek records, the new president intended his empowering of Kissinger and the NSC to, in Nixon's words, "give the people of this country the foreign policy they want," through a system that returned power from the insular bureaucracy to its rightful home in the White House.[6] This democratic ambivalence would pervade Nixon's presidency, as he alternated between cultivating and channeling, and disregarding and disdaining, public opinion concerning his statecraft.

A Revolution in Transition

In the impossibly short period of just over two months between the election victory and inauguration, every president-elect and national security adviser-designate receives a deluge of advice, briefing memos, reports, and studies on how to organize the White House and the broader administration. A few of these papers are solicited, some others are welcome, and the largest amount are neither invited nor read. The Nixon transition was no exception. However, among the flood of written advice there appear to have been a few documents that Kissinger (and occasionally Nixon) found of value.

One prominent report came from the Institute for Defense Analyses on "National Security Staffing in the White House." Its observation on the Johnson administration's NSC system aptly crystallizes the complex relationship between world events, American policies, and the organization and instruments of government:

> Beginning in 1965 Vietnam occupied a major portion of the time and energy of the President and his principal advisers, sometimes at the expense of attention to policy problems in other areas of the world. The demands of the war affected the President's way of doing business with his principal advisors in a number of ways, drawing them together in a tightly restricted inner circle varying from the Secretary of State alone, to the four or five who normally attended the Tuesday Lunch at the White House.[7]

Nixon and Kissinger shared this critique of the Johnson administration. They strategized to reorient American policy away from the Vietnam morass, which mirrored their organizational intention to strengthen the NSC system to address a much broader array of policy issues. A short memo from Kissinger to president-elect Nixon on December 13, 1968, captures these intentions well. Reporting on his recent lunch with venerable columnist Walter Lippmann, in advance of Nixon's upcoming meeting with Lippmann, Kissinger wrote in a section on "U.S. role in the world" that "Mr. Lippmann believes that we are vastly overcommitted and have not adjusted to the fact that the immediate post-war situation was most unusual. I told him that one of your principal concerns was a systematic review of American policy in order to relate our commitments to our interests and that you were proposing to use the NSC to bring this about."[8]

In addition to being flooded with reports, memos, and letters offering recommendations on how to structure the NSC, during the transition period Kissinger also took the initiative to seek out counsel. His files contain a fascinating seven-page typewritten set of notes from a December 9, 1968, dinner meeting in Cambridge, Massachusetts, on NSC organization. The list of dinner attendees is not included, so the names of Kissinger's dinner counselors that night remain a historical mystery. Fortunately the advice he received does not and is recorded in considerable detail. Pervading the notes is the theme of strengthening the NSC and consolidating control in the White House. For example, the notes contain the recommendation that the Interagency Working Groups (IWG) "be agencies of NSC, not State, and chairmen are Presidential appointees, not departmental ones"—a demonstrable departure from the State Department's chairmanship of these groups in the previous administration. Similarly, the dinner notes reveal some explicit suspicions about the Defense Department and CIA. On the former, the notes comment that "the new Armed Forces aide will need useful things to do other than mucking into HK's information channels. Finding useful work for this colonel should be a charge on HK's own colonel (providing HK owns him)." Regarding the intelligence community, the notes caution that Kissinger "will need a CIA man on his own staff, but check carefully with others (like Hughes) before accepting bodies from CIA. As in the case of the Armed Forces aide, CIA may hanker to play its own information games." Furthermore, "HK's staff must know what goes on in intelligence-gathering CIA activities and other related activities also."[9] The candor in these notes is striking. Even before formally entering government, Kissinger already envisioned the CIA and Pentagon as bureaucratic adversaries and potential impediments to the grand strategy that he and Nixon planned to implement.

Kissinger's dinner interlocutors also reinforced the preexisting inclinations he and Nixon shared to consolidate control and minimize opportunities for bureaucratic rivals to spy or otherwise gather information from Nixon and Kissinger, or alternatively to withhold information from the president and national security adviser. They appreciated a bureaucratic art that Nixon and Kissinger would soon master: information is not just knowledge, not just insight, but also a source of control. Kissinger put it succinctly in his memoirs: "In Washington knowledge was power."[10] Controlling the flow of information, often blocking it all together, would become a favored method by which Nixon and Kissinger would cultivate their power and exert it over bureaucratic adversaries (real and imagined) in the State Department, Pentagon, and CIA—and sometimes even against each other. This should not be dismissed as mere conniving, though deviousness no doubt played a part. It also reflected their strategic design. As John Lewis Gaddis argues, Nixon and Kissinger resolved "to isolate the bureaucracy from the policymaking process almost entirely, centralizing decisions to an unprecedented degree in their own hands. . . . 'Linkage' was central to the new administration's strategy, but achieving it required the ability to evaluate separate issues in relation to each other, a sense of timing and priority, and the discipline to enforce decisions with firmness. The bureaucracy possessed none of these qualities."[11]

Kissinger also reached out to General Andrew Goodpaster, who had served eight years in the White House as Eisenhower's staff secretary and one of the president's most influential foreign policy advisers and thus was also well known by Nixon. Taking a hiatus from his responsibilities as deputy commander of US forces in Vietnam, Goodpaster responded enthusiastically, writing four memos for Kissinger totaling sixteen pages with a description of how the Eisenhower NSC had functioned and offering detailed recommendations for the development of the Nixon NSC system. Goodpaster recalled that Eisenhower had divided national security staffing responsibilities between two individuals, the special assistant to the president for national security affairs and the staff secretary. In the Nixon White House, "a pattern heading up in a single individual can offer evident advantages of unified and coordinated effort, particularly if the single individual is a man suited to large conceptions and broad-reaching formulations and interpretations designed to have validity over a considerable period of time."[12] No doubt Goodpaster wrote this mindful of his primary reader and intended to flatter as well as to inform.

Goodpaster also arranged for Kissinger to meet with Eisenhower, despite the former president's hospitalization and frail health. As Rodman recalls, Kissinger was "stunned by the vehemence" of Eisenhower that the State Department should not control the NSC process as it had in past administrations. "The system had to be pulled into the White House, he emphasized; the Pentagon would never accept interagency coordination under State Department control."[13]

Eisenhower's words reinforced Kissinger's existing predilections toward a White House–centered system. As his biographer Niall Ferguson describes, at Harvard, Kissinger had already devoted considerable intellectual energy to reflecting on how best to organize the American national security system. As a member of the Harvard Study Group on Presidential Transition, along with his faculty colleagues Ernest May, Phillip Areeda, and Frank Lindsay, Kissinger had co-authored a series of reports on how to organize the next presidency, with a special focus on national security functions. The report cautioned against giving the State Department too much responsibility in co-ordinating interagency policy and instead favored upgrading the National Security Council's stature as the primary venue for presidential deliberations, replacing the intentional informality of President Lyndon Johnson's Tuesday lunch group with his secretaries of state and defense and the national security adviser. Ironically, the Harvard report also "caution[ed] against the other extreme—concentration of the coordination function under a single Special Assistant," which was precisely what Kissinger would do when he assumed the position.[14]

While Kissinger favored a strong NSC serving an assertive president, Nixon himself had already arrived at the same conviction, a point made in Kissinger's own memoir. Describing his first meeting with president-elect Nixon, Kissinger recalled that the subject "was the task of setting up his new government. . . . He had very little confidence in the State Department. Its personnel had no loyalty to him; the Foreign Service had disdained him as vice president and ignored him the moment he was out of office. He was determined to run foreign policy from the White House." Regarding his own posture, Kissinger notes, "When I was appointed, I did not have any organizational plan in mind. My major concern was that a large bureaucracy, however organized, tends to stifle creativity."[15]

An early January bureaucratic squabble—merely the first of many that would beset the Nixon administration—both clarified Nixon's preference for the primacy of the NSC and anticipated the subsequent fierce divisions that would afflict the Nixon administration's national security leadership. With assistance from Goodpaster, his Harvard colleague Morton Halperin, and Lawrence Eagleburger, a foreign service officer detailed to the NSC, Kissinger drafted a proposed national security organization plan for Nixon's approval. It evaluated the purported strengths and weaknesses of the Eisenhower, Kennedy, and Johnson systems, respectively, averring that the Eisenhower NSC had been well organized and thorough; "participants had the benefits of fully staffed papers, and a systematic effort was made to give all interested parties a hearing." However, the memo also noted, likely channeling Goodpaster's recollections, that "if there is any criticism to make of this system it is that its very formality tended to demand too much of the principals' time, while giving insufficient priority to issues of primary Presidential concern." In contrast, the memo lauded the existing Johnson administration system for "its flexibility and the speed with which decisions can be made. The absence of formal staffing for the Tuesday lunch, for example, permits a free and frank discussion unencumbered by a large group of second-level staff." Yet, not surprisingly, all was not well with this approach, as "the discussants are frequently inadequately briefed and often unfamiliar with the nuances of the issue before them." Moreover, "since there is no systematic follow-up, it is often unclear exactly what has been decided or why. Nor is there any formal method for assuring that decisions are adequately implemented."[16]

Not surprisingly, the memo intoned that "the present task is to combine the best features of the two systems." A suggested blueprint laid out for the president-elect envisioned an expansive role for an NSC that would address "middle and long-range issues as well as current matters" (i.e., everything, and perceptive readers would have realized this included some of the operational and implementation issues that ordinarily would be the preserve of the State Department and the Pentagon).[17] Crucially, the "NSC Review Group" that Kissinger called for would be chaired by the national security adviser, replacing the "Senior InterDepartmental Group" that had been chaired by the State Department in the Kennedy and Johnson administrations. Peter Rodman describes this as "an innocuous-sounding but very pregnant 'note'" that effectively eviscerated "the last effort of the Kennedy-Johnson team to give the State Department the leadership role in coordinating and integrating national policy."[18]

The Kissinger memo did not eliminate the State Department entirely from any meaningful role, designating the under secretary of state as the chair for the "Ad Hoc Under Secretary's Committee" which, in an artful bit of understated bureaucratic condescension, was given a mandate to handle "matters referred to it by the NSC Review Committee deemed of insufficient importance to bring before the NSC." Indicating his support for Kissinger's proposed new National Security structure, Nixon initialed the "approve" line on each page.[19]

Nixon's initials did not end the bureaucratic fight, and if anything exacerbated it. As Rodman records, "The State Department professionals fought

a tenacious rearguard action to change Nixon's mind before inauguration day. The distinguished senior diplomat U. Alexis Johnson, tapped by
Nixon to be undersecretary of state for political affairs, did his best to argue
the matter with Kissinger—and simultaneously to explain to his new boss,
William Rogers, a foreign policy novice, why all this was important from the
department's point of view."[20] On January 7, Kissinger sent Nixon an acerbic
memo informing the president-elect that "the State Department has now
begun to object to the NSC procedures which you approved in Florida. (Bill
Rogers had agreed to the general outline in Key Biscayne, but now—in light
of the objections of his Foreign Service subordinates—wants to reserve judgment.)" Having engaged in a passive-aggressive skewering of Rogers for being
subservient to those at State that Rogers was supposed to oversee, Kissinger
then laid out his summary of the arguments for and against State's remon-
strance. His cover memo concluded with a warning that delay in resolving
the dispute would also delay Nixon's plans to begin addressing the many
urgent national security issues confronting his new presidency. Moreover,
warned Kissinger, "It would not be helpful to begin the Administration with
a bureaucratic disagreement—particularly since it would be over an issue
you had already decided at Key Biscayne."[21]

Nixon's response was swift and clear. Less than a week later, Nixon replied
that he had read the arguments submitted by Kissinger for a strong NSC and
by Elliott Richardson (another under secretary of state–designate) on behalf of the State Department's appeal to retain its interagency authority. The
president-elect directed Kissinger to "please inform all concerned that I adhere to my plan as previously provided and as set forth in the implementing
documents; that this is my firm and definite decision and that I want all necessary preparatory action taken immediately to put this organization and
system into effect on January 20."[22] Nixon could not have been more em-
phatic: Kissinger had won. It may be tempting to ascribe this early bureaucratic victory to Kissinger's cleverness in knowing how to manipulate Nixon
and appeal to his insecurities and vanities, such as by accusing Rogers of already having succumbed to the career foreign service officers he was supposed to control, or by subtly needling Nixon that the State Department
was defying his authority. Such messages likely did resonate with the thin-
skinned president-elect. But this should not overlook the simpler and more
fundamental explanation: Nixon agreed with Kissinger on the substance and
had all along wanted a stronger White House–centered system. Kissinger
himself makes this point in his memoirs. Reflecting on this dispute, he

observes that "the true origin of our policymaking procedures lay in Nixon's determination—antedating my appointment—to conduct foreign policy from the White House, his distrust of the existing bureaucracy, coupled with the congruence of his philosophy and mine and the relative inexperience of the new Secretary of State."[23]

One other moment from the transition merits notice. Nixon read the afore-mentioned Harvard study and made some notes on it, offering a revealing window into what caught his attention. His chief of staff Bob Haldeman sent a copy of the report with Nixon's annotations to Kissinger, and another copy to Rogers, along with the cover memo drawing Rogers's attention to Nixon's handwritten underlining and exclamation points. To Kissinger, Nixon added a note (in his inimitable manner of referring to himself in the third-person): "To H.K., note on page 17, RN thinks this is a good idea—see if Goodpaster agrees—if so set-up with Laird." On page 17, Nixon had checked the report's recommendation that "we would urge that you find several early occasions to see all the Joint Chiefs, in company with the Defense Secretary." Nixon also underlined the additional recommendation that "you could make a point of occasionally joining your Defense Secretary for a briefing given in the Pentagon by the Joint Staff, [and] you could indicate your own interest in and respect for the military profession by visiting the National War College and, if possible, some of the service War Colleges and academies." In the margins next to each of these, Nixon also wrote "good."[24] That he directed this guidance to Kissinger—rather than directly to secretary of defense-designate Laird—is a small but revealing indication that he was already ele-vating Kissinger as primus inter pares among his national security principals.

Even more interesting are Nixon's annotations directed to Rogers. The sections of the report devoted to the State Department (partly authored by then-professor Henry Kissinger) were unsparing in their criticism of Foggy Bottom. Passages that Nixon highlighted included "The Secretary and his aides have relatively little power of initiative. . . . The Secretary of State has rel-atively little leverage within his department. Unlike the Secretary of Defense, the Secretary of State has not found a means of compelling career officials to explain and justify their recommendations." Lest Rogers be too dispirited by these presidential annotations, Nixon also underlined and directed Rogers to take note of the report recommendation that the top management personnel at State, such as the deputy under secretary for administration and head of the secretariat, "be neither a congressional nor a Foreign Service nom-inee but instead that he be chosen by, and be exclusively responsible to, the

Secretary and Under Secretary." If nothing else, Rogers was made aware of the diplomat-in-chief's endemic suspicion of the nation's diplomatic corps.

Finally, all who received Nixon's annotated copy of the report would notice his marks highlighting some concluding passages. Especially revealing is the report's observation that while other reports make recommendations on how a president can best gather information and make decisions, "we have been equally concerned in this memorandum with the problem of how to get your government to execute the decisions you make. As we read the history of the Presidency in the last quarter-century, it contains many fewer examples of decisions unsoundly based than of decisions misinterpreted, misunderstood, or deliberately not carried out."[25] Such was Nixon's overriding preoccupation as he assumed the duties of office.

Taking Office and Taking Charge of Implementation

Upon Nixon's inauguration and Kissinger's formal start in office, they began operating the new system. Their organizational chart gave the impression of clarity, coherence, balanced interagency participation, and a smooth operational flow. On the chart, each department and agency had an opportunity to present its views, issues were deliberated by relevant agency representatives, options were presented to the president for consideration, and then presidential decisions were communicated and implemented. In practice, like virtually every presidency before and after, Nixon and Kissinger often deviated from this organizational model. Their deviations only further revealed the growing influence of the national security adviser and concomitantly the NSC staff. It is but a slight exaggeration to say that an organizational revolution in American foreign policy was under way: for the first time in the modern era of America's global power, the State Department was relegated to the margins of statecraft while the NSC assumed pride of place.[26]

In his study of Nixon and Kissinger's design of policy structures for crisis management, Asaf Siniver observes "The more interesting question is why did they bother devising a sophisticated advisory system which they had no intention of using in the first place?"[27] Siniver's assumption is somewhat unfair. As former Kissinger aide Peter Rodman recalls, "Nixon and Kissinger continued for the first few years to rely on the NSC process to elicit the best thinking that was available in the government." However, the State

Department almost immediately either resisted or disregarded several clear Nixon policy decisions, which Rodman describes as "a series of missteps committed by the department in the first two years of the administration, over both the procedure and the substance of policy, which compounded Nixon's suspicions and led him to strengthen White House dominance even beyond the White House–centered bureaucratic process he had started with."[28] Foggy Bottom's deliberate deviations from Nixon's stated policies included unilateral efforts to resume Strategic Arms Limitation Talks (SALT) with the Soviets, unilateral gestures to resume negotiations with North Vietnam, and pungent criticisms leaked to the media of Nixon's outreach to Romania. Rodman observes that such resistance from State extended beyond individual issues to a broader rejection of Nixon and Kissinger's strategic concept of linkage. What was said of Georgetown elite society's disposition toward Nixon was also true of the State Department: just because he was paranoid does not mean that they did not despise him.

Nixon's use of the NSC for centralization of control sometimes found tangible expression in NSC-organized bodies that were created along the way, such as the Washington Special Action Group and others of its ilk that formed a veritable acronym soup. Sometimes it manifested itself in unorthodox ways, such as clandestine negotiating trips or the use of "backchannel" diplomatic arrangements for sensitive negotiations. Nixon first established the famous backchannel between Kissinger and Soviet ambassador Anatoly Dobrynin on February 17, 1969, less than a month after Nixon's inauguration.[29] Other backchannels developed throughout his administration, most famously the multilayered ones employed in the years leading up to the China opening. For the purposes here it is enough to note that the backchannel was not an aberration from the broader NSC system that Nixon and Kissinger established. Rather, it was consistent with their preferences for secrecy, control of information, and tight presidential centralization of grand strategy and its implementation.

As any policymaker will appreciate (or lament!), office location bears directly on perceived influence and effectiveness. Accordingly, in the summer of 1970 the office of the national security adviser experienced a literal elevation that carried symbolic as well as substantive importance. A West Wing renovation included the move of the NSA's office upstairs from the basement to one of the most coveted pieces of real estate in the world: a large corner office just steps away from the Oval Office. The meaning was unmistakable: no longer a mere staff member, the national security adviser now stood as an architect of American foreign policy in his own right.[30]

Conclusion

As Nixon and Kissinger began implementing their strategic designs and centralized system, not coincidentally, the marginalization of the State Department and corresponding elevation of the national security adviser drew the attention and sharp commentary of former secretary of state Dean Acheson. In a 1971 *Foreign Affairs* article titled "The Eclipse of the State Department," Acheson contended that the position of secretary of state had, with rare exceptions under Truman and Eisenhower, seen its power erode over the past seventy-five years. He thus found it unsurprising that presidents such as Nixon would turn to another position such as national security adviser to ensure the faithful executive of the presidential will in affairs of state. Perhaps anticipating the limits of even someone of Kissinger's legendary energy and work ethic, he did not believe this rendered the State Department entirely irrelevant:

> Another fear is that a presidential adviser in the White House will usurp the functions of the Secretary and the Department, leaving for them only formal and administrative duties. This bugaboo is constructed out of ignorance. No matter how ambitious an empire builder he may be, an adviser in the antechamber is restricted by limitations of time and staff to participation in formulation of policy—and few policies at that—to helping with speeches and messages expounding them, and to scrutinizing their execution. For the rest, both formulation and execution remain, and must remain, in the departments. What has been occurring has not been that the White House advisers have edged the foreign office out of functions being competently performed but that they have been needed to do what is not being done anywhere to the satisfaction of the man responsible, the President. . . . However, it is a mistake to believe that present arrangements are a disaster, or ill serve the public interest, or are due to presidential whimsy, or personal ambitions.[31]

Acheson made clear that his sympathies lay with Nixon and Kissinger. State had consigned itself to the sidelines, he contended, due to its bureaucratic torpor, its lack of strategic vision, and its failure to attend scrupulously to the chief executive's preferences and priorities. As a contemporaneous account from a Democrat and former secretary of state—in other words, one whose loyalties would presumably run in the opposite direction—Acheson's article reveals that Nixon and Kissinger's consolidation of control over national security policy may have been as much from necessity as by design. Hence Rodman's conclusion that "the pattern emerged that Nixon and Kissinger looked to the bureaucracy for technical expertise, but not for strategy."[32]

For all of the successes of the Nixon-Kissinger approach, it was not without its costs, some of them considerable. As Gaddis writes in an otherwise sympathetic treatment, "The price was an uninformed, sullen, and at times sabotage-minded bureaucracy, a Congress determined to reassert its eroded constitutional authority without any sense of how far that authority could feasibly extend, and, ultimately, the resignation of a president certain otherwise to have been impeached and convicted for abusing the overwhelming power his own system had given him."[33]

Nonetheless, the ultimate verdict on a grand strategy is rendered not by its conceptual design, nor its organization, nor its implementation, but by its results. In its policy consequences, the Nixon-Kissinger model can claim some notable successes, including the strategic opening to China, reduced tensions and arms control agreements with the Soviet Union, and a strengthened American posture in the Middle East. It produced some notable organizational consequences too, in establishing a new paradigm for the National Security Council. With a brief and partial exception during the Reagan presidency, every successive presidential administration adopted the Nixon-Kissinger model of a strong national security adviser and an NSC staff that controlled the interagency process. The fact that most future presidents eschewed Nixon and Kissinger's realpolitik grand strategy yet embraced their NSC organizational model testifies to what may be Nixon and Kissinger's most enduring legacy.

Notes

1. The scholarly literature on the Nixon/Kissinger years is voluminous. Just to begin, the memoirs written by Nixon and Kissinger are incomparable resources, often quite insightful though of inconsistent reliability. See Richard Nixon, *RN: The Memoirs of Richard Nixon* (New York: Grosset and Dunlap, 1978); Henry Kissinger, *White House Years* (Boston: Little, Brown, 1979); Henry Kissinger, *Years of Upheaval* (Boston: Little, Brown, 1982); and Henry Kissinger, *Years of Renewal* (New York: Simon and Schuster, 1999). Thoughtful scholarly and journalistic assessments include, but are not limited to, David Milne, *Worldmaking: The Art and Science of American Diplomacy* (New York: Farrar, Straus and Giroux 2015); Daniel Sargent, *A Superpower Transformed: The Remaking*

of American Foreign Relations in the 1970s (New York: Oxford University Press, 2015); Peter Rodman, *Presidential Command: Power, Leadership, and the Making of Presidential Foreign Policy from Richard M. Nixon to George W. Bush* (New York: Knopf, 2009); Evan Thomas, *Being Nixon: A Man Divided* (New York: Random House, 2015); John Alyosius Farell, *Richard Nixon: The Life* (New York: Doubleday 2017), Walter Isaacson, *Kissinger: A Biography* (New York: Simon and Schuster, 1992); Niall Ferguson, *Kissinger, 1923–1968: The Idealist* (New York: Penguin Press, 2015); Jeremi Suri, *Henry Kissinger and the American Century* (Cambridge, MA: Harvard University Press, 2007); David Greenberg, *Nixon's Shadow: The History of an Image* (New York: W.W. Norton, 2003); Richard Thornton, *The Nixon Kissinger Years: The Reshaping of American Foreign Policy* (St. Paul, MN: Paragon Press, 2001); Hal Brands, *What Good Is Grand Strategy? Power and Purpose in American Statecraft from Harry S. Truman to George W. Bush* (Ithaca, NY: Cornell University Press, 2014); Robert Dallek, *Nixon and Kissinger: Partners in Power* (New York: HarperCollins, 2007); and Greg Grandin, *Kissinger's Shadow: The Long Reach of America's Most Controversial Statesman* (New York: Metropolitan Books, 2015).

2. Richard Nixon, "Asia after Viet Nam," *Foreign Affairs*, October 1967, 111–125.

3. Rodman, *Presidential Command*, 37.

4. Note that the formal title for the position is "assistant to the president for national security affairs" (APNSA), but this chapter will use the more familiar "national security adviser" (NSA). These authors include Nixon and Kissinger themselves. For just a sampling of accounts, see Nixon, *RN*, 340–341; Kissinger, *White House Years*, 9–16; Thomas, *Being Nixon*, 190–193; Isaacson, *Kissinger*, 134–139; and Ferguson, *Kissinger*, 850–855.

5. Brands, *What Good Is Grand Strategy?*, 62, 64.

6. Dallek, *Nixon and Kissinger*, 84.

7. Institute for Defense Analyses, "National Security Staffing in the White House," in *The National Security Process*, November 1968 report, box: National Security Council Files; Henry A. Kissinger Office Files; HAK Administrative and Staff Files— Transition; box 2; folder: National Security Planning Material [3 of 4], Nixon Library.

8. December 13, 1986, memo to President-Elect from HAK, in Box: National Security Council Files; Henry A. Kissinger Office Files; HAK Administrative and Staff Files— Transition; box 2; folder: Memoranda to President-Elect [2 of 2], Nixon Library

9. Notes of Dinner Meeting, December 9, 1968, (10 Traill Street, Cambridge), in folder: NSDM 1; box: National Security Council Institutional Files; Records of the Staff Secretary (1969-1974); National Security Decision Memorandum Working Files; Box H-284, Nixon Library.

10. Kissinger, *White House Years*, 37.

11. John Lewis Gaddis, *Strategies of Containment: A Critical Appraisal of American National Security Policy during the Cold War* (New York: Oxford University Press 2005), 299–300.

12. December 15, 1968, Memorandum from Goodpaster to Kissinger, in folder: Gen. Goodpaster, box: National Security Council Files; Henry A. Kissinger Office Files; HAK Administrative and Staff Files—Transition; box 1, Nixon Library.

13. Rodman, *Presidential Command*, 38.

14. Ferguson, *Kissinger*, 845–848.

15. Kissinger, *White House Years*, 11, 39.

16. Memorandum for the President-Elect from Kissinger [undated] in folder: NSDM-1, from box: National Security Council Institutional Files; National Security Decision Memorandums; box H-209, Nixon Library. See also very similar documents (copies or drafts?) in folder: Memoranda to President-Elect [1 of 2] in box: National Security Council Files; Henry A. Kissinger Office Files; HAK Administrative and Staff Files—Transition; box 2, Nixon Library. Note that, in its effort to draw insights from the three most recent presidencies, the Kissinger memo represented one particular way of learning from history (albeit very recent history) and applying those lessons to current policy. I have described this type elsewhere as the use of history for "institutional guidance." See William Inboden, "Statecraft, Decision Making, and the Varieties of Historical Experience: A Taxonomy," *Journal of Strategic Studies* 37 (April 2014), 291–318.

17. Ibid.

18. Rodman, *Presidential Command*, 39.

19. Memorandum from Kissinger to the President-Elect, Nixon Library.

20. Rodman, *Presidential Command*, 39.

21. January 7, 1969, Memo for the President-elect from Kissinger re: NSC Procedures in folder: NSDM-1, from box: National Security Council Institutional Files; National Security Decision Memorandums; box H-209, Nixon Library.

22. January 13, 1969, Memo for Kissinger from Nixon, in folder: NSDM-1, from box: National Security Council Institutional Files; National Security Decision Memorandums; box H-209, Nixon Library.

23. Kissinger, *White House Years*, 47.

24. Note to Sec Rogers on task force report noting "RN's underlinings"; Memo to Kissinger from Haldeman's office on "attached memo to Mr. Nixon, subj: National Security organization"; November 1, 1968, Memorandum for Mr Nixon on "National Security Organization" in folder: Task Forces, box: National Security Council Files; Henry A. Kissinger Office Files; HAK Administrative and Staff Files—Transition; box 3, Nixon Library.

25. Note to Sec Rogers on task force report noting "RN's underlinings"; November 1, 1968 Memorandum for Mr Nixon on "National Security Organization" in Folder: Task Forces, Box: National Security Council Files; Henry A. Kissinger Office Files; HAK Administrative and Staff Files – Transition; Box 3, Nixon Library.

26. President Woodrow Wilson's occasional marginalization of the State Department and reliance on Colonel Edward House may be a partial exception to this that proves the rule.

27. Asaf Siniver, *Nixon, Kissinger, and U.S. Foreign Policy Making: The Machinery of Crisis* (New York: Cambridge University Press 2008), 69–70.

28. Rodman, *Presidential Command*, 42.

29. Rodman, *Presidential Command*, 50.

30. The only subsequent deviation from this was the exception that proved the rule, when Reagan's short-lived experiment in 1981 of demoting National Security Adviser Richard Allen in both rank and office location ended in failure and led to the position's restoration in 1982 under Judge Bill Clark.

31. Dean Acheson, "The Eclipse of the State Department," *Foreign Affairs*, July 1971, 593–606. Of course, Kissinger's appointment as secretary of state in 1973 would restore the Department's authority.

32. Rodman, *Presidential Command*, 53.

33. Gaddis, *Strategies of Containment*, 273.

14

George H. W. Bush

Strategy and the Stream of History

Jeffrey A. Engel

George Bush governed during remarkable times, which he negotiated through a grand strategy of restraint. President from 1989 until 1993, on his watch the Cold War ended, taking with it the international system's most durable foundation posts, in place since 1945. Bipolarity collapsed. The Iron Curtain crumbled. Divided since World War II, Germans reunited. Under Soviet control for equally as long, Eastern Europe collectively turned toward democracy. More remarkable still, those aforementioned changes took place largely without war or violence, in a manner so smooth it is today recalled for being like velvet. But not everywhere. The People's Republic of China, having first broken from Soviet dogma in previous decades and then raced past it by embracing market reforms, aborted a commensurate pro-democracy movement under the treads of tanks in 1989. Thousands died; more were imprisoned or exiled; Tiananmen Square, the center of the protest and its demise, transformed in global consciousness from a place to an event, as China itself lurched closer to unrest and potentially even civil war than at any time since 1949.

Beijing's government survived. Others did not. Ripped by secessionist and democratic winds alike, the Soviet Union first lost its empire during Bush's time in office, then its reason for being, its disparate republics refusing first to hold together, then to continue their union altogether. The Warsaw Pact it once led self-destructed as well. "The jury is still out" on the very notion of reform behind the Iron Curtain, Bush had said while a candidate for office in 1988.[1] Four years later as his sole term in office neared its end, he publicly accepted history's verdict. "Today, by the grit of our people and the grace of God, the Cold War is over. Freedom carried the day."[2]

Changes on Bush's watch did not end there. He ordered Manuel Noriega's capture in late 1989, removing the Panamanian despot from office in the largest American military operation since Vietnam. Pivoting from Europe to the Middle East less than nine months after the Berlin Wall fell, he subsequently oversaw a military operation rivaled only by Vietnam in the post-1945 era, orchestrating a broad international coalition to defend Saudi Arabia from potential Iraqi assault, and then to liberate Kuwait from Iraq's earlier aggression. Add in the development of international environmental accords to limit acid rain, tense economic negotiations with Japan and other rising industrial juggernauts, the break-up of Yugoslavia, and the North American Free Trade Act largely negotiated during his tenure, and it is fair to say that Bush faced more complex and intertwined international issues during his sole term in office than any American president save for Franklin Roosevelt at the height of World War II.

He succeeded because he, and we, survived. Any of the aforementioned crises in Europe or Asia might have spun dangerously into war, as so often in history occurred whenever great powers implode. Bush did not prevent war on his own. That would be a preposterous suggestion. Yet his adroit crisis management prioritizing calm, stability, and patience made war less likely. He succeeded as a grand strategist in large measure by identifying and preserving that which he considered fundamental to American power and influence around the world, and more broadly to a fully functioning world as well. "Amid the triumph and the tumult of the recent past, one truth rings out most clearly than ever," Bush said as his time in office came to a close, speaking on the campus where his presidential library would soon be erected. "America remains today what Lincoln said it was more than a century ago: 'the last best hope of man on earth,' because of a truth made indelible by the struggles and the agonies of the 20th century and in the sacrifice symbolized by each towering oak on Simpson Frill Field here at Texas A&M University. The leadership, the power, and yes, the conscience of the United States of America, all are essential for a peaceful, prosperous international order, just as such an order is essential to us."[3]

This was more than mere rhetoric or the words of a recently defeated leader hoping to stamp some final imprint on history. It was more too than a reflexive American exceptionalism. Such words instead revealed the central plank of Bush's intertwined ideology and strategy, and they offer a means of gauging his performance. Evaluating a strategist's accomplishments is never easy, the task made all the more difficult by our ever-evolving sense of the consequences of their work with the passage of time. Victory so often sows the seeds of future conflict, and the successes of one generation's day may easily generate another's demise.

Scientific advances demonstrate the way success is itself a malleable judgment more clearly than politics. We could in the same breath praise Albert Einstein for providing a general theory of relativity while damning him for contributing a key element of the ensuing pox of nuclear weaponry. Perhaps pausing to breathe once more, we might decide to praise him anew for the possibility of nuclear power his work advanced, though this is praise the residents of Fukushima, Chernobyl, or Three Mile Island would find difficult to unreservedly grant. By the same token, American botanist Norman Borlaug was once cited by the Nobel Peace Prize committee as the man who had saved more lives than any other human in history following his development of genetically modified grains capable of sustaining Earth's blossoming mid-twentieth-century populations. Those billions saved, however, now speed global consumption of water and other valuable resources potentially past the breaking point, making him in the acerbic words of one critic, "aside from Kissinger, probably the biggest killer of all to have got the peace prize."[4] To fully evaluate and judge accomplishments, in science as well as in strategy, one must therefore consider not only the short- and long-term results but also the time frame for evaluation. The evolution of events, in other words, directly affects our judgments of decisions and accomplishments long past. They are static; our sense of their meaning changes.

How then to judge a strategist's skill and success if we know the effects of their actions and our own appreciation of them will invariably evolve over time? A nihilist would not try, neither would the average sophomore. Lest we find ourselves too hamstrung by consideration of myriad long-term and oftentimes unintended outcomes to render any useful historical judgment on any policy decision or policymaker, a simpler formula for evaluating a strategist's achievements can nonetheless offer insights. One might merely evaluate a strategist's effectiveness in conceiving and then accomplishing particular goals.

Simply put, does the strategist have a plan, and then accomplish it? Failure to plan is an indictment of its own. Hope is not a strategy, and too great a reliance on its timely appearance is not the mark of an effective strategist. Having identified goals, one does not attain high marks for failure. The effective strategist both plots and achieves.

Evaluating Bush as a Grand Strategist

Bush ranks high by this standard. Determined above all else to preserve the elements of traditional American power amid a tumultuous world and to prevent as much as possible a rapidly transforming world from descending into chaos, he successfully achieved the markers he set in pursuit of this goal. These included sustaining relations with an ustable China wracked by pro-democracy movements and the ensuing crackdown upon them (known colloquially and collectively as the Tiananmen Square protests), reeling China, preserving NATO, uniting Germany, negotiating a continent-wide free trade zone designed to counter the rise of Asian and European economic consolidation, and protecting the sanctity of international sovereignty and the import of the United Nations in a post–Cold War world. Each of these, and their intertwined nature, will be explored below.

Bush ranks well if the parameters of success are expanded beyond evaluation of a strategist's planning and achievement of plans, but also if those goals are attained in rank of importance. One gets more points for touchdowns than for field goals in football, attaining more for fully achieving the desired goal (moving the ball into the opponent's end zone) than a secondary option employed only after having been stymied in attaining the first (kicking the ball between the goal posts positioned at the end zone's back line). One in this metric receives greater reward for accomplishing big things than cursory ones. Surely, some quests matter more than the rest combined. In this metric, Bush showed himself a grand strategist of the highest order when he left his successors the fundamentals of American power, as he saw them, intact and unsullied: American international leadership as a first among equals within the Western alliance; American dominance of the international economy; and an American military presence in any of the world's major strategic hotspots including its global commons.

Other standards for evaluating strategic success and failure lead, not surprisingly, to a different assessment. These should in good conscience be acknowledged even if not this author's preferred metric. For example, if the mark of a great strategist lies in his ability to conceptualize and achieve something new, not merely securing goals but in transforming the world, Bush would receive low grades indeed. He was no man's radical or revolutionary, nor did he ever aspire to those roles. He would have gladly embraced any evaluation that noted he utterly failed to be a revolutionary or that made radicalism the sole mark of achievement, because his ultimate strategic goal, as he saw it, lay in recognizing and preserving the true foundation of American power and of global order, both of which he considered intertwined and set on a common course toward the future. Novelty was not his standard; continuity was his stock-in-trade.

Bush in this sense embodied a sense of leadership uttered by the great nineteenth-century Prussian statesmen Otto Von Bismarck. "The stream of history flows inexorably along," Bismarck once said of the statesman's role. "By plunging my hand into it, I am merely doing my duty. I do not expect to change its course." Indeed, "man can neither create nor direct the stream of time," he often told visitors. "He can only travel upon it and stream with more or less skill and experience; he can suffer shipwreck and go around and also arrive in safe harbors."[5]

Truly perceptive leaders, the Prussian argued, did not row against the tide. They instead recognized the stream's direction, course, and ultimate destination, seeing into the future to note where the great trends of their age were likely to result. They thereby position their ship of state within its current, ensuring safe arrival at their ultimate destination, avoiding rocky shoals even amid rapids (periods of flux and dramatic change). This ability to perceive the world's true direction even in swirling currents was Bush's best attribute as a strategist, though he was helped mightily by the tide's general flow in a direction he innately endorsed. It was also his greatest flaw.

Bush never cited Bismarck nor fully trusted his ability to cite philosophers of any stripe. "My problem, very frankly," Bush said in 2000, "was that I wasn't articulate. I didn't feel comfortable with some of the speech-writers' phrases, so I would cross them out. I didn't quote Shelley and Kant. I don't remember exactly what Thucydides had meant to me when I was only twelve."[6] He was, nonetheless, Bismarckian in spirit, at least when it came to placing his faith in the stream of time. Just as the Prussian thought history flowed toward industrialized and centralized power, and thus toward any who could consolidate central Europe under Berlin's banner, the tide in Bush's day seemed to flow in Washington's direction, toward the democratic capitalist order it had championed since the Second World War in particular. Ironically the nation's last veteran of that war to subsequently serve as commander in chief, he took office in 1989 convinced not only of the centrality of American power for the international system's success but also of its essential goodness. The stream of history dictated by American leadership was, in his mind, not only the fastest but the best. "I will never apologize for the United States," he boasted from the campaign trail in 1988. "Not even when its wrong."[7]

More than jingoism, the statement revealed instead Bush's fundamental faith in the ultimate logic of the American system as he had come to define it by the close of the 1980s: one based on democracy, free markets, and similarly amorphous terms and institutions rarely defined but better simply embraced, words like "freedom," "liberty," "enterprise," and "justice." Born into wealth and privilege, inculcated with a strong sense of noblesse oblige and having never known what it meant to have freedom withheld—though he knew from wartime service what it meant to fight under its banner and to lose comrades in its pursuit—Bush had prospered from the American system personally and came of age during the apex of American global power. He also lived to see American power questioned and its institutions waver, moments such as the Vietnam loss or the Watergate scandal with which he was remotely involved, and which he believed occurred only when Americans came to doubt their central tenets and deviated from their fundamental values. While witnessing Chinese celebrations of the communist victory in Vietnam in 1975, when he was de facto United States Ambassador to Beijing, he wrote in his diary: "As soon as America doesn't stand for something in the world, there is going to be a tremendous erosion of freedom."[8]

More than a decade later, after directing the CIA and serving eight years as vice president to a man who longed to transform America along more radical lines, Bush joined his innate conservatism and trust in Americanism together as a statement of faith: "We don't need radical new directions," he explained when opening his formal campaign for the White House in late 1987. "We don't need to remake society—we just need to remember who we are." No further elaboration seemed necessary for a man who thought such points not just obvious but obviously right. "I like what's real," he explained. "I'm not much for the airy and abstract; I like what works. I am not a mystic, and I do not yearn to lead a crusade."[9]

Gorbachev: The Grandest Strategic Question of them All

Bush had every reason to think, upon entering office in early 1989, that the world had finally come to accept his long-held faith in the superiority of the American system. Mikhail Gorbachev's reforms shook the Soviet bloc, in particular his embrace of market forces and democratic urges best described by his intertwined terms *perestroika* and *glastnost*, each in their own way a means of salvaging the Soviet Union's brand of communism that had grown staid and unproductive by the 1970s. The first of Gorbachev's ideals is best understood as change, in particular the Soviet Union's willingness to accept new ideas (including once-heretical democratic ones), whereas the second conveyed a concurrent new openness to discussing its own problems and potential solutions, again much like a democratic society. To save socialism, Gorbachev explained to the dismay of his critics—and there were plenty of them—they had to face the reality that democracy and markets proved more efficient, and what the Soviet Union needed most of all in the latter half of the 1980s was greater efficiency. As Bush took office, even America's adversaries seemed ready to endorse the ideals he so fervently espoused.

But how sincere was the Soviet conversion? Gorbachev's reforms coupled with President Ronald Reagan's newfound willingness to negotiate (the doctrinaire Reagan of his first term showed little in common with the flexible and trusting man of the second) significantly cooled superpower tensions by the time Bush took office. Some even quietly whispered the era of Soviet-American tensions might be nearing an end. The Cold War was "all over but the shouting," Reagan's secretary of state proclaimed as he handed his department over to his successor. Reagan's closest international partner said much the same.[10] "We're not in a Cold War now," Britain's Margaret Thatcher declared mere moments after meeting with the new president-elect in Washington.[11]

Bush and those around him, skeptical realists at least in their own minds, were less trusting, reasoning that democracy's rise would not necessarily bring peace, or long-term Soviet acquiescence, in its wake. The first point seemed self-evident, even if its implications potentially took one's breath away. Bush took office at nearly the precise moment an obscure political scientist and mid-level policymaker named Francis Fukuyama would famously declare "the end of history." By year's end the scholar would be a household name, having best articulated what others thought, that the long arc of humanity had passed an important milestone. "What we may be witnessing is not just the end of the Cold War, or the passing of a particular period of postwar history," Fukuyama explained in a published version of his paper first delivered in late February 1989 at the University of Chicago. Instead it might be "the end point of mankind's ideological evolution and the universalization of Western liberal democracy as the final form of human government."[12] Time was not at an end, nor would humans cease to create events. History's real purpose and endpoint, he argued, more specifically its *democratic* endpoint, had been revealed. The United States and its allies, in winning the Cold War by turning the Soviets democratic, had in fact won history's grand prize, as the Cold War was in fact history's final ideological competition. As the editor of the *New York Times Magazine* summed it up, "In other words, we win." [13] Speaking from the far right, the editor of the *National Interest*, which published Fukuyama's work, verily gloated: "We may have won the Cold War, which is nice," but as Fukuyama showed, "it's more than nice, it's wonderful."[14]

Fukuyama became famous for saying with greater eloquence and clarity something others had said before, including the incoming president of the United States. Peoples throughout the world were "moving toward democracy through the door to freedom," Bush had declared the previous month mere moments after taking the oath of office. "Men and women of the world move towards free markets through the door to prosperity. The people of the world agitate for free expression and free thought through the door to the moral and intellectual satisfactions that only liberty allows." In short, "the day of the dictator was over."[15]

More than mere victory was at hand, Bush added. What the world truly faced in dictatorship's erosion was instead the dawn of a new democratic day. "We don't need to talk late into the night about which form of government is better," he explained. "We don't have to wrestle justice from the kings. We only have to summon it from within ourselves" because in the final analyses, they already had all the answers to peace and prosperity before them. "We know what works," Bush said. "Freedom works. We know what's right: freedom is right. We know how to secure a more just and prosperous life for man on Earth: through free markets, free speech, free elections, and the exercise of free will unhampered by the state."[16]

But having achieved a democratic victory, could they secure it for their posterity? "There is a new world out there," Brent Scowcroft, Bush's close intellectual partner and national security adviser, told his staff upon taking office. "We just might stand at the door of a new era," provided they could ensure the things that had made their own era come so close to democracy's final victory.[17] The United States alone wielded such power and responsibility. This was history's central lesson for Bush and those around him, at least, the history of the twentieth century which they thought mattered most, especially when it came to Europe, home to the greatest political transformations of their age, and the centerpiece of American strategic thinking. Twice in that century Europe had plunged the world into war. Twice, in the way of thinking dominant in Washington and among Bush's incoming circle,

Americans had crossed the ocean to save civilization. Twice they had won, at great cost. The first time, however, they had returned home, only to be forced to travel once more across the Atlantic on a new crusade for freedom. Having stayed at war's end this time round, peace ensued. The complex reasons for that long Cold War cantonment across the sea after 1945 mattered less in this reading of history than the results. "The burdens were—and are—difficult to bear," Bush's secretary of state, close friend, and longtime tennis partner James Baker explained in late 1989. "But we upheld our values. And we prevented war in Europe" and thus helped make the new democratic age possible.[18]

The pronoun mattered. "We" won. Yes, the United States had allies, without whom it could not have succeeded. By the same token American force was to their eyes the crucial stabilizing factor within European politics, and more broadly throughout the world. Its absence would conversely invite instability's return—and with it, perhaps, war. "The basic lesson of two world wars was that American power is essential to any stable equilibrium on the continent," Scowcroft reminded Bush in March of 1989. "The postwar era's success is founded on recognition of this fact."[19]

Bush needed no convincing. No matter what happened with *perestroika* and *glastnost*, or for that matter with the embryonic European Community then coming into sharp focus, American power had to remain if peace were to prevail. He made this point bluntly only weeks into his administration, with France's president Francois Mitterrand at his side. "We must never forget that twice in this century American blood has been shed over conflicts that began in Europe," Bush explained. "That is why the Atlantic alliance is so central to our foreign policy. And that's why America remains committed to the alliance and the strategy which has preserved freedom in Europe. We must never forget that to keep the peace in Europe is to keep the peace for America."[20]

The central element of Bush's grand strategy, indeed underlying his pro-democracy rhetoric, was therefore nothing less than American indispensability and American power, which explains his response to the paramount foreign policy issue of his day: how to deal with Soviet decline and the potential Pandora's box of new strategic issues it posed, not least of which was the prospect of a reunified Germany. As deputy national security adviser Robert Gates frequently told his colleagues, never before in modern history had a great empire collapsed without an ensuing great-power war, and they naturally feared the outcomes a power vacuum might spawn.[21]

Gorbachev, by striving to save socialism, had inadvertently destabilized the entire Soviet sphere of influence, setting the very conditions of a power vacuum that American policymakers—imbued with the responsibility for ensuring stability—deemed so very dangerous. This is why Bush and those around him viewed these changes with cautious optimism, and with a premium on the first word of that description. Innately skeptical by nature, they neither trusted Gorbachev's sincerity nor relished the instability ingrained in any revolution. Scowcroft in particular feared the Soviet leader might be foisting upon the West a "peace offensive" through his talk of openness and reform, fearing in particular that the architecture of his proposed common European home purposely held no wing for the Americans and thus no long-term rival for Soviet power.[22] Other key Bush advisers such as Gates had already put their fear of the implications of a Soviet collapse on record. "After three years of reform, restructuring and turmoil, there has been little, if any, slowing in the downward spiral of the Soviet economy," he had publicly stated in 1988. When coupled with the ingrained ethnic and racial tensions ever-present within the amalgamated Soviet state scattered across ten time zones in which more than 75 million ethnic Russians resided amid a broader population twice that size, Gates noted that all this added up to an ominous conclusion: "While Gorbachev's bold political moves and radical rhetoric have shaken the Soviet system, he has not yet really changed it," and "it is by no means certain—I would even say it is doubtful—that Gorbachev can in the end rejuvenate the system." Ultimately, "whether Gorbachev succeeds, fails, or just survives, a still long competition and struggle with the Soviet Union lie before us."[23]

Primacy and American Power

European fluidity demanded American stability, Bush argued in turn, reemphasizing on taking office the necessity of strong transatlantic ties. "We've arrived at this historic point by maintaining a strong partnership with our European allies," Bush thus announced in early May of 1989, calling for a new NATO summit designed to look anew at the organization's key missions. To start the bidding, he announced curtailment of the short-range nuclear missile deployment that had been such an irritant to Atlantic relations when he had first taken office, while pledging an overhaul of the organization's priorities and mission.[24]

Questioning its very existence, however, was not in the cards. "NATO will remain vital to America's place in Europe," he vowed, setting the parameters of what he thought the summit might reasonably engage. "The future of the United States cannot be separated from the future of Europe, and so along with our allies we must prepare for the magnificent opportunities that lie ahead. In these times of uncertainty and hope, NATO will continue to be vital to America's place in Europe and a bulwark of democratic values and security."[25] It will have to expand, conceptually at least, Bush told Mitterrand in advance of his formal announcement. "Its role will be different. The organization must be flexible," he explained. "It will be guaranteeing against instability," even as it helped former adversaries like the Soviets take comfort that it was no longer organized against them.[26]

He made the same point in public. "Who's the enemy?" veteran White House reporter Helen Thomas asked after Bush and Gorbachev met in Malta in early December of 1989. During the previous three weeks the Berlin Wall had fallen and talk of the once unthinkable—German unification—filled the air. Surely, Thomas asked, American forces couldn't still be focused on defending against a Soviet bloc that had just embraced the very democracy we espoused. "Who [in Europe] are they [American troops] supposed to be fighting against?" Bush replied, "The U.S. troops are there as a stabilizing factor. Nobody can predict, Helen, with total certainty, what tomorrow's going to look like. I've been wrong. You've been wrong. He's been wrong. She's been wrong—on how it's going to go. . . . Our European allies want us there. I have a feeling that some of the Eastern Europeans want us there because they know that the United States is there as a stabilizing factor."[27]

How then to keep Americans onsite and with oversight, or in other words to maintain a heavy hand on the rudder as the world flowed down history's stream? Bush had already mentioned the answer and his paramount strategic goal: to ensure continuation of the instruments of American power and influence that made the peace possible and allowed the stream of history to carry Europe toward its inevitable rendezvous with democracy, free markets, and freedom. In practical terms, this meant NATO, whose existence ensured an ongoing American invitation to participate in European affairs. Bush thus made NATO's survival his singular requirement for backing German chancellor Helmut Kohl's vision of rapid unification following the collapse of the German Democratic Republic and its long-despised Berlin Wall. He made Germany's full membership in the organization the one thing he could not do without, and the one thing he told his French and British allies he valued more than his individual relationship with each. He also made clear that he would part ways with Gorbachev if need be to secure German NATO membership, regardless of the growing warmth of Soviet-American relations as 1990 progressed, and he set this as the litmus test for future ties with Moscow. NATO, Bush argued time and again, was key to everything, because it allowed the United States to steady European instability.

"I've got to look after the U.S. interest in all this without reverting to a kind of isolationist or stupid peace-nik view on where we stand in the world," he recorded in his diary in the early spring of 1990. But given all the successes of the past year, "Who's the enemy? I keep getting asked that. It's apathy; it's the inability to predict accurately; it's dramatic change that can't be foreseen.... There are all kinds of events that we can't foresee that require a strong NATO," he ultimately wrote. "And there's all kinds of potential instability that requires a strong U.S. presence."[28]

Only one thing could derail instability so long as Americans remained on site, and that was chaos itself. Fear of chaos remained the other touchstone of Bush's grand strategy. Put simply his was a Hippocratic diplomacy. When faced with no clear choice or with international turmoil more generally, Bush invariably fell back on the central principle that he first should do no harm. This is why he refused, in his words, to "dance on the wall" when others in Washington urged him to travel to Berlin to celebrate the West's Cold War triumph in late 1989. He did not want to further instigate a crackdown, or further destabilize Gorbachev and other clearly stressed and strained communist leaders. This too is why he refused to fully endorse China's democratic movement in the summer of 1989, Hungarian or Polish crowds that year, or secessionist movements in the Baltic the following one. He sympathized with each. But he also feared his words could incite violence and revolution, and more of each in reprisal, leading to a cascade toward the very chaos he feared and loathed, the one thing capable of derailing the West's inevitable journey down the stream of time. "I keep hearing critics saying we're not doing enough on Eastern Europe," he complained to his diary, ironically mere days before the Berlin Wall's unexpected breach. "Here the changes are dramatically coming our way, and if any one event—Poland, Hungary, or East Germany—had taken place, people would say this is great."[29]

"But it's all moving fast—moving our way," he continued. "And [yet] you've got a bunch of critics jumping around saying we ought to be doing more. What they mean is, double spending. It doesn't matter what, just send money, and I think it's crazy." It had been five months since the bloodshed at

Tiananmen, which he had been unable to prevent or even really influence from abroad, and an incessant fear that his tempered praise of the student protestors had somehow contributed to the violence. "If we mishandle it [Eastern Europe], and get way out looking like an American project," he continued, "you would invite crackdown, and . . . that could result in bloodshed," the end of perestroika, and the end more profoundly of all this talk of the Cold War's end.[30]

His answer: do nothing, at least while cameras rolled and the world anxiously watched. When things were going one's way, and the stream of time seemed to flow in one's direction, the less one paddled or interfered the better. Even when criticized. "We're seeing it move, aren't we," he quickly returned when a reporter asked yet again why his White House was not doing more to openly support democracy behind the Iron Curtain. "We're seeing dynamic change, and I want to handle it properly." Pundits and legislators might rail, but their words mattered for little in the end. His, conversely, echoed globally. "The United States can't wave a wand and say how fast change is going to come to Czechoslovakia or to the GDR," he exclaimed. What mattered was the direction of change. Asked yet again the same question, he finally burst out in anger. "I knew exactly what I wanted to do, and knew how I wanted to go about doing it," he blustered in response. "And that's why I didn't need the advice of others on this particular subject. I knew how I wanted to do it."[31]

Which was calmly, cautiously, and conservatively to ensure stability by ensuring the continued existence of the institutions, like NATO, that he believed had most contributed to their present good fortune. So long as those continued, he felt confident his grand strategy would succeed. Indeed, the same rationale explained his most radical move, his decision to authorize what ultimately became a half-million person expedition to the Middle East. Americans still bore the emotional scars of Vietnam. Indeed the Oval Office seemed haunted by its memory. "I know you're aware of the fact that this has all the ingredients that have brought down three of the last five presidents," Baker privately told Bush in the aftermath of Iraq's occupation of Kuwait. "A hostage crisis, body bags, and a full-fledged economic recession caused by forty-dollar oil."[32]

"I know that, Jimmy, I know that," Bush calmed his friend and chief diplomat. "But we're doing what's right; we're doing what is clearly in the national interest of the United States."[33] And—he did not say at that moment, though he had said it previously and repeatedly—he believed what they were doing was in the global interest as well. The Gulf War can only be understood as the final coda of the Cold War, because American policymakers, within Bush's inner circle especially, moved quickly after their initial surprise over Hussein's move to realize that their response would reverberate beyond the Middle East. If they were ever to ensure stability, returning the world to the vision of the post–1945 generation that founded the United Nations whose global order they believed the Cold War had interrupted, this was the time. "The Soviets have come down hard," acting secretary of state Lawrence Eagleburger told the National Security Council the day after the Iraq invasion. "Saddam Hussein now has greater flexibility because the Soviets are entangled up in domestic issues," Eagleburger continued. "If he succeeds, others may try the same thing. It would be a bad lesson."[34]

Such a blow to basic respect of national sovereignty could, in fact, disrupt the stream of time. This Bush would not tolerate. "Nothing of this importance," he therefore explained of the Gulf War in 1990, in the hope of rallying popular support for the military expedition he had already ordered, had occurred in the world "since World War II." Considering all that had occurred since that war, it was an audacious statement indeed.[35] But it was also a deliberate one. It was time for the United States, now secure in its place in Europe due to his work ensuring Germany's solid place in NATO and thus the organization's critical survival, to initiate a "new world order," where "the United Nations, free from Cold War stalemate, is poised to fulfill the historic vision of its founders. A world in which freedom and respect for human rights," or in other words the American system as he understood it, "find a home among all nations." A world ready, in other words, to join the broad American-led flotilla down the stream of time. "A hundred generations have searched for this elusive path to peace, which a thousand wars raged across the span of human endeavor." It was now their generation's rare opportunity to forge "a world quite different from the one we've known."[36]

Even if it was one previous generations would have found remarkably familiar. A world in which American power mattered, democracy's appeal widened, and sovereignty as defined by international organizations like the United Nations reigned supreme. A world, in other words, new yet with nothing new within it. This ultimately is why Bush ranks low on any scale for evaluating grand strategists predicated upon novelty. His vision was not new. He never intended it to be so. It was, quite explicitly, the vision of Franklin Roosevelt, his own commander in chief back when Bush had sailed aboard an aircraft carrier in the Pacific, who had never had opportunity to see his ideas fully implemented. Bush's grand strategy was in this sense conservative;

it was not new. But it was, he believed, both timely and within the current of time.

Grading This Grand Strategist

When evaluating Bush's time in office and his work as a strategist, metrics matter. With the exception of a second term in office, he achieved all he desired. Few can make that claim. He handed his successors the tools he considered necessary for America's long-term success. NATO endured, and with it Washington's reason for being on-site in Europe. The Chinese-American relationship remained, strained but not broken, after Tiananmen, keeping the world's most powerful nation at least on speaking terms with its most populous one as the twenty-first century approached. International trade remained on track with fewer restraints, and Washington retained the economic entry point in Europe its military superiority ensured.

Each would prove strained in the twenty-first century. NATO expanded, albeit under Bush's successors, straining Russian-American relations. China's growing economy fueled heightened strategic aspirations, and Europe struggled in the twenty-first century to remain united. Most tragically, the version of Middle Eastern stability Bush secured in 1991 led directly to widespread resentment of America's on-site presence, directly fueling the religious radicalism that inspired the terrorist attacks of September 11, 2001, and another generation (so far) of American direct engagement in a region at best uncomfortable and more often outwardly hostile to any American-led occupation. Those attacks occurred precisely twenty-one years to the day after Bush had first declared the quest of a "new world order." Gauging George H. W. Bush's success in 1991, or in 2001, or in 2011, therefore, produces different answers. A hero in the first instance, perhaps the reason Americans faced problems in the Middle East in the second, he was by the third date largely celebrated for the restraint his son never exhibited. Times changed, his actions in office did not, nor did the central tenets as a strategist he embraced and embodied: he faced instability, believed in the stream of history, and by acting hippocratically and by ensuring the American stability he considered paramount to security, helped keep chaos at bay. And he ensured that subsequent presidents wielded the authority and the mechanisms to keep American power the world's dominant guarantor of the peace and global prosperity. His was never a pacifistic vision, nor a fully cooperative one. It rested on American power, unabashedly so. It also rested on foundations he inherited and never questioned. As an innovator he was less a failure than one who had never tried. Because he already knew "what worked."

Notes

1. Jeffrey A. Engel, "When Bush Believed the Cold War Ended, and Why that Mattered," in *41: Inside the Presidency of George H. W. Bush*, ed. Michael Nelson and Barbara Perry (Ithaca, NY: Cornell University Press, 2014), 109.
2. "Robert J. McMahon, "'By Helping Others, We Help Ourselves': The Cold War Rhetoric of American Foreign Policy," in *Critical Reflections on the Cold War: Linking Rhetoric and History*, ed. Martin J. Medhurst (College Station: Texas A&M University Press, 2000), 233.
3. Public Papers of the President, "Remarks at Texas A&M University in College Station, Texas," December 15, 1992, UCSB Presidency Project.
4. Alexander Cockburn, "Al Gore's Peace Prize," *Counterpunch*, October 13, 2007.
5. Otto Pflanze, *Bismarck and the Development of Germany* (Princeton, NJ: Princeton University Press, 1963), 17.
6. Catherine L. Langford, "George Bush's Struggle with the 'Vision Thing,'" in *The Rhetorical Presidency of George H.W. Bush*, ed. Martin Medhurst (College Station: Texas A&M University Press, 2006), 35.
7. Michael Kinglsey, "Rally Round the Flag Boys," *Time*, September 12, 1988, 86.
8. Jeffrey A. Engel and George H. W. Bush, *The China Diary of George H. W. Bush* (Princeton, NJ: Princeton University Press, 2008), 451.
9. Owen Ullmann, "Bush Era Promises to Be Low-Key Practical Affair," *Philadelphia Inquirer*, January 20, 1989.
10. George Shultz, *Issues on My Mind* (Palo Alto, CA: Hoover Institute Press, 2013), 1949.
11. "Gorbachev Policy Has Ended the Cold War, Thatcher Says," *New York Times*, November 18, 1988.
12. Francis Fukuyama, "The End of History?," *National Interest*, 16 (Summer 1989), 3–18.
13. James Atlas, "What Is Fukuyama Saying? And to Whom Is He Saying It?," *New York Times Magazine*, October 22, 1989.
14. The same National Interest volume included full commentaries by notable conservative thinkers and critics incliuding Alan Bloom, Peirre Hassner, Irving Kristol, Gertrude Himmelfarb, Stephen Sestanovich, and Daniel Patrick Moynihan can be found at *The National Interest*, 16, Summer 1989, pp. 19–35.
15. Public Papers of the President, "Inaugural Address," January 20, 1989. For on-line access to all published presidential papers, I have employed the University of California, Santa Barbara American Presidency Project, https://www.presidency.ucsb.edu/. Hereafter UCSB Presidency Project.
16. Ibid.

17. Frances Fitzgerald, *Way Out There in the Blue* (New York: Simon & Schuster, 2001), 469.
18. "Address by James A. Baker Before the Center for Strategic and International Studies," May 4, 1989, https://www.c-span.org/video/?7351-1/challenge-change-us-soviet-relations, accessed October 15, 2020.
19. Bush Library, NSC Papers, Arnold Kanter Files, Subject Files, NATO Summit-May 1989, "Brent Scowcroft to POTUS, Re: The NATO Summit," March 20, 1989.
20. "Remarks at the Boston University Commencement Ceremony in Massachusetts," May 21, 1989, UCSB Presidency Project.
21. Robert Gates Oral History, Miller Center for Public Affairs, University of Virginia, Charlottesville, July 23–24, 2000, 101.
22. John Broder, "'Cold War Is Not Over,' Bush Adviser Cautions," *Los Angeles Times*, January 23, 1989.
23. Michael R. Gordon, "C.I.A. Aide Sees Soviet Economy Failing to Gain," *New York Times*, October 15, 1988.
24. President's News Conference, May 3, 1990, UCSB Presidency Project.
25. "Evolution in Europe," *New York Times*, May 4, 1990.
26. George Bush and Brent Scowcroft, *A World Transformed* (New York: Vintage Books, 1999), 267.
27. "The President's News Conference," February 12, 1990, UCSB Presidency Project .
28. George Bush, *All the Best, George Bush: My Life in Letters and Other Writings* (New York: Scribners, 2014), p. 461.
29. Ibid., 441–442.
30. Ibid.
31. UCSB Presidency Project, "The President's News Conference," October 31, 1989.
32. James A. Baker and Thomas DeFrank, *The Politics of Diplomacy: Revolution, War, and Peace, 1989–1992* (New York: G.P. Putnam's Sons, 1995), p. 277.
33. Ibid.
34. Bush Library, NSC Papers, Richard Haass Papers, box 43, File: Iraq-August 2, 1990-December 1990 (8), Minutes of the NSC Meeting, August 3, 1990.
35. Christopher Maynard, *Out of the Shadow: George H.W. Bush and the End of the Cold War* (College Station: Texas A&M University Press, 2008), 80.
36. UCSB Presidency Project, "Address before a Joint Session of the Congress on the Persian Gulf Crisis and the Federal Budget Deficit," September 11, 1990.

PART IV
NEW APPROACHES

15

Foreign Missions and Strategy, Foreign Missions as Strategy

Emily Conroy-Krutz

In 1829, a committee met to decide whether to send a young American man to China. He was not expected to have any short-term success in advancing their interests. In time, though, they hoped he might become incredibly important. He would help open relations between China and the United States, paving the way for future connections. He would work to teach the Chinese about America and the West and, at the same time, to inform the West about Chinese history and culture. Increased knowledge, he was sure, would assist western efforts to "open" China. This was an important goal for the committee. They had been trying to gain access to China for over a decade, sure that connections there would be the key to advancing their global vision for their country in the world. They were certain that America was designed to play a particular role in global affairs, to be a leader in morality and "civilization," partnering with Great Britain in advancing these ideals internationally. China would be an important step in this process. For almost twenty years, this committee had worked tirelessly toward their grand vision, carefully weighing options and strategically embarking on new projects only in the places where they believed success toward this larger goal was possible. As the committee made its decisions, was it practicing grand strategy?

That terminology certainly never would have passed their lips, and yet thinking about this group in connection with grand strategy is instructive. These evangelical Protestant men from the Northeast were the Prudential Committee of the American Board of Commissioners for Foreign Missions (ABCFM). They were not diplomats or statesmen. Where they did have power, however, was in shaping the early American foreign mission movement, and they did so with a strategic vision that surpassed that of their country's contemporary diplomatic apparatus. The early history of American foreign missions perhaps seems an awkward fit in a volume about grand strategy. Political, not religious, figures generally populate the pages of such studies. And yet thinking about missions and strategy—or missions as strategy—provides productive lessons for "rethinking grand strategy."

Thinking about missions provides an essential reminder of the sometimes hidden or overlooked role of religion in the history of foreign relations and policy. Historians are increasingly attentive to this fact, exploring the explicit and implicit ways that religion has affected particular events or the decision making of particular individuals in the history of foreign relations.[1] Even outside these studies of events and individuals, foreign missions are important to this discussion. For the nineteenth century in particular (but also for the twentieth) missionaries held an important and often overlooked role.[2] As a significant portion of the Americans who made their lives abroad, missionaries were positioned to provide information to decision makers and strategists about foreign peoples and places. In this role, the particular priorities and strategies of the mission movement could have important and sometimes hidden effects on American foreign relations more generally. Accordingly, attention to foreign missions reveals the multiple ways that religious belief and priorities could shape political strategies.

Once attention is paid to these missionaries, it is quite clear that they themselves worked strategically. In foreign missionaries, we can see a group of early nineteenth-century Americans who had a grand plan for the role of the United States in the world. The United States was, in their view, one of the two seats of "true religion" in the world (England being the other) and accordingly it had a duty to lead the rest of the world toward a particular type of Christianity and "civilization." The missionaries confidently proclaimed the right and duty of Americans to be active in the world as leaders in a worldwide religious movement. Through the mission movement, evangelicals in the generations after the American Revolution attempted to enact their vision for their country and for the world. They sought to make their nation a leader in the work of spreading civilization and, in so doing, making the world ever more interconnected.[3] This can be seen in the ABCFM's general process of location selection as well as their early efforts in China, which they saw as a key strategic location in the overall project of the conversion of the world. Similar dynamics were at work in all of the board's mission stations, but the particular interest that missionaries, merchants, and diplomats had in relations with China make it a particularly apt location for considering missionary and grand strategy.

Missionary stories are often compartmentalized as American religious history, not as a part of American diplomatic history. Not only does this create a misunderstanding of the role of religion in foreign relations and an inaccurate dichotomy between "domestic" and "foreign" affairs, but it also creates a false sense of unity when talking about American ideals, goals, and priorities on the world stage. Incorporating missions into a discussion of foreign relations and grand strategy is a reminder of the multiplicity of groups that claim the mantle of "American" and the right to define American goals in the world. Rethinking American grand strategy requires paying attention to this diversity of strategists and their visions for American foreign relations.

Selecting Missionary Locations

Missionaries of the early nineteenth century saw themselves as engaged in the work of the Great Commission of the New Testament to go out into the world and bring the Gospel to all people.[4] Their goal was the conversion of the world. That this project was quite ambitious and perhaps impossible was not lost on their contemporaries or even the missionaries themselves. Missionaries were sure, though, that they were being guided by Providence, that the time had come for action, and that, with strategic choices about where to go and when, they could make a profound difference. The first decades of American foreign mission work were marked by discussions about strategy as missionary organizations decided where their efforts would be most useful and how they could most effectively reach those populations. Researching potential locations with British correspondents, merchants, diplomats, and eventually missionaries stationed in the field, American missionary societies mapped the world and ranked its peoples in respect to their likelihood for conversion. As they did so, they revealed a vision for American religion, politics, and economics: they sought an active empire that would enable the spread of Protestantism and civilization, improving the lives of foreigners and Americans alike. They did not always agree with the vision of the American state or that of American capitalists, but they shared a general assumption that core American democratic and economic values were part and parcel of the religious change they were offering and that trade and political connections would benefit everyone.

Some of this strategizing work is visible in the 1818 publication by two of the board's first missionaries, Gordon Hall and Samuel Newell. They published *The Conversion of the World, or the Claims of 600 Millions* to explain their understanding of the duty of American Christians to the non-Christian "heathen" around the world. Much of their plan focused on prioritizing certain places in the world over others as potential recipients for American evangelization efforts. "Some parts of the world have a greater claim to our immediate attention than others," they wrote. To demonstrate this, they provided an example to their readers in the early American republic: Louisiana or Ceylon. Which place deserved more American attention? The answer was rather obvious. Clearly, it was Ceylon.[5]

From the perspective of the twenty-first century, the choice might seem less straightforward than it was to Hall and Newell. But the missionaries had very clear reasons for their emphasis on the globe over the continent. Since there were not enough missionaries to actually preach to the entire world, Hall and Newell insisted that their duty was "to select the most important places first." As they laid it out for their readers, these selections came down to the extent to which the missionaries could expect Christianity to be spread once it was planted. Because of the relative population densities and the presumed civilization of Ceylon and Louisiana, the missionaries were sure that Ceylon was the more prudent choice for their efforts.[6]

Just as Hall and Newell did in this text, the members of the American Board worked to create order out of seeming chaos as they planned where to focus their evangelizing efforts. They created a hierarchy of heathenism, a system that brought together their ideas about culture, race, and religion with the geopolitical realities of the world in which they lived.[7] The hierarchy of heathenism considered a variety of factors: population size and density, proximity to other "heathen countries," climate, existing educational infrastructure, "condition of the people," and finally, level of civilization. When missionaries spoke of civilization, they referred to a whole constellation of attributes that they believed could convey the position of a society on a grand historical narrative of development. For missionaries, civilization was central to conversion. They might debate the direction of causality, but they were all convinced of the close links between Protestantism and civilization. Accordingly, in the first half century of American missionary work, the introduction of Christianity to a "heathen" culture seemed to require the introduction of civilization. Missionaries thus prioritized places close to British or American imperial or commercial expansion, assuming that empires and missions could work hand in hand to ensure the spread of both Christianity and civilization.[8]

As the American Board began its research into potential mission sites, its members assumed that the first mission would be somewhere in South Asia. Everything that Americans heard about India and its surrounding region made it appear to be their ideal sort of place: relatively civilized, with a large and dense population. Proximity to British colonies meant both that the area could be expected to become more civilized and, they hoped, that missionaries could expect protection. American evangelical readers could easily access the writings of British missionaries who were already active in the field and of British travelers and chaplains who wrote about the progress of religion in the Empire.

These texts drew missionary attention to Burma, which at this time remained independent of the British East India Company. In the texts that were available to American readers, British authors expressed optimism about the potential in Burma for high rates of conversion.[9] This, combined with the New England understanding of the refined goods that could be found in Burma, suggested a level of civilization that would be welcoming to mission work.[10] After missionaries arrived in Calcutta in 1812, though, they determined that Burma was not the civilized empire they had expected but was ruled by a "tyrannical" emperor who was far from friendly to their work. They then began to survey the rest of the Indian Ocean region to find a new location. It was, in short, the civilization issue that kept them from Burma. And it was that same issue that would keep them within the British Empire, eventually establishing the first American foreign mission in Bombay in 1814. Bombay, with the influence of the British, seemed to possess everything that the Americans were looking for in a mission population: civilization and a supportive government, a sizable population, and access to even more places once the initial entry point was successful.

These same guidelines shaped how the board approached its Native American missions at the time. By the end of the War of 1812, there were, board secretary Samuel Worcester insisted, "indications of Providence" that missionary success in North America might indeed be possible. Just as it had described Asia earlier in the decade, the board was using biblical language to call this region "white already to the harvest" by 1817.[11] Here, too, the example of other missions suggested the beginning of what one missionary described as "civilization taking the ground of barbarism." The Cherokee seemed to be becoming "civilized," but they were not yet Christians. In many ways, then, the Cherokee Nation appeared to be ideal. There was much for the missionaries to do, but the way had been prepared. The Cherokee, further, had a sizable population and a centralized location, both of which were important factors for the board. Above all, it was the proximity to white settlement and the perceived progress in "civilization" that drew the board's attention to the Cherokee nation, where they established a mission in 1816.[12]

In the missionary excitement over Asia and certain parts of North America, though, there was a decided lack of interest in working in other regions. Africa, for example, was generally rejected in the 1810s, only to be called "among the most important and accessible fields" globally by the mid-1820s.[13] This changing evaluation of Africa represented a shift in American knowledge (or asserted knowledge) about Africa, its peoples, and its religious culture. Whereas missionaries in India were attempting to convert "heathen" from one religion to another, American missionaries were convinced that the "heathen" of Africa were without religion entirely: they saw them as a blank slate on whom the missionaries could impart the truth of the Gospel. This new understanding was largely a result of the spread of the British Empire into West Africa. Sierra Leone inspired American missionaries, who saw it as an imperial project that was undertaken on benevolent and even evangelical grounds. They were delighted to read news of the colony, in particular of the success of its educational and agricultural programs. This inspired the board to join with the American Colonization Society in sending missionaries to Liberia.[14] In planning this new mission, the board referred to colonies as "important auxiliaries" that would "greatly facilitate our entrance among the several tribes of the interior" through "the information they collect, the roads they open, and their commercial intercourse."[15]

As the board evaluated potential mission sites, they marked the world according to commercial networks, imperial spaces, and differing levels of "heathenism." The specificity that might be expected to guide their efforts was largely diminished in this process. "Likely" locations began to look more and more alike, and missionaries were regularly told to peruse the formal instructions issued to earlier missionaries, even at far distant stations. Missionaries to West Africa might be told to look to the instructions for missionaries to Hawaii, places with very different cultures and histories that, according to missionary logic, could be approached in similar ways.[16] Specific strategies were mostly devoted to determining where to go. Once a station was selected, what actually happened there, at least in the view from Boston, would be quite similar to the procedure in other stations. Preaching, teaching, translating, and printing the Gospel would consume the energy of missionaries around the world. The skills of civilization would, they assumed, be effective in all spaces that were ready to receive them.

Waiting to be received, though, was the difficult part. Missionaries generally assumed that the physical ability to go somewhere was all that was necessary. They spent less time worrying about their welcome. Working largely within Anglo-American imperial and commercial networks, this often worked out well enough, with physical access leading to some type of permission to work. One exception loomed large: China. The full complexity of missionary strategy is evident in the movement's discussions of China, which early missionaries saw as the key to the conversion of the whole world. Its large population, high literacy rate, history of civilization, and prominent role in global trade gave it incredible significance. Yet American missionaries had limited access to China. They spent significant energy, accordingly, strategizing their work in Asia so that they would be able to take advantage as soon as they could gain entry to that country.

Strategies for China

The American Board opened its mission to China in 1829 when it quietly sent Elijah Bridgman to Canton. Bridgman joined Robert Morrison of the London Missionary Society, who had been there since 1807. Even as Americans sent Ira Tracy and Samuel Wells Williams to assist the mission in 1833, the political context in China made it very difficult for American Protestants to imagine entering China in the early nineteenth century. They could, however, imagine a future in which they would be able to support broad-scale missions in China. In the early decades of the century, American missionaries strategized ways to make the most of what opportunities they did have and to be ready when the time came for China to open its doors to them.

Before the Opium Wars of the 1840s, China limited Westerners to Canton, where they were subject to a factory system that controlled their interaction with goods and people. In this, they were not alone: the government also strictly controlled merchants and diplomats, all of whom hoped to gain increased access to China. It was a deeply significant destination for many Americans and British subjects abroad in these years; all were seeking ways to reach this population of potential converts and trading partners. American merchants had long valued their ability to take part in the lucrative China trade. The *Empress of China*, the first American ship to reach Canton, had left New York harbor in 1784 on the same date that Americans sent word to Britain of Congress's ratification of the Treaty of Paris, formally ending the American Revolution. The US-China trade, then, was an early and significant interest.[17] As was the case in other locations, commercial interest in a space was closely connected to missionary interest. The goods that drew in American merchants—tea, chinaware, furniture, and more—also signaled to the missionaries evidence of a civilization that might give way to Christianization.

The directors of the American Board described this push and pull they felt toward China in 1833. Here they saw a densely populated space, with "mountains, plains, rivers, and canals . . . covered with people; while millions of the busy race are scattered over the neighboring country and islands." These millions of people, further, were "not barbarians: they have arts and sciences, and among them are more persons who are able to read and write, probably, than in Great Britain and America, combined." Yet this was still a place in need of transformation. "The sun of their civilization," the writers continued, "has never exceeded to the zenith" and had indeed been in retrograde for thousands of years. By the logic of the hierarchy of heathenism, in other words, this was an ideal population for missionary endeavors. China had the population, the literacy, and the roots of civilization that American missionaries prized. It also had a government that did not want missionaries to enter the country and that had the power to keep them out.[18]

It was a group of evangelical merchants who had first seen this opportunity for American participation in 1827. Writing to Morrison and the American Board, they echoed the central logic of the hierarchy of heathenism that had brought American missionaries to India a decade earlier. Providence had opened the way for Christianity in China at the port of Canton, and the merchants saw work for two initial missionaries: one focused on sailors who visited Canton and could then bring the gospel home with them, and the other working within Canton itself. The latter missionary would "gain acquisitions for eventual usefulness as a more direct laborer for the establishment of Christianity in China." It was a long-term goal that the board supported, and this was the role that Bridgman was expected to fill. Importantly, this evangelistic work would not consist of preaching alone. The missionary in Canton would have a printing press, allowing for the creation of texts that could spread the missionary message far and wide. The merchants expected, too, that the missionary could rely on the British presence for some form of protection.[19]

At times, these merchant connections could be uncomfortable, as not all (or even most) merchants had the evangelical enthusiasm that brought the missionaries to China. The two groups shared some objectives (increased access to China) but also differed in their vision. Merchants' primary interest in China was profit. Increased access to China would bring additional goods and markets. While missionaries shared an understanding of the importance of trade for creating and enforcing connections between countries, they were in China for very different reasons. Missionaries were warned against forming too close relations with merchants. Bridgman was told to "be frank, courteous, and affectionate, but do not, at any time, lose, or appear to lose, the seriousness and solicitude for their spiritual welfare, which become the ambassador of Christ to sinners."[20] By the time Tracy and Williams were sent, they were reminded that they had "no mercantile, no political designs," but their "only aim is to be instrumental in publishing the gospel."[21]

This emphasis on the separation between the missionaries and other groups of American and non-American merchants and diplomats was essential because of the opium trade. Missionaries were early opposed to the trade for humanitarian reasons; they saw it as a harmful drug and were troubled to see western merchants enriching themselves through it. Further, for practical reasons they hoped the illegal trade would cease. Smuggling complicated the ability of all Westerners to gain a foothold in China and challenged missionaries' understanding of the linked goals of the two groups. Some of the major donors to the China mission and its philanthropic institutions were smugglers, making it difficult for missionaries to speak out against the trade. It took several years for Bridgman to voice his opposition in print to American audiences, but when he did speak out against the trade, it had some impact. In 1839, he was able to push American merchants to agree to Chinese demands to give up the trade. Missionaries had some influence over US governmental policy as well. When missionary Peter Parker toured the United States, he met with the president, secretary of state, and several senators and wrote a report for them on his recommendations for America's China policy.[22] After the Opium Wars opened up new ports to Westerners, Bridgman and Parker assisted in the 1844 framing of the Treaty of Wanghsia and were able to include articles that would protect missionary efforts in these new treaty ports. This gave missionaries their long-sought ability to evangelize more openly in China and initiated a new era in the complex relations between missionaries and merchants.[23] In the years between missionary arrival and the conclusion of the Opium Wars, though, missionaries had to delicately and strategically balance long-term and short-term goals as they approached their work in Asia.

If their long-term goal, shared with merchants and diplomats, was open access to China, missionaries also sought short-term strategies for getting the word of the Gospel into China even when they could not physically bring it. In this context, translation and printing became central aspects of the work missionaries did in China. Everywhere that missionaries went, the written word was important. Globally, missionaries used a metaphor of seeds planted when talking about print. They trusted that their translated scriptures, tracts, and catechisms could yield long-term effects, even in the absence of missionary labors. Missions to India frequently described encounters on itinerancy tours where they would come upon people who, while not having met actual missionaries, had come into contact with missionary texts. The words themselves had done important work. A young girl might have a catechism memorized. An old man might be able to discuss the scriptures. Based on these experiences and their general faith in the written word of God, missionaries had long been committed to the work of translation. With China, though, that work took on a distinctly strategic end. As early as 1825, the board understood that the press would be a prime method for evangelism in the absence of missionaries' ability to itinerate. Even before the arrival of the Americans, the *Missionary Herald* reported that Morrison could distribute as many as 4,000 tracts within a four-month period.[24] These numbers were expected to rise with the arrival of Bridgman and other American missionaries.[25]

The mission used the press to distribute more than sacred texts to the Chinese, however. Before Westerners had access to mainland China, the mission press was also busy printing information that would help ease the way for increased relations between the West and China. Accordingly, missionaries not only worked on explicitly evangelical tracts but also sought to provide Chinese language secular histories of the West through organizations such as the Society for the Diffusion of Useful Knowledge. The goal of this organization was to open up increased exchanges between the West and China: diplomatic, commercial, and religious. Working alongside merchants, the missionaries were a minority in the group, but they were influential and quite vocal in their support of reform to Chinese foreign relations. For his part,

Bridgman authored a *Concise Account of the United States of America*, the first Chinese-language history of the nation, in 1836.[26]

The other side of this work was providing information about China to the West. Bridgman stressed the importance of missionaries and other Westerners learning Chinese and also the literary and philosophical heritage of China.[27] "Accurate observation will be among your most important duties," the board had instructed Tracy and Williams. While they did not need to travel for the express purpose of gathering information about China, they were to describe as much as possible what they observed about the Chinese.[28] While some of this information was for the benefit of the mission movement, it had broader purposes. Through the *Chinese Repository*, first published in 1832, missionaries were to provide information about China for Western audiences more generally. This periodical, published on the mission press and largely authored by missionary personnel, gave British and American audiences with various interests in China a window onto its culture, history, and politics. It represented another link between missionary and merchant networks, not only in authors and readers but also in its financing. The *Repository* was able to run only because of the support of D. W. C. Olyphant, a merchant who had guaranteed all losses from the journal. Although Bridgman aimed for an unbiased approach, the China depicted in the pages of the *Repository* was in desperate need of western influence and intervention. In addition to subscribers in Asia and elsewhere, the *Repository* was sent to western periodical offices, which would occasionally reprint articles or mention receipt of the issues in their pages.[29]

Those missionaries actually stationed in Canton found much of their time consumed with this type of writing. Other missionaries in the region, particularly those in Singapore, were also expected to work primarily in translation and writing to serve the goals of the mission. These linguistic skills were important. In the 1830s, it was clear that missionaries going to China would need to be doing this work primarily; consequently, candidates, such as James T. Dickinson, evaluated their ability to serve based on their language skills. Dickinson, who would eventually serve in Singapore, had initially expressed a willingness to work in China but expressed a "doubt whether I am enough of a scholar and linguist" for that station.[30] In Singapore, Dickinson would indeed need to do translation work.

The Singapore mission itself was a strategic move in the long-term project of converting China. Only recently incorporated into the British Empire,

322 RETHINKING AMERICAN GRAND STRATEGY

Singapore was quickly becoming a major trading center for the region, and not only among western traders. Huge numbers of ships passed through the port city from South, East, and Southeast Asia, and missionaries believed that a printing press and text distribution there would allow for unprecedented reach, particularly into China. Missionaries themselves would hardly need to itinerate, they felt, if they could simply hand out texts to an eager literate population of Asian mariners who would carry the tracts home with them. Through print, they would spread the word of God throughout Asia.[31]

In addition to print and linguistic study, the American Board had another long-term plan for eventual entry into China: the preparation of missionary children as the next generation of missionaries. While never an explicit policy of the board, the strategy can be glimpsed in correspondence between the board and missionary parents. In their discussions about the education of missionary children, the board clearly hoped that they would eventually follow in their parents' footsteps. This next generation of missionaries would be uniquely skilled. Raised abroad, they would have linguistic abilities that American-born missionaries simply could not acquire. They would have an understanding of culture that would allow them to evangelize more effectively. And, importantly, once Americans were granted permission to station more missionaries in China, they would already be in the region, ready to serve. Though many missionary parents in this era shared those goals, they also worried about the health and cultural implications of raising their children overseas, and this was an ongoing source of tension for many years.[32]

Translation, printing in multiple languages, establishing satellite missions, and hoping for a second-generation of missionaries all represented the short-term strategies that the American Board employed in the service of its goal of full entry into China and the eventual conversion of the world. At times, their interests overlapped with other Americans in the region who hoped to gain access to the mainland. At times, as with the controversy over the opium trade, there could be some serious tensions. These would continue well after the end of the Canton system and the increased access of Americans to China. Missionaries and merchants may have had similar short-term goals, but they also had divergent long-term goals. How those dynamics worked out in China, as in other mission locations around the world, is similar to the challenges of conceiving American foreign relations in the framework of grand strategy.

Missionary Strategy, American Strategy

The missionary approach to the world is not only important for missionary strategy and religious history. Missionaries also helped to shape the ways that other Americans saw the world. Missionaries were important as representatives of American culture abroad as well as key sources of information about the rest of the world for many American Protestants at home: they provided Americans with a specific way of thinking about the role of their country in the world. Those connections could be felt in multiple ways, whether it was in the monthly prayer concerts that sought to spiritually connect Christians in the United States and missionaries abroad, or, more important for discussions of foreign relations, in the regular writings of the missionaries that appeared in the American press.

Alongside the voices that more commonly populate diplomatic histories (British informants, American merchants, diplomats), missionaries, sometimes acting as diplomats themselves, provided dispatches that were eagerly read by their evangelical audience and beyond as Americans attempted to make sense of events around the world such as the Opium Wars. In China and beyond, their hands can be seen not just in official missionary dispatches but also in regional histories and even diplomatic treaties. With their long-term residences in foreign spaces, missionaries became trusted American informants about the world. Accordingly, scholars of America's engagement with the world are increasingly ready to incorporate their voices more fully.[33]

The previous reluctance to do so is largely due to the fact that American missionary organizations are, of course, not state directed. While many China missionaries did serve the US government in various roles during their time in China, they saw this consular, translation, and occasional advising work as separate from their evangelism. Yet missionaries also saw themselves as speaking for their country and representing its interests around the world in various ways. Supporters saw them as an important face of the United States abroad. The importance of the conversion of the world was first and foremost religious, but supporters also expected it to have important political implications. If Christianity brought "civilization," it would also bring about cultures that were more interested in trade partnerships and more open connections with the West. Missionaries, further, were connected in complex ways to merchants and political actors as they thought about where to go, when, and how. They could be vocal critics of other Americans overseas, not least because foreigners were not always interested in acknowledging the differences between groups of Americans abroad, seeing them as collectively representative of their country and its people. Throughout their global endeavors, these overlapping networks determined the ways in which missionaries went about their work, and the ways that they understood that work to be connected to larger American goals abroad.

This is an important feedback loop in considering a grand strategy for American foreign relations. Missionaries in this period were strategic thinkers. They had an ambitious long-term goal (the conversion of the world), and they made strategic choices as they sought to realize that goal. As they selected where to go, they carefully weighed political and cultural possibilities and attempted to determine the "most likely" sites for their success.

This was difficult in part because a range of different priorities and interests was shaping American diplomatic actors. The China example highlights divergent understandings of what America was, or ought to be, as a global actor, and what its major goals were. Was it the promotion of free trade, or the promotion of American prominence among world powers, or the spread of civilization, or the Christianization of the world? Was it all of these things, or some combination? The ways that individuals answered those questions were deeply significant for determining the appropriate American response to, for example, the Opium Wars. Foreign missionaries were an important group of players in this conversation about America's role abroad, and their answers to those questions would influence not just what happened on the ground in China but how Americans at home talked about those events.

Those questions about America's role in the world were important to historical actors and should also drive the modern reader's attention to the contested nature of America's role abroad. Rethinking grand strategy should involve questioning the assumption of a unified American identity and a unified American strategy. At any given moment, as the stories of foreign missionaries show, there were multiple groups of Americans debating these questions and at times reaching different answers. Prioritizing the conclusions of one group over another as historically significant is a choice that ultimately limits historical understanding of the United States in the world.

The early history of American foreign missions in general, and the early missionary experience in China in particular, directs attention to the importance of religion in American foreign relations and to some particular limitations of the grand strategy model. As non-state actors, missionaries seem unlikely figures for a discussion of grand strategy. Yet their strategizing reveals a different sort of vision for the position of the United States in the world than is evident from looking at American diplomats or merchants alone. They expected their country to become an active power in the world, not only interested in making a profit in Asia but also in transforming Asian culture to embody a Christian civilization. Their vision and their work reveal strategies that seem far more consistent and, indeed, grand than those of their contemporaries in the American government. They expected the government to share their vision and were frustrated whenever the government more closely followed the merchants' competing understanding of the role of the United States in China.

Seeing missionaries as strategists with a distinctive clear and overarching vision of the American role on the world stage that at times supported but at times challenged the vision of the American state demands rethinking any unified definition of grand strategy. Missionaries' often underappreciated role in shaping domestic American ideas about the world should invite further discussion about the links between diplomacy and all sorts of groups of Americans connected to, but distinct from, the state. Scholars ought to ask which thinkers' visions matter in this conception, which voices are overlooked, and what unseen influences are shaping policy?

The American foreign mission movement was certainly strategic, and it does not feel like much of a stretch, after all, to talk about it in terms of grand strategy. If grand strategy is an intellectual architecture that shapes complex and diverse long- and short-term decisions in service of an overarching vision, then that is what the missionaries were building. Missionaries thought in the long term, with ambitious goals and a broad vision that drove their decisions in a wide range of places and contexts. They were selective of where to spend their resources (financial, personnel, and temporal) and developed methods that they expected to be relatively easily exportable from place to place. As the early planning for a China mission reveals, this could be very piecemeal, with missionaries understanding that it would be many years before their plans bore fruit. As they tried to make their policy decisions in service of that long-term goal of world conversion, they found themselves working at times with, and at times against, other Americans in the region who had different priorities and different long-term goals of commerce and diplomacy. Their experiences are a necessary reminder of the diversity of American ideas about what America is and the complexity of identifying an encompassing strategy that could meet the demands and priorities of the country's interests overseas. Once China did begin to open up to an increased American presence later in the century, this earlier missionary strategy would turn out to have important implications for US-China relations. Many years of planning and experience had prepared missionaries to be the authorities that the government could trust in shaping the treaties and policies that would determine the role of the. United States in China for decades to come.

Notes

1. Andrew Preston, *Sword of the Spirit, Shield of Faith: Religion in American War and Diplomacy* (New York: Knopf, 2012).
2. On the twentieth century, see David A. Hollinger, *Protestants Abroad: How Missionaries Tried to Change the World but Changed America* (Princeton, NJ: Princeton University Press, 2017); Melani McAlister, *The Kingdom of God Has No Borders: A Global History of American Evangelicals* (New York: Oxford University Press, 2018); and Matthew Avery Sutton, *Double Crossed: The Missionareis who Spied for the United States During the Second World War* (New York: Basic Books, 2019).
3. Emily Conroy-Krutz, *Christian Imperialism: Converting the World in the Early American Republic* (Ithaca, NY: Cornell University Press, 2015).
4. Mark 16:15–16 (King James Version).
5. Gordon Hall and Samuel Newell, *The Conversion of the World or the Claims of Six Hundred Million and the Ability and Duty of the Churches Respecting Them*, 2nd ed. (Andover: Printed for the American Board of Commissioners for Foreign Missions, by Flagg and Gould, 1818), 32–33.
6. Hall and Newell, *The Conversion of the World*, 32–33.
7. Conroy-Krutz, *Christian Imperialism*, ch. 1.
8. William R. Hutchison, *Errand to the World: American Protestant Thought and Foreign Missions* (Chicago: University of Chicago Press, 1987), especially ch. 2.
9. Frank N. Trager, *Burma from Kingdom to Republic: A Historical and Political Analysis* (New York: Frederick A. Praeger, 1966), 24. For an example of these texts, see Michael Symes, *An Account of an Embassy to the Kingdom of Ava, in the Year 1795*, 2 vols. (Edinburgh: Printed for Constable and Co., 1827), vol. 1, 251 and vol. 2, 40 .
10. Samuel Eliot Morison, *The Maritime History of Massachusetts, 1783–1860* (Boston: Houghton Miflin, 1921), 92; Courtney Anderson, *To the Golden Shore: The Life of Adoniram Judson* (Boston: Little, Brown, and Co., 1956), 132; John L. Christian, "American Diplomatic Interest in Burma," *Pacific Historical Review* 8:2 (1939), 139; Susan Bean, *Yankee India: American Commercial and Cultural Encounters with India in the Age of Sail, 1784–1860* (Salem, MA: Peabody Essex Museum, 2001), 40, 78–79.
11. Samuel Worcester to Jeremiah Evarts, Salem, July 1, 1815, Papers of the American Board of Commissioners for Foreign Missions, Houghton Library, Harvard

University (Hereafter ABC) 1.5, vol. 2. Worcester is quoting from John 4:35–36. Samuel Worcester to Elisha Swift, Salem, October 22, 1817, ABC 1.01, vol. 1.

12. Conroy-Krutz, *Christian Imperialism*, 34–36

13. "Foreign Establishments," *Missionary Herald*, January, 1827, 6.

14. Christopher Leslie Brown, *Moral Capital: Foundations of British Abolitionism* (Chapel Hill: University of North Carolina Press, 2006), 261; Conroy-Krutz, *Christian Imperialism*, ch. 6.

15. Rufus Anderson, "Instructions of the Prudential Committee to the Rev. John Leighton Wilson, missionary to West Africa; read at a public meeting, held at Philadelphia, Sept. 22, 1833," ABC 8.1, v. 2.

16. "Instructions to Revs. Daniel Lindley, Alden Grant, Henry J. Brenable, George Champion, Dr. Alexander E. Wilson, and Dr. Newton Adams, and their wives," ABC 8.1, v. 2.

17. Kariann Akemi Yokota, *Unbecoming British: How Revolutionary America Became a Postcolonial Nation* (New York: Oxford University Press, 2011), ch. 3; John Rogers Haddad, *The Romance of China: Excursions to China in U.S. Culture, 1776–1876* (New York: Columbia University Press, 2008); John Rogers Haddad, *America's First Adventure in China: Trade, Treaties, Opium, and Salvation* (Philadelphia: Temple University Press, 2013); John Kuo Wei Tchen, *New York before Chinatown: Orientalism and the Shaping of American Culture, 1776–1882* (Baltimore: Johns Hopkins University Press, 2001); Paul Arthur Van Dyke, *The Canton Trade: Life and Enterprise on the China Coast, 1700–1845* (Hong Kong: Hong Kong University Press, 2005); Jacques M. Downs, *The Golden Ghetto: The American Commercial Community at Canton and the Shaping of American China Policy, 1784–1844* (Bethlehem, PA: Lehigh University Press, 1997); Leonard Blussé, *Visible Cities: Canton, Nagasaki, and Batavia and the Coming of the Americans* (Cambridge, MA: Harvard University Press, 2008).

18. ABCFM, "To the Rev. Ira Tracy, and Mr. Samuel Wells Williams, Appointed to Labor in Connection with the China Mission," June 6, 1833, ABC 8.1, v. 1.

19. Dr. W. Oliphant, Walter Crocker, and Charles B. Brintuaer, in "Account of the Origin of the China Mission," ABC 85.11.

20. "Instructions to Mr. Bridgman," in ABCFM Annual Report (1829), 94.

21. Instructions to Tracy and Williams, ABC 8.1, v. 1.

22. Despite the pledge, few American merchants in fact disengaged from the practice of smuggling. Michael Lazich, "American Missionaries and the Opium Trade in 19th Century China," *Journal of World History* 17:2 (June 2006), 197–223.

23. Haddad, *America's First Adventure in China*, 151–152.

24. "China," *Missionary Herald*, August, 1825, 250.

25. Murray A. Rubinstein, *The Origins of the Anglo-American Missionary Enterprise in China, 1807–1840* (Lanham, MD: Scarecrow Press, 1996).

26. Lazich, "Placing China in Its 'Proper Rank Among Nations': The Society of the Diffusion of Knowledge in China and the First Systematic Account of the United States in Chinese," *Journal of World History* 22;3 (September 2011), 529–530.

27. Ibid., 532.

28. ABCFM Instruction to Tracy and Williams, ABC 8.1, v. 1.

29. Elizabeth L. Malcolm, "The *Chinese Repository* and Western Literature on China, 1800 to 1850," *Modern Asian Studies* 7:2 (March 1973), 165–178; Murray A. Rubinstein, "The Wars They Wanted: American Missionaries' Use of 'The Chinese Repository' before the Opium War," *American Neptune* 48:4 (1988), 271–282.

30. James T. Dickinson to Wisner, Norwich, CT, May 27, 1834. ABC 6, Vol. 8.

31. Conroy-Krutz, *Christian Imperialism*, ch. 6.

32. Lisa Joy Pruitt, *A Looking-Glass for Ladies: American Protestant Women and the Orient in the Nineteenth Century* (Macon, GA: Mercer University Press, 2005), 69–71; Patricia Grimshaw, *Paths of Duty: American Missionary Wives in Nineteenth-Century Hawaii* (Honolulu: University of Hawaii Press, 1989), ch. 6; Joy Schulz, *Hawaiian by Birth: Missionary Children, Bicultural Identity, and US Colonialism in the Pacific* (Lincoln: University of Nebraska Press, 2017).

33. On information sources for American media coverage of the Opium Wars, see Dael Norwood, "Trading in Liberty: The Politics of the American China Trade, c. 1784–1862," PhD dissertation, Princeton University, 2012, ch. 4. On treaties: Haddad, *America's First Adventure in China*, 151–154; Francis Wayland, *Memoir of the Life and Labors of Adoniram Judson* (Boston: Sampson, and Company, 1853), 116–117. For histories, see, for example, John Leighton Wilson, *Western Africa: Its History, Condition, and Prospects* (New York: Harper and Brothers, 1856). On this theme for the Middle East, see Christine Heyrman, *American Apostles: When Evangelicals Entered the World of Islam* (New York: Hill and Wang, 2015).

16

The Unbearable Whiteness
of Grand Strategy

Adriane Lentz-Smith

The problem for grand strategy, to misquote W. E. B. Du Bois, is the problem of the color line. The field melds inquiry and application—often treating the study of how the powerful have pursued national interest as a prescription for how they *should* do so. For policymakers, grand strategy is, as political scientists have noted, "a nation-state's theory for how to produce security for itself."[1] For scholars of the United States keen "to get the ear of power," grand strategy is a metanarrative of foreign relations in which individual decision makers have primacy of place and anthropomorphized states develop patterns of behavior.[2] Like most big narratives, grand strategy offers some useful fictions. Useful, because it reassures policymakers and the scholars who work with them that nation-states are what they seem, that they have enough coherence in composition and purpose to serve as historical actors. Fictive, because the world conjured up by scholars of grand strategy can get so abstracted that it bears only passing resemblance to the one in which most people live and make meaning; history's rough edges—process and complexity—get smoothed for propulsive action. Indeed, for most students and practitioners of grand strategy, the nation remains a self-evident truth; negotiations over national interest remain spirited but relatively bloodless; and tracing causation involves psychologizing the actions of political elites rather than examining the culture and structures that set their horizons of possibility. Race and other forms of social difference go unremarked and their constitutive relationship to power go uninterrogated. White supremacy as political program and governing ideology is rarely, if ever, named.

Despite the field's willful self-positioning above the messy terrain of race, few things have remained more consistent across centuries of American history than state hostility to people of color.[3] More than an indictment of racism, this fact structures how power gets enacted, represented, and seen as legitimate. Inasmuch as this observation presumes that "ideational milieu[x]" do indeed structure behavior, choice, and what people conceive as possible, it makes an assertion about culture and ideology.[4] Yet, I am less concerned with extracting and asserting a strategic culture of states or state actors than I am with culture as varied (and contested) "meanings and values" expressed in "institutions and ordinary behavior."[5] Race is a "metalanguage," to use historian Evelyn Brooks Higginbotham's formulation, "that has a powerful and all-encompassing effect on the constitution and representation of power relations." Often functioning as analogy, it "impregnates the simplest meanings we take for granted" and thus masks its ideological—and by extension political—work.[6] Thinking through the relationship between race, ideology, and the practice of power is an epistemological problem and one of the aims of this chapter.

The chapter explores grand strategy as an intellectual and cultural project by considering its willful blindness to so fundamental a social cleavage as race as a political project. To ignore race is to misapprehend how power works in the United States and how domestic formulations of subjectivity, difference, and racialized power imbue American foreign relations. From the carceral state to the security state, establishing certain populations as the racialized rightless—subjected to laws but "refused the legal means" and denied "the political legitimacy and moral credibility" to contest them—can determine not just who gets "rendered . . . ineligible for personhood," in the words of scholar Lisa Marie Cacho, but who becomes "disentitled to life."[7] Deciding how far rights extend, and with that what forms of violence are allowable and on whom they are allowed, sets the frame for an array of other, vital decisions. Even, perhaps especially, in the realm of high policy, questions of means and ends—of what can be done and what it will mean—are inextricable from contests over who democracy encompasses and how power may be exercised. African Americans in the civil rights era voiced this insight in the vernacular of the black freedom struggle, consistently identifying white supremacy as constitutive not just of southern segregation but of state, economy, and society in the United States and beyond.[8]

To examine what work grand strategy does domestically and abroad, this chapter focuses on African Americans in the era of Cold War civil rights. But race-making, rights-making, and allocating power were never solely struggles between black and white, neither in the United States nor elsewhere. For Carl Rowan and Sam Greenlee, however, the two African American veterans who provide concrete cases for thinking about the

United States and the world, their blackness and ambitions for their people would color how they interpreted America's role in political and military struggles in the Third World and beyond. As with other people of color, their encounters with white supremacy shaped their understandings of liberation, violence, and the United States security project. Their perspectives challenge scholars' conceptions of the Cold War as a period of "defined clear national interests" and "public consensus." Centering the stories of Rowan and Greenlee highlights not simply ongoing contestation over the myth and history of the Cold War but, more fundamentally, the unthinking whiteness of grand strategy itself.[9]

Carl Rowan's American Dilemma

"Race is the key to history," black journalist and diplomat Carl Rowan asserted in *Ebony* magazine in late summer 1965.[10] Writing in the magazine's special issue on "The White Problem in America," Rowan was echoing an assertion that Great Britain's prime minister Benjamin Disraeli had made in his autobiographical novel *Endymion* some eighty-five years earlier. For Disraeli, an aggressive proponent of British empire in the previous century, race mattered. No statesman should remain "insensible" to it, he wrote in his novel, "whether you encounter its influence in communities or in individuals."[11]

Disraeli spoke of European races such as "the Teutons, the Sclaves, and the Celts" and more alien "Semites," "Arabs," and "Tatars" at a moment when imperial encounters were changing what European and American thinkers understood race to be.[12] In Victorian Britain, closer embrace of their settler colonies—"white men's countries," as two historians would later label them—coupled with the contests borne of new administrative and territorial claims in Asia and Africa would serve to dampen Britons' emphasis on racial difference between Europeans.[13] In the Gilded Age United States, similar struggles over how to classify, incorporate, or control foreign peoples at home and abroad would link up with bitter, often deadly, contests over African Americans' place and prospects. As old-stock white Americans sorted out what to do with the Slavs, Semites, Arabs, and others in their midst, whiteness would emerge as the definitive racial category.[14] By 1906, when W. E. B. Du Bois observed that "the color line belts the world," the projects of race-making and empire-making would be intricately bound.[15]

By the time Carl Rowan appropriated Disraeli's words eight decades on, the landscape had changed. The "rising tide of color" about whom white supremacist scholars had been sounding the alarm since the First World War had become a mighty force by the Second. Although racial identity largely hardened during these civil rights years—nothing tempers whiteness better, after all, than the forge of massive resistance—racial hierarchy stood on trembling earth. Writing in this age of anti-colonial struggle abroad and at home, Rowan argued that the United States could "scarcely afford for a moment to 'treat with indifference the principle of race.'" A former United States ambassador to Finland—posted "at the red border" with the Soviet Union, *Ebony* would breathlessly report—and current director of the United States Information Agency (USIA), Rowan knew full well that questions of race shaped both America's Cold War legitimacy and the emerging postcolonial order.[16] As he put it, race was the "key to the country's future in a world where a couple billion black, brown and yellow people have risen up in explosive revolution." Long after even the Cold War had faded, he argued, race would remain "the key to the fateful issue of war and peace."[17]

For Rowan, the problem of race was more precisely a problem of racism. "Race" served as a shorthand for the grossly unequal distribution of power, rights, and respect that people in power had long justified through theories of heritable difference, rooted in bloodline and mostly made visible by color. Thus he did not concern himself with racism as affect or emotion—although he did label "racial bitterness" and "racial arrogance" the "ugly and ominous time bomb that spells danger to mankind"—but as the creation of social difference and political hierarchy, and their perpetuation through violence.[18] Too politic a representative of the Johnson administration to call white supremacy out by name in the pages of *Ebony*, he nonetheless identified both the ideology and political program of what southern Democrats in the pre–World War II years would have proudly called white supremacy.

Rowan knew firsthand the pain and peril of such white supremacy. Raised in desperate, Depression-era poverty in a small town near the foot of Tennessee's Cumberland mountains, he had experienced Jim Crow as "grotesque bigotry" that left him in physical and economic peril: jobs scarce and debased, racial etiquette intricate and fraught.[19] If one had no "usefulness" in McMinnville, Tennessee, an increasingly restless Rowan realized as he began to chafe at Jim Crow, then one could quickly find himself in a "foolish and rather dangerous predicament."[20] He had escaped his predicament through military service and challenged the system through journalism and diplomatic service.

Even as Rowan lived Jim Crow, he also experienced the benefits of a state grown marginally less hostile to African American lives. Indeed, Rowan believed in and had benefited from the promise of the liberal order: his father's World War I bonus had saved his family from starvation during the Great Depression; his enlistment in the Navy in the 1940s—"the great turning point in the life of a green country kid"—had shown him a world beyond Tennessee; and the GI Bill had financed the education that set him on the path that led to ambassadorship and the USIA.[21] He was not naïve, he would explain late in his life, and had "never believed that any American boy can grow up to be president." He did believe, however, that with the system stacked against certain peoples and populations, "some of us" could still "beat the system to a satisfying degree."[22]

The occasional African American could beat the system because white supremacy was on the defensive in the postwar world. It had been damaged, as publisher John Johnson wrote in introducing *Ebony*'s special issue, by international upheavals: "World War II, the Communist conspiracy," and "the black nations' fight for freedom from colonialism."[23] So entangled were the fates of foreign peoples and African Americans that the NAACP in the late 1940s briefly considered changing its name from the National to the International Association for the Advancement of Colored People. Although the NAACP board tabled the proposal, they also reiterated "the pressing need for us to lift our sights and see the world problem of race and color in its overall significance." To approach it as anything other than a world problem would be "short-sighted and futile."[24] Even with the 1954 Supreme Court ruling in *Brown v. Topeka Board of Education* opening up nation-state-based tactics for attacking Jim Crow, many African Americans believed that securing black civil rights required tamping down white supremacy worldwide.

Yet if African Americans' grand strategy was to contain Jim Crow, folks like Rowan saw doing so as an integral part of fighting the Cold War. Decolonization, nonalignment, and challenges to white supremacy launched from an emerging Third World could threaten Jim Crow, but if the United States did not distance itself from segregation, they could also threaten American power. Sorting through his own impressions not long after reporting on the 1955 Asia-Africa Conference in Bandung, Indonesia, Rowan balanced "loyalty to country—to color—to religion" against "loyalty to those bonds 'that tie together the oppressed.'" In the wake of Bandung, he felt "keenly and acutely aware" that "the awakening" of Asia "may yet be our salvation," but, even more, he felt consternation over how much South Asians' and others' conviction that "the United States is incurably addicted to racism" damaged America's international standing and bolstered communist propaganda.[25] By inclination and occupation, Rowan's primary concern was to secure the nation's international position. The first step in doing so was facing "the grim fact that the United States' most critical domestic problem is also our most worrisome international problem."[26]

For Rowan, the answer to these pressing problems lay in the state's fulfilling its promise. President Lyndon Johnson raised the cause of black legal rights "to the level of a national imperative," Rowan would write decades later (in one of the few unqualified compliments he would pay the president), by going before Congress and requesting passage of the 1965 Voting Rights Act.[27] In the decade following Bandung, a powerful combination of direct action, community organizing, and urban uprising in the United States had spurred Lyndon Johnson to make firmer commitments to expanding civil rights. Rowan encouraged protest in certain moments, advised moderation in others, and occasionally excoriated voices he saw as too radical; but he always saw the protests as crucial, as he told a group of college students in North Carolina, to extending "the sphere of democracy in the U. S. in the eyes of the world."[28] As he put it in *Ebony*, "In an era where Western wealth and military power are of themselves not enough to guarantee Western leadership the future hangs in our ability to breathe enough life into the ideal of equal justice under the law to fire the imagination of the world's angry masses."[29]

In other words, appearances mattered. Maintaining American power meant convincing folks in Africa and Asia that Jim Crow no longer reigned in the United States. In this, he argued, the United States' treatment of African Americans served as a bellwether of how the country would conduct itself in the world. This was not about solidarity for Rowan; it was about American influence. Whereas activists like John Lewis of the Student Nonviolent Coordinating Committee (SNCC) felt "a sense of communion, a sense of fellowship" with "the young men and women" of Africa, Rowan approached "the world's angry masses" with both political and emotional distance.[30] As members of SNCC and other organizations increasingly articulated their critique of American empire and solidarity with Third World movements through the language of black power, Rowan derided the notion as "a plain old-fashioned hoax."[31] Black power and its reimagining of racial identity as political kinship had "less force in our real, cruel world than a fantasy born of a good slug of LSD."[32] Indulging that fantasy not only weakened the civil rights cause, he felt, but also ran the danger of giving succor to the enemy.[33]

At the end of the day, Rowan was an *American Dilemma* sort of fellow, one who believed as did its author Gunnar Myrdal that "what America is constantly reaching for is democracy at home and abroad."[34] Even after he had resigned from diplomatic service, Rowan found himself making the same arguments that he had made to international skeptics two decades before— that "the society that had given me a break was in the process of taking great strides for racial justice."[35] His rejoinder to proponents of black power relied on a vision of America as "continuously struggling for its soul," to borrow another phrase from Gunnar Myrdal, but ultimately united around a universalist political creed that promised more than any other nation on earth.[36] Reaping the fruits of that promise required buying in. "To gain freedom, the Negro . . . needs the help of the courts," he wrote. "He needs the power of the Justice Department and the prestige of the White House and the pocket of the federal treasury. He will need the pressure that can be exerted by a large portion of white America."[37] Race remained the key to war and peace, to be sure, but for Rowan, solving the white problem in America required the indulgence and resources of white America. Faith placed elsewhere looked to him like "hopelessness."[38]

Sam Greenlee's Revolutionary Blues

Sam Greenlee dreamed of revolution. Even as Carl Rowan took to the press to decry black power as thought and practice, Greenlee produced poetry and prose as part of black power's cultural front. "We were baaaad, writing about revolution," he would say of himself, editor Hoyt Fuller, and other members of Chicago's Organization of Black American Culture (OBAC) Writer's Workshop, "and if words were incendiary, we would have started another Great Chicago Fire!" Greenlee described himself and his compatriots as "warriors, revolutionaries devoted to providing a solution to the pollution of Western Imperialism, racism, oppression and exploitation." Reflecting back on his Cold War–era politics in his memoirs, he conceded that he and his colleagues were "naïve, maybe" but more important they were "totally committed!"[39] He carried that commitment into old age, explaining, "I do not consider myself a victim because a victim submits. Nor am I appalled by Euro-American 'history' because I consider it a racist fiction."[40] For Greenlee, whose most famous novel featured an African American ex-CIA agent who trained gang members for armed revolution on the south side of Chicago, Rowan and his defense of the American creed likely would have sounded delusional.

Rowan and Greenlee shared similar profiles but hewed to different narratives. Both descendants of black soldiers who had become soldiers themselves—a lieutenant in the Korean War–era army, in Greenlee's case— both had used the benefits from the GI Bill to finance graduate study. Like Rowan, Greenlee broke barriers in the foreign service: in 1957 after earning an MA in International Relations from the University of Chicago, he secured a position as one of the first three African Americans hired into the USIA. Rowan was moving from journalism into diplomacy in those years, rising to succeed Edward R. Murrow as Greenlee's boss in the USIA.

Yet unlike Rowan, who presented his military service as the dramatic ful-crum of his Horatio Alger story, Greenlee found his assignment to the aptly named Thirty-First Infantry "Dixie Division" to be a different kind of cru-cible. He had known "closet bigotry" as a college student at the University of Wisconsin but "the open contempt that southerners offered 'colored people' " caught him unawares. Although "raised and conditioned in patriotism" and subjected as a child to "the Pavlovian conditioning that all nations lay on its citizens," Greenlee grew certain after repeated encounters with racists in the army that he owed no "allegiance to a country that treated black people as scum."[41] Rather than identify as an American soldier, he began to think of himself as "a guerrilla fighter against the pervasive racism" that surrounded him.[42] Where Rowan offered himself up as proof positive of the potential of American liberalism, Greenlee told stories based on his experiences that were at once pulpy, satirical, and deadly serious. From the 1960s on, both his novels and memoirs offer an account of Greenlee becoming, to borrow a phrase from poet and veteran Amiri Baraka, "post American."[43]

Sam Greenlee was decidedly *not* an *American Dilemma* kind of guy. Like Baraka, Haki Madhubuti, and other black veterans who would go on to par-ticipate in the Black Arts Movement, military service fed in Greenlee what literary scholar James Smethurst has called a "wide-ranging and inchoate political and artistic radicalism."[44] Travel in the decolonizing and postcolo-nial world would intensify that radicalism as he came to believe that "Black Americans are no more citizens of the U.S. than were the Algerians citizens of metropolitan France."[45] The comparison worked for Greenlee because experience taught him to view the multiethnic liberal nation-state, like American history itself, as a fiction.

Indeed, linking an ever-expanding national body to a liberal state struck him as a fiction as well. Where Rowan saw promise, Greenlee saw a white supremacist state system centered in a government committed to preserving power and its spoils for a select few. Those select "White Folks and their pet Negro flunkies" preserved that system through violence even as they obscured its workings by linking the idea of an abstract, universalizing national body to an *idea* of a liberal state—a powerful narrative, both messianic and teleological, in which the United States, especially, tended toward expanding rights and freedoms for its peoples.[46] Such obfuscation, Greenlee felt certain, was an imperial project; having labored in service to that project, he saw in action what scholars like Abrams strove to emphasize, that reifying the state as such made it harder to see the "real relations of domination within the state-system and between it and other interest and institutions and groups."[47]

A self-described "professional propagandist in the foreign service of the United States Information Service," Greenlee knew a hustle when he saw one—and could run one when he wished to. He did the job well, so well that he won a meritorious service award for his work, but, he was quick to say in his reminiscences, always as a skeptic.[48] Working for the USIA offered him an alternative to the low-paying debasing jobs he found in Chicago, a way to travel the world, and a chance to use his graduate training; but his memoirs insistently frame the job as a means to an end. Like any effective hustle, it required him to lie with ease. When asked in his job interview how he would explain American race relations to an American audience, he gave a response that would have done Carl Rowan proud. "I might draw a comparison" to "the caste system in India," he answered. "I would maintain that no right-thinking Indian could support the indignities and discrimination of the caste system, nor Americans of comparable discrimination. I would conclude by saying that I believed great social strides were being made in both India and America." Greenlee considered his answer to be "stone bullshit, of course," but it was also exactly what his interviewers wished to hear.[49]

Greenlee got by in the USIA by handling white people expertly enough to not pierce their fictions. He both "sold the United States like toothpaste" to Iraqis, Bengalis, and Indonesians and sold his white colleagues on their own high-mindedness.[50] Posted to Baghdad in 1957, he found himself socially ostracized by his white colleagues even as, at work, they trotted him around at parties "like an organ grinder and his pet monkey" to assure Iraqi guests that the United States did not discriminate. Alienated but tactical, Greenlee "learned to take a low profile" at work, to "keep [his] political opinions to [himself], attempt a good little nigger stance," and to parry his social invisibility among white Americans into more meaningful encounters with local people among whom his blackness was, by and large, viewed as an asset. Although these encounters convinced him that revolution in Iraq was "imminent," he understood that saying so would sink his career. "A strong and stable Iraq," he had discerned from his boss's reluctance to complicate any narratives coming out of Washington, was the only "illusion permitted by State Department dogma."[51] Whatever tweaks came to American foreign policy would be delivered top-down; there was no refining strategy from the bottom up.

An astute and acerbic observer of the day-to-day enactment of United States foreign policy, Greenlee came to believe that one of its primary functions was to convince white Americans that their understanding of the world made sense. When events departed from narrative, as when revolution finally came to Iraq in July 1958, he "marveled at how easily the most arrogant people on the planet could fall apart." His colleagues' whiteness—an amalgam of class, national, and professional identity—took a hit. Coworkers seemed less "self-assured, confident, and ready to patronize anyone who's [sic] class ring did not match their own." Disoriented and "bewildered," they moved about with "their cord suits wilted, faces stubbled, pouches beneath their eyes, their crew cuts less jaunty." For Greenlee, these physical transformations arose not just from his colleagues' fear for their safety but also from the shock of glimpsing a reality in which foreign service work was not easy, in which Iraqis "were as good at the put-on as Black folks are," and in which a nationalist coup could take them by surprise.[52] To regroup, his colleagues began searching for communist influence. As one colleague explained to Greenlee, "We've built the Communists up to be masters of deception, duplicity and revolution. If it's a communist takeover, everything is forgiven" by the higher-ups in Washington. A nationalist coup, the colleague continued, the "kind of thing we're witnessing? Heads will roll!" Nationalism was untenable given their understanding of locals as child-like, but communist subversion fit a narrative into which Americans had already invested plenty of time and resources.[53]

Greenlee responded to his time in the foreign service by spinning fictions of his own. When he resigned from the agency to become a full-time writer, his eight years of sojourning for the American century provided ample fodder. His observations in Baghdad were reinforced by experiences in Dhaka, Jakarta, and Thessaloniki, where he watched local people attempt to turn US-backed rebellions to their own ends. Don Freeman, the main character in his first and best-known novel, *The Spook Who Sat by the Door*, reflected the wily watchfulness of Greenlee and the rebels who inspired him. Freeman succeeded as a spy because, as he notes in one passage, a black person made for "a natural agent in the United States," given that his or her life "might depend, from childhood, on becoming what whites demanded, yet somehow maintaining what he was as an individual human being."[54] Part of the inspiration for Freeman, a more liberated stand-in for Greenlee, came straight out of Iraq. "The cat who planted the seed in my mind was a guy named Abdul Kharrim Kassim" who had risen to general before launching the coup that ended the Baghdad Pact. "That cat kept undercover and organized and planned and plotted for 21 years," Greenlee marveled.[55] If Kassim could pull that off, what would such a feat look like in the ghetto? Writing *Spook* allowed Greenlee a way to plot a rebellion from within the civil service, not just laying bare the relations of domination that underpin the state system and foreign policy but imagining a method of effectively meeting its violence with violence.

Spook was at once a satire, an indictment, and a revolutionary manual. Having seen racialized power at work, indeed having been part of the institutional structure that brought that power to ground, Greenlee produced a novel that traced the relationship between the United States security project and uprisings at home and abroad. The book directly linked the economic marginalization and state violence visited on African Americans to the domination and exploitation that the United States visited on the Third World. "They call them gooks and us niggers in Vietnam and Korea," a Chicago gang member in *Spook* observes about white American leaders, "And they don't see any reason why gooks and niggers shouldn't kill each other for whitey's benefit."[56] Upon realizing this, the gang members become willing recruits in Don Freeman's campaign to turn urban riots into guerrilla insurrections.

Greenlee could not have written the book, he would say four decades later, if he "hadn't been out there among revolutionaries" in the Third World, folks "who had gotten nose to nose with the White folks and kicked their ass." He also was out there watching "them desperately trying to rebuild nations that had been systematically destroyed by their colonial masters. And they're still struggling."[57] To readers still processing working-class rebellions in cities from Los Angeles to Newark, neither the book's plot nor the sense of perpetual struggle seemed unfamiliar. In fact, the book seemed so "real" to one reviewer that he cautioned readers "to remember that this is a work of fiction and not a statement of fact."[58] A theologian in the *Christian Century* worried that the movie adaptation, co-authored by Greenlee, would spur "future use by the state of excessive force to put down every racial disorder but thought the risk worth it because "in a paradoxical way," the movie "dealt more *realistically* with the terrifying but logical extension of black response to oppression than did the actual events of the 60s."[59] As Americans struggled to articulate the relationship between black power, working-class protest, and inchoate internationalisms, *Spook* pointed to the revolutionary potential of folks who, like Greenlee, "traveled the road" from state-bound reformist to "Third World revolutionary."[60]

The White Problem in Grand Strategy

The point of discussing Carl Rowan and Sam Greenlee is not to argue that they belong in a pantheon of great grand strategists. Rather, it is to ponder what they thought race was, how they saw racialized power at work, and what they believed it meant for the United States in the world. For all their profound differences in temperament, trajectory, and solidarities, both men understood that, as scholar Nikhil Pal Singh has written, "black skin has historically demarcated and condensed what lies outside the protection of the nation-state and its cultures of citizenship and civility."[61] Greenlee and Rowan diverged sharply in how they approached the nation-state, but each knew that white supremacy mattered to American foreign policy, that other nations recognized and reacted to American investment in white supremacy, and that the work of dismantling it would be vital, brutal, and long incomplete.

The charge to take such insights seriously is not a matter of representation—mentioning a black secretary of state here, or citing an African American diplomat there—but a matter of thinking. Foregrounding how Greenlee and Rowan used race as a tool of analysis is a reminder to approach grand strategy's whiteness as an epistemological problem; it ought not remain a given, an unspoken norm that requires no acknowledgment or consideration. To do so is to ignore the relationship between subjectivity and structure in the United States, the ways that "race neutral" in foreign and domestic policy has largely meant "white," and the extent to which the investment in whiteness-as-norm has conditioned how American policymakers have defined partner and ally, client and vassal, enemy and threat. Normalizing whiteness does ideological work—masking racialized power while declaring the United States to be blessedly free of ideology. If we treat grand strategy as "the intellectual architecture that gives form and structure to foreign policy" or a "coherent set of ideas about what a nation wishes to accomplish in the world," then we must think about the ideas—understandings of self, of what makes a nation, of what constitutes an interest—that mix with the construction material.[62] We also must accept that ideology does not exist separate from statecraft; it is what legitimizes the practice of power.

Thinking through race—divining the relationship between statecraft and what scholars Barbara and Karen Fields have labeled "racecraft"—forces us to articulate how the entwined sociopolitical constructions of "race" and "state" motivate and inform American actions.[63] Doing so allows for sharper analyses of the history of United States in the world, and, for scholars of grand strategy, a richer language for talking about how the United States exercises power, on whom, and to what effect. As political scientist Robert Vitalis has written in his intellectual history of international relations, "In the first few decades of the twentieth century in the United States, international relations meant race relations." That this statement seems self-evident to many scholars of African American studies and "strange and wrong" to many scholars of international relations or diplomatic history underscores how much of the ideal of colorblindness comes down to willful unseeing.[64] It highlights how much the fields' self-perception comes down to what Vitalis calls, inspired by Toni Morrison, the "norm against noticing."[65] For the sake of scholarship and policy, I propose that we disrupt the norm against noticing in order to rethink grand strategy, that we inspect its intellectual architecture, and allow—to tweak Carl Rowan's language, "No 'Whitewash'" for the United States in the world.

Notes

1. Barry Posen, *Restraint: A New Foundation for U. S. Grand Strategy* (Ithaca, NY: Cornell University Press, 2014), 1.
2. The phrase "to get the ear of power" comes from advice given by historian John Lewis Gaddis to a group of Yale graduate students to "try to get the ear of power" in the fall

of 1998. For a helpful discussion of how scholars of grand strategy define the term, see Nina Silove, "Beyond the Buzzword: The Three Meanings of 'Grand Strategy,'" *Security Studies*, 27 (January–March 2018), 27–57.

3. On race as constitutive of American state and nation, see Reginald Horsman, *Race and Manifest Destiny: The Origins of American Racial Anglo-Saxonism* (Cambridge, MA: Harvard University Press, 1981); Matthew Frye Jacobson, *Whiteness of a Different Color: European Immigrants and the Alchemy of Race* (Cambridge, MA: Harvard University Press, 1998); Mae Ngai, *Impossible Subjects: Illegal Aliens and the Making of Modern America* (Princeton, NJ: Princeton University Press, 2004); Gary Gerstle, *American Crucible: Race and Nation in the Twentieth Century* (Princeton. NJ: Princeton University Press, 2001). For an extended review of the vital and extensive scholarly literature on race, power, and transnational United States histories, see Paul F. Kramer, "Shades of Sovereignty: Racialized Power, the United States and the World," in *Explaining the History of American Foreign Relations*, 3rd ed., ed. Frank Costigliola and Michael J. Hogan (New York: Cambridge University Press, 2016), 245–270.

4. Alistair Iain Johnston, "Thinking about Strategic Culture," *International Security* 19 (Spring 1995), 46.

5. Raymond Williams, *The Long Revolution* (New York: Harper and Row, 1966), 61–62.

6. Evelyn Brooks Higginbotham, "African-American Women's History and the Metalanguage of Race," Signs 17 (Winter 1992), 252; 255.

7. Lisa Maria Cacho, *Social Death: Racialized Rightlessness and the Criminalization of the Unprotected* (New York: New York University Press, 2012), 6, 98.

8. See, for example, Tim Tyson, *Radio Free Dixie: Robert F. Williams and the Roots of Black Power* (Chapel Hill: University of North Carolina Press, 1999); Barbara Ransby, *Eslanda: The Large and Unconventional Life of Mrs. Paul Robeson* (New Haven, CT: Yale University Press, 2013); or Sean Malloy, *Out of Oakland: Black Panther Party Internationalism during the Cold War* (Ithaca, NY: Cornell University Press, 2017.

9. Jeremy Suri, "America's Grand Strategy from Cold War's End to 9/11," *Orbis* 53:4 (Fall 2009), 613.

10. Carl T. Rowan, "No 'Whitewash' for U.S. Abroad," *Ebony* 20 (August 1965), 56.

11. Benjamin Disraeli, Earl of Beaconsfield, *Endymion* (New York: D. Appleton, 1880), 252.

12. Ibid., 253.

13. Marilyn Lake and Henry Reynolds, *Drawing the Global Colour Line: White Men's Countries and the International Challenge of Racial Equality* (Cambridge: Cambridge University Press, 2008).

14. See Matthew Frye Jacobson, *Barbarian Virtues: The United States Encounters Foreign Peoples at Home and Abroad, 1876–1917* (New York: Hill and Wang, 2000), and Nell Irvin Painter, *The History of White People* (New York: Norton, 2010).

15. W. E. B. Du Bois, "The Color Line Belts the World," *Collier's Weekly*, October 20, 1906, reproduced in David Levering Lewis, *W. E. B. Du Bois, A Reader* (New York: Henry Holt, 1995), 42.

16. "Youngest U. S. Ambassador," *Ebony* 19 (January 1964), 52.

17. Rowan, "No Whitewash," 57.

18. Ibid.

19. Carl T. Rowan, *Breaking Barriers: A Memoir* (Boston: Little, Brown, 1991), 15.

20. Carl T. Rowan, *South of Freedom* (New York: Knopf, 1952), 3.

21. Biographical info comes from Rowan, *Breaking Barriers*. Quote comes from Carl T. Rowan, "What Jimmy Carter's Election Will Mean," in *Landon Lecture Series on Public Issues: The First Twenty Years, 1966–1986* (Manhattan: Kansas State University Press, 1976), 389.

22. Rowan, *Breaking Barriers*, 15.

23. John H. Johnson, "Publishers Statement," *Ebony* 20 (August 1965), 27. On African American internationalism and the black freedom struggle in the postwar era, see Penny von Eschen, *Race against Empire: Black Americans and Anticolonialism, 1937–1957* (Ithaca, NY: Cornell University Press, 1997); Nikhil Pal, *Black Is a Country: Race and the Unfinished Struggle for Democracy* (Cambridge, MA: Harvard University Press, 2004); and James Meriwether, *Proudly We Can Be Africans: Black Americans and Africa, 1935–1961* (Chapel Hill: University of North Carolina Press, 2002).

24. Walter White, "A Suggestion for Change in the Name of the NAACP," *Chicago Defender*, September 3, 1949, 7. See also, Carol Anderson, *Bourgeois Radicals: The NAACP and the Struggle for Colonial Liberation, 1941–1960* (New York: Cambridge University Press, 2015), 331.

25. Carl T. Rowan, *The Pitiful and the Proud* (New York: Random House, 1956), vii, 147. On Rowan's and other African Americans' tours of the emerging Third World, see Michael Krenn, *Black Diplomacy: African Americans and the State Department, 1945–1969* (Armonk, NY: M. E. Sharpe, 1999), 75–77.

26. Rowan, "No Whitewash," 57. On extending civil rights as Cold War strategy, see Mary L. Dudziak, *Cold War Civil Rights: Race and the Image of American Democracy* (Princeton, NJ: Princeton University Press, 2000); and Mary L. Dudziak, "Desegregation as a Cold War Imperative," *Stanford Law Review* 41:1 (November 1998), 61–120. On nonalignment and the Third World as a political project, see Vijay Prashad, *The Darker Nations: A People's History of the Third World* (New York: New Press, 2007). For rich discussions of African Americans' engagements with decolonization and postwar nationalism, see Anderson, *Bourgeois Radicals*; Robeson Taj Frazier, *The East Is Black: Cold War China in the Black Radical Imagination* (Durham, NC: Duke University Press, 2014); Brenda Gayle Plummer, *In Search of Power: African Americans in the Era of Decolonization, 1956–1974* (New York: Cambridge University Press, 2013); and Kevin K. Gaines, *American Africans in Ghana: Black Expatriates and the Civil Rights Era* (Chapel Hill: University of North Carolina Press, 2006.

27. Rowan, *Breaking Barriers*, 249.

28. "Rowan Declares Sit-Ins Benefit Negroes, Whites," *Chicago Daily Defender*, April 18, 1962, 5. On the importance of the black freedom struggle to the Cold War, see Dudziak, *Cold War Civil Rights;* Thomas Borstelmann, *The Cold War and the Color line: American Race Relations in the Global Arena* (Cambridge, MA: Harvard University Press, 2001); Carol Anderson, *Eyes off the Prize: The United Nations and the African American Struggle for Human Rights, 1944–1955* (New York: Cambridge

University Press, 2003); Penny von Eschen, *Satchmo Blows Up the World: The Jazz Ambassadors Play the Cold War* (Cambridge, MA: Harvard University Press, 2004); and Jonathan Rosenberg, *How Far the Promised Land? World Affairs and the American Civil Rights Movement* (Princeton, NJ: Princeton University Press, 2006).

29. Rowan, "No Whitewash," 57.
30. John Lewis, quoted in Fanon Che Wilkins, "The Making of Black Internationalists: SNCC and Africa before the Launching of Black Power, 1960–1965," *Journal of African American History* 92 (Fall 207), 468. On SNCC's internationalism, see also Julia Erin Wood, "Freedom Is Indivisible: The Student Nonviolent Coordinating Committee (SNCC), Cold War Politics, and International Liberation Movements," Ph.D. dissertation, Yale University, 2011.
31. "Rowan Calls Black Power a Phony Cry; Says It Only Divides Race," *Chicago Defender*, November 7, 1966, 27.
32. Ibid; Carl T. Rowan, "Crisis in Civil Rights Leadership: Isolation Is a Trap; 'Black Power' Is a Phony Cry, a Plain Old-Fashioned Hoax," *Ebony* 22 (November 1966), 37.
33. See, for example, Rowan's chastisement of Martin Luther King for his statement criticizing the Vietnam War, "Martin Luther King's Tragic Decision," *Reader's Digest*, September 1967. Reprinted in C. Eric Lincoln, *Martin Luther King, Jr.: A Profile* (New York: Hill and Wang, 1984), 212–218.
34. Gunnar Myrdal, *An American Dilemma: The Negro Problem and American Democracy* (New York: Harper and Row, 1962 [1944]), 3. Quoted in Nikhil Pal Singh, *Black Is a Country: Race and the Unfinished Struggle for Democracy* (Cambridge: Harvard University Press, 2004), 39.
35. Rowan, *Breaking Barriers*, 124. Also quoted in Singh, *Black Is a Country*, 178.
36. Myrdal, *An American Dilemma*, 4.
37. Rowan, "Crisis in Civil Rights Leadership," 36.
38. Ibid., 37.
39. Sam Greenlee, "Weary Warrior Blues," 2–3; and "Prologue," both in "Sam's Blues: The Adventures of a Traveling Man," in box 1a, folder 1, Samuel Greenlee Papers 1965–2005, Rare Books and Special Collections Library, University of Rochester River Campus Libraries
40. Greenlee, "Sam's Blues," Prologue; Greenlee uses nearly the exact same language on back cover of his 1971 book of poetry, *Blues for An African Princess*. See Sam Greenlee, *Blues for an African Princess* (Chicago: Third World Press, 1971).
41. Greenlee, "Sam's Blues," 233, box 1a, folder 4.
42. Greenlee, "Sam's Blues," 229, box 1a, folder 4.
43. Baraka, quoted in Sohail Daulatzai, *Black Star, Crescent Moon: The Muslim International and Black Freedom Beyond America* (Minneapolis: University of Minnesota Press, 2012), 19.
44. James Smethurst, *The Black Arts Movement: Literary Nationalism in the 1960s and 1970s* (Chapel Hill: University of North Carolina Press, 2005), 34.
45. Sam Greenlee, *Ammunition: Poetry and Other Raps* (London: Bogle-L'Ouverture Publications, 1975), back inside cover; Sam Greenlee, "Sam's Blues," Prologue.
46. Greenlee, "Sam's Blues," Prologue.

47. Abrams, "Notes on the Difficulty of Studying the State," 88 fn 47. See also Singh, *Black Is a Country*, 202–206.
48. Greenlee, *Ammunition*, back inside cover.
49. Greenlee, "Sam's Blues," 283–284, box 1a, folder 1.
50. Cheryl Aldave, "The Revolution," Interview with Sam Greenlee, *Wax Poetics*, 2011, http://www.waxpoetics.com/features/articles/the-revolution (accessed July 20, 2016).
51. Greenlee, "Sam's Blues," 293, 297, 307, box 1a, folder 5.
52. Ibid., 330–331, box 1a, folder 5. Greenlee's observation about "the put-on" comes from page 294.
53. Ibid., 333, 307, box 1a, folder 5.
54. Sam Greenlee, *The Spook Who Sat by the Door* (Detroit: Wayne State University Press, 1990 [1969]), 109–110.
55. Jim Cleaver, "'The Spook Who Sat by the Door' Exposes Black Tokenism in the CIA," *Los Angeles Sentinel*, January 29, 1970, B4A.
56. Greenlee, *The Spook Who Sat by the Door*, 102.
57. Aldave, "The Revolution."
58. Cleaver, "The Spook Who Sat by the Door."
59. Cornish Rogers, "How the Riots Might Have Turned Out," *Christian Century*, October 3, 1973, 964. Emphasis in original.
60. Greenlee, "Sam's Blues," Prologue.
61. Singh, *Black Is a Country*, 204.
62. Hal Brands, *What Good Is Grand Strategy? Power and Purpose in American Statecraft from Harry S. Truman to George W. Bush* (Ithaca, NY: Cornell University Press, 2014), 4.
63. Karen E. Fields and Barbara J. Fields, *Racecraft: The Soul of Inequality in American Life* (New York: Verso Books, 2012).
64. Robert Vitalis, *White World Order, Black Power Politics: The Birth of American International Relations* (Chapel Hill: University of North Carolina Press, 2015), 1.
65. Robert Vitalis, "The Graceful and Generous Liberal Gesture: Making Racism Invisible in American International Relations," *Millennium: Journal of International Studies* 29 (2000), 333.

17

Rival Visions of Nationhood

Immigration Policy, Grand Strategy, and Contentious Politics

Daniel J. Tichenor

Immigration control rests at the intersection of domestic and international politics, presenting a compelling policy tool available to generations of US leaders who could use it to build a strong nation at home and to advance that nation's power and ideals abroad. In the abstract, state regulation over the entry and membership of newcomers gives these decision makers a potent means of shaping the country's demographic landscape. This power to literally constitute the nation suggests how immigration policy can be deployed as a key instrument of grand strategy, a site where state actors might use the levers of immigrant and refugee admissions to advance both a comprehensive and an integrated set of social, economic, and security goals at home. Equally important, these policy levers also may enable political leaders to pursue crucial geopolitical goals, such as enhancing economic competitiveness, gaining or maintaining superiority in science and technology, influencing diplomacy with sending countries, providing humanitarian relief to refugees fleeing rival states and ideologies, and strengthening the nation's image in the world. A diverse array of US presidents, lawmakers, and activists have had grand strategies in mind as they pursued major immigration reform, from nativist designs in the early twentieth century to establish a national origins quota system to liberal-internationalist plans during the Cold War to open the gates for larger numbers of European refugees and immigrants.[1] Larger national interests also are pivotal in contemporary debates over family reunification, border enforcement, legalization for undocumented immigrants, levels of refugee relief and grants of asylum, and ways to attract skilled immigrants.

Despite its allure as a means of pursuing larger national purposes, however, US immigration policy generally has proven frustrating to those with the best-laid plans for governing immigrant admissions and rights. Indeed, the politics and history of immigration control in the United States are not readily understood through the lens of grand strategy. This is largely because American immigration politics and policymaking routinely defy at least two major features of grand strategy. First, grand strategy is expected to focus on how to secure the national interests of a state or country rather than partial ones that advance the goals of specific partisan, ethnic, religious, business, labor, or single-issue groups.[2] Yet a welter of special interests traditionally has pervaded US immigration policymaking, each pressing their particular agendas on elected officials. When policy change occurs, as political scientist Gary Freeman aptly observes, organized interests are frequent winners of concentrated benefits at the expense of larger collective goals and preferences.[3] But policy innovation is in fact quite rare in this arena. Over the course of US political history, major immigration reform regularly has produced polarizing conflicts, sending activists on a tortured path of false starts, prolonged negotiations, and vexing stalemates.[4]

Second, grand strategy also reflects a comprehensive, cohesive, and flexible blueprint of government action, one that effectively connects the varied means of a nation-state to broader ends.[5] In this context, actors can be opportunistic in advancing their plan amid shifting constraints and openings in order to realize national interests and higher moral purposes (something Charles Edel calls "tactical flexibility"). However, because immigration politics is so contentious and gridlock is so commonplace, it is often hard for policymakers to act decisively when opportunities arise. Even when presidents use unilateral power on immigration and refugee matters, the polarizing nature of the issue raises the specter of legislative, judicial, and popular sanctions. Furthermore, when lightning has struck for passage of comprehensive immigration reform, it typically has been anything but cohesive or well integrated. As we shall see, US immigration policy historically has been shaped by competing interests and visions of nationhood. Consequently, major reform has hinged on the formation of "strange bedfellow" alliances that are unstable and that demand difficult compromises. The result often has been policy innovation that incorporates rival goals and interests in often incoherent and bedeviling ways.

This is not to say, however, that these formidable challenges have prevented key presidents, lawmakers, and other political actors from seeking immigration policies consistent with higher forms of statecraft. Each major period of US immigration politics and policy has seen leaders attempting strategically to use the means at their disposal for reshaping immigration policy to serve far-sighted, comprehensive, and national ends. This enterprise was complicated from the start of the American republic and became increasingly so as soon as newcomers began arriving in large numbers. Popular mobilizations for and against new immigration have produced pitched battles that make the conception and pursuit of grand strategies all the more elusive. Nevertheless, the allure of immigration policy as a tool for nation building has attracted more than a few political leaders and activists with grand designs. This chapter focuses on a particularly significant effort to remake the US immigration system—the 1960s struggle to dismantle national origins quotas and reopen US gates to immigrants and refugees—in order to illuminate the possibilities and limitations of grand strategizing in this policy realm. One can discern these dynamics in immigration reforms and executive actions from the 1920s to the present, but the successful battle for the Immigration and Nationality Act of 1965 provides an especially illuminating example. Before turning to this case, however, let us first consider immigration control and grand strategy in the early American republic, and the rise of rival interests and ideals that make significant policy innovation contingent on incongruous coalitions and uneasy compromises.

Immigration, Rival Interests, and Strange Bedfellow Politics

Some of the most pristine views of immigration policy as grand strategy can be seen during the early American republic, when the country's first political leaders had freer rein to contemplate immigration and naturalization within a larger intellectual framework for advancing national interests and ideals. At a time when newcomers were few (roughly 3,000 to 6,000 per year) and the country's resources and territories were vast, anti-immigrant voices generally were overshadowed by those who welcomed European laborers and their families to spur national economic development and territorial expansion. Madison, Hamilton, Franklin, and others noted that states which endorsed robust immigrant admissions and rights were the most advanced in wealth, territory, and the arts. These founders also saw European immigration and refugee relief as consistent with their natural rights philosophy and republican ideals, a view expressed in George Washington's 1783 pledge that "America is open to receive not only the Opulent and respectable Stranger, but the oppressed and persecuted of all Nations and Religions." In later decades, however, the use of immigration policy as a tool for nation building became far more complicated as the size and sources of new immigration expanded. Indeed, political conflict, rival interests, and policy contradictions became defining features of US immigration governance from the nineteenth century onward.

During the past quarter-century, immigration has been one of the most salient and polarizing issues on the national agenda. In fact, immigration policy helps define the partisan divide in contemporary US politics, with Republicans associated with hardline restrictions and enforcement and Democrats linked to expanding immigrant admissions and rights. These perceptions have been powerfully reinforced by the ability of Donald Trump, both as a Republican candidate and president, to energize his base with promises to "build the wall," pursue a Muslim ban, and end chain migration of families. Yet in truth, the partisan contrasts may be less dramatic than is often presumed. For instance, the administration of George W. Bush pursued immigration reforms that were far friendlier toward undocumented immigrants (including pathways to "earned legalization") than some might assume from a contemporary Republican president. Likewise, the Obama administration was far more vigorous in detaining and deporting undocumented immigrants than some might expect from a contemporary Democratic president. Obscured by the pitched battles between Republicans and Democrats in recent elections is the fact that immigration is a powerful cross-cutting issue that creates important conflicts within party coalitions that often rival those between them. Whereas the most vocal conservative Republicans in recent years demonize new immigrant groups, pro-immigration conservatives long have welcomed newcomers as vital to meet the labor needs of US businesses, to fuel national economic growth and prosperity, and to serve American geopolitical interests. Ronald Reagan, the revered icon of the modern Republican Party, embraced immigrants as hard-working and entrepreneurial while depicting the United States as a "city on a hill" for refugees escaping enemy regimes.

In similar fashion, liberal Democrats have prominently highlighted the universality of the American experiment, professing deep faith in the social, economic, political, and foreign policy benefits of diverse, large-scale immigration. But the American left also has featured protectionists who view new immigrants as economic competitors providing employers with tractable labor that undercuts sound wages and working conditions. For example, former congresswoman Barbara Jordan, who chaired the Commission on Immigration Reform during the Clinton years, made it clear that she supported reduced immigration to provide economic opportunity for disadvantaged citizens.[6] In this way, she echoed Frederick Douglass who lamented during the Gilded Age that "every hour sees the black man elbowed out of employment by some newly arrived immigrant."[7]

While inspiring considerable partisan polarization in the contemporary era, US immigration policymaking also continues to fuel tensions between liberal cosmopolitans and economic protectionists on the left, and between pro-immigration conservatives and cultural protectionists and border hawks on the right. This has meant that US immigration policymaking has spurred fierce political conflicts and stalemate between powerful decision makers from these competing ideological camps. In the end, major policy innovation almost invariably has required the building of incongruous left-right alliances or "strange bedfellow" coalitions. That is, a crucial consequence of political warfare and strange bedfellow politics in immigration policymaking is the necessity of painful compromises and the codification of rival interests and moral visions in major reforms. These political patterns have presented key challenges for various architects of US grand strategy but not necessarily insurmountable ones. To better evaluate the possibilities and limitations of grand strategy for understanding the politics and history of American immigration policy, let us focus on an especially revealing case: the 1960s battle over major immigration reform that culminated in the landmark Immigration and Nationality Act (INA) of 1965.

Reopening the Gates

When he became president in late 1963, Lyndon Johnson (LBJ) knew well that nearly all of his predecessors from the Gilded Age onward found immigration policy to be politically perilous. Over time, few occupants of the Oval Office sought to leave their mark on how immigrant admissions and rights were governed and even fewer had a measure of success in doing so. It was Congress, not the American presidency, which dominated immigration policymaking for most of the nation's history.[8] Presidents who resisted Chinese exclusion to serve broader US geopolitical interests in the late nineteenth century, for instance, were castigated by mass publics in the West and ignored by large House and Senate majorities eager to curry favor with the Sinophobic vote.[9] Woodrow Wilson vetoed literacy test legislation designed to discourage southern and eastern European immigration during his first term, only to have his veto of similar legislation overridden by large bipartisan majorities in 1917.[10] In the 1930s, a period when draconian national origins quotas barred entry for most newcomers, and demagogues like Representative Martin Dies (D-TX) blamed unemployment on past immigration policies, Franklin Roosevelt avoided clashes with congressional immigration restrictionists in order to guard larger domestic and international goals.[11] When Eleanor Roosevelt and Frances Perkins considered endorsing a Wagner-Rogers bill in 1939 that would have provided asylum to 20,000 German Jewish children, the White House insisted they maintain silent neutrality as nativist lawmakers blocked action.[12]

Cold War presidents like Harry Truman and Dwight Eisenhower were far more aggressive in challenging draconian immigration policies they saw as damaging to US geopolitical interests. Both administrations enjoyed some success in winning temporary refugee relief for European "displaced persons" and Hungarian insurgents, either taking independent executive action or gaining passage of modest refugee relief laws.[13] However, neither president was able to secure significant changes in federal immigration policies that explicitly favored northern and western Europeans. In fact, congressional defenders of immigration restriction gained passage of the McCarran-Walter Act of 1952 (over a Truman veto) that fortified the exclusionary national origins quota system begun in 1924 and established new bars based on ideology and sexual preference.[14] "In no other realm of our national life," Truman lamented during his battle with congressional restrictionists, "are we so hampered and stultified by the dead hand of the past, as we are in this field of immigration."[15] Eisenhower fared no better during his two terms, lecturing Congress during his final year in office about the need to liberalize federal immigration laws.[16]

Perhaps no president was more closely identified with the cause of liberal immigration reform than John F. Kennedy. During his senate tenure, Kennedy joined with pro-immigration colleagues like Philip Hart (D-MI) and Kenneth Keating (R-NY) in proposing unsuccessful bills to replace the McCarran-Walter Act. He also celebrated America's immigration traditions as author of *A Nation of Immigrants* in 1958, ghost written by adviser Meyer Feldman and promoted by the Anti-Defamation League.[17] His 1960 victory invigorated pro-immigration reformers. Despite their high expectations, however, Kennedy got nowhere on plans to alter US immigration law due to potent opposition from conservative Democrats like Senator James Eastland

(D-MS) and Representative Frances Walter (D-PA), who controlled the immigration subcommittees of both houses. It was not until 1963, after Walter's death, that JFK proposed legislation to dismantle national origins quotas with a new preference system giving top priority to immigrant job skills and education.[18] The White House soon discovered that Walter's successor as chair of the House immigration subcommittee, Michael Feighan (D-OH), strongly opposed the administration's blueprints for reform.[19]

Some immigration scholars have argued that the nation's grief over Kennedy's assassination combined with Johnson's prowess as a legislative leader "meant the end of the quota system and its replacement by a preference system was virtually inevitable."[20] But few Washington insiders shared this conviction in the first stages of the Johnson administration.[21] Although LBJ famously insisted "there was not time to rest" in pursuit of his Great Society agenda, it was unclear early on whether he wanted immigration reform to figure prominently on that agenda.[22] In fact, he was all too familiar with the legislative headaches that immigration reform posed by the time he became president, having been whipsawed by rivals on the issue for years in the Senate. When Johnson was Senate majority leader in 1955, reporters noted that he "exploded with invective" when pressed about holdups on progressive immigration reform.[23] He was well aware of the challenges of leading Senate Democrats who were deeply divided between conservatives opposed to any opening of the gates and liberals committed to dismantling national origins quotas.

During his first days as president, Johnson's willingness to pursue immigration reform was an open question. Acutely aware of his silence on the issue while mobilizing on a broad slate of civil rights, anti-poverty, and other initiatives, White House officials who worked on immigration policy during Kennedy's tenure urged LBJ to support the dismantlement of national origins quotas. However, Johnson initially refused the idea when urged by former Kennedy advisers like Meyer Feldman, who were told that immigration was an explosive issue that could hurt other reform plans.[24] He also worried about being assailed for flip-flopping on the issue by championing Kennedy's proposal after having voted for the McCarran-Walter Act of 1952. To his own close adviser, Jack Valenti, Johnson voiced grave reservations about backing immigration reform legislation that enjoyed little public support.[25]

Behind the scenes, administration officials who had been appointed by Kennedy and who favored sweeping immigration reform persuaded close LBJ advisers such as Valenti and Bill Moyers to make their case to an unconvinced president.[26] Three arguments for reform were particularly compelling to Johnson. First, advocates of policy innovation underscored that JFK had described his immigration proposal in 1963 as "the most urgent and fundamental reform" of a New Frontier agenda that Johnson had pledged to advance. Second, reform proponents insisted that Johnson's endorsement of new immigration legislation would yield electoral premiums in the 1964 campaign. White ethnic voters in the Northeast and Midwest, they insisted, were more likely to vote on immigration than were other mass publics for whom the issue was less salient. Finally, numerous White House advisers and State Department officials told Johnson that national origins quotas hurt American credibility abroad as much as Jim Crowism did. Cold War imperatives also loomed large in these calculations, since, as Senator Philip Hart (D-MI) put it, discriminatory immigration quotas "needlessly provide grist for the propaganda mills of Moscow and Peiping."[27] The persistence of the national origins quota system also clearly contradicted Johnson's pledge "to eliminate from this Nation every trace of discrimination and oppression that is based upon race or color."[28] "The President eventually recognized that existing immigration law, and in particular, national origins quotas, created many decades before on racist grounds, was inconsistent with civil rights and racial justice," recalls Valenti.[29] According to Feldman, LBJ could not ignore the obvious connections between immigration reform and the administration's most important foreign and civil rights goals. Johnson ultimately became a late convert to immigration reform.[30]

For advocacy groups who had waited for decades to dismantle national origins quotas, Johnson's first State of the Union Address in 1964 was cause for celebration. In this speech, the president outlined a civil rights agenda that championed for all citizens access to public facilities, equal eligibility for federal benefits, an equal chance to vote, and "good public schools" for all children. Then he added, "We must also lift by legislation the bars of discrimination against those who seek entry into our country."[31] An administration bill was soon introduced that would increase annual immigration to 165,000 and replace discriminatory per-country quotas in favor of a preference system allocating 50 percent of visas on the basis of special occupational skills or education that benefited the national economic interests. Remaining visas would be distributed to refugees and those with close family ties to US citizens or legal permanent residents.

The Battle for Immigration Reform: Conflict and Fateful Compromises

When Ohio Democrat Michael Feighan became chair of the House immigration subcommittee in 1963, many reformers hoped that he would be more receptive than his predecessor, Francis Walter, to revising immigration policy. Yet he soon made headlines by charging that the Central Intelligence Agency had been infiltrated by Soviet spies, and by calling on the State Department to ban Richard Burton from entering the country due to "immoral conduct" with Elizabeth Taylor. Republicans reveled that the once obscure, twenty-year veteran of the House was proving to be an embarrassment to their partisan opponents.[32] Backed by a bipartisan majority of subcommittee members, Feighan introduced his own bill, a substitute for the Johnson proposal, in August of 1964.[33] As his staffers put it, the substitute bill was designed "to avoid charges of inaction by the Subcommittee" which "would have opened the door to ramming through the Administration bill."[34] Feighan's bill promised to "preserve the national origins quota formula," to give a preference to immigrants with family ties under the quotas, to maintain exclusions for ideology and sexual preference, and to guarantee that "the principle of the Asia-Pacific Triangle remains as is."[35] Whereas the Johnson administration worked its magic to neutralize a normally obstreperous James Eastland, the unexpectedly deft resistance mounted by Feighan and his nativist allies ensured that no action would be taken on the Kennedy-Johnson bill until after the 1964 election.

During the 1964 campaign, Democrats highlighted immigration reform as one of the key "progressive" goals in their platform.[36] Republican candidates generally said little about the issue. Barry Goldwater promised to revive a Mexican guest worker program, while his running mate, Representative William Miller (NY), occasionally suggested that immigration reform would produce increased unemployment and welfare dependency. Yet there is little indication that immigration had much political salience for most of the electorate.[37] Gallup polls found that less than 1 percent of Americans ranked immigration among the most important problems facing the nation. Nevertheless, shortly after the Democratic electoral windfall of 1964, Johnson sent a Special Message to lawmakers again endorsing the dismantlement of national origins quotas. When the 89th Congress convened in 1965, administration experts testifying before Congress stressed the "urgency" of immigration reform "in terms of our self-interest abroad. In the present ideological conflict between freedom and fear, we proclaim to the world that our central precept is that all are born equal. . . . Yet under present law, we choose among immigrants on the basis of where they are."[38] Even with improved prospects for immigration reform in the new Congress, however, major challenges still loomed. In particular, immigration restrictionists in the House and Senate demanded two important concessions from liberal reformers and the Johnson administration in exchange for abolishing the national origins quota system.

The Johnson team began its renewed 1965 push for the INA in the House, where seventy-seven-year-old Emanuel Celler, the longtime champion of immigration reform, introduced the administration's bill as H.R. 2580. Yet an important barrier stood in the way. Celler, as chair of the House Judiciary Committee, was locked in an epic feud with Feighan, who still chaired the committee's Subcommittee on Immigration and Nationality. Celler initially sought to have Feighan removed from the subcommittee, but he soon discovered that the subcommittee majority sided with their obstreperous chair. As Kentucky Democrat Frank Chelf explained, "I have been on this subcommittee now some eighteen years. I have always been a rather strong believer in the national-origins theory."[39] When Celler scolded Feighan publicly for perpetuating policies that unfairly discriminated against would-be immigrants and kept out desperate refugees, Feighan retorted, "How about giving the welfare of the American people first priority for a change?"[40] For two months, Feighan dominated hearings on H.R. 2580, peppering administration officials with questions about a new merit-based preference system and its potential impact on the number and diversity of newcomers. According to Johnson's chief liaison to Congress, Lawrence O'Brien, "he had his own views and he was going to be disruptive procedurally to accomplish his objectives." O'Brien added that "there's nothing worse than to have a subcommittee chairman . . . get his nose out of joint."[41]

Frustrated by Feighan's roadblocks, LBJ and House Democratic leaders successfully maneuvered in the spring of 1965 to expand the immigration subcommittee to add Johnson loyalists like Jack Brooks (D-TX) as crucial swing votes. Despite this tactical blow, Feighan privately told anti-immigrant lobbyists that he enjoyed enough bipartisan backing to seriously limit radical policy change. "There is no need for you to be worried about developments because there is no possibility of the opposition here opening 'Pandora's box'" and dramatically expanding immigration opportunities, he reassured anxious nativists.[42] Yet Feighan also understood that Johnson and reformers now had enough political momentum to overcome delaying tactics. It was time, he concluded, for supporters of the national origins quota system and McCarran-Walter restrictions to try to influence inevitable legislation. "My greatest concern is that the people who advocate the 'sitting duck' approach to national issues will open the 'box.' "[43] Reporters noted at the time that new political realities—"the pro-administration majorities and a genuine Presidential push"—persuaded opponents of reform that their best strategy was to shape a compromise plan.

In the end, Feighan and his allies agreed to abolish national origins quotas and the so-called Asiatic Barred Zone in exchange for a significant alteration in the administration's proposed preference system for immigrant admissions. The Kennedy-Johnson blueprints for reform consistently envisioned replacing national origins quotas with high-skilled immigration. "At present, [the national origins system] prevents talented people from applying for visas to enter the United States," Kennedy observed in 1963. "It often deprives us of immigrants who would be helpful to our economy and our culture." Legal preferences, he argued, "should be liberalized so that highly trained or skilled persons may obtain a preference without requiring that they secure employment here before emigrating."[44] Immigrant merit and skills were to trump discriminatory restrictions based on race, ethnicity, religion or nationality. In May 1965, however, Feighan proposed a compromise with the White House that profoundly altered these plans to make family reunification, rather than occupational skills and education, the centerpiece of a new preference system for immigrant admissions. Feighan was convinced (incorrectly, as he later discovered) that reserving most visas for immigrants with family ties to US citizens and legal permanent residents would decidedly favor European applicants and thus maintain the nation's ethnic and racial makeup.[45] Feighan and other House opponents of the Hart-Celler bill agreed to dismantle the national origins quota system and the so-called Asiatic-Barred Zone. However, in exchange Johnson would have to sacrifice the administration's emphasis on individual merit. Convinced that family-based immigration was far preferable to discriminatory national origins quotas, the White House eventually acceded to Feighan's demand to make immigrant skills, education, and professional occupations far less important than family ties.[46]

The administration bill's new legal preference system established four preference categories for family reunification, which were to receive nearly three-quarters of total annual visas. Spouses, minor children, and parents of

US citizens over the age of twenty-one were granted admission without visa limits. Two preferences were established for economic goals, including a preference not to exceed 10 percent of the annual visas for "qualified immigrants who are members of the professions, or who because of their exceptional ability in the sciences or the arts will substantially benefit prospectively the national economy, cultural interests, or welfare of the United States." The revised bill left a quarter of annual visas for economic-based admissions and refugee relief.[47] This revised preference system was well received by conservative Democrats in the Senate, most of whom opposed Johnson's original immigration proposal, introduced by Philip Hart (D-MI) as S. 500.

The compromise plan's emphasis on family-based immigration even reassured Senator Strom Thurmond of South Carolina, who switched to the Republican Party in 1964 and vigorously opposed a new merit-based admissions process that he believed would trigger seismic shifts in the volume and composition of US immigration. "The preference which would be established by this proposal," Thurmond told colleagues and constituents, "are based on sound reasoning and meritorious considerations, not entirely dissimilar in effect from those which underlie the national origins quotas of existing law."[48] In other words, as the Japanese American Citizens League and other Asian groups protested, the new system was designed to perpetuate racial biases codified in federal immigration law for generations:

> Inasmuch as the total Asian population of the United States is only about one half of 1 percent of the total American population, this means that there are very few of Asia-Pacific origin in this country who are entitled to provide the specific preference priorities to family members and close relatives residing abroad. . . . Thus, it would seem that, although the immigration bill eliminated race as a matter of principle, in actual operation immigration will still be controlled by the now discredited national origins system and the general pattern of immigration which exists today will continue for many years yet to come.[49]

Along with the legal preference system, the "non-quota status" of Mexican immigration in particular and Latin American admissions in general were a prominent concern for restrictionists in both houses of Congress during the legislative wrangling of 1965. In the House, Feighan pointed out that no numerical limitations were placed on Western Hemisphere immigration in the 1920s because the numbers were so small; in 1965, he warned colleagues that

Latin American entries have "shown a steady increase each year" and that demographic research indicated that the Latin American population was sure to grow "from some 69 millions to some 600 millions."[50] In negotiations with Feighan and other House stalwarts, however, Johnson was unwilling to budge on this issue. The notion of a cap on Western Hemisphere immigration was adamantly denounced by Secretary of State Dean Rusk and other foreign policy advisers, who argued that taking such a step would be a huge setback to relations with Central and South American countries. Indeed, Rusk warned the president that such a measure would alienate Latin American nations already outraged by Johnson's decision to send US troops into the Dominican Republic on April 28, 1965. "We will vex and dumbfound our Latin American friends," Rusk told key White House advisers, "who will now be sure we are in final retreat from Pan Americanism."[51]

The administration's stand on Western Hemisphere immigration came under withering attack in the Senate, however. In particular, southern Democrats led by Sam Ervin Jr. (NC) threatened to block action on S. 500 in the Senate immigration subcommittee unless concessions were made. Public opinion also presented a challenge for liberal immigration reformers. Consistent with other surveys, a June 1965 Gallup poll found that only 7 percent of respondents favored increasing immigration opportunities, while 72 percent preferred decreased or unchanged immigration levels.[52] Facing a major logjam and eager to convince the public that his reform plan was not "a revolutionary bill," Johnson and pro-immigration lawmakers compromised with Ervin and his restriction-minded colleagues on an annual ceiling for Western Hemisphere immigration. As O'Brien explained, "Listen we're not going to walk away from this because we didn't get a whole loaf. We'll take half a loaf or three-quarters of a loaf."[53]

Buoyed by compromises on the admissions preference system and a new ceiling on Western Hemisphere immigration, the Immigration and Nationality Act of 1965 passed both houses with large bipartisan majorities. The new immigration system provided 170,000 visas for immigrants originating in the Eastern Hemisphere (no country was to be allotted more than 20,000 visas), and 120,000 visas for Western Hemisphere immigrants (no per-country limits). Spouses, minor children, and parents of American citizens were exempted from these numerical ceilings. All other persons from the Eastern Hemisphere were placed on waiting lists under seven preferences: four preference categories and 74 percent of visas were reserved for family reunification, two preference categories and 20 percent for needed professionals and unskilled workers, and one preference category and 6 percent of visas for refugees. During the televised signing ceremony at the base of the Statue of Liberty in October 1965, Johnson celebrated the legislation for repairing "a deep and painful flaw in the fabric of American justice."[54] Yet if the INA proved to be one of the hardest-won reforms of the Johnson presidency, its significance barely registered for most Americans. A Harris poll conducted at the end of 1965 found that in sharp contrast to broad public interest in Medicare, civil rights, and other legislative initiatives, only 3 percent described the new immigration law as important to them.

Conclusion

The power to regulate immigrant and refugee admissions is an alluring instrument of grand strategy for policymakers, a site where state actors might advance both a comprehensive and integrated set of national interests at home and abroad. Yet the contentious and uneven character of immigration and refugee control in American politics often has frustrated the best-laid plans of leaders pursuing larger national purposes in domestic and international relations. This was certainly the case for a succession of Democratic and Republican presidents and congressional leaders in the post–World War II era, who failed in their efforts to make US immigration and refugee policy more consistent with liberal internationalist blueprints of an "open society."[55] As much as in the contemporary era, comprehensive immigration reform in the Cold War years was polarizing and extraordinarily elusive. Independent executive actions served as a temporary and piecemeal means for the Truman, Eisenhower, and Kennedy administrations to advance national interests in this policy realm despite roadblocks from congressional nativists.

Even by the outsized standards of Lyndon Johnson and his Great Society juggernaut, the Immigration and Nationality Act of 1965 was monumental. The new law marked a dramatic break from immigration policies of the past by abolishing eugenics-inspired national origins quotas that barred nearly all Asian and African newcomers and reserved about 70 percent of visas for immigrants from just three countries: Great Britain, Ireland, and Germany. In their place, the INA established a preference framework that continues to guide American immigrant admissions, with family ties receiving highest priority followed by occupational skills and political refugee status.[56] The

product of contentious political wrangling, this immigration reform ultimately transformed the demographic makeup of the country. Although few
historians believe that the INA's champions anticipated just how profoundly
it would change the US demographic landscape,[57] Johnson recognized that
its passage was especially significant—enough so that he oversaw the staging
of an elaborate signing ceremony at the base of the Statue of Liberty. White
House staffers were given strict instructions by the president to physically
block political rivals like New York governor Nelson Rockefeller from the
cameras assembled on the dais at Liberty Island.[58] Hinting at the INA's potential impact, Johnson predicted that the new law would "strengthen us
in a hundred unseen ways."[59] Fifty years later, this sweeping immigration
reform is being commemorated alongside the Voting Rights Act as one of
the crowning—and most controversial—achievements of the hard-driving
Johnson years.[60]

It is revealing that in the end, Johnson's success in winning passage of
the Immigration and Nationality Act depended significantly on painful
compromises, including cross-cutting reform packages that both expanded and restricted immigration opportunities in new ways. Whether
one celebrates or condemns the INA, it is clear that the Hart-Celler Act
defies simple characterization precisely because it is an intricate law with
multiple meanings and impacts. The headlines then and now are not
wrong: the INA marked a monumental watershed in US immigration
policy by ending a draconian national origins quota system that was explicitly rooted in eugenicist notions of northern and western European
superiority. The fact that it took twenty years after the defeat of Nazi
Germany for Congress to remove these barriers in American immigration
law speaks to how effectively Cold War nativists knitted together racial hierarchy and national security fears. This history made it especially fitting
that the Johnson administration coupled the INA with the Civil Rights
and Voting Rights Acts.

It is equally true, however, that opponents of diverse immigration left
their imprints on the INA by winning new limits on Western Hemisphere
immigration and by making family ties rather than individual skills the
keystone of the legal preference system. The dramatic and unanticipated
demographic shifts that these restriction-minded provisions helped
spur underscore the INA's transformative, yet variegated, influence on
American life. Rather than a straightforward sea change in US immigration governance, the INA is better understood as a mosaic of reforms with

cross-cutting implications that continue to influence American immigration political life.

True to form, Johnson's successful pursuit of major immigration reform hinged on the formation of strange bedfellow politics aligning a left-right coalition behind a variegated set of policy innovations. As would be the case for major reforms in later years, such as the Immigration Reform and Control Act of 1986 and the Immigration Act of 1990, the INA incorporated rival goals and interests in often incoherent and bedeviling ways. In the end, Johnson and various immigration reform champions in Congress and his administration saw themselves as advancing policies consistent with higher forms of statecraft. Many of their goals were sacrificed or constrained by crucial bargains with opponents, yet Johnson and his Great Society adherents realized important gains with the new immigration system they helped build.

Immigration and refugee policy remain an alluring tool for state actors and other leaders to strategically use the means at their disposal to promote the nation's long-term interests at home and abroad. It promises to pursue crucial geopolitical goals, such as enhancing economic competitiveness, gaining or maintaining superiority in science and technology, influencing diplomacy with sending countries, providing humanitarian relief to refugees fleeing rival states and ideologies, and strengthening the nation's image in the world. Yet American immigration politics and policymaking routinely defy at least two major features of grand strategy. Whereas grand strategy focuses on how to secure larger national interests, the policy struggles presented in this chapter highlight the dominance of a welter of competing partisan, ethnic, religious, business, and labor interests. Equally important, to the extent that grand strategy reflects a comprehensive, cohesive, and flexible blueprint of government action, this chapter underscores how often immigration reform incorporates cross-cutting innovations and goals. Looking forward, as popular nativism and partisan gridlock continue to derail much-needed comprehensive policy corrections, it is likely that US immigration politics and policy will continue to humble even the most skilled architects of grand strategy.

Notes

1. Daniel J. Tichenor, *Dividing Lines: The Politics of Immigration Control in America* (Princeton, NJ: Princeton University Press, 2002); Aristide Zolberg, *A Nation by Design* (Cambridge, MA: Harvard University Press, 2004).

2. See, for example, Christopher Hemmer, *American Pendulum: Recurring Debates in U.S. Grand Strategy* (Ithaca, NY: Cornell University Press, 2015), 2–3.

3. Gary Freeman, "Modes of Immigration Politics in Democratic States," *International Migration Review* (Winter 1995), 881–902.

4. Daniel Tichenor, "The Demise of Immigration Reform," in *Congress and Policymaking in the 21st Century*, ed. Jeffrey Jenkins and Erik Pitashnik (New York: Cambridge University Press, 2016), 242–272.

5. Hemmer, *American Pendulum*, 2–5; Charles Edel, *Nation Builder: John Quincy Adams and the Grand Strategy of the Republic* (Cambridge, MA: Harvard University Press, 2014), 4–6.

6. U.S. Commission on Immigration Reform, *U.S. Immigration Policy: Restoring Credibility* (Washington, DC: US Government Printing Office, 1994).

7. Douglass is quoted in Adrian Cook, *The Armies of the Streets* (Lexington: University Press of Kentucky, 1974), 205.

8. Daniel Tichenor, "The Transformation of American Immigration Policy," in *The American Congress: The Building of Democracy*, ed. Julian Zelizer (New York: Houghton Mifflin, 2004), 395–410.

9. Rutherford B. Hayes, for instance, elicited public outrage and was burned in effigy when he vetoed the Fifteen Passenger Bill that was designed to restrict Chinese immigration. See *Diary and Letters of Rutherford B. Hayes*, ed. Charles Richard Williams (Columbus: Ohio State Historical Society, 1924, vol. 3, 525–526.

10. Woodrow Wilson, "The Literacy Test Condemned," in *Immigration as a Factor in American History*, ed. Oscar Handlin (Englewood Cliffs, NJ: Prentice-Hall, 1958), 187–188; John Higham, *Strangers in the Land* (New Brunswick: Rutgers University Press), 192–193.

11. Martin Dies, "Nationalism Spells Safety," *National Republic*, March 1934, 2; Daniel Tichenor, *Dividing Lines: The Politics of Immigration Control* (Princeton, NJ: Princeton University Press, 2002), 156–167.

12. Frances Perkins to Cornelia Bryce Pinchot, December 31, 1939, Frances Perkins Papers, 1939 Correspondence File, General Records of the Labor Department, Record Group 174, National Archives, Washington, DC; David Wyman, *The Abandonment of the Jews* (New York: Pantheon Books, 1984), 89–96.

13. Harry S. Truman, "State of the Union Address to Congress," January 6, 1947, *Public Papers of the Presidents of the United States: Harry S. Truman* (Washington, DC: Government Printing Office, 1963), 10; Gil Loescher and John Scanlan, *Calculated Kindness: Refugees and America's Half-Open Door, 1945 to Present* (New York: Free Press, 1986), 17–62.

14. Robert Divine, *American Immigration Policy, 1924–1954* (New York: Da Capo Press, 1972), 177–191; David Reimers, *Still the Golden Door: The Third World Comes to America* (New York: Columbia University Press, 1992), 54–56.

15. *Public Papers of the Presidents of the United States: Harry S. Truman* (Washington, DC: Government Printing Office, 1953), 443–444.

16. *Public Papers of the Presidents of the United States: Dwight D. Eisenhower* (Washington, DC: Government Printing Office, 1961), 308–310.

17. John F. Kennedy to Lyndon B. Johnson, June 29, 1955, Senate Files, Pre-Presidential Papers of John F. Kennedy, John F. Kennedy Library, Boston, Massachusetts; Author's interview with Meyer Feldman, December, 1994, Washington, DC.
18. Edward Kennedy, "The Immigration Act of 1965," *Annals of the American Academy of Political and Social Science* 367 (September 1966), 137–138.
19. Abba Schwartz to Theodore Sorenson, November 6, 1963, Theodore Sorenson Papers, Legislative Files, Legislation 1963 Folder, May 21–November 13, 1963, John F. Kennedy Library; Abba Schwartz, *The Open Society* (New York: William and Morrow, 1968), 116.
20. See, for example, Michael LeMay, *From Open Door to Dutch Door* (New York: Praeger, 1987), 111.
21. Lawrence O'Brien Oral History Interview; Paul Douglas Oral History Interview, November 1, 1974, LBJ Library; author's interview with Meyer Feldman; author's interview with Jack Valenti, December 1994; Schwartz, *The Open Society*, 116–121.
22. William Leuchtenberg, *In the Shadow of FDR* (Ithaca, NY: Cornell University Press, 1985), 132; Lyndon Johnson, *The Vantage Point* (New York: Holt, Rinehart, and Winston, 1971), 161.
23. Robert Dallek, *Lone Star Rising* (New York: Oxford University Press,1992), 485.
24. Author's interview with Meyer Feldman.
25. Author's interview with Jack Valenti.
26. Author's interviews with Feldman and Valenti; Schwartz, *The Open Society*.
27. Hart is quoted in Nationalities Services Center, "A New Immigration Proposal: A Fact Sheet on S.3043," copy in the author's files.
28. *Public Papers of the Presidents of the United States: Lyndon B. Johnson, 1963–1964*, vol. 1, November 27, 1963 (Washington, DC: Government Printing Office, 1965).
29. Author's interview with Jack Valenti.
30. Author's interview with Meyer Feldman.
31. Lyndon B. Johnson, "State of the Union Address," *Public Papers of the Presidents of the United States: Lyndon B. Johnson*, vol.1, 116.
32. Paul Duke and Stanley Meisler, "Immigration: Quotas vs. Quality," *The Reporter*, January 14, 1965, 30–31.
33. John P. Leacacos, "Feighan Argues Merits of His Immigration Bill," *Cleveland Plain Dealer*, August 13, 1964; and John Leacacos, "Feighan Upsets Administration," *Cleveland Plain Dealer*, August 12, 1964, Press clippings file, Michael Feighan Papers, Seely Mudd Manuscript Library, Princeton University, box 5.
34. "Points to Be Covered in Brief" Memo, August 13, 1964, "Immigration" folder, Feighan Papers, box 5.
35. "Highlights of Proposed Congressional Action," staff memorandum, no date, Feighan Papers, box 5.
36. "Building a Great Society," Democratic Study Group, 1964 Campaign Cards, Papers of the Democratic Study Group, Library of Congress, Washington, DC, box 54.
37. Schwartz, *The Open Society*, 120–121.
38. Nicholas deB. Katzenbach, Testimony on Immigration Reform, Hearings before the Subcommittee on Immigration and Naturalization, Senate Judiciary Committee,

89th Congress, 1st Session, pt. 1 (Washington, DC: US Government Printing Office, 1965), 8.

39. Duke and Meisler, "Immigration: Quotas vs. Quality," 31.
40. "Celler—Calling for Hold-Up," Staff Memorandum, September 22, 1964, Feighan Papers, box 5.
41. Lawrence O'Brien Oral History Interview, LBJ Library.
42. Jean Kerbs to Michael Feighan, Western Union telegram, no date; and Feighan to Kerbs, letter, no date, "Immigration" folder, Feighan Papers, box 5.
43. Jean Kerbs to Michael Feighan, Western Union telegram, no date; and Feighan to Kerbs, letter, no date, "Immigration" folder, Feighan Papers, box 5.
44. Congressional Record, July 23, 1963, 13132–13133.
45. Bon Tempo, 2008, 96.
46. Reimers, *Still the Golden Door*, 69–74.
47. William S. Stern, "H.R. 2580: The Immigration and Nationality Amendments of 1965—A Case Study," PhD dissertation, New York University, 1974.
48. *The Congressional Record*, September 17, 1965, 24237.
49. Reimers, *Still the Golden Door*, 73, and *Congressional Record*, September 20, 1965, 24503; Robert Goldfarb, "Occupational Preferences in U.S. Immigration Law," in *The Gateway: Issues in American Immigration*, ed. Barry Chiswick (Lanham, MD: Rowman and Littlefield, 1981), 412–448.
50. Michael Feighan, "Highlights of the Immigration Issue," January 18, 1965, copy on file with the author.
51. Irving Bernstein, *Guns or Butter: The Presidency of Lyndon Johnson* (New York: Oxford University Press, 1996), 256.
52. Carl Bon Tempo, *Americans at the Gate: The United States and Refugees during the Cold War* (Princeton, NJ: Princeton University Press, 2008), 92–94.
53. Lawrence O'Brien Oral History Interview, LBJ Library; Tichenor, *Dividing Lines*, 215.
54. Lyndon Johnson, "Remarks on the Immigration Law," *Congressional Quarterly* (October 1965), 2063–2064.
55. Schwartz, *The Open Society*.
56. Schwartz, *The Open Society*; Reimers, *Still the Golden Door*; Ellis Cose, *A Nation of Strangers* (New York: William and Morrow, 1992); Roger Daniels, *Guarding the Golden Door* (New York: Hill and Wang, 2004).
57. Higham, *Strangers in the Land*; Eirka Lee, "A Nation of Immigrants and a Gatekeeping Nation," in Reed Ueda, ed., *A Companion to American Immigration*, ed. Reed Ueda (New York: Wiley Blackwell, 2011), 5–36; Mae Ngai, *Impossible Subjects* (Chicago: University of Chicago Press, 2004). For an interesting perspective on this question, see Gabriel Chin, "Were the Immigration and Nationality Act Amendments of 1965 Antiracist?," in *The Immigration and Nationality Act of 1965*, ed. Gabriel Chin and Rose Cuison Villazor (New York: Cambridge University Press, 2015), 11–54.
58. Lawrence O'Brien, Oral History Interview, September 18, 1985, LBJ Library.
59. Lyndon Johnson, "Remarks on the Immigration Law," *Congressional Quarterly* (October 1965, 2063–2064.

60. Ceclia Munoz, "Celebrating the 50th Anniversary of the Immigration and Nationality Act," *Whitehouse.gov Blog*, October 16, 2015; Tom Gjelten, "The Immigration Act That Inadvertently Changed America," *The Atlantic*, October 2, 2015; Philip Wolgin, "The Immigration and Nationality Act Turns 50," *Center for American Progress*, October 16, 2015.

18

Disastrous Grand Strategy

US Humanitarian Assistance and
Global Natural Catastrophe

Julia F. Irwin

The Congress, recognizing that prompt United States assistance to
alleviate human suffering caused by natural and manmade disasters
is an important expression of the humanitarian concern and tradition of the people of the United States, affirms the willingness of the
United States to provide assistance for the relief and rehabilitation of
people and countries affected by such disasters.
—Section 491, Chapter 9, Foreign Assistance Act of 1961, as
amended by the International Development and
Food Assistance Act of 1975

In December 1975, the US federal government first established its authority
to provide international disaster relief. This date may strike readers as rather
late, with legitimate reason. Since the early twentieth century, the US government had routinely allocated cash, food, military assistance, and other state
resources to foreign disaster victims. Since the 1950s, moreover, Congress
had adopted several key pieces of foreign aid legislation with provisions related to disaster assistance, while the State Department, USAID and its predecessor agencies, and the Defense Department had all developed procedures
and bureaucratic arrangements to guide their actions in the wake of international catastrophes. Yet until the mid-1970s, no federal laws specifically and
affirmatively authorized the US government's involvement in this sphere of
humanitarian assistance.

Public Law (P.L.) 94–161, the International Development and Food
Assistance Act of 1975, brought an end to this ambiguous situation. More

precisely, this legislation amended the 1961 Foreign Assistance Act to add an entirely new chapter on "International Disaster Assistance." Avowing the United States' readiness to provide humanitarian relief in the wake of foreign catastrophes, it empowered the president (or his appointed delegates) to furnish relief and short-term rehabilitation assistance to any country affected by "natural or manmade disasters." It also created a fund expressly for this purpose, financed with an initial congressional appropriation of $25,000,000 per year. With this act, US international disaster assistance—carried out for decades in an ad hoc albeit increasingly formal manner—was officially codified as an instrument of US foreign policy.[1]

But why, in the 1970s, did US policymakers conclude that international disaster assistance should form part of the state's foreign affairs arsenal? What steps in this direction had their predecessors taken during previous decades? And finally, how can the study of grand strategy help us to make sense of these developments? What can it tell us, in other words, about the origins of the United States' contemporary system of foreign disaster aid? Taking these questions as a starting point, this chapter first traces the evolution of the US government's international disaster assistance policy, beginning at the dawn of the nineteenth century and culminating with the landmark enactment of P.L. 94–161 in 1975. It then analyzes the state's gradually expanding role in this humanitarian sphere in light of the shifting architecture of nineteenth- and twentieth-century US grand strategy.

Grand strategy, as Hal Brands has defined it, represents "an integrated scheme of interests, threats, resources, and policies." It is "the intellectual architecture that lends structure to foreign policy" and "the logic that helps states navigate a complex and dangerous world."[2] Its function, as political scientist William C. Martel puts it, "is to prioritize among different domestic and foreign policy choices and to coordinate, balance, and integrate all types of national means—including diplomatic, economic, technological, and military power—to achieve the articulated ends."[3] If one accepts these definitions, it follows that by thinking about grand strategy, historians can better comprehend why past leaders adopted certain policies and what they hoped to achieve as a result. In the case of US international disaster assistance, a consideration of grand strategy promises to shed light on three related historical questions: First, why did US government officials decide to devote limited state resources to aiding the victims of catastrophes in other sovereign nations? Second, how did policymakers come to believe that providing international disaster assistance would advance the United States' most essential interests while also warding off threats to those same core interests? And finally, why did policymakers see the short-term action of providing international disaster relief as a means to attain the United States' long-term objectives? Together, the answers to these core questions of grand strategy help to clarify how and why international disaster assistance became an official instrument of US foreign policy.[4]

If a grand strategy framework can help make sense of US international disaster assistance, studying the history of catastrophes and disaster relief—and the history of humanitarian aid, more broadly—also stands to say something new about US grand strategy itself. Disasters are, quite often, unforeseen events. Although "creeping" disasters caused by droughts and famine unfold gradually over time, "sudden-onset" catastrophes caused by earthquakes, tropical storms, tsunamis, or flash floods tend to catch both their victims and US policymakers by surprise.[5] Even if the risk and probability of these hazards can be predicted or calculated, the exact moment they will occur, the levels of death and destruction they will cause, and the precise types of secondary problems they will trigger are largely unknowable. If a nation's grand strategy is to be successful, it must be able to accommodate such contingent events and adjust accordingly—particularly when they occur in areas of the world that are of key strategic concern.

Studying the history of US international disaster assistance policy, it follows, represents one way to gauge the effectiveness of US grand strategy at different periods of time. In any given era, were US government officials in a position to execute a flexible, adaptable response to catastrophes in other nations? Did they formulate systems and procedures to deal with the effects of disasters in a more structured, organized manner? Were they forward-thinking enough to undertake prevention and risk-reduction measures that would mitigate the harms of future foreign disasters? Just as thinking about grand strategy promises to provide important insights into the history of US international disaster assistance policy, the answers to these questions stand to inform the history of American grand strategy itself.

At its most fundamental level, this chapter makes two central contributions to this volume. First, it argues for the importance of expanding the conventional analytical boundaries of grand strategy and of integrating less traditional subjects—in this case, international disaster relief—into studies of grand strategic thinking. Second, it demonstrates the value of viewing state-led humanitarian actions within a grand strategy framework. Such an approach, this chapter contends, allows us to better understand policymakers' motivations for contributing (and in many cases, failing to provide) foreign disaster aid and other types of humanitarian assistance.

Origins of the US International Disaster Assistance Policy, 1812–1975

The history of US governmental assistance for international disasters arguably dates to 1812. That May, following a devastating earthquake in Venezuela, Congress authorized President James Madison to purchase and send provisions for the "relief of citizens who have suffered" and allocated $50,000 to fund this aid effort.[6] This act marked the first instance of the US government committing state resources to survivors of a foreign natural disaster. Rather than establishing a precedent or a consistent policy for future disaster aid, however, this assistance is better understood as an anomaly. For the remainder of the nineteenth century, US government outlays for overseas humanitarian crises proved extremely rare. Of the handful of relief measures that Congress did pass, all represented responses to either political strife or enduring famine (rather than abrupt natural or technological disasters). All, moreover, were limited to allowing US Navy ships to transport privately donated aid and did not include appropriations of cash or supplies.[7] US international disaster assistance may have been born in 1812, but its maturation as an official instrument of foreign policy would be decades in the future.

Not until the early twentieth century did the US government began to contribute disaster assistance to other countries on a consistent basis. In 1902, Congress made its first cash appropriation for an international natural disaster since 1812, allocating $200,000 to aid survivors of a volcanic eruption in Martinique and St. Vincent and authorizing President Theodore Roosevelt to procure and distribute food, clothing, and other relief provisions.[8] From this moment forward, US governmental commitments to international disaster assistance steadily increased. Over the next forty years, the federal government regularly expended state resources for foreign disaster survivors, usually in the form of supplies from its military stores. The State, War, and Navy departments also routinely assigned embassy and consular officials and military personnel to provide relief and short-term assistance in other countries, authorizing the use of naval ships and, by the 1930s, military aircraft to deliver US aid abroad. Among the most noteworthy examples of such assistance were a congressional allocation of $800,000 for survivors of a 1908 earthquake and tsunami in southern Italy and the granting of $8,000,000 worth of army and navy supplies and services, for victims of a 1923 earthquake in Japan.[9] These acts, though, were by no means isolated events. By the end of World War II, the US government had provided tens of millions of dollars' worth of cash, supplies, and logistical assistance to dozens of disaster-stricken countries from Europe to Asia to Central and South America.[10]

But if the US government had begun to devote more resources to foreign disaster aid during the first four decades of the twentieth century, its precise role in this sphere remained rather ambiguous. In many cases, rather than contributing aid directly, US government officials instead opted to support and promote the humanitarian work of the quasi-governmental American Red Cross and other voluntary organizations, actively facilitating their efforts to provide monetary and material assistance in the name of the United States. When the War Department, State Department, and Congress did provide disaster assistance to other countries, they did so on an ad hoc basis. With few written procedures to guide them, without designated state agencies to respond to catastrophes, and with no affirmative legislative authority for their actions, the federal government's mechanisms for providing foreign disaster assistance could hardly be considered systematic or structured.

In the thirty years after World War II, however, this situation was completely transformed. From the mid-1940s to the mid-1970s, US international disaster assistance evolved from an unofficial and limited tool of US foreign affairs into a formal and critical instrument of US foreign policy. Such significant changes, however, did not occur overnight. In fact, compared with many other facets of the government's postwar foreign aid program, US international disaster assistance policy developed relatively slowly.

During Harry Truman's presidency, from 1945 to 1953, federal government spending on foreign military, economic, and technical assistance all increased exponentially, while a broad slate of foreign aid legislation—including most notably the 1948 Economic Cooperation Act (Marshall Plan), the 1950 Foreign Economic Assistance Act (Point IV), and the 1951 Mutual Security Act—enshrined foreign assistance as a critical element of US international relations.[11] Yet significantly, none of this landmark foreign aid legislation contained language expressly related to international disaster assistance. Focused first on postwar relief and reconstruction, and then on longer-term economic, military, and technical assistance, American policymakers neglected to address the specific issue of natural and man-made catastrophes. The effect, as far as US foreign policy was concerned, was that disasters remained contingencies, treated in federal law and policy as unforeseeable events. Accordingly, the US government continued to respond to them on an unsystematic, case-by-case basis, just as it had in previous decades. This early legislation did, however, include one provision with implications for international disaster assistance: it authorized the federal government to reimburse approved American voluntary agencies for the expense of shipping relief supplies overseas. Though originally intended to support private humanitarian efforts for postwar Europe, these ocean freight subsidies soon became a major source of state spending on foreign disaster aid, to the tune of millions of dollars per year.[12]

While early US foreign aid policy remained silent on international disaster assistance, the federal government began to make its role in this field more explicit during Dwight D. Eisenhower's presidency, from 1953 to 1961. A first clear shift in this direction came in 1954, with the passage of Public Law 480: The Agricultural Trade Development and Assistance Act. This legislation, a landmark in the history of US foreign aid, authorized the president to dispose of hundreds of millions of dollars' worth of surplus agricultural commodities annually as international assistance. Title II of the legislation, notably, related directly to disaster assistance. It empowered the president to grant food assistance up to $300 million in value for the victims of "famine or other urgent relief requirements," namely, natural and manmade catastrophes. Title III of the law, moreover, authorized the government to transfer surplus commodities to voluntary organizations "for use in the assistance of needy persons outside the United States." As with ocean freight subsidies, these food grants to private agencies soon became a principal channel for US governmental commitments to foreign disaster aid. With this legislation, Congress had greatly increased the federal government's annual commitments to international disaster assistance and had professed the government's authority to respond to situations requiring "urgent relief."[13]

Congress was not the only branch of the federal government involved in shaping foreign disaster assistance policy during the 1950s. In 1956, Eisenhower's Operations Coordinating Board, the body responsible for synchronizing security activities across various federal agencies, produced a manual titled "Foreign Disaster Relief Operations." The manual spelled out, for the first time, "inter-agency guidelines in connection with emergencies occurring overseas in which US Government assistance may be of importance." Defining "emergencies" to include "all types of natural disasters such as flood, earthquakes, hurricanes, fires, volcanic eruption, and pestilence, as well as major explosions and accidents," it defined procedures for the International Cooperation Agency (ICA),[14] the Departments of State, Defense, and Agriculture, and the United States Information Agency to follow in the aftermath of such crises.[15] In 1958, further elaborating on these policies, Secretary of State John Foster Dulles issued a secret set of instructions for all US overseas diplomatic missions, which outlined their duties in the event of "a disaster . . . resulting from phenomena of nature such as flood, hurricane, typhoon, earthquake, fire, volcanic eruption or pestilence." In this memorandum, Dulles charged all chiefs of mission with the responsibility of determining whether outside assistance was necessary, what specific needs existed, and whether it was "in the interest of the United States to assist in meeting such initial emergency needs." He also authorized mission chiefs to commit up to $10,000 for emergency relief in any disaster event, to be drawn from a new ICA Foreign Disaster Emergency Relief Account. While the US State Department, military, and Congress regularly committed additional assistance beyond this amount, this new measure enabled diplomats to respond more effectively and swiftly to sudden calamities as soon as they occurred.[16] Together, the ICA's manual and Dulles's guidelines established lasting precedents for future US disaster aid operations.

By the end of the 1950s, the federal government was providing cash, food, military support, and other forms of assistance to dozens of disaster-stricken countries per year and was doing so on a far more structured basis than in the past. During the 1960s, its role in global disaster relief expanded further still, as US policymakers took additional steps to formalize the government's role in this sphere of humanitarian aid. Developments in this field, however, continued to lag behind other foreign aid initiatives. Most notably, although passage of the Foreign Assistance Act of 1961 completely overhauled the existing structures of US foreign aid, it had few immediate effects on the country's international disaster assistance policy. Like previous foreign aid legislation, the 1961 Foreign Assistance Act focused primarily on long-term development and technical assistance, making no specific mention of aid for natural or manmade disasters. The legislation did, however, establish a "contingency fund" for use in unspecified events that were determined "to be important to the national interest."[17] This fund soon underwrote most of the foreign disaster assistance activities of the new US Agency for International Development (USAID), the US Armed Forces, and US diplomatic and development missions. The new foreign aid system also retained earlier disaster-related provisions, including ocean freight subsidies for voluntary agencies, government grants of surplus commodities for disaster survivors, and the $10,000 available to chiefs of mission for emergency assistance. Still, none of this constituted a major sea change in the US government's international disaster assistance policy.

It was not until 1964 that US international disaster assistance policy began to transform appreciably. In January of that year, the administrator of USAID established a new position within the agency: the Foreign Disaster Relief Coordinator (FDRC). This individual and his staff were responsible, as the title suggested, for coordinating all US governmental and military, and certain voluntary, disaster response activities. For the first time, select US government personnel had been charged with the sole and explicit task of responding to overseas calamities. Later that year, USAID also increased the emergency funds it made available to US diplomatic missions, from $10,000 to $25,000 per disaster event, and drafted updated manuals to guide military, diplomatic, and foreign assistance personnel in disaster relief operations.[18] Further developments in disaster assistance policy came in the late 1960s and early 1970s. In these years, the administrator of USAID expanded the size of the FDRC's staff, enabling this office to devote greater attention not only to disaster response but also to such complementary tasks as prevention and risk reduction. USAID also began stockpiling large quantities of disaster relief supplies on US military bases in the Canal Zone, Guam, Livorno, and Singapore, a measure that allowed American forces to respond more rapidly and effectively to foreign disasters in various parts of the world.[19]

The clearest articulation of US foreign disaster aid policy came with the passage of the International Development and Food Assistance Act of 1975. This legislation amended the 1961 Foreign Assistance Act to include a chapter on "International Disaster Assistance." Transforming long-standing precedents, tacit agreements, and unstructured policies into federal law, the act affirmatively established the US government's authority and willingness to provide international disaster relief, defined the state's role in coordinating and planning overseas disaster response and prevention activities, and allocated funds exclusively for such purposes. Just a few months later, in an act that further reflected the formalization of US international disaster assistance policy, the office of the FDRC was renamed the Office of Foreign Disaster Assistance (OFDA), the title that it still holds today.[20] Although the system has evolved in critical ways since that time, the mid-1970s arguably marks the origins of the contemporary legal and bureaucratic system of US foreign disaster aid.

International Disaster Assistance and US Grand Strategy

During the twentieth century—and especially during the three decades after the Second World War—US policymakers thus transformed international disaster assistance from a routine yet unsystematic activity of the federal government into an official instrument of foreign policy. With the outlines of how this process occurred laid out, it is now worth contemplating the reasons it did. Why did US government officials come to regard international disaster assistance as such a critical policy initiative, one worth formalizing and incorporating into federal law? The explanation for this development can be attributed to a wide variety of factors, among them diplomatic objectives, economic aims, domestic political pressures, and moral convictions. Yet, as this chapter contends, thinking about grand strategy can offer a particularly valuable framework for understanding this history. By taking into account the United States' core interests, the major threats to those interests, and the resources at its disposal—key foci of grand strategy—one can better comprehend the relationship of international disaster aid to US foreign relations.

Looking back to the nineteenth century, the federal government's initial aversion to expending state resources for the victims of foreign disasters makes sound sense from a grand strategy perspective. The United States' overarching grand strategy for much of the nineteenth century, as William Martel has summarized it, was concerned with "building the domestic foundations of natural power."[21] To protect against foreign threats and promote US interests in the long term, most American leaders believed, they first needed to develop the United States' political, military, economic, and territorial strengths. Accordingly, nineteenth-century US policymakers directed what resources they had chiefly toward such ends as continental expansion, consolidating federal power, developing a modern industrial economy, and building a stronger army and navy.[22] Attaining these objectives, for many, would have understandably taken priority over aiding the anonymous victims of foreign catastrophes.

The federal government's later expansion of US international disaster assistance policy, on the other hand, can be understood with reference to the seismic shifts in US grand strategy that occurred during the twentieth century. By the early 1900s, the United States had assumed a very different position in the world from the one it had occupied throughout much of the nineteenth century. It entered the twentieth century with a strong and sizable navy and a robust industrial economy; with the project of continental expansion complete, US overseas expansion had commenced. The United States, in other words, had emerged as a world power and an empire, a status that only grew stronger following World War I. In this context, most scholars of the subject agree, US grand strategy was characterized by two overarching objectives: first, projecting and expanding US power and influence in the world, and second, restraining sources of international disorder that might threaten US interests.[23] If these aims shaped the United States' interactions with the early twentieth-century world, they became all the more central to its grand strategy in the aftermath of World War II. The United States had become a political, economic, and military superpower, and its leaders—facing the dual geopolitical challenges of the Cold War and decolonization—embraced new beliefs about their nation's international role and responsibilities. In the years from 1945 to 1975, US policymakers widely agreed on the necessity of containing (if not rolling back) communism. Most shared, too, a commitment (avowedly, if not always in practice) to preserving and promoting the principles of representative democracy, individual freedom, and private enterprise. Securing these goals lay at the heart of postwar grand strategy, and they fundamentally influenced the US government's interactions with the world.[24]

In light of the nation's ambitions and interests in twentieth-century international affairs, both before and after 1945, the decision to use disaster assistance as an instrument of foreign policy was logical for several reasons. First, as many twentieth-century policymakers recognized, international disaster assistance represented a potent form of public diplomacy. Through such actions as delivering relief supplies, rescuing survivors, or funding rehabilitation projects, various US officials observed, the US government stood to promote "goodwill," to "strengthen our prestige," and to have a "marked and lasting beneficial effect on relations" with other countries.[25] Beyond demonstrating US humanitarian concern, dispatching Navy ships or "flights of airplanes on missions of mercy" also provided visible evidence of the United States' military capabilities and its financial might.[26] To make doubly sure that disaster aid recipients understood the message, Congress went so far as to require that all disaster aid supplies "shall be clearly identified . . . as being furnished by the people of the United States of America."[27]

Foreign disaster aid, then, served as valuable propaganda, but this was by no means its only function. A second benefit to disaster assistance, in US policymakers' minds, was its potential to promote American economic and political objectives in the world. In this sense, humanitarian relief shares noteworthy parallels with global development and modernization initiatives.[28] By contributing to the rehabilitation of agriculture, industry, and trade in disaster-stricken nations, US officials believed, the United States could nurture the economic conditions required for capitalism and free markets to flourish and, by extension, stave off communism. Motivated in part by such goals, American officials sent hundreds of thousands of dollars' worth of seeds and agricultural equipment to Haiti following Hurricane Hazel in 1954, loaned $3,000,000 to Iran "to rehabilitate agricultural production capability" after a major earthquake there in 1962, and offered $50 million in grants and loans to Yugoslavia in 1963 to assist in rebuilding housing and industry when a catastrophic earthquake destroyed the city of Skopje.[29] Moreover, by making disaster relief grants and loans contingent on certain conditions—as they did, for instance, when lending $100 million to Chile following a devastating 1960 earthquake[30]—US policymakers could exert considerable pressure on foreign leaders, compelling them to adopt desired fiscal or political behaviors in exchange for much-needed assistance. As these examples (and many others like them) attest, US international aid not only benefited disaster survivors; it also served core US interests.

Considering the threats, real and perceived, that the United States faced in the twentieth-century world, foreign disaster aid proved useful for additional reasons. For policymakers concerned with external disorder and the risk it might pose to US investments, military installations, or diplomatic agendas, providing aid presented a way to minimize unrest and restore political and economic stability within disaster-stricken nations.[31] Finally, contributing disaster aid represented a way for the United States to outshine its rivals on the world stage. By giving more disaster aid than other countries and by delivering that aid more rapidly—figures that US officials closely monitored and routinely trumpeted[32]—the United States stood to best its adversaries in the global battle for hearts and minds.

Disaster assistance, in sum, represented an activity with the potential to promote a variety of US interests in the world and to circumvent threats to those same interests. For a government focused on projecting its power, expanding its influence, winning friends, and overcoming its geopolitical rivals, delivering swift and liberal international disaster assistance offered a theoretical means to each of these ends.

If foreign disaster assistance were to succeed in achieving these various outcomes, however, it had to function as smoothly and flawlessly as possible. It did not always do so. When the US government provided international disaster assistance on an ad hoc basis, as it did for much of the twentieth century, its efforts were often hampered by delays, duplication of effort, and inconsistent or unpredictable funding. These issues made US aid efforts less helpful for disaster survivors and created embarrassments for US policymakers. To maximize the effectiveness of disaster assistance as a tool of foreign affairs, policymakers increasingly came to recognize, they would need to formalize their approach. It was this reasoning that led policymakers to create interagency guidelines for international disaster relief in the 1950s, to establish the position of the Foreign Disaster Relief Coordinator in 1964, and to add the "International Disaster Assistance" amendment in the Foreign Assistance Act in 1975, among other reforms. With these policy changes, US officials were endeavoring to make international disaster assistance more systematized and structured, to mold it into a policy instrument that would be maximally positioned to serve national interests.[33]

An analysis of US global objectives thus goes a long way toward explaining the twentieth-century evolution of US international disaster assistance policy. Abstract goals alone, however, cannot fully account for its development; on a material level, this process was also determined by the resources that the federal government had at its disposal. In the nineteenth century, even if policymakers had wanted to provide international disaster relief on a regular basis, they would have found themselves rather stymied. Lacking considerable finances, a significant physical footprint in the world, and a sizable navy, the US government was ill equipped to contribute generous or rapid relief to other countries. By contrast, providing disaster assistance to other countries became far more feasible in the early twentieth century, due to the greater strength of the economy and the presence of US territories, ships, aircraft, and diplomatic and military personnel stationed throughout the world. By the post–World War II decades, it became easier still. In command of the world's richest treasury, the US government was far more capable of funding foreign disaster relief operations than it ever had been in the past. With new foreign assistance agencies, sizable diplomatic missions in all parts of the world, thousands of overseas military installations, and hundreds of thousands of troops stationed globally, the US government possessed a bureaucratic infrastructure capable of carrying out major foreign disaster assistance operations. While a calculus of interests and threats may have motivated US policymakers to provide international disaster assistance, in other words, it was the abundant resources of the twentieth-century state that ultimately made such actions possible.[34]

Thinking about grand strategy—about means and ends, and about interests, threats, and resources—helps to clarify how and why US policymakers chose to make international disaster assistance an official element of twentieth-century US foreign affairs. In turn, the study of US foreign disaster assistance policy also has something important to suggest about twentieth-century American grand strategy. If it is to be effective, a nation's grand strategy cannot be rigid and inflexible; it must be able to react to unforeseen events and surprising developments—natural disasters chief among them.

As early as 1812, while debating whether to send earthquake aid to Venezuela, at least some US policymakers recognized that such humanitarian actions could be in "the interests of the United States."[35] Over the course of the twentieth century, US policymakers became ever more aware that responding swiftly, liberally, and professionally to catastrophes in other countries might well be in the United States' interest. In the three decades after World War II, this recognition led them to devise the procedures, policies, and legislation they would need to respond to foreign disasters in a more structured and consistent manner. Rather than treating disasters as unpredictable contingencies, policymakers began to regard them as events that they could plan for and mitigate in advance. Perhaps, it could be argued, the development of these new mechanisms of foreign disaster assistance made US grand strategy itself more effective—more adaptable in the face of unforeseen crises and forward-thinking enough to help prevent those crises from occurring in the first place. By constructing an official system of international disaster assistance, US leaders devised a new means of navigating and accommodating the upheavals of the twentieth-century world.

Conclusions: Avoiding a Disastrous Grand Strategy for the Twenty-First Century

To achieve their short-term aims and long-term ambitions, twentieth-century US policymakers interacted with the world through a wide variety of channels. They waged overt wars and engaged in covert operations; they pursued policies of defense, diplomacy, and development; and, on an increasingly regular and official basis, they directed state resources toward foreign disaster assistance. By the mid-1970s, international disaster aid had become an official tool in the United States' foreign affairs arsenal, one means of achieving desired foreign policy ends.

Since that time, the US government has continued to respond regularly to natural and technological disasters in other countries. Currently, the US government provides hundreds of millions of dollars' worth of food, cash grants, medical supplies, and recovery assistance annually to millions of people affected by global catastrophes. Much of this aid flows through the US Office of Foreign Disaster Assistance, whose staff responds to dozens of international catastrophes each year and helps other nations prepare for future calamities. The US military, too, remains a major player in delivering emergency relief and performing life-saving rescue operations in the wake of disasters around the world.[36] Through legislative initiatives, meanwhile, Congress continues to enumerate and refine the government's role in foreign disaster assistance.[37] Well into the twenty-first century, foreign disaster assistance has endured as a critical instrument of US foreign policy and an important form of US global engagement.

The procedures and policies that policymakers developed in the three decades after World War II were supposed to make the United States a far more effective provider of international disaster aid. By certain measures, these reforms have achieved their purpose. And yet, one need only recall the problems that arose during recent crises, including the 2004 Indian Ocean tsunami, 2010 Haitian earthquake, the 2011 Tōhoku earthquake and tsunami, and the 2017 hurricanes Irma and Maria in the Caribbean, to realize that the United States' system of foreign disaster aid remains far from perfect—and, at times, is deeply problematic. Myriad issues—delays and funding constraints, a lack of support for foreign assistance among many American politicians and citizens, a lack of intra-agency cooperation within the United States, political and cultural tensions and misunderstandings on the ground in other countries, and disagreements on the international stage over whether US aid should flow through unilateral or multilateral channels—together continue to limit both the diplomatic and the humanitarian potential of US foreign disaster assistance.

Given these concerns and constraints, perhaps a grand strategy for the twenty-first-century United States ought to focus less on traditional realms of defense and diplomacy and more on preparing for the challenges that disasters will invariably pose, both to the United States and to the world. In coming years, disaster experts predict, such factors as global population growth, the rise of megacities, and climate change will all create greater

vulnerability to catastrophes globally. If US policymakers want to successfully promote the nation's political, economic, and strategic interests through
disaster aid—and if they sincerely believe that "alleviat[ing] human suffering
caused by natural and manmade disasters . . . is an important expression of
the humanitarian concern and tradition of the people of the United States,"
as the Foreign Assistance Act declares[38]—they must continue working to
improve the mechanisms of US international disaster assistance. Utilizing
the nation's vast material and financial resources, they must make US global
response, recovery, and risk-reduction efforts as effective, equitable, and
ethical as they can possibly be. With a more intent focus on international humanitarian relief, twenty-first-century US policymakers will be less at risk of
pursuing a disastrous grand strategy.

Notes

1. International Development and Food Assistance Act of 1975, Public Law 94–161, 89
   Stat. (1975): 849–869.
2. Hal Brands, *What Good Is Grand Strategy? Power and Purpose in American Statecraft
   from Harry S. Truman to George W. Bush* (Ithaca, NY: Cornell University Press,
   2015), 3, 1.
3. William C. Martel, *Grand Strategy in Theory and Practice: The Need for an Effective
   American Foreign Policy* (New York: Cambridge University Press, 2015), 31–32.
4. This chapter builds on the scholarship of many historians and political scientists of
   US foreign aid. See, for example, Merle Curti, *American Philanthropy Abroad* (New
   Brunswick, NJ: Rutgers University Press, 1963); Michael Latham, *The Right Kind
   of Revolution: Modernization, Development, and US Foreign Policy from the Cold
   War to the Present* (Ithaca, NY: Cornell University Press, 2011); David Ekbladh, *The
   Great American Mission: Modernization and the Construction of an American World
   Order* (Princeton, NJ: Princeton University Press, 2009); Nick Cullather, *The Hungry
   World: America's Cold War Battle against Poverty in Asia* (Cambridge, MA: Harvard
   University Press, 2010); Daniel Immerwahr, *Thinking Small: The United States and the
   Lure of Community Development* (Cambridge, MA: Harvard University Press, 2015);
   David Engerman, *The Price of Aid: The Economic Cold War in India* (Cambridge,
   MA: Harvard University Press, 1998); David Lumsdaine, *Moral Vision in International
   Politics: The Foreign Aid Regime, 1949–1989* (Princeton, NJ: Princeton University
   Press, 1993); Carol Lancaster: *Foreign Aid: Diplomacy, Development, Domestic Politics*
   (Chicago: University of Chicago Press, 2007). For US foreign disaster aid specifi-
   cally, see William Tilchin, "Theodore Roosevelt, Anglo-American Relations, and the
   Jamaica Incident of 1907," *Diplomatic History* 19 (1995), 385–406; John F. Hutchinson,
   "Disasters and the International Order II: The International Relief Union,"

International History Review 23:3 (2001), 253–298; A. Cooper Drury, Richard Stuart Olson, and Douglas Van Belle, "The Politics of Humanitarian Aid: US Foreign Disaster Assistance, 1964–1995," *Journal of Politics* 67 (2005), 454–473; Alexander Poster, "A Hierarchy of Survival: The United States and the Negotiation of International Disaster Relief, 1981–1989," PhD dissertation, Ohio State University, 2010.

5. For "creeping" and "sudden-onset" disasters, see Damon P. Coppola, *Introduction to International Disaster Management*, 3rd ed. (Oxford: Butterworth-Heinemann, 2015), 34.

6. An Act for the Relief of the Citizens of Venezuela, Chapter LXXIX, 2 Stat. (1812): 730.

7. These claims (along with others throughout this section) draw from my ongoing research, but see also Merle Curti, *American Philanthropy Abroad*; List of Acts and Resolutions of Congress Granting Relief to the People of Foreign Nations on Account of Earthquakes, Fire, Famine, Etc., Senate Document 629, 60th Congress, 2nd Session (1909).

8. An Act for the relief of citizens of the French West Indies, Public Law 57–112, 32 Stat. (1902): 198.

9. An Act for the Relief of Citizens of Italy, Public Law 60–184, US Statues at Large, 35 Stat. (1909): 584; Charles Burnett, Report on Relief Activities in Japan, January 31, 1924, Central Decimal File (CDF) 894.48 (1910–1929), Records of the Department of State, Record Group (RG) 59, National Archives and Records Administration, College Park, MD (NARA).

10. Julia Irwin, "Connected by Calamity: The United States, the League of Red Cross Societies, and Transnational Disaster Assistance after the First World War," *Moving the Social: Journal of Social History and the History of Social Movements* 57 (2017), 57–76; Julia Irwin, "The 'Development' of Humanitarian Relief: US Disaster Assistance Operations in the Caribbean Basin, 1917–1931," in *The Development Century: A Global History*, ed. Stephen Macekura and Erez Manela (New York: Cambridge University Press, 2018), 40–60.

11. Raymond Geselbracht, ed., *Foreign Aid and the Legacy of Harry S. Truman* (Kirksville, MO: Truman State University Press, 2015); Economic Cooperation Act of 1948, Public Law 80–472, 62 Stat. (1948): 137; Foreign Economic Assistance Act of 1950, 64 Stat. (1950): 204; Mutual Security Act of 1951, Public Law 82–165, 65 Stat. (1951): 373.

12. Rachel McCleary, *Global Compassion: Private Voluntary Organizations and US Foreign Policy since 1939* (New York: Oxford University Press, 2009); Joshua Mather, "Citizens of Compassion: Relief, Development, and State-Private Cooperation in US Foreign Relations, 1939–1973," PhD dissertation, Saint Louis University, 2015.

13. The Agricultural Trade Development and Assistance Act of 1954, Public Law 83–480, 68 Stat. (1954), 454–459. See also Kristin Albergh, *Transplanting the Great Society: Lyndon Johnson and Food for Peace* (Columbia: University of Missouri Press, 2009); Julia Irwin, "Raging Rivers and Propaganda Weevils: Transnational Disaster Relief, Cold War Politics, and the 1954 Danube and Elbe Floods," *Diplomatic History* 40:5 (2016), 893–921.

14. The ICA, which operated from 1955 to 1961, was the predecessor agency to the US Agency for International Development (USAID).

15. Operations Coordinating Board, "Foreign Disaster Relief Operations," September 14, 1956, rev. August 22, 1958, box 1660, Records of the American National Red Cross, RG ANRC, Series 4, NARA.

16. John Foster Dulles, Department of State Instruction CA-11026, June 16, 1958, Office of the Director, Subject Files of the Director, 1948–1966, box 58, Records of US Foreign Assistance Agencies, RG 469, NARA.

17. Foreign Assistance Act of 1961, Public Law 87-195, 22 USC. 2371 (1961).

18. USAID, "Foreign Disaster Emergency Relief: Introduction and Definition," M.S. 1562.1, October 9, 1964, box 1660, RG ANRC, Series 4, NARA.

19. Jarold Kieffer, Report from the Task Force on Enhancement of the A.I.D. Disaster Relief Function, October 12, 1974, Records Relating to Organizations, box 7, P/Entry 115, Records of the Agency for International Development, RG 286, NARA.

20. International Development and Food Assistance Act of 1975; American Red Cross, Committee on International Disaster Assistance Report, December 13, 1976, box 65, RG ANRC, Series 5, NARA.

21. Martel, *Grand Strategy in Theory and Practice*, 167.

22. Ibid., 167–208.

23. Martel, *Grand Strategy in Theory and Practice*, 209–243.

24. Brands, *What Good Is Grand Strategy?*, 17–101; Martel, *Grand Strategy in Theory and Practice*, 244–299.

25. Herbert Hoover Jr. to Andrew Goodpaster, October 22, 1955, Official File 113-F, Box 476, White House Central Files, Dwight D. Eisenhower Presidential Library, Abilene, KS; Paul Jameson to Paul Reinsch, August 12, 1916, CDF 893.48 (1910–1929), RG 59, NARA; Cyrus Woods to Department of State, December 1, 1923, CDF 894.48 (1910–1929), RG 59, NARA.

26. Norman Davis to General Malin Craig, February 15, 1939, box 1228, RG ANRC, Series 3, NARA.

27. The Agricultural Trade Development and Assistance Act of 1954, Public Law 480, 83rd Congress, 2nd Session, enacted July 10, 1954.

28. Irwin, "The 'Development' of Humanitarian Relief."

29. John Foster Dulles to Dwight Eisenhower, November 1, 1954, CDF 838.49 (1950–1954), RG 59, NARA; Julius Holmes to Secretary of State, September 16, 1962, CDF 888.49 (1960–1963), RG 59, NARA; Eric Kocher to Secretary of State, August 12, 1963, SNF-10 Yugoslavia, box 4224, RG 59, NARA.

30. An Act to provide for assistance in the development of Latin America and in the reconstruction of Chile, and for other purposes, Public Law 86-735, 86th Congress, 2nd Session, enacted September 8, 1960.

31. I discuss this more fully in Irwin, "Raging Rivers and Propaganda Weevils."

32. See, for instance, War Dept., Press Release, February 14, 1939, box 1228, RG ANRC, Series 3, NARA; US Army Attaché in Santiago Chile to Department of the Army, June 1, 1960, box 22, Entry 163, RG 59, NARA.

33. For a discussion of these problems and policies developed in response, see Foreign Disaster Relief Coordinator, "US Foreign Disaster Relief," September 23, 1975, Material Resources Committee/Disaster Files, box 101, Records of the American Council of Voluntary Agencies for Foreign Service, Rutgers University Special Collections, New Brunswick, NJ.

34. For a good synthesis of these developments, see George Herring, *From Colony to Superpower: US Foreign Relations since 1776* (New York: Oxford University Press, 2015).

35. John Rhea, *Annals of Congress*, House of Representatives, 12th Congress, 1st Session, April 29, 1812, 1348–1352.

36. For more specifics on these operations, see the Annual Reports of the Office of Foreign Disaster Assistance, https://www.usaid.gov/what-we-do/working-crises-and-conflict/crisis-response/resources/annual-reports (last accessed September 29, 2018).

37. For these amendments, see the Foreign Assistance Act of 1961, as Amended through P.L. 115–141, enacted March 23, 2018.

38. International Development and Food Assistance Act of 1975.

19

Denizens of a Center

Rethinking Early Cold War Grand Strategy

Ryan Irwin

Grand strategy is commonly defined as the alignment of unlimited aspirations with limited capabilities. "Whatever balance you strike," John Lewis Gaddis explains in *On Grand Strategy*, "there'll be a link between what's real and what's imagined: between your current location and your intended destination."[1] This chapter rethinks this balance by exploring how culture informs the way people perceive reality and imagination. It reaches back into the most commonly utilized historical example of grand strategy—the early Cold War—and revisits the period's most frequently analyzed protagonists: George Kennan, Walter Lippmann, and Dean Acheson.

However, the chapter is not about that era's seminal strategic doctrine: containment. Instead, it explores the relationship between law and power and argues for a new understanding of the intellectual architecture of the early Cold War.[2] At mid-century, American liberals shared a particular vocabulary about strategy—about realism itself—that reflected specific claims about natural law, sovereign interdependence, and World War I. Drawing on rarely examined primary documents, this chapter excavates this conversation and suggests that these assumptions informed how American leaders defined their aspirations and their capabilities. The United States might have waged the Cold War with a different set of assumptions and these undoubtedly became unpopular after the 1960s. However, they should not be glossed over for they elucidate how our predecessors once understood politics. At a time when US leaders are profoundly divided over the country's foreign policy, there is value in revisiting the concepts that animated and circumscribed an earlier generation's strategic thought.

Old Man and the Sea

This story begins in 1995 in a community called North Haven. Situated about half way up Maine's coastline, North Haven is a small island, reachable by ferry. Fewer than 400 people live there year-round, though the population swells in July and August. In August of that year, George Kennan retreated to North Haven to enjoy the ocean and catch up on some correspondence and reading. "Among the books that our hostess left in this cottage," he wrote in his diary on the evening of August 25, was "a [volume] of taped interviews," which he opened at random—he explained to himself (and anyone who might read his diary in the future)—whereupon he discovered interviews with Felix Frankfurter, Walter Lippmann, and Dean Acheson, "all older men and celebrities of the time when I was in my Planning Staff period" in the 1940s.[3]

The interviews prompted memories. In those "long-gone days," Kennan wrote, he had been "impressed by the reputations and authority" of these three individuals. However, he was "now something of a minor celebrity [himself]" and one who regarded himself "as the intellectual equal" of any of them. "It amuses me to think back on the deference with which I treated them all." Frankfurter, Kennan continued, was a "wily and formidable denizen of a political center dominated by lawyers, but neither a philosopher nor an impressive personality." Lippmann was a "fine writer with a brilliant mind" who "wrote too often and too much, his formidable critical quality carrying him around in circles until he found himself chasing his own tail." (Lippmann also resented Kennan, Kennan wrote, because he had penned the famous X-article.) Meanwhile, Acheson was "in every inch a man of the law," but he knew nothing about the American Foreign Service and failed to defend those who had been maligned by McCarthyism.[4]

The entry is both revealing and ironic. It is revealing because it confirms what many scholars have said of George Kennan. We tend to think of him at the center of the Establishment—the sage whose ideas "suffused" America's Cold War grand strategy, as Henry Kissinger put it in his review of John Lewis Gaddis's Kennan biography.[5] Yet Kennan saw himself as an outsider and he carried that mark with some resentment. Even better, the passage hints at why Kennan saw himself as an outsider. Age and style were factors; Kennan was a pensive, boyish-looking forty-year-old, surrounded, in his own mind, by self-assured fifty- and sixty-year-old "celebrities." However, more important was Kennan's craft. In his own words, Frankfurter and Acheson were men of the law, and Lippmann swam confidently in those waters. These were charismatic older men, but more specifically they were denizens of a center dominated by lawyers. Kennan was not a lawyer.

The entry indicates that Kennan opened this book of interviews at random on that late summer day and that he just happened to stumble on these interviews, which prompted his reflections. Irrespective of whether this claim is true, it is undoubtedly ironic—because if Kennan clumped these individuals together randomly, it was serendipitous. He may not have appreciated it, but the life paths of Frankfurter, Lippmann, and Acheson were profoundly entwined. Frankfurter and Lippmann had lived together during World War I. They met in Boston in 1914 and corresponded regularly, mostly arguing about the *New Republic*, a magazine that Lippmann edited in those years and Frankfurter shaped behind the scenes. When America entered the war in 1917, both men relocated to Washington to work for the Wilson administration. They had rooms together in a home owned by a mutual friend, dubbed the "House of Truth" by Oliver Wendell Holmes Jr., who frequently dined there with Lippmann and Frankfurter and other young progressives who hoped to change the world.[6]

In this same period, Frankfurter was mentoring Dean Acheson, who graduated from Harvard Law School in 1918, where Frankfurter taught. Frankfurter got Acheson a position clerking for Louis Brandeis at the Supreme Court, then secured Acheson his first government job in Franklin Roosevelt's Treasury Department, and was single-handedly responsible for getting Acheson back into government just before World War II. When Frankfurter became a Supreme Court justice in the late 1930s and relocated to Washington permanently, the two men walked from their homes in Georgetown to Foggy Bottom every morning, gossiping about their colleagues and debating the nature of power and the lessons of history.[7]

During the early Cold War, Dean Acheson and Walter Lippmann loomed larger in public debates about US foreign policy than any two Americans alive. Kennan authored the X-article, but Lippmann named the Cold War and published the most widely read books about the topic. Kennan had a staff at the State Department, but Acheson ran the place—he was the face of Truman's foreign policy after 1947 and arguably the architect of US grand strategy. Lippmann and Acheson did not get along, making Kennan's pairing, if truly random, surprisingly evocative. These were the heavyweights of Henry Luce's "American Century."[8]

Kennan's diary entry is useful because it reveals an assumption, which raises a question and clarifies this chapter's argument. The assumption is my own. In historiographical terms, this chapter takes for granted historian Robert Beisner's claim: "It is clearly an error to lump Acheson with Kennan as coeval advocates of containment, or, worse, to see Kennan as its founder and Acheson its executor."[9] Kennan saw himself as an outsider because he *was* an outsider. From this assumption comes the question: If Kennan wasn't really an insider in the early Cold War, who was?

While this chapter is interested in policy, it is principally about ideas, specifically the ideas of Acheson, Frankfurter, and Lippmann. It will argue that they were important insiders, and that the tension framed by Kennan—a tension rife with meaning—is a superb departure point to rethink the relationship between culture and grand strategy.

Man of the Law

About thirty years before Kennan found himself in North Haven, Maine, reflecting on those long-gone days, Dean Acheson delivered a speech to policy scholars at Indiana University in March 1965. Acheson had chosen a relevant question to unpack that day: What did it mean to be a man of the law? He was talking specifically about the relationship of law to US foreign policy and trying to historicize America's world role. His theme was ambivalence— "Ambivalences in American Foreign Policy" was the talk's title—and a good portion of what he had to say might be characterized as a lament against change.

It was not Acheson's finest hour. To the extent that historians have lingered on his words, they have focused on the racism they expressed. Acheson told his audience that young people reached maturity faster in warm climates and that the United Nations was becoming an orphanage run by "children whose development had been retarded." He lectured that non-white people needed to control their populations and give up their dreams of steel mills and airlines.[10] Those who have cited this speech and others like it have tended to zero in on these offensive and therefore quotable words. In them, this individual who is widely credited as a great statesman exposed his racial paternalism, warts and all.[11]

But the lecture, in Acheson's mind, was not about race—it was about law and power. He was complaining about change, specifically decolonization, but doing so to make a more capacious point, namely, that the rapid expansion of sovereign states after the mid-1950s had left American elites disoriented. Stripped of pretense, his argument was that too many people were saying too many things, and in the context of a truly global Cold War, his successors in Washington had become too comfortable accepting the path of least resistance—that is, more aid, more guns, fewer conditions—rather than pursuing a coherent grand strategy. More noteworthy, perhaps, was his suggestion that Americans themselves were responsible for their disorientation, and much of his talk was an attempt to explain how this confusion had come about.

For answers, Acheson looked to history. Since the nineteenth century, he argued, US foreign policy had been organized around a project: the creation of an interdependent, rule-based community of sovereign states. Acheson introduced this claim with a quote from Tennyson's *Locksley Hall*, and then laid out a fairly teleological narrative, underscoring the point that while the exact form of America's commitment had changed, this project—the establishment of an interdependent, rule-based community of sovereign states—had been the lodestar of United States history. His logic was somewhat muddled that day, but he had explained this lodestar clearly in other talks and articles. This project resonated because of the lessons of the nineteenth century, when the United States had proved that a cross-section of sovereign states could—albeit with some difficulty—create a durable union. If one did not appreciate American history, one could not really grasp what it meant to be a man of the law, because the law, in Acheson's formulation, is what held this interstate union together.[12]

This hinted at the source of American ambivalence in 1965. The legal profession in the United States had undergone a sea change during the interwar years, and not enough people, in Acheson's mind, understood this transformation, hence America's inability to orient itself to the tumult of the 1960s.[13] Of course this does not negate Acheson's racist words, but it does raise the question: What was he talking about? Up until the early twentieth century, Acheson continued, American lawyers had tended to tackle "community making" through the prism of natural law. In layman's terms, proponents of natural law believed that certain truisms—about sovereignty, property, and race—transcended politics. Because certain things were universally true, they had to be legally binding everywhere and always. American expansion on the frontier, in this regard, had created new states by extending law's geographic domain. Acheson believed this to be an unsustainable mindset.[14]

"The disciple of Natural Law seemed to Justice Holmes"—Acheson's muse in all things—"to be like the knight of romance." It was "not enough that you agreed that his lady was a very nice girl." No, "if you did not admit that she was the best girl that God ever made (or would make), you must fight." Because truth was True, resistance was futile.[15]

Acheson disavowed knights of romance because their aspirations outstripped their capabilities. But he took this criticism a step further by attacking natural law at its roots, emphasizing that no principle could ever create a "celestial city on earth."[16] In the United States—where judges, politicians, and industrialists dined at the same table—this mindset had actually prevented checks on powerful people. It was wiser to begin from the premise that conflict was an essential feature of human existence. Law should never try to transcend politics. It was a tool created by man, wielded by men, and its highest purpose was to canalize conflict between men.[17] Good lawyers, therefore, were consensus makers, not truth-tellers, and if America wanted to create an environment where sovereigns accepted their interdependence, it followed that legal declarations and universalist proclamations were useless. *Good* lawyers used institutions to cultivate "habits of productive dialogue," since unions only worked if conflict and negotiation were woven into their sinews.[18]

This made Acheson's conclusion somewhat ironic, because the problem America faced in 1965, in his mind, was that too many people disagreed with him. His theory of law—rooted in the distinction between truth-telling and consensus-making—had not squashed the natural law tradition, and because Acheson's viewpoint was contested, disorientation was inevitable. The real nut was the UN Charter. Some Americans (incorrectly) saw the United Nations through a universalist lens—they viewed the charter as a binding constitution that reflected True principles—while others (rightly) felt that it was merely a tool that facilitated negotiation between the United States and other sovereign powers. And if US elites themselves had not come to terms with this schism, how could policymakers adopt a coherent response to the demands of the decolonized world? Solving the ambivalences of American foreign relations did not require Americans to cast countries out of the United Nations, and Acheson did not want Americans to remove themselves from that organization.[19] In this particular setting on this particular day, he cast himself as an educator with two points. First, the United States needed to eschew universalism. Second, the United Nations was not a sacred cow. "The ambivalence in our foreign policy," Acheson concluded, "did not come from our tendency to swing between idealism and Machiavellianism." American ambivalence stemmed from the fact that not enough people were realists. Not enough people understood the law correctly.[20]

What did it mean to be a man of the law? Acheson's was a fairly thorough response: men of the law were leaders who used institutions to cultivate dialogue in order to avoid cataclysmic war, thereby nurturing sovereign states into accepting a status quo that assumed America's preponderance. Law did not enforce truth or justice; law held unions together. In other words, it was a tool, which, if used correctly, had the ability to guide how politics happened. Acheson wasn't really saying, "The United Nations had become an orphanage," even if the quip remains quotable.[21] His point was more nuanced. "People believe for some incomprehensible reason that the U.N. is some disembodied moral force apart from ourselves," he had explained to former president Truman in the late 1950s. "There can be no U.N. without guts and guns from us."[22] Acheson returned to this theme often in retirement, and he obviously sensed that his worldview was out of step with the times in 1965. Bloody Sunday, the turning point of the voting rights movement, unfolded just days before Acheson's Indiana University talk, and civil rights activists were unquestionably rehabilitating the universal rights tradition.

Denizen of the Center

Would anyone—in 1965 or earlier—have grasped the distinctions hidden within Acheson's lecture? Where did Acheson's ideas come from? Acheson wasn't just delivering speeches in 1965; he was also mourning his best friend's death. Felix Frankfurter had suffered a stroke in 1962, and while he regained some mobility afterward, his final years had been difficult. Nudged off the Supreme Court in 1962, his reputation was sullied by the perception that he had undercut the *Brown* decision.[23] Frankfurter passed in February 1965, but Acheson rarely left his side in those final years. Just days before traveling to Indiana, he had written a friend: "I thought I was prepared—[Felix] had been ill for so long—but found that I was not." In another letter, he wrote, "Ours was the most joyous association of my life. . . . Almost every day something happens which I immediately remind myself to tell Felix about."[24]

Acheson's ideas came from Frankfurter, which Acheson admitted openly and often. Although it may be more accurate to say that Frankfurter introduced Acheson to a contest—the fight against natural law—that Acheson embraced with considerable enthusiasm. Regardless, to appreciate the nature of their friendship requires going back in time another twenty years to a moment in October 1943. Frankfurter was arguably at the height of his influence in the 1940s. He had arrived in the United States from Austria as a child in 1890s—he spoke no English—and grew up in modest circumstances in New York City. Yet he distinguished himself in school and went to Harvard Law School, and then distinguished himself further as Henry Stimson's right hand during the Theodore Roosevelt and William Taft administrations, and then distinguished himself further still as a law professor at Harvard. From his nest in Cambridge, Frankfurter became one of Franklin Roosevelt's most trusted advisers, and while he declined to return to Washington in 1933, he exercised considerable influence over the new president's staffing and policy decisions. Frankfurter's influence eventually landed him a spot on the Supreme Court in 1939 and to a home in Georgetown around the corner from Acheson.[25]

On this particular day in 1943, the two men did what they did almost every day—they walked to work together. Frankfurter and Acheson did not record their conversations, but they occasionally sent notes to each other after they arrived at work, and on October 27 they had evidently had a stimulating back-and-forth about the relationship between legitimacy and power. Frankfurter was an excitable conversation partner, and he was still humming about a position he had staked out that morning. "Even a people's war," he wrote, "precludes cognizance by the people—[defined as] the press—of the deliberations and decisions of the Joint Staffs." Frankfurter and Acheson had debated World War II that morning, specifically how the US government should balance the ideal of transparency—a cornerstone of democratic governance—with the strategic imperatives of war. "All that the people are entitled to," he continued, "is assurance that the guiding considerations for military decisions is vanquishment of aggression . . . [so that] democracy may proceed secure from aggression and the fear of its reappearance."[26]

This is a simple enough concept to grasp. Less straightforward was Frankfurter's next point: this principle, he argued, could be elaborated to understand politics itself. The great travesty of World War I, Frankfurter suggested, had been Woodrow Wilson's commitment to "open covenants openly arrived at."[27] For Wilson, legitimacy came from ideas, hence his emphasis on the Fourteen Points. In Wilson's mind, in Frankfurter's retelling, if one laid down a True idea, foreign diplomats would be compelled to accept this principle as legitimate and coalesce around it, which would lead ipso facto to more power for the United States. This approach hadn't worked; Versailles was a disaster. The Allies had rejected Wilson's plan, the Senate had rejected Wilson's treaty, voters had rejected Wilson's party, and here were Acheson and Frankfurter, walking to work in the midst of a second "people's war." The unasked question of this note—which must have been the focus of their morning walk—seemed to be, How does one lead in a way that's both legitimate and effective? Wilson's answer, to lead from the front, had failed, and Hitler's alternative was a non-starter.

Frankfurter was answering the question head-on, and he articulated three distinct claims. First, legitimacy required communication and consistency. Week after week, American leaders had to establish a balance: "Precisely because so much [information] isn't open to the public, enough know-ledge must be conveyed so that confidence is established, and so that [the public] can be critical or at least raise questions, even though [the public] is disqualified from making constructive suggestions." Second, legitimacy did not come from ideas but from a style of exchange—or the act of being open without being transparent. "That's the rub, Dean. Because—as no one knows better than you—[governance] does not consist of abstractions." Maintaining this balance over time required a back and forth, not some uni-fied theory or grand proclamation. America's Grandest Strategy had nothing to do with moving from one place to another. It was, third, the establish-ment of an arena that cultivated conflict as a means to prevent aggression, nudging the public, in the process, to trust its leaders. "This presents us with one of the most exigent aspects of democracy, namely, how can the people be given enough knowledge to judge the validity of the policies pursued by their government when . . . the material that makes up that policy is necessarily withheld from them."[28]

Frankfurter drove his point home with an example. "To be spe-cific . . . I should say that the success of the [United Nations] Food Conference"—which had taken place earlier in 1943—"was due to the treat-ment of the smaller nations as real sharers, and not merely as third party bene-ficiaries vel non." This approach, this style of engagement, represented, in Frankfurter's mind, a clear departure from America's efforts in the previous world war. And "if I am right about the Food Conference, it indicates the kind of thing" that the United States might build upon going forward.[29] To state the obvious, Frankfurter was giving his former student a lecture. Equally ob-vious is the fact that some of these lessons stuck, since Frankfurter's phrase-ology animated some of Acheson's later writing. Less obvious, Frankfurter's comments hinted toward a playbook for achieving an objective that Acheson (and others) often acknowledged but rarely explained. If law was a tool created by man and wielded by men, so that smart leaders might avoid cataclysmic war and cultivate a community of sovereigns that accepted their interdependence with America, Frankfurter was answering an obvious question with surprising candor: How do you use this tool? How might leaders foster habits of productive dialogue? The answer wasn't straightforward but it was clear enough: be open but not transparent, avoid declarations, and delimit conflict to prevent aggression.[30]

Frankfurter's logic actually sheds useful light on Acheson's earlier distinction between idealism and Machiavellianism. If idealism was a code word for natural law—the idea that truths were self-evident and that their recognition would alter human behavior for the better—Machiavellianism evoked an era before Tennyson's *Locksley Hall*. The phrase conjured a time before the quest for a rule-based community of sovereigns took hold of America's imagination. Machiavellianism suggested a ruthlessness that felt Hitlerian to these denizens of the center. Acheson did not juxtapose idealism and realism—the more familiar contrast today—because realism for him was what Frankfurter was talking about on that October morning. It was the middle way between having the wrong definition of law (a la Wilson) and a world without law (a la Machiavelli). Or in Acheson's actual words, realism was the act of "keep[ing] one's wits and perceptions sharp"—of "employing one's native instinct for orderly work" by using the instruments at one's disposal.[31] Acheson's theory of law saturated this definition, shaping how he understood politics and the meaning of orderly work.

Bringing Acheson's speech and Frankfurter's note into dialogue gestures toward a wider claim. Despite the obvious differences between these artifacts—and they were written at different times for different audiences—there is a generational specificity to them. The shadow of World War I is present in the way Acheson framed his history lesson; it's there in Frankfurter's backhanded dismissal of Wilson's peace treaty. In the mind of its progenitors, realism—or whatever we call it—did not exist in dialectic opposition to Wilsonianism, but it was rooted in a debate about Wilson's presidency. For Acheson and Frankfurter, American world power was assumed. They did not need the twenty-eighth president of the United States to tell them that the United States was big and influential and connected to everything after World War I.[32] The issue—the only issue that mattered—was how America governed. And Acheson and Frankfurter's ideas about this question, expressed publicly and scribbled privately, were woven into a story that had 1919 at its center.

Chasing One's Tail

At the center of this story is one final moment, plucked from World War I. Did anyone share Frankfurter's and Acheson's worldview? An answer reveals itself if we turn to Walter Lippmann, arguably the most influential, widely read columnist of the twentieth century. He occupied a unique place in this milieu. Frankfurter and Lippmann were close friends during World War I. They met in 1914, thanks mostly to a New York State judge named Learned Hand, who saw Frankfurter and Lippmann as rising stars of the progressive movement.[33] At thirty-two years old, Frankfurter had just joined the faculty at Harvard Law, and he was a force of nature—combative, connected, and confident. At twenty-five years old, Lippmann had just become an editor at the *New Republic*. His first book had won him acclaim; Theodore Roosevelt announced in a review that Lippmann was the "brightest young mind in America."[34] Lippmann and Frankfurter were enormously ambitious; they were both Jewish; they were progressive nationalists who took cues from Herbert Croly and James Bryce, and idolized Oliver Wendell Holmes Jr.; and, most important, they saw themselves as intellectuals who could swim in the world of politics—in the world as it was.[35]

It's not hard to see why they enjoyed each other's company. Frankfurter had a brilliant sense of how things worked. He had served in government and possessed an intuitive grasp of power and how the US government operated, as well as a sharp legal mind that relished the minutiae of complex problems. Lippmann, in contrast, saw the big picture effortlessly. He was a better writer than Frankfurter and he used prose to clarify the stakes of the issues that interested him. If Frankfurter lost himself in details, Lippmann possessed that rare quality of being able to peer around new corners. When the United States entered the war in 1917, Frankfurter leaped at the opportunity to rejoin the War Department and dragged Lippmann with him to Washington. The two men worked as special assistants to Secretary of War Newton Baker. Frankfurter dealt initially with labor issues in the American West and then traveled to Paris, while Lippmann allied with Edward House and eventually became an adviser to President Wilson, who made him the principal interlocutor of the Inquiry that drafted America's peace plan.[36]

Lippmann and Frankfurter's correspondence from this period dwarfed the exchanges they had in writing with other people, and in subsequent years both men framed this period as formative. It was a time when their service forced them to reconsider their assumptions. In debating how to prevent a recrudescence of world war, for example, they elaborated arguments about American history. "Would it not be [wise] to take the specific countries involved [in the war] and study the nature and origin of Unions as well as the forces which call for separation," Frankfurter suggested to Lippmann in October 1917. "If American history revealed anything it was how to organize a union." Historically, he continued, successful unions had (1) protected their members against a common enemy; (2) maintained commercial relations or free trade; and (3) exploited conquered territory. This narrative of the American union—internalized by Acheson many years later—came within a free ranging back-and-forth about Frankfurter's experiences in Arizona, where he had been dispatched to ensure that copper miners did not strike. In Frankfurter's own mind, he was on the front lines of point three, since Arizona had joined the union only five years earlier.[37] "I'd like to bring you back east," Lippmann replied. "The moment I see a break in the line"—the moment a position opened on the Inquiry—"I will telegraph you."[38]

Colonel House ensured that that did not happen, and the war eventually left Frankfurter and Lippmann deeply frustrated about their president. In his *Reminiscences*, Frankfurter concluded, "Wilson was a great fellow for laying down postulates and avowing principles, but not for translating . . . these general principles into actual governance."[39] Lippmann wrote an entire book about the events of 1918.[40] The volume was an act of catharsis—he had been sidelined when Wilson arrived in Paris and he watched with dismay as the Fourteen Points were dismantled. His friend Harold Laski concluded that the "process of statesmanship left [Lippmann] . . . more critical, less facile. . . . He possesses a deeper [appreciation] that you don't find truth by skimming milk."[41] There is no question that Lippmann returned from Paris in a critical mood. His *New Republic* set the progressive world on fire by announcing its opposition to Wilson's peace treaty in May 1919, two months before Wilson returned home, and much of Lippmann's public writing from the time focused on the peace treaty's supposed fallacies: it blocked the triumph of industrial democracy, entrusted France with mastery of mainland Europe, and employed America's economic power to maintain the status quo.[42]

In private, Lippmann obsessed over a different issue—a deeper issue—of why Wilson had failed. This was the question that occupied Lippmann and

Frankfurter's correspondence during the summer of 1919. Lippmann was in New York and Frankfurter was still in Paris. "The bottom fact," Frankfurter wrote, in providing his autopsy of the just-signed treaty, "is that neither the President nor the Colonel had an adequate conception of what the problem of peace-making was." He continued, "I do not mean the actual detailed questions"—the questions handled by Lippmann's Inquiry in 1917 and 1918. No, for Frankfurter, America had failed because of Wilson's "technique." Wilson had no process to deal with the schemes he encountered in Paris—no way to co-opt his rivals into America's fold.[43]

Lippmann's response came a few days later. "You are quite right in saying that the bottom fact of the whole failure was a failure of technique." Wilson's intentions were "good enough," but "Paris [had] demonstrated that you cannot . . . improvise a structure of good will." Goodwill came from communication and consistency. "The United States should have secured a general agreement about the war's aims before it entered the war," rather than creating its postwar plans in secret, and the country desperately needed to create a "diplomatic service capable of diagnosing Europe." Without steady contact it would be impossible to translate America's economic influence into political power. "We never negotiated but simply enunciated," Lippmann concluded, and "what diplomatic service we had was insulated from the President, who worked by intimation from Colonel House, who had his own irresponsible, haphazard diplomatic coterie."[44]

Some historians might take issue with this conclusion that Wilson's style had foiled the treaty. What is more interesting than whether Lippmann and Frankfurter were correct is the fact that they obviously thought they were. And their conclusion about technique marked the beginning of an intellectual debate about power, one that resonated among young liberals after World War I. "The bottom fact of the whole failure was a failure of technique." This claim became a lodestar for denizens of a political center dominated by law, and it gestures toward a set of assumptions.

These assumptions animated mid-century liberal internationalism. Any knight of romance could invent a grand strategy, or some pristine concept on a piece of paper that claimed to be universally true. What the United States needed was not doctrine but a framework for being powerful. America's factories, its mines, its farms, its banks—its conquered territory—made it the Essential Nation. However, there was a difference between having power and being powerful, and this was the lesson of World War I, a lesson that politicized this cross-section of smart, ambitious, young lawyers. What the United

States needed was a strategic culture to understand its national power and a technique to bind sovereign states into some sort of functional union. This project was as old as the Northwest Ordinances, and it was a project whose historical urgency had been proved by the United States' rise after the Civil War. It was a project that rebuffed the Machiavellianism of a bygone age, just as it rejected Wilsonianism in 1919. The United States needed a workable union, not a celestial city on a hill. This project was rooted in institutions, yes, but anchored by a particular understanding of power: a paradigm that embraced openness (or public diplomacy) even as it eschewed transparency; a paradigm that treated smaller states as real sharers, not third party beneficiaries; a paradigm that welcomed conflict in order to temper aggression.

At the center of this story is a question that every young generation asks of those who came before: How will we do it better that our predecessors? Why does this particular answer matter? If we circle back to Kennan, perhaps the utility of a story like this one comes into sharper relief. First, Kennan wrote history and he has been the muse for some of the most influential historians of the late twentieth century. European geopolitics organized his ideas about the past—not nineteenth-century America—and they informed his vocabulary of grand strategy. There is some value in simply acknowledging a different conversation because, as Kennan admitted, Acheson, Frankfurter, and Lippmann mattered. Second, the story told here invites us to reflect on the Cold War's beginning stages and the lessons of that time for today. America's relationship with the Soviet Union was enormously important and containment obviously influenced many Washingtonians, but American elites might have tackled the Cold War with a very different set of ideas. This cohort's assumptions about power and strategy—about realism itself—stemmed from an ongoing, complex conversation about law and history.

If American grand strategy is reduced to anti-communism and history is presumed to start in 1945, then it is too easy to miss the fact that Americans constructed a truly mad number of institutions during the mid-twentieth century. This effort was not the opening act of a new story—these people were halfway through their lives. If we want to understand what American leaders meant when they talked of the "Free World," we should understand their assumptions about these institutions. Early Cold Warriors were builders determined to codify US power and they used institutions crafted by lawyers who had a very particular understanding of what they were doing and why. These were employees of Acheson, students of Frankfurter, and readers of Lippmann—individuals who cultivated interdependence even as they repudiated universalism, and did so while reveling in doubleness, contradiction, and irony. This particular cohort undoubtedly used coercive methods to ensure that these institutions worked in particular ways. But focusing on that fact alone overlooks the Cold War's relationship to this bigger, older, more interesting question: How do you govern an interdependent world? Describing mid-century liberals as "pragmatic" without unpacking the intellectual legwork here—without explaining where these ideas came from and why they resonated—distorts this past in profound ways. It makes complex things seem obvious.

Who cares? Mid-century liberals had blind spots, especially when it came to race and gender, and they were hubristic. They were self-proclaimed anti-imperialists, committed unapologetically to American power, which became an increasingly untenable intellectual premise in the decades after the 1960s. But they lived in a fact-based world, and their record—the way they understood national power, the way they crafted this center rooted in law—invites reexamination today, especially for anyone invested in the question: Can we do it better?

Notes

1. John Lewis Gaddis, *On Grand Strategy* (New York: Penguin, 2018), 21.
2. Hal Brands, *What Good Is Grand Strategy? Power and Purpose in American Statecraft from Harry S. Truman to George W. Bush* (Ithaca, NY: Cornell University Press, 2014), 1.
3. Frank Costigliola, ed., *The Kennan Diaries* (New York: Norton, 2014), 646.
4. Ibid., 647.
5. Henry Kissinger, "The Age of Kennan," *New York Times*, November 10, 2011; John Lewis Gaddis, *George F. Kennan: An American Life* (New York: Penguin, 2011).
6. Brad Snyder, *The House of Truth: A Washington Political Salon and the Foundations of American Liberalism* (New York: Oxford University Press, 2017); Jeffrey O'Connell and Nancy Dart, "The House of Truth: Home of the Young Frankfurter and Lippmann," *Catholic University Law Review* 35:1 (1985), 79–95.
7. Dean Acheson, *Morning and Noon: A Memoir* (Boston: Houghton Mifflin, 1965), especially chapters 3 and 9; Liva Baker, *Felix Frankfurter* (New York: Coward-McCann, 1969), 216. For context, Gregg Herken, *The Georgetown Set: Friends and Rivals in Cold War Washington* (New York: Alfred A. Knopf, 2014).
8. For reflections, David Milne, *Worldmaking: The Art and Science of American Diplomacy* (New York: Farrar, Straus and Giroux, 2015), chapter 4; Alan Brinkley, *The Publisher: Henry Luce and His American Century* (New York: Knopf Doubleday, 2010).

9. Robert Beisner, "The Secretary, the Spy, and the Sage: Dean Acheson, Alger Hiss, and George Kennan," *Diplomatic History* 27:1 (2003), 13.

10. "Ambivalences in American Foreign Policy," March 5, 1965, box 52, Dean Acheson papers, Yale University Manuscripts & Archives.

11. Douglas Brinkley, *Dean Acheson: The Cold War Years, 1953-1971* (New Haven, CT: Yale University Press, 1992), chapter 10; as well as Robert Beisner, *Dean Acheson: A Life in the Cold War* (New York: Oxford University Press, 2009), 128–134, 529–533, 625–626; James Chace, *Acheson: The Secretary of State Who Created the American World* (New York: Simon & Schuster, 1998), 107–108.

12. "Ambivalences in American Foreign Policy."

13. For context, Edward Purcell Jr., "American Jurisprudence between the Wars: Legal Realism and the Crisis of Democratic Theory," *American Historical Review* 75:2 (1969), 424–446.

14. For introduction, Morton J. Horwitz, *The Transformation of American Law, 1780–1860* (Cambridge, MA: Harvard University Press, 1977).

15. "Ambivalences in American Foreign Policy."

16. Ibid.

17. Jonathan M. Zasloff, "Dean's List: Power, Institutions, and Achesonian Diplomacy," *Public Law & Legal Theory Research Paper Series, Research Paper No. 08-15* (2008), 1–19; Jonathan M. Zasloff, "More Realism about Realism: Dean Acheson and the Jurisprudence of Cold War Diplomacy," *Public Law & Legal Theory Research Paper Series, Research Paper No. 07-01* (2007), 1–47; Jonathan M. Zasloff, "Power and International Law," *Public Law & Legal Theory Research Paper Series, Research Paper No. 06-29* (2006), 64–87.

18. "Ambivalences in American Foreign Policy." For context, Morton J. Horwitz, *The Transformation of American Law, 1870–1960* (New York: Oxford University Press, 1992); William W. Fisher III, Morton J. Horwitz, and Thomas A. Reed, eds., *American Legal Realism* (New York: Oxford University Press, 1993).

19. "Ambivalences in American Foreign Policy."

20. Ibid.

21. Brinkley, *Dean Acheson*, 301.

22. Harry Truman and Dean Acheson, *Affection and Trust: The Personal Correspondence of Harry S. Truman and Dean Acheson, 1953-1971* (New York: Knopf, 2010), 156–157.

23. Leonard Baker, *Brandeis and Frankfurter: A Dual Biography* (New York: New York University Press, 1984), chapter 24.

24. Acheson to Noel Gilroy, March 15, 1965, and Acheson to Erwin Griswold, March 22, 1965, in David McLellan and David Acheson, *Among Friends: Personal Letters of Dean Acheson* (New York: Dodd, Mead, 1980), 265–266.

25. For context, Max Freedman, ed., *Roosevelt & Frankfurter: Their Correspondence, 1928-1945* (Boston: Little, Brown, 1967); Joseph Lash, *From the Diaries of Felix Frankfurter: With A Biographical Essay and Notes* (New York: Norton, 1975); Sujit Raman, "Felix Frankfurter and His Protégés: Re-examining the 'Happy Hot Dogs,'" *Journal of Supreme Court History* 39:1 (2014), 79–106; Peter Irons, *The New Deal Lawyers* (Princeton, NJ: Princeton University Press, 1982); and Jeremy Kessler, "The

Administrative Origins of Modern Civil Liberties Law," *Columbia Law Review* 114:5 (2014), 1083–1166.

26. Felix Frankfurter to Dean Acheson, October 27, 1943, box 19, Felix Frankfurter papers, Library of Congress (LoC).

27. Ibid.

28. Ibid.

29. Ibid.

30. For context, Jeffrey Hockett, *New Deal Justice: The Constitutional Jurisprudence of Hugo L. Black, Felix Frankfurter, and Robert H. Jackson* (New York: Rowman & Littlefield, 1996).

31. "Ambivalences." Acheson elaborated this theme in "Ethnics in International Relations Today" and "The Real and Imagined Handicaps of Our Democracy in the Conduct of Its Foreign Relations," in *This Vast External Realm* (New York: Norton, 1973).

32. Adam Tooze, *The Deluge: The Great War and the Remaking of Global Order* (New York: Penguin, 2014)

33. Constance Jordan, ed., *Reason and Imagination: The Selected Correspondence of Learned Hand* (New York: Oxford University Press, 2013), 9–66.

34. Ronald Steel, *Walter Lippmann and the American Century* (Boston: Little, Brown, 1980), 63–64.

35. Charles Forcey, *The Crossroads of Liberalism: Croly, Weyl, Lippmann and the Progressive Era, 1900–1925* (New York: Oxford University Press, 1961); Edward Stettner, *Shaping Modern Liberalism: Herbert Croly and Progressive Thought* (Lawrence: University of Kansas Press, 1993).

36. Michael Parrish, *Felix Frankfurter and His Times: The Reform Years* (New York: Free Press, 1982), chapters 5–6; Steel, *Walter Lippmann*, chapters 10–13.

37. Felix Frankfurter to Walter Lippmann, December 3, 1917, box 77, Frankfurter papers, LoC.

38. Walter Lippmann to Felix Frankfurter, in John Morton Blum, ed., *Public Philosopher: Selected Letters of Walter Lippmann* (New York: Ticknor and Fields, 1985), 75–76.

39. Harlan Phillips, *Felix Frankfurter Reminiscences: An Intimate Portrait* (New York: Reynal, 1960), 159.

40. Walter Lippmann, *The Political Scene: An Essay on the Victory of 1918* (New York: Henry Holt, 1919).

41. Harold Laski to Oliver Wendell Holmes Jr., in Mark DeWolfe Howe, ed., *Holmes-Laski Letters* (New York: Antheneum, 1963).

42. Walter Lippmann to Raymond Fosdick, August 15, 1919, box 9, Walter Lippmann papers, Yale University Manuscripts and Archives (YUMA).

43. Felix Frankfurter to Walter Lippmann, July 11, 1919, box 77, Frankfurter papers, LoC.

44. Walter Lippmann to Felix Frankfurter, July 20, 1919, box 10, Lippmann papers, YUMA.

20

Reproductive Politics and Grand Strategy

Laura Briggs

In the summer of 2017, the Trump administration was skewered in the press following a *New York Times* story about Donald Trump Jr. meeting with Russian lawyer Natalia Veselnitskaya during the presidential campaign in order to get negative information about Hillary Clinton. Asked about the meeting for the article, the White House denied that it was even about Clinton: initially, the president declared that the response would be to "describe the meeting as unimportant. He wanted the statement to say that the meeting was about . . . the adoption of Russian children," the *Washington Post* reported.[1]

Although minimizing the significance of the meeting proved difficult, and it figured prominently in the Mueller Report and subsequent impeachment hearings, in this chapter I am interested in the adoptions. Why would saying it was "just" about adoptions seem to Trump like a good strategy for making the meeting go away as a political problem? Russia's ban on allowing children to be adopted by US residents was that country's retaliation for the Magnitsky Act, an Obama administration law that imposed financial and travel sanctions on certain Russian officials. This US restriction was a response to human rights abuses and corruption that had led to the death of Sergei Magnitsky, a Russian lawyer allegedly beaten to death in prison for his cooperation with a US businessman in exposing Russian fraud. The New York meeting involving Donald Trump Jr. and Natalia Veselnitskaya apparently was concerned with the question of renegotiating the economic sanctions of the Magnitsky Act imposed by a sitting president (Obama) against representatives of a major world power (Russia), and the meeting's major players were campaign members of the opposition party's candidate (Trump)—all of which would seem to underscore rather than minimize the importance of the meeting. But the Trumpian strategy of saying it was "just" about adoptions relied on an old and familiar gendered logic for rendering certain kinds of politics, stories, and economic relations irrelevant to the work of states: it was about the private world of reproduction and families—in a word, feminine.

This chapter seeks to go beyond the Magnitsky Act or even impeachment to argue that, *pace* Donald Trump, transnational adoption and reproductive politics more broadly have actually been quite important to US foreign policy, and are, in fact part of US grand strategy. They do much more political work than is generally acknowledged, in ways that merit scholarly attention. Too often, scholars of grand strategy have relied on the same gendered logic that Trump did, in which reproductive politics belong to a feminized, private world of children and families rather than to the robust, masculine world of politics, militaries, and foreign policy. That logic has made the signal importance of things like transnational adoption, overpopulation, and birth control invisible in studies of grand strategy. This chapter seeks to rectify that oversight, restoring reproductive politics to its rightful place as a real and important element in grand strategy.

Although feminist scholarship on overpopulation and the role of the US government in pushing birth control on other nation's populations has been raising these issues for decades, it was Foucault's notion of biopolitics that most nearly brought the attention of significant numbers of scholars to the work of reproductive politics in statecraft. Biopolitics refers to the role of states in fostering (and measuring) the life of some and the death of others—to make live and let die. It is why the United States has a decennial census, for example—to quantify the "life" it governs. It can also be about building the right kind of nation. Latin American policies of "whitening" their populations, for example, were concerned with who reproduced with whom, as was the global project of eugenics, extending across many nations, including, importantly, the United States and Nazi Germany. Miscegenation laws in the United States tried to limit unruly, interrracial reproduction as a threat to the racial logic of governance. *Jus soli* (birthright citizenship) and even more, *jus sanguis* (the acquisition of citizenship through ancestry), and *partus sequitur ventrem* (in which the enslaved or free status of offspring follow the condition of their mothers) are all key legal doctrines about citizenship and freedom that derive from relations of reproduction. If we think of reproduction beyond the mere fact of producing offspring, to attend to their care and raising—social reproduction, in Marx's term—we find that questions of public schooling, health, and welfare are very much on the agenda of states.[2]

This chapter argues that reproductive politics has long been part of US grand strategy. It offers a three-part chronology, borrowing a definition of grand strategy from Hal Brands, as part of the "logic that guides leaders seeking security in a complex and insecure world."[3] Brands's argument about grand strategy as a *logic* is important, because it adds a necessary layer of complexity, insisting that grand strategy is more than just a set of principles from on high that govern foreign policy—uniting the military, the economic, the diplomatic, and the humanitarian—that emerged full-blown from the head of a Henry Kissinger or a George Kennan. In this sense, grand strategy may extend beyond what is embedded in policy documents; it can also be a cultural logic that provides a general framework of what makes sense in any particular time or place. It may be reliant on private actors as well as policymakers, and it takes in a broad swath of political leaders, including those implementing the kinds of humanitarianism that has been increasingly privatized since the 1980s.

Building on Brands's notion, then, this chapter offers a narrative of how reproductive politics became grand strategy. First, there was birth control as a technological fix for overpopulation that was embedded in a national security memo advocated by Henry Kissinger as part of containment policy. Birth control was advanced as a remedy for civil strife and regional conflicts, identified as a contest over resources caused by too many people—overpopulation. This national security effort put the US government in the birth control business, which became controversial under Ronald Reagan, who advanced the 1980 Mexico City policy—a gift to evangelical Christian supporters—that halted any aid to organizations that supported abortion rights in its public statements. In this second phase, the Republican Party explicitly allied itself with international evangelical Christian and Catholic efforts to use abortion (and later "gender ideology") as a political issue, particularly in Latin America and Eastern Europe, to affect elections and hone a new kind of transnational right, organized in relation to anti-communism and gender politics. Bill Clinton reinstated the historic national security-based support for birth control organizations internationally, inaugurating an era in which Democrats backed reproductive health groups; then, with George W. Bush, Republicans opposed it. The third issue considered here is the forced disappearance of children and transnational adoptions. Beginning with the Ford administration and Kissinger and continuing through Clinton, the United States supported Latin American regimes—from Argentina to El Salvador to Guatemala—that disappeared children and offered them in adoptions to the United States and Europe in order to prevent the rearing of a new generation of communists. Beginning in the postwar 1950s and continuing through the era of soft power, a doctrine of free trade, libertarianism, and downsizing of state welfare measures from South Korea to Guatemala relied in part on compelling desperate single mothers to place their children in international adoptions rather than turning to state supports. As private organizations and evangelical Christian religious groups assumed greater power in influencing US foreign policy, adoption and the movement of refugee children were increasingly the responsibility of private actors. It is worth exploring in detail the process through which that came to be, as it holds important lessons about the interrelationship between official foreign policy and what Elizabeth Bernstein calls, in a different context, "militarized humanitarianism."[4]

Overpopulation and Family Planning

Truman set the stage for thinking about overpopulation with his 1949 inaugural address. It was expressly a grand strategy blueprint—bringing together economic, military, diplomatic, and other means to attain foreign policy ends—to contain communism in the aftermath of World War II. Diplomatically, he said, the United States would uphold and strengthen the authority of the United Nations. Economically, the United States would support the European recovery from the war and encourage free trade policies. Militarily, the United States would support a collective defense pact among the nations that would become NATO as well as a parallel one in the Western Hemisphere—and, setting up the problem that would come in Viet Nam, he promised "military advice and equipment" to nations that would advance "freedom." Finally—and this is where birth control entered—Truman's fourth point advanced the notion of a development policy and the transfer of scientific and economic knowledge to the impoverished of the world:

> More than half the people of the world are living in conditions approaching misery. Their food is inadequate. . . . Their economic life is primitive and stagnant. Their poverty is a handicap and a threat both to them and to more prosperous areas. . . . I believe that we should make available to peace-loving peoples the benefits of our store of technical knowledge in order to help them realize their aspirations for a better life. . . . Our aim should be

to help the free peoples of the world, through their own efforts, to produce more food, more clothing, more materials for housing, and more mechanical power to lighten their burdens.[5]

The notion that technical assistance could alleviate poverty—including "inadequate food"—was the seed of an overpopulation policy that ultimately centered on birth control as precisely that kind of technological fix.

However, it was another twenty years before the United States took up the promotion of family planning as a foreign policy. Following what was subsequently known just as (Truman's) Point Four, some began to argue for a US population policy, although Truman's own administration did not. The Eisenhower administration, fearing backlash from the Catholic Church and other sexual conservatives, was also reluctant. Indeed, Eisenhower himself said that he could not "imagine anything more emphatically a subject that is not a proper political or government activity or function or responsibility. . . . This government will not, so long as I am here, have a positive policy doctrine in its program that has to do with this problem of birth control. That's not our business."[6] After he retired from office, however, he came around, and told a Senate committee in 1965 that overpopulation was "one of the most, if not the most, critical problems facing mankind today," and that the United States government should be in the family planning business after all.[7] It took a Catholic, John F. Kennedy, to open the door to funding population control, and Johnson and then Nixon made birth control a cornerstone of foreign aid in the 1960s and '70s.

Throughout this period, advocates of family planning lobbied these administrations. Scholars, funders, and activists sought to persuade the foreign policy establishment that containment was more than a military policy; it also referred to population and children—"containing" the number of children would lead to less poverty, and more wealth meant people would be less inclined to "go over" to communism and its seductive promises to the poor. In 1948, two bestselling books framed overpopulation in Trumanesque terms: Fairfield Osborn's *Our Plundered Planet* and William Vogt's *Road to Survival*. While eugenics was undergoing its postwar nosedive in respectability, and Malthusianism had been in disrepute since the early twentieth century, these two environmentalists helped revive both. Vogt urged the Truman administration to link overpopulation to foreign aid, arguing that "any aid we give should be made contingent on national programs leading toward population stabilization."[8] Together, they made "overpopulation" a household word; reinvigorated the Malthusian concept that population would overrun resources; and put it to work on a global scale, building the concept that not just nations or regions but the planet itself was under siege by a "population explosion."[9] Others, like Elmer Pendell, wrote, "Population causes frequently lead to political consequences. Sometimes people have bartered their freedom for the promise of food. Sometimes people have rebelled against government because their poverty was too bitter."[10] Another influential group in tilting public opinion toward family planning was the Hugh Moore Fund; this organization gave money and a catchy title to Stanford biologist Paul Ehrlich to write what became a bestseller, *The Population Bomb*, which argued that world population growth represented a political and ecological threat. (His wife, Anne Ehrlich, was an uncredited co-author.)[11] Famine, said the Ehrlichs, would become widespread by 1970, because food production couldn't possibly keep up with the birth rate. Together with *Famine 1975!*, published by William and Paul Paddock in 1967, the overpopulation popularizers were full of attention-getting apocalyptic language. The Paddocks argued for the United States to triage the places that could be saved, offering food and other foreign aid only to those places where the birth rate showed signs of declining. India, for example, should be written off.[12]

While these intellectuals and outsiders did not move the needle on policy, they did build considerable broad support for a foreign policy that linked aid to birth control. Changing federal policy received a massive assist when, as critic Steve Weissman put it, "the Population Bomb became a Rockefeller baby." John D. Rockefeller III organized the powerful Population Council, which brought together conservationists, Planned Parenthood leaders, and social scientists. He quickly involved other prominent foundations—Ford, Carnegie, Mellon, the Mott Trust—to urge national action on overpopulation. Rockefeller was concerned about decolonization leading to communism. "The restlessness produced in a rapidly growing population is magnified by the preponderance of youth," according to the Rockefeller Brothers Fund's *Prospect for America*, the final report of a project directed by Henry Kissinger, whose goal was "to clarify national purposes and objectives." The report added, "In a completely youthful population, impatience to realize rising expectations is likely to be pronounced. Extreme nationalism has often been the result."[13]

The Population Council persuaded John F. Kennedy's administration to begin quietly laying the groundwork for a population policy. The US military began offering birth control to service members' families, and the National Institutes of Health started research on human reproduction.[14] Meanwhile, the council was gaining influence with the Planned Parenthood Federation of America (PPFA) and began urging the organization to launch some "experiments" that would make the case for international family planning efforts, including one targeting "Depressed Socio-Economic Groups in New York City" (which is to say, black and Puerto Rican residents) and another "To Make Family Planning Available to the Southern Negro through Education, Motivation, and Implementation of Available Services." PPFA reached out to the civil rights group, the Southern Christian Leadership Council, and together they formed a joint program in Philadelphia.[15]

"Family planning," as both an anti-poverty measure in the United States and an important part of foreign aid, took root and then flourished in the Johnson administration. Within months after Kennedy's assassination in 1963, Johnson signed off on allowing the US Agency for International Development (USAID) to provide health services and population surveys in developing countries. In 1965, two things happened: a widely discussed famine in India seemed to give lie to the possibility of industrialization as a way out of poverty, and Ernest Gruening held Senate hearings on over-population (a concern he had developed as head of the Puerto Rico Reconstruction Administration from 1935 to 1937). By 1967, the Johnson administration had made the US government the largest supplier of birth control in the world, through the combined efforts of the Department of Health, Education, and Welfare (HEW) and foreign aid. That year, he said in his State of the Union speech: "Next to the pursuit of peace, the really great challenge of the human family is a race between food supply and population." In Indochina, the USAID distributed birth control pills to halt the spread of communism in South Vietnam, while the Defense Department dropped na-palm and bombs.[16]

In Nixon's White House, population matters were considered an im-portant question of national security and the subject of internal palace in-trigue and warring factions (like so much else). In 1969, Nixon sent a Special Message to Congress that it in turn endorsed, calling for a broad range of activities related to population growth, including measures to increase re-search on birth control methods, to encourage social science study of pop-ulation growth and food supply, to train more people in the population and family planning fields, and to make more family planning money available domestically. Most significantly, John D. Rockefeller finally got his official commission, chairing a twenty-four-member presidential Commission on Population Growth and the American Future. It spent two years preparing a report, released in 1972, that advocated widespread sex education, particularly in schools; availability of birth control for all, including minors, subsidized by the government; abortion on demand; the passage of the Equal Rights Amendment (ERA); increased research on population control; and measures to halt the employment of undocumented immigrants.[17] At the ceremony to accept the Rockefeller commission's report, Nixon instead denounced it—particularly its advocacy of abortion and birth control for minors (although not the draconian measures against immigrants). Rockefeller blamed this sudden lack of faith from Nixon and his advisers on activism by Catholics, which was likely right—the Catholic Church was very concerned about overpopulationist rhetoric, believing that the analysis was wrong and that the remedy was sinful at best and coercive at worst.[18] (In this, they were actually in agreement with the feminist and non-feminist left.)

A couple of years later, though, members of Nixon's administration tried again—and this time, the results were lasting. The second time around, family planning was urged not as a quasi-feminist social policy linked to the ERA but as a national security measure, most likely led by Kissinger himself. Kissinger chaired a new joint study, together with representatives from the departments of Defense and Agriculture, the CIA, and USAID to study the impact of population on "U.S. security and overseas interests." While Nixon was impeached before the committee finished its work, the final product was presented to Brent Scowcroft—national security adviser to both Gerald Ford and George H. W. Bush, the latter a protégé of Kissinger. The resulting National Security Memo 200 argued that rapid population growth resulted in exceeding the capacity of states to provide services, resulting in slums. The committee wrote that urban slum dwellers, could be "a volatile, violent force that threatens stability," and it blamed "separatist actions" and "revolutionary actions" generated by these factors. Further, the committee argued that the root causes of many "violent conflicts in developing areas" were not political, as they appeared on the surface, but demographic. It was an influential report, and led Scowcroft and Ford to release National Security Decision Memorandum 314, which addressed the issues that had been raised and remained in force through the Carter administration and beyond.[19]

The Kissinger-Scowcroft memoranda had a profound effect on US foreign policy, ensuring that "family planning assistance" would be a significant part of foreign aid and continue to grow, up to the present day. Initially a containment measure, it stayed in force even as US grand strategy changed. Much of it was routed through the International Planned Parenthood Federation, with additional funds flowing through the United Nations Fund for Population Activities. The largest single source of funds to family planning, however, was USAID, which by the time of the Carter administration was allocating hundreds of millions of dollars to international family planning organizations in the name of political stability.[20]

The problem with the overpopulation thesis, it bears noting, is that it isn't true. In the intervening half century since it was elaborated by demographers and policymakers, the global population has doubled, but famine and air and water pollution—the things that were supposed to make us concerned about overpopulation, according to its mid- and late twentieth-century proponents—have declined precipitously, and overall living standards have risen. Even in the 1960s and '70s, the Malthusian argument—that population would outstrip the food supply—was sharply criticized by the left, from feminists concerned about the coercive use of birth control to Marxists who pointed out—quiet correctly, in hindsight—that famine had nothing to do with absolute food supply and everything to do with political questions of its distribution, including price gouging, hoarding, and the influence of foreign imperialism.[21] Overpopulation, like the Green Revolution and development in general, reproduced modernization's blind spot: it promoted technology without context, inventing solutions to problems it only dimly understood, made worse by the desire to find one-size-fits-all solutions for the whole "underdeveloped" world. It identified the cause of "Third World" poverty not as the history of colonialism or economic forms but as ignorant women and too-large families, and found solutions in suburban American-style domesticity and liberal democracy. In this way, birth control provided a response to the Soviet Union's accusations of US imperialism and a grounding for a patriotic American nationalist overreach, following the US military to Indochina and advisers to the installation and support of authoritarian regimes in Latin America.

Predictably, policymakers' demands about what impoverished US Americans and people overseas did while they were having sex did not work well. When people did not seem to be doing what policymakers thought was right for them, states—including the United States—resorted to force. Reports of forced sterilization in HEW facilities and Indian Health Services hospitals quickly began to surface, as did reports of infection and death.[22] In India, sterilization camps, mostly for rural woman (after an abortive attempt to sterilize men ended Indira Gandhi's political career) have been the cornerstone of India's population policies since the 1970s, with the government funding about 4 million tubal ligations a year this way, with periodic crises about coercion, consent, and safety. (A recent crisis, following the serious illness and death of dozens of women from infection in 2014, reinvigorated calls to replace this approach with one favoring injectable contraceptives. The usual mix of humanitarian and state organizations stepped in to back the shots—the Bill and Melinda Gates Foundation, USAID, and the government of India. It's a measure of how much has stayed the same since the mid-1970s pronouncements about security and global stability—or rather, how much the population and "family planning" establishment has grown.)[23]

Yet if all these years of alarmist overpopulation rhetoric have left a legacy of state policies of sterilization and even coercion, it has also been a means through which feminist movements throughout the world have won for women new opportunities to control their own fertility through the availability of contraceptives. As I argue in *Reproducing Empire*, in Puerto Rico, alongside the rhetoric about the need for fertility limitation in the service of modernity and the nation, we find a feminist movement demanding that women have the ability to limit their fertility in order to be freed from endless childbearing, have greater roles in the public sphere, and have less onerous responsibilities at home. And while Kissinger may not have cared much about women's rights, not only US global security empires but also women's rights were wounded by what was to come: Reagan's Mexico City policy.[24]

By the 1980s, the most alarmist of the Malthusian, overpopulationist discourse was in decline. No books on the bestseller list argued for an imminent danger of babies causing shocks to the food supplies. With the election of Ronald Reagan seven years after the federal legalization of abortion with *Roe v. Wade* in 1973, a new formation was on the horizon: the globalization of evangelical Christian concerns about abortion, and somewhat later, Catholic concerns about "gender ideology." While the Catholic Church had long put the brakes on birth control and abortion (voluntarily and coercive), white evangelicals were a newly emergent player.[25] Further, in 1980 China had finally taken the step proposed by overpopulationists: to offer a combination of incentives and fines to restrict couples to having one child. In the context of US anti-communism, that was sufficient to push the tide of public opinion in the opposite direction in the United States. While the hundreds of millions of dollars of family planning money passing through the State Department and USAID to foreign NGOs had never encompassed funding for abortions,

some NGOs had included pregnancy termination among their array of services, albeit with strictly separated monies. In the face of conservative and
Christian right pressure to do something about China's one-child policy
abroad and legal abortion at home, the Reagan administration settled on the
Mexico City Policy, announced in 1984 at a population conference in that
global city. It said: "The United States will no longer contribute to separate
nongovernmental organizations which perform or actively promote abortion as a method of family planning in other nations." Since it also limited
funds for any organization that advocated abortion legalization or routinely
informed its clients about abortion services elsewhere, it became known as
the "global gag rule" for its limitations on speech. Since much of the money
was run through the International Planned Parenthood Federation, which
frequently worked with women's rights advocates to liberalize abortion laws,
the policy clamped down on a great deal of activity.[26]

In subsequent years, the Mexico City policy became a key Republican
issue. Where Reagan and then Bush kept it in force through executive order,
Bill Clinton rescinded it in 1993. Congressional Republicans passed a law
that put it back in effect from 1999 to 2000, but since then, it has seesawed
as US policy depending on the party affiliation of the president. In 2017,
as Donald Trump renewed it, the Mexico City policy had been in effect
for seventeen of the previous thirty-two years. While the now-declassified
Kissinger-Scowcroft policy related to overpopulation, National Security
Decision Memorandum 314, is still officially US policy in ways that matter
for the Mexico City policy, overpopulation has largely passed into the dor-
mant lexicon of containment as US grand strategy.

As containment, anti-communism, and birth control to remedy overpopulation declined as grand strategy, at least on the Republican side, an emergent soft power doctrine placed anti–birth control activism in relationship
to a complicated formation on the Christian right: opposition to so-called
gender ideology. Although gender ideology is an unfamiliar phrase to most
in the United States, it is a way of characterizing the purported evils of feminist and trans movements—akin to claiming the importance of "traditional
family values"—that has played a surprisingly large role in diverse locations
in Eastern Europe and Latin America. The term—which has no real, fixed
meaning—emerged in response to discussion of birth control at the Cairo
Conference on Population and Development in 1994 and the Fourth World
Women's Conference in Beijing in 1995 (famously attended by Hillary
Clinton as First Lady). These conferences identified a rather anodyne notion

of "gender equality" (including things like the education of women) as a major factor in reducing birth rates. As a result, the term "gender" (as opposed to sex) appeared for the first time in intergovernmental documents.

These developments were attacked by Pope John Paul II and US conservative Catholic writer Dale O'Leary, who responded with a book, *The Gender Agenda*. They saw "gender" as a new front in their war against birth control and abortion. Despite the original association with Catholicism, gender ideology has proven a flexible concept for many right-leaning Christian formations to rally around. It has offered fertile ground for many rightist authoritarian populist formations, playing a role in the election of Jair Bolsonaro in Brazil and Viktor Orban in Hungary (both pledged their opposition to gender ideology); upended the plebiscite on the peace accords in Colombia (where the FARC was said to support forced abortion and gender ideology); and consolidated right political formations from Poland to Chile. It has even appeared, albeit in muted form, in the Donald Trump administration in the United States, as the rejection of the existence of transgender people and opposition to international treaties protecting women from "gender-based" violence.[27]

From overpopulation to the Mexico City policy to "gender ideology," then, arguments about birth control have advanced US foreign policy. Reproductive politics in this sense have been part of the cultural logic that emerged as US grand strategy.

Adoption

If population policy and family planning began as a private, Rockefeller-funded effort and became a state one, transnational adoption had the opposite trajectory: it began as a state issue and became more privatized, although still less so than most people think. Transnational adoption is not even approximately the series of individual and family decisions that many people consider it to be; it requires visas and state-to-state agreements under any circumstances. During and after World War II, the transnational movement of children without their parents was done in accordance with broader state policies—anti-fascism and anti-communism were the ideologies that determined what children went where, and which ones stayed put. By the mid-1980s, as the United States engaged in semi-clandestine warfare in Central America (think, for example, of Iran-Contra as an indication of how it was both overt and cloaked), militaries and paramilitaries led by people trained at the School of the Americas in Fort Benning, Georgia, engaged in the disappearance of children in El Salvador and Guatemala as a counterinsurgency tactic—children who were sometimes transnationally adopted. The real explosion of the numbers of children involved in transnational adoption, however, took place in the aftermath of trade liberalization in the 1990s as children followed other goods in being both highly profitable and readily available (at least in Guatemala and China, significant coercion and even kidnapping assured their availability.)[28] Those same numbers began an abrupt collapse in 2008, however, with the US ascension to the Hague Convention on International Adoption, which mandated more state involvement in adoptions and expanded the rights of birth parents to challenge the expatriation of their children. Finally, the most intriguing suggestion that some prominent players saw transnational adoption as part of US grand strategy was the Families for Orphans Act—an ambiguous but highly suggestive piece of proposed legislation that attempted to link trade, debt, and other financial assistance to a country's willingness to send their children abroad in adoptions.[29]

The idea of transnational adoption was born out of relief programs in and after World War II. In Europe, the Kindertransport of mostly Jewish refugee children from Nazi-controlled areas to Britain and the evacuation of Basque children from fascist Spain were two of the best-known efforts. The United States mostly refused Jewish child-refugees from fascism, even as it accepted British children, relying on a rhetoric that Jewish children were prevented from being admitted because they were "likely to become a public charge" (no matter that they were minors who would have sponsors).[30] After the war, Truman brought 1,300 children mostly from Hungary, but also Poland, Germany, and Czechoslovakia, to protect them from the Soviet army. Anticommunism was also the ideology behind Operation Pedro Pan ("Peter Pan" to its critics in Cuba), which authorized a Miami priest, Monsignor Bryan O. Walsh, to bring more than 14,000 children from Castro's Cuba, from 1960 to 1962, to be fostered in families and wherever room could be found for them—military barracks, refugee camps, monasteries, and homes for troubled children. While the effort was long portrayed as simple humanitarianism, after a Freedom of Information Act search, historian Maria de los Angeles Torres found what Walsh's critics long suspected: Pedro Pan was part of a CIA effort to protect the children of the anti-Castro underground resistance by creating a mass exodus of children in which they could hide. From

Guatemala, the CIA's propaganda organ, Radio Swan, spread rumors that the government would "nationalize" children, while others circulated fears that they would be killed and turned into tinned meat. That Cuban parents were so afraid of Castro that they would send their children to relatives or even strangers in Miami also, not incidentally, made terrific anti-communist propaganda for the press.[31]

Not long afterward, the Christian right—in the person of Harry Holt most prominently, but through a complex evangelical Christian network—began a humanitarian program in Korea as an alternative to the scourge of communism. Other groups brought Amerasian children to the United States from China and Vietnam, the offspring of the liaisons (and rape) that occurred between US soldiers and civilians during World War II, Korea, and then the Vietnam War. Coming out of the war in Korea, the United States doubled down on its development efforts there; the appearance that cooperating with the United States led to prosperity—or at least material assistance—had its desired effect. Adoption from South Korea began as an evangelical Christian effort, fitting that group's slow emergence at mid-century into politics. Holt and other evangelicals made headlines for their adoption efforts, ultimately persuading Congress to pass enabling legislation and ease visa restrictions from Asia, and putting pressure on more established international organizations to make transnational adoption simpler. Ultimately, the Holt family established their own organization to, as historian Arissa Oh put it, "save the children of Korea." While the Holt operation was private and sometimes exceeded what Congress or the State Department wanted, it was in many ways as clearly in harmony with US anti-communist grand strategy as Monsignor Walsh's was in relationship to Cuba. It also, from the 1950s to 2017, solved a significant problem for South Korea's government: how to grow the economy without building a welfare state, specifically without providing for the children of single mothers.[32] Over the subsequent decades, the Holt family effort became Holt International, and war refugees and Amerasian children became children that couldn't be cared for by their families—usually single mothers—often working in factories and otherwise contributing to Korea's "development" efforts.[33]

In Guatemala and El Salvador in the 1960s, '70s and '80s, kidnapping the children of those suspected of being associated with leftist rebels and adopting them out—including to the United States—became part of US-backed counterinsurgency efforts. Although the disappearances of children were initially portrayed as just accidental casualties of a brutal war, organizations like Salvador's Pro Busqueda took seriously the insistence of parents that they saw their children taken alive by the military, and ultimately uncovered a secret Salvadoran military program to disappear children from communities thought to be sympathetic to the rebels, the Farabundo Martí National Liberation Front (FMLN). Hundreds of disappeared children were left in orphanages or placed in families, sometimes adopted by people associated with the military; others, however, were just dropped off at the Red Cross, from which they were placed in international adoptions.

An InterAmerican Court case prosecuted against the Salvadoran military points to the role of the United States in the forcible disappearance of children. Both Salvador's and Guatemala's militaries and paramilitaries were honed into a terrorizing force in significant part through training by US military and intelligence advisers. The court found in 2005 that the Atlacatl Battalion, a notorious counterinsurgency unit created at the US Army's School of the Americas, disappeared two girls aged three and seven, Ehrlinda and Ernestina Serrano Cruz, in 1982 as part of a coordinated strategy of terrorizing and disrupting the reproduction of those associated with the left.[34] The *New York Times* called the battalion "the pride of the United States military team in San Salvador."[35] While the question of US knowledge of or involvement in the taking of children remains unanswered, it is all but certain that US advisers were aware of it. Some forcibly disappeared children were even living in Salvadoran military barracks, and every child who was adopted transnationally to the United States passed through the US embassy in San Salvador. Robert White, US ambassador to El Salvador in 1980 and '81, commented on the efforts of the Reagan administration and to a lesser extent the Bush and Carter administrations to cover the horrors of death squads that left bodies in the streets, and forced the disappearance, torture, and massacres of civilians: "The Salvadoran military knew that we knew, and they knew when we covered up the truth. It was a clear signal that, at a minimum, we tolerated this."[36] Human rights groups estimate that between 800 and 1,000 children were forcibly disappeared by the military during the Salvadoran civil war.

The Guatemalan program was even larger. In a war that often pitted small indigenous communities against their neighbors, paramilitary groups were instructed to take children to other nearby communities, where they would be placed with families from other indigenous or Ladino linguistic and cultural groups, so that they were estranged from their mother tongue. Thousands of Guatemalan children were forcibly disappeared and raised this way, while others were dropped off in cities, joined Spanish-speaking Ladino families, or were sent in international adoptions to Europe or the United States.[37] After the Peace Accords were signed, this largely internal-to-Guatemala counterinsurgency program became an international adoption marketplace, as many of the same Guatemalan state actors seamlessly slipped into roles as adoption brokers, judges, social workers, and notaries, creating one of the most notoriously lax adoption programs in the world, with high fees and persistent allegations that the kidnappings continued, as making a child available to a waiting US couple required only a stamp from a notary and a visa from the United States embassy. From the early 1990s to 2008, transnational adoption to the United States in particular became relentlessly privatized and a multimillion-dollar transnational enterprise. As report after report detailed, children continued to be coercively separated from their parents, always impoverished, often indigenous, through midwives and other middle figures who persuaded and sometimes paid them, social workers and judges who used the law to force them, and mafias that kidnapped them.[38] This regime came crashing down in 2008, when the US accession to the Hague Convention on Intercountry Adoption halted this high-rolling and sometimes profoundly exploitative business by giving more power to birth parents and creating a Guatemalan adoption authority that a new, more sympathetic government allowed to actually start documenting the decades of abuse.

Although there has been debate about whether the United States has even had a grand strategy after Reagan, few would dispute that free trade and the Washington Consensus on economics have been a key part of what Joseph Nye called "soft power" in this era, updating and intensifying the Cold War framework on trade. More recently, through organizations like the World Trade Organization (WTO) and free trade agreements, a neoliberal or libertarian ideology has opened borders to goods and finance, although it has also corresponded with growing extremes of wealth and poverty and immigration restriction that has kept labor from following high wages even as it has allowed finance and capital to move freely to maximize its benefits.

In the post–Cold War era, liberalization of trade with countries like China and Russia has been foundational to US foreign policy, and from the mid-1990s to 2008, transnational adoption expanded directly alongside free trade measures. And as in Guatemala, China and Russia (along with other major sending countries in transnational adoptions) saw dramatic expansions of their programs following the liberalization of trade between those countries and the United States. Russia, for example, began sending children to the United States in 1991, when the Soviet Union collapsed, and saw an abrupt rise in numbers between 2001, when it acceded to the World Trade Organization, and 2008, when the United States joined the Hague Intercountry Adoption treaty community. (Those numbers crashed to zero in 2011 with the US passage of the Magnitsky Act.) China, similarly, reduced tariffs and trade barriers significantly in the period from 2001 to 2004 and joined the WTO; this was also the period of dramatic expansion of its transnational adoption programs to the United States and the EU.[39]

Even as numbers of transnational adoptions shrank, powerful advocates of transnational adoption in the United States did not lose hope, and their map of reform suggests a great deal about how they understood the politics of transnational adoption. In 2009, Mary Landrieu (with an assist from Harvard professor Elizabeth Bartholet) proposed the "Families for Orphans Act" (attempting to play on a misunderstanding of the "orphan" data produced by the United Nations Children's Fund (UNICEF), which counted the children of single mothers as orphans). They proposed that, in contrast to the multilateral framework of the Hague, the US State Department have unilateral power to develop global child welfare strategies by providing financial incentives to other nations (including debt and trade relief) to send their children abroad for international adoption. It defined orphans even more broadly than UNICEF, potentially including even children living away from home in boarding schools (and hence in institutional care), and insisting on a sharply time-limited period for family reunification, thus in fact producing new "orphans" essentially by defining their parents out of existence. It favored international solutions to local ones. Although sending countries would thus technically be free to refuse to send its "orphans" to the United States, there would be conspicuous financial and even diplomatic costs to doing so.[40] Although the bill failed, and even garnered opposition from John Kerry as secretary of state, it is not actually difficult to imagine a different outcome under a more conservative administration. Landrieu and Bartholet, significant players in promoting and advocating transnational adoption for decades, understood the system as precisely one that moved and changed in response to diplomacy and trade. From the evangelical anti-communism to Central American paramilitaries to trade liberalization and human rights treaties, transnational adoption was a state matter of reproductive policy.

Transnational adoption belongs to a gray area, criss-crossing back and forth across the line between state policy and privatized humanitarianism, in contrast to overpopulation, which moved clearly in one direction, from humanitarianism to foreign (and domestic) policy. It belongs to a post-Reagan era when all sorts of things were being privatized, up to and including the military work of "contractors" who have been crucial to the US wars in Iraq and Afghanistan. What adoption does represent, above all, is a shift in US understanding of the relationship of economics, reproduction, and privatization. Overpopulationist beliefs, however coercive they might have been, belonged to a now past development logic: children clearly belonged to the people who gave birth to them; the application of US technological know-how, industrialization, and loans was designed to raise the standard of living of a whole community. If "they" didn't understand that birth control was good for them, it might be surreptitiously slipped into water supplies or there might be coercive sterilization, but ultimately, there was no way as a matter of policy to separate mothers from their children. Adoption belongs to a different imaginary: US individuals or families can rescue children one by one, airlift them from their conditions of poverty and give them better schooling and flute lessons. Here, the coercive limit case—represented by the failed Families for Orphans Act—operated differently: if nations or communities or individual parents don't understand that taking their "orphans" to the United States is in their best interest, then the law can separate them by force.

Ultimately, though, both kinds of policies were only things that could be done to women—and men, but usually women—who were understood to be fundamentally different somehow from those who were making the policies. In the United States, two images have a striking—if opposite—resonance that reminds us what is at stake in terms of suffering when others control women's fertility. One is the "desperate infertile" woman/couple that is the subject of so many reproductive technology narratives—the grief and stress of not being able to have the children one wants. The second is the idea that losing a child is the worst pain that one can experience—by which is meant, inevitably, death—because the idea that you could lose your child to state violence or disappearance is simply outside the emotional vocabulary of the United States.

Conclusion

So is there a reproductive politics of US grand strategy? Absolutely. This chapter has only alluded to the parallel effort by conservative religious groups to insist on anti-abortion and, in HIV prevention, "abstinence only" as part of the US government's reproductive politics abroad, but that would also provide a case study of reproductive politics as grand strategy. But even leaving those aside and looking only at overpopulation, family planning, and transnational adoption, the United States—particularly through the State Department and the Agency for International Development, but also Defense—have used birth control and adoption to advance US grand strategy goals, including containment, development, free trade, soft power, and anti-communist proxy wars. Reproductive politics have been hidden from most of our accounts of US foreign policy—with some exceptions[41]—in part through the work of imagining an absolution distinction between public/private, which renders reproduction part of the private sphere, and hence not meaningfully the subject of policy.

Under the influence of Kissinger's National Security Memo 200, the United States has acted to prevent regional conflicts in overpopulationist terms, by attempting to help lower birth rates to reduce pressure on resources. In Cuba, we also have good evidence that the CIA was involved in a massive effort to relocate 14,000 children, largely without their parents, as part of its anti-Castro program. In Salvador and Guatemala, we know that a US-backed counterinsurgency effort kidnapped children as a tactic of terror and to prevent the rearing of a next generation of "reds." After the end of the Cold War, transnational adoption became more privatized but followed the larger movements of trade and tariff liberalization, producing a kind of free trade in children, until an international human rights treaty (and, in the case of Russia, the aftermath of the Magnitsky Act) halted it. Were the Donald Trumps (père and fils) correct when they tried to say they were not really meeting with a Russian-government figure to talk about Trump's election, but "just" adoption? Of course not. Adoption is US grand strategy too.

Notes

1. Aaron Blake, "Trump Aides' Stunning Cry for Help: Admitting the President Misled the American People," *Washington Post* (August 1, 2017).
2. Foucault only briefly touched on the concept of biopolitics, but this handful of references has been of intense interest to his subsequent interlocutors. See Michel Foucault, *Society Must Be Defended: Lectures at the Collège de France, 1975–1976* (New York: St. Martin's Press, 1997), 243. On whitening in Latin America, see, for example, Thomas Skidmore, *Black into White: Race and Nationality in Brazilian*

Thought (Durham, NC: Duke University Press, 1974). On eugenics, see, for example, Alexandra Minna Stern, *Eugenic Nation: Faults and Frontiers of Better Breeding in Modern America*, 2nd ed. (Berkeley: University of California Press, 2015). On social reproduction, see Karl Marx, *Capital: A Critique of Political Economy*, vol. 1, *The Process of Capitalist Production* (New York: International Publishers, 1967).

3. Hal Brands, *What Good Is Grand Strategy? Power and Purpose in American Statecraft from Harry S. Truman to George W. Bush* (Ithaca, NY: Cornell University Press, 2014).

4. Elizabeth Bernstein, "Militarized Humanitarianism Meets Carceral Feminism: The Politics of Sex, Rights, and Freedom in Contemporary Antitrafficking Campaigns," *Signs: Journal of Women in Culture and Society* 36:1 (2010), 45–71.

5. Harry S. Truman, "Truman's Inaugural Address," January 20, 1949. Available from Harry S. Truman Presidential Library and Museum, https://www.trumanlibrary.org/whistlestop/50yr_archive/inagural20jan1949.htm.

6. Elizabeth Siegel Watkins, *On the Pill: A Social History of Oral Contraceptives, 1950–70* (Baltimore: Johns Hopkins University Press, 1998), 67.

7. Donald Critchlow, *Intended Consequences: Birth Control, Abortion, and the Federal Government in Modern America* (New York: Oxford University Press, 1999), 244–245.

8. Kari Boyd Brooks, *The Environmental Legacy of Harry S. Truman* (Kirksville, MO: Truman State University Press, 2009), 37.

9. Fairfield Osborn's "'Our Plundered Planet' and William Vogt's 'Road to Survival' in Retrospect," *Electronic Journal of Sustainable Development* 1:3 (2009), 37–61.

10. Elmer Pendell, *Population on the Loose* (New York: W. Funk, 1956), 21.

11. Paul Ehrlich and Anne Ehrlich, "The Population Bomb Revisited," *Electronic Journal of Sustainable Development* 13:1 (2009).

12. Paul [and Anne] Ehrlich, *The Population Bomb* (New York: Ballantine, 1968); William Paddock and Paul Paddock, *Famine 1975: America's Decision: Who Will Survive?* (New York: Little, Brown, 1975).

13. Rockefeller Brothers Fund Archives, Finding Aid, http://rockarch.org/collections/rbf/; Steve Weissman, "Why the Population Bomb Is a Rockefeller Baby," *Ramparts Magazine*, May 1970, 42–47.

14. Donald Critchlow, *Intended Consequences: Birth Control, Abortion, and the Federal Government in Modern America* (New York: Oxford University Press, 1999), 48–49.

15. As a critic put it: "Where birth controllers once went begging, now guest lists at Planned Parenthood banquets read like a cross between the Social Register and Standard and Poor's Directory of Corporation Executives" (Weissman, "Why the Population Bomb Is a Rockefeller Baby," 44). For the history of PPFA, see James Reed, *The Birth Control Movement and American Society: From Private Vice to Public Virtue* (Princeton, NJ: Princeton University Press, 1978), 225–280, and Johanna Schoen, *Choice and Coercion: Birth Control, Sterilization, and Abortion in Public Health and Welfare* (Chapel Hill: University of North Carolina Press, 2005).

16. Thomas Robert, *The Malthusian Moment: Global Population Growth and the Birth of American Environmentalism* (Newark, NJ: Rutgers University Press, 2012), 85–94; Neil Sheehan, *A Bright Shining Lie: John Paul Vann and America in Vietnam* (New York: Random House, 1988).

17. Stephen D. Mumford, "Overcoming Overpopulation: The Rise and Fall of American Political Will" (Buffalo, NY: Council for Democratic and Secular Humanism, 1994).

18. Richard Nixon, "Statement about the Report of the Commission on Population Growth and the American Future," May 5, 1972. Online by Gerhard Peters and John T. Woolley, *The American Presidency Project*, http://www.presidency.ucsb.edu/ws/?pid=3399.

19. National Security Study Memorandum 200, National Security Council, Washington, DC, April 24, 1974, http://schillerinstitute.org/strategic/NSSM200.htm.

20. Hobart Rowan, "Global Overpopulation," *Washington Post*, February 1985; declassified National Security Decision Memorandum 314, November 26, 1975, Ford Library, https://www.fordlibrarymuseum.gov/library/document/0310/nsdm314.pdf.

21. Amartya Sen, *Poverty and Famines: An Essay on Entitlement and Deprivation* (New York: Oxford University Press, 1982).

22. Bonnie Mass, *Population Target: The Political Economy of Population Control in Latin America* (Toronto, Canada: Women's Educational Press, 1977); Mahmood Mamdani, *The Myth of Population Control: Family, Caste, and Class in an Indian Village* (New York: Monthly Review Press, 1972); Laura Briggs, *Reproducing Empire: Race, Sex, Science and US Imperialism in Puerto Rico* (Berkeley: University of California Press, 2002).

23. Ellen Barry and Sushasini Raj, "12 Women Die after Botched Government Sterilizations in India," *New York Times*, November 11, 2014; Ellen Barry and Celia Dugger, "India to Change Its Decades-Old Reliance on Female Sterilization," *New York Times*, February 20, 2016.

24. Briggs, *Reproducing Empire*.

25. R. Marie Griffith, *Moral Combat: How Sex Divided American Christians and Fractured American Politics* (New York: Basic Books, 2017); Daniel K. Williams, *God's Own Party* (New York: Oxford University Press, 2012).

26. Hobart Rowen, "Global Overpopulation," *Washington Post*, February 17, 1985, https://www.washingtonpost.com/archive/business/1985/02/17/global-overpopulation/fc36dd10-7184-4935-a50a-15209411f1cd/?utm_term=.babec11a7a23; Kaiser Family Foundation, *The Mexico City Policy: An Explainer*, http://www.kff.org/global-health-policy/fact-sheet/mexico-city-policy-explainer/#footnote-217066-1; Tessa Berenson, "Here's How China's One-Child Policy Started in the First Place," *Time*, October 29, 2015, https://time.com/4092689/china-one-child-policy-history/#:~:text=In%201979%2C%20the%20Chinese%20government,the%20Communist%20Party%20of%20China.

27. Sonia Correa, "Gender Ideology: Tracking Its Origins and Meanings in Current Gender Politics," *Engenderings*, December 11, 2017; Márcia Tiburi, "The Functionality of Gender Ideology in the Brazilian Political and Economic Context," In *In Spite of You: Bolsonaro and the New Brazilian Resistance*, ed. Foley Conor, 134–146 (New York: OR Books, 2019); Mariana Pradini Assis and Ana Carolina Ogando, "Gender Ideology and the Brazilian Elections," *Public Seminar*, November 13, 2019; Eliza Apperly, "Why Europe's Far Right Is Targeting Gender Studies," *Atlantic*, June 15, 2019; Isis Geraldo, "The 'Gender Ideology' Menace and the Rejection of the Peace

Agreement in Colombia," *Discover Society*, December 6, 2017; Julian Borger, "Trump Administration Wants to Remove 'Gender' from UN Human Rights Documents," *The Guardian*, October 25, 2018..

28. For more on kidnapping and coercion, see my *Somebody's Children: The Politics of Transracial and Transnational Adoption* (Durham, NC: Duke University Press, 2012).

29. Sarah Park, "The Foreign Adopted Children's Act (FACE) and Families for Orphans Act," July 29, 2009, blog post at https://readingspark.wordpress.com/2009/07/27/the-foreign-adopted-childrens-act-face-and-families-for-orphans-act/ preserves the original posting and analysis of the Families for Orphans Act from Ethica in 2009, from their now-defunct excellent site.

30. David S. Wyman, *Paper Walls: America and the Refugee Crisis, 1938–1941* (Amherst: University of Massachusetts Press, 1968), 4–9.

31. Maria de los Angeles Torres, *The Lost Apple: Operation Pedro Pan, Cuban Children in the U.S and the Promise of a Better Future* (Boston: Beacon Press, 2004); Susan S. Forbes and Patricia Fagan Weiss, "Unaccompanied Refugee Children: The Evolution of U.S. Policies," *Migration News* 3 (1985): 3–36.

32. Eleana J. Kim, *Adopted Territory: Transnational Korean Adoptees and the Politics of Belonging* (Durham, NC: Duke University Press, 2010); Tobias Hübinette, "Comforting an Orphaned Nation: Representations of International Adoption and Adopted Koreans in Korean Popular Culture," PhD dissertation, Stockholm University, 2005.

33. See, for example, Arissa H. Oh, *To Save the Children of Korea: The Cold War Origins of International Adoption* (Palo Alto, CA: Stanford University Press, 2015); Kim Park Nelson, *Invisible Asians: Korean American Adoptees, Asian American Experiences, and Racial Exceptionalism* (Brunswick, NJ: Rutgers University Press, 2016); Sara K. Dorow, *Transnational Adoption: A Cultural Economy of Race, Gender, and Kinship* (New York: New York University Press, 2006); Barbara Yngvesson, *Belonging in an Adopted World: Race, Identity, and Transnational Adoption* (Chicago: University of Chicago Press, 2010); Kay Ann Johnson, *Wanting a Daughter, Needing a Son: Abandonment, Adoption, and Orphanage Care in China* (St. Paul, Minn: Yeong and Yeong, 2004).

34. Maya Rozov, "The Serrano-Cruz Sisters v. El Salvador," *Loyola of Los Angeles International and Comparative Law Review* 36:5 (2014), 2071–2087; *Serrano Cruz Sisters v. El Salvador*, Inter-American Court of Human Rights, Merits, Reparations and Costs, March 1, 2005.

35. Clifford Krauss, "How US Actions Helped Hide Salvadoran Human Rights Abuses," *New York Times*, March 21, 1993.

36. Lea Marren, *Salvador's Children: Song for Survival* (Columbus: Ohio State University Press, 1992); Margaret Ward, *Missing Mila: Finding Family* (Austin: University of Texas Press, 2011).

37. Human Rights groups have worked tirelessly to document these disappearances. See, for example, Asociación Pro-Búsqueda de Niñas y Niños Desaparecidos, *El día más esperado* (San Salvador: UCA Editores, 2001); Liga Guatemalteca de Higiéne Mental, *A voz en grito: Testimonios de familiares de niñez desaparecida durante el*

conflicto armado interno en Guatemala (Guatemala: Magna Terra Editoriales, 2003); Oficina de Derechos Humanos de Arzobispado de Guatemala (ODHAG), *Hasta encontrarte: Niñez desaparecida por el conflicto armado interno en Guatemala*, 3rd ed. (Guatemala: ODHAG, 2005).

38. Casa Alianza and Myrna Mack Survivors Foundation, "Adoptions in Guatemala: Protection or Business?" With support from the Social Movement for the Right of Children and Adolescents, Human Rights Office of the Archbishop of Guatemala and Guatemalan Social Welfare Secretariat. Translation by UNICEF. Guatemala City, Guatemala, 2007,.

39. Barry Naughton et al., "A Political Economy of China's Economic Transition in China's Great Transformation," in *China's Great Transformation*, ed. Loren Brandt and Thomas G. Rawski (Cambridge: Cambridge University Press, 2008); State Department historical adoption data, compiled by William Robert Johnson, http://www.johnstonsarchive.net/policy/adoptionstatsintl.html.

40. Sarah Park, "The Foreign Adopted Children's Act (FACE) and Families for Orphans Act," July 29, 2009, blog post at https://readingspark.wordpress.com/2009/07/27/the-foreign-adopted-childrens-act-face-and-families-for-orphans-act/, preserves the original posting and analysis of the Families for Orphans Act from Ethica in 2009, from their now-defunct site.

41. Matthew Connelly, *Fatal Misconception: The Struggle to Control World Population* (Cambridge, MA: Belknap Press, 2010); Alison Bashford, *Global Population: History, Geopolitics, and Life on Earth* (New York: Columbia University Press, 2016); Derek Hoff, *The State and the Stork: The Population Debate and Policy Making in U.S. History* (Chicago: University of Chicago Press, 2012.

PART V

REFLECTIONS FROM THE
AMERICAN CENTURY

21

Casualties and the Concept of Grandness

A View from the Korean War

Mary L. Dudziak

How do the casualties of strategy matter? Are the human consequences of strategic choices a distraction, or should they be centered? Grand strategy seeks to set particularities aside and focus on the big picture, so that a broad theory of strategy can be conceptualized. Understood as "the use of power to secure the state," national security scholar R. D. Hooker Jr. explains, grand strategy "exists at a level *above* particular strategies intended to secure particular ends."[1] The "grandness" of grand strategy relates both to the scale of strategizing, and to the ideas that inform it. For American policymakers, it proceeds from a broad theory of the United States' role in the world. Specific problems and facts on the ground are not grand strategy, but are the contexts that strategy is applied to.[2] At the conceptual level, particularities can be distractions that undermine the search for essence. But what if the essence cannot be untangled from the details? Can the search for grandness obscure elements that strategy should require?

Casualties usually matter to the cost and consequences of different approaches. When armed force is a strategic option, policymakers consider how much "blood and treasure" the American public is willing to bear. The blood that matters to grand strategists is often US military casualties, and the reason these casualties matters is concern that they could undermine political support for the use of force.[3] Blood, death, and lasting injury are not usually conceptualized as the objective of strategy but instead as unavoidable consequences. Death and destruction are war's methods, but are thought of as side-effects.[4]

Casualties are most commonly represented in numbers, but this abstracts casualties and obscures them.[5] The numbers themselves are misleading when military deaths are privileged while non-lethal casualties and the deaths of civilians are ignored.[6] Civilian casualties are thought of as collateral to armed conflict, and atrocities are considered aberrations.[7] Paul Thomas Chamberlin shows, however, that the majority of Cold War casualties were civilians and that atrocities were systemic.[8] Sidelining war's corporeality thus shields strategy-makers from the nature and consequences of military options.

When considering how casualties affect American perceptions of the cost of war, the Korean War is instructive. It was the first large-scale overseas US war that was not declared or authorized by Congress, and the war's greatest impact was on Korean civilians. Using the example of Korean War casualties, this chapter explores the tension between the idea of "grandness" in grand strategy and the importance of granular, concrete consequences. Because armed force can be a strategic option, an understanding of the concrete human experience of the death and destruction of war should be firmly incorporated into grand strategy—both the practice and the pedagogy.

US Casualties in Korea

Before dawn on June 25, 1950, North Korean forces crossed the 38th parallel, a border between North and South Korea created only five years earlier. The ensuing war began as an intensification of preexisting conflict. Occupied by Japan from 1910 to 1945, Korea was divided after World War II. The Soviet Union initially controlled the northern half of the peninsula, and the United States occupied the south. What was planned as a temporary division became entrenched as Cold War tensions heightened. The United Nations and the United States supported the formation of the Republic of Korea (ROK) in the South, and the Soviets supported the formation of the Democratic People's Republic of Korea (DPRK) in the North. US and USSR troops largely withdrew in 1948. This resolution did not bring peace to Korea. There were brutal political purges on both sides of the border as well as border skirmishes. Broader conflict, at some point, was expected. Still, the North's large-scale military offensive on the morning of June 25 surprised the South Korean leadership and their American allies.[9]

Reports of the invasion reached Washington, DC, late in the evening of June 24. President Harry Truman and Secretary of State Dean Acheson quickly planned to bring North Korean aggression before the United Nations Security Council the next day. With the Soviet Union absent and unable to use its veto, the Security Council passed a resolution objecting to North

Korean action and demanding its withdrawal.[10] Over the next two days, North Korean forces, armed with Soviet tanks and weaponry, advanced quickly. South Korean forces lacked the anti-tank weapons that might stop them. South Korean President Syngman Rhee and his government would soon evacuate south, as would thousands of refugees.[11]

The Truman administration focused on a military response during the first twenty-four hours after the invasion. On the evening of June 26, the president ordered General Douglas MacArthur to use the US Navy and Air Force to "offer fullest possible support to South Korean Forces." Previous restrictions on the use of the US Far East Air Forces to help defend South Korean territory were "lifted for operations below the 38th Parallel." Military targets were "cleared for attack." The goal was to eliminate the North Korean threat to the South.[12] The next day, at American urging, the UN Security Council adopted a resolution calling on member nations to assist an effort to repel the North Koreans. General MacArthur was appointed commander of UN forces. Even as American troops stationed in Japan were quickly deployed into combat, President Truman did not ask Congress to authorize the use of military force. This unconstitutional deployment without authorization would become a crucial precedent for the unilateral use of force by future presidents.[13]

American troops' first battle was a military disaster. Lieutenant Colonel Charles B. Smith, a thirty-four-year-old infantry officer and veteran of World War II, was asleep in his quarters near Kumamoto, Kyushu, Japan, on June 30, 1950, when he was awakened by a phone call. "The lid has blown off— get on your clothes and report to the CP," his Commanding Officer, Colonel Richard W. Stephens, ordered. Smith would soon be on the way to Korea with his battalion, the first American ground troops deployed in the Korean War. Only about one in six of his 406 men had previous combat experience. Most were twenty years of age or younger. Their orders were to stop the North Koreans as far north of Busan, South Korea, as possible, providing support to ROK forces. "All we need is some men up there who won't run when they see tanks," explained Brigadier General John H. Church in Korea. But Smith's troops were ordered into service without the most effective weapons for stopping a tank because the US military had none in Korea at the time.[14]

As Smith and his troops headed north, the roads were crowded with Koreans fleeing south. Five hundred forty Americans were in position in Osan by the early morning of July 5 when a North Korean tank column approached in the distance. American artillery began firing, but the tanks continued to advance. When they were 700 yards from the infantry positions, the infantry opened fire, but direct machine gun hits did not damage them. The US troops employed more firepower, and finally two damaged tanks stopped their advance. One caught fire, and three men emerged. Two surrendered, but the third fired at American machine gunners, killing possibly the first US ground soldier killed in the Korean War. Eventually a total of thirty-three tanks passed through, killing or wounding about twenty Americans. This turn of events defied expectations. "Everyone thought the enemy would turn around and go back when they found out who was fighting," an artilleryman said.[15]

Smith and his troops dug in deeper in steady rain as they waited, expecting DPRK ground troops to follow the tanks. After about an hour, a column of trucks and foot soldiers about six miles long, led by three tanks, could be seen in the distance. Far outnumbered, General MacArthur would later call the US forces an "arrogant display of strength" that might cause the enemy to believe that there was greater US troop strength. In the ensuing battle, poor weather ruled out air support, so it was only a matter of time before the battered American troops would need to withdraw. They had to leave behind their dead and seriously wounded. From Smith's infantry battalion, 150 men were killed, wounded, or missing from this "arrogant display," and the war had barely begun.[16]

Even as more troops readied to deploy, President Truman called Korea a "police action," not a "war." As casualties mounted, however, the war-like character of the conflict was undeniable. Having launched American troops into this action without authorization from Congress, the president hewed to forms of official denial. Over and over he called it the "Korean Situation." Folders in Truman's archival records are titled "Korean Emergency."[17]

After United Nations forces pushed the DPRK back to the 38th parallel, General McArthur's disastrous decision to attack North Korea in the fall of 1950 led China to join the war.[18] The fighting in frigid conditions was brutal. Chinese troops encircled UN troops near the Chosin Reservoir in North Korea. Under desperate conditions, they abandoned their dead in an effort to survive.[19] The UN forces retreated, and the war settled into an ongoing stalemate near the 38th parallel, the pre-war dividing point. Public support in the United States slipped away. In this context, the impact of war on American bodies did not generate a call to arms. Instead, it provoked political division and undermined the president's political power.[20]

By December 1950, it was clear that casualties from the Korea "police action" required government action to help disabled soldiers. President

Truman asked Congress to extend World War II–era rehabilitation to disabled veterans of Korea. In the end, 54,249 American military personnel were killed (combat and non-combat) and 103,284 injured. Over 10,000 US troops were missing or prisoners of war, many of whom were surely dead soldiers whose bodies had not been recovered.[21]

The Work of the Dead

War produces death, injury, and destruction. The cost of war is most commonly measured in the numbers of dead. Names of many thousands of dead line the pathway into the War Memorial of Korea in Seoul. They are divided by country and by US state and then listed alphabetically.[22] "Freedom isn't free," visitors are told at both the War Memorial of Korea and the Korean War Veterans Memorial in the United States.[23] The "price" of this freedom is the military dead.[24] War's cost is also represented in the gravestones at Arlington National Cemetery that seem to extend into infinity.[25] It is to the dead that we are asked to extend our reverence and gratitude.

Death is at the center of the cultural memory of war, but that memory is fractured and distorted by which bodies we count and what is obscured. The focus in the United States is on American combatants, but the Korean War was multinational. The United Nations Cemetery in Busan, South Korea, is dedicated to UN forces killed in the war, and troops from the United Kingdom, Turkey, and many other countries are buried there. (The American part of the UN Cemetery is sparsely occupied, the bodies having been returned to the United States for burial.)[26] We are not asked to mourn the millions of Korean civilians killed.[27] Civilian casualties are thought to be collateral, and this marginality extends to memorialization. Although war is a tragedy for all sides, we are not asked to mourn North Korean or Chinese deaths. It is as if the souls continue the conflict in the netherworld.

War death is politically generative. The nation had a duty to the dead at Gettysburg, President Abraham Lincoln argued. It could be repaid through "a new birth of freedom."[28] The dead do particular cultural work for the living—they have a purchase on culture that living beings do not.[29] Historian Drew Gilpin Faust has shown the experience with death during the US Civil War generated a "Republic of Suffering"—a polity shaped through the experience with death.[30] Korea could not generate this kind of societal connection with war. In the Civil War, American civilians were often vulnerable, and civilians far from the battle zone would see the returning injured. Many visited battlefields and graveyards in search of a loved one's body. The sheer number of deaths—over 600,000—meant that mourning was ubiquitous.[31]

Compared with the Civil War, American losses in Korea were private tragedies. "Why doesn't someone tell the people what it's really like over there?" a soldier asked Senator Robert Taft, who opposed Truman's decision to go to war without Congress.[32] Parents of soldiers agonized. "Do you have a son in Korea, outnumbered 10 to 1?" asked G. H. Wynne.[33] Rosella M. Goldsborough of Decatur, Illinois, was not a constituent, but she felt Senator Taft "was one to whom I could write." Her son, Private First Class Paul D. Goldsborough, had been missing in action since late November 1950. She thought, correctly, that he had been captured. "There are questions which continually go through my mind, day and night. Where is Paul, does he have food, does he have a place to sleep, does he have warm clothing, now that winter is coming on." Was he tortured, she wondered. "I would rather have Paul than all of Korea." Private First Class Goldsborough would never come home and is assumed to have died in captivity.[34] "No one knows what it's all about and how hard it is unless you have one of your own among the missing or among the dead," Mrs. Donald Baker wrote.[35]

Death is not the only human casualty of war, however. The casualty of war lives on in the minds and bodies of those who are injured.[36] The names of the injured are not inscribed on walls, so that survival accomplishes a kind of erasure, at least when we are called on to reflect on war's human cost and to honor those who have borne the burden.[37] When persons disabled by war are excluded from society—by architectural barriers or prejudice—this accomplishes a second erasure. The effect is twofold. The corporeal injury is compounded with a social injury, further harming the veteran, and the polity is sheltered from understanding the full effects, the "costs" of what its country's armed conflicts have accomplished.

Disabled Bodies

In May 1952, two years into the war with no end in sight, Mrs. R. A. Raines of Chicago sent a pair of newspaper clippings to President Truman. They were captioned photographs of two injured soldiers at Walter Reed Hospital. "Look at the enclosed," she wrote. Maybe these images would "take some of the cockiness out of you and also your swaggering attitude. You and you alone are to blame for these boys and thousands of others who are crippled, blinded and wrecked humanly for the rest of their lives." The ink in her letter had run, as if she wrote it while crying. "You will, for the rest of your life be able to wash your hands in the blood of young American boys who are needlessly sent to their doom in Korea."[38]

The young men did not look angry in their photographs. James Bashman looked downward from his hospital bed, his head supported, his thin arms dangling. He was paralyzed by a sniper's bullet. This awkward position was how he could read a Christmas letter from home.[39] Private First Class H. Edward Reeves faced the camera from his wheelchair, holding in his arms paper poppies for sale for veterans' relief. His fingerless hands were bandaged, and the stumps where his feet had been were not visible in the photograph.[40]

For Mrs. Raines, the soldiers' disabled bodies were an anti-war statement. Bodies of disabled veterans can serve to reveal the terribleness of war, historian David A. Gerber writes. As in " 'Look! This is what war does!' "[41] Reeves did not feel the way Raines described him, however: wrecked humanly for the rest of his life. At nineteen years of age, he was the only survivor of a doomed convoy surrounded by Chinese troops near the Chosin Reservoir in North Korea. When it was clear that his unit was in mortal danger, Reeves could not escape because his legs were injured by shrapnel. A Chinese soldier shot him in the head at short range and left him for dead, but the bullet only grazed his scalp. When enemy soldiers later realized he was alive, they again tried to kill him, brutally beating him with rifle butts, and then threw him into a pile of dead along the road. Reeves later crawled down the mountain alone on his elbows and knees—his hands were broken—leaving a trail of blood on the snow. Temperatures dipped to 35 below zero Fahrenheit. He was wearing a lightweight summer uniform underneath his parka. The cold hurt more than his injuries. After he was finally rescued, he lost his fingers and feet to frostbite.[42]

As Edward Reeves experienced, enemy fire power was only one source of injury and disability. Frostbite was the largest single cause of admissions at the US military hospital in Osaka, Japan. One survivor remembered that when he removed his boots his toes simply fell off. Blackened limbs meant amputation.[43]

In later years, Reeves's survival, not the limbs he lost, was at the core of his identity. He used both a wheelchair and prosthetic legs, and he had no fingers, but he thought of his absent feet as beautiful. He married at nineteen, got his GED, went to college, had a long career working with computers, and had seven children, two adopted from Korea. He viewed his experience as life affirming and not tragic, attributing his survival to God's will.[44]

Reeves's self-identity is in tension with the way war casualties are often portrayed. His story reflects the focus of disability studies scholars outside of war, who concentrate more on the agency of people with disabilities. For example, Rosemarie Garland Thompson's pathbreaking scholarship highlights "disability's generative force, what disability *makes* in the world, as opposed to the more standard descriptions of disability as an occasion for oppression and discrimination."[45] It is the other-ness of war-related disability—the conceptualization of disability as less than whole, as the source of stigma[46]—that has generative force in war politics. The availability of disabled persons as an "other," in a category the rest of society wishes not to occupy, enables regret about war, and the desire to minimize its impact.

American war is an especially "effective creator of disability," Gerber writes. Higher survival rates have two long-term impacts: they create new populations of disabled veterans, and they also keep names off memorial walls.[47] Narratives of the dead are encased within their wars, in static monuments and graveyards. Disability is persistent and becomes, in effect, an unwelcome reminder of war, an affront to peacetime.[48] These living casualties retain a generative force, as Garland Thompson puts it, but are most often sidelined in memorialization.

Unseen Injury

Not all war disabilities can be seen. One of the best-known photographs from the war is of a soldier caressing another soldier who is grieving after seeing a friend killed in action. It is used to portray psychiatric distress.[49] In the official tally of Korean War non-lethal casualties, the numbers could not capture the psychological and brain injuries stemming from war but only diagnosed years afterward.

In the last year of his life, Korean War veteran Raymond A. Kasten decided to talk about his war experience for the first time. Kasten was drafted into the army in December 1952, only seven months before the Korean War armistice. Though trained as a medic, he was ordered to drive a truck in Korea. As he described his duties, Kasten began to cry. It was a difficult time in the war, he explained. UN troops had been overrun by the Chinese. His job was to drive replacements to the front. Some of the men were close to the end of their enlistment. What so upset Kasten was that he believed he had taken them to their deaths.[50]

Kasten was diagnosed with post-traumatic stress disorder (PTSD) thirty-seven years after his discharge from service in 1954. He had a troubled family life, and he suffered from anxiety, but it was only after he retired and had time on his hands that he became dysfunctional and sought help. "Battle fatigue" was a familiar concept during the Korean War, but the modern diagnosis of PTSD emerged after Vietnam.[51] Kasten was 50 percent disabled, but his outward appearance was unremarkable. The effect of his disability slipped through in asides when he mentioned his broken family. The cost of war, for Kasten, was internalized, invisible to the public.[52]

Korean War veteran Raymond E. Metcalf was more emotional in his oral history interview. As an aviation photographer's mate, he spent much of his time stationed on an aircraft carrier where he developed photographs taken by planes with cameras underneath for targeting. What he saw traumatized him. After developing photographs of a North Korean train to reveal whether it was carrying war materiel, Metcalf next processed film of the aftermath of bombing the train. They had "blasted the hell out of it," and there were many dead civilians beside the tracks, he said, crying, and many dead caribou.[53]

Metcalf was angry that solders went to war and became a time bomb that "never gets defused." Fifty-six years later, he still had nightmares, and he often broke down. He once rented a Cessna plane planning to fly it until it ran out of gas. In a second suicide attempt, he took pills but was found and hospitalized in time.[54] War caused his emotional pain, and this pain is a war injury that will not heal.

There is no grandness in the voices of these anguished veterans, but the on-the-ground experience doesn't disrupt grand narratives about war. In the study of strategy, Kasten's and Metcalf's pain is collateral rather than central. It was not the war's purpose to psychologically maim them, of course. Instead, the purpose was to drive North Korean forces from South Korea and to uphold the United Nations, which had, in essence, created the southern Republic of Korea. The broadest purpose for the proponents of US action was to halt Soviet aggression in Asia and elsewhere (though their assumption that Stalin was the protagonist in Korea was not borne out in the archival record).[55] War's broad global objectives are the candidates for grandness, not its carnage.

The Uncounted

If disabled American veterans often disappear from calculations of the cost of war, civilian casualties are even harder to see. Millions of civilians perished in the Korean War. An unknown number were injured. All lived through terror and horror, dirt and blood, hunger and sorrow.[56]

In the first weeks of the war, life was precarious for refugees. The Han River snaked along the southern boundary of the city of Seoul in 1950. Bridges across the river were the escape route for civilians and ROK military before the city fell just days after the invasion began. In the early morning hours of June 28, with the North Koreans advancing quickly, ROK soldiers blew up the crowded bridges to block the DPRK from crossing the river. About a thousand civilians and soldiers were killed, and countless others were trapped.[57]

Civilian deaths in large numbers were unfortunately not new in Korea. In 1948–49, ROK government efforts to suppress an uprising on Cheju Island led to an official count of 28,000 deaths. Seventy percent of the island's villages were burned. [58] The Truman administration defended its Korea intervention as an effort to protect freedom and democracy, but it came to the aid of a government that had massacred its ideological opposition.

The US military also knowingly killed Korean civilians. Noncombatants always die in wars, and in that sense the killing of civilians is known and intended, though often regretted, in any war. Lawful civilian deaths are "collateral damage"—destruction that is not the core purpose but an ancillary result. Contemporary targeting decisions weigh these "costs" against the value of the target.[59]

The concept of collaterality is illustrated by the US air war in Korea. Air crews received orders to bomb, strafe, or napalm particular locations. Collateral damage would include the civilians along the railroad track that Raymond Metcalf saw when developing photographs. The train was the legitimate target. The civilians were thought of as unavoidable consequences.[60]

Mistakes happened, of course. United Nations forces used napalm in Korea. The answer to out-manned and under-supplied US, UN, and South Korean forces, napalm could be terribly destructive without precisely hitting the target. If napalm hit close enough to splatter a tank, it was enveloped in flames.[61] An American plane mistakenly dropped napalm too close to James Ransone Jr.'s unit, but somehow missed him. He saw men with their skin "burned . . . to a crisp" and "peeled back from the face, arms, legs. It looked as though the skin was curled like fried potato chips." Some men begged Ransome to shoot them.[62]

Karl L. Rebman saw napalm's effects from the air. "The pilot let me put my first air strike in!" he wrote in his diary. "We really burnt the top off of the hill. The napalm hits and splashes along the tops of the ridges and runs into the caves and trenches. You can see the enemy soldiers jumping out of the gun emplacements and trenches. Their clothing burning and smoking." Napalm "is a terrible weapon," he thought, "but very effective."[63] Crews could never precisely identify from the air that burning people were enemy forces, however, and bombing of North Korea was widespread and indiscriminate.[64]

Civilian killings were not always a mistake or a collateral consequence. During the chaotic weeks just after the North Korean invasion began, the United States attempted to establish a battle line to prevent the North Korean advance. Some soldiers were told that North Koreans used guerilla tactics, dressing like civilians, and hiding among them. Concerned about enemy infiltrators, on July 24, 1950, General Johnnie Walker, commander of the Eighth Army in Korea, assured General MacArthur that "no movement of refugees will be permitted through the battle lines of our forward area." He requested that leaflets be dropped to assist this effort.[65]

On July 26, 1950, near the village of No Gun Ri, hundreds of refugees walked in a dense column, wearing sandals and carrying small children and whatever belongings they could manage. American forces initially shepherded them away from their homes, and some recalled being told to gather on railroad tracks. The next day, they heard American soldiers blow whistles. Then planes dove and strafed them. "The ground was shaking and both of my legs shook like walking on a small boat," Chun Choon-ja later remembered. "It looked like the heaven crashed on us." Refugees ran, panicked, dragging small children. Others lay crying in the dirt amid blood, dust, and severed body parts. Choon-ja found her mother dying, with part of her head missing.[66]

For US 7th Cavalry troops in hillside positions, it was the first time they had seen an airstrike up close. Some thought it was a mistake, while others thought it was intentional. "The attack fit the policy the air force was pursuing at the army's request, to 'strafe all civilian refugee parties that are noted approaching our positions,'" wrote Charles J. Hanley, Sang-Hun Choe, and Martha Mendoza, investigative reporters awarded a Pulitzer Prize for their exposure of the attack decades later.[67]

Prodded by troops, surviving civilians gathered under a railroad bridge. They were then fired on from American machine gun positions and hit with aircraft fire. "We just annihilated them," soldier Norman Tinkler remembered. "It was about like an Indian raid, back in the old days."[68] Ten-year-old Yang Hae-chen tried to build a protective wall of dead bodies around his mother. Other children attempted to burrow underneath dead parents for protection. Survivors recalled that this went on for three days, until the Americans retreated.[69]

The United States and South Korea investigated the No Gun Ri massacre after its exposure in 1999, but the gap of five decades leaves some facts unclear. How many were killed remains in dispute, anywhere from a low estimate of under 200 to over 400. A US Army report stressed that the troops were young and unprepared for battle. The report found that civilians were killed and injured, but indicated that what exactly had transpired could not be accurately determined. It stated, nevertheless, that "the deaths and injuries of civilians, wherever they occurred, were an unfortunate tragedy inherent to war and not a deliberate killing."[70] President Bill Clinton expressed American regret and condolences for the deaths, but without acknowledging American responsibility.[71]

Six years later, historian and archivist Sahr Conway-Lanz revealed a letter he located in the US National Archives that was not mentioned in the Pentagon report.[72] US ambassador to South Korea John Muccio wrote to Dean Rusk on July 26, 1950, regarding army concerns that the enemy was infiltrating refugees. In response, the army planned leaflet drops and other warnings "that no one can move south unless ordered, and then only under police control, that all movement of Korean civilians must end at sunset or those moving will risk being shot when dark comes."[73] New documents have not led the US government to revisit No Gun Ri, and survivors still hope for an apology. Even as the US government supported the creation of a memorial park and museum at the site of the massacre, the incident is largely forgotten in the United States, and a battle over its memory continues.[74]

Conway-Lanz argues that No Gun Ri was not an isolated event but "part of a larger pattern" in Korea.[75] The army report found that such events are "inherent to war." If it is the case that atrocities are inescapable in war, then it is important for the human experience of the Korean War, in all its horror, to be remembered. Americans need to understand just what their government is authorizing. Grand strategizers must find a way to make the experience of war palpable to decision makers. The abstraction of numeric casualty estimates simply can't capture the consequences of what happened at No Gun Ri and in the rest of Korea.

Toward Humility

A 1953 armistice ended the fighting in Korea but not the palpable consequences for Koreans. On the journey home to her village, sixteen-year-old Park Doosung found that there were so many dead it was impossible not to step on them. "There were US soldiers, North Korean People's Army's soldiers," she recalled in a 2013 oral history interview. "Every village's forest was piled up with bodies." She could not pass though without walking over them.[76] It is a privilege that American civilians no longer encounter war dead along the roadside, as did Civil War Americans, but the distance of war turns casualties into abstractions.

Famed World War II journalist Ernie Pyle once rebuked American civilians for their inability to understand war death. "There are so many of the living who have had burned into their brains forever the unnatural sight of cold dead men scattered over the hillsides and in the ditches along the high rows of hedge throughout the world," he wrote in his final column, which was found on his body after he was killed during the US invasion of Okinawa near the end of World War II. "Dead men by mass production—in one country after another—month after month and year after year. Dead men in winter and dead men in summer. Dead men in such familiar promiscuity that they become monotonous." To civilians at home, they were simply "columns of figures, or he is a near one who went away and just didn't come back."[77]

Pyle focused on the deaths of American soldiers. It is their bodies that appear in columns of numbers accounting for the costs of US wars. The mechanization of war now enables the United States to use force remotely, and increased reliance on contractors puts fewer American in war zones.[78] This raises the crucial question of whether less risk for American lives has enabled less restraint in the use of force.[79]

The Korean War's history requires us to recognize the profound limits on our ability to perceive the carnage that is war's methodology. It also requires us to expand Pyle's frame to the bodies of foreign civilians and soldiers. For Koreans, the war has never ended, and in spite of peace efforts, the peninsula remains divided by a militarized border. The war lives on in the bodies and minds of elderly Koreans. Skyscrapers today hover over old battlefields, but traces of war can still be seen. There are still bullets wedged in concrete at No Gun Ri. Remembering war, and accounting for its costs, requires humility about what Americans can know of their own country's faraway conflicts. The question for strategy is whether that necessary humility can coexist with the idea of grandness.

Notes

1. R. D. Hooker Jr., *The Grand Strategy of the United States* (Washington, DC: National Defense University Press, 2014), 1.
2. For example, the Yale Brady-Johnson Program in Grand Strategy's focus is "large-scale, long-term strategic challenges of statecraft, politics, and social change," while Hal Brands defines grand strategy as "an intellectual architecture that gives form and structure to foreign policy." Brady-Johnson Program in Grand Strategy, https://grandstrategy.yale.edu/about; Hal Brands, *What Good Is Grand Strategy? Power and Purpose in American Statecraft from Harry S. Truman to George W. Bush* (Ithaca, NY: Cornell University Press, 2014), 1. See also Peter Feaver, "What Is Grand Strategy and Why Do We Need It?," *Foreign Policy*, April 8, 2009, https://foreignpolicy.com/2009/04/08/what-is-grand-strategy-and-why-do-we-need-it/ (defining grand strategy as "the collection of plans and policies that comprise the state's deliberate effort to harness political, military, diplomatic, and economic tools together to advance that state's national interest. Grand strategy is the art of reconciling ends and means").
3. See, for example, Christopher Gelpi, Peter D. Feaver, and Jason Reifler, *Paying the Human Costs of War: American Public Opinion and Casualties in Military Conflict* (Princeton, NJ: Princeton University Press, 2009).
4. See, for example, Denis Winter, *Death's Men: Soldiers of the Great War* (London: Penguin Books, 1979).
5. On counting, see Jacqueline Wernimont, *Numbered Lives: Life and Death in Quantum Media* (Cambridge, MA: MIT Press, 2018), 19–49; Peter Andreas and Kelly M. Greenhill, eds., *Sex, Drugs, and Body Counts: The Politics of Numbers in Global Crime and Conflict* (Ithaca, NY: Cornell University Press, 2010).
6. John Tirman, *The Deaths of Others: The Fate of Civilians in America's Wars* (New York: Oxford University Press, 2011); Marilyn B. Young, "Counting the Bodies in Vietnam," in *Body and Nation: The Global Realm of US Body Politics in the Twentieth Century*, ed. Emily Rosenberg and Shannon Fitzpatrick, 230–240 (Durham, NC: Duke University Press, 2014).
7. On the idea of "collateral damage," see Helen Kinsella, *The Image before the Weapon: A Critical History of the Distinction between Combatant and Civilian* (Ithaca, NY: Cornell University Press, 2011); Sahr Conway-Lanz, *Collateral Damage: Americans, Noncombatant Immunity, and Atrocity after World War II:* (New York: Routledge, 2006).

8. Paul Thomas Chamberlin, *The Cold War's Killing Fields: Rethinking the Long Peace* (New York: HarperCollins, 2018), 14.

9. James I. Matray, "Koreans Invade Korea," in *The Ashgate Research Companion to the Korean War*, ed. James I. Matray and Donald W. Boose Jr. (Surrey, UK: Ashgate, 2014), 309–320; Bruce Cumings, *The Korean War: A History* (New York: Random House, 2010).

10. Security Council official records, 5th year: 473rd meeting June 25, 1950, New York, 1–2, http://dag.un.org/handle/11176/86697.

11. Steven Casey, *Selling the Korean War: Propaganda, Politics, and Public Opinion, 1950–1953* (New York: Oxford University Press, 2008), 19–40; Larry Bloomstedt, *Truman, Congress, and Korea: The Politics of America's First Undeclared War* (Lexington: University Press of Kentucky, 2016), 24–53. Relevant primary sources documenting these events are accessible at *Foreign Relations of the United States, 1950, Korea*, vol. 7, https://history.state.gov/historicaldocuments/frus1950v07; *The Korean War and Its Origins*, Harry S. Truman Presidential Library and Museum, https://www.trumanlibrary.org/whistlestop/study_collections/koreanwar/index.php.

12. Teleconference with MacArthur, 270217Z, June 26, 1950, folder: Korea—June 26, 1950, box 71, George M. Elsey Papers, Harry S. Truman administration, Subject File, Harry S. Truman Presidential Library, Independence, MO.

13. Elsey to Smith, July 16, 1950, Subject: Congressional Resolution, folder: Korea—July 1950, box 71, George M. Elsey Papers, Harry S. Truman administration, Subject File, Harry S. Truman Presidential Library, Independence, MO. The United Nations Security Council subsequently passed a resolution supporting military action, but this did not obviate Truman's constitutional obligation to seek congressional authorization. The impact of Truman's actions in the Korean War on the authority of future presidents to use military force without a war declaration or authorization is detailed in Mary L. Dudziak, "The War Powers Pivot: How Congress Lost Its Power in Korea" (unpublished manuscript, 2020, on file with author).

14. Roy E. Appleman, *The United States Army in the Korean War: South to the Naktong, North to the Yalu (June–November 1950)* (Washington, DC: US Government Printing Office, 1961), 60–61, 72, https://history.army.mil/books/korea/20-2-1/SN06.HTM; T. R. Fehrenbach, *This Kind of War: The Classic Korean War History* (Lincoln, NE: Potomac Books, 2008), 65–71.

15. Appleman, *South to the Naktong, North to the Yalu*, 65–70.

16. Appleman, *South to the Naktong, North to the Yalu*, 72–76; Janet G. Valentine, "To the Pusan Perimeter," in *The Ashgate Research Companion to the Korean War*, ed. James I. Matray and Donald W. Boose Jr. (Surrey, UK: Ashgate, 2014), 321–332.

17. Folder: Disabled Veterans (Korean Emergency), box 1479, OF 471-B, Official File, Papers of Harry S. Truman, Harry S. Truman Presidential Library, Independence, MO.

18. Michael Sheng, "Chinese Intervention," in *The Ashgate Research Companion to the Korean War*, ed. James I. Matray and Donald W. Boose Jr. (Surrey, UK: Ashgate, 2014), 359–370.

19. Hampton Sides, *On Desperate Ground: The Marines at the Reservoir, the Korean War's Greatest Battle* (New York: Doubleday, 2018); *The Battle of Chosin* (documentary

film), *American Experience* (2016), https://www.pbs.org/wgbh/americanexperience/films/chosin/.

20. Casey, *Selling the Korean War*; Paul G. Pierpaoli Jr., *Truman and Korea: The Political Culture of the Early Cold War* (Columbia: University of Missouri Press, 1999).

21. Michael Clodfelter, *Warfare and Armed Conflicts: A Statistical Encyclopedia of Casualty and Other Figures, 1494–2007*, 3rd ed. (Jefferson, NC: McFarland, 2008), 709.

22. The War Memorial of Korea, https://www.warmemo.or.kr/LNG/main.do?lan=en. I visited the War Memorial of Korea in Seoul and the United Nations Cemetery in Busan, South Korea, in September 2018.

23. Korean War Veterans Memorial, Washington, DC, http://www.koreanwarvetsmemorial.org/the-memorial/.

24. Steven Casey, *When Soldiers Fall: How Americans Have Confronted Combat Losses from World War I to Afghanistan* (New York: Oxford University Press, 2014). A major exhibition at the National Museum of American History, Washington, DC, is based on the idea that US military deaths and suffering are the price paid to enable Americans to enjoy the freedom of their daily lives. See *The Price of Freedom: Americans at War*, National Museum of American History, http://americanhistory.si.edu/exhibitions/price-of-freedom). On the idea of the "price of freedom," see Daniel Y. Kim, "Nationalist Technologies of Cultural Memory and the Korean War: Militarism and Neo-Liberalism in the Price of Freedom and the War Memorial of Korea," *Cross-Currents* 4:1 (2015), 40–70.

25. Micki McElya, *The Politics of Mourning: Death and Honor in Arlington National Cemetery* (Cambridge, MA: Harvard University Press, 2016).

26. United Nations Memorial Cemetery in Korea, http://unmck.or.kr/eng_index.php. The thirty-six Americans buried at the UN Cemetery died after the war and had requested burial at the cemetery.

27. Tirman, *The Deaths of Others*, 91-92

28. Abraham Lincoln, Gettysburg Address (November 19, 1863), in The Avalon Project, http://avalon.law.yale.edu/19th_century/gettyb.asp.

29. Thomas W. Laqueur, *The Work of the Dead: A Cultural History of Mortal Remains* (Princeton, NJ: Princeton University Press, 2015).

30. Drew Gilpin Faust, *"This Republic of Suffering": Death and the American Civil War*. See also Thomas W. Laqueur, *The Work of the Dead: A Cultural History of Mortal Remains* (Princeton, NJ: Princeton University Press, 2015); Mary L. Dudziak, "Death and the War Power," *Yale Journal of Law and the Humanities* 30 (2018), 25–61.

31. Faust, *"This Republic of Suffering."*

32. Soldier to Robert A. Taft, folder: Robert A. Taft, Subject File, War—General, 1951, box 1078, Robert A. Taft Papers, Library of Congress.

33. G. H. Wynne to Robert A. Taft, January 3, 1951, folder: RAT, Subject File, War—General, 1951, Robert A. Taft Papers, Library of Congress.

34. Rosella M. Goldsborough (Decatur, IL) to Robert A. Taft, September 25, 1951, folder: RAT Subject File, Casualties, 1951, box 947, Robert A. Taft Papers, Library of Congress.

35. Mrs. Donald Baker to Robert A. Taft, June 20?, 1952, folder: RAT Subject File, Casualties 1953, box 1209, Robert A. Taft Papers, Library of Congress.

36. John M. Kinder, *Paying with Their Bodies: American War and the Problem of the Disabled Veteran* (New York: Oxford University Press, 2015).

37. There is a beautiful but obscure American Veterans Disabled for Life memorial in Washington, DC, https://www.nps.gov/nama/planyourvisit/american-veterans-disabled-for-life.htm. Steven Lubar discusses the very limited portrayal of disability in monuments. "Memorializing Disability: Lessons for Museums," August 17, 2018 (unpublished essay), https://medium.com/@lubar/memorializing-disability-lessons-for-museums-b50e5e03bc27.

38. Mrs. R. A. Rainier to Harry S. Truman, May 20, 1952, folder: Disabled Veterans (Korean Emergency), box 1479, OF 471-B, Official File, Papers of Harry S. Truman, Harry S. Truman Presidential Library, Independence, MO.

39. "Christmas Letter" newspaper clipping, enclosure, Raines to Truman.

40. "Buy One," *Chicago Daily News*, May 19, 1952?, enclosure to Raines to HST; Hubert Edward Reeves Oral History, Hubert Edward Reeves Collection (AFC/2001/001/18290), Veterans History Project, American Folklife Center, Library of Congress, http://memory.loc.gov/diglib/vhp/story/loc.natlib.afc2001001.18290/; testimony of Ed Reeves, America at War, https://www.youtube.com/watch?v=HPhXCFLvlp0.

41. David A. Gerber, "Preface to the Enlarged and Revised Edition: The Continuing Relevance of the Study of Disabled Veterans," and "Introduction: Finding Disabled Veterans in History," in *Disabled Veterans in History*, enl. and rev., ed. David A. Gerber (Ann Arbor: University of Michigan Press, 2012), xiv, 14.

42. Reeves Oral History, Veterans History Project, Library of Congress; *Shot and Beaten, A Marine Crawls from Chosin to Safety, Chosin*, https://www.youtube.com/watch?v=EdtSDoKHZQU; Patricia Brennan, "The 'Forgotten' Conflict," May 28, 2000, *Washington Post*, https://www.washingtonpost.com/archive/lifestyle/tv/2000/05/28/the-forgotten-conflict/ea2cd870-8e1c-4fc4-9142-a8d6e45f0758/?utm_term=.2a873b9cd462; Beverly and Ed Reeves, *Beautiful Feet & Real Peace* (Prescott, AZ: Melcher Printing, 1997).

43. Albert E. Cowdry, *The US Army in the Korean War: The Medics' War* (Washington, DC: US Government Printing Office, 1987), 282–283; *The Battle of Chosin* (documentary film).

44. Reeves Oral History, Veterans History Project, Library of Congress; Reeves, *Beautiful Feet & Real Peace*.

45. Rosemarie Garland Thomson, "Disability Studies: A Field Emerged," *American Quarterly* 65:4 (December 2013), 918; Rosemarie Garland Thomson, *Extraordinary Bodies: Figuring Physical Disability in American Culture and Literature*, 20th anniversary ed. (New York: Columbia University Press, 2017), x–xi.

46. The classic work on this is Erving Goffman, *Stigma: Notes on the Management of Spoiled Identity* (New York: Simon and Schuster, 1963).

47. David A. Gerber, "The Continuing Relevance of the Study of Disabled Veterans," x. Gerber is illuminating the tensions in the literature between disability studies and histories of war and disability/disabled veterans, xii–xii.

48. Kinder, *Paying with Their Bodies.*
49. US Army Korea Media Center official Korean War online video archive, https://www.flickr.com/photos/imcomkorea/2920380608/in/set-72157607808414225/. Psychological injury during the Korean War is discussed in Megan Fitzpatrick, *Invisible Scars: Mental Trauma and the Korean War* (Vancouver: University of British Columbia Press, 2017).
50. Raymond A. Kasten Collection (AFC/2001/001/57057), Veterans History Project, American Folklife Center, Library of Congress, https://memory.loc.gov/diglib/vhp/bib/loc.natlib.afc2001001.57057.
51. The American Psychiatric Association added it to the *Diagnostic and Statistical Manual of Mental Disorders* in 1980. PTSD "is a technical name for a complex of symptoms that arise in the wake of a trauma, an experience that causes feelings of 'fear, helplessness, or horror.'" A formal diagnosis requires that a person experience one of three things: reexperience of trauma, such as flashbacks; avoidance or numbing in an effort to avoid remembering the trauma; or hyperarousal, such as agitation or hypervigilance. Erin P. Finley, *Fields of Combat: Understanding PTSD among Veterans of Iraq and Afghanistan* (Ithaca, NY: Cornell University Press, 2011), 5–6. See also David Kieran, *Signature Wounds: The Untold Story of the Military's Mental Health Crisis* (New York: New York University Press, 2019).
52. Kasten Collection, LOC.
53. Raymond Eldred Metcalf Collection (AFC/2001/001/69684), Veterans History Project, American Folklife Center, Library of Congress. The devastating effect of American bombing on Korean civilians is detailed in Marilyn Young, "Bombing Civilians from the Twentieth to the Twenty-First Centuries," in *Body and Nation: The Global Realm of U.S. Body Politics in the Twentieth Century,* ed. Emily Rosenberg and Shanon Fitzpatrick, 230–40 (Durham, N.C.: Duke University Press, 2014).
54. Metcalf Collection, LOC.
55. Chamberlin, *Cold War's Killing Fields,* 112–122; James I. Matray, "Conflicts in Korea," in *A Companion to Harry S. Truman,* ed. Daniel S. Margolies (West Sussex, UK: Blackwell, 2012), 498.
56. Su-kyoung Hwang, *Korea's Grievous War* (Philadelphia: University of Pennsylvania Press, 2016).
57. Chamberlin, *Cold War's Killing Fields,* 117.
58. Hwang, *Korea's Grievous War,* 26–58; Chamberlin, *Cold War's Killing Fields,* 109–111.
59. For critical analysis of collateral damage, see Kinsella, *The Image before the Weapon;* ; Conway-Lanz, *Collateral Damage..* See also David Kennedy, *Of War and Law* (Princeton, NJ: Princeton University Press, 2006).
60. Metcalf Collection, Library of Congress.
61. Robert M. Neer, *Napalm: An American Biography* (Cambridge, MA: Harvard University Press, 2013), 56–61, 75–86, 92–93.
62. Donald Knox, *The Korean War, An Oral History: Pusan to Chosin* (New York: Harcourt Brace Jovanovitch, 1985), 552.

63. SFC Karl L. Rebman, "Chunchon Diary: A Chronological Narrative," 10, folder: A.35, box 1, Center for the Study of the Korean War Records, Harry S. Truman Presidential Library, Independence, MO. This document is a reconstructed memoir based on Rebman's diaries and letters.
64. Tirman, *The Deaths of Others*, 99-110.
65. Charles J. Hanley, Sang-Hun Choe, and Martha Mendoza, *The Bridge at No Gun Ri: A Hidden Nightmare from the Korean War* (New York: Henry Holt, 2001), 120–121; Sahr Conway-Lanz, "Beyond No Gun Ri: Refugees and the United States Military in the Korean War," *Diplomatic History* 29:1 (January 2005), 49–81.
66. Hanley, Choe, and Mendoza, *Bridge at No Gun Ri*, 122.
67. Ibid., 124.
68. Ibid., 134.
69. Ibid., 136, 141.
70. US Department of the Army No Gun Ri Review Report (2001), https://en.wikisource.org/wiki/US_Department_of_the_Army_No_Gun_Ri_Review_Report#Executive_summary.
71. William J. Clinton, "Statement on the Korean War Incident at No Gun Ri," January 1, 2001, *The American Presidency Project*, ed. Gerhard Peters and John T. Woolley, https://www.presidency.ucsb.edu/documents/statement-the-korean-war-incident-no-gun-ri.
72. Charles J. Hanley and Martha Mendoza, "Pentagon Withheld Document from Report on No Gun Ri Killings," *New York Times*, April 15, 2006, https://www.nytimes.com/2007/04/15/world/americas/15iht-military.1.5293259.html.
73. John Muccio to Dean Rusk, July 26, 1950, No Gun Ri Digital Archive, http://nogunri.rit.albany.edu/omeka/items/show/2.
74. Charles J. Hanley, "In the Face of American Amnesia, the Grim Truths of No Gun Ri Find a Home," *Asia-Pacific Journal* 13, Issue 10, Article 4, March 9, 2015.
75. Conway-Lanz, "Beyond No Gun Ri," 62. See also Chamberlin, *Cold War's Killing Fields*.
76. Hangugjeonjaeng iyagi jibseong: 2. Jeonjaen sog-eul sal-anendanuen il, *A Compilation of Korean War Narratives*, 6, *The Burden, Surviving in War*, ed. Donghuen Shin, Gyeongsup Kim, Guiok Kim, Myeongsoo Kim, Myeongja Kim, Minsoo Kim, Jeongeun Kim, Jonggoon Kim, Jinhwan Kim, Hyosil Kim, Kyeongwoo Nam, Gyeongryeol Park, Sami Park, Hyunsook Park, Hyejin Park, Woojang Shim, Jungmee Oh, Hyochoul Yoo, Buwhui Lee, Seungmin Lee, Wonyoung Lee, Jinah Jung, Hongyoon Cho, Sanghyo Han, Seungup Hwang (Seoul: Pag Ijong, 2017), 279–281. I am grateful to Diana Dahye Shin for her assistance in translating this interview.
77. Ernie Pyle, "On Victory in Europe," n.d., *Ernie Pyle* (online archive), Indiana University, accessed August 24, 2017, http://mediaschool.indiana.edu/erniepyle/1945/04/18/on-victory-in-europe/. See also Mary L. Dudziak; "You Didn't See Him Lying . . . beside the Gravel Road in France": Death, Distance, and American War Politics, *Diplomatic History* 42:1 (January 2018), 1–16, https://doi.org/10.1093/dh/dhx087.

78. *Targeted Killings: Law and Morality in an Asymmetrical World*, ed. Claire Finkelstein, Jens David Ohlin, and Andrew Altman (Oxford: Oxford University Press, 2012).

79. Samuel Moyn, "A War without Civilian Deaths? What Arguments for a More Humane Approach to War Conceal," *New Republic*, October 23, 2018, https://newrepublic.com/article/151560/damage-control-book-review-nick-mcdonell-bodies-person.

22

American Grand Strategy

How Grand Has It Been? How Much Does It Matter?

Fredrik Logevall

In considering these questions it should be said up front that in *relative* terms the United States has fared quite well geo-politically over its history. One would be hard-pressed to identify a great power that has had a better 240-year run or has done better over any given century, or half-century, within that span. Then again, we're not grading on a curve. In a great-power world of Cs, Ds, and Fs, it may just mean the United States musters a C+. Moreover, this relative foreign-policy success over the long duration has less to do with grand strategy and more to do with geographical good fortune and demographic advantages. For most of its history, the United States did not need to concern itself with the specter of military invasion that haunted its European cousins. The Atlantic and Pacific oceans acted as vast moats, making it all but impossible for European or Asian rivals to consider sending their armies to conquer the US homeland. America's immediate neighbors, meanwhile, were geo-politically weak. At times, too, European balance of power politics played a role; if Germany, say, determined it would send a large force across the Atlantic to try conquer the vast territory of the United States, it would inevitably have been opposed by one or more of its European rivals, and in particular by the Royal Navy.

Historian C. Vann Woodward coined the term "free security" to describe this fortuitous geo-strategic condition.[1] For Woodward, and for most other analysts, the condition of free security ended in the 1930s, or certainly with the Pearl Harbor attack, with the shrinking of the world through the advent of transoceanic military technologies. My argument, which Campbell Craig and I developed in our book *America's Cold War*, is that free security continued beyond 1941 and into the twenty-first century, with major consequences for US foreign policy. After the perilous first few decades of its existence, the United States was objectively safe from external attack, as safe as any nation could realistically hope to be. Its security was seldom directly imperiled, and this essential reality warped American foreign policy in key ways. Even with the traumatic and destructive attacks on September 11, 2001, the basic condition did not change—the geo-political world the United States inhabited in the two decades thereafter was a remarkably secure and safe place. The nation continued to operate in a largely benign international environment, with few serious enemies or rivals to speak of, and none that could match America's military might. Not since the days of the Roman Empire had a great power enjoyed such geo-political fortune.[2]

Nor was it just about geography: demography mattered as well. Americans' numbers multiplied more than twelvefold over the course of the nineteenth century, the new arrivals constituting an enormous source of enterprise, vigor, and ability. More than 30 million Europeans took their ambition, energy, intelligence, and skills to the United States in the century or so after 1820. Foreign investment, too, especially from Britain, found the United States enticing and provided the capital for the creation of much of the nation's industrial and agricultural infrastructure. By the beginning of the twentieth century the United States already had more than 200,000 miles of railway track—more than all of Europe. It was the world's greatest debtor nation, but seemed untroubled by that burden. By 1914 the United States had the greatest manufacturing output in the world.[3]

None of this is to say that statesmen in early decades of the Republic necessarily had it easy, as Charles Edel's chapter in this volume makes clear. But an interesting question is whether the nation's astonishing growth to great-power status over its first century and a half owed much to *grand strategy* as such. Alexis de Tocqueville, that sagacious foreign observer, described a nation that was uninterested in pursuing grand strategy as the rest of the human race understood it and yet seemed destined to achieve astonishing success in terms of growth, security, and power that no other state in the world, save perhaps Russia, could match.

Tocqueville indeed anticipated that the US-Russian relationship would come to dominate world affairs, predicting already in 1835 that "each of them seems marked out by the will of Heaven to sway the destinies of half the globe."[4] So it came to be, though not for another century and only with the advent of the Cold War. The superpower confrontation dominated global politics for four-plus decades after 1945, ending in the Soviet Union's defeat and subsequent dissolution. One hears the lament these days that the containment followed by the United States in the Cold War was the grand strategy par excellence and that what we need is a new George Kennan who, like Samuel Beckett's Godot, never shows.

If this is the most successful, or at least most celebrated, grand strategy the United States has ever pursued, it is worthy of a closer look. Specifically, let us consider two foundational writings from the early Cold War: Kennan's "X" article, published in *Foreign Affairs* in 1947 (under the pseudonym "X") that laid out the containment policy—that is to say, the containment of Soviet power—and National Security Council Memorandum 68 (NSC-68) of April 1950. Both of these documents are held to have played major roles in shaping the grand strategy that helped the United States deal successfully with the Soviet threat and ultimately win the Cold War. Each has indeed been referred to as the "blueprint" for US policy in the struggle.

If "containment" in the formal sense originated with the X article, the basic concept emerged earlier. Already at the Potsdam Conference of July 1945, mere weeks after the war in Europe ended and while fighting still raged in the Pacific, American officials understood that Kremlin leaders were intent on dominating the areas the Red Army had conquered. US planners determined that they would not try to thwart these Soviet designs but would resist any effort by Stalin and his lieutenants to move farther west, to those parts of Europe that the Allied powers controlled. Likewise, the Soviets would not be allowed to interfere in Japan or be permitted to take over Turkey and Iran. By early 1946, the Grand Alliance was already a fading memory. By then, anti-Soviet hostility was a staple of much US policy documentation and much journalistic reporting.

Whereas this early containment policy applied to particular areas, Kennan in his article spelled out a general strategy, one with globalist application. To counter the Soviet threat, he wrote, it would be necessary to pursue "a policy of firm containment, designed to confront the Russians with unalterable counter-force at every point where they show signs of encroaching upon the interests of a peaceful and stable world." The task would not be easy, and the West could expect perpetual crises and ceaseless efforts by the Soviet Union "to make sure it has filled every nook and cranny available to it in the basin of world power." Stalin's aggressive actions stemmed not from historic Russian fears of invasion, Kennan continued, but from the nature of communist ideology and the Kremlin's domestic needs. "There is ample evidence that the stress laid in Moscow on the menace confronting Soviet society from the world outside its borders is founded not on the realities of foreign antagonism but in the necessity of explaining away the maintenance of dictatorial authority at home." Stalin was not adventurous, however. Indeed he was cautious, which for Kennan meant that the United States could afford to be patient, secure in the knowledge that strains on Soviet society would inevitably increase until they caused either the mellowing or the collapse of the Soviet system.[5]

One imagines *Foreign Affairs* readers nodding in agreement as they read these words. Few of them, one can assume, would have troubled themselves over the article's lack of a specific policy prescription or its failure to explain how the Soviets could be at once fanatical and cautious. But some commentators took exception, none more strongly than columnist Walter Lippmann, who assailed the X article in a remarkable series of columns in the *New York Herald Tribune* in September and October, to be scrutinized in chancelleries the world over—for such was Lippmann's international influence. The columns were then gathered together in a slim book whose title, *The Cold War*, gave a name to the Soviet-American competition. Whereas Kennan had emphasized Marxist ideology as the foundation of Soviet foreign policy, Lippmann saw Stalin's government as a successor to the czarist regimes that, seeking to protect their western flank against European foes, had pushed into Eastern Europe and had also sought power in the Mediterranean. "Mr. X has neglected even to mention the fact," he wrote, "that the Soviet Union is the successor of the Russian empire and that Stalin is not only the heir of Marx and Lenin but of Peter the Great, and the Czars of all the Russians."[6]

Lippmann did not question the need to contain the expansion of Soviet power, but he rejected Kennan's expansive plan for doing so. "Containment" as outlined by Kennan would, the journalist claimed, draw the United States into defending any number of far-flung areas of the world. Military entanglements in such remote places might bankrupt the treasury and would in any event do little to enhance American security at home. American society would become militarized in order to fight a "Cold War." What's more, Lippmann maintained, the containment doctrine wrongly gave the strategic initiative to the Soviets, permitting them to choose for confrontation those areas where they were stronger. To compensate for this weakness, Washington would be forced to recruit a "heterogeneous array of satellites, clients, dependents, and puppets," any number of whom could be expected to pull the United States in to defend them when problems arose.[7] Thus there was but a short step between containment, as articulated in the X article, and an indiscriminate globalism certain to bring untold problems to the United

States. For Lippmann, Kennan's article missed the fundamental reality that American power, no matter how great in relative terms, was ultimately limited. Containment, in other words, failed the test of realism.

Lippmann's critique had power, both at the time and in retrospect—in one of the ironies of the age, Kennan himself from an early point privately shared its basic precepts—but it failed to move top planners in Washington. In succeeding months, containment took firm hold as America's guiding strategy. Which brings us to NSC-68. That document, penned in early 1950 in the wake of the so-called Twin Shocks of 1949—the Soviet detonation of an atomic device and the victory in the Chinese civil war of Mao Zedong's revolutionary forces—called for an ambitious effort to counter, and indeed turn back, Soviet power. The strategy, the paper declared, would be "to check and to roll back the Kremlin's drive for world domination." Such an endeavor would involve "calculated and gradual coercion" which would "retract" Soviet power and cause the USSR to "recede."

Hence the explicit call in NSC-68 for a huge US military buildup. Merely fighting communism by political and economic means would not be enough. And merely balancing Soviet military power would be insufficient; it was necessary to create such an enormous preponderance of power that the Soviet Union would back off on its own accord, without American military force having to be used. The United States must project its own armed forces to all four corners of the world in order to meet the Kremlin's pressure with countervailing American power. It would have to train foreign armies and equip them with advanced weaponry. It would have to deploy US soldiers and materiel not only in Europe but anywhere on the globe where communists threatened to prevail. This would of course mean raising a huge peacetime army and massively expanding the national security institutions involved in running such a project. The report, in short, made all interests "vital" and made negotiations possible "only on the basis of Soviet capitulations.[8]

Never mind that by 1949—months before NSC-68 had even been written—containment had largely succeeded. Western Europe was by then firmly in the American camp, as was Japan, which meant that Kremlin leaders could no longer contemplate a retreat by the United States to its own hemisphere, leaving Eurasia open to the Kremlin's territorial designs. The political balance Kennan had said was necessary before negotiations with Moscow could begin had been achieved.[9] To the extent it hadn't, the scale tilted toward the United States and the West. Yet Washington declined to pursue a general political settlement at mid-century, or in the decades thereafter. The Cold War

raged on, and Europe remained divided into armed camps. America repeatedly projected its military power into far-flung corners of the world, in the
name of Cold War imperatives and at huge material and human cost. Despite
a thermonuclear standoff predicated on the Orwellian notion of mutual assured destruction, the nation continued to spend billions on new weapons
systems. And despite the fact that the American strategic arsenal surpassed
that of the Soviet Union in all but one category—the number of men under
arms—Washington politicians and lobbyists warned of present dangers, of
windows of vulnerability, of imminent doom.

For the latter-day George Kennan, reflecting back from the 1970s and
1980s, this state of affairs seemed to suggest something extraordinary about
America's Cold War: that it had begun for necessary geo-political reasons
and had been waged effectively in its early years, but that it had been pro-
tracted for another thirty-five years for reasons largely internal to the United
States rather than in response to external pressures and perils. The USSR, he
firmly believed, had long since ceased being a plausible threat to America
and its allies. Yet American foreign policy was still dominated by political
grandstanding and alarmist militarism.[10]

Year after year, decade after decade, this alarmist and highly militarized
approach to East-West relations was hammered into the popular imagination, long after any justification for it had withered, until the malevolent
Russian became the archetypal villain of the Hollywood spy thriller and
the stock monster of children's nightmares. It coasted along on its own in-
trinsic energy, its course changing only in the mid-1980s when a Soviet
leader arrived who was bold enough to declare that the rationale for the
Cold War was preposterous and acted accordingly. It was an approach that
spoke to Americans' moralistic proclivity to see any hostility directed toward their nation as inherently false and to want to frame those conflicts
that arose in stark dualistic terms, as pitting angels against devils, good
against evil, with the very existence of civilization hinging on the outcome.
After all, a wicked adversary is a total adversary; no meaningful dialogue—
never mind good-faith bargaining based on mutual concessions—is
possible with such a being until he disappears or is wholly transformed,
abandoning his enmity. Or as historian Richard Hofstadter put it, for many
Americans international politics was a struggle against an enemy who is "a
perfect model of malice."[11]

Kennan came to puzzle over this chronic American penchant for inflating
threats. In a speech in 1984 he wondered whether the tendency was not

compounded by certain deeply ingrained features of our political system. . . . I am thinking first of all about what I might call the domestic self-consciousness of the American statesman. By this I mean his tendency, when speaking or acting on matters of foreign policy, to be more concerned for the domestic political effects of what he is saying or doing than about their actual effects on our relations with other countries. . . . Every statesman everywhere has to give some heed to domestic opinion in the conduct of his diplomacy. But the tendency seems to be carried to greater extremes here than elsewhere.[12]

This is an extraordinary set of claims—about political structure, about American exceptionalism, and about the degree to which domestic politics drives grand strategy. And Kennan got it basically right. Power, many scholars have noted, is more widely dispersed in the US political system than in relatively more centralized parliamentary arrangements, where control over foreign policy is usually firmly concentrated in the executive. American political parties are weak, and leaders depend for their positions on popular backing. From the emergence of the two-party system in the 1790s to the current day, the parties have maneuvered for advantage; frequently leaders have found that the best way to get the attention of a generally parochial public and Congress, and to score points against the other party, is to exaggerate a given threat and portray it in the most vivid terms possible.

What I'm suggesting, then, is that from an early point in the Cold War, key players in American society realized that their fundamental interest lay in denying that the United States was secure, no matter what was happening overseas. Talking up the threat, perpetuating "the politics of insecurity," became the mission.[13] The result was a militarization of American politics. Each new generation of politicians in Washington rediscovered the winning political formula of talking tough on communists, both foreign and domestic, often irrespective of what was actually happening in the world. Meanwhile, politicians who were accused of being insufficiently vigilant against the Reds were put on the defensive and often found it irresistible to call for a more militaristic waging of Cold War, whatever they actually thought about the merits of such a policy.

A dynamic took hold that would persist through the end of the Cold War and beyond. A great many powerful interests stood to benefit from a vigorous prosecution of the struggle and from increased military spending—individual politicians and the party they represented, the armed forces themselves, civilian officials associated with defense issues, arms industrialists, labor unions associated with weapons industries, universities and businesses that benefited from military research. Few organizations—at least few powerful ones—had reason to fight such a rise.[14]

Thus came into being a permanent defense establishment. Whereas during the world wars US corporations had quickly converted from military to commercial production at the conclusion of hostilities, this did not happen after World War II. NSC-68 and the Korean War institutionalized a military-industrial complex that grew and grew, as corporations such as Lockheed, McDonnell, Pratt & Whitney, and General Dynamics—many of them clustered in California and Texas—became both hugely profitable and hugely dependent on military contracts. The congressional representatives in the home districts and states of these companies often became key players on the House and Senate committees that determined defense expenditures. A kind of iron triangle developed that linked these congressional panels with the armed services and the military firms.

In my judgment, historians of US foreign policy don't pay enough attention to this foreign-domestic nexus and to the inclination of politicians, operating in a condition of free security, to play politics with foreign policy and engage in wholesale threat-mongering.[15] Politics did not stop at water's edge in the Cold War. Far from it.

Fair enough, a skeptical reader may be thinking at this point, but even if we grant that grand-strategy documents like the X article and NSC-68 were flawed and had detrimental long-term consequences, couldn't that be specific to the case rather than flowing from the very nature of the grand-strategy enterprise? Couldn't one say that containment as it developed had serious flaws, that global dominance (or deep engagement, as some call America's post–Cold War grand strategy) is likewise seriously deficient, and nonetheless endorse the concept of grand strategy?

It's a fair question. A principal problem with grand strategy is that it moves consideration of policy from the realm of the specific to the general, from thinking about how best to tackle a particular policy concern to articulating a broad explanation for what is driving international politics, or at least what lies at the root of the crisis one is confronting. And since the strategy needs to be simple and clear, there is a tendency, as historian and political scientist Marc Trachtenberg has noted, for it to be framed in rather extravagant terms—that is, for the strategy to overanalyze and overstate the problem and, in any case, to take attention away from the core concern.[16]

This is the problem with American Cold War strategy as it took hold, as well as with the global dominance strategy that the United States has followed since the Cold War ended: it became all-encompassing, it became grandiose, it became much too alarmist, it became overly militarized and left far too little room for diplomacy, for good-faith bargaining based on mutual concessions. Walter Lippmann's trenchant concern, articulated already in 1947, that the Truman Doctrine's sweeping scope portended interventions in far-flung and non-vital corners of the world was to a significant extent realized. It bolstered what would become known as the domino theory (always an odd theory, with little application in the real world) and helped lead, most notably, to the disaster of Vietnam.

Of course, the United States ultimately prevailed in the Cold War, albeit for reasons that had relatively little to do with grand strategy and a great deal to do with the systemic and long-standing weaknesses of the Soviet system, in particular the chronic inability of Kremlin leaders to give their own people and those of Eastern Europe more of what they wanted—in economic, social, and cultural terms. Which brings me to the second of my two questions in this chapter: How much does grand strategy matter in the context of American history? My answer is, again, not as much as we might think, at least in broad geo-political terms. (For the victims in Southeast Asia and elsewhere and for the families of the US soldiers who lost their lives in Vietnam and Iraq, it mattered a great deal.) History suggests that grand strategies do not alter the trajectory of great-power politics all that much. In the case of the United States, even radically imperfect strategies have not fundamentally affected its rise and fall. The United States could have taken a more active role in world affairs after World War I (it had the means) but chose not to. Successive presidents took the United States deeper and deeper into the morass of Vietnam, beyond what any strategic logic would have dictated. They chose war. The George W. Bush administration did the same with Iraq in 2003, with disastrous consequences.

All three of these strategic mistakes were rooted in coherent strategic narratives popular with both policymakers and the public. (It bears noting, parenthetically, that this did not mean policymakers or other elite observers always endorsed the narratives privately, behind closed doors. On Vietnam, we now know, three US presidents—Kennedy, Johnson, and Nixon—secretly doubted the prospects in the war and, more important, doubted the geo-political importance of the outcome, as did key advisers such as Robert McNamara and Henry Kissinger.)[17] What is striking, however, is that none of these missteps really altered the trajectory of US power. The relative inaction of the interwar era did not prevent the United States from committing itself to primacy after the Second World War. The nation's misadventure in Vietnam did not lead to a collapse in American credibility or change the outcome of the Cold War. Operation Iraqi Freedom was costly in every sense, but the United States remains today far and away the biggest player on the geo-political stage.

What then to make of all this? I've suggested here that I take a skeptical view of the entire grand-strategy undertaking, but I am not arguing that one should ignore the core issues of national policy. The argument, rather, is that the analysis will be more skillful, more effective, if it focuses on real problems and avoids grandiose theorizing. I like Marc Trachtenberg's formulation: "Certainly there are basic issues that have to be thought through on a fairly abstract level, but in dealing with them the goal should be to develop the conceptual framework for handling specific problems with a degree of sophistication." Historical thinking has much to offer here, showing us how policymakers in the past confronted difficult problems and sought to overcome them. If one commits to such historical investigation, Trachtenberg astutely remarks, "certain general principles emerge: one reaches conclusions about what would have been better in particular situations, and those conclusions are almost bound to have certain points in common. Those principles then define a general framework for dealing with new problems."[18]

Barack Obama is interesting in this regard. Implicit in the chapter by David Milne is the notion that Obama during his time in office seemed skeptical of grand-strategic analysis. He appeared to recognize that taking things more or less as they come is a logical course for a world power facing no major global rivals and enjoying remarkable physical security. It's a principled pragmatism leery of doctrine and dogma and built on a desire, in a hugely complicated and interconnected world, to frame foreign policy on a case-by-case basis. That is to say, there's an incrementalism and ad-hocism at work, and though derided by many in the East Coast foreign policy establishment, it has much to recommend it. If it loses a certain overarching conceptual coherence as a result, it gains from husbanding the power upon which American primacy rests and minimizing the fear that this power provokes.[19]

I find similarities here between Obama and John F. Kennedy. Kennedy too was wary of doctrine and dogma, and became more so in his final months. He always had a sense—even as a young man—of the vagaries of history and, from an early point in his career, saw the limits of military power to solve problems that are at root political. Like Obama he was a cautious pragmatist, notwithstanding the soaring "pay any price, bear any burden" rhetoric of his often-misinterpreted inaugural.[20]

Now, I don't think either Kennedy or Obama can be considered outright opponents of grand strategy per se. Both maintained the broad strategic objectives they inherited upon taking office. Both believed in American primacy, in the need for the United States to be able to project its power globally. Both were, in their way, liberal internationalists. But they had a sense, I argue, of the limitations of grand strategy, of its capacity to distort, to constrict. They had a sense of the opportunity cost. Maybe that should be our takeaway too.

Grand strategy can help fashion a response to emerging threats or prospective challenges beyond a nation's borders, and it can in the American case provide a framework for utilizing US power to shape that external environment. And there may be moments when grand strategies really can make an important difference: during times of radical uncertainty in international affairs or when an all-consuming threat emerges. But the rest of the time—which is most of the time, thank goodness—we should be mindful that strategizing of that sort may not do all that much for us and sometimes may do more harm than good.

Notes

1. C. Vann Woodward, "The Age of Reinterpretation," *American Historical Review* 66 (October 1960), 2–8. See also Campbell Craig, "The Not-So-Strange Career of Charles Beard," *Diplomatic History* 25 (Spring 2001), esp. 253.
2. Campbell Craig and Fredrik Logevall, *America's Cold War: The Politics of Insecurity* (Cambridge, MA: Harvard University Press, 2009). I also draw in this chapter on my article, "A Critique of Containment," *Diplomatic History* 28 (September 2004): 473–499.
3. Paul Kennedy, *The Rise and Fall of the Great Powers* (New York: Random House, 1987), 202.
4. Alexis de Tocqueville, *Democracy in America*, ed. J. P. Mayer and Max Lerner (New York, 1966), 559.
5. "X" (George F. Kennan), "The Sources of Soviet Conduct," *Foreign Affairs* 25:4 (July 1947).
6. Walter Lippmann, *The Cold War: A Study in U.S. Foreign Policy* (New York: Harper & Brothers, 1947). There were fourteen columns in all, published between September 2 and October 2.
7. Lippmann, *The Cold War*, 11–16.

8. The text of NSC-68, along with numerous scholarly assessments of the document and its importance, is in Ernest R. May, *American Cold War Strategy: Interpreting NSC-68* (New York: Bedford Books, 1993).

9. Kennan declared in a 1987 speech marking the fortieth anniversary of the Policy Planning Staff: "Now, many people seem to have difficulty understanding that the purpose of the concept of containment as put forth in the 1940s was to prepare the ground for a wider political negotiation and accommodation, designed to overcome, if only by sensible compromise, the extremely serious East-West misunderstandings that had been permitted to develop during the war and now threatened to grow into a full Cold War situation." Quoted in George F. Kennan, *At a Century's Ending: Reflections, 1982–1995* (New York: Norton, 1996), 139.

10. See, for example, Kennan, *At a Century's Ending*, 121, 154–155.

11. Kennan, *At a Century's Ending*, 117–121; Richard Hofstadter, *The Paranoid Style in American Politics and Other Essays* (New York: Knopf, 1965), 31.

12. Kennan, *At a Century's Ending*, 135.

13. This is the subtitle of *America's Cold War* by Craig and Logevall.

14. Ibid.

15. Fredrik Logevall, "Domestic Politics," in *Explaining the History of American Foreign Relations*, 3rd ed., ed. Frank Costigliola and Michael J. Hogan (New York: Cambridge University Press, 2016), 151–167. On this point, see also Thomas Alan Schwartz, "'Henry, . . . Winning an Election Is Terribly Important': Partisan Politics in the History of U.S. Foreign Relations," *Diplomatic History* 33 (April 2009), 173–190; Jussi M. Hanhimäki, "Global Visions and Parochial Politics: The Persistent Dilemma of the 'American Century,'" *Diplomatic History* 27 (September 2003), 423–447; Julian E. Zelizer, *Arsenal of Democracy: The Politics of National Security—From World War II to the War on Terrorism* (New York: Basic, 2010); Andrew L. Johns and Mitchell Lerner, eds., *The Cold War at Home and Abroad: Domestic Politics and U.S. Foreign Policy since 1945* (Lexington: University Press of Kentucky, 2018); Melvin Small, *Democracy & Diplomacy: The Impact of Domestic Politics on U.S. Foreign Policy, 1789–1994* (Baltimore: Johns Hopkins University Press, 1996).

16. Marc Trachtenberg, "American Grand Strategy during the Cold War and After," unpublished paper in author's possession. A version of the paper is available at www.sscnet.ucla.edu/polisci/faculty/trachtenberg/cv/ISA.doc.

17. The high-level gloominess could be detected already in the Pentagon Papers but has been more strongly underscored in more recent literature. See, for example, Fredrik Logevall, *Choosing War: The Escalation of War in Vietnam and the Lost Chance for Peace* (Berkeley: University of California Press, 1999); Daniel Ellsberg, *Secrets: A Memoir of Vietnam and the Pentagon Papers* (New York: Viking, 2002); Ken Hughes, *Fatal Politics: The Nixon Tapes, the Vietnam War, and the Casualties of Reelection* (Charlottesville: University Press of Virginia, 2015).

18. Trachtenberg, "American Grand Strategy during the Cold War and After."

19. See Jeffrey Goldberg, "The Obama Doctrine," *The Atlantic*, April 2016.

20. Fredrik Logevall, *JFK: Coming of Age in the American Century* (New York: Random House, 2020).

Index

For the benefit of digital users, indexed terms that span two pages (e.g., 52–53) may, on occasion, appear on only one of those pages.

abortion, 403–4, 407–8, 410–12, 418–19
Acheson, Dean
  "Ambivalences in Foreign Policy"
    and, 387–90
  containment doctrine and, 387
  decolonization lamented by, 387–88
  on distinction between idealism and
    Machiavellianism, 393
  Frankfurter and, 386, 390–94
  Kennan and, 385–86, 387
  Korean War and, 428–29
  Lippmann and, 386
  natural law tradition and, 388–91, 393
  racism and race theories of, 387
  on relations between Nixon State
    Department and National Security
    Council, 287–88
  rule-based community of sovereign
    states advocated by, 388
  United Nations and, 387, 389–90
ACT UP organization, 68–69
Adams, Henry, 256–57
Adams, John, 84–85
Adams, John Quincy, 84, 95, 99–100, 106–
  7, 110, 165
Addams, Jane, 179, 183, 185–86,
  188, 191–92
adoption. *See* transnational adoption
Afghanistan, 40, 166–67, 233, 417–18
Africa
  AIDS crisis in, 5–6, 63, 65–66, 68–70, 74
  Christian missionaries in, 316
  European imperialism in, 116–17, 188
African Americans
  Kennan on, 263
  New Deal and, 203, 211

  World War II and, 225–26,
    227–28, 230–31
Agricultural Trade Development and
  Assistance Act of 1954, 371
Agriculture Department, 371–72, 408
Ahuja, Anjana, 9
Albany Plan of 1754, 93
Albright, Madeleine, 162–63
Alexander I (tsar of Russia), 158
Alien and Sedition Acts, 94
Alinsky, Saul
  institution-building emphasized
    by, 57–58
  labor movement and, 54
  Machiavelli and, 54–55
  Marxism and, 55
  mass action and, 56
  means *versus* ends questions and, 55–56
  military history examples offered
    by, 56–57
  Rules for Radicals and, 54–55,
    56–57, 60–61
  Tea Party and, 60–61
Al Qaeda, 164
Alsop, Joseph, 266–67
Alvarez, José, 209–10
"Ambivalences in American Foreign
  Policy" (Acheson), 387–90
America First doctrine, 167–68, 212, 225
American Board of Commissioners for
  Foreign Missions (ABCFM), 311–12,
  313–15, 317–19, 322
American Colonization Society, 316
American Enterprise Institute, 165
American Revolutionary War, 93, 115
Anderson, Carol, 189–90, 208

Anti-Ballistic Missile (ABM) Treaty
      (1972), 163–64
Antifederalists, 86, 94
Arab Spring uprisings (2011), 32–33, 60
Areeda, Phillip, 281
Argentina, 403–4
Arms Control and Disarmament
      Agency, 275
Arrangement de Rome (1907), 71–72
Articles of Confederation, 91, 93
al-Assad, Bashar, 15, 166–67
Atlantic Charter (1941), 204, 205–7
Austro-Hungarian Empire, 9–10, 187–88

Bacevich, Andrew, 164
Baker, James, 299–300, 304–5
Baker, Newton, 394
Balch, Emily, 179
Bandung Conference (1955), 190, 333–34
Bannon, Steve, 167–68, 211–12
Baraka, Amiri, 336–37
Bartholet, Emily, 417
Bashman, James, 433
Beard, Charles, 146
Beisner, Robert, 387
Bensel, Richard Franklin, 125
Berinsky, Adam, 221, 233
Berlin Wall, 154–55, 292–93, 302–3
Bernstein, Elizabeth, 403–4
Betts, Richard, 3, 36
Biddle, Francis, 208–9
biopolitics (Foucault), 402
birth control. See also overpopulation
   anti-poverty policies and, 407
   Bush (George W.) administration
      and, 403–4
   Cairo Conference on Population and
      Development (1994) and, 411–12
   Catholic Church and, 403–4, 405,
      410–11, 412
   Clinton administration and, 403–4, 411
   Eisenhower administration and, 405
   Fourth World Women's Conference
      (1995) and, 411–12
   Health, Education and Welfare
      Department (HEW) and,
      407, 409–10
   India and, 409–10

Johnson administration and, 405, 407
Kennedy administration and,
      405, 406–7
Kissinger's policymaking regarding,
      403–4, 406, 408–9, 419
Nixon administration and, 405, 407–8
Planned Parenthood and, 262, 406–7,
      408–9, 410–11
State Department and, 410–11, 418–19
sterilization and, 409–10
Truman administration and, 405
US military and, 406–7
Bismarck, Otto von, 296
Black Arts Movement, 336–37
Blain, Keisha, 188–89
Blower, Brooke, 222–23, 226–27
Bocock, Thomas, 113–14
Bodnar, John, 230–31
Bolsonaro, Jair, 228
Bono (musician), 68–69
Bonus Army veterans (interwar era), 211
Borah, William, 179–82, 185,
      192–93, 194–95
Borgwardt, Elizabeth, 194
Borlaug, Norman, 294
Bourne, Randolph, 185
Boyd, Douglas, 176
Bradley, Mark, 194
Brady-Johnson Program in Grand
      Strategy (Yale University), 49–50,
      51–53, 59–60
Brandeis, Louis, 386
Brands, Hal
   on foreign policy as a "lonely, heroic
      endeavor," 277–78
   on grand strategy and the structuring
      of foreign policy, 1, 108, 143,
      194, 367–68
   on grand strategy as "logic that guides
      leaders seeking security," 403
   on the "what" and "how" of grand
      strategy, 64
Brazil, 110–11, 116–17, 212, 412
Bretton Woods system
   establishment of, 143, 149,
      204, 220–21
   General Agreement on Tariffs and
      Trade and, 209

global economic stability and,
    201–2, 208–9
  Keynes and, 149, 206, 208–9
  liberal capitalist system and, 149
  Roosevelt and, 201–2, 204
Brevern, Maxim von, 246–47
Brewer, Susan, 225
Bridgman, Elijah, 317–21
Brooks, Jack, 355–56
Brown v. Topeka Board of Education,
    333, 390
Bryce, James, 394
Buchanan, James, 109–10
Buchanan, Patrick, 161
Burma, 315
Burton, Richard, 354
Bush, George H.W.
  Central American wars and, 415
  China and, 295, 303–4, 306
  Cold War's end and, 161–62, 292,
    297–301, 303–5
  German reunification and, 295,
    300, 302–3
  Gorbachev and, 302–3
  Gulf War (1991) and, 292–93, 304–5
  Mexico City policy and, 411
  North American Free Trade Agreement
    and, 292–93, 295
  North Atlantic Treaty Organization
    and, 295, 301–3, 304–7
  Panama intervention (1989)
    and, 292–93
  United Nations and, 295
  on the US role in the two world
    wars, 300
  Vietnam War and, 297
  Watergate scandal and, 297
  Yugoslavia and, 292–93
Bush, George W.
  Anti-Ballistic Missile Treaty withdrawal
    by, 163–64
  birth control as aspect of foreign policy
    under, 403–4
  Defense Policy Guidance (DPG) Report
    (1992), 161
  democratization in the Middle East
    and, 165–66
  Evangelical Christianity of, 65–66

  immigration policy and, 349
  Iraq War and, 3–5, 15, 164, 455
  National Security Strategy of the United
    States (2002) and, 165
  preemptive defense doctrine and, 165
  President's Emergency Plan for AIDS
    Relief and, 5–6, 63, 65–71, 73–74
  September 11 terrorist attacks and, 3–4,
    41–42, 164
  "Surge" strategy in Iraq (2007) and, 4–5
Bush, Roderick, 189

Cacho, Lisa Marie, 330
Cairo Conference on Population and
    Development (1994), 411–12
Calhoun, John C.
  federal government power in foreign
    affairs and, 112–13
  on neutrality and US foreign
    policy, 114–16
  slavery in Texas and, 109
  Southern dominance of United States
    desired by, 107–8
  Tariff of 1828, 94
  US cabinet positions held by, 109–11
  US-Mexico War and, 115–16
Cambodia, 156
Canada, 130–31, 161–62, 240–41
Canaday, Margot, 211
Canton (China), 317–19, 321, 322
Carter, Jimmy, 157–59, 408–9, 415
Castro, Fidel, 38, 413–14, 419
casualties
  civilians and, 427–28, 431–32, 436–39
  Civil War and, 431–32, 439
  disabilities resulting from, 432–34
  government aid for victims of non-
    lethal forms of, 430–31
  Iraq War (2003-12) and, 455
  Korean War and, 428, 429–40
  non-lethal forms of, 427–28, 432–35
  psychiatric distress and, 434–35
  US public's willingness to accept, 427
  Vietnam War and, 455
  War Memorial of Korea and, 431
  World War II and, 439
Catholic Church, 263, 403–4, 405, 407–8,
    410–11, 412

Celler, Emanuel, 355
Central America, 114, 117, 412–13, *See also specific countries*
Central Intelligence Agency (CIA), 154, 164, 408, 413–14, 419
Chamberlin, Paul, 154–55, 427–28
Chatham House, 144–45
Chelf, Frank, 355
Cheney, Dick, 161
Cherokee Nation, 315–16
Chile, 375–76, 412
China
    authoritarian nature of regime in, 38
    Bush (George H.W.) and, 295, 303–4, 306
    Communist Revolution (1949) and, 451
    Five-Year Plans of, 30
    Great Britain and, 317–19
    Korean War and, 43–44, 260–61, 430, 431, 434–35
    maritime disputes during twenty-first century and, 44
    market reforms in, 292
    May Fourth Movement in, 177
    Nixon's normalization of US relations with, 155, 156–57, 274, 286, 288
    one-child policy in, 410–11
    Open Door Policy and, 130, 145–46
    Opium Wars and, 317–18, 319–20, 323, 324
    Sino-Japanese War (1937-45) and, 248–49
    Tiananmen Square massacre (1989) in, 292, 303–4, 306
    transnational adoptions and, 412–13, 414, 416–17
    US missionaries in, 311, 312, 317–26
    Vietnam War and, 156–57
    Wanghsia Treaty (1844) and, 319–20
Choe, Sang-Hun, 437
Chollet, Derek, 39
Choon-ja, Chun, 437
Christian right, 410–12, 414
Church, Frank, 256–57
Church, John H., 429
Churchill, Winston, 56–57, 204, 205, 209–10
Civil Rights Act of 1964, 360

Civil Rights movement, 60, 330–32
Civil War, 94, 106–7, 117–18, 431–32, 439
Clark, Christopher, 176
Clausewitz, Carl von, 7, 36, 57–58, 64, 102, 238–39
Clemenceau, Georges, 144–45, 177
Clinton, Bill
    birth control as aspect of foreign policy under, 403–4, 411
    defense spending under, 162
    international democratization and, 161–62
    Iraq and, 163
    Kennan and, 256–57, 261–62
    Kosovo War (1999) and, 162–63
    Latin America and, 403–4
    NATO expansion and, 161–62
    North American Free Trade Agreement and, 161–62
    North Korea and, 163–64
    skepticism regarding grand strategy expressed by, 36
    statement on No Gun Ri massacre (1950) by, 438
    United Nations and, 162
Clinton, Hillary, 15–16, 269–70n5, 401, 411–12
Cold War. *See also* Soviet Union
    Afghanistan War (1980s) and, 40
    Bush (George H.W.) and, 161–62, 292, 297–301, 303–5
    Civil Rights movement and, 60, 330–31, 332
    containment strategy by United States and, 30, 32–34, 38–42, 43, 397
    détente policies and, 41–42, 60, 155–57
    Eisenhower Doctrine and, 32–33
    end of, 30–31, 39, 160, 161–62, 292, 297–301, 303–5, 455
    humanitarian aid and, 376
    ideological conflict between US and Soviet Union, 148–49
    Munich Conference (1938) and, 162, 219, 229
    NSC-68's zero-sum framing of, 152–53, 154–55, 156
    nuclear weapons and, 40, 451–52
    realism in foreign policy and, 266–67

Soviet control over Eastern Europe
and, 148, 154–55, 209–10, 258, 292,
304, 449
US partisan political debates
regarding, 41
US public opinion regarding,
229–30, 231–32
US race relations and, 189–90
Colombia, 412
Commission on Population Growth and
the American Future, 407–8
Concert of Europe system, 184
Congress of Industrial Organizations
(CIO), 54
Constitution of the United States
Article 4 of, 95
consolidation of state power and, 91
executive power and, 91
federalism and, 93–94
ratification of, 86
Tenth Amendment of, 94
US territorial expansion and, 95
containment doctrine (Cold War)
asymmetrical *versus* symmetrical
methods in, 33–34
domino theory and, 455
Dulles's criticism of, 43
Kennan and, 107, 156, 254–55, 258,
260–61, 387, 450–52
Kissinger's criticisms of, 156
success of, 38–39, 41
Truman and, 32–33, 38–42, 229, 260,
404, 455
Vietnam War and, 260, 261, 404, 455
Conway-Lanz, Sahr, 438–39
Coolidge, Calvin, 145
Corbett, Julian, 7
Costigliola, Frank, 254–55
Council on Foreign Relations
(CFR), 144–45
COVID-19 epidemic, 9
Craig, Campbell, 447–48
Craig, Gordon A., 246
Croly, Herbert, 394
Cruz, Ehrlinda and Ernestina Serrano, 415
Cruz, Ted, 159–60
Cuba
authoritarian nature of regime in, 38

Kennedy and, 165
Obama and, 15, 16
Operation Pedro Pan (1960-62) and,
413–14, 419
potential independence during 1850s
of, 111–12
slavery and, 110–12, 116–17
sugar production in, 116–17
Culbertson, Jane, 230

Dallek, Robert, 277–78
Daulaire, Nils, 70
Davis, Jefferson
as Confederate president, 117–18
Cuba and, 111–12
federal government power in foreign
affairs and, 112–14
grand strategy and, 107
on neutrality and foreign policy,
115, 118
Southern dominance of United States
desired by, 108
as US secretary of war, 109–10, 111, 113
Dawes Plan, 145–46
De Bow, James D.B., 110, 112, 114
Declaration of Independence, 93, 206
Defense Department
birth control policies in foreign affairs
and, 418–19
humanitarian aid and, 366,
369–70, 371–72
Kissinger and, 277, 279–80, 284
National Security Council and, 280
Nixon and, 273, 274–75, 277, 279–80, 284
Defense Policy Guidance (DPG) Report
(1992), 160–61, 162, 165
Democracy in America (Tocqueville), 37
Democratic Party
antebellum South and, 109
immigration policy and,
349–50, 354–55
reproductive politics and, 403–4
US-Mexico War and, 115–16
US regional variation and, 125–26, 132
World War II and, 221–22
Dennery, Étienne, 245–46
détente policies (Cold War), 41–42,
60, 155–57

Dewey, George, 130–31
Dewey, John, 185
Dickinson, James T., 321
Diehl, Jackson, 212
Dies, Martin, 222, 350–51
Dillon, Douglas, 154
Dionysius, 213
disaster aid. *See* humanitarian aid
Disraeli, Benjamin, 56–57, 331–32
Dobbin, James, 113
Dobrynin, Anatoly, 286
Dominican Republic, 186, 357–58
Douglass, Frederick, 349–50
Drezner, Daniel, 16
Du Bois, W.E.B.
    African travels (1923) of, 188
    anticolonialism and, 187–88, 189–90
    black internationalism and, 17–18, 179,
        183, 188–90
    the color line in the analysis of, 189,
        329, 331
    Garvey and, 188–89
    Ku Klux Klan, 189–90
    League of Nations and, 189–90
    National Association for the
        Advancement of Colored People and,
        179, 188, 189
    pan-Africanism and, 179, 189–90
    Russian Revolution and, 189
    on slaveholders as US
        ambassadors, 108
    World War I and, 188–89
Dudziak, Mary, 154–55, 189–90, 229–30
Duedney, Daniel, 207–8
Dulles, John Foster
    containment policy criticized by, 43
    humanitarian aid and, 371–72
    Kennan and, 154, 259
    massive retaliation doctrine and, 154
    rollback of communism emphasized by,
        153–54, 259, 266–67
    Suez War (1956) and, 261
Durant, Will, 224–25
Dybul, Mark, 67–68

Eagleburger, Lawrence, 281–82, 304–5
Earle, Edward Mead
    Gaddis on, 238–39

grand strategy concept developed
    by, 7–8, 238, 239–40, 241–42, 243,
    247–48, 249
grand strategy defined by,
    123–24, 238–39
on industrialization and global
    power, 134–35
Institute for Advanced Study seminar
    convened (1939-43) by, 240–41,
    243–46, 248–49
Kennedy (Paul) on, 238–39
national security concept and, 239–40,
    241–47, 248–49
publication record of, 240
on totalitarian states and
    industrialization, 134
Weinberg and, 243–48
Eastland, James, 351–52, 354
Economic Bill of Rights, 208, 210–11
Economic Cooperation Act. *See*
    Marshall Plan
Edel, Charles, 347, 448
Edinburgh world missionary conference
    (1910), 176
Egypt, 60, 177, 186, 261
Ehrlich, Paul, 405–6
Einstein, Albert, 294
Eisenhower, Dwight D.
    Agricultural Trade Development and
        Assistance Act of 1954 and, 371
    birth control and population policy
        under, 405
    containment strategy and, 43
    defense budget under, 153
    Dulles's emphasis on rolling back of
        communism and, 153, 154, 259
    Eisenhower Doctrine and, 32–33
    Guatemala and, 154
    immigration policy and, 351, 359
    inaugural address (1953) of, 153
    Iran and, 154
    Kissinger and, 280–81
    military-industry complex criticized
        by, 152–53
    National Security Council and, 154,
        276, 280, 281–82
    Operations Coordinating Board
        and, 371–72

on overpopulation problems, 405
Solarium exercise and, 32, 33–34
State Department and, 280
Suez War (1956) and, 261
Ekbladh, David, 239, 241
El Salvador, 159, 403–4, 412–13,
    414–15, 419
Elsey, George, 150
Emerson, Ralph Waldo, 166–67
Engelbrecht, H. C., 145
Engler, Mark and Paul, 58–59
environment, 34–35, 64, 212, 379–80
Equal Rights Amendment (ERA), 407–8
Ervin Jr., Sam, 358
European Community, 300
European Recovery Plan (ERP). *See*
    Marshall Plan
Evangelical Christians
    abortion policies and, 403–4, 410–11
    Christian right and, 410–12, 414
    missionary activities by, 311–12, 318–19
    President's Emergency Plan for AIDS
        Relief and, 65–66
    transnational adoption and, 414

Fallon, William J., 5
Families for Orphans Act, 412–13, 417–18
Farabundo Martí National Liberation
    Front (FMLN, El Salvador), 414–15
Fauci, Anthony, 68
Faulkner, Charles, 113–14
Faust, Drew Gilpin, 431–32
Feaver, Peter, 1, 41–42
The Federalist Papers
    centralization of state power and, 91
    domestic unity emphasized by, 88,
        92, 95–96
    Federalist 5 and, 88
    Federalist 9 and, 88
    Federalist 10 and, 88, 96
    Federalist 11 and, 84
    Federalist 23 and, 91–92
    Federalist 41 and, 86, 91
    origins of, 86
    on the United States' geographic
        advantages, 86–87
    on US commercial power, 88–89, 90, 92,
        97, 100

US grand strategy and, 85, 87, 102
on US naval power, 90, 92, 100
on US policy neutrality in European
    affairs, 89, 90, 92, 98, 100
on US territorial expansion, 88, 92, 95–
    96, 100, 102
Federalists, 86, 89, 101
Feighan, Michael, 351–52, 354–58
Feith, Douglas, 4–5
Feldman, Meyer, 351–53
Fergie, Dexter, 240–41
Ferguson, Niall, 15–16, 281
Fields, Barbara and Karen, 341
Fish, Hamilton, 222
Flynn, John, 206–7
Ford, Gerald, 35, 157–58, 403–4, 408
Foreign Assistance Act of 1961,
    366–67, 372–73
Foreign Assistance Act of 1975,
    376–77, 379–80
Foreign Disaster Relief Coordinator
    (US Agency for International
    Development), 373, 376–77
Foreign Economic Assistance Act of
    1950, 370–71
Forrestal, James, 150
Foucault, Michel, 402
Fourteen Points (Wilson)
    capitalism and, 184
    The Inquiry's role in drafting, 144
    League of Nations and, 184, 187
    liberal internationalism and, 179,
        180, 184
    open diplomacy emphasized in, 183,
        184, 391–92, 393–94
    Paris Peace Conference and, 395
Fourth World Women's Conference
    (1995), 411–12
Fousek, John, 231–32
France
    empire of, 84, 90, 93, 95, 111–12, 187–88
    Great Britain and, 87, 89–90, 93, 98–99
    industrialization and, 129
    interwar period and, 146
    Kellogg-Briand Pact and, 193–94
    Libya War (2011) and, 16
    Paris Peace Conference and, 144–45
    revolution in, 98–99

France (*cont.*)
  Suez War (1956), 261
  US "Quasi War" with, 98–99, 100
  Versailles Treaty and, 395
  World War I and, 144
  World War II and, 146–47, 247, 248–49
Frankfurter, Felix
  Acheson and, 386, 390–94
  death of, 390
  on effective leadership, 391–93
  Kennan and, 385–86
  Lippmann and, 386, 394–96
  natural law doctrine and, 390–91
  New Republic and, 386
  Roosevelt (Franklin) and, 390–91
  as Supreme Court justice, 386, 390–91
  Versailles Peace Treaty criticized
    by, 395–96
  on Wilson's emphasis on open
    diplomacy, 391–92, 393–94
  World War I and, 386, 394–95
Franklin, Benjamin, 93, 348–49
Freeman, Gary, 346–47
French and Indian War, 93
Fromm, Erich, 254, 256–57
Fugitive Slave Law, 109
Fukuyama, Francis, 158, 160, 298–99
Fuller, Hoyt, 335–36

Gaddis, John Lewis
  on aspirations and capabilities, 1, 50–
    51, 220, 223–24, 384
  on authoritarianism's quixotic
    illusions, 41–42
  on democracy and international
    alliances, 38
  Earle and, 238–39
  Kennan and, 254–55, 258–59,
    263–64, 385–86
  on Nixon, 279–80, 288
  on the non-linear nature of history, 137
  Wisconsin school and, 127
Gadsden Purchase, 95–96
Gandhi, Indira, 409–10
Gandhi, Mahatma, 58–59, 177
Gardner, Lloyd, 127
Garland Thompson, Rosemarie, 434
Garvey, Marcus, 188–89

Gates, Robert, 300–1
Gates Foundation, 226
gender
  Catholic Church and, 412
  Latin America and, 411–12
  transnational adoption and, 401–2
  Trump and, 412
General Agreement on Tariffs and Trade
    (GATT), 209
Gerber, David A., 433, 434
Germany
  Cold War's end and, 303–4
  Great Britain and, 130, 132, 135
  industrialization and, 129, 135
  Kellogg-Briand Pact and, 193–94
  Nazism and eugenics in, 402
  North Atlantic Treaty Organization
    and, 150, 302–3, 305
  Paris Peace Conference and, 144
  reunification (1991) of, 292, 295,
    300, 302–3
  World War I and, 97, 132, 144, 183–84
  World War II and, 38, 148, 223–25, 227–
    29, 247, 261–62
GI Bill of 1944, 210–11, 333, 336
Gilbert, Felix, 241–42, 246
glasnost (Soviet political reform policies),
    159–60, 297–98, 300
Global Fund to Fight AIDS, 65–66, 68–69
globalization, 125–26, 136
Global War on Terror, 3–4, 65–66, 232
Goldgeier, James, 39
Goldsborough, Rosella and Paul, 432
Goldwater, Barry, 354–55
Goldwater-Nichols Act of 1986, 32
Goodman, David, 225
Goodpaster, Andrew, 280–82, 284
Gorbachev, Mikhail, 159–60, 297–98,
    301, 302–3
Graham, Franklin, 65–66
Graham, James, 159–60
Grandin, Greg, 157
Gray, Colin, 11–12
Great Britain
  Atlantic Charter (1941) and,
    204, 205–6
  Central America and, 114
  China and, 317–19

empire of, 84, 90, 93, 95, 111–12, 134–
    35, 187–88, 315–16, 321–22, 331
France and, 87, 89–90, 93, 98–99
geographical advantages of, 86–87
Germany and, 130, 132, 135
industrialization and, 123,
    128–29, 134–36
influenza pandemic of 1918-19 and, 10
interwar period and, 145–46
Jay Treaty (1795) and, 89–90
Kellogg-Briand Pact and, 193–94
Korean War and, 431
Libya War (2011) and, 16
missionaries and, 311, 313, 315
nineteenth-century financial and
    commercial power of, 129–30
North Atlantic Treaty Organization
    and, 150
Oregon Treaty (1846) and,
    95–96, 114–16
Paris Peace Conference and, 144–45
Royal Navy and, 87, 129, 130–31,
    134–36, 447
Seven Years War and, 87
slavery abolished (1833) by, 110, 112–
    13, 115, 116
Suez War (1956), 261
US trade with, 97–98, 125–26
War of 1812 and, 94, 97–98, 101, 115
World War I and, 10, 132, 144
World War II and, 146–47, 148
Great Depression, 145, 202–3, See also
    New Deal
Great Society legislation, 352, 359–60, 361
Great War. See World War I
Greece, 260
Green, Duff, 110
Greenlee, Sam
    anti-racism of, 335–37
    decolonization and, 335–37
    in Iraq, 337–39
    Organization of Black American
        Culture and, 335–36
    The Spook Who Sat by the Door
        and, 338–40
    United States Information Agency and,
        336, 337–39
    US Army service of, 336–37

Green Revolution (agricultural
    engineering processes), 409
Green Revolution (Iran, 2009), 256
Grinnell, Josiah, 108
Gruening, Ernest, 407
Guatemala, 154, 159, 403–4, 412–13,
    414–16, 419
Guevara, Che, 55
Gulf War (1991), 161–62, 292–93, 304–5

Haass, Richard, 232–33
Hadley, Stephen, 4–5
Hae-chen, Yang, 438
Hague Convention on Intercountry
    Adoption, 412–13, 415–17
Hague Conventions (1899 and 1907), 176
Haiti, 99–100, 186, 189, 375–76, 379
Haldeman, H. R. ("Bob"), 284
Hall, Gordon, 313–14
Halperin, Morton, 281–82
Hamilton, Alexander
    centralization of state power and, 91
    decision to write Federalist Papers
        and, 86
    domestic unity emphasized by, 88
    Federalist 11 and, 84
    Federalist 23 and, 91–92
    Federalist 41 and, 86
    on immigration and economic
        development, 348–49
    Jay Treaty (1795) and, 89–90
    on means versus ends, 91–92
    territorial expansion of the United
        States and, 88
    on the United States as "arbiter of
        Europe in America," 84
    on the United States's geographic
        advantages, 86–87
    US commercial power and,
        88–89, 90, 97
    US naval power and, 89, 90
    US policy neutrality in European affairs
        and, 89–90
Hand, Learned, 394
Hanighen, F.C., 145
Hanley, Charles J., 437
Harding, Warren, 145
Hardt, Michael, 59

Hart, Philip, 351–53, 356–57
Hartford Convention, 94
Harvard Study Group on Presidential
    Transition Report (1968),
    281, 284–85
Hay, John, 130
Health, Education and Welfare
    Department (HEW), 407, 409–10
Health and Human Services Department
    (HHS), 70
Health Organization of the League, 72
Helms, Jesse, 65–66
Hemmer, Christopher, 190–91
Herring, George, 175
Higginbotham, Evelyn Brooks, 329–30
Hill, Charles, 175, 182
History of the Peloponnesian War
    (Thucydides), 37
Hitler, Adolf, 134, 208, 223–24,
    225, 391–92
Ho Chi Minh, 177
Hofstadter, Richard, 107–8, 452
Holderness, Lord, 87
Holmes Jr., Oliver Wendell, 386,
    388–89, 394
Holt, Harry, 414
Hooker Jr., R.D., 427
Hoover, Herbert, 145, 222
Hopkins, Anthony, 126–27
Hopkins, Harry, 205
House, Edward "Colonel," 144, 394–96
Howard, Michael, 137–38
Hugh Moore Fund, 405–6
human rights
    Carter and, 157–58
    Magnitsky Era and, 401–2
    Obama and, 256
    Roosevelt and, 204–5
    State Department and, 157–58
    Trump and, 212
humanitarian aid
    Agricultural Trade Development and
        Assistance Act of 1954 and, 371
    Caribbean hurricane relief (2017)
        and, 379
    Chile earthquake relief (1960)
        and, 375–76
    Cold War rivalry and, 376

Defense Department and, 366,
    369–70, 371–72
Foreign Assistance Act of 1961 and,
    366–67, 372–73
Foreign Assistance Act of 1975
    and, 376–77
Foreign Economic Assistance Act of
    1950 and, 370–71
free market capitalism and, 375–76
Haiti earthquake relief (2010) and, 379
Haiti hurricane relief (1954)
    and, 375–76
International Development and
    Food Assistance Act of 1975 and,
    366–67, 373
Iran earthquake relief (1962)
    and, 375–76
Italy earthquake relief (1908)
    and, 369–70
Japan earthquake relief (1923)
    and, 369–70
Japan earthquake relief (2011) and, 379
Martinique and St. Vincent volcano
    relief (1902), 369–70
Mutual Security Act of 1951
    and, 370–71
Office of Foreign Disaster Assistance
    (OFDA) and, 373, 379
public diplomacy and, 375
State Department and, 366,
    369–70, 371–72
US Agency for International
    Development and, 366, 372–73
US Navy and, 369–70, 377
Venezuela earthquake relief (1812) and,
    369, 378
Yugoslavia earthquake relief (1963)
    and, 375–76
Humphrey, Hubert H., 43–44, 276
Hungary, 212, 303, 351, 412, 413–14
Hunter, Robert M.T., 109–10,
    114, 117–18
Huntington, Samuel, 160
Hussein, Saddam, 3–4, 38, 161–62, 163–
    64, 166, 304–5
Hyten, John, 59–60

Ikenberry, G. John, 38, 207–8, 212

immigration policy
   Asiatic Barred Zone and, 356
   Chinese exclusion acts and, 350–51
   competition among workers
      and, 349–50
   Democratic Party and, 349–50, 354–55
   Eisenhower and, 351, 359
   family reunification provisions and,
      354, 356–61
   Immigration Act of 1990 and, 361
   Immigration and Nationality Act of
      1965, 347–48, 350, 355, 358–61
   Immigration Reform and Control Act
      of 1986 and, 361
   Johnson and, 350–51, 352–61
   Kennedy and, 351–53, 356, 359
   liberal internationalist approaches to, 346
   McCarran-Walter Act of 1952 and,
      351–52, 355–56
   merit-based preference systems
      and, 355–57
   "Muslim Ban" (Trump administration)
      and, 211–12, 349
   national origins quotas and, 346,
      347–48, 350–60
   Obama and, 349
   occupational skills and education as
      factors in, 353, 356–57, 358–61
   public opinion regarding, 358–59
   realist approach to foreign relations
      and, 267
   refugees and, 347–48, 350–51, 356–57,
      359–60, 413–14
   Republican Party and, 349, 354–55
   Roosevelt and, 350–51
   Truman and, 351, 359
   Western Hemisphere immigration and,
      357–59, 360–61
   Wilson and, 350–51
India
   anticolonial nationalism during
      interwar era in, 177, 186
   birth control and sterilization campaign
      sin, 409–10
   caste system in, 337
   Christian missionaries in, 315, 320
   famine (1965) in, 407
   overpopulation and, 405–6

Indivisible (organization), 60–61
industrialization
   France and, 129
   geopolitical power and, 134–35
   Germany and, 129, 135
   Great Britain and, 123, 128–29, 134–36
   Russia and, 134
   totalitarian states and, 134
   US economic development (1815-1914)
      and, 123, 128–29, 448
   US regional variation and, 125
influenza pandemic of 1918-19, 9–10
The Inquiry (foreign policy advisory group
      for Woodrow Wilson), 144–45, 394–95
Institute for Defense Analyses, 278
Interagency Working Groups, 279
Intermediate-Range Nuclear Forces Treaty
      (INF), 212
International Congress for Women
      (1915), 185
International Cooperation Agency
      (ICA), 371–72
International Court of Justice, 202
International Criminal Court, 202,
      208–9, 212
International Development and Food
      Assistance Act of 1975 (P.L. 94–161),
      366–67, 373
International Health Conference
      (1946), 72–73
International Labor Organization, 201–2
International Monetary Fund (IMF), 149,
      201–2, 208–9
International Sanitary Conferences, 71–72
internationalism
   Du Bois and, 17–18, 179, 183, 188–90
   Kellogg–Briand Pact and, 179–80,
      187, 193–94
   Wilson and, 179, 180, 184
Iran
   Cold War and, 449
   coup (1953) in, 154
   earthquake (1962) in, 375–76
   Green Revolution (2009) in, 256
   nuclear nonproliferation agreement
      in, 212
   Obama administration and, 15, 16, 256
   shah's autocratic regime in, 158–59

Iraq
    authoritarian nature of Hussein
        regime in, 38
    chemical and biological weapons
        programs in, 163, 164
    Clinton administration policy and, 163
    Gulf War (1990), 161–62, 304–5
    Kurdish population in, 163
    revolution (1958) in, 338–39
    United Nations sanctions and no-fly
        zones (1991-2003) in, 163
    US invasion and occupation (2003-12)
        of, 3–5, 14–16, 43–44, 49, 51, 164,
        165–67, 266, 417–18, 455–56
Iriye, Akira, 12–13, 182
Iron Curtain, 209–10, 292, 304., See also
        Cold War
Isaacson, Walter, 254–55
Islamic State, 34–35
Ismay, Lord, 150
isolationalism
    interwar period in United States and,
        145–46, 179–80, 191–94, 205–6
    Kellogg–Briand Pact and, 193–94
    Roosevelt on, 205–6
    Vietnam War and, 158–59
    World War II and, 221, 225
Israel, 4, 164, 261
Italy, 193–94, 369–70

Jackson, Andrew, 84–85
James, William, 167
Japan
    Cold War and, 449, 451–52
    earthquake (1923) and, 369–70
    earthquake and tsunami (2011) in, 379
    Kellogg-Briand Pact and, 193–94
    Pearl Harbor attack (1941) and, 221,
        223–24, 225–26, 241–42, 248, 447–48
    Sino-Japanese War (1937-45)
        and, 248–49
    United States and, 135
    World War I and, 176
    World War II and, 38, 221, 223–24, 225–
        26, 228–29, 241–42, 248, 447–48
Japanese American Citizens League, 357
Jay, John, 86–88
Jay Treaty, 89–90

Jefferson, Thomas
    avoidance of foreign entanglements
        advocated by, 146, 192
    Embargo of 1807 and, 97–98
    military budget and strategy during
        presidency of, 101
    Missouri Compromise (1820)
        and, 96–97
    Napoleonic Wars and, 84–85
    Virginia and Kentucky Resolutions
        (1798-99), 94
John Paul II, 412
Johnson, John, 333
Johnson, Lyndon B.
    birth control and population policy
        under, 405, 407
    civil rights for African Americans and,
        334, 352, 360
    Dominican Republic military
        intervention (1965) and, 357–58
    election of 1964 and, 352–53, 354–55
    Great Society legislation and, 352,
        359–60, 361
    immigration policy and,
        350–51, 352–61
    McCarran-Walter Act of 1952 and, 352
    National Security Council and, 276,
        278–79, 281–82
    NSC-68 and the zero-sum framing of
        Cold War by, 154–55
    State Department and, 282
    Vietnam War and, 260, 278–79, 455–56
Johnson, Robert, 193–94
Johnson, U. Alexis, 282–83
Jomini, Antoine-Henri, 7
Jordan, Barbara, 349–50

Kagan, Robert, 107
Kassim, Abdul Kharrim, 338–39
Kasten, Raymond A., 434–35
Katznelson, Ira, 210–11
Keating, Kenneth, 351–52
Kellogg-Briand Pact (1928), 179–80,
        187, 193–94
Kennan, George
    Acheson and, 385–86, 387
    on American penchant for inflating
        threats, 452–53

anti-semitism of, 261–63
on Clausewitzian friction and grand
    strategy, 36
Clinton and, 256–57, 261–62
containment doctrine and, 107, 156,
    254–55, 258, 260–61, 387, 450–52
democracy criticized by, 265–66, 267
Democratic Party and, 256–57
Dulles and, 154, 259
Frankfurter and, 385–86
Gaddis and, 254–55, 258–59,
    263–64, 385–86
homophobia of, 263–64
Institute for Advanced Study and,
    257, 259
Kissinger and, 155–56
Korean War and, 260–61
Lippmann and, 151–52, 260,
    385–86, 450–51
"Long Telegram" and, 150, 258–59
Marshall Plan and, 67–68, 259
McCarthyism condemned by, 254–55
misanthropy toward American masses
    expressed by, 264–65, 267
misogyny of, 263–64
North Atlantic Treaty Organization
    and, 255–56
pessimism of, 254, 256–58, 259
Policy Planning Staff work (1947-48) by,
    32, 259, 386
racism and race theories of, 262–63
realist approach to foreign policy
    and, 266–67
Russia expertise developed by,
    257–59, 268
socialism and, 254
on Stalin's strategic approaches,
    150, 449–50
Suez War (1956) and, 261
on tension between grand strategy and
    democratic institutions, 37
Truman Doctrine and, 260
Vietnam War criticized by,
    254–56, 260
"X" article and, 150–51, 258–59, 260,
    385, 386, 449–51, 454
Kennedy, John F.
assassination of, 43–44, 351–52

birth control and population policy
    under, 405, 406–7
Cuba policy and, 165
grand strategy approach to foreign
    policy criticized by, 456–57
immigration policy and, 351–53,
    356, 359
Kennan and, 256–57
National Security Council and,
    276, 281–82
NSC-68 and the zero-sum framing of
    Cold War by, 154–55
State Department and, 282
Vietnam War and, 455–56
Wilson and, 154–55
Kennedy, Paul, 1, 135, 136, 238–39
Kerry, John, 417
Keynes, John Maynard, 149, 201, 206
Khalilzad, Zalmay, 160
Kindertransport (evacuation of Jewish
    children during World War
    II), 413–14
King, William Rufus DeVane, 109–10
King Jr., Martin Luther, 59
Kirkpatrick, Jeane, 158–60
Kissinger, Henry
birth control policy, 403–4, 406,
    408–9, 419
Central Intelligence Agency and,
    277, 279–80
China, 155, 156–57
Defense Department and, 277,
    279–80, 284
détente policies supported by, 155, 157
Dobrynin and, 286
Eisenhower and, 280–81
Ford administration and, 35
"Great Man" theory of history and, 17
Harvard Study Group on Presidential
    Transition and, 281, 284–85
Interagency Working Groups and, 279
Kennan and, 155–56
Latin America and, 403–4
linkage doctrine and, 274, 285–86
Lippmann and, 278–79
National Security Council and,
    273, 274–75, 276–77, 278–84,
    285–86, 287–88

Kissinger, Henry (*cont.*)
Nitze and, 155–56
NSC-68 and, 155, 156
the Philippines and, 159
State Department and, 277, 279–81,
282–85, 287–88
on tension between grand strategy and
democratic institutions, 37
Vietnam War and, 155–56,
278–79, 455–56
Kloppenberg, James, 167
Kohl, Helmut, 302–3
Korean War
armistice (1953) and, 439
casualties in, 428, 429–40
China and, 43–44, 260–61, 430,
431, 434–35
Great Britain and, 431
Kennan and, 260–61
MacArthur and, 43–44, 429–30
military-industrial complex and, 454
napalm and, 436–37
No Gun Ri massacre (1950) and, 437–40
NSC-68 and, 152–53
refugees during, 428–30, 436, 437–38
Smith's US Army battalion in, 429–30
Soviet Union and, 260–61, 428–29
Truman and, 43–44, 428–29, 430–31,
432–33, 436
United Nations and, 428–29, 430, 431,
434–35, 436–37
US public opinion regarding, 230, 430
War Memorial of Korea and, 431
Kosovo War (1999), 162–63
Krasner, Stephen, 34, 35, 39
Krauthammer, Charles, 160
Ku Klux Klan, 189–90
Kuwait, 161–62, 292–93, 304

LaFeber, Walter, 123, 127
Laing, Edward, 206
Laird, Melvin, 284
Landrieu, Mary, 417
Laos, 156
LaRocque, Gene, 230–31
Laski, Harold, 395
Latin America. *See also specific countries*
abortion policies and, 403–4

biopolitics in, 402
gender ideology and, 411–12
immigration to the United States from,
357–59, 360–61
US commercial power and, 129–30
US interventions during interwar
period and, 145–46
Lauterbach, Albert T., 245–46
Layne, Christopher, 175, 220, 223–24
League of Nations
Americans involved in work of, 191–92
Health Organization of the League
and, 72
influenza pandemic of 1918-19
and, 9–10
The Inquiry's role in establishing, 144
international trafficking of narcotic
substances and, 186
mandate system and, 187
national sovereignty and, 182–83
self-determination doctrine and, 187
United States' refusal to join, 72, 145,
175, 179–80, 193
Wilson and, 147–48, 160–61, 179, 184,
186–87, 190–91
League to Enforce Peace (LEP), 184–85
Leites, Nathan, 152
Lenin, Vladimir, 55, 164
Lewis, C.S., 213
Lewis, John, 334–35
Libby, I. Lewis "Scooter," 160
Liberia, 316
Libya, 16, 166–67
Liddell Hart, Basil, 7–8, 50, 123–24, 125
Lincoln, Abraham, 56–57, 106–7, 117,
293, 431–32
Linderman, Gerald, 228
Lindsay, Frank, 281
Lippmann, Walter
Acheson and, 386
Frankfurter and, 386, 394–96
Kennan and, 151–52, 260,
385–86, 450–51
Kissinger and, 278–79
on maintaining equilibrium between
power and objectives, 91–92
New Republic and, 386, 394, 395
Paris Peace Conference and, 395

Roosevelt and, 148
Soviet Union and, 148–49
United Nations and, 148
Versailles Peace Treaty
    criticized, 395–96
World War I and, 386, 394–96
World War II and, 148, 248
List, Friedrich, 134
Liu, Eric, 59–61
Lloyd George, David, 177
"Long Telegram" (Kennan), 150, 258–59
Louisiana Purchase (1803), 95–96
Luce, Henry, 7–8, 218, 386
Lundestad, Geir, 150

MacArthur, Douglas, 43–44, 429–30
Machiavelli, Niccolo, 54–55, 57–58, 59,
    389–90, 393, 396–97
Mackinder, Halford, 134–36
Macmillan, Harold, 146–47
Madhubuti, Haki, 336–37
Madison, James
    agrarian production
        emphasized by, 97
    Constitutional Convention call by, 93
    decision to write *Federalist Papers*
        and, 86
    Federalist 10 and, 88, 96
    Federalist 41 and, 91
    on immigration and economic
        development, 348–49
    iterative nature of national security
        decisions and, 91
    Napoleonic Wars and, 84–85
    territorial expansion of the United
        States and, 88, 96
    on the United States' geographic
        advantages, 87
    Venezuela earthquake relief (1812)
        and, 369
    Virginia and Kentucky Resolutions
        (1798-99), 94
Magnitsky Act of 2011, 401–2,
    416–17, 419
Mahan, Alfred Thayer, 7, 123–24, 134–35,
    146, 206
Mallory, Stephen, 109–10, 113–14, 117–18
Manela, Erez, 177–78

manifest destiny ideology, 112, 243–44,
    246–47, 248
Mann, A. Dudley, 114
Mann, James, 164
Mao Zedong, 55, 177, 451
Marcos, Ferdinand, 159
Marshall, George C., 67–68, 259
Marshall, T.H., 210–11
Marshall Plan, 41, 143, 209, 211, 370–71
Martel, William C., 106–7, 367–68, 374
Martinique and St. Vincent volcano
    disaster (1902), 369–70
Mason, James Murray, 109–10, 117–18
Maury, Matthew Fontaine, 110, 113
May, Ernest, 281
McAlevey, Jane, 59–60
McCarran-Walter Act of 1952,
    351–52, 355–56
McCarthy, Eugene, 256–57
McCarthyism, 254–55, 385
McDougall, Walter, 123
McMaster, H.R., 59–60, 167–68
McNamara, Robert, 455–56
Mead, Walter Russell, 38–39, 107
Meaney, Thomas, 51, 124
Mearsheimer, John, 160
Mendoza, Martha, 437
Merriam, Charles, 203–4, 208
Metcalf, Raymond E., 435–36
Metternich, Klemens von, 158
Mexico
    abolition of slavery and, 112–13, 115
    immigration to the United States
        from, 357–58
    North American Free Trade Agreement
        and, 161–62
    US intervention (1910s) in, 186
    US war (1846-48) with, 95–96, 115–16
Mexico City policy, 403–4, 410–12
Middle East. *See also specific countries*
    Arab Spring uprisings and, 32–33, 60
    democratization efforts in, 164–65
    Eisenhower Doctrine and, 32–33
    Nixon administration and, 276, 288
    US invasion and occupation of Iraq
        (2003-12) and, 164, 165
    US military presence during 1990s in, 97
    World War I and, 176

Mikolajczyk, Stanislaw, 258
Millennium Development Goals
 (MDGs), 64–66
Miller, William, 354–55
Milne, David, 16, 220–21, 456
Milosevic, Slobodan, 162–63
Milton, John, 83
missionaries
 Africa and, 316
 American Board of Commissioners for
  Foreign Missions and, 311–12, 313–
  15, 317–19, 322
 Burma and, 315
 Ceylon and, 313–14
 children of, 322
 China and, 311, 312, 317–26
 civilization and conversion emphasized
  as priorities among, 311, 312–14,
  315–17, 318, 323–24
 Edinburgh world missionary
  conference (1910) and, 176
 Evangelical Christians and,
  311–12, 318–19
 Great Britain and, 311, 313, 315
 India and, 315, 320
 merchants and, 313, 319–21, 322
 Native American communities
  and, 315–16
 opium trade and, 319–20, 322
 in Singapore, 321–22
 Society for the Diffusion of Useful
  Knowledge and, 320–21
 translation and printing work by, 320–22
 US diplomacy and, 312–13, 323–26
Missouri Compromise (1820), 96–97
Mitterrand, Francois, 300–2
Monroe Doctrine (1823), 84–85, 95–96,
 98–100, 192
Morgenthau, Hans, 231–32
Morris, Toni, 341
Morrison, Robert, 317, 320
Moyers, Bill, 352–53
Muccio, John, 438
Mueller Report (2019), 401–2
Munich Conference (1938), 162, 219, 229
Murray, Williamson, 6
Mutual Security Act of 1951, 370–71
Myrdal, Gunnar, 335

Napoleonic Wars, 84–85
National Association for the Advancement
 of Colored People (NAACP), 179,
 188, 192–93, 333
National Institute of Allergy and
 Infectious Diseases (NIAID), 68
National Resources Planning Board
 (NRPB), 208
National Security Council (NSC)
 Defense Department and, 280
 Eisenhower and, 154, 276, 280, 281–82
 Interagency Working Groups and, 279
 Iraq War (2003-12) and, 3–4
 Johnson and, 276, 278–79, 281–82
 Kennedy and, 276, 281–82
 Kissinger and, 273, 274–75, 276–77,
  278–84, 285–86, 287–88
 Nixon and, 273, 274–75, 276–77, 278–
  80, 281–84, 285–88
 Obama and, 15
 State Department and, 280
 Washington Special Action Group
  and, 286
National Security Memo 200, 408, 419
National Security Memo 314, 408, 411
National Security Strategy reports, 3–4,
 32, 165
Native Americans, 315–16
Negri, Antonio, 59
Nehru, Jawaharlal, 177
neutrality
 Calhoun and, 114–16
 Davis and, 115, 118
 The Federalist Papers and, 89, 90, 92,
  98, 100
 Hamilton and, 89–90
 Monroe Doctrine and, 98–100
 US public opinion during interwar era
  and, 222–23
 Washington's proclamation (1792)
  of, 98–99
New Deal
 African Americans and, 203, 211
 Economic Bill of Rights and,
  208, 210–11
 Republican Party opposition to, 202,
  210–12, 222, 226–27
 Social Security, 202–3

trial-and-error policy approaches
in, 201
US foreign policy influenced by, 203–4,
205, 207–8, 220
Newell, Samuel, 313–14
New Left movement, 54–55, 266–67
Nicaragua, 117, 158–59, 192, 212
Niebuhr, Reinhold, 231–32, 248–49
Ninkovich, Frank, 181
Nitze, Paul
Dulles's anti-communism policies
and, 154
Eisenhower defense budget and, 153
Kissinger and, 155–56
Leites and, 152
NSC-68 and, 152–53, 155
NSC-141 and, 153
Nixon, Richard M.
birth control and population policy
under, 405, 407–8
Central Intelligence Agency and, 273,
274–76, 277–78, 279–80
China and, 155, 156–57, 274, 286, 288
Defense Department and, 273, 274–75,
277, 279–80, 284
détente policies with Soviet Union and,
274, 288
Eisenhower administration and,
276–77, 281
Harvard Study Group on Presidential
Transition, 284–85
Kennan and, 256–57
linkage doctrine and, 274, 275,
279–80, 285–86
Middle East and, 276, 288
National Security Council and,
273, 274–75, 276–77, 278–80,
281–84, 285–88
Rogers and, 276–77
Romania and, 282–83, 285–86
State Department and, 273, 274–78,
279–80, 281, 282–86, 287–88
Strategic Arms Limitation Talks and,
275, 285–86
Vietnam War and, 274, 276, 278–79,
285–86, 455–56
No Gun Ri massacre (1950), 437–40
Non-Aligned Movement, 190

Noriega, Manuel, 292–93
North American Free Trade Act (NAFTA),
161–62, 292–93
North Atlantic Treaty
Organization (NATO)
Bush (George H.W.), 295, 301–3, 304–7
establishment of, 143
expansion during 1990s of, 161–62
Germany and, 150, 302–3, 305
Great Britain and, 150
Kosovo War (1999) and, 162–63
United Nations and, 209
North Korea, 163–64, 428–29, See also
Korean War
Northwest Ordinance of 1787,
95–96, 396–97
NSC-68 (1950)
containment doctrine and, 451–52
Defense Policy Guidance Report (1992)
compared to, 160
drafting of, 152
Kennedy and, 154–55
Kissinger's criticisms of, 155, 156
Korean War and, 152–53
military budget recommendations in,
153, 451, 454
preemptive defense doctrine and, 165
Soviet intentions described in, 152, 153
Truman administration's
implementation of, 32
zero-sum framing of Cold War in, 152–
53, 154–55, 156
NSC-141 (1952), 153
NSC 162/2 (1953), 154
NSDD-32 and NSDD-75 (Reagan
administration), 32
nuclear weapons
Anti-Ballistic Missile Treaty of 1972
and, 163–64
Cold War and, 40, 451–52
Dulles and, 154
grand strategy implications of, 8
Intermediate-Range Nuclear Forces
Treaty (INF), 212
Soviet atomic bomb test (1950) and,
40, 451
Strategic Arms Limitation Talks and,
275, 285–86

Nuremberg Charter and War Trials, 202, 204, 206, 208–9
Nye, Gerald P., 145
Nye, Joseph, 416

Obama, Barack
    Afghanistan War and, 166–67
    Arab Spring uprisings and, 32–33
    Cuba and, 15, 16
    grand strategy approach to foreign policy criticized by, 14–16, 166–67, 256, 267, 269–70n5, 456–57
    immigration policy and, 349
    Iran and, 15, 16, 256
    Iraq War (2003-12) and, 166
    Libya War (2011) and, 16, 166–67
    Magnitsky Act of 2011 and, 401–2
    National Security Council and, 15
    "Pivot to Asia" policies of, 15, 166–67
    pragmatism in foreign policy and, 167
    Syrian civil war and, 15–16, 166–67
O'Brien, Lawrence, 355, 358
Occupy Wall Street, 60–61
Office International d'hygiene Publique (OIHP), 71–72
Office of Foreign Disaster Assistance (OFDA), 373, 379
Oh, Arissa, 414
O'Leary, Dale, 412
Olney Note (1895), 130
Olyphant, D.W.C., 321
Open Door Policy, 130, 145–46
Operation Pedro Pan (Cuba, 1960-62), 413–14, 419
Operations Coordinating Board, 371–72
Opium Wars, 317–18, 319–20, 323, 324
Orban, Viktor, 412
Oregon Treaty (1846), 95–96, 114–16
Organization of Black American Culture (OBAC), 335–36
Orlando, Vittorio, 177
Osborn, Fairfield, 405–6
Ottoman Empire, 71, 99, 187–88
Outlawry of War movement, 179, 187
overpopulation. See also birth control
    China's one-child policy and, 410–11
    Commission on Population Growth and the American Future and, 407–8

    Eisenhower on, 405
    eugenics and, 405–6
    famine and, 405–6, 409
    Gruening hearings at US Senate (1965) and, 407
    Hugh Moore Fund and, 405–6
    India and, 405–6
    Malthusianism and, 405–6, 409, 410–11
    Marxist interpretations of, 409
    National Security Memo 200 and, 408, 419
    National Security Memo 314 and, 408, 411
    Planned Parenthood and, 262, 406–7, 408–9, 410–11
    Population Council and, 406–7

Packer, George, 160–61
Paddock, William and Paul, 405–6
pan-Africanism, 190, 193
Panama, 292–93, 373
pandemics, 9–10, 30–31, 64–65, 73–74
Paris Climate Accord (2015), 212
Paris Peace Conference (1919), 144–45, 181, 190, 395–96
Park Doosung, 439
Parker, Peter, 319–20
Parran, Thomas, 72–73
Pearl Harbor attack (1941), 221, 223–24, 225–26, 241–42, 248, 447–48
Pedersen, Susan, 176, 187
Pendell, Elmer, 405–6
perestroika (Soviet economic reform policies), 159–60, 297–98, 300, 303–4
Perkins, Frances, 350–51
Perkins, John, 114
Perle, Richard, 160, 166
The Philippines, 159, 212
Pierce, Franklin, 109–10, 111, 113
Pitt the Elder, William, 87
Planned Parenthood, 262, 406–7, 408–9, 410–11
Poland
    Cold War's end and, 303
    democratic decline in, 212
    German invasion (1939) of, 225
    government-in-exile during World War II and, 258

refugee children during World War II
from, 413–14
right-wing parties in, 412
Versailles Treaty and, 144
Polk, James K., 84–85, 106–7,
109–10, 114–16
Poole, DeWitt, 246–47
Population Council, 406–7
Posen, Barry, 6–7
Potsdam Conference (1945), 449
Power, Samantha, 15–16
President's Emergency Plan for AIDS
Relief (PEPFAR)
abstinence education and, 68–69
African countries' role in
implementing, 67
antiretroviral drugs and, 65–66,
68, 73–74
budget for, 63, 65–66, 68–70
contraception and, 68–69
effectiveness of, 69–70, 73–74
Evangelical Christians and, 65–66
grand strategy implications of, 5–6,
64, 73–76
implementation challenges facing, 69
limitations of, 74
Marshall Plan compared to, 67–68
Millennium Development Goals
and, 65–66
origins of, 5–6, 63, 65–66
sex workers and, 68–69
United Nations and, 69
US Agency for International
Development and, 63
Pro Busqueda, 414–15
Protestantism, 311–12, 313, 314, 317, 323.,
See also Evangelical Christians
public health, 9–10
Puerto Rico, 410
Putin, Vladimir, 15, 37, 166–67
Pyle, Ernie, 439

Quitman, John, 111

racism
Acheson and, 387
Cold War and, 332, 333–35
Greenlee's opposition to, 335–37

Kennan and, 262–63
Wilson and, 186
World War II and, 225–26,
227–28, 230–31
Radio Swan (CIA propaganda operation
in Guatemala), 413–14
Raines, Mrs. R.A., 432–33
Rajchman, Ludwik, 72
Ransone Jr., James, 436–37
Reagan, Ronald
Central American wars and, 159, 415
Cold War grand strategy and, 34, 41–42
defense spending under, 162
Gorbachev and, 159–60, 298
immigration policy and, 349
Kennan and, 256–57
Kirkpatrick and, 159
Mexico City policy and, 403–4, 410–11
NSDD-32 and NSDD-75, 32
The Philippines and, 159
Rebman, Karl L., 437
Red Cross, 176, 370, 414–15
Reeves, H. Edward, 433–34
Republican Party
abortion policies and, 403–4, 411
immigration policy and, 349, 354–55
New Deal opposition and, 202, 210–12,
222, 226–27
opposition to slavery and the origins of,
108, 117–18
President's Emergency Plan for AIDS
Relief and, 68–69
Tea Party and, 60–61
US regional variation and, 125–26
World War II and, 221–22
Responsibility to Protect doctrine, 224
Reynolds, David, 176
Rhee, Syngman, 177, 230, 428–29
Rhodes, Ben, 14–15
Rice, Condoleezza, 4–5
Richardson, Elliott, 283–84
Riesman, David, 254, 256–57
Rockefeller, Nelson, 276, 359–60
Rockefeller III, John D., 406,
407–8, 412–13
Rodman, Peter, 276, 282–83,
285–86, 287–88
Roe v. Wade, 410–11

Rogan, Eugene, 176
Rogers, William, 276–77, 282–85
Romania, 282–83, 285–86
Roosevelt, Eleanor, 350–51
Roosevelt, Franklin D.
    Atlantic Charter and, 204, 205–7
    Bretton Woods system and, 201–2, 204
    Four Freedoms Address (1941) and,
        204–5, 206, 208, 220
    free trade and, 147–48
    human rights and, 204–5
    immigration policy and, 350–51
    improvisation and personal diplomacy
        emphasized by, 147–48, 166–67, 201
    Lippmann and, 148
    national security concept invoked
        by, 239–40
    New Deal and, 201, 202–3, 208
    United Nations and, 148, 201,
        204, 208–9
    Wilson and, 147–48, 149, 201
    World War II and, 41–42, 146–47, 148,
        206–7, 208, 218, 219–20, 221–22,
        223–24, 225, 227–29, 248–49
Roosevelt, Theodore, 184–85, 369–70,
    390–91, 394
Roosevelt Corollary, 130
Root, Elihu, 184–85
Rosenberg, Emily, 186
Rosinski, Herbert, 245–46
Rowan, Carl
    civil rights movement and, 334
    decolonization movement and, 333–35
    on race as the key to history, 331–32
    segregated childhood of, 332–33
    United States Information Agency and,
        332, 333, 336
    as US ambassador to Finland, 332, 333
    US Navy service of, 333, 336
    US racism during the Cold War era,
        332, 333–35
Royal Navy (Great Britain), 87, 129, 130–
    31, 134–36, 447
Rules for Radicals (Alinsky), 54–55,
    56–57, 60–61
Rumsfeld, Donald, 4–5
Rusher, William, 156
Rusk, Dean, 357–58
Russia. See also Soviet Union

Bolshevik Revolution in, 189
democratic decline in, 212
empire of, 84, 95, 187–88
industrialization and, 176
Intermediate-Range Nuclear Forces
    Treaty (INF) and, 212
Magnitsky Act of 2011 and, 401–2
Napoleonic Wars and, 158
Syria and, 15
Tocqueville on, 448–49
transnational adoptions and,
    401–2, 416–17
US trade with, 416–17
World War I and, 144, 176
Ryskind, Allan, 156

Sakharov, Andrei, 157–58
Sanders, Bernie, 60–61
Sanders, Elizabeth, 125
Schelling, Thomas, 58–59
Schlesinger Jr., Arthur M., 267
School of the Americas (Fort Benning,
    Georgia), 412–13, 415
Scowcroft, Brent, 161, 299–301, 408–9, 411
Sebelius, Kathleen, 70
Sender, Toni, 224–25
September 11 terrorist attacks (2001), 3–
    4, 41–42, 164, 306–7, 447–48
Serbia, 162–63
Seven Years War, 87
sexuality, 68–69, 263–64, 351, 354,
    405, 407–8
Sharp, Gene, 58–59
Shawn, Wallace, 261–62
Sierra Leone, 316
Silove, Nina, 12
Singapore, 321–22, 373
Singh, Nikhil Pal, 340
Siniver, Asaf, 285–86
Slaughter, Anne-Marie, 59–60, 259
slavery
    abolitionist movement and, 51, 53–54
    federal government power in federal
        affairs and, 112–14
    Fugitive Slave Law and, 109
    Great Britain's abolition (1833) of, 110,
        112–13, 115, 116
    Missouri Compromise (1820)
        and, 96–97

Republican Party and, 108, 117–18
US national unity threatened by, 84
US territorial expansion and, 96–97,
    109, 116–17
Whig Party and, 109–10
Slidell, John, 109–10, 117–18
Sluga, Glenda, 182–83
Smethurst, James, 336–37
Smith, Charles B., 429–30
Smith, Gerald L.K., 212
Snyder, Jack, 11–12
social movement theory
    Alinsky and, 54–61
    grand strategy and, 50–51,
        53–54, 57–58
    labor movement and, 53–54
    mass action and, 50, 56, 59
    nonviolence and, 58–59
    social media and, 60
Social Security, 202–3
Society for the Diffusion of Useful
    Knowledge, 320–21
Solarium exercise, 32, 33–34
Somoza, Anastosio, 158–59
Sorensen, Annelise, 257–58
South Africa, 69, 158–59, 263
Southern Christian Leadership
    Council, 406–7
South Korea. See also Korean War
    establishment (1945) of, 428
    No Gun Ri Massacre investigation
        and, 438
    Sunshine Policy of engagement with
        North Korea and, 163–64
    transnational adoptions and, 403–4, 414
    United Nations Cemetery in, 431
    United States and, 428–29
    welfare policies in, 403–4, 414
Soviet Union. See also Cold War
    Afghanistan War (1980s) and, 40
    atomic bomb test (1949) by, 40, 451
    authoritarian nature of regime in, 38
    Baltic secessionist movements in, 303
    China's normalization of relations with
        United States and, 156–57
    dissidents in, 157–58
    Eastern Europe controlled by, 148, 154–
        55, 209–10, 258, 292, 304, 449
    economic decline during 1980s in, 301

fall (1991) of, 161–62, 212, 292, 301,
    304, 448–49
Five-Year Plans of, 30
glasnost policies in, 159–60, 297–98, 300
Korean War and, 260–61, 428–29
perestroika policies in, 159–60, 297–98,
    300, 303–4
Suez War (1956) and, 261
World War II and, 148
Spain
    empire of, 9–10, 84, 93, 95, 99, 111–12
    evacuation of Basque children during
        fascist era in, 413–14
    Spanish-American War (1898) and, 131
    World War I and, 9–10
The Spook Who Sat by the Door
    (Greenlee), 338–40
Sprout, Harold and Margaret, 134–36
Stalin, Josef
    Eastern Europe and, 258, 449
    Kennan's analysis of, 150, 449–50
    Korean War and, 435
    Lippmann's approach to, 148–49
State Department
    birth control policies and,
        410–11, 418–19
    Bureau of Human Rights and
        Humanitarian Affairs at, 157–58
    Eisenhower and, 280
    humanitarian aid and, 366,
        369–70, 371–72
    Johnson and, 282
    Kennedy and, 282
    Kissinger and, 277, 279–81,
        282–85, 287–88
    McCarthy's accusations of communist
        infiltration of, 41
    National Security Council and, 280
    Nixon and, 273, 274–78, 279–80, 281,
        282–86, 287–88
    Office of Soviet Affairs and, 275
    Strategic Arms Limitation Talks
        and, 285–86
    transnational adoptions and, 414, 417
    Truman and, 287
    United States Information Agency
        and, 337–38
    Vietnam War and, 285–86
Stebbins, Richard P., 245–46

Steill, Benn, 149
Stephens, Alexander, 109, 111–12, 117–18
Stephens, Richard W., 429
Stevenson, Adlai, 256–57
Stimson, Henry, 390–91
Strachan, Hew, 11
Strategic Arms Limitation Talks (SALT),
    275, 285–86
Student Nonviolent Coordinating
    Committee (SNCC), 334–35
Suez War (1956), 261
suffragist movement, 53–54
Sumner, William Graham, 256–57
Sunstein, Cass, 208–9
Syria, 15–16, 44, 166–67, 256

Taft, Robert A., 222, 432
Taft, William Howard, 184–85, 390–91
Talbott, Strobe, 36
Tariff of 1828, 94
Taylor, Elizabeth, 354
Tea Party, 60–61
Tenet, George, 164
Terkel, Studs, 230–31
Texas
    military-industrial complex and, 451
    Republic of Texas era and, 110–11,
        112, 115
    slavery in, 109, 110–11, 112,
        115–16, 117
    US annexation (1845) of, 95–96, 111,
        112, 116
Thatcher, Margaret, 298
Thomas, Evan, 254–55
Thomas, Helen, 302
Thomas, Norman, 192–93, 254
Thompson, John A., 146, 248–49
Throntveit, Trygve, 186, 190–91
Thucydides, 37, 57
Thurmond, Strom, 357
Tiananmen Square massacre (China,
    1989), 292, 303–4, 306
Tillman, Ben, 131–32
Tinkler, Norman, 438
Tocqueville, Alexis de, 37, 448–49
Tokyo War Trials, 202, 208–9
Tooze, Adam, 176
Torres, Maria de los Angeles, 229–30

Trachtenberg, Marc, 454, 456
Tracy, Ira, 317, 319, 321
Transcontinental Treaty of 1819, 95–96
transnational adoption
    China and, 412–13, 414, 416–17
    Evangelical Christians and, 414
    Families for Orphans Act and,
        412–13, 417–18
    forced disappearances in Central
        America and, 403–4, 412–13,
        414–16, 419
    gendered logics regarding, 401–2
    Hague Convention on Intercountry
        Adoption and, 412–13, 415–17
    Red Cross and, 414–15
    Russia and, 401–2, 416–17
    State Department and, 414, 417
    Trump administration and, 401–2, 419
transnationalism, 180–81, 182,
    183, 191–92
Trans-Pacific Partnership, 44
Trescot, William Henry, 110, 111–12
Trubowitz, Peter, 126
Truman, Harry S.
    birth control and population policy
        under, 405
    defense budget and, 153
    Foreign Economic Assistance Act of
        1950 and, 370–71
    immigration policy and, 351, 359
    Korean War and, 43–44, 428–29, 430–
        31, 432–33, 436
    "Long Telegram" and, 150
    Marshall Plan and, 67–68, 259, 370–71
    Mutual Security Act of 1951
        and, 370–71
    North Atlantic Treaty Organization
        and, 404
    NSC-68 and, 32
    State Department and, 287
    on transfer of scientific knowledge to
        developing world, 404–5
    Truman Doctrine (containment) and,
        32–33, 38–42, 229, 260, 404, 455
    United Nations and, 404
Trump, Donald
    "America First" policies of, 167–68, 212
    authoritarian leaders praised by, 167–68

gender ideology and, 412
immigration policy and, 349
Mexico City policy and, 411
"Muslim Ban" immigration policy and, 211–12, 349
Paris Climate Accord abrogated by, 212
Tea Party and, 60–61
trade policies and, 167–68
transnational adoption policies and, 401–2, 419
Trans-Pacific Partnership rejected by, 44
Trump Jr., Donald, 401–2, 419
Tufekci, Zeynep, 60
Turkey, 150, 260, 431, 449
Tyler, John, 109–10, 111
Tyler, Patrick, 160–61
Tyrrell, Ian, 186

United Nations (UN)
Atlantic Charter and, 205–6
birth control and population policies at, 408–9
charter of, 204, 206, 390
Cold War's end and, 304–6
collective security and, 201, 206
decolonization and, 209–10
Defense Policy Guidance Report's criticisms (1992) of, 160–61
establishment of, 143, 204, 220–21
Korean War and, 428–29, 430, 431, 434–35, 436–37
Kosovo War (1999) and, 162–63
Millennium Development Goals and, 64–66
national sovereignty and, 182–83, 209
North Atlantic Treaty Organization and, 209
President's Emergency Plan for AIDS Relief and, 69
Roosevelt and, 148, 201, 204, 208–9
Security Council of, 65–66, 429
UN Charter and, 209–10
United Nations Children's Fund (UNICEF) and, 417
UN Relief and Rehabilitation Association and, 209
US public opinion regarding, 228, 229–30

World Health Organization (WHO) and, 72–73
United Nations Cemetery (Busan, South Korea), 431
United Negro Improvement Association (UNIA), 188–89
United States Information Agency (USIA), 332, 336, 337–38, 371–73
Upshur, Abel P., 113
US Agency for International Development (USAID), 63, 366, 372–73, 407–10
US Global Health Initiative, 70
US-Mexican War (1846-48), 95–96, 115–16
US Navy
basing infrastructure and, 130–31
battleships and, 131–32, 134–35
disaster relief and, 369–70, 377
domestic politics and, 131–32
Federalist Papers on expansion of, 90, 92, 100
grand strategy and, 123–24
Korean War and, 429
Naval Appropriations Act of 1916 and, 132–33
Naval War College and, 136
nineteenth-century expansion of, 123, 126, 128
Spanish-American War (1898) and, 131
Wilson and, 132–33
Wisconsin School and, 135–36

Vagts, Alfred, 245–46
Valenti, Jack, 352–53
Vandenberg, Arthur, 40–41
Venezuela, 212, 369, 378
Versailles Treaty, 144, 181, 243, 391–92, 395
Veselnitskaya, Natalia, 401–2
Vietnam War (1954–75)
birth control policies and, 407
casualties in, 455
China and, 156–57
containment doctrine and, 260, 261, 404, 455
domestic opposition to, 231–32, 266–67
Johnson and, 260, 278–79, 455–56
Kennedy and, 455–56

Vietnam War (1954–75) (*cont.*)
   Kissinger and, 155–56, 278–79, 455–56
   Nixon and, 274, 276, 278–79,
     285–86, 455–56
   post-traumatic stress disorder (PTSD)
     and, 435
   US collective memory and, 304
   US grand strategy goals challenged
     by, 16, 37
   US interventions in Cambodia and Laos
     during, 156
   US troop deployment levels in, 154–55
Vinogradradov, N. A., 73
Virginia and Kentucky Resolutions
   (1798-99), 94
Vitalis, Robert, 341
Vogt, William, 405–6
Vonnegut, Kurt, 201, 213
Voting Rights Act of 1965, 211–12,
   334, 359–60

Walker, Johnnie, 437
Wallace, Henry, 218
Walsh, Bryan O., 413–14
Walt, Stephen, 1
Walter, Frances, 351–52, 354
Wanghsia Treaty (1844), 319–20
Warburg, James P., 218, 232–33
War Department. *See* Defense
   Department
War Memorial of Korea, 431
War of 1812, 94, 97–98, 101, 115
Washington, George, 93–94, 98–100, 146,
   192, 348–49
Washington Naval Conference (1921–22),
   179, 243
Wasserman, Harriet, 261–62
Watergate scandal (1972-74), 37, 297
Watts, Barry, 34–35
Webb-Pomerene Act of 1918, 132–33
Webster, Daniel, 93–94, 242
Weinberg, Albert K., 243–48
Weissman, Steve, 406
Wertheim, Stephen, 51, 124, 184
Western Hemisphere
   European imperial claims in, 84, 98
   Monroe Doctrine (1823) and, 84–85,
     95–96, 98–100, 192

   slavery and, 110–11, 112, 116–18
Westphalia Treaty (1648), 184
Whig Party, 89, 109–10, 115–16
White, Harry Dexter, 149
White, Micah, 59–60
White, Robert, 415
Wilhelm II (kaiser of Germany), 130
Wilkerson, Lawrence, 164
Williams, Samuel Wells, 317, 319, 321
Williams, William A., 127
Williams, William Appleman, 127, 145–46
Willkie, Wendell, 212–13
Wilson, James Graham, 159–60
Wilson, Woodrow
   critics of the foreign policy and, 146
   death of, 180–81
   Fourteen Points of, 144, 179, 180–81,
     183–84, 187, 391–92, 395
   immigration policy and, 350–51
   influenza pandemic (1918-19)
     and, 9–10
   The Inquiry (foreign policy advisory
     group) and, 144–45, 394–95
   League of Nations and, 147–48, 160–61,
     179, 184, 186–87, 190–91
   Paris Peace Conference (1919) and,
     144–45, 181, 190, 395–96
   presidential election of 1916 and, 184
   racism of, 186
   Roosevelt (Franklin) and, 147–48,
     149, 201
   self-determination doctrine and, 17–18,
     177–78, 183, 186
   stroke suffered by, 43–44
   US Navy and, 132–33
   Versailles Treaty and, 395–96
   World War I and, 41–42, 132–33, 145,
     183, 184
Winter, Jay, 181
Wisconsin school, 123, 127, 130, 135–36
Wise, Henry A., 109–11, 117
Wohlstetter, Albert, 160
Wolfowitz, Paul
   Anti-Ballistic Missile Treaty withdrawal
     and, 163–64
   Bush (George W.) and, 163–64
   Carter administration and, 157–58
   Clinton foreign policy and, 162–63

Defense Policy Guidance Report (1992)
 and, 160–61, 162, 165
Iraq policy and, 163–65, 166
Kissinger and, 158
National Security Strategy of the United
 States (2002), 165
North Korea and, 163–64
September 11 terrorist attacks and, 164
Wilson and, 158, 160–61
Women's International League for Peace
 and Freedom (WILPF), 179–80,
 185, 191–93
Women's March (2017), 60
Women's Peace Party (WPP), 179
Woodward, C. Vann, 83, 447–48
Worcester, Samuel, 315–16
World Bank, 149, 208–9
World Court, 145, 179–80
World Health Organization
 (WHO), 72–73
World Trade Organization (WTO),
 208–9, 416–17
World War I
 commercial shipping rights and, 97
 Eastern Front of, 176
 France and, 144
 Germany and, 97, 132, 144, 183–84
 Great Britain and, 10, 132, 144
 Hague Conventions (1899 and 1907)
  and, 176
 influenza pandemic of 1918-19 and, 10
 Japan and, 176
 Middle East and, 176
 Red Cross and, 176
 Russia and, 144, 176
 Spain and, 9–10
 US causalities in, 144

US public opinion regarding, 222–23
Wilson and, 41–42, 132–33, 145,
 183, 184
World War II
 African Americans and American
  racism during, 225–26,
  227–28, 230–31
 anti-semitism in the United States and,
  227–28, 230–31
 casualties and, 439
 France and, 146–47, 247, 248–49
 Germany and, 38, 148, 223–25, 227–29,
  247, 261–62
 Great Britain and, 146–47, 148
 The Holocaust and, 227–28
 Japanese American internment
  during, 227–28
 Pearl Harbor attack (1941) and, 221,
  223–24, 225–26, 241–42, 248, 447–48
 Roosevelt and, 41–42, 146–47, 148,
  206–7, 208, 218, 219–20, 221–22,
  223–24, 225, 227–29, 248–49
 Soviet Union and, 148
 US casualties during, 228
 US Congress and, 226–27
 US public memory regarding, 219, 221,
  228, 230–31
 US public opinion during, 221–28, 247
Wynne, G.H., 432

"X" (Kennan). See under Kennan, George

Yale University, 49–50, 51–53, 59–60, 136
Young, Marilyn, 130
Young, Nancy Beck, 226
Young Plan, 145–46
Yugoslavia, 292–93, 375–76